BARRON'S

HOW TO PREPARE FOR THE

SAT II

UNITED STATES HISTORY

11TH EDITION

David A. Midgley
Former Head, History Department, Albany Academy for Boys
Former Adjunct Professor, Russell Sage College and Siena College

and

Phillip Lefton
Former Principal, Theodore Roosevelt High School, New York City
Former Assistant Principal, Franklin Delano Roosevelt High School, New York City

BARRON'S

ACKNOWLEDGMENTS

Grateful acknowledgment is made to the following organizations for permission to include their materials in this publication:

Chicago Sun Times for the cartoon, "Drag Race"

Long Island Press for the cartoon, "Stricter Enforcement of Gun Law"

Newsweek Magazine for the graph, "Estimated Average Age of Plant and Equipment"

New York Convention & Visitors Bureau for the drawing of the Verrazano-Narrows Bridge

New York State Education Department for some questions from *Sourcebook of Test Items for the Advanced Placement Program in American History*

The New York Times Copyright © 1977 for the graph "Percent of population in each age group"

The New Yorker for the cartoon, "Founding Fathers"

The Oregonian for the cartoon, "World Leadership Role"

Time, Inc. for the chart, "Popularity Highs and Lows"

Times-Picayune for the cartoon, "Either one's poison to me!"

U.S. News and World Report for the chart, "Immigrants to the U.S."

Washington Post Writers Group for the Herblock cartoons, "Want a Lift?" and "The Other Road"

All inquiries should be addressed to:
Barron's Educational Series, Inc.
250 Wireless Boulevard
Hauppauge, NY 11788
http://www.barronseduc.com

Library of Congress Catalog Card Number 2002033228

International Standard Book Number 0-7641-2023-9

Library of Congress Cataloging-in-Publication Data
Midgley, David A.
   How to prepare for the SAT II. United States history / David A. Midgley and Phillip Lefton.—11th ed.
      p. cm.
   Rev. ed. of: How to prepare for the SAT II. American history and social studies. c1998.
   At head of title: Barron's.
   Includes index.
   ISBN 0-7641-2023-9 (alk. paper)
      1. United States—History—Outlines, syllabi, etc.   2. United States—History—Examinations, questions, etc.   I. Title:
Barron's how to prepare for the SAT II. United States history.   II. Lefton, Phillip.   III. Midgley, David A. How to prepare for the SAT II. American history and social studies.   IV. Title.

E178.2 .M63 2003
973′.076—dc21

                                                                                              2002033228

PRINTED IN THE UNITED STATES OF AMERICA
9 8 7 6 5 4

CONTENTS

INTRODUCTION TO THE TEST

SAT II: United States History is a one-hour examination consisting of 90 to 95 multiple-choice questions. It is used by colleges as one of the measures in selecting students for admission. It is also used, although less frequently, to determine placement in college history courses.

The test is administered five times a year (in November, December, January, May, and June) at SAT Test Centers. For specific dates and addresses of testing centers, see your school's college guidance counselor, or call or write the Educational Testing Service, Princeton, New Jersey 08541, (609) 921-9000; for the western United States call (510) 596-5500 in California.

The United States History test is designed to measure students' knowledge of American history from the pre-Columbian period to the present; the main emphasis is on the period after 1789. The related social studies areas covered in the examination are political science, economics, sociology, geography. The main emphasis is on political history, although economic, social, intellectual and cultural history, and foreign policy are also covered (see the chart). The test measures not only your knowledge of United States history, but also your ability to analyze and interpret facts, apply concepts, and judge information.

If you do not know the answer to a question, random guessing is not recommended. However, if you have some knowledge about a particular question, eliminating the choices you know to be incorrect can help in choosing the correct answer. It is inadvisable to spend too much time on any single question, since the test lasts only one hour. The best approach is first to answer the questions you feel confident about, and then, if you have time, to go back and ponder the more difficult questions. Don't worry if you do not have time to finish all of the questions. No one is expected to get a perfect score.

Scores on SAT II: Subject Tests are based on the number of correct answers minus a fraction of the number of the incorrect answers. All correct answers count equally toward the total score, which can range from a low of 200 to a high of 800; there are no "passing" or "failing" scores.

The best time to take the test is as soon as possible after completeing a course in American history and/or carefully reviewing the material in this book. Last-minute cramming is unadvisable. As you take the test, remember to pace yourself with the one-hour time limit in mind, and to read each question carefully so that you clearly understand what is being asked. The eight tests in this book provide excellent practice. They are valuable study tools for preparing for SAT II: United States History.

Material Covered	*Approximate Percentage of Test*
Political History	32–36
Economic History	18–20
Social History	18–22
Intellectual and Cultural History	10–12
Foreign Policy	13–17
Social Science Concepts, Methods, and Generalizations are incorporated in the material above	

Periods Covered	
Pre-Columbian History to 1789	20
1790 to 1898	40
1899 to the Present	40

> **Note:** Unless designated otherwise, double and single asterisks throughout the text represent material that deserves special emphasis.

TYPES OF QUESTIONS USED ON THE TEST

The types of questions used on the United States History SAT II test are designed to measure several skills and abilities. According to the information provided by the College Board, the questions may be presented as separate items or in sets based on quotations, maps, pictures, graphs, or tables. The College Board also indicates that the questions on the test fall into four general categories.

One type of question tests your recall of facts, terms, concepts, and generalizations. The following question from the Diagnostic Test is a sample of this type.

1. The British colony that was first settled by the Swedes was

    (A) Delaware
    (B) Georgia
    (C) New Jersey
    (D) North Carolina
    (E) South Carolina

The **second type** of question requires you to analyze and interpret information. The following question from the Diagnostic Test is a sample of this type.

2. "I disapprove of what you say, but I will defend to the death your right to say it." This statement suggests that the speaker would be most opposed to

    (A) media censorship
    (B) the right of petition
    (C) civil disobedience
    (D) formation of monopolies
    (E) abortion rights

The **third type** of question requires you to relate ideas to given data. The following question from Practice Test 1 is a sample of this type.

3. One of President Wilson's "Fourteen Points" was reduction of armaments. Which of the following is closest to his stated goal in this respect?

    (A) All nations should reduce their armaments by 25 percent three times at five-year intervals. Then they should hold a conference to decide how further to reduce them.
    (B) The defeated nations should disarm immediately. The Allies should maintain their armaments until the stability of the postwar period was assured.
    (C) Armaments should be reduced to the point where nations had only sufficient forces to maintain police protection against smuggling, piracy, etc., and to maintain domestic tranquility within their borders.
    (D) The United States should make the first substantial move toward disarmament as an encouragement for other nations to follow suit.
    (E) The United States and Great Britain should pledge sharp reduction in their naval power as an inducement to other nations to move in the same direction.

The **fourth type** of question requires you to evaluate data for a specific purpose. The following question from Practice Test 1 is a sample of this type.

4. These topics—efforts of the War Hawks, the Fenian raids, filibustering in Central America, and the Ostend Manifesto—might all be cited in an essay dealing with

    (A) our relations with Great Britain
    (B) wars in which the United States has been involved
    (C) influences on our foreign policy prior to the Mexican War
    (D) attempts to extend the boundaries of the United States
    (E) incidents ultimately settled by arbitration

HOW TO USE THIS BOOK

This book has been carefully planned to assist you in the most effective manner in preparing for SAT II: United States History. The following approach is recommended:

1. Familiarize yourself with the scope and organization of the book by reviewing the detailed Contents. Note that an outline of each chapter is included, so you can quickly determine which topics you may need to review in greater detail.
2. After reading "Introduction to the Test," take the Diagnostic Test. Score it and review the Answer Explanations, for a thorough understanding of the material tested.
3. Complete the Answer Analysis Chart on page 16. Study it to determine in what eras of history you need the most review. (Because the greater part of the test covers the two periods from 1790–1898 and 1899 to the present, you should obviously pay more attention to these eras.) Use the Contents, which clearly indicates which chapters cover each of the historic periods, to plan your review schedule.
4. Take the Practice Tests, following the same procedures as you did for the Diagnostic Test: review the Answer Explanations and complete the Answer Analysis Charts, followed by the indicated review. You should see a definite improvement in your overall scores, as well as in those periods that you have identified as needing study.

Just prior to the actual test date, you should review the material in the Introduction, page X. Then approach the test with complete confidence that you have done everything possible to assure your very best performance.

TEST-TAKING TECHNIQUES

1. Make certain that you understand what the question is asking. Read the stem of the question (the part before the choices) very carefully to make certain you know what the examiner is asking.
2. Always read all of the choices before you select an answer. Don't fall into the trap of picking the wrong answer because it was a good distractor and it came before the correct choice. Read all choices!
3. Never make a choice based on frequency of previous answers. Some students pay attention to the pattern of answers when taking an exam. *There are no secret patterns.* Tests are checked carefully for this, and any patterns that someone sees are *imagined*. Always answer the question without regard to what the previous choices have been.
4. Eliminate choices you know are wrong. As you read the choices, put a slash mark through any choice you know is wrong. Reread only the ones you did not eliminate the first time. Many times, when you read the remaining choices again, the answer is clear. If you know the answer, mark it in the space provided. If you still do not know the answer, reread the stem of the question and make sure you understand the question. Then go through the choices again.
5. Do not dwell too long on any one question. Simply skip the question, but put a mark by it so that you can find it quickly when you return to it later.
6. Check your time periodically.
7. Once you have answered all of the questions you were sure of, go back to the ones you did not know and read them again.
8. Change answers only if you are sure they are wrong. Unless you have a good reason, do not change an answer once you have chosen it. Studies show that people generally change an answer from the right one to the wrong one.

Reprinted with permission from *Barron's Regents Exams and Answers, Global Studies.* Barron's Educational Series, Inc., Hauppauge, 1990.

PART ONE
DIAGNOSTIC TEST

ANSWER SHEET : DIAGNOSTIC TEST

1. Ⓐ Ⓑ Ⓒ Ⓓ Ⓔ 16. Ⓐ Ⓑ Ⓒ Ⓓ Ⓔ 31. Ⓐ Ⓑ Ⓒ Ⓓ Ⓔ
2. Ⓐ Ⓑ Ⓒ Ⓓ Ⓔ 17. Ⓐ Ⓑ Ⓒ Ⓓ Ⓔ 32. Ⓐ Ⓑ Ⓒ Ⓓ Ⓔ
3. Ⓐ Ⓑ Ⓒ Ⓓ Ⓔ 18. Ⓐ Ⓑ Ⓒ Ⓓ Ⓔ 33. Ⓐ Ⓑ Ⓒ Ⓓ Ⓔ
4. Ⓐ Ⓑ Ⓒ Ⓓ Ⓔ 19. Ⓐ Ⓑ Ⓒ Ⓓ Ⓔ 34. Ⓐ Ⓑ Ⓒ Ⓓ Ⓔ
5. Ⓐ Ⓑ Ⓒ Ⓓ Ⓔ 20. Ⓐ Ⓑ Ⓒ Ⓓ Ⓔ 35. Ⓐ Ⓑ Ⓒ Ⓓ Ⓔ
6. Ⓐ Ⓑ Ⓒ Ⓓ Ⓔ 21. Ⓐ Ⓑ Ⓒ Ⓓ Ⓔ 36. Ⓐ Ⓑ Ⓒ Ⓓ Ⓔ
7. Ⓐ Ⓑ Ⓒ Ⓓ Ⓔ 22. Ⓐ Ⓑ Ⓒ Ⓓ Ⓔ 37. Ⓐ Ⓑ Ⓒ Ⓓ Ⓔ
8. Ⓐ Ⓑ Ⓒ Ⓓ Ⓔ 23. Ⓐ Ⓑ Ⓒ Ⓓ Ⓔ 38. Ⓐ Ⓑ Ⓒ Ⓓ Ⓔ
9. Ⓐ Ⓑ Ⓒ Ⓓ Ⓔ 24. Ⓐ Ⓑ Ⓒ Ⓓ Ⓔ 39. Ⓐ Ⓑ Ⓒ Ⓓ Ⓔ
10. Ⓐ Ⓑ Ⓒ Ⓓ Ⓔ 25. Ⓐ Ⓑ Ⓒ Ⓓ Ⓔ 40. Ⓐ Ⓑ Ⓒ Ⓓ Ⓔ
11. Ⓐ Ⓑ Ⓒ Ⓓ Ⓔ 26. Ⓐ Ⓑ Ⓒ Ⓓ Ⓔ 41. Ⓐ Ⓑ Ⓒ Ⓓ Ⓔ
12. Ⓐ Ⓑ Ⓒ Ⓓ Ⓔ 27. Ⓐ Ⓑ Ⓒ Ⓓ Ⓔ 42. Ⓐ Ⓑ Ⓒ Ⓓ Ⓔ
13. Ⓐ Ⓑ Ⓒ Ⓓ Ⓔ 28. Ⓐ Ⓑ Ⓒ Ⓓ Ⓔ 43. Ⓐ Ⓑ Ⓒ Ⓓ Ⓔ
14. Ⓐ Ⓑ Ⓒ Ⓓ Ⓔ 29. Ⓐ Ⓑ Ⓒ Ⓓ Ⓔ 44. Ⓐ Ⓑ Ⓒ Ⓓ Ⓔ
15. Ⓐ Ⓑ Ⓒ Ⓓ Ⓔ 30. Ⓐ Ⓑ Ⓒ Ⓓ Ⓔ 45. Ⓐ Ⓑ Ⓒ Ⓓ Ⓔ

46. Ⓐ Ⓑ Ⓒ Ⓓ Ⓔ 61. Ⓐ Ⓑ Ⓒ Ⓓ Ⓔ 76. Ⓐ Ⓑ Ⓒ Ⓓ Ⓔ
47. Ⓐ Ⓑ Ⓒ Ⓓ Ⓔ 62. Ⓐ Ⓑ Ⓒ Ⓓ Ⓔ 77. Ⓐ Ⓑ Ⓒ Ⓓ Ⓔ
48. Ⓐ Ⓑ Ⓒ Ⓓ Ⓔ 63. Ⓐ Ⓑ Ⓒ Ⓓ Ⓔ 78. Ⓐ Ⓑ Ⓒ Ⓓ Ⓔ
49. Ⓐ Ⓑ Ⓒ Ⓓ Ⓔ 64. Ⓐ Ⓑ Ⓒ Ⓓ Ⓔ 79. Ⓐ Ⓑ Ⓒ Ⓓ Ⓔ
50. Ⓐ Ⓑ Ⓒ Ⓓ Ⓔ 65. Ⓐ Ⓑ Ⓒ Ⓓ Ⓔ 80. Ⓐ Ⓑ Ⓒ Ⓓ Ⓔ
51. Ⓐ Ⓑ Ⓒ Ⓓ Ⓔ 66. Ⓐ Ⓑ Ⓒ Ⓓ Ⓔ 81. Ⓐ Ⓑ Ⓒ Ⓓ Ⓔ
52. Ⓐ Ⓑ Ⓒ Ⓓ Ⓔ 67. Ⓐ Ⓑ Ⓒ Ⓓ Ⓔ 82. Ⓐ Ⓑ Ⓒ Ⓓ Ⓔ
53. Ⓐ Ⓑ Ⓒ Ⓓ Ⓔ 68. Ⓐ Ⓑ Ⓒ Ⓓ Ⓔ 83. Ⓐ Ⓑ Ⓒ Ⓓ Ⓔ
54. Ⓐ Ⓑ Ⓒ Ⓓ Ⓔ 69. Ⓐ Ⓑ Ⓒ Ⓓ Ⓔ 84. Ⓐ Ⓑ Ⓒ Ⓓ Ⓔ
55. Ⓐ Ⓑ Ⓒ Ⓓ Ⓔ 70. Ⓐ Ⓑ Ⓒ Ⓓ Ⓔ 85. Ⓐ Ⓑ Ⓒ Ⓓ Ⓔ
56. Ⓐ Ⓑ Ⓒ Ⓓ Ⓔ 71. Ⓐ Ⓑ Ⓒ Ⓓ Ⓔ 86. Ⓐ Ⓑ Ⓒ Ⓓ Ⓔ
57. Ⓐ Ⓑ Ⓒ Ⓓ Ⓔ 72. Ⓐ Ⓑ Ⓒ Ⓓ Ⓔ 87. Ⓐ Ⓑ Ⓒ Ⓓ Ⓔ
58. Ⓐ Ⓑ Ⓒ Ⓓ Ⓔ 73. Ⓐ Ⓑ Ⓒ Ⓓ Ⓔ 88. Ⓐ Ⓑ Ⓒ Ⓓ Ⓔ
59. Ⓐ Ⓑ Ⓒ Ⓓ Ⓔ 74. Ⓐ Ⓑ Ⓒ Ⓓ Ⓔ 89. Ⓐ Ⓑ Ⓒ Ⓓ Ⓔ
60. Ⓐ Ⓑ Ⓒ Ⓓ Ⓔ 75. Ⓐ Ⓑ Ⓒ Ⓓ Ⓔ 90. Ⓐ Ⓑ Ⓒ Ⓓ Ⓔ

91. Ⓐ Ⓑ Ⓒ Ⓓ Ⓔ
92. Ⓐ Ⓑ Ⓒ Ⓓ Ⓔ
93. Ⓐ Ⓑ Ⓒ Ⓓ Ⓔ
94. Ⓐ Ⓑ Ⓒ Ⓓ Ⓔ
95. Ⓐ Ⓑ Ⓒ Ⓓ Ⓔ

Diagnostic Test

The following exam will test your knowledge of the topics included on the actual United States History achievement test, and give you an indication of your strengths and weaknesses.

Directions: Each of the questions or incomplete statements is followed by five suggested answers or completions. Select the one that is best in each case and then blacken the corresponding space on the answer sheet.

Questions 1-2 refer to the following cartoon.

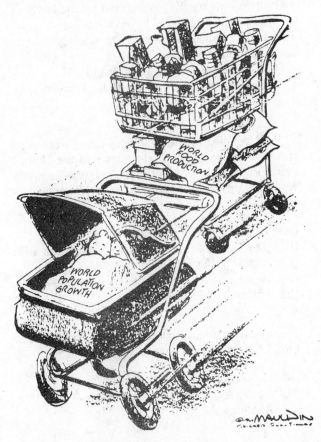

Drag Race
©1964 *The Sun-Times and Bill Mauldin*

1. Which current problem does this cartoon portray?

   (A) The prosperous nations of the world are not attempting to increase world food production.
   (B) The ability of nations to produce enough food to meet their needs is threatened by a rapid increase in population.
   (C) World food production is accelerating at a faster rate than world population growth.
   (D) Although there is a food surplus, inadequate transportation prevents delivery to the world's hungry people.
   (E) Population control is controversial; increasing food output is not.

2. In which area of the world is the problem portrayed in the cartoon most acute?

   (A) Asia   (D) the United States
   (B) eastern Europe   (E) Africa
   (C) western Europe

Questions 3-4 refer to the following graph.

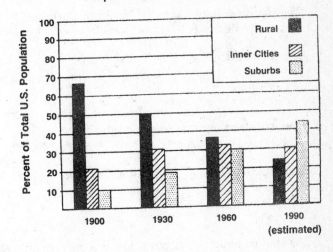

People Move to Cities and Suburbs

3. Which conclusion is best supported by the graph?

  (A) Suburbs may need urban-renewal programs by the 1980s.
  (B) Farmers received greater subsidies from the federal government in 1900 than in 1960.
  (C) As the population shifts toward suburban areas, inner cities will find it easier to raise necessary tax revenue.
  (D) In 1990, a greater percentage of the total population will live in rural areas than in 1930.
  (E) Economic development of suburbs is a priority item.

4. Which statement about future governmental activities could most logically be made from the trends indicated on the graph?

  (A) Cities will adopt the city manager form of government.
  (B) County governments will be solely responsible for financing welfare programs.
  (C) The federal government will need to play an important part in attempting to solve the problems of metropolitan areas.
  (D) State governments will reduce the number of interstate compacts and agreements.
  (E) Suburbs should have a greater voice in state government.

5. The British colony where the House of Burgesses was established was

  (A) Connecticut   (D) Pennsylvania
  (B) Georgia   (E) North Carolina
  (C) Virginia

6. The British colony that was first settled by Swedes was

  (A) Delaware   (D) North Carolina
  (B) Georgia   (E) South Carolina
  (C) New Jersey

7. As applied to the American colonial scene, which one of the following statements BEST explains the term salutary neglect?

  (A) Colonials neglected to pay taxes as required by law.
  (B) England neglected to support the war against the French and Indians until Pitt took over.
  (C) France neglected to put forth strenuous efforts to back up her settlers in America.
  (D) American settlers neglected to enter whole-

heartedly into the French and Indian War.
  (E) England did not enforce, either strictly or regularly, the trade and navigation acts.

8. Which weakness of the Articles of Confederation was most closely associated with the Mount Vernon and Annapolis Conventions?

  (A) No courts to handle interstate disputes
  (B) No authority to regulate interstate commerce
  (C) No power to collect the taxes it levied
  (D) No power to recruit an adequate armed force
  (E) No power to change its constitution except by unanimous approval of all thirteen states

9. An ex post facto law is one that

  (A) punishes a crime that was legal when committed
  (B) makes an act illegal that, before the law was passed, was legal
  (C) makes punishable an act that was legal when committed
  (D) is so unjust as to be intolerable
  (E) neither the states nor the federal government may pass

10, 11. All but *two* of the following items were controversial between the Federalists and the Democratic Republicans during President Washington's administrations. Which two were NOT controversial?

  (A) Whiskey Rebellion
  (B) Handling state debts by the Assumption Bill
  (C) Handling the foreign debt
  (D) Genêt and the Treaty of Alliance of 1778
  (E) Pinckney Treaty

12. The engineer in charge of building the Panama Canal for the United States was

  (A) Goethals   (D) Pauncefote
  (B) Verrazanao   (E) de Lesseps
  (C) Roebling

Questions 13-14: One item in each of these groups lacks a factor common to all the other items in the group. Select the ODD item in each.

13. (A) George Westinghouse
    (B) Eli Whitney
    (C) Benjamin Franklin
    (D) Cyrus McCormick
    (E) George Norris

14. (A) Thomas E. Dewey   (D) John Hay
    (B) Frank B. Kellogg   (E) Dean Acheson
    (C) Henry Stimson

15. All of the following items first became important before 1861 EXCEPT

    (A) American Federation of Labor
    (B) Brook Farm
    (C) New Harmony
    (D) Lucretia Mott
    (E) Rochdale Cooperatives

16. All of the following were associated with the period from 1861 to 1900 EXCEPT

    (A) Haymarket Square riot
    (B) Homestead, Pennsylvania massacre
    (C) Knights of Labor
    (D) Pullman strike
    (E) State "right-to-work" laws

17. All of the following were associated with the period from 1901 to 1929 EXCEPT

    (A) U.S. Department of Labor established
    (B) Pure Food and Drug Act passed
    (C) Sherman Antitrust Act passed
    (D) Clayton Antitrust Act passed
    (E) Anthracite coal strike led by John Mitchell

18. All of the following were associated with the period since 1929 EXCEPT

    (A) Formation of the CIO
    (B) Molly Maguires most active
    (C) Sit-down strike at General Motors
    (D) Taft-Hartley Act passed
    (E) Wagner-Connery Act enacted

19. All of the following is *provided* for by the Taft-Hartley Act EXCEPT

    (A) Unions are made subject to suit for breach of contract.
    (B) Employers are made subject to suit for breach of contract.
    (C) Union officials must take an oath that they are not members of the Communist party.
    (D) Management officials bargaining with unions must take an oath that they are not members of the Communist party.
    (E) An injunction can be obtained to postpone a strike for 80 days.

Questions 20-22 are based on the following map. Use the map and your knowledge of history to answer each of the questions.

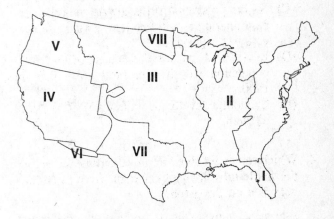

20. Which item represents the largest territory acquired from Great Britain?

    (A) II   (D) V
    (B) III   (E) VII
    (C) IV

21. Of those named below, which U.S. territory was acquired last?

    (A) Florida
    (B) Gadsden Purchase
    (C) Mexican Cession
    (D) Oregon
    (E) Texas

22. Which of the following is true about United States' acquisition of the territories shown in this map?

    (A) V was purchased from Russia by Secretary of State William Seward
    (B) I and II were won from Great Britain in the American Revolution
    (C) I and III were purchased from Spain
    (D) I and IV were ceded by Mexico
    (E) II and IV were won by force of arms

23. Which tariff bill protected scores, perhaps hundreds, of infant manufacturing establishments in the United States?

    (A) Tariff of 1816   (B) Tariff of 1833

(C) Tariff of 1838   (E) Tariff of 1930
(D) Tariff of 1890

24. Which tariff bill resulted in massive foreign retaliation against American protectionism?

(A) Tariff of 1824   (D) Tariff of 1913
(B) Tariff of 1833   (E) Tariff of 1930
(C) Tariff of 1890

25. Which tariff clearly illustrated for the first time the sharp sectional cleavage on the tariff issue between the South and the Northeast?

(A) Tariff of 1816   (D) Tariff of 1890
(B) Tariff of 1824   (E) Tariff of 1930
(C) Tariff of 1833

26. When the United States' frontier settlement first reached the Native American tribes of the Great Plains, these tribes had undergone major social and political changes that had been brought about by the introduction of

(A) gunpowder   (D) horses
(B) iron tools   (E) liquor
(C) Christianity

27. An important immediate result of the American Revolution was that it

(A) turned attention away from Europe to internal problems
(B) strengthened the doctrine of nationalism over states' rights
(C) further developed the American doctrine of isolationism
(D) accelerated the trend toward the abolition of entail and the law of primogeniture
(E) improved American commerce with foreign nations

28. One reason it was difficult for a President before Clinton to cooperate with reformers who wished to limit "pork barrel" legislation is that earlier Presidents lacked the power to

(A) veto individual items in an appropriation bill
(B) make proposals that infringe on the power of the House of Representatives to introduce appropriation bills
(C) return any appropriation bill with a veto
(D) confer with the Director of the Budget on proposed expenditures

(E) have members of the Executive branch testify before a Senate committee after the bill has passed the House

29. Which statement was NOT used by the British to justify taxing the colonies after 1763?

(A) The British debt had increased as a result of the French and Indian War.
(B) There were heavy administrative expenses associated with maintaining the empire.
(C) The colonies should contribute to the expenses involved in providing for their defense.
(D) The colonies had representation in Parliament.
(E) Taxes were uniform throughout the empire.

30. Considered in its modern meaning, there was no such thing as a labor problem in the American colonies because

(A) there was no wage-earning class as such
(B) wages were good
(C) there were many skilled workers
(D) a steady stream of cheap immigrant labor was available
(E) slavery existed throughout the colonies

31. One reason for the development of the system of indenture employed in the early colonial period was

(A) a desire to reduce the traffic in slaves
(B) Parliament's refusal to allow skilled craftspeople to emigrate
(C) the lack of trained domestic help on the large estates
(D) the desire to assist religious refugees
(E) the scarcity of labor in the colonies

32. The major reason Napoleon decided to sell Louisiana to the United States was that he

(A) feared he could not retain Louisiana if France became involved in a war with England
(B) wished to placate the United States because of its loss of the "right of deposit"
(C) believed such a sale would provide a maritime rival for England in future years
(D) expected the addition of western territory would ultimately divide the United States into two separate nations
(E) feared he could not hold Louisiana as the result of his loss of Haiti

33. The Articles of Confederation provided that

    (A) each state have one vote in Congress
    (B) the Chief Executive be responsible to Congress
    (C) Congress consist of two houses
    (D) members of Congress be elected directly by qualified males
    (E) a unanimous vote by Congress be required to pass a law

34. In the United States the idea of a "fixed" or rigid Constitution emerged most directly from

    (A) the writings of Thomas Paine
    (B) the theories set forth by John Dickinson in his "Letters from a Farmer"
    (C) the experience under the Articles of Confederation
    (D) Massachusetts' colonial experience under the Mayflower Compact
    (E) the quarrel between the colonists and parliament in the decade preceding the Revolution

35. Charles A. Beard's interpretation of the Constitutional Convention differed from previous studies in stressing that the delegates were most concerned with designing a government that would

    (A) maintain essential states' rights
    (B) provide for the general welfare
    (C) safeguard property rights
    (D) prevent the rise of a tyrant
    (E) prove the superiority of republican government

36. The ratification of the U.S. Constitution was opposed by the

    (A) people in the frontier farming districts
    (B) clergy and the people in areas where religious interests were strong
    (C) large plantation owners in the South
    (D) financial interests and businessmen of the North
    (E) merchants and commercial classes

37. The LEAST likely source of support for the Federalist party in 1800 would have been

    (A) Providence shipbuilders
    (B) Mohawk Valley farmers
    (C) Boston coppersmiths
    (D) Philadelphia merchants
    (E) New Jersey tradespeople

38. Which contributed LEAST to the downfall of the Federalist party?

    (A) Its policy of neutrality
    (B) Its opposition to extension of the suffrage
    (C) Disagreement within the party
    (D) Obnoxious taxation
    (E) The unpopularity of laws infringing on civil liberties

39. By the end of 1816 the adoption of Federalist principles by the Republicans was so complete that there was no longer a need for the Federalists. Which policy of the Republican party best illustrates this theory?

    (A) Increasing the ad valorem duties on certain goods
    (B) Making internal improvements at federal expense
    (C) Removing Native Americans to reservations
    (D) Granting preemption rights to western lands
    (E) Approving disarmament on the Great Lakes

40. The party platform proposed "adequate protection to American industry, uniform internal improvements by the general government, the settlement by the Supreme Court of constitutional questions"; and it opposed "indiscriminate removal of public office holders." The platform just described expresses the aims of the

    (A) National Republicans in 1832
    (B) Jacksonian Democrats in 1836
    (C) Democrats in 1852
    (D) Populist party in 1896
    (E) Republicans in 1912

41. Which group did NOT include supporters of the new Whig party in the 1830s?

    (A) National Republicans
    (B) States' rights groups and advocates of nullification
    (C) Southern planters and Northern industrialists
    (D) Followers of Senator Thomas H. Benton and his land policy
    (E) Advocates of a system of state banks

42. Which political party advocated policies that were most similar to those of the Populists?

    (A) Whig   (D) Democratic-Republican
    (B) Know-Nothing   (E) Bull Moose
    (C) Republican

Questions 43-51: Five speakers were discussing trends in American history during the period 1820-1840. The following statements were made:

Speaker A: This era was important because it marked the beginning of the rise of the common man in government.

Speaker B: The political changes were important, but even more significant were the humanitarian reforms that occurred.

Speaker C: The most significant historical development was the rise of nationalism.

Speaker D: This period is unique in American history because two opposing movements developed, namely sectionalism and nationalism.

Speaker E: Actually, this was a period of consolidation that provided the basis for "manifest destiny."

43. A sociologist would be most likely to agree with Speaker

    (A) A   (B) B   (C) C   (D) D   (E) E

44. Decisions of the Supreme Court during this period would tend to support Speaker

    (A) A   (B) B   (C) C   (D) D   (E) E

45. Will Rogers would have been most likely to agree with Speaker

    (A) A   (B) B   (C) C   (D) D   (E) E

46. Which speaker is being most general in his interpretation?

    (A) A   (B) B   (C) C   (D) D   (E) E

47. Which can be cited in support of Speaker D?

    (A) The attempt to recharter the Second United States Bank and the Tariff of Abominations
    (B) The movement for extension of slavery and internal improvements at federal expense
    (C) The Monroe Doctrine and the death of the Federalist party
    (D) The *South Carolina Exposition and Protest* and *Gibbons* v. *Ogden*
    (E) The dependence on state banks and liberal immigration laws

48. Andrew Jackson would most likely have agreed with Speaker

    (A) A   (B) B   (C) C   (D) D   (E) E

49. The political defeats suffered by John C. Calhoun in the period 1820-1840 could be used to support the statement of Speaker

    (A) A   (B) B   (C) C   (D) D   (E) E

50. The influence of the frontier, according to Turner, would tend to support Speaker

    (A) A   (B) B   (C) C   (D) D   (E) E

51. Lyman Beecher's contributions can be cited in support of Speaker

    (A) A   (B) B   (C) C   (D) D   (E) E

52. "Cannonism" contributed to the demand of the reformist wing of the Republican party for

    (A) impeaching the Speaker of the House, Joseph Cannon
    (B) providing for the election of the Speaker by party caucus
    (C) convincing Theodore Roosevelt to bring pressure on Speaker Cannon to liberalize his procedures
    (D) compelling Speaker Cannon to resign
    (E) providing for election of the rules committee by the House

53. In the presidential election of 1848, which candidate supported the point of view expressed by the statement, "The free grant of land to actual settlers, in consideration of the expenses they incur in making settlement in the wilderness...is a wise and just measure of public policy"?

    (A) Zachary Taylor   (D) Martin Van Buren
    (B) James G. Birney   (E) Lewis Cass
    (C) John C. Fremont

54. The federal fiscal system that prevailed from 1846 until the Civil War was the

    (A) Independent Treasury System
    (B) National Banking System
    (C) policy of managed currency
    (D) policy of high protective tariff
    (E) regulation of state banks

55. In the 1840s, a characteristic common to both major political parties was their

    (A) inclusion of conflicting class and sectional interests
    (B) concentration on national issues and elections
    (C) use of the legislative caucus to nominate their presidential candidates
    (D) restriction of the spoils system to high salaried positions
    (E) advocacy of "manifest destiny" in their platforms

56. The first United States Bank was most satisfactory to the advocates of

    (A) private control of banking
    (B) a decentralized banking system
    (C) government control of banking
    (D) government ownership of banking
    (E) government policy of laissez faire in banking

57. The prosperity of the United States merchant marine during the 1840s and 1850s was greatly stimulated by the

    (A) invention of the screw propeller
    (B) rapid development of steamships
    (C) reopening of the British West Indies trade
    (D) construction of American clipper ships
    (E) granting of federal subsidies for ship construction

58. During the period 1855-1865, which factor had the LEAST influence on the growth of manufacturing in the United States?

    (A) Increase in exports
    (B) Development of natural resources
    (C) Expansion of the population
    (D) Growth of cities
    (E) The Civil War

59. The growth of trusts in the period following the Civil Was is best explained as the result of the

    (A) application of mass-production techniques to industry
    (B) prevalence of intense competition among producers
    (C) invention of labor-saving devices
    (D) failure of government to outlaw monopolistic practices
    (E) demands of stockholders for lower prices

60. James J. Hill's special contribution to the development of the United States was

    (A) pushing the first railroad to the Pacific Coast
    (B) spreading the ownership of railroads by means of public stock sales
    (C) encouraging people to settle in the area served by his railroad
    (D) convincing Congress that land grants should be offered to railroads to stimulate construction
    (E) providing special freight rates to farmers to encourage railroad usage

61. Which industries did labor find most difficult to organize in the late 19th century?

    (A) Those employing a large proportion of foreign-born workers
    (B) Those engaged in intrastate commerce
    (C) Those providing various fringe benefits for employees
    (D) Those depending on a protective tariff for prosperity
    (E) Those requiring more skilled than unskilled workers

62. Theodore Roosevelt's regard for the interests of labor was shown when he

    (A) secured legislation to outlaw the use of the injunction in labor disputes
    (B) obtained legislation to prohibit child labor in interstate commerce
    (C) secured legislation to restrict immigration
    (D) succeeded in getting a substantial reduction in tariff rates on items that the working class used most
    (E) coerced the anthracite coal operators into arbitrating a labor dispute

63. The major strikes in the latter part of the 19th century show that the

    (A) demands of the workers were limited to the goal of higher wages
    (B) federal government's intervention better served the interests of the employer than those of the unions
    (C) strikers were usually successful in winning their demands
    (D) use of violence in strikes was steadily diminishing
    (E) public was generally unsympathetic toward capital

64. The Coal Strike of 1902 is sometimes considered a turning point in labor history because it marked the first time that

(A) a national union won recognition and the right to bargain collectively
(B) federal intervention resulted in a setback for the employers
(C) the Supreme Court halted the use of troops in an industrial dispute
(D) an industrial dispute was settled to the satisfaction of both labor and management
(E) the nation's economy was seriously crippled by an industrywide strike

65. Which of the following events occurred FIRST?

(A) Beginning of the Berlin Airlift
(B) Truman Doctrine
(C) Formation of NATO
(D) Formation of the Marshall Plan
(E) Potsdam Conference

66. Which of the events in question 65 occurred LAST?

67. In all of the pairs below, the words or phrase in parentheses help to bring into effect, to support, or to make more effective the item with which it is paired EXCEPT

(A) Judicial review of federal laws (John Marshall)
(B) The success of the Democrats in the election of 1844 (the Liberty party)
(C) Seward's "higher law" point of view (Personal Liberty Laws)
(D) The Tweed Ring (*Harper's Weekly* and *The New York Times*)
(E) The slogan, "He kept us out of war" (Sussex Pledge)

68. Which of the following items was FIRST in chronological order?

(A) First law excluding Chinese laborers
(B) Peak of Irish immigration resulting from famine
(C) McCarran-Walter Act
(D) Gentlemen's Agreement
(E) National Origins Formula

69. Which of the items in question 68 was LAST in chronological order?

70. Which of the following acts was FIRST in chronological order?

(A) Wagner-Connery Act
(B) Interstate Commerce Act
(C) Clayton Antitrust Act
(D) Taft-Hartley Act
(E) Sherman-Antitrust Act

71. Which of the acts in question 70 was LAST in chronological order?

Questions 72-76: Five investment brokers were carrying on the following discussion concerning the stock market with special reference to the Jones Corporation:

Speaker *A*: The capital structure of the corporation is weak because the firm is overcapitalized. I also dislike the relationship between income and expenses. I'm buying the debenture bonds.

Speaker *B*: I like the preferred stock because it can't be retired, and the 8 percent rate is better than I can get in a bank.

Speaker *C*: The preferred stock is sound, but I don't like the requirement that the dividend must be paid during the year that it is earned. However, since I think we are going into a bear market, the preferred is my choice.

Speaker *D*: Since we are in a bull market, the common stock is a good buy because it is selling at ten times its earnings.

Speaker *E*: The mortgage bonds are paying a higher rate than the collateral bonds, and I think I'll invest in those.

72. Which speaker is most likely to have information as to the number of shares of stock and the number of bonds the Jones Corporation has outstanding?

(A) *A*   (D) *D*
(B) *B*   (E) *E*
(C) *C*

73. Which speaker would be most likely to engage in short selling?

(A) *A*   (D) *D*
(B) *B*   (E) *E*
(C) *C*

74. Which speaker will be a creditor of the corporation and will have securities backed only by the good-

will, income, reputation, and general assets of the corporation?

(A) A   (D) D
(B) B   (E) E
(C) C

75. If the Federal Reserve bank decreases the rediscount rate and starts to buy up government bonds from individuals, which speaker will benefit most?

(A) A   (D) D
(B) B   (E) E
(C) C

76. If the Jones Corporation liquidates, which speaker will be paid first?

(A) A   (D) D
(B) B   (E) E
(C) C

77. "I disapprove of what you say, but I will defend to the death your right to say it." This statement suggests that the speaker would be most opposed to

(A) media censorship
(B) the right of petition
(C) civil disobedience
(D) formation of monopolies
(E) abortion rights

Questions 78-84 are based on the following map. For the description in each question, select the appropriate location on the map.

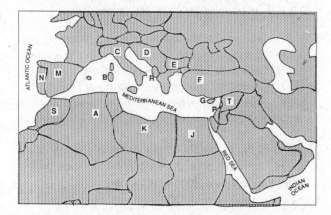

78. This nation, once the heart of the Ottoman Empire, provided air bases for U.S. use during the Gulf War in 1991.

(A) D   (D) T
(B) E   (E) J
(C) F

79. This was the birthplace of Napoleon Bonaparte.

(A) A   (D) D
(B) B   (E) M
(C) C

80. This country became independent in 1962 after a long and bloody revolt against France.

(A) A   (D) M
(B) J   (E) N
(C) K

81. U.S. troops have served as United Nations peacekeepers here in the 1990s civil war in Bosnia.

(A) C   (D) D
(B) R   (E) T
(C) E

82. Once an Italian colony, this country's support of international terrorism led to a U.S. air strike against it in 1986.

(A) S   (D) K
(B) A   (E) J
(C) C

83. This small Middle Eastern country, supported by the United States, has been bitterly opposed by most of the Arab world.

(A) R   (D) P
(B) E   (E) T
(C) G

84. As a reward for making peace with Israel in 1978, this country has received large amounts of U.S. aid.

(A) N   (D) D
(B) M   (E) C
(C) J

85. During the latter half of the 19th century, farmers practiced extensive farming, primarily because

(A) scientific assistance was readily available from agricultural colleges
(B) there was an increase in foreign demand for farm products
(C) the increase in demand for farm products threatened to outstrip production
(D) fertilizers and insecticides were inexpensive
(E) land was readily available

86. Which did NOT contribute to the expansion of farm production from 1870-1890?

    (A) Increase in population
    (B) Liberal land policy
    (C) Transportation subsidies
    (D) Federal loans to agricultural cooperatives
    (E) Establishment of land-grant colleges

87. Which was most responsible for the decline of the Granger movement?

    (A) Organization of the Non-Partisan League
    (B) Supreme Court decision in *Wabash* v. *Illinois*
    (C) Rise of the Populist party
    (D) Passage of the Gold Standard Act of 1900
    (E) Passage of the Resumption Act of 1875

88. State legislation regulating the working hours of women was delayed because

    (A) state legislators felt uniform national legislation was necessary
    (B) the invention of textile machinery decreased the bargaining power of women
    (C) courts interpreted state laws as improper because they limited the rights of women to decide on their own working conditions
    (D) industrialists feared state legislation would pave the way for far more drastic social legislation
    (E) labor unions preferred to get the credit for improving work conditions

89. Why did the United States lag behind many European nations in adopting social legislation?

    (A) The success of welfare capitalism in the United States made social legislation unnecessary.
    (B) Judicial interpretations limited the powers of the federal government in this field.
    (C) The United States lacked national labor parties in the 19th century.
    (D) Utopian philosophers made such a movement unnecessary.
    (E) Trade unions in the United States were weaker than those in Europe.

90. A characteristic of European government insurance plans that had NOT been adopted by the United States by 1960 is provision for

    (A) joint contribution by employers and employees
    (B) government control of the insurance program

    (C) unemployment insurance
    (D) protection against medical expenses incurred from prolonged illness
    (E) financial aid for widows and orphans

91. On the basis of the neutrality legislation in the 1930s, one could generalize that Congress acted on the assumption that the best way to keep out of war was to

    (A) seek allies among nations of similar aims
    (B) discourage aggressors by threatening economic reprisals
    (C) maintain superior land and naval strength
    (D) restrict loans to and trade with belligerents
    (E) support international organizations designed to prevent war

92. The neutrality policy of the United States tended to favor

    (A) France in 1793
    (B) Mexico in 1835
    (C) Imperial Germany in 1915
    (D) Nazi Germany in 1937
    (E) Loyalist Spain in 1937

93. Congressional legislation of the 1930s reflected an abandonment of America's historic position on

    (A) the Open Door policy
    (B) the Good Neighbor policy
    (C) the Monroe Doctrine
    (D) freedom of the seas
    (E) entangling alliances

94. Among the foreign policy successes for which President George Bush could justly take credit were all of the following EXCEPT

    (A) Start of the Arab-Israeli peace talks
    (B) End of the Cold War
    (C) Ouster of Iraqi troops from Kuwait
    (D) Ouster of Manuel Noriega from Panama
    (E) Aid to starving victims of civil war in Somalia

95. President Franklin D. Roosevelt's decision in 1933 to recognize the Soviet Union was probably LEAST influenced by

    (A) a need to increase U.S. exports
    (B) the rise of militarism in Italy and Germany
    (C) Japanese expansion policies in the Pacific
    (D) a changing attitude on the part of the American public toward the Soviet Union
    (E) the danger of a Russian-German treaty of alliance

ANSWER KEY: DIAGNOSTIC TEST

1.	B	20.	A	39.	A	58.	A	77.	A
2.	E	21.	B	40.	A	59.	B	78.	C
3.	A	22.	E	41.	E	60.	C	79.	B
4.	C	23.	A	42.	E	61.	A	80.	A
5.	C	24.	E	43.	B	62.	E	81.	D
6.	A	25.	B	44.	C	63.	B	82.	D
7.	E	26.	D	45.	A	64.	B	83.	D
8.	B	27.	D	46.	E	65.	E	84.	C
9.	C	28.	A	47.	D	66.	C	85.	E
10.	C or E	29.	E	48.	A	67.	D	86.	D
11.	E or C	30.	A	49.	C	68.	B	87.	B
12.	A	31.	E	50.	A	69.	C	88.	C
13.	E	32.	E	51.	B	70.	B	89.	B
14.	A	33.	A	52.	E	71.	D	90.	D
15.	A	34.	E	53.	D	72.	A	91.	D
16.	E	35.	C	54.	A	73.	C	92.	D
17.	C	36.	A	55.	A	74.	A	93.	D
18.	B	37.	B	56.	A	75.	D	94.	B
19.	D	38.	B	57.	D	76.	E	95.	E

ANALYSIS CHART: DIAGNOSTIC TEST

Taking diagnostic and practice tests and studying and understanding the explanations afterward are important steps in becoming acquainted with typical SAT II: United States History Subject Test questions and successful approaches to the questions. Another benefit of practice tests is analyzing and understanding the kinds of errors you are making, thus enabling you to work to minimize them. For instance, if a very high percentage of your incorrect answers is due to careless errors or misreading the problem, perhaps you are working too fast and you should slow your pace accordingly. Conversely, if you find that you aren't completing a number of questions because of lack of time, you may need to increase your speed. If your incorrect answers are due primarily to lack of knowledge, then a careful rereading of the appropriate material in this book may be in order.

This kind of analysis of the Diagnostic Test will enable you to identify your particular weaknesses and thus remedy them.

It is important that you read every answer explanation, even though your answer was correct.

If after reading the explanation of the correct answer, you still do not fully understand the reasoning, or if you want to study that topic more thoroughly, refer to the Index or Table of Contents of this book to find a further discussion of the particular subject.

CHARTING YOUR ANSWERS

Era	Number of Questions	Number Right	Number Wrong	Number Unanswered
Pre-Columbian to 1789: 5-8, 27, 29-36	13			
1790 to 1898: 10, 11, 15, 16, 21-23, 26, 37-41, 43-51, 53-61, 63, 65-68, 70, 71, 73-75, 77, 78, 84-87	47			
1899 to present: 1-4, 12, 17-20, 28, 42, 52, 62, 64, 69, 72, 80-83, 89-91, 93-95	26			
Cross period: 13, 14, 24, 25, 42, 79, 92	7			
Nonchronological: 9, 21, 88	3			

FINDING THE REASONS FOR INCORRECT ANSWERS

Be sure to check the answer explanations before completing the following chart.

Era	Number Wrong	Lack of Knowledge	Misunderstand Problem	Careless Error	Not Answered
Pre-Columbian to 1789					
1790 to 1898					
1899 to present					
Nonchronological					

ANSWER EXPLANATIONS: DIAGNOSTIC TEST

1. **B** The cartoon is titled "Drag Race." The baby carriage represents world population growth, and it is moving faster than the supermarket wagon, which represents increasing world food production. The carriage also contains two babies, not just one.

2. **E** In recent years, drought in Africa south of the Sahara has caused famine in many developing nations.

3. **A** The graph shows a marked decline in the percentage of rural population and increases in the percentage of Americans in both inner cities and suburbs since 1900. As suburbs of large cities continue to grow, the unplanned urban sprawl may require the kind of government programs to meet the problems of deteriorating areas in the suburbs that have already been used in inner cities.

4. **C** Metropolitan areas consist of the largest cities and their immediately surrounding areas. These face the problem of obtaining money to carry on their usual functions, as well as special urban programs (e.g., urban renewal). As many substantial taxpayers move out and as poorer families with many problems move into the metropolitan areas, local tax receipts are inadequate to meet the need. The federal government, as receiver of the lion's share of taxes, is increasingly being called upon by city, county, and state governments to assume a larger share of the burden of metropolitan expenses, including the costs of welfare and employment programs.

5. **C** The election of the Virginia House of Burgesses in 1619 marked the beginning of representative government in America and established the idea of popularly elected colonial assemblies.

6. **A** Delaware was first settled by Swedes in 1638. They called their colony New Sweden.

7. **E** Those acts, which were harmful to colonial trade, were not enforced. Thus, salutary neglect was beneficial both to England and to its American colonies. The picture changed after the French and Indian War.

8. **B** In the post-Revolutionary period, each of the thirteen states erected tariff walls against imports from any other state, creating a condition where there was little trade for anyone. Political and business leaders had a meeting in 1785 at Mount Vernon, where Virginia and Maryland delegates hoped to abolish or modify tariffs. Since these two states by themselves could do nothing effective, a meeting was planned for Annapolis, Maryland. There, five states met about the depressed interstate commerce. Then a third meeting was arranged, which turned out to be the Philadelphia Convention of 1787.

9. **C** The Constitution expressly prohibits both national and state governments from passing ex post facto laws—in Article I, Section 9, Clause 3, and Section 10, Clause 1, respectively.

10. **C and E** There was no organized opposition to paying the foreign debt, which was owed chiefly to friendly nations, France and Holland. The Pinckney Treaty with Spain in 1795 gave the United States better terms than expected, including free navigation of the Mississippi River and the right of deposit at New Orleans. That permitted Americans to ship goods down the river on flat boats for transshipment by sailing vessels to foreign ports.

12. **A** A United States colonel in the Corps of Engineers, George W. Goethals was in charge of constructing the Panama Canal.

13. **E** George Norris was a 20th-century United States Senator from Nebraska, who was important in promoting the Tennessee Valley Authority in the 1930s. Each of the other four choices was an inventor.

14. **A** Thomas E. Dewey was the New York Governor who ran against President Truman and lost in 1948. Each of the others was a United States Secretary of State.

15. **A** The American Federation of Labor was organized by Samuel Gompers in 1881.

16. **E** The Taft-Hartley labor law of 1947 gave states the right to pass "right-to-work" laws permitting workers to hold a job without being required to join a union. Such laws outlaw the union shop and are found mostly in some states of the South and Midwest.

17. **C** The Sherman Antitrust Act, the nation's oldest, was passed by Congress in 1890.

18. **B** The Molly Maguires were a secret group of disgruntled coal miners who took part in the bloody fighting in the Pennsylvania anthracite fields in the 1870s.

19. **D** Union officials in the bargaining process must take such an oath; management is not required to do so, under that law.

20. **A**   This was the area between the original thirteen states and the Mississippi River, ceded to the United States by the Treaty of Paris, 1783, following the American Revolution.

21. **B**   This strip of land south of the Gila River in Arizona and New Mexico was to provide a very favorable route for a southern transcontinental railroad. It was purchased from Mexico in 1853.

22. **E**   Area II was referred to in the explanation of question 20, above. Area IV was the Mexican Cession, yielded by Mexico under the treaty ending the Mexican War in 1848.

23. **A**   The Tariff of 1816 was needed to protect cottons, woolens, iron, and other manufactured goods stimulated by the War of 1812. It was part of Henry Clay's "American system," which also favored internal improvements for the West and the South at federal expense.

24. **E**   The Hawley-Smoot Tariff of 1930 pushed protection to a new high and brought protests from importers, bankers, and others. A petition signed by a thousand economists urged President Hoover to veto it. He did not. Foreign reaction was swift and negative, as 25 nations put up tariff barriers against American goods, and our foreign trade was cut in half.

25. **B**   This tariff drove up the prices of manufactured goods that Southerners had to buy, since the South had little manufacturing.

26. **D**   The use of horses made it easier for the nomadic Plains Indians to hunt for buffalo, to move from place to place, to carry supplies, and to defend themselves.

27. **D**   Those undemocratic practices were a holdover from European feudalism. Entail prevented the division of an estate, and primogeniture was the right of the first-born son to inherit his father's lands.

28. **A**   Clinton was the first President to have available and to use the **line item veto.** It became law as part of a complex Taxpayer Relief Act of 1997. The item veto permits the President to eliminate, within five days, specific measures from legislation he has signed.

29. **E**   This statement is clearly false, while each of the others was part of the British rationale for ending salutary neglect and imposing new taxes.

30. **A**   There was no laboring class. Each blacksmith's helper and clerk in a general store aspired to own his own shop one day. Only with the creation of the factory system did a permanent laboring class develop in Europe and in America.

31. **E**   The voluntary indentured servants sold themselves—actually, their labor—for a period of from three to seven years to shipmasters or emigration brokers in payment of passage to America. Involuntary indentured servants were usually debtors, vagrants, or criminals deported by the courts in England—"His Majesty's Seven-Year Passengers."

32. **E**   Napoleon's action was partly a result of a successful slave revolt in Haiti against French control, which upset his dreams of an American empire, and partly his need for funds to finance the expected renewal of war with Britain.

33. **A**   The voting scheme emphasized the equality and independence of the states in their loose union.

34. **E**   Fearing government, especially a national government, the framers of the Constitution designed a national government that could handle the tasks facing the nation but that would not be able to seize or wield too much power. To check national power, they depended on these two devices: (1) fair and free elections, so that nobody could take elective office unless acceptable to a majority of the voters, and (2) an elaborate system of balancing power. In addition, the fixed Constitution was to be flexible, to admit amendments needed to meet new demands.

35. **C**   In his influential work *An Economic Interpretation of the Constitution*, Beard contends that people's political behavior reflects their broad economic interests.

36. **A**   A map of Anti-Federalist sentiment shows that feeling prevalent in the western areas of New York State and in Pennsylvania, Virginia, the Carolinas, Tennessee, and most of Kentucky in 1787-1788.

37. **B**   The Mohawk Valley lies west of Albany, New York, in the area described in answer to question 36.

38. **B**   This policy coincided with that of the Anti-Federalists.

39. **A**   A protective tariff was one of Hamilton's original financial programs. The Tariff of 1816 was a protective tariff proposed by the Democratic-Republicans and supported nationwide.

40. **A**   Note that two points are directed against Jackson: one over his clash with Chief Justice Marshall about Indian removal in Georgia; and the other over his right to remove political appointees—"throw the rascals out."

41. **E** They would vote for Jackson and the Democrats. Jackson withdrew federal deposits from and opposed recharter of the Second Bank of the United States. He put government money in state banks ("pet banks").

42. **E** Theodore Roosevelt's Progressive party, or Bull Moose party, of 1912 was in the mainstream of progressivism, asking for more direct democracy through such means as initiative and referendum, conservation of natural resources, votes for women, and an inheritance tax.

43. **B** As one who studies the development of human society, the sociologist would be most interested in the reform movements of the period.

44. **C** Important Supreme Court decisions during this period strengthened the power of the national government.

45. **A** Will Rogers, the cowboy philosopher, was America's favorite humorist in the 1920s and 1930s. He won Americans' hearts by gently mocking their prejudices. He epitomized the common man.

46. **E** The speaker gives no examples of what "provided the basis" for his generalization.

47. **D** The South's fear of becoming a permanent political minority in Congress gave rise to Calhoun's *South Carolina Exposition and Protest*, which supported states' rights and nullification. The Supreme Court decision in *Gibbons* v. *Ogden* was an example of developing nationalism. In it, the Court ruled that Congress alone, not the states, had the right to regulate interstate commerce.

48. **A** This was the era of Jacksonian Democracy. Jackson favored having all elected officials, including the President, directly responsible to the people. He also believed that any intelligent person was capable of holding any government office.

49. **C** Only choices C and D apply. Between them, nationalism helps explain Calhoun's defeat on the tariffs of 1824, 1828, and 1832, and his resignation as Jackson's Vice-President. See also the explanation of question 47.

50. **A** Frederick Jackson Turner's 1893 address, "The Significance of the Frontier in American History," showed that the ability of frontier farmers to clear the land, tend their crops, and protect their families was more important than their prior social standing or wealth.

51. **B** Lyman Beecher was an early 19th-century Protestant minister and preacher of temperance. His children, Harriet Beecher Stowe, author of *Uncle Tom's Cabin*, and Henry Ward Beecher, one of the great speakers of his time, were champions of the antislavery and women's rights movements.

52. **E** Joseph G. Cannon was Speaker of the House of Representatives from 1903 to 1911. He ruled the House dictatorially in the interest of Old Guard Republicans until a bill reforming House rules broke his power.

53. **D** In 1848, Northern Democrats who favored the Wilmot Proviso joined with "Conscience Whigs" and members of the Liberty party to form the Free Soil party and nominate Martin Van Buren for President. The party slogan was "free soil, free speech, free labor, and free men."

54. **A** The failure to recharter the second Bank of the United States ended the attempt to control the currency by means of a central bank. Van Buren proposed that the government establish an independent treasury to care for its own funds, to divorce the government from the business of banking, and, by paying only in specie, to lessen the demand for bank notes.

55. **A** Both the Democratic party and the Whig party were severely divided over the slavery issue. See also the explanation of answer 53.

56. **A** The Bank of the United States, a central bank, was established by Congress in 1791. It was privately owned and managed, 80 percent of its stock being reserved for private individuals and the remaining 20 percent owned by the government.

57. **D** The clipper ships—tall, graceful, and built to carry cargoes of high value and small volume—were the fastest oceangoing sailing vessels built at that time. They were later replaced by steamships.

58. **A** Wartime conditions are not conducive to the growth of exports. Large additional amounts of food, fiber, and manufactures were then demanded by the military for the Civil War. The North blockaded Southern ports to prevent the export of cotton to Europe.

59. **B** The purpose of the trusts was to eliminate competition and maximize profits. The holders of controlling shares in competing firms would turn over their shares to a group of trustees in exchange for trust certificates. The shareholders gave up their control of the companies in exchange for the profits they expected from the elimination of competition.

60. **C**   Creator of the Great Northern Railway Company, Hill started to build it in 1879, without federal grants or land subsidies. Financing his railroad would depend on encouraging settlers to come to the Northwest as quickly as possible. He offered them free transportation, low-interest loans, inexpensive tools, and farm machinery if they would settle in the region.

61. **A**   Differences in language, religion, and customs among the immigrants made it hard to organize and join them into an effective labor union. Also, many foreign workers were unskilled, and labor unions during the 19th century were successful only in organizing skilled workers, such as cigar workers and machinists.

62. **E**   In May 1902, 140,000 Pennsylvania anthracite coal workers went on strike to protest working conditions. When the mine operators refused to meet with United Mine Workers' representatives, President Roosevelt intervened, threatening to seize the mines.

63. **B**   The Sherman Antitrust Act of 1890 was used to deny labor unions the right to strike, as in the Pullman strike of 1894. Unions were treated as conspiracies in restraint of interstate commerce, injunctions were issued to prevent striking, and union leaders were jailed for violating such injunctions.

64. **B**   As a result of arbitration, the miners received a 10 percent raise and a few other improvements. However, for the people of 1902, the important point was that the federal government had played a major role in bringing about a settlement of a strike, rather than joining the fight to assure victory to one side, as in the Pullman strike of 1894. See the answer to question 63.

65. **E**   Of the items listed, only the Potsdam Conference of July 1945 took place before the end of World War II. There, President Truman, Marshal Joseph Stalin, and British prime minister Clement Atlee met to draw up details of the occupation and administration of defeated Germany, while calling upon Japan to surrender.

66. **C**   In 1947 the United States formulated the Marshall Plan to help rebuild war-torn western Europe, and began to provide economic and military aid to Greece and Turkey through the Truman Doctrine. The Berlin airlift was begun in 1948, and NATO (the North Atlantic Treaty Organization) was formed in 1949.

67. **D**   The two publications attacked the corruption of "Boss" William Tweed and his Tammany Hall political organization that cost New York City several hundred million dollars in the 1860s and 1870s.

68. **B**   The failure of the Irish potato crop in the 1840s brought famine to that land and millions of immigrants to the United States. Chinese laborers were first prohibited by the Chinese Exclusion Act of 1882 because they supposedly undercut American wage rates. Japanese immigration was ended by the 1907 Gentlemen's Agreement, and the National Origins Formula of 1929 further restricted immigration from southern and eastern Europe.

69. **C**   The 1952 McCarran-Walter Act continued the National Origins system and extended a small quota to the Far East and Pacific areas.

70. **B**   The Interstate Commerce Act of 1887 was the earliest federal legislation to regulate the railroads or any business activity. The Sherman Antitrust Act passed in 1890, the Clayton Act in 1914.

71. **D**   The Taft-Hartley Act of 1947 was supposed to correct the pro-labor bias of the Wagner-Connery (National Labor Relations) Act of 1935.

72. **A**   Such information would be necessary for the speaker to discuss "overcapitalization."

73. **C**   One is most likely to sell short in a bear market of declining securities prices. In selling short, a speculator tries to profit from a decline in the price of given securities. He sells borrowed securities and when their price has fallen, buys them to return them to the lender.

74. **A**   Every bondholder is a creditor. This question describes the backing of debenture bonds, which excludes more specific property as security.

75. **D**   Such action by the Federal Reserve will increase the amount of money and credit in circulation, generating inflationary pressure. Prices of common stock tend to rise during a period of inflation, and a bull market is one in which securities prices are rising.

76. **E**   As a *creditor* (as explained in answer 74), the bondholder must receive the principal and interest on his investment before any stockholders can be paid.

77. **A**   The speaker urges freedom of speech and of the press.

78. **C**   Turkey was an ally of the United States in the Gulf War against Iraqi aggression.

79. **B**   Sardinia, once Italian, then French, was the place.

80. **A**   Beginning in 1954, the largely Muslim population of Algeria began guerrilla warfare to win independence from France.

81. **D**   Yugoslavia has been splintered in a civil war and ethnic cleansing involving Christian Serbs, Christian Croats, and Moslem Bosnians.

82. **D**   Libya, led by Colonel Muammar Quadaffi, became a training ground for the most extreme Arab terrorists, and shielded known murderers from international justice.

83. **D**   Israel has been at war with its Arab neighbors from the time of its declaration of independence from British control in 1948. Only Egypt has made peace with the state of Israel. In 1993, Israel and the PLO signed accords recognizing each other.

84. **C**   President Anwar Sadat of Egypt and Prime Minister Menachem Begin of Israel signed the *Camp David Accords* with President Carter in September, 1978.

85. **E**   The frontier was available until about 1890. The other choices are flagrantly wrong.

86. **D**   Such federal assistance was not available until the 20th century.

87. **B**   This 1886 ruling invalidated many of the Granger laws, by stating that where railroads and other forms of commerce ran across state lines, the states could not restrict them. The decision reversed *Munn* v. *Illinois* and led Congress to pass the 1887 Interstate Commerce Act.

88. **C**   While writing decisions as if protecting the rights of women to freedom of contract, judges were actually legitimizing the greed of employers and ignoring the health consequences to a nation. See also the explanation of question 89.

89. **B**   In *Lochner* v. *New York*, the Supreme Court in 1905 held unconstitutional a New York law limiting bakers to a ten-hour day and a sixty-hour week. In condemning a supposed violation of liberty under the 14th Amendment, Justice Peckham used the words "unreasonable, unnecessary and arbitrary" in striking down the law in question. An Oregon law to keep women from working more than ten hours a day in factories and laundries met a similar fate.

90. **D**   Such "socialized medicine" was widely debated in this country after World War II until Congress passed the Medicare Act in 1965, providing medical care for the aged under Social Security. In addition, Congress provided for Medicaid, or state aid to the indigent. Also, private medical and hospital insurance plans have been widely used by the rest of the population.

91. **D**   The Neutrality Acts of 1935 and 1937 placed an embargo on the sale or transportation of munitions to belligerents and forbade loans to nations at war.

92. **D**   By 1937, the United States government had secret information showing that the Axis powers were bent on war. Yet, American isolationism simply reinforced British and French appeasement. That led President Franklin D. Roosevelt to call on our nation to help cure the "epidemic of world lawlessness" by joining with other powers to "quarantine" aggressor nations.

93. **D**   The neutrality laws of the 1930s prohibited travel by American citizens on the ships of nations at war.

94. **B**   The major reason for the end of the 45 years of international competition and conflict between the communist states and the western powers was the breakup of the Soviet bloc of eastern European nations, followed by the dissolution of the Soviet Union into 15 independent nations.

95. **E**   Nazi Germany under Hitler bitterly denounced communism and persecuted communists at home. Soviet Russia under Stalin reciprocated those feelings.

PART TWO

REVIEW OF AMERICAN HISTORY

PRE–COLUMBIAN HISTORY
America and Americans

Our Country's Name

A reasonable beginning for the study of American history is an inquiry into the meaning of *America* and *Americans*. From the Rio Grande and the Gulf of Mexico to the Canadian border, more than 200,000,000 people think of the United States as being America. Some people of Central and South America are mildly irritated when citizens of the United States call themselves Americans; it suggests to them that the United States is considered by its own people to be the only nation of importance in the Americas. Of course, we Americans have no such idea in mind; we have merely fallen into a pattern of terminology. Two of our best loved patriotic songs, "America" and "God Bless America," are about the United States. To us, American history begins in 1492 when Columbus landed at San Salvador (Watling Island) in the Bahamas. In 1499 and 1501 Amerigo Vespucci, an Italian explorer (he would have called himself a merchant of Florence), sailed along the north and east coasts of South America and discovered it to be a continent. This Florentine merchant was employed by the king of Portugal. A professor in Lorraine, Martin Waldseemüller, helped make a map of the New World. This German professor put the name, America, on the map. Now we have a North, a South, and a Central America. The origin of the name of our country is mixed enough to make it "typically American." The exact meaning of America can be determined only in the context in which it is used.

Migrations from Asia

Now, how about Americans? Some 50,000 to 100,000 years ago, people from Asia crossed from Siberia to Alaska over a land bridge that existed then. On a clear day, land is still continuously visible as one crosses the Bering Strait. Today's maps show Uelen in Siberia and Wales in Alaska on opposite sides of the strait. Just about midway between them is Diomede Island, which rises over 1,500 feet above the sea. Alaska offered abundant supplies of salmon and seal. Some scientists believe that the earliest migrations occurred during a cold period when the polar ice cap extended southward, causing a receding of the waters to form a land bridge from Siberia to Alaska. We can guess why these people left Siberia for Alaska. Hunger, due to a prolonged period of poor hunting, pressure from hostile tribes, changes in climate, or just the restless meanderings of people could have been the reasons. From Alaska these people from Asia spread in all directions. When Columbus arrived, the Native Americans were distributed throughout the Americas. It is thought that the first Asians to cross to Alaska were Mongols, but the migrations covered so long a period of time and the types of Indians and Eskimos are so varied that it is probable that several kinds of Asians crossed the Bering Strait.

Today's scholars most interested in the origins of human life in the Americas and most curious about these very early settlers are the *ethnologists*, the *anthropologists*, and the *archeologists*. They are the experts. Ethnologists study races and groups of people to determine their distinctive characteristics and their relationships to one another. Anthropologists study humans; they delve into their physical and psychological characteristics. The archeologists uncover history by seeking buried relics of the remote past. These authorities support the conclusion that nowhere in the Americas did civilization begin. The Americas have no true natives. All the people who ever lived in the Western Hemisphere have been descended from people whose origins go back to one of the "cradles of civilization," such as the Nile Valley, the Tigris-Euphrates Valley, the Ganges-Indus Valley, and the Hwang Ho Valley—or possibly other cradles yet to be found. From the historical view, this makes Columbus a recent arrival. He started a new stream of people to America, this time primarily from Europe. That Columbus started such a continuous movement of peoples gives him undisputed rank as first among the explorers, and justly the most renowned.

The Native American

When he made his first voyage, Christopher Columbus thought he had reached the part of Asia then known as the Indies, and he called the people he found there "**Indians.**" Since most of the "Indians" had no form of writing, they lacked the written records to explain their history. We now know quite a bit about their past through the scientific studies of anthropologists and archeologists who find and examine ancient remains such as human bones, artifacts (tools and ornaments), and the bones of animals.

As small groups of these earliest Americans migrated from Siberia to Alaska, they walked eastward in search of game. They were nomadic hunters who had spears tipped by stone points, and spear throwers to help them throw the spears farther. They probably knew how to make a fire, which kept them warm and cooked their food. We also think they knew how to tame dogs to help them hunt.

Over the centuries, bands of hunters spread through North America and down into South America. Their cultures became more complex as they invented the bow and arrow and many other specialized tools. They learned to farm, and then formed settled communities. They domesticated corn, which became the most important staple crop for all Indians and grew other native American plants, including pumpkins, other squash, potatoes, beans, peppers, tomatoes, cotton, and tobacco. Some groups developed the complicated arts of basketry, pottery making, and weaving.

Some groups of Native Americans created advanced cultures of great wealth and power. These included the **Aztecs**, who built cities and huge stone pyramids in Mexico; the **Maya**, architects and astronomers of Central America who developed a form of writing (*quipus*); and the **Incas** of Peru, whose complex system of roads stretched for hundreds of miles through the Andes.

By the time the Europeans arrived, there were anywhere from 8 to 75 million Native Americans in the Americas. They spoke 1200 different languages, in more native language families than were present in all the rest of the world combined. Native Americans are usually classified (grouped) by language, by tribe, or by culture areas. The descriptions that follow provide some information about the culture groups of the Native Americans of the United States.

The Eastern Woodlands Native Americans

The area of the Eastern Woodlands extended from the east coast of the United States to the Mississippi River. The Iroquois tribes, known as the **Five Nations**, controlled the Northeast. That group included the **Mohawk**, the **Oneida**, the **Onondaga**, the **Cayuga**, and the **Seneca**. Major tribes of the Southeast included the **Cherokee, Chickasaw, Choctaw, Creek**, and **Natchez.** Tribes that lived around the Great Lakes were the **Fox, Illinois, Menominee, Miami, Potawatomi, Sauk, Shawnee, Winnebago, Chippewa**, and **Cree**. Most Woodlands Native Americans hunted the game that was plentiful in the forests, and they also did some farming. They had a simple tribal organization and shared many similar religious beliefs.

Some of the Native Americans of the eastern United States were **Mound Builders**, who built extensive bur-ial and temple mounds. They lived mainly in the Ohio and Mississippi valleys, were primarily farmers, had a more complicated political organization, and created fine arts and crafts.

The Plains Native Americans

The **Plains Native Americans**, such as the **Cheyenne**, the **Crow**, and the **Sioux**, lived on the Great Plains—a dry, almost treeless area extending from the Mississippi River to the Rocky Mountains and from Canada to Mexico. Few lived in this vast grassland area before the arrival of the Spaniards, who brought the horse and the gun to the region in the 1600s. On horseback, the Plains Native Americans, who had always been hunters, could follow and take what they needed from the great herds of buffalo. Buffalo meat became their main food, and the buffalo skins were used for clothing, bedding, and tepees. The bones and horns were made into tools and utensils, and dry buffalo manure was used for fuel. Forced westward by the advancing white settlers, other tribes adopted the Plains way of life. The **Apache, Arapaho, Blackfeet**, and **Comanche** were among the late arrivals.

Native Americans of the Southwest

The **Pueblo** tribes, most of whom descended from the early **Anasazi** Native Americans, had one of the most highly developed civilizations in North America. The Pueblo lived in villages and farmed along rivers that provided enough water to irrigate their crops. The word **"Pueblo,"** the Spanish word for "village," refers both to the people and to their communities. The **Hopi** and **Zuni** are two of the Pueblo peoples. The pueblo dwellings found in New Mexico and Arizona were built with wooden frames covered with stone and adobe (sun-dried brick of clay and straw) and might contain hundreds of rooms. Two groups of nomadic hunters later entered the Southwest. The **Apache** plundered the Pueblo, while the **Navajo** settled down and imitated the arts of the Pueblo. Navajo weaving became world-famous.

The Basin-Plateau Native Americans

The home of the **Shoshone, Bannock, Ute**, and **Paiute** was the Great Basin between the Rockies on the east and the Cascade Mountains and the Sierra Nevada Mountains on the west. The land is poor and too dry for farming. It includes Nevada, Utah, southern Idaho, and western Wyoming. The Plateau is a high, level tableland north of the Great Basin, stretching from

Canada down through northern Idaho and eastern Washington and Oregon. Two great rivers furnish life-giving water: the Columbia and the Snake. There was salmon in the big rivers and game on the Plateau. Mostly, the Basin-Plateau Native American Indians were food-gatherers, picking berries, nuts, seeds, and roots. The Plateau tribes included the **Cayuse, Coeur d'Alene, Flathead**, and **Nez Perce**. They had to move about constantly, usually in small bands, in search of food.

Native Americans of the Northwest Coast

The **Tlingit, Haida, Kwakiutl, Nootka**, and **Chinook** were among the tribes living along the Pacific Coast from southern Alaska to northern California. Blessed with natural resources, they had fish and wood in abundance. The ocean and rivers provided salmon, shellfish, halibut, cod, herring, and smelt. Forests of cedar grew down to the water's edge. There were also groves of alder, hemlock, spruce, pine, and yew. Northwest crafts were very beautiful. The Native Americans of the Northwest carved masks, drums, and animal figures of wood for use at religious ceremonies. They made fine hunting equipment and canoes. They built sturdy houses and large totem poles. The totems and door posts were decorated with carved and painted designs of fish and animals.

The California Native Americans

California's mild climate and abundance of food attracted many tribes. They hunted small game, fished in the rivers, and collected wild plants, seeds, and nuts. The area had one of the largest Native American populations in North America. At about the time of the American Revolution, Spanish explorers, soldiers, and missionaries began moving up from Mexico. Spanish missionaries established many Roman Catholic missions in California. They tried to convert the Native Americans to Christianity and to teach them farming and cattle-raising. By 1800 most of the southern California Native Americans lived on the missions, which had become ranches. The missions broke up in the 1830s after Mexico became independent of Spain, and many Native Americans settled in the mountains. In the northern area there was conflict with the United States government after the Civil War, when the Native Americans refused to be moved onto reservations. The Modoc and the Nez Perce Wars of the 1870s brought a tragic end to a way of life that was in harmony with nature.

(For further information, you may wish to read *Indians of North America* by Paula A. Franklin, published by David McKay Co., New York, 1979.)

Indians of the United States and Canada:
Major Culture Groups

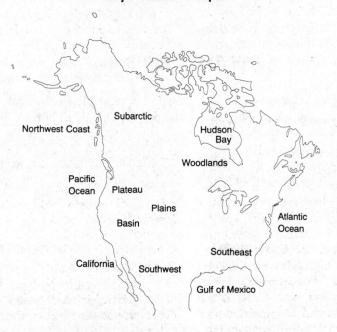

The Age of Exploration

Factors Favoring Exploration

It is difficult to explain with certainty why the period of exploration occurred when it did. We can be sure that certain facts were common knowledge among the navigators and map makers who gathered around and worked with Prince Henry "the Navigator" of Portugal during the first half of the 1400s. These facts were as follows.

1] Aristotle had concluded that the earth was a sphere, and another Greek, Eratosthenes, had calculated the circumference to be 28,000 miles, an over estimate of about one-seventh. This speculation, while not commonly known, had been kept alive by scholars throughout the centuries between Aristotle (350 B.C.) and Prince Henry the Navigator (1450).

2] Marco Polo had lived in China (Cathay) for seventeen years. He had taken four years to go from Constantinople to Peking.

3] Johann Gutenberg's printing press, invented in 1450, made Marco Polo's book of truth and tall tales common knowledge among navigators.

4] The magnetic compass had made navigation beyond the sight of land and without the sight of the stars a more certain art.

5] The astrolabe was a new device for determining latitude.

6] The caravel (such as the *Santa Maria*, *Nina*, and *Pinta*) was a new Portuguese invention. Its sails were a great improvement for sailing against the wind. It was the fastest large ship of its day.

7] More important perhaps then all other facts, but less easy to explain, was the ferment in people's minds during the 1400s. The dull rehash of ancient learning and the preoccupation of scholars with religious thought had given way to a fresh outlook. A vital curiosity about humans, nature, and things scientific had developed.

THE EXPLORERS

The following list of explorers has many dates. It is suggested that you learn those that are underlined. Develop the habit of noticing dates in order to place the event in its proper relation to other events.

The explorers are grouped according to the nation sponsoring the expedition. Within each national group the listings are in chronological order.

Explorers often worked for nations other than their own. For example we may call Amerigo Vespucci an Italian. He thought of himself as a citizen of Florence. His first exploration was in the service of Spain, and his second in the service of Portugal. Henry Hudson was English, but he worked for the Netherlands. Both Cabots, father and son, were citizens of Venice, but they explored for England.

NATION	DATE	EXPLORER	ACCOMPLISHMENT
Norway	<u>1000</u>	Leif Ericson	Atlantic coast from Nova Scotia to Rhode Island. First European to land in America. Unimportant because there was no chain of events as a result.
Portugal	**1488**	Bartholomeu Dias	Rounded southern tip of Africa, the Cape of Good Hope. Turned back.

NATION	DATE	EXPLORER	ACCOMPLISHMENT
Portugal	**1498**	Vasco da Gama	Rounded the Cape of Good Hope. Crossed Indian Ocean to India. Started continuous trade by sea between Europe and the Far East.
Portugal	**1501**	Amerigo Vespucci	Second trip. Sailed along much of the eastern coast of South America. On his first trip in 1499, working for Spain, he had sailed along much of the northern coast. Both trips together gave geographers a good idea of the size of the continent from north to south.
Spain	**<u>1492</u>**	Christopher Columbus	August 3, 1492, the *Santa Maria*, *Pinta*, and *Nina* sailed from Palos. On October 12 they arrived at the Bahama Islands. Columbus called the island San Salvador (probably Watling Island). He explored the islands of Cuba and Haiti (Hispaniola).
Spain	**<u>1493</u>**	Christopher Columbus	Explored the Leeward Islands and Puerto Rico. Made the settlement of Santo Domingo on the island of Haiti headquarters for further explorations.
Spain	**1498**	Christopher Columbus	Explored the Island of Trinidad and the nearby coast of South America.
Spain	**<u>1502</u>**	Christopher Columbus	Coast of Central America from Panama to Honduras.
Spain	**1499**	Amerigo Vespucci	See above: 1501—Vespucci.
Spain	**1513**	Ponce de Leon	Explored Florida searching for the "fountain of youth."
Spain	**<u>1513</u>**	Vasco Nuñez de Balboa	Saw the Pacific Ocean from the Isthmus of Panama on September 25, 1513. This led to the idea that North and South America might be about as wide as Panama.
Spain	**<u>1519-1521</u>**	Hernando Cortez	Conquered the Aztec Indians of Mexico under their king, Montezuma. Great wealth in gold and silver shipped to Spain.
Spain	**<u>1519-1522</u>**	Ferdinand Magellan	First circumnavigation of the world. Left Spain September 20, 1519; killed in the Philippines April 27, 1521. Expedition returned to Spain September 6, 1522. Claimed Philippines for Spain.
Spain	**1530-1536**	Francisco Pizarro	Conquered the Inca Indians of Peru and founded a settlement at Lima.
Spain	**1539-1542**	Hernando de Soto	Explored the Gulf coast from Florida to the Mississippi River. Went into what is now Georgia, Alabama, Mississippi, Arkansas, and Oklahoma. Died of fever and was buried in the Mississippi River.
Spain	**1540-1542**	Francisco Vasquez de Coronado	Discovered the Grand Canyon of Arizona. Also explored New Mexico, the Panhandle area of Texas, and Kansas.

NATION	DATE	EXPLORER	ACCOMPLISHMENT
France	1524	Giovanni da Verrazano	Explored the coast from Carolina to Nova Scotia. Also entered New York Harbor and Narragansett Bay.
France	1534	Jacques Cartier	Explored the St. Lawrence Gulf and River to Montreal.
France	1608-1615	Samuel de Champlain	West up the St. Lawrence and through the Great Lakes to Lake Huron. Discovered Lake Oneida and Lake Champlain. Made 11 trips. Established fur trade with the Indians. The "Father of New France."
France	1673	Père Marquette & Louis Joliet	Explored Mackinac Strait, Lake Michigan, Green Bay, Wisconsin River, and Mississippi River to the Arkansas River.
France	1682	Robert, Sieur de LaSalle	Went from the Great Lakes to the Mississippi River and down to its mouth.
England	1497	John Cabot	Sailed along the coast from Newfoundland to Maine.
England	1498	John Cabot	Sailed from Newfoundland to Chesapeake Bay.
England	1509	Sebastian Cabot	Explored northeast coast.
England	1577-1580	Sir Francis Drake	Second circumnavigation of the world.
Netherlands	1609-1611	Henry Hudson	Explored the Hudson River and Hudson Bay. A mutinous crew set him adrift in Hudson Bay in June 1611.

In the very early period of these explorations, the Spanish government urged the pope, Alexander VI, who was himself a Spaniard, to issue an edict or "papal bull" concerning the New World. In 1493 the pope declared that all lands west of a line of longitude 100 leagues (about 300 miles) west of Azores and the Cape Verde Islands should belong to Spain. This, of course, brought a reaction from Portugal, and the original papal bull was modified by a treaty. In its modified form the agreement set the "**demarcation line**" at 320 leagues west of the Cape Verde Islands (about 1,110 miles). This line cut off a part of the hump of Brazil east of the line for Portugal, and left all the rest of the Western Hemisphere to Spain. In 1493 no one knew how such a line would in fact divide the New World. But line or no line, the period of exploration was destined to be followed by a struggle for empire. The big question was not who found it but who could settle it and hold on to it.

Viewing the list of explorers not merely as something to remember but as a factual record to be interpreted, we can form certain conclusions:

1] Portugal was early but did more navigating than exploring of land areas;

2] Spain was almost as early as Portugal and much more active in supporting expedition;

3] England was early but made only a weak effort;

4] France was a bit late but put forth a substantial effort;

5] The Netherlands was late and apparently disinterested. (The East Indies and the "spice trade" were more attractive.)

6] Spain explored the Bahamas, West Indies, Central America, Florida, Mexico, Peru, the Philippines, Georgia, Alabama, Mississippi, Arkansas, Oklahoma, Texas, Kansas, and Arizona;

7] The French went into the St. Lawrence River, through the Great Lakes, into Green Bay, down the Wisconsin River, and down the Mississippi River to the Gulf of Mexico. They went down into New York State to Lake Oneida and to Lake Champlain close to the Mohawk and Hudson rivers;

8] the English hired two Italian navigators who sailed along the North Atlantic Coast of North America no farther south than Chesapeake Bay.

The Spanish, French, and English were to be the nations to build empires based on the explorations. This pattern of exploration was roughly repeated in the settlements made by these contenders for empire in the New World. Spain dominated the south and west. France dominated the great waterways entering North America at the St. Lawrence River and preceding by way of the Great Lakes into the heart of the continent and out southward by way of the Mississippi River. Henry VIII (1509-1547), Queen Elizabeth (1558-1603), the Spanish Armada (1588), the first two Stuart kings, James I and Charles I (1603-1649), combined to supply England with national power, hatred of Spain and France, and a constant flow of English settlers willing, and often eager, to leave their homeland. And there was the eastern seaboard of North America waiting for them.

*Some European Influences and Rivalries in Colonial America

When settlements were made in North America, the people who came here brought with them their points of view about government and religion; they brought with them their homeland customs. For the French, Spanish, and Dutch, this meant acceptance of autocratic, absolute government with all power centered in the sovereign or the sovereign's representative. It would not occur to them to have a legislature made up of settlers. The French and Spanish were Roman Catholics. They would easily accept both church and king as authorities generally to be obeyed and certainly not to be questioned. Although church and government had their rivalries and jealousies, nevertheless they worked reasonably well together. Their joint supervision of the people was accepted as a matter of course. The position of the Dutch settlers in these respects was not very different, even though there was no official church. Their government was absolute. Almost all of the Dutch settlers were Protestants whose church affiliation was a dominant factor in their lives.

The English were different. **Magna Carta** (the Great Charter) of 1215 and the **Model Parliament** of 1295 had sown seeds of liberty that could not be completely killed. Popular monarchs (Henry VIII and Queen Elizabeth I) could ignore Parliament and rule as dictators, but unpopular kings ran into difficulties. Charles I had his head cut off in 1649. By 1600 the "divine right of kings" theory either was dead or dying as far as the English were concerned. Having had representative government in England, English settlers had assemblies in the English colonies. The "Tree of Liberty" found more favorable soil in the New World even though it took a great deal of cultivating and required time to develop. The English settlers were accustomed to private ownership of land by ordinary people as well as by the landed aristocracy. The French, Dutch, and Spanish were much closer to feudalism in the distribution of land; the **Patroon** system of the Hudson Valley with its tenant farmers illustrates the point.

The French settlements were strung so thinly along the major waterways (St. Lawrence, Great Lakes, Mississippi) that land ownership was not a problem. The French were fur traders, hence nomads, circulating from tribe to tribe of Native Americans. There were comparatively few French women in America. There were few towns but many forts and trading posts. By and large, the French and the Native Americans liked one another; the French did not want their land, and the trading supplied both with what they wanted.

The Spanish explorers struck it rich in Mexico and Peru. This was, in spite of its initial appearance, a misfortune for them and their nation. This taste of success kept later Spanish expeditions intent upon fruitless searches for more treasure. The English "seadogs" such as Drake, Cavendish, Davis and Frobisher harassed the Spanish treasure-laden ships on their homeward journey. The Spanish took in so much treasure that they spent it importing merchandise, most of it from England. Spanish arts and crafts languished while England's flourished. Spain poured its treasure into the greatest armament program of the day, the building of the **Great Armada.** In 1588 this was a total loss when it was defeated by a picked-up English merchant marine with a few cannon aboard (England had no navy), the superior seamanship of the English sea dogs, the comparative clumsiness of the large Spanish ships, and stormy seas. This catastrophe was Spain's quick start on a prolonged decline as a world power. Thus, the real struggle for North America was left to England and France.

In comparison with today's rapid pace, events moved slowly in the 1600s and 1700s. Then, as now, international politics, economics, and religious turmoil in Europe had their repercussions in North America. Without attempting any detail, we can get an appreciation of this intermingling of European and American affairs by listing a series of wars between France and England. Many other nations were involved, but the primary opponents were England and France. Notice the dates. Figure out the intervals between the wars.

THE WARS IN EUROPE		THE SAME WARS IN AMERICA	
1]	War of the League of Augsburg (also called War of the Palatinate)	1689-1697	King William's War
2]	War of the Spanish Succession	1701-1713	Queen Anne's War
3]	War of the Austrian Succession	1740-1748	King George's War
4]	Seven Years War	1756-1763	French and Indian War
5]	France, Holland, and Spain at war with England during the American Revolution	1775-1783	American Revolution
6]	Napoleonic Wars (intermittent)	1798-1815	War of 1812 (1812-1815)

By the end of the first four of these six wars, the French had been driven out of North America and the Spanish had lost Florida. The last two wars were unsuccessful attempts by France to reestablish its position in North America. At the end of the American Revolution, Spain did make a slight recovery by regaining Florida.

Unless otherwise indicated, provisions throughout this book with one or more asterisks (*) denote items worth special attention.

The English Colonies

Two of the earliest permanent English colonies established in America were **Jamestown** in Virginia in the South and the **Massachusetts Bay Colony** in Massachusetts in the North—one in sympathy with England regarding politics and religion, and the other at odds with England in these respects. Each represented the economic and social structure typical of its area. By 1775 both had wealth and population. For these two colonies a rather detailed account of their early days is provided—about the first hundred years.

* Virginia at Jamestown, 1607—Basic Facts

1] Three vessels arrive in Virginia on April 26, 1607; 105 settlers established themselves at Jamestown on May 24.

2] Captain John Smith, according to his own account in "A True Relation" (relation of events), led the colony through the first eight months.

3] The winter of 1609-1610 was the terrible starving time.

4] Lord De La Warre rescued the colony in the spring of 1610. Governor Thomas Dale's harsh but wise rule maintained the colony. Governors Gates and Yeardley succeeded Dale and continued a similar tough, practical policy.

5] John Rolfe introduced West Indian tobacco to Virginia.

6] Sir Edwin Sandys, treasurer of the London Company, formed Virginia's first General Assembly, the House of Burgesses, in 1619.

7] Misfortune from many directions drove the London Company into bankruptcy in 1622. Virginia became a royal colony in 1624.

8] In 1675 Nathaniel Bacon led a rebellion against Governor Berkeley.

Some of the Virginia Story

The **London Company** was a private stock company that sold shares of stock which raised the money to finance the venture. Very few shareholders were also settlers. As a business venture, the colony was a failure; as a factor in establishing an empire, it was a success.

The Virginia story is a harsh one: 120 men (no women) were on 3 vessels that set sail for Virginia. Although accounts differ, it seems safe to accept as fact that about 50 percent of those who left England for Virginia survived the first year. Although instructed by the officers of the London Company to select a high, dry site on a river, the settlement was made on low ground in a swampy region about 30 miles up the James River. This group of about 100 men were mainly gentlemen, not laborers. They were the wrong type and they did the wrong things, such as searching for treasure instead of planting crops.

The first crude houses they built let in rain and cold. The long trip over had exhausted the ships' food supplies. Hunger, disease (especially malaria), bickering among themselves, and fighting with the Indians made life miserable. What food was raised was put into a common storehouse to be given out as needed in the winter. Such a plan might have been necessary for the first season. But, as time went on, the fact that how much food one received had no relation to how much one had done to maintain the colony resulted in less food produced.

During the first year **Captain John Smith** managed to keep food production to at least the minimum required. He was captured by the Indians, but his life was spared through the intercession of the Indian maiden **Pocohontas**, daughter of the chief. However, his influence was lost to the colony, which slacked off in its one important task—the raising of food.

More ships arrived in Virginia in 1608 and 1609, so about 900 had come to the colony by Christmas of 1609. Yet by the next spring only 60 people were alive. These were the few who survived the terrible "starving time" of the winter of 1609-1610. These miserable, half-starved men were ready to leave Jamestown when **Lord De La Warre** arrived with new settlers and more supplies. Lord De La Warre soon returned to England and left Governor Thomas Dale in charge. The London Company was reorganized, with Governors Thomas Gates and George Yeardley succeeding Dale. Under all three governors much the same policy was followed. Men were marched under armed guard to work in the fields twice a day. The basic rule was: those who don't work, don't eat. The common storehouse could be kept reasonably well supplied if enough force could be applied to keep the men at work. Another reorganization of the London Company brought **Sir Edwin Sandys** in as treasurer in 1619. Reforms were instituted. The common storehouse had given way to individual farms. A general assembly was formed. Twenty-two members represented groups of settlers (two from each group). This is the famous **House of Burgesses,** the first representative government in the New World. The two delegates represented a **hundred** or a **town** or a **plantation.** These three terms meant an area where enough settlers lived to warrant two delegates.

Tobacco gave a great economic lift to Virginia. **John Rolfe** introduced West Indian tobacco plants, a great improvement over the local variety. From 1616 to 1619, the tobacco exported from Jamestown rose from under 3,000 pounds to over 50,000 pounds.

The year 1619 not only found Virginia eating well, enjoying a thriving tobacco trade, and inaugurating the House of Burgesses, it also witnessed the arrival at Jamestown of the first Africans (20 of them) and of the first women (90 of them). The Africans were sold as indentured servants, but by the 1640s **slavery** had been introduced. One of Virginia's great weaknesses during its first dozen years had been the lack of family life and the many civilizing influences it brings.

The year 1622 might be called Virginia's year of misfortunes. Disease, especially malaria, poor crops, a slump in the tobacco trade, and increased Indian troubles combined to drive the colony into a desperate situation and the London Company into financial collapse. When the London Company gave up, the king took over, and in 1624 Virginia became a royal colony directly under the authority of the king.

The House of Burgesses continued under the royal governors. Virginia grew in strength. Small farms worked by their owners lined the James, York, and Rappahannock rivers. Life was still simple and hard.

Just a century before the thirteen colonies had their revolution against England, the colony of Virginia had its rebellion against a royal governor. In 1675 **Nathaniel Bacon** led a rebellion against Governor Berkeley. By this date Jamestown had spread out. The poorer farmers lived on the outer fringes of the colony and were from time to time the victims of Native American raids. In 1675 a series of raids on isolated farms accounted for over 30 deaths. Families left their homes in fear of further attacks, but Governor Berkeley made no move to handle the problem. It was charged that the reason for the governor's lack of action was his private fur trade with the Native Americans.

Nathaniel Bacon led an unofficial armed force of about 500 men against the Native Americans, and Governor Berkeley branded him an outlaw. Bacon then attacked Jamestown, where he drove the governor and his militia from the town. Much of Jamestown was burned during this fight. Bacon died suddenly and the rebellion collapsed. Berkeley reestablished his authority, rounded up some of Bacon's most prominent supporters, and executed 23 of them. King Charles II was disgusted with Berkeley and called him back to England.

* Massachusetts Bay Colony at Boston, 1630—Basic Facts

1] **John Winthrop** was elected Governor before the colonists embarked from Southampton, England.

2] In 1630, eleven ships sailed from Southampton and others from Bristol and Plymouth. Over 1,000 colonists, some in family groups, settled in and near Boston.

3] By October 1630 a representative government was organized. It was made up of Governor Winthrop, a Governor's council (which was also a court and the upper house of the legislature), and an assembly.

4] For about 35 years the right to vote and to hold office was restricted to church members in good standing (**theocratic** government).

5] Harvard College was founded in 1636. Its main purpose was to maintain a well-educated clergy for the Puritan church (later the Congregational denomination).

6] In 1636 **Roger Williams**, a minister in Salem, was tried and ordered banished to England. He escaped to Narragansett Bay, where he started the Rhode Island colony at Providence. Here, complete religious freedom was established.

7] In 1636 **Ann Hutchinson** persuaded some clergy and many others to accept unorthodox religious ideas. She was excommunicated. With her family she went to Providence. She established a settlement at Portsmouth, Rhode Island, and soon thereafter started another settlement on Long Island.

8] In 1636 the Reverend **Thomas Hooker** was at odds with Boston's theology. He and some of his congregation settled in Hartford. In 1639 they drew up the **Fundamental Orders,** the first written constitution in the New World.

9] In 1638 the Reverend John Davenport was also unhappy about the religious setup in Boston. He founded a colony at New Haven.

10] In 1643 the **New England Confederation** was formed to give more effective defense against the Indians and to guard against encroachment by the Dutch from the Hudson Valley. The four members were Massachusetts Bay, Plymouth, New Haven, and Connecticut (Hartford).

11] In 1665 four commissioners from King Charles II came to New England. Their reception by Boston officials led three of them to advise the king to revoke the Massachusetts charter.

12] King Philip's War in 1675-1676 spread all over New England. It was the Indians' last great effort in New England to stop the spreading white settlements. About half of the towns were attacked and twelve were wiped out, but the Indians really had no chance to succeed.

13] In 1684 King James II made Massachusetts a royal colony. (See the list of items under "Massachusetts Irritates the King".

14] **Sir Edmund Andros** arrived in Boston in December 1686 as the appointed royal governor of New England. He was to unite New England, New York, New Jersey, and Pennsylvania under his command as a precaution against war with France. (See "Rule of Andros.")

15] In 1689 news of the expulsion of James II and the coming to power of William and Mary (William III) led to the arrest of Andros and his being shipped back to England. This was the **Bloodless** or **Glorious Revolution,** as it was known in England.

16] In 1691 King William III granted a new charter that kept Massachusetts a royal colony, rescinded all punitive acts taken against it, forbade religious qualification for political rights, and made Maine and Plymouth part of Massachusetts Bay Colony.

* Massachusetts Irritates the King

1] In 1630 the first settlers and Governor Winthrop brought the charter of the colony to Boston with them. This put the charter beyond easy reach of the king and

gave Massachusetts a sense of independence it could not otherwise have had.

2] In the 1640s and 1650s Massachusetts annexed the New Hampshire towns Nashua, Exeter, Dover, and Hampton, and also the Maine towns Kittery and York. Massachusetts aided these nearby towns against the Indians but acted without the king's permission and in violation of charter rights.

3] In 1643 the **New England Confederation** was formed. It was a defense against Indians and a precaution against encroachment by the Dutch. Massachusetts organized and dominated it. This union was made without the king's permission and against his wishes. Any union of colonies could be turned against the king.

4] In 1653 Massachusetts refused to aid England in its conflict with Holland. Every colony's first duty was to come to the aid of the mother country in time of war.

5] In 1665 the king's commissioners were rudely treated and their demands rejected. Massachusetts refused to

   a. allow all orthodox churches freedom to observe their religion;
   b. have all heads of families take an oath of allegiance to the king;
   c. repeal all local laws repugnant to the king.

The Rule of Andros (December 1686 to January 1689)

1] Rhode Island and Connecticut were declared to be royal colonies. Connecticut hid its charter in an oak tree (Charter Oak). In 1691 King William II declared this change in the status of Rhode Island and Connecticut to have been illegal and of no effect.

2] New England, New Jersey, New York, and Pennsylvania were united under Andros in anticipation of war with France.

3] The Old South Meeting House was changed to an Anglican Church.

4] All land titles were to be reexamined. Any quit-rents still due must be paid if the landholder was to keep his property.

5] The only town meetings permitted without the special consent of Andros were the annual meetings for the election of officers.

6] Andros levied taxes without any action by the legislature.

All of these measures were resisted. The president of Harvard College, Reverend **Increase Mather**, stole off to England to lodge a protest. The hostile climate of opinion greatly hindered Andros in getting his program actually established. He had created bitterness and chaos before the Glorious Revolution ended this episode.

* Some of the Massachusetts Story

Much of this story has been covered under the previous heading, *Basic Fact* (Massachusetts Irritates the King) and (The Rule of Andros). In addition, the atmosphere, character, and spirit of Massachusetts, as well as New England in general, deserves attention.

The **Pilgrims** who settled at Plymouth had deep religious convictions as their reason for leaving England. First they went to Leyden, Holland. Because their children were becoming Dutch, they made arrangements to return to England in preparation for the trip to America. They were **Separatists**, so-called because they wished to separate entirely from the Anglican Church. The *Mayflower* with its 101 colonists, 35 of them from the Leyden group, arrived at Cape Cod in early November 1620. Before landing, 41 men representing themselves and their families signed the **Mayflower Compact**.

This was an agreement to make "just and equal laws" to which they promised "all due submission and obedience." Hence, the Mayflower Compact is often called the first example of self-government in the New World. About half of those who arrived on the *Mayflower* died during the first winter, yet none of the survivors decided to return to England in the spring. **William Bradford** was their governor for 30 of the first 36 years.

The **Puritans**, who established the Massachusetts Bay Colony settling in Boston and nearby areas also had a religious difference with the Anglican Church, but they did not wish to separate from it. They wished to purify it; hence the name, Puritans.

The Puritans did not believe in religious tolerance, let alone religious freedom. They demanded that the church be run their way and that everyone conform. Non-church members could live in Boston only if they were careful not to speak of religious matters. Some Quakers were hanged. Ministers who failed to subdue differences of religious belief found it wise to found other colonies. The Puritan church restricted political rights to its own members. Despite this narrow view the Puritan communities had great strength and many virtues. Puritan clergy and Puritan public officials set high standards of personal and official conduct that were reflected by, or were the result of, a similar level of conduct by the populace. Integrity, simplicity, and industry characterized this society more than most.

List of Colonies

Colony	*Date Place Founder	Type a) When founded b) In 1775	Important Information
Virginia	1607 Jamestown London Co.	a) Charter to stock company b) Royal	See text discussion.
Plymouth	1620 Plymouth Pilgrims	a) Self-governing b) Royal	Leyden, Holland Wm. Brewster—first leader Separatists Miles Standish—military leader Wm. Bradford—early governor
New Hampshire	1623 Portsmouth John Mason	a) Massachusetts claimed it; the title was obscure. Charles II made it royal in 1679. b) Royal	Very weak settlement. Southern towns taken over by Massachusetts
Maine	1623 Portland Sir Ferdinando Gorges	a) Proprietary; claimed by Mass. b) Royal	Became part of Mass. in 1691.

Colony	*Date Place Founder	Type a) When founded b) In 1775	Important Information
New York	1624 Albany and New Amsterdam Dutch	a) Proprietary in 1664 when the Duke of York took it for England. b) Royal	N. Y. harbor and the Hudson River separated the English colonies. This was an intolerable situation to the empire-minded British.
New Jersey	1624	a) Same as N. Y.	For a period it was divided into East and West Jersey. For several years New York's governor also governed N.J., although the courts and the legislature were separate. Not until 1738 was N.J. definitely made a separate unified colony.
Massachusetts	1630 Boston Mass. Bay Co.	a) Charter to stock Company b) Royal	See text discussion.
Maryland	1634 St. Mary's Province Cecilius Calvert, the 2nd Lord Baltimore	a) Proprietary b) Proprietary	Started as a Catholic colony. The Toleration Act of 1649 gave freedom of religion to all Christians to protect Catholics from interference by other Christians.
Rhode Island	1636 Providence Roger Williams	a) Self-governing b) Self-governing	Freedom for all religions and for nonbelievers. Ann Hutchinson founded the settlement of Portsmouth.
Connecticut	1636 Hartford Thomas Hooker	a) Self-governing b) Self-governing	In 1639 Fundamental Orders was the first written constitution in the New World. Davenport's colony at New Haven became part of Conn. in 1662.
Delaware	1638 Wilmington Swedes	a) Proprietary after conquest by England in 1664. b) Proprietary	First settled by Swedes.
North and South Carolina	1665 Albemarle Eight Noble Lords	a) Proprietary b) Royal	Albemarle Sound and Charleston Harbor, where the the earliest settlements were made, are 300 miles apart. They had little contact with each other. Started with an impractical government based on John Locke's ideas. There was almost continual political strife. North and South Carolina became separate colonies in 1711.
Pennsylvania	1683 Philadelphia William Penn	a) Proprietary b) Proprietary	Quaker settlement. Also many Germans (Pennsylvania Dutch). In the buying of the land from the Indians and allowing complete religious freedom PA. followed the good example of R.I. Penn's colony was called "The Holy Experiment."
Georgia	1733 Savannah James Ogelthorpe	a) Proprietary b) Royal	A mismanaged attempt at human rehabilitation. Many debtors and other unfortunates were among the first settlers. At first the rum trade and slavery were prohibited. It had the unavailable location to serve as a buffer between Spanish Florida and the Carolinas.

*Colonial Governments

As noted in the preceding list of colonies, there were three types of government: **proprietary, royal**, and **self-governing**. The colonies that were to become the original thirteen states represented all three types. Rhode Island and Connecticut started out as self-governing and remained that way right up to the American Revolution in 1775. Pennsylvania, Maryland, and Delaware began as proprietary and remained so. The other eight—Massachusetts, New Hampshire, New York, New Jersey, Virginia, North Carolina, South Carolina, and Georgia—had become royal colonies by 1775, although they had not all started as such.

All three types had a **governor** and **legislature**. Pennsylvania had a **unicameral** (one-house) legislative body, which was unusual. The typical colonial legislature was **bicameral** (two-house). The **council**, a small group of advisors to the governor, was the upper house. Sometimes, if it was a royal colony, the council was appointed by the king, sometimes by the governor or the proprietor, and in some cases the lower house, the **assembly**, elected the council. Besides being an upper house of the legislature, the council was usually also a court. A not uncommon provision in the charter of a colony was that the king's privy council in England could, within a specified time, veto an act of the colonial legislature. Governors could veto laws. The trump card held by the colonial legislatures was the power of the assemblies to appropriate money; they held the **"power of the purse."** Even the governors of royal colonies, except for Virginia, depended on the assembly for their salaries. This often put the royal governor in a difficult position. When the king's policy ran counter to colonial wishes, what would the governor do? Ignore the king and lose his job or ignore the colonists and lose his salary? Royal governors got directives from the king which they simply could not carry out; they had the legal authority but lacked the actual means necessary in the situation. In short, a royal governor had responsibility without adequate power.

The right to vote was restricted to those who met the property qualifications. Property qualifications differed from colony to colony, and over periods of time there were changes within each colony. The significant fact is that nowhere else in the world except in England was there a comparable degree of popular, representative government. As the New England colonies grew to contain several towns within a single colony, the famous **town meeting** developed. This political device was **direct democracy**, which permitted taxpayers to go to meetings and vote their local ordinances into effect.

The significant point to be learned from the several colonial governments is that they were wonderful training schools for those who were to become revolutionists in 1775. This experience in political know-how accompanied by the belief in the "Immemorial Rights of English Subjects" prepared our people to set up and operate a government of their own.

Mercantilism in the English Colonies 1650-1763

To understand this period, it is important to keep two facts in mind:

1] The **mercantile theory of trade** was accepted as the guide for building the strength of a nation.

2] **North America** was a **battleground for empire** between **England** and **France**.

Mercantile Theory of Trade

A basic concept of this theory of trade was that a nation must sell abroad (export) goods of greater money value than it buys from abroad (imports). In this way a nation will have a **favorable balance of trade** because it will collect more in payments from foreigners than it will pay to foreigners.

The mercantile theory of trade meant that something had to be done to bring about and maintain an excess of exports, in terms of money value, over imports. Whatever was done had to be done by government. In England laws had to be passed that would encourage exports from England and discourage imports. However, England needed many goods that it could not produce. To buy such goods from France, Holland, Sweden, Spain, etc., would have increased their exports and strengthened those nations. Such a result was to be avoided.

Any goods obtained from one's own colonies, however, would make the colonies prosper, keep the trade away from other nations, and supply England with goods it could not produce. Any goods commonly produced in England must not be produced in the colonies. Colonies were naturally sources of raw materials: forest products, minerals, fish, and whatever agricultural products were best suited to them. Mercantilism dictated that the colonies be encouraged in these commercial pursuits and restricted to them. For example: skin the beavers in Albany, New York, sell the skins to a London furrier, sell the beaver caps and capes wherever there is a market for them, but don't allow manufacturing of beaver caps and capes in the colonies. Was this a ruinous policy for the colonies? Not at all. As long as the supply of beaver skins held out, the beaver trade could grow and grow, provided the English furrier could find purchasers for caps and capes. Of course, if the supply of beavers was exhausted, the situation would be different. But during this period of about a hundred years, the colonial supplies of raw materials did not run out; in fact, the tremendous wealth of the American colonies was hardly more than scratched on the surface. This sort of regulation could be applied to many products. Lumber and iron ore from the colonies must be sent to England only in a crude state. The processing must be reserved for the craft workers and manufacturers in England.

Invisible items of international trade must be regulated. All ships owned by British subjects and engaged in the business of transportation constituted the British merchant marine. Whenever these ships were hired by foreigners, the transaction was a British export. Under mercantilism this transportation service by ship was so important a business that it must be closely controlled by laws. Every effort must be made to favor the British ships and discourage the foreign ships. Notice the British included the people throughout the empire, not only the people of England.

List of the Provisions of Some of the Trade and Navigation Acts, 1650-1764

The provisions with an asterisk (*) are worth special attention.

*1] 1650: No foreign ships could trade in a British colony without a license.

2] 1651: Ships entering English ports with goods from Asia, Africa, or America had to be owned by British subjects, captained by a British subject, and operated by a crew that was mostly British.

3] 1651: No foreigners could import fish into England, Ireland, or any British colony.

4] 1651: No foreign ship could carry cargo from one English port to another; that is, no coastal trade.

*5] 1660: No goods, no matter where they originated, could enter or leave a British colony except in a British ship with a British captain and a crew that was at least three-fifths British.

*6]   1660: Certain enumerated (listed) products from the colonies had to be shipped only to England or to other British colonies (sugar, indigo, tobacco,† and a few others).

7]   1696: All colonial laws in opposition to English navigation laws were void.

8]   1699: No wool products could be exported from the colonies.

*9]   No beaver hats could be exported from one colony to another. Making beaver hats was put under severe restrictions.

  a. Only those who served an apprenticeship of seven years could make beaver hats.

  b. No more than two apprentices could be employed in each establishment.

*10]   1733: Rum, spirits, sugar, and molasses from foreign West Indies to America were taxed.

†Laws forbade the growing of tobacco in England, required the American tobacco colonies (Virginia and Maryland) to export tobacco only to England, and forbade the importation into England of tobacco from Spain and Portugal.

*11]   Several times throughout the 1700s, **bounties** were granted on certain colonial products. A bounty was a sum of money paid to the colonial shipper by the English government to encourage the flow of certain goods into England. From time to time there were bounties paid on tar, pitch, turpentine, masts, rice, indigo, and a few other items.

*12]   1750s: Smelting furnaces, rolling mills, and forges were prohibited in the colonies. Pig and bar iron could be sent to England duty-free.

*13]   1764: The duties on sugar and molasses were lowered from the levels set by the law of 1733. Importation from the foreign West Indies of rum and spirits was prohibited.

These triangular trips with a payload on each leg of the triangle were lucrative.

The Triangular Trade

New England *rum*	→	Africa *slaves*	→	West Indies *sugar* *molasses*	→	back to New England
New England *fish* *lumber*	→	England *handicraft* *and factory* *goods*	→	West Indies *sugar* *molasses*	→	back to New England
New England *fish* *lumber*	→	West Indies *rum* *sugar* *molasses*	→	England *handicraft* *and factory* *goods*	→	back to New England
Middle Colonies *grain* *flour*	→	West Indies *rum* *sugar* *molasses*	→	England *handicraft* *and factory* *goods*	→	back to Middle Colonies

* How English Legal Restrictions Affected American Colonial Commerce up to 1764

Colonial trade was aided by some of the trade and navigation laws. It would have been hurt by other laws had they been enforced. The laws restricting shipping to British ships, captains, and crews helped New England shipyards and enabled many to "follow the sea." Restrictions on manufacturing in the colonies undoubtedly prevented the formation of many enterprises, even though a few smelting furnaces operated illegally. The Tobacco laws guaranteed American colonies a monopoly in selling to the British Isles, but did not allow the colonies to sell tobacco to Europe. Much American tobacco got to Europe, the English merchant being the middleman. The duties on sugar and molasses from foreign West Indies, had they had enforced, would have severely hurt the distilleries in Massachusetts, Connecticut, and Rhode Island. Making rum in New England had grown to such proportions that the manufacturers needed more sugar and molasses than the British West Indies could supply. Without foreign supplies, production would have been curtailed. The trade and navigation acts that helped the colonists were obeyed; those that made their businesses less profitable were violated more often than not.

* Salutary Neglect

It was during this period that England followed a policy of **salutary neglect**, which was beneficial to England and to its colonies. By and large, the trade and navigation acts that were harmful to colonial trade were not enforced. The government was aware of the situation but made no appreciable effort to correct it. Official graft accounted for some of the laxness. A political favorite in London would be appointed customs officer for a colonial port. He wished to live in England, so he hired someone in the colonies to do the job. To this local "deputy" he paid part of his salary. The local "deputy" was naturally sympathetic to his friends and neighbors, and London was many weeks and 3,000 miles away. It became customary not to notice smuggling. The navigation law requiring a ship with a cargo from Europe to America to stop at England to have the cargo transferred to an English vessel was also commonly evaded. It is easy to see why the colonists evaded these laws, but why did England permit such evasion?

The presence of the French in North America is the best single answer. England needed the settlers for the final show-down that was certain to come. The king and parliament did not wish to create a hostile spirit in America toward England. It worked both ways. The colonists were very conscious of the presence of the French along the Great Lakes and the Mississippi River. They were anti-French and generally anti-Catholic. They were aware of how important the British navy was to their safety. When the final test of strength arrived, they would need the leadership, wealth, and power of England. So the colonists accepted the many trade and navigation laws without organized protests and with little grumbling. The regulations irked them but were rated more as a nuisance than a grievance, especially in view of the policy of salutary neglect.

Another point should be noted: trade within the British empire was less thoroughly regulated than that of the French, Dutch, and Spanish empires. Had the British colonials looked around, they would have seen that under the control of England they enjoyed more freedom of commerce than did the colonists of their rival nations.

The French and Indian War 1754-1763

Native Americans Helped the French

In Europe the French and Indian War was called the **Seven Years' War** (1756-1763). It was the fourth in a series of six wars, with France and England opposing one another (see p.33). Most of the Native American tribes from Canada to Florida were allied with the French; hence, to the English colonists in America, this was a war against the French and the Native Americans. The Iroquois of central New York were anti-French, so they gave some support to the English. This war was decisive and forced the French off the continent of North America.

Below are dates, people, places, and events that are associated with the war.

1753 Governor Dinwiddie and George Washington

Governor Dinwiddie of Virginia sent **George Washington**, a 21-year-old major in the Virginia militia, to tell the French to leave the Allegheny-Monongahela rivers area. Washington delivered the message and returned to Richmond.

1754 Washington Led Troops Against the French

The French had erected Fort Duquesne at the junction of the Allegheny and Monongahela rivers. Washington built Fort Necessity nearby. The ensuing battle at Great Meadows opened the war with a victory for France. Fort Necessity was surrendered to the French on July 4.

* 1754 Albany Plan of Union (The Albany Congress) Benjamin Franklin

In early summer, delegates from the colonies and the Iroquois gathered at Albany, New York. For months the Iroquois, encouraged by the French, had made raids from Florida to Canada. The Albany meeting was called in part to deal with this situation. **Benjamin Franklin** from Pennsylvania submitted a plan to centralize and unify the handling of defense problems and Native American affairs. The plan called for a Grand Council elected by the colonial assemblies. Each colony could have from two to seven delegates. A President-General appointed by and paid by the king would preside over the Grand Council. Taxes would be levied to pay for a single armed force to represent all the colonies to regulate trade agreements with the Native Americans, to make treaties with them, settle boundary disputes with them, and to take care of those matters that were obviously of common concern to the colonies as a group.

This plan, though accepted by the delegates at the Albany Congress, was rejected by the colonies. Each colony was reluctant to place its armed men in a force it could not control and under the command of someone from another colony. At this point, 1754, the individual colonies were more fearful of losing the power of independent action than they were of being wiped out by the French and Native Americans. The king of England, George II, rejected the plan for a different reason. He felt that such a union with an armed force representing the several colonies constituted at least a potential threat against the crown. Some of the features of Franklin's plan reappeared when the Articles of Confederation were drawn up.

* 1755 General Braddock and Washington

General Braddock made a second attack on Fort Duquesne. Lieutenant Colonel Washington was second in command. They were badly defeated at the Battle of the Wilderness within ten miles of Fort Duquesne. Braddock was killed. Washington led the retreat to Fort Cumberland, Maryland.

1756 The War Spreads to Europe

Prussia lined up with England; Austria sided with France.

1757   General Montcalm Took Fort William Henry at Lake George, New York.

* 1757 William Pitt Headed a New Ministry

The war in Europe and in America was not going well for England. War loans were raised, new taxes levied, men and supplies were thrown into the struggle. New commanders of outstanding ability, Lord Jeffrey Amherst and James Wolfe, replaced those who had failed.

1758   Amherst and Wolf Took Fort Louisbourg, Cape Breton Island

1758   The English Captured Forts Frontenac and Duquesne

Fort Duquesne was renamed Fort Pitt. It is now Pittsburgh, Pennsylvania.

1759   The English Captured Fort Niagara

General Amherst's superior manpower led to French withdrawal from Ticonderoga and Crown Point.

* 1759 General Wolfe Defeated General Montcalm on the Plains of Abraham to Take the Great Fortress of Quebec

This was the decisive battle; England had won the war.

1760   General Amherst Took Montreal

A few days later Detroit fell to the English and thereafter other French forts on the Great Lakes were deserted.

1762   The Treaty of San Ildefonso

France transferred to Spain all French territory west of the Mississippi River and New Orleans. Spain had been drawn into the war as an ally of France. It had lost to the English some of its possessions in the Far East and in the West Indies. To compensate Spain for these losses, France ceded the lands in North America that England had not yet taken.

* 1763 Treaty of Paris

1]   France gave up all of Canada to England. (By the Treaty of Utrecht, 1713, England had taken much of northern Canada.)

2]   France and Spain gave all lands east of the Mississippi River except New Orleans to England. (Spain had owned Florida).

3]   The West Indies were unscrambled and re-divided much as they had been before the war.

4]   France got two small islands, St. Pierre and Miquelon, off the south coast of Newfoundland. They were not to be fortified. The French needed them as a base for fishing fleets. France was guaranteed fishing rights off Newfoundland.

5]   Spain's title to New Orleans and lands west of the Mississippi River as arranged in the Treaty of San Ildefonso was recognized.

* Significance of the French and Indian War

As far as the American colonists were concerned, the war was over with the fall of Montreal. The colonies had contributed very substantially of their manpower and wealth. England and the colonists rejoiced together for the French had been driven from North America. The changed circumstances brought about by this victory rather clearly foreshadowed separation of the American colonies from England.

With the French out of North America, the colonists had no need of the British fleet, of British soldiers, or of British wealth to preserve their way of life. England was victorious and financially broke. Since no foreign power now threatened the empire, the British no longer needed to humor the colonials with "salutary neglect." The British believed that since the American colonies had benefited greatly by the late war they should carry much of the tax load to pay for it. This view seemed reasonable in London at the time.

True historical insight pointed in another direction. There were about 3 million people in the American colonies. Philadelphia, Boston, New York City, and Charleston ranged in population from about 10,000 to 25,000. Still, 90 percent or more of the people lived in rural areas and hence were widely scattered. London was too far away in both time and distance to enforce unpopular laws, whether just or not.

Heading into the American Revolution
1765-1775

1763   The Proclamation Line

The western edge for colonial settlement was set at the Alleghenies. The land west of the Alleghenies was reserved for the Native Americans.

When the Great Lakes forts held by the French collapsed after the fall of Detroit, the British tried in vain to make trade agreements with the Native Americans. Negotiations broke down. **Pontiac,** Chief of the Ottawas, destroyed most of the English forts in the Ohio Valley area. By midsummer Pontiac agreed to peace terms, but this uprising explains, in part, why the **Proclamation Line** seemed to King George III and his ministers a good way to keep peace with the Native Americans. To maintain a chain of forts would have taken thousands of soldiers and tremendous expenditures.

To the colonists the problem seemed quite different. Thousands of settlers were already west of the Alleghenies in the Ohio region. The Proclamation directed such settlers "forthwith to remove themselves." The real trouble with the Proclamation Line was that it simply could not be enforced and it angered the colonists.

1764-1765   The Grenville Program

1764   Sugar Act

This act, which placed a duty on molasses and sugar and other products imported from outside the British empire, was proposed by the Chancellor of the Exchequer (treasurer), **George Grenville**, in the British ministry.

1764   Ending the Policy of "Salutary Neglect"

1]   A vice-admiralty court was established in Halifax where tax cases could be taken for trial without a jury. Local colonial courts had a history of being sympathetic toward tax evaders.

2]   Shippers were required to post heavier bond (larger sums of money) so that, when found guilty of tax evasion, the money to pay the fine would be readily available.

3]   Tax collectors could no longer live in England and have a deputy in America do their work. The local "deputies" gave way to tax officials from England.

4]   Soon after the new tax officials arrived in America, an increase in the number of soldiers was evident. About 10,000 came allegedly to strengthen the defenses of the colonies against the Indians. As most of the soldiers were stationed in the cities and towns along the coast, the colonists got the idea that their real purpose was to back up the tax collectors.

5]   Tax officials were given **writs of assistance** (blanket search warrants).

* 1765 The Stamp Act Passed

Stamps had to be affixed to about 50 items such as legal documents, insurance policies, playing cards, newspapers, pamphlets, and licenses. These stamps varied in cost from a half-penny to two pounds (1 cent to $10).

American colonials were to be given the jobs as tax-stamp distributors, and the income from the tax was to be used to pay the expense of defending the colonies.

1765   The Stamp Act Congress

James Otis persuaded the Massachusetts legislature to call a protest meeting. Letters were sent to all the colonies suggesting that the meeting be held in New York City. In October the **Stamp Act Congress**

met. Nine colonies were represented (Massachusetts, South Carolina, Rhode Island, Connecticut, New Jersey, Delaware, New York, Pennsylvania, Maryland). Their petition to the king and parliament brought up the issue of **taxation without representation** and stated their conviction that only their own assemblies could levy taxes for revenue purposes.

1765   Boycott—Sons of Liberty—Stamp Tax Repealed

Just days after the Stamp Act Congress adjourned, merchants in New York City, Boston, Philadelphia, and Charleston signed pledges not to buy anything shipped from England. In many towns, groups calling themselves **"Sons of Liberty"** organized to use violent means, if necessary, to punish merchants found violating the boycott. They attacked the colonials who had been appointed tax distributors. In Boston the vice-admiralty court records were burned; homes of unpopular officials were entered and ransacked. In New York City the royal governor's coach was overturned in the street and burned.

The boycott so damaged the business of merchants in England that they petitioned parliament for a repeal of the Stamp Tax. The protest alone was probably enough to convince parliament. Added to the general furor in America, it resulted in the repeal of the Stamp Tax on May 1, 1766.

* Evaluating Grenville and His Program

Lord Grenville was a conscientious treasurer whose job was to raise money. Grenville thought in terms of bookkeeping and economics, not in terms of people. The big difficulty was a political one. The question was not *what* to tax or *how* to tax—it was, How could taxes be levied in such a manner that the colonists would accept them? Perhaps there was no effective answer. Grenville seemed not to appreciate the problem, and blundered into a hornet's nest. The purpose of the Grenville program was to improve "the *revenue* of this Kingdom." The **Stamp Tax** was levied on items originating wholly within each colony and not intended to go out of the colonies. It openly proposed *to raise revenue* for a stated purpose. Colonial assemblies quickly seized upon this new direction the Grenville program had taken. Up to 1764 the laws of Parliament regulating the colonies had been for the **control of intercolonial and foreign trade.** If such regulations incidentally created revenue, that too was acceptable. But the Grenville program was openly a revenue-raising scheme. If accepted, it would expand; and if it ex-

panded, it would take the "power of the purse" from the colonial assemblies.

1766   Declaratory Act

At the same time the Stamp Act was repealed, Parliament passed the **Declaratory Act.** It stated that Parliament had the right to make any laws that would hold the colonies and the British government together. This was a flat rejection of the colonial arguments about taxation without representation, about taxation for revenue, and about any distinction between internal and external taxes. In celebrating the repeal of the Stamp Tax, the colonists paid no attention to the Declaratory Act. But it was apparent that a cleavage of opinion, probably an irreconcilable one, was in the making.

1766   Quartering Act

General Gage had more troops stationed in New York City than barracks to house them. At his request, Parliament had passed a **Quartering Act**, which required the colony in which troops were stationed to supply living quarters for those troops not accommodated by the military authorities. Inns, any vacant public buildings, and private homes could be used. New York resented the presence of the soldiers, as did all the coastal cities and towns. They also resented the expense. The populace erected liberty poles (a mast or staff with a liberty cap on top) as a symbol of derision and defiance toward the soldiers. The Redcoats pulled them down. The Sons of Liberty were leaders in such disorders.

1767   The Townshend Acts (Charles Townshend, Chancellor of the Exchequer)

While Townshend denied there was any legal distinction between internal and external taxes, he was wise enough to make all the new taxes external ones. This would irritate the colonists less and provide them with less on which to base objections. The new taxes on imports into America were to make up for the loss in British taxes to pay salaries of officials stationed in America, to pay for operating new vice-admiralty courts, and to establish an American Board of Commissioners of Customs. The new customs commissioners in Boston would be colonists but they would be responsible directly to the British treasury. The new import taxes were on glass, tea, lead, paint, and paper.

* 1767 John Dickinson's "Farmer's Letters"

These letters appeared in the Pennsylvania Chronicle. They were an attack on the Townshend duties, their main point being that import duties levied for the purpose of raising revenue could not legally be levied by Parliament. Only duties levied to control trade or to regulate the affairs of empire were within the proper sphere of the king and Parliament. Dickinson then pointed out that the Townshend duties were, as the laws themselves plainly stated, revenue taxes. This argument was widely circulated throughout the colonies and favorably received. But Franklin said something at this time which had more the flavor of insight and the tang of common sense. He said, "Either Parliament has the power to make *all laws* for us, or Parliament has the power to make *no laws* for us; and I think the arguments for the latter more numerous and weighty than those of the former."

* 1768 Circular Letters—Samuel Adams—Boston

Samuel Adams drew up a series of statements protesting the Townshend Acts and reiterating the slogan, "Taxation without representation is tyranny." He also called for united action by all the colonies. The Massachusetts House of Representatives adopted this document and provided that it be sent to the other colonial assemblies. The royal governor declared the circular Letter seditious. The ministry in England approved the governor's attitude and suggested that any assemblies adopting such measures be dissolved. But the idea had caught on. Within three months, Connecticut, New Hampshire, New Jersey, and Virginia had passed similar resolutions. It was a natural step from this Circular Letter by Sam Adams to the much more effective **Committees of Correspondence**, also started by Sam Adams only four years later.

1768   The Second Boycott

Items on the Townshend list were not to be bought by the colonial merchants. The plan was initiated in Boston and after a few months had spread to most of the colonies. It reduced appreciably the volume of trade, much as had the boycott of 1765, but there was no petition for relief this time to Parliament by English merchants. It so happened that trade with Europe was unusually brisk. Nevertheless, by the spring of 1769, word had been sent to the colonial governors that a modification of the Townshend duties was imminent.

1770   Townshend Duties Repealed, Except on Tea

About the middle of April, the new prime minister, **Lord North**, came into power and repealed all of the Townshend duties except the tax on tea. The **tea tax** was retained to emphasize the point that Parliament had the right to levy such taxes. No new taxes were levied. The Quartering Act, which had a two-year time limit written in it, expired and was not renewed. These moves so eased tensions that colonial merchants dropped the boycott. Only in Boston was there an organized attempt to continue the boycott, but it failed.

* 1770 The Boston Massacre (March 5) Five Killed

British soldiers and Bostonians frequently exchanged other than complimentary greetings. A fistfight occurred between a soldier and a civilian on March 5. The onlookers participated in a small riot before order was restored. That evening an altercation started between a sentry and some civilians. People gathered; the sentry was joined by British **Captain Thomas Preston** and a squad of soldiers. Stones and snowballs flew, the crowd pressed closer, the soldiers with fixed bayonets raised their guns, and someone shouted, "Fire!" Five civilians were killed. Who gave the command to fire? Certainly not Captain Preston and probably not the more or less disciplined soldiers.

Seven months later, Captain Preston and four of his soldiers were tried. Two were convicted of manslaughter but given a rather mild penalty. They were branded on the hand and allowed to go free. The others were acquitted. **John Adams**, cousin of Sam Adams, and **Josiah Quincy** were the defense lawyers for Captain Preston and his men. Both lawyers were unsympathetic with the British authorities; hence their action displayed both professional integrity and personal courage.

1770   (April) to 1773 (December) The Quiet Period)

For over three years business was good. The import duties, even the tea tax, were being collected. Leaders in all walks of life throughout the colonies as well as the royal governors welcomed both the prosperity and the quiet.

A few sour notes marred this three-year period of comparative quiet. In Rhode Island the British revenue ship *Gaspee* pursued a suspected smuggler in

Narragansett Bay. The smaller local ship led the *Gaspee* onto a sandbar. That evening, June 9, 1772, several small boats attacked the stranded *Gaspee*, forced its crew ashore, and burned it.

Much less exciting but nevertheless disturbing was the news, a few days after the burning of the *Gaspee*, that Governor Hutchinson in Boston was henceforth to be paid by the king, not by the Massachusetts assembly. The colonials were quite aware that "he who pays the fiddler calls the tune."

There were at least three very important people in the colonies who were not at all pleased with peace and quiet—**Samuel Adams, Patrick Henry**, and **Thomas Jefferson**. The decision to have the king pay Governor Hutchinson's salary set Sam Adams to work. He persuaded a Boston town meeting to set up a committee of 21 men to form **committees of correspondence** in every Massachusetts town. **James Otis** was chairman of the Boston committee. From Boston, Sam Adams sent a rehash of every complaint and violated right of the past eight years throughout the colony. It was a propaganda campaign to fan the fires of rebellion. The idea spread. Thomas Jefferson and Patrick Henry took hold of it in Virginia. Early in 1774 the Committees of Correspondence were in high gear in all the colonies except North Carolina and Pennsylvania.

* 1773 The Boston Tea Party (December 16)

The British East India Tea Company was almost bankrupt. To help the company, Lord North's ministry permitted the tea to be shipped directly from the British East Indies to America and thus bypass the English import tax. With this tax relief, the company could reduce the price of the tea and still make a good profit. In addition, England had given the British East India Tea Company a **monopoly** of the tea trade within the empire. The arrangements permitted legal British tea to be sold in America at prices below that of tea smuggled in from the Dutch East Indies.

The colonists protested this new plan, even though it meant the price of tea was lower. England had given a monopoly to a company. If this could be done with tea, why not with other items? Colonial merchants could not compete with the lower price, and the colonists feared other such monopolies could be established. Also, the colonists opposed all taxes passed by Parliament. While Boston was more violent in its reactions, a similar sentiment was evident in all the seaports from Massachusetts to Virginia. The colonists reacted by refusing to buy the tea. In Charleston the tea was stored in damp cellars and not sold. In Annapolis, Maryland, a ship with a cargo of tea was burned. In Philadelphia and New York, British ships carrying tea were refused entry to the harbors and turned back. In Boston three tea ships had been in the harbor for days. Mass meetings in Boston demanded that the ships be sent back still unloaded. Governor Hutchinson refused to permit the ships to leave the harbor unloaded. The Sons of Liberty, who were more popular and hence stronger than ever made it clear that any attempt to unload the tea and store it in warehouses would almost certainly result in burned warehouses. A group of colonists, disguised as Indians, boarded the three tea ships and 342 chests of tea, valued at about $70,000, were dumped into the harbor. Colonial reaction to the **Boston Tea Party** was mixed. Some colonists approved while others deplored the violence.

* 1774 The Intolerable Acts

After the Boston Tea Party, Parliament followed King George III's lead. His objective was to make the colonies accept the tea tax even if it took force to do it. The king's program resulted in the passage of the following laws. Not only in Massachusetts, but throughout the colonies, they were so strongly resented that they became known as the **Intolerable Acts**.

1]   **The Boston Port Bill:** No ships could enter or leave Boston harbor except those with military supplies and whatever food ships the customs officials at Salem permitted. The restrictions could be lifted by the king after the East India Tea Company had been paid for the tea.

2]   Any official of the king charged with a capital crime in connection with enforcing official duties was to be tried in England.

3]   The upper house (Council) of Massachusetts Assembly was to be appointed by the king instead of elected by the lower house (House of Representatives).

4]   There were to be no town meetings without the governor's consent, and even such meetings were confined to an agenda approved by the governor.

5]   Quebec province was extended southward to the Ohio River.

6]   The Quartering Act was again put into effect.

7]   General Gage was to replace Governor Hutch-inson.

All of these changes took effect within three months, in March, April, and May of 1774. The Virginia House of Burgesses declared a "day for fasting, humiliation, and prayer" as a protest against closing the port of Boston. Any measures taken by the king to change the government of Massachusetts were considered threats to all the American colonies. If it could happen to Massachusetts, it could happen to them. On May 27, 1774, the Virginia House of Burgesses called for a meeting of all the colonies at Philadelphia. Ten days earlier, the Rhode Island Assembly had urged an intercolonial meeting. Pennsylvania and New York had also suggested joint consideration of the situation by all of the colonies. Arrangements were made for a meeting at Philadelphia in 1774.

* 1774 First Continental Congress (September 5 to October 26)

Fifty-six delegates attended the Congress held in Carpenters Hall, Philadelphia. Georgia was the only colony not represented. The Congress, each colony having one vote, adopted the **Suffolk Resolves**. They resolved to:

1]   keep trade with England at a minimum by a boycott on imports, by a drastic curtailment of exports, and by refusal to wear, use, or consume English products;

2]   consider null and void all of the punitive measures taken against Boston and Massachusetts since the Tea Party;

3]   approve the efforts of Massachusetts to operate a colonial government separate from royal control until the punitive measures had been repealed;

4]   urge all colonies to raise and train a militia of their own.

To enforce these resolutions an association was organized with a committee in each colony. These committees working under the association were more closely knit and under better control than was the case with the Sons of Liberty, but their function was pretty much the same. The trade restrictions were most effectively carried out. Drilling of local militias became common practice in most of the colonies.

After showing that it stood firmly behind Massachusetts, the First Continental Congress voted upon the **Galloway Plan of Union**. This plan set up a Grand Council for all the colonies similar to the Albany Plan of 1754. This council would act as an adjunct to the British Parliament. Measures dealing with the colonies would have to pass both Parliament and the Grand Council. The king was to appoint a president-general with authority to veto acts of the Grand Council. This plan recognized the right of the king and Parliament to regulate external trade and any matters that were clearly affairs of empire; it also denied the right of king and Parliament to levy revenue taxes or interfere with the internal affairs of the colonies. By a one-vote margin the Galloway Plan failed to pass.

The First Continental Congress sent a petition to the king requesting the repeal of all regulatory acts since 1763 and informing him of the economic restrictions that were being taken against England. Before they adjourned, the Congress set May 10, 1775, for another meeting.

* 1775 The King's Reply, Lexington and Concord (April 19)

While the boycott and other economic moves against England were very effective in reducing trade, they had no effect upon the determination of George III and Parliament to make the colonies pay the tea tax and force them to abide by the coercive regulations that followed the Tea Party.

General Gage was ordered to enforce the laws. His first move was to send troops to Concord to seize stores of arms from which the rapidly forming companies of militia were being supplied. On the night of April 18, the British started from Boston. **Paul Revere** and **William Dawes**, riding by different routes, aroused the whole countryside along the fifteen miles to Lexington. A third rider, **Dr. Samuel Prescott**, got the warning to Concord so that when the British arrived, the colonials were expecting them.

At dawn, on April 19, **Captain John Parker** had 70 **Minutemen** in formation on the Village Green at Lexington. **Major Pitcairn**, in command of a much larger British force, ordered the colonials to disarm and disperse. At this point a shot was fired; no one knows from which side. There then followed a quick burst of shots from the British and a few scattered shots from the colonials. One British soldier was wounded, eight colonials were killed and ten wounded. This was the **Battle of Lexington**. The British marched on to Concord.

At the North Bridge in Concord a small group of colonial militiamen fired a volley into the British troops ("the shot heard 'round the world"). The British destroyed military stores and food supplies and at about noon were ready to march back to Charlestown and Boston. By this time the countryside was swarming with colonial militia and they were angry. From Concord back to Lexington, the British redcoats were easy targets for the colonial soldiers shooting from behind trees and stone walls. The British were saved from utter rout by the arrival of reinforcements at Lexington. April 19 cost the British about three times the casualties suffered by the colonials,—about 93 to 275 killed, wounded, and missing.

1775   Ticonderoga Captured by Ethan Allen (May 10)

On the very day that the Second Continental Congress met, **Ethan Allen** and his **Green Mountain Boys** captured Fort Ticonderoga, which was so taken by surprise that the only casualty was one British soldier wounded. The cannons captured here were dragged to Boston, where they became a decisive factor in persuading the British to leave Boston harbor in March of the next year.

* 1775 Second Continental Congress

The meetings were held in Independence Hall, Philadelphia. Again the radicals were in control. **John Hancock** was president. **Thomas Jefferson** and **Benjamin Franklin** were delegates and favored complete independence. **John Dickinson** was an effective spokesman for the conservative faction among the delegates who wished to send more petitions and appeals to the king. The decision in favor of a war for independence was made outside of the Congress by the events of 1775 and Thomas Paine's **Common Sense** pamphlet of January 1776.

Events at Lexington and Concord occurred before the Second Continental Congress convened. **Bunker Hill** was five weeks after the opening meeting of the Congress. This battle, actually fought on **Breed's Hill**, cost the British over 1,000 casualties and the colonials about 400. The news of the capture of Ticonderoga and Crown Point arrived in Boston about the same time the Battle of Bunker Hill took place. In the summer of 1775, colonial troops under **General Philip Schuyler** and later under **General Richard Montgomery** were in Canada. In September they had occupied Montreal, which the British had evacuated, and were forming an expedition to attack Quebec. In short, by the end of 1775, war was well under way. King George III in England said (August 1775) in a formal proclamation that the colonies in America were in a state of rebellion. Nevertheless, it was still true that in January 1776, there was still a rather heavy haze of indecision concerning the exact state of the American-English relationship.

1775   Washington Appointed Commander-in-Chief (June 15)

Events from April 19 through May pushed the Second Continental Congress into acts that transformed it from an organization of protest to one of revolution. After Lexington and Concord, the Massachusetts militia, numbering several thousands, hemmed in the British on the land sides of Boston. The Congress called for more militia from Virginia, Pennsylvania, and Maryland. A full week before Bunker Hill the Congress was considering uniting all colonial forces into a Continental Army under a unified command. John Adams had suggested **George Washington** as the man to head this army.

Perhaps no single act begins to compare in importance with the choice of Washington as the factor in the war that contributed most to victory. The choice was not only a superb one because it selected a man with the right character and abilities; it also displayed political know-how. Boston and Massachusetts had been so much the area of violent incidents, so much the victim of British retaliation, so much the instigator of boycotts and anti-English propaganda that there was some danger that the revolution would appear to be a Massachusetts rather than an American revolution. It was therefore politically important to give prominence early in the war to some colony other than Massachusetts. Virginia had **Patrick Henry**, a flaming revolutionist, and **Thomas Jefferson**, the most effective spokesman for self-government in the colonies. It was strong in wealth and manpower. Its social and economic structure differed from that of New England; it represented the Southern area much as Massachusetts represented the Northern. It was a political necessity that Virginia be brought into as prominent a position as possible at the very beginning of the war.

The Ideology of the American Revolution

* 1776 Common Sense by Thomas Paine (January)

The American colonies were, with hesitancy and with troublesome doubts, moving toward independence. Paine's pamphlet, *Common Sense,* was definite, tough, clear, uncomplicated common sense to the people. If anything was read by every literate person in the colonies, it was *Common Sense.* Paine attacked the institution of hereditary monarchy in principle, called the British monarchy corrupt, and cited George III in particular. He called for the colonists to separate themselves from Britain and to make America the one place in the world where freedom and love of humankind could flourish. Through Paine's pamphlet, popular opinion caught up with and further stimulated the radical leadership in the Second Continental Congress. Six months after its publication the Congress would adopt the **Declaration of Independence** signed by representatives of each of the 13 colonies.

1776 Declaration of Independence (July 4)

On June 7 Richard Henry Lee of Virginia made a motion, which was seconded by John Adams of Massachusetts. Lee was acting in accordance with instructions from his state. The motion contained three parts: that the American colonies are independent states, that foreign aid should be sought, and that a confederate form of government be prepared for submission to the several states. The motion was discussed for four days, and then it was decided to postpone a vote until July 1. In the meantime, a committee was appointed to draw up a declaration of independence and another committee to work on a **constitution** for a confederation. The members of the committee on the declaration of independence were **Thomas Jefferson** (Virginia), **Benjamin Franklin** (Pennsylvania), **John Adams** (Massachusetts), **Robert Livingston** (New York), and **Roger Sherman** (Connecticut). The committee asked Jefferson to write the first draft of the declaration. With very few changes, Jefferson's work was presented to the Congress. From July 1 to July 4, consideration was given to Lee's motion and to the proposed Declaration of Independence. Some changes were made in Jefferson's work by the Congress, and then on July 4, by a vote of 12 to 0, the Declaration of Independence was adopted. New York abstained from voting. On July 9 the New York Provincial Congress formally approved the Declaration.

** The Nature and Content of the Declaration of Independence

Jefferson set out to express effectively ideas commonly held. The job was so well done that it not only served the occasion for which it was written, the **American Revolution**, but has continued to be a source of inspiration throughout the world. Wherever freedom through independence is sought, the American Declaration of Independence is a guiding star.

The Declaration falls into three main divisions. First there is a statement of the **"natural rights"** of people. This is packed into four not very long sentences. Many of the key ideas Jefferson wrote into this section came from the writings of John Locke (1632–1704), an English philosopher. Almost a century earlier, Locke expressed the following ideas in his *Treatise on Civil Government:* (1) Man is granted certain rights by nature. (2) Among these rights are life, liberty, and property. (3) The purpose of government is to protect these rights. (4) If a government fails to protect those rights of mankind, the people have the right and duty to alter or abolish that government. Jefferson changed "life, liberty and property" to "life, liberty and the pursuit of happiness." These ideas define the purpose of American government and the relationship between the people and their government. Next is a long list of complaints about the king and a statement or two about the humble patience of the American colonies under such treatment; and finally, there is the declaration that the colonies are now independent states.

For all the generations since the establishment of our nation, the statement of belief in "natural rights" and **unalienable rights** is the heart of the Declaration. Not only is there recognition of, but there is insistence upon, belief in the dignity and importance of the individual. There is no such thing as an unimportant person. "All men are created equal" is not a statement of fact revealing truth; it is a statement of faith displaying wisdom.

The second part of the Declaration is a list of complaints and blames George III for almost everything, in spite of the fact that much of our quarrel was with Parliament. Certainly it was effective in convincing most of its readers of the wickedness and obstinacy of the king; it served well the cause of revolution.

For its time, July 1776, the high point of the Declaration was the ringing statement, "We, therefore, the representatives of the United States of America, in General Congress assembled, appealing to the Supreme Judge of the world for the rectitude of our intentions, do, in the name and by the authority of the good people of these colonies, solemnly publish and declare, that these united colonies are, and of right ought to be, free and independent states....And, for the support of this declaration, with a firm reliance on the protection of Divine Providence, we mutually pledge to each other our lives, our fortune, and our sacred honor."

Note that the full Declaration of Independence can be found in the Appendix, beginning on page 417.

The American Revolution 1775-1783

** The Great Experiment in Self-Government

The social and economic status of the people of America did not change markedly as a result of the war. The families that were in positions of leadership in social, economic, and political affairs before the war were also in such positions after the war. Of course, the king's agents and their appointees were thrown out of power, but the colonials prominent in the local governments of 1763 were, by and large, still the leaders in 1784. **Loyalists** lost their property in many instances.

In a more significant sense, the American Revolution was an experiment in the field of politics and government. A whole people were to govern themselves through a representative framework of officeholders chosen by the sovereign people. Could a large republic be established? Could it live if established? Did people really have "natural rights" just because they were human beings? Could a people govern themselves? Would not freedom breed chaos, and chaos necessitate dictatorship to restore order? What if the experiment in republican government did work, would American success then mark the beginning of the disintegration of monarchies? Imagine that you are back in 1770 and try to answer each of the preceding questions. It might give you a fuller appreciation of how great a faith our founders had in humankind; it might put greater meaning in **Thomas Paine's** words, "These are times that try men's souls." The ideology emphasizing the "natural rights" of individuals and the right of a people to govern themselves through their chosen officials had permeated colonial America. People with a cause fight with tenacity; the more noble the cause, the greater the tenacity.

Because our cause was great, we were able to recruit several notable personages with special military skills. The **Marquis de Lafayette** helped America before his country became our ally. Later he was a leader in the French Revolution. The famous French *Declaration of the Rights of Man* was Lafayette's adaptation of Jefferson's Declaration of Independence. **Major General Johann de Kalb,** a German, died fighting for the American cause, as did **Count Casimir Pulaski** of Poland. **Colonel Thaddeus Kosciusko,** also Polish, and **General Friedrich Baron von Steuben** of Prussia also joined the American forces because they deemed the cause worth the risk of life itself.

Strengths and Weaknesses of England and America

England's Strong Points
It had a great navy, a well-equipped army, and money.

There was considerable Loyalist support in America.

England's Weak Points
Its supply line included 3,000 miles of ocean requiring four to six weeks to cross.

Pitt, Burke, and Fox opposed in Parliament the war policy of King George III.

A large segment of English opinion (Whig party members) were more pleased with the failure of the king's policies than distressed by failure in war.

The English were slow to develop techniques of fighting to suit conditions in America.

America's Strong Points
George Washington's leadership was superb.

American rifles were superior to those of the English.

American soldiers had gained experience in the French and Indian War.

To hasten victory, they were determined to avoid capture and continue resistance.

Defensive tactics served the American cause; attack could be reserved for favorable circumstances.

America's Weak Points
Discipline was often poor.

Enlistments were for short terms.

Desertions were frequent. (Soldiers would be temporarily "A.W.O.L." during planting and harvesting seasons.

The Americans lacked military supplies, money, and an adequate navy.

It had a poorly organized government.

* What Made Washington "First in War"?

Persistence in rebellion and avoidance of capture

were the two *musts* for American success. Time and again, Washington slipped away when the British expected a fight under circumstances favorable to them. From the British point of view, the exasperating thing about Washington was that, even though he could be beaten, he couldn't be caught. He would not give up. The following list of only a few of the trials and troubles Washington experienced makes the tenacity of the man apparent.

1] The Continental Army totaled less than 10,000 ready for duty at any one time. (There were probably 250,000 men in the colonies, widely scattered, of course.)

2] The militias of the states totaled about 20,000. They fought well in defense of their own towns. Discipline was usually poor. They deserted and returned to service as they saw fit.

3] Much of the time soldiers had no uniforms. Lack of proper footwear was a major problem.

4] Pay was seldom on time for the soldiers, and when it arrived the Continental currency was of little value. The soldiers were not too far wrong when they said that their pay was $20 a month in worthless money.

5] Political intrigue was aimed at displacing Washington. The Conway Cabal in 1778 revealed letters by General Gates attacking him.

6] Generals **Charles Lee** and **Benedict Arnold** were traitors.

7] Shortages that caused the intense suffering at **Valley Forge** were more the result of mismanagement than of genuine shortages.

8] In 1780 two Connecticut regiments at Morristown paraded under arms demanding full rations (they had been on one-eighth rations) and back pay. Pennsylvania troops held them in check.

9] In 1781 over 1,000 Pennsylvania troops broke away from the encampment at Morristown. Several officers were wounded. The men were bent upon marching to Congress to demand back pay. About half of these soldiers returned.

10] The Newburg Letters attempted to stir up rebellion against Congress over back pay, short rations, etc. Major John Armstrong, General Gates, and Assistant Attorney-General Barber were instigators of this conspiracy.

This list could be expanded to many times this length. Only the dedication of a great man to a great cause can explain why Washington did not resign in disgust.

* Summary of Major Campaigns of the American Revolution

The first major American campaign was to end the British plan to take New England. The British were determined to end the war in 1777. Their plan was to use three British armies to converge upon Albany, New York, from the north, south, and west and separate New England from the other colonies. On paper the plan was sound. However, one who knew the distances and the terrain might have recognized how difficult its execution would be and realized that communication during the operation would be impractical. This campaign has been called the "British Blunder of 1777." The blunder was not in the plan but in its execution. **Sir William Howe** left New York for Chesapeake Bay and Philadelphia with one army at the very time he should have been starting up the Hudson for Albany. **General Burgoyne** with a second army found the forests of northeastern New York State very difficult terrain for his overburdened troops. He never reached Albany. Instead, he was trapped at Saratoga and surrendered on October 17, 1777. This led to an alliance with France. Saratoga is considered to be the turning point of the war.

Colonel St. Leger with the third army came up the St. Lawrence River and across Lake Ontario to Fort Oswego and laid siege to Fort Stanwix on the Mohawk River. General Benedict Arnold arrived in the vicinity and by trickery persuaded the Indians to desert the British. St. Leger gave up the attack on Fort Stanwix and retreated to Canada. So a military plan that looked very good on a map was turned into a complete failure by mismanagement, difficult terrain, long distances, plus American generals and several thousand sharp-shooting Americans.

The other major American campaign was the setting of the trap to capture **Cornwallis** at **Yorktown**. Washington received word that the French fleet under **Admiral DeGrasse** was leaving the West Indies for Chesapeake Bay. Cornwallis was on the York peninsula, a perfectly good position so long as the British fleet controlled Chesapeake Bay. Washington slipped away with his troops and went south to combine with French troops under **Lafayette** and **Rochambeau.** The combined French-American forces held Cornwallis at Yorktown while DeGrasse entered Chesapeake Bay. With retreat by sea cut off, Cornwallis was under siege and he surrendered, ending the war on October 19, 1781.

In addition to these two campaigns, General Washington in 1776 and into January of 1777, led a masterly retreat from Long Island, up the Hudson, across to New Jersey, and south to Trenton where he suddenly stopped retreating and made his surprise attacks at Trenton and Princeton. Washington set up winter quarters in northern New Jersey at **Morristown** in January 1777. The following September and October he tried unsuccessfully to prevent the British from taking up quarters at Philadelphia (**Brandywine** and **Germantown**). In December 1777 and the rest of the winter, the troops were half starved and half frozen at **Valley Forge**. For the rest of the war until Yorktown, the main winter quarters were at **Morristown**, New Jersey. Washington had his forces around New York while the British enjoyed the comforts in the city with the fleet insuring their safety. DeGrasse's plan to come to Chesapeake Bay set up the Yorktown campaign.

CHRONOLOGICAL LIST OF BATTLES AND OTHER IMPORTANT EVENTS DURING THE WAR

The symbol (GW) indicates a battle involving forces where George Washington was in direct command, or other forces in the immediate area acting in conjunction with him.

The symbol (HM) indicates battles that were part of the Hudson-Mohawk rivers "British Blunder of 1777."

There are more items listed than you will care to remember. They are for easy reference.

1775   (April 19) Lexington and Concord

Major John Pitcairn was sent by Governor Gage of Massachusetts to seize military supplies at **Concord. Paul Revere, William Dawes,** and **Dr. Samuel Prescott** aroused the countryside. Skirmishes at **Lexington (Captain John Parker** in command of the colonials) and at Concord.

1775   (May 10) Fort Ticonderoga taken by Ethan Allen

1775   (May 12) Crown Point taken by Ethan Allen

Crown Point and Ticonderoga were important control points on the southern end of Lake Champlain.

1775   (June 15)

The Second Continental Congress voted unanimously to appoint George Washington Commander-in-Chief of the Continental Army. Washington accepted the commission on June 16.

1775   (June 17) Bunker Hill (fought on Breed's Hill)

To prevent the British from occupying Dorchester Heights, 1,200 colonial troops under **Colonel William Prescott** secretly took positions the night of June 16 on Breed's Hill and by the next morning the colonists had 1,600 men on the hill. The attacking force numbered 2,400. Two frontal attacks failed. The third one succeeded only because the defenders' ammunition gave out. British casualties included many officers and totaled about 1,050, over three times the colonial losses. This defeat was immediately a source of pride. Raw colonial militia had met the best soldiers the British had.

1775   (August through December) Expedition Against Quebec

General Richard Montgomery invaded Canada and forced the British to leave Montreal, which he then occupied. His forces were strengthened by joining with a second invading force led by **Benedict Arnold**. The combined attack on Quebec on the last day of the year was a complete failure. Montgomery was killed, Arnold wounded, and about one-third of the colonial troops were killed or captured.

1776   (March 17) Howe Evacuates Boston

Cannon and other artillery captured at Ticonderoga were mounted on **Dorchester Heights,** bringing most of the town and harbor within effective range. The British decided to evacuate. About 1,000 Loyalists of the Boston area went with the fleet to Halifax.

1776   (July 4) Declaration of Independence

1776   (August 27) Long Island (Brooklyn Heights)

*GW   Having left Boston, **General William Howe** went to New York City to set up headquarters. Washington knew of this move and went to Long Island to interfere with these plans. On the island Howe took possession of Brooklyn Heights and apparently had Washington trapped. Here the war might have ended in favor of the British had Howe pressed his advantage without delay. During the night, Washington got his troops onto Manhattan Island so that by daylight General Howe had no one to fight.

1776   (September 16) Harlem Heights

GW   The British had occupied the city, and Washington slowed them down as best he could. At **Harlem Heights** he made a successful temporary stand and was allowed to stay behind fortified positions in the area for about three weeks.

1776   (October 28) White Plains

GW   Washington retreated north along the east side of the Hudson. As General Howe attempted to encircle him, Washington hastened north to White Plains. Again Howe managed to gain a superior position on high ground. Again he delayed, awaiting reinforcements, and again, while Howe waited, Washington slipped away.

1776   (November 15) Fort Washington Fell to the British

GW   Howe sent a force of about 13,000 to take Fort Washington which they did.

1776   (November 15) Fort Lee Fell to the British

GW   Cornwallis forced **General Greene** to evacuate **Fort Lee**, while Greene saved his men, he

gave up a large amount of sorely needed military supplies.

1776   (December 26) Trenton

GW   Washington crossed the Hudson into New Jersey to join forces with General Greene. They proceeded southward not too far ahead of the pursuing Cornwallis. After a few days the British gave up the chase. By mid-December they went into winter quarters but left defense forces at **Trenton, Princeton,** and a few other places. Washington had crossed the **Delaware River** going south, but he surprised the British by turning north, recrossing the Delaware, and entering Trenton early in the morning the day after Christmas, where he attacked a force of **Hessians**, mercenary troops from the German state of Hesse. This sudden victory after a string of defeats was a tonic to the depressed spirits of the army and of Congress.

1776   (January 3) Princeton

The British were stung by the surprise at Trenton. Cornwallis caught up with Washington a few miles east of Trenton on January 2. Both sides prepared for battle, but heavy reinforcements were nearby, so Cornwallis chose to delay until the next morning. Again Washington slipped away overnight. At dawn, he ran into the British reinforcements just south of Princeton and defeated them. Three days later Washington settled down in winter quarters in the hills of Morristown, New Jersey.

1777   (June 14) The United States Adopts a Flag

The Second Continental Congress voted to have an official flag for the United States of America, "thirteen stripes alternate red and white, that the Union be thirteen stars white in a blue field..."

1777   (August 6) Oriskany

Oriskany is on the Mohawk River, southeast of **Fort Stanwix**. General Herkimer was ambushed while going to the relief of Fort Stanwix. Word that General Benedict Arnold

---

* A situation in which Washington was a major factor.

was coming frightened the Native Americans into deserting the British under St. Leger. This *HM stopped St. Leger's attack on Fort Stanwix and put an end to his advance toward Albany.

1777   (August 16) Bennington, Vermont

HM General Burgoyne, while on his way south from the St. Lawrence River to Albany, sent General Baum to Bennington, Vermont, to seize military supplies stored there. General John Stark captured almost the entire British force. Reinforcements arrived for both sides, and in a second encounter, the Americans again won.

1777   (September 11) Brandywine

GW Sir William Howe left New York City for Chesapeake Bay and Philadelphia to establish winter quarters. Washington came south from Morristown to prevent him from entering Philadelphia. At Brandywine (about 25 miles from Philadelphia) Washington suffered a severe defeat.

1777   (October 4) Germantown

GW Howe had most of his troops encamped at Germantown, north of Philadelphia. In an attempt to force the British out of Philadelphia, Washington was again defeated. He then retired to winter quarters at Valley Forge.

1777   (October 16) Kingston Burned by the British

HM Burgoyne had been having trouble for weeks as he headed south through the rough terrain of northeastern New York. General Clinton in New York City received a call for reinforcements and started up the Hudson. He got as far as Kingston, burned the town, and returned to New York City. At the time he burned Kingston (only one day before Burgoyne's surrender), he was 90 miles from Saratoga.

1777   (October 17) Saratoga

HM Burgoyne had suffered a series of setbacks in encounters throughout the ten days immediately preceding the surrender at Saratoga. He had already turned back when his forces were practically surrounded by American troops about three times as numerous as his own. Burgoyne surrendered his entire army of about 5,700 men.

1777   (November 15)

The Second Continental Congress voted to adopt the Articles of Confederation, which had been submitted to them as early as July 12, 1776. The Articles would become the official government of the United States of America only when all of the thirteen states ratified them. This did not occur until March 1, 1781.

1777   (December—On Through the Winter) Valley Forge

GW After defeats at Brandywine and Germantown, Washington retired to Valley Forge. Shortages of food, clothing, and blankets made the winter one of intense suffering. The shortages were due more to inefficient management and poor logistics than to genuine shortages.

1778   (June 17) France Becomes Our Ally

HM The victory at Saratoga set off negotiations in Paris toward a formal alliance. As early as February 1777, it was agreed that, if and when England and France were at war, the military alliance between America and France would automatically come into effect. A clash at sea between the British and French occurred on June 17, 1778. It was agreed that neither America nor France would make a truce or sign a peace until the other consented.

1778   (June 17) England Offers Peace ("Extends the Olive Branch")

The catastrophe at Saratoga clearly invited an American-French alliance. Parliament and King George III realized it. In February they began arranging terms to offer to America. Their

* A situation which is part of the Hudson-Mohawk River campaign.

terms were that Parliament would impose no revenue taxes upon the colonies, that the Coercive Acts and the tea tax would be repealed, and that all acts by Parliament affecting the colonies passed since 1763 would be suspended. On June 17 Congress announced that it would agree to no terms other than the complete withdrawal of British soldiers from American soil and the recognition by England of the complete independence of the United States of America.

1778   (June 28) Monmouth (about 25 miles east of Trenton)

GW Washington attempted to intercept General Clinton's forces, which were going from Philadelphia to New York City. Through the treachery of **General Charles Lee**, who was later found to have been a traitor, a major American victory was prevented.

1778   (July 4) Kaskaskia (Cahokia and Vincennes)

George Rogers Clark carried the war as far west as the Mississippi River. Starting out with 175 men, he went down the Ohio river to within a few miles of the Mississippi, then cut across to **Kaskaskia**.   This cross-country march was extremely difficult. Surprise was the chief element in Clark's success. Kaskaskia was so remote and inaccessible that its defenders were not alert. During the following few months, Clark took the British forts at **Cahokia** and **Vincennes**. These operations are sometimes called the "war in the West."

1779   (June 21) Spain Declared War on England

Congress sent **John Jay** to try to get money and supplies from Spain. He had very little success. Spain refused to recognize American independence and refused to pledge to continue at war with England until American independence was, in fact, established.

1780   (May 12) Charleston Captured by the British

General Clinton took 4 American ships and about 5,000 prisoners when he occupied the city.

1780   (August 16) Camden

Washington advised Congress to send General Greene to oppose the British in the South, but Congress sent General Gates instead. Gates was thoroughly defeated at Camden, South Carolina. Gates had been as much a hindrance as a help at Saratoga even though he had been in command. He encouraged disaffection against Congress and Washington. It was at this battle that Baron de Kalb lost his life.

1780   (September 21) Benedict Arnold's Treason

Benedict Arnold was given command of West Point on August 5, 1780. On September 21 he met the British officer Major John Andre and gave him the plans of West Point with suggestions as to its weak points. Andre was caught with these papers at Tarrytown before he got back to British lines. On September 30, Andre was hanged.

1780   (October 7) King's Mountain (Borderline of North and South Carolina)

The British **Major Ferguson** lost almost all of his force of about 1,100 men to a group of sharp-shooting frontiersmen. This American victory lifted morale in the Carolina and throughout the South.

1781   (March 1) The Articles of Confederation Went Into Effect

Maryland finally ratified the Articles, the last of the states to do so.

1781   (August 14) News from Admiral De Grasse

The French **Admiral De Grasse**, sent word to Washington that he was bringing his fleet to Chesapeake Bay from the West Indies. Washington then made plans to bottle up Cornwallis in Virginia on the York Peninsula.

1781   (October 19) Yorktown (The War Is Virtually Ended)

Washington left troops around the land sides of New York City and maintained activity to deceive the British into expecting an offensive action against the city. Meanwhile, he went south with his main force to join with **Lafayette**, **Rochambeau**, and **De Grasse** to trap Cornwallis. The position of Cornwallis at **Yorktown** was a good one so long as the British fleet had control of Chesapeake Bay. Cornwallis had no inkling that the French fleet was about to hem him in. The siege began on October 9. By the 18th the British position was hopeless. Cornwallis and his 8,000 men surrendered on the 19th.

1782 (March 5) Parliament Acts to Bring the War to a Close

The House of Commons passed a bill against any further prosecution of the war against America. It further directed that peace terms be arranged.

1782 (November 30) Peace Terms Arranged

Our ministers, **John Adams**, **Benjamin Franklin**, and **John Jay**, signed a separate treaty with England, not waiting for France to agree. This was a source of irritation to France, but Franklin was able to smooth things over. Although the terms were agreed upon between England and the United States, they were not to go into effect until France and England had come to terms. The agreements reached were as follows.

1] The independence of the United States of America was recognized.

2] The northern border would be the St. Croix River, the St. Lawrence-Atlantic watershed divide (not easily determined), the 45th parallel to the St. Lawrence River, the Great Lakes, and from Lake Superior to the Mississippi River (not very definite).

3] The western border was the Mississippi River as far south as the 31st parallel.

4] The southern border was the 31st parallel to the St. Mary's River to the Atlantic Ocean. (This line was disputed by Spain.)

5] Debts existing between British subjects and Americans were valid.

6] Congress would recommend restoration of property and rights to the Loyalists.

7] The British would evacuate American soil "with all convenient speed."

1783 (September 3) Peace Treaty Signed at Paris

The treaty was ratified by our Congress on January 14, 1784.

American Naval Operations During the War

The Continental Navy was made up of ships built or bought by order of Congress and paid for by the United States. This Navy had seven ships at the end of the war. Some of the states had navies of their own, but their services were uncoordinated and were of very little account. There were over a thousand privateers. Privateers were privately owned ships whose captains carried letters of marque and reprisal, which certified that they were acting with the permission of their government against ships of an enemy nation. Privateers got whatever they captured and privateering often paid handsomely. This was a great hindrance to recruiting sailors for the Continental Navy since the pay was low. Serving in the Navy was more dangerous than privateering, as well as much less profitable. The privateers raised havoc with British commerce.

If we had no really effective Navy, we did have a spectacular naval hero, **John Paul Jones**. He made raids on coastal towns near his boyhood home in Scotland, took a few prisoners, and burned a few houses. His raids kept many British ships roving the waters of the North and Irish seas when they might otherwise have been doing more important work. Jones took many prizes, outmaneuvered British warships too powerful for him to fight, and he defeated those he did engage. His most spectacular victory was at the battle between the *Bonhomme Richard* and *H.M.S. Serapis* when he said "I have not yet begun to fight."

*The Articles of Confederation
March 1, 1781-March 4, 1789

Confederation and Federation

The first constitution of the United States of America was the **Articles of Confederation**, which went into effect in 1781. In a confederation each state retains the major powers of government; each state guards its sovereignty to such an extent that the central government is unable to force any state to act against its own will. A confederation emphasizes the rights of states and holds, to a minimum, the power of the central government.

Facts to Know About the Articles of Confederation

1] There was no chief executive.

There was a **"Committee of States"** made up of one delegate from each state. But this committee existed only during the intervals between the sessions of the Congress. This committee could, in the absence of Congress, perform routine governmental functions. It was specifically denied the power to make any policy decisions or to do anything which required a majority of nine of the thirteen states when the Congress was in session.

2] There was no judicial department.

There was no court to handle disputes between or among the states. If a dispute arose that could not be resolved by the states involved, then Congress was authorized to establish a court to judge the dispute. While the decision of this court was stated to be "final and conclusive," there was no provision for the enforcement of the verdict. It is important to know that there was an adequate court system in each of the thirteen states.

3] A majority of nine votes was required to pass important laws.

A few routine matters of minor importance could be settled by a simple majority vote, and it was these few and minor powers that were also possessed by the "executive department" previously described. Nine votes out of thirteen is a two-thirds majority. Passing laws was a slow and difficult process. The Congress was **unicameral** (one house), and each state had from two to seven delegates but only one vote.

4] Congress could requisition taxes from the states but could not force their collection.

Based on the value of "all land within each state, granted to or surveyed for any person," the Congress told each state what it should pay in taxes toward the support of the United States of America. It was left to the states to collect this money and turn it over to the central government. As one might well guess, the states did not pay the amounts requisitioned. For example, in 1781 a total of $8 million was requisitioned. Over two years later, less than $1.5 million had been paid.

5] The Congress could requisition men into the armed forces but could not draft men into the service of the United States.

Based upon population "in proportion to the number of white inhabitants in each state," Congress told each state how many men to supply for the armed forces. It was up to the states to raise the quota "clothed, armed and equipped" and march them "to the place appointed." This worked about as ineffectively as did the raising of money.

6] The members of Congress were paid by the states, and a state could recall any delegate at any time.

This arrangement made the members of Congress think and act as ambassadors for their states. They did not serve the United States nor, under this system, should they have done so. Their function was to protect and advance the interests of their own states and to cooperate for the welfare of the United States only when such cooperation coincided with this objective.

7] Congress was not given exclusive power to regulate interstate and foreign commerce.

Each state set its own import duties, and soon each state tried to protect its own internal trade by levying tariffs against goods from other states. Thus, effective trade agreements between the United States and any foreign nation were impossible, and internal trade across state borders reached a very low volume.

8] Congress was not given the exclusive power to issue paper money.

Congress did fix the value of coins by setting the weight and the alloy used regardless of whether the coins were "struck by their own authority, or by that of the respective states." But the paper money situation became utterly chaotic.

9] Treaties made by the United States could be nullified by the action of the states.

If any provision in a treaty required the cooperation of the states, there was no way the central government could guarantee such cooperation.

10] Amending the Articles of Confederation required the unanimous vote of the thirteen states.

This provision expresses the concern sovereign states have whenever they form a league or common government. The right to exercise a veto power at some critical point is each state's protection against being coerced by the combined will of several other states.

Some Worthwhile Sidelights on the Articles of Confederation

Soon after the Second Continental Congress appointed the committee to draw up a declaration of independence, it also formed another committee to draw up a constitution for the new nation. This second committee reported several days later by submitting to the Congress of the Articles of Confederation. Several of the concepts written into the Articles of Confederation stemmed directly from Benjamin Franklin's **"Albany Plan of Union"** of 1754. From time to time, the Second Continental Congress considered the original draft of the Articles and made revisions. By November 1777 the Articles had been approved and submitted to each of the thirteen states for ratification. The Articles would become the official government of the United States of America when ratified by all of the thirteen states. All but one state ratified them rather quickly. Maryland held out until March 1781, which is only about seven months before the Yorktown campaign that ended the Revolutionary War. So, for a war that lasted about five and one-half years as far as fighting was concerned, we had a makeshift government except for the last seven months. Much has been made of the mismanagement of the Revolutionary War by the Second Continental Congress, but perhaps the fact that is really surprising is that a loosely organized Congress not intended for the purpose did prosecute a war and win it.

Maryland refused to ratify the Articles of Confederation because it was a small state and feared union with so many large states that might become larger. Only Rhode Island, Delaware, and New Jersey were smaller, and all four of these small states had no claims to western lands. Their boundaries were fixed; they could become no larger. Maryland withheld ratification until it was assured that the states having claims to vast western areas lying roughly between the Allegheny Highland and the Mississippi River and from the Great Lakes to Spanish Florida would relinquish them. Perhaps more than could have been realized at the time, Maryland performed a service to our country. Pressure from Maryland induced the states to cede their western lands to the United States. The acquisition of these lands by the central government set the stage for the **Northwest Ordinance of 1787**, and greatly aided the solution of the financial problems during the first shaky years of our republic under the present Constitution.

** Understanding and Appreciating the Articles of Confederation

The ten weaknesses of the Articles of Confederation previously listed were not mistakes; that is, not mistakes in the sense that they were not intended. Each protection of the sovereign power of the states and each limitation on the power of the United States was deliberately and carefully calculated. Had the power of the central government been made greater, the states would have refused to form the union. With the Declaration of Independence and the reforming of the colonial governments into state governments, each of the thirteen states became a **republic**, an independent sovereign power. Modifying sovereignty is perhaps the most difficult of all political necessities to bring into effect. And no sovereign power is induced to sacrifice sovereignty until the painful necessity to do so is less painful than the penalty for not doing so.

The Critical Period 1781-1789

or

The United States Under the Articles of Confederation

The Crisis

The historian John Fiske gave the period between the American Revolution and the adoption of the Constitution the title **"Critical Period."** The crisis that built up during these years was the issue of life and death for our republic. Washington, who could not be discouraged during the Revolution, was on the verge of despair over the prospects for its survival. Jefferson, then our ambassador to Paris, reported to Congress that the French government simply wouldn't take this country seriously; he concluded with, "We are the lowest and most obscure of the whole diplomatic tribe."

* A Sampling of Conditions During the Critical Period

Shays' rebellion in Massachusetts made plain the desperate condition of the debtors. **Captain Daniel Shays**, a farmer, had seen service at Bunker Hill. He knew that the farmers, many of them veterans of the Revolution, were unable to pay their debts and that their farms were being taken from them by court action so that creditors could be satisfied. Many of these farms had been family homes for years. Shays didn't know what to do and he thought it must be the government's fault, or, at least, that the government should do something about it.

Seen through Shays' eyes, the Revolutionary War was fought for "liberty," for "independence," for a "republic." Shays felt that an end should be put to the foreclosure of mortgages on farms and homes, more paper money should be printed, and creditors should be forced by law to accept paper money in payment of debts. **Governor Bowdoin** and the Massachusetts legislature refused to pass such laws. Protest meetings were held in many rural towns throughout Massachusetts. In September, mobs formed; violence broke out in the Worcester, Springfield, and Berkshire areas of central and western Massachusetts. Shays led the larg-

est and most persistent armed group. Mobs prevented judges from holding court. From early September 1786 to early February 1787, rural Massachusetts was in a turmoil. Militia from Boston finally rounded up the leaders, the resistance fell apart, and order was restored. The central government had played no part in restoring order. Many Americans were alarmed by Shays' Rebellion because it showed the weakness of the nation and the inability of the central government to maintain law and order.

During this time, there was a depression. The adjustment from war to peace is upsetting to business, but it should have been a minor factor in the simple and overwhelmingly agricultural economy of the post-Revolutionary period. Tariff walls had been erected by each of the thirteen states against imports from any other state. Trying by laws to confine trade to their own people, the states had created a condition where there was precious little trade for anyone. Virginia and Maryland sent representatives to a meeting at Mt. Vernon in 1785, hoping to abolish or modify tariffs. They planned a meeting at Annapolis, Maryland, where more states might meet to do something about the depressed interstate commerce. Five states, Delaware, New Jersey, New York, Pennsylvania, and Virginia, attended this second effort at planning to improve trade. But five states were too few to act effectively, so a third meeting was arranged where an effort would be made to get all the states represented. This turned out to be the **Philadelphia Convention of 1787.** All states but Rhode Island were there. At the Annapolis meeting, **Alexander Hamilton** suggested that the third meeting consider all problems, not just commerce, that confronted the states. Congress acted upon Hamilton's idea late in February 1787 by calling a convention "for the sole and express purpose of revising the Articles of Confederation."

In the field of foreign relations, our government was having its troubles. England would not get its subjects out of the Ohio River Valley, where they continued their fur trading in competition with Americans. Spain had closed the Mississippi River to American commerce. As part of the British Empire, we had enjoyed certain protections and favors in trade, but these evaporated when we became an independent nation. In addition, all the major powers of the world were monarchies, and this new republic was, by its very existence, a threat to their system of government. Under the best of conditions, it would have been difficult for a new nation to break through the trade barriers that mercantilism had established.

There was one glittering success story written by the Congress under the Articles. This stemmed from Maryland's refusal to ratify the Articles until the other states had agreed to abandon their claims to western lands and cede the areas to the central government. Roughly this was an extensive area east of the Mississippi river, west of the present boundaries of the original thirteen states, south of the Great Lakes, and north of Spanish Florida. This great national domain was a source of financial strength. But much more important in the long run was the foresight and wisdom shown by Congress when it passed the **Land Ordinance of 1785** and the **Northwest Ordinance of 1787**. Both of these laws applied to the **Northwest Territory**, but they also served as a pattern for other public lands.

In 1785 the Northwest Territory was the northwest corner of the United States; now it is the states of Ohio, Indiana, Illinois, Michigan, Wisconsin, and an adjacent corner of Minnesota. Under the Ordinance of 1785 the Northwest Territory was cut into square townships measuring six miles on each side. Each township was cut into 36 square miles. The government would sell no less than 1 square mile, 640 acres, at a price no less than $1 per acre. An individual settler could rarely pay as much as $640, but land companies, states, and banks could. When resold to settlers, the one square mile, 640 acres, could be sold in plots no smaller than 40 acres. One square mile, called a **section**, in each township was reserved so that any income received therefrom could be used for public education. This was the first United States law granting aid to education.

The Ordinance of 1787 made the Northwest Territory one political unit ruled by a governor and judges appointed by Congress. When 5,000 male adults lived in the territory, it could organize a bicameral legislature and send a delegate to Congress. A territorial delegate could speak but not vote in Congress. Three to five states could be formed in the Northwest Territory. The formation of a state required a population of 60,000. The Ordinance guaranteed trial by jury, freedom of worship, forbade slavery, and provided for support of public education. By far the most significant provision was that every state carved out of the Northwest Territory would enter the Union on an equal footing with the original thirteen. Thus, a pattern was set that permitted us to grow into a strong unified nation of 50 states. The development of the United States into a great power rests largely on the concept that new states were extensions of the United States, with each new state having full rights and dignity with every other state.

**The Constitutional Convention

The Founders

Congress had set May 14 as the date for the opening of the convention at **Independence Hall, Philadelphia.** By May 25, seven states were represented, so the convention was able to get under way with a majority present. Each state, no matter how many delegates, was to have one vote. Within a few days delegates from four other states arrived and, finally the New Hampshire delegates arrived in late July. Rhode Island was not represented.

Fifty-five delegates in all attended the convention. The average daily attendance was between 30 and 35 delegates. Ages ranged from eighty-one to twenty-six; the average was in the low forties. Twenty-nine had attended college; 29 were lawyers; 17 were prominent in business (banking, insurance, shipping, merchants); 15 were slave owners (owning from 6 to 200 slaves); 11 were large landowners; and 7 held high public office (governors, judges, legislators). The delegates were of superior talents, recognized leadership, and ample property.

Thomas Jefferson, much more inclined to protect liberty than property, gave these founders too extravagant praise; he called them demi-gods. Looking back upon the work of the Convention, **James Madison** wrote, "...there never was an assembly of men, charged with a great and obvious trust, who were more pure in their motives, or more exclusively and anxiously devoted to the object committed to them than were the members of the Federal Convention of 1787." Professors Morison and Commager, in writing of the founders over 150 years after the event, expressed a judgment accepted with practical unanimity among historians: "Seldom has a class acted more wisely for the good of the whole, than ... the property owners, publicists, and professional men that framed the Federal Constitution...." The delegates were aware of historical importance of the work of the Convention.

Chosen unanimously because his prestige would help immeasurably to gain acceptance among the people for anything done by the Convention, **George Washington** was the chairman of the Constitutional Convention. **Benjamin Franklin**, who was 81 and the most renowned of Americans throughout the world, wielded influence in informal conferences and in committees.

James Madison made very fine and full notes of all the proceedings. All delegates were instructed not to discuss the convention business except during the meetings. Secrecy was well kept. The notes written by Madison were not made public until 1840, four years after his death. These notes and **The Federalist Papers** by **Hamilton**, **Madison**, and **Jay** are invaluable for the light they shed on the Constitution and the thinking of those who created it. For purposes of secrecy, Washington ordered that the official minutes kept by the secretary be merely a record of motions made and the vote taken. It was felt that had all the details of debate been made public, the members of the Convention would be unable to speak their minds as their best judgment directed. Honest, constructive deliberation can best be accomplished free from the pressures of public opinion.

The Convention Decides to Draw Up a Constitution and Adopt Compromises

The big problem was one of **representation**, which caused a serious divergence of opinion between the large and the small states. **Edmund Randolph** presented the Virginia Plan, which called for a bicameral legislature with representation in both houses based on population. **William Paterson** presented the **New Jersey Plan**. It provided for equal representation for each state in both houses of the legislature. The debate continued for about three weeks. It was then decided that a new constitution was more practical than amending the Articles of Confederation. Another month of meetings passed before **Roger Sherman** presented the **Connecticut Plan**. This compromise proved acceptable to both large and small states. It provided for a bicameral legislature with representation in the lower house (House of Representatives) according to population, and equal representation for each state in the upper house (Senate). After this agreement, the rest of the convention's business presented difficulties, but eventual success was never in doubt. Hence, the Connecticut Plan was called the **Great Compromise**.

Another compromise was over economic matters. The Southern states with their export of tobacco and naval stores led the agricultural interests in demanding that a two-thirds vote be required to pass laws regulating foreign commerce. Their principal fear was that there might be an export tax. The Northern states with a strong commercial interest wished to have import taxes levied to stimulate the growth of manufacture, so they opposed the two-thirds vote requirement. The agricultural interests were placated by two provisions: export taxes were made illegal, and Congress could pass no law interfering with the importation of slaves until 1808. In return for these two concessions, the commercial states of the North were favored by a provision permitting import taxes, or tariffs, to be levied by a simple majority vote.

Still a third important compromise was required to modify the differences between the slave and the free states. The slave states wanted slaves counted as part of the population when determining how many representatives they could have in the House of Representatives, but not counted when Congress levied direct taxes according to population. The free states wanted just the opposite arrangement. The compromise reached was that for both purposes of representation and taxation, the population of a state would be determined by counting all free people plus three-fifths of "all other persons," meaning slaves.

Ratification of the Constitution

Article VII of the Constitution reads, "The ratification of the conventions of nine States, shall be sufficient for the establishment of this Constitution between the States so ratifying the same." It was the Congress that had called the meeting at Independence Hall in Philadelphia to "amend the Articles of Confederation." It was to the Congress that the Philadelphia Constitutional Convention submitted the Constitution on September 20, 1787. On September 28, Congress sent copies of the Constitution to each state legislature with instructions that they submit the new government to the people through statewide conventions.

On December 7, 1787, Delaware was the first state to ratify the Constitution. On June 21, 1788, New Hampshire was the ninth state to ratify, and therefore the Constitution, in accordance with Article VII, became the government of the United States for the nine states. A committee of Congress, under the Articles of Confederation, named New York City as the capital, made February 4 the date for the presidential electors to vote for President, and set March 4 as the opening of the first Congress under the Constitution. North Carolina and Rhode Island entered the Union in the late fall of 1789 and the spring of 1790, respectively, after Washington had been inaugurated.

Just what part the people played in the ratification of the Constitution has been pretty well determined. The state of New York was the only one that made a special arrangement for this occasion by allowing universal manhood suffrage for the election of delegates to the state convention. In the other states, the usual qualifications for electing delegates were the same as required for voting for members of the lower house of the state legislature. That meant owning a certain amount of property. Less than 5 percent of the population lived in towns of 8,000 or more. Rural America, with relatively few exceptions, was made up of small farmers, and such men met the property qualifications for voting. Professor Charles Beard has estimated that between two-thirds and four-fifths of the male adults were enfranchised. But many qualified voters did not vote. Towns and cities organized rallies and parades, which kept interest high and got out the vote. Newspapers and pamphlets were circulated almost exclusively in urban areas and tended to keep interest alive. The **Federalist party** in supporting the Constitution worked much more effectively than the **Anti-Federalists** in working against it. This ratification campaign was a memorable, historical event. Citizens, not public officials, had gathered together and drawn up a framework of government, which had then been submitted to a vote of the people in each of the thirteen states. To determine the will of the voters, the most representative political machinery then known, the convention, was used. In accordance with this vote, a new government was set in motion. For its day, this was a tremendous political achievement.

Vote of the States on Ratification of the Constitution

The states are listed in the order in which they ratified the Constitution.

	VOTE OF THE DELEGATES	
	FOR	AGAINST
Delaware	unanimous	
Pennsylvania	46	23
New Jersey	unanimous	
Georgia	unanimous	
Connecticut	128	40
*Massachusetts	187	168
Maryland	63	11
South Carolina	149	73
*New Hampshire	57	47
*Virginia	89	79
New York	30	27
*North Carolina	194	77
Rhode Island	34	32

*These states proposed amendments which, in each case, amounted to a bill of rights.

**The Constitution

An Approach to the Constitution

The Constitution is a legal document, not just laws, but basic or fundamental law. It is legal framework upon which all other laws rest. **William E. Gladstone**, several times prime minister of England in the latter half of the 1800s, referred to our Constitution as "...the most wonderful work ever struck off at a given time by the brain and purpose of man." When, in 1887, we celebrated the 100th anniversary of the adoption of the Constitution, Gladstone wrote to the committee in charge this more subdued statement, "I have always regarded that Constitution as the most remarkable work known to me in modern times to have been produced by the human intellect, at a single stroke (so to speak), in its application to political affairs." This Constitution has been in continuous operation longer than any other basic law written for the government of a people.

The full Constitution with annotations can be found in the Appendix, beginning on page 427.

The Preamble

The Preamble grants no power, either to the government or to anyone. It is a statement of purposes. One way to estimate the success of the Constitution is to consider each of the six purposes listed, and form an opinion as to how well each purpose has been accomplished.

1] "To form a more perfect union"
Success here is 100 percent. The union formed is more perfect than that under the Articles of Confederation. The union was severely, but unsuccessfully, challenged by the Civil War.

2] "To establish justice"
Courts throughout the United States operate in a manner that approximates justice to a commendable degree. There is room for improvement.

3] "To insure domestic tranquility"
Violence between states, since the Civil War, seems outside the realm of the most remote possibility. Violence between the federal government and a state or states seems almost as unlikely. Violence associated with labor problems and organized crime are usually, though not always, state problems.

4] "To provide for the common defense"
That includes preparation against foreign enemies and domestic terrorists.

5] "To provide for the general welfare"
Measured by the standard of living of its people, the United States is among the very top few nations, possibly at the very top. Was "standard of living" what "general welfare" meant to those who wrote the Constitution? What does general welfare mean now?

6] "To secure the blessings of liberty to ourselves and our posterity"

That this is the "land of liberty" has not been an empty phrase. Our people do (and always have, under the Constitution) possess religious, political, and economic liberty to a high degree. Liberty is as unstable and fragile as it is precious. No generation can guarantee it to its posterity. "Eternal vigilance is the price of liberty."

Did "we the people" ordain and establish this Constitution? The people had no direct voice in sending the delegates to the Constitutional Convention. State legislatures chose most of them. The question of choosing delegates to the convention was not an issue in any state election. The meetings of the Constitutional Convention were secret. The people played no part in the framing of the Constitution.

In the ratification of the Constitution the issue was presented by each state to its people. Conventions in each state were formed by the vote of the people. The percentage of adult males who qualified as voters was high, far superior to any other place on earth then or ever before. The campaigning was on the one issue of ratification, publicity by both sides was unhindered, and voting was unimpaired. The ratification campaign was a major political achievement, a milestone along the hard road toward self-government. The people were as free to reject the Constitution as to accept. They accepted it.

A Bicameral Legislature

The **Senate** (upper house) and the **House of Representatives** (lower house) constitute **Congress**. Each state has two Senators. The number of members each state has in the House of Representatives is directly in proportion to its population.

The small states are protected in their equal representation in the Senate by the clause in Article V, which says, "...no State, without its consent, shall be deprived of its equal suffrage in the Senate." This clause is the only one in the Constitution not subject to change unless every state agrees. There must be a federal census every ten years so that seats in the house of Representatives may be reapportioned according to population changes. The first census was in 1790, and each state was allowed one representative for every 30,000 people. To keep the house from becoming too large, Congress, in 1912, restricted the membership to 435. As each census is taken, the total population is divided by 435 to determine each state's quota in the House. Today, each congressional district contains about 500,000 people. Every state has at lease one representative in the House. With 50 states, there are 100 Senators; hence the total membership of Congress is 535 and will remain so unless more states are created.

Qualifications for Senators

AGE   Thirty years old or over

CITIZENSHIP   Must have been a citizen of the United States for at least nine years

RESIDENCE   Must reside in the state he or she rep resents

Qualifications of Members of the House of Representatives

AGE   Twenty-five years old or over

CITIZENSHIP   Must have been a citizen of the United States for at least seven years

RESIDENCE   Must reside in the state he or she represents

Powers of the Senate (These Powers Are Not Given to the House of Representatives)

1] May ratify treaties (requires a two-thirds vote)

2] May elect the Vice-President if the Electoral College fails to do so

3] May try officials who have been impeached and, by a two-thirds vote, may dismiss them from office

4] May ratify presidential appointments to certain high offices as specified in the Constitution or by Congress. The approval by a simple majority vote is required for the appointment of ambassadors, consuls, judges of the Supreme Court, and Cabinet officials

Powers of the House of Representatives (These Powers Are Not Given to the Senate)

1] May introduce revenue bills

2] May elect the President when the Electoral College fails to do so

3] May impeach public officials

To impeach an official means to decide that the official should be tried on charges that have been made against him or her. Only the House of Representatives can make such a decision; it requires a simple majority vote. Impeachment does not imply guilt; it does show that, in the opinion of the House, the charges made and the prevailing circumstances make trial before the Senate desirable.

How Bills Become Laws

In order to pass Congress and then get to the President, a bill must meet three conditions: pass each house of Congress in identical form by a simple majority vote.

Identical form means exactly what it states: any changes in punctuation, in spelling, in wording, no matter how minor, require the bill to be submitted again to the house that passed it before such alterations occurred. To prevent endless shuttling of bills between the House and Senate, bills are referred to **joint committees** made up of members of both houses. These committees smooth out the form of a bill and then submit it to Congress. Most of the serious work of lawmaking is done in committees.

After a bill has passed each house of Congress in identical form by a simple majority vote, it then is submitted to the President. At this point four things may happen to it.

1] The President may sign it. It is then law.

2] The President may ignore it. If Congress continues in session for more than ten days after the bill has been sent to the President, the bill automatically becomes law on the eleventh day. Sundays are not counted.

3]   The President may veto the bill. The President does so by attaching in writing objections to the bill and sending it back to the house in which it originated. If each house then passes the bill by a two-thirds vote, taken by roll call, it becomes law. This is **overriding a veto**. Unless the vetoed bill is passed by the two-thirds majority, it is dead.

4]   If the President ignores the bill and Congress adjourns within the next ten days, not counting Sundays, the bill is dead. This is a **pocket veto.**

Special Privileges of Members of Congress

1]   Except for a felony, treason, and breach of the peace a member of Congress cannot be arrested during a session of Congress or on his or her way to or from Congress. Arresting legislators for minor offenses, real or imagined, was once a device used to keep them away from the legislature for political advantage to the opposite party.

2]   No action for libel, no charges, no official questioning is permitted against a member of Congress concerning anything he or she may have said in Congress or in any committee of Congress. This permits members of Congress to voice suspicions that, if true, might uncover corruption; if false, might be libelous. This unusual completeness of freedom of speech is a substantial protection to members of Congress as it enables them to seek the public good without fear of libel suits. Obviously this privilege is subject to abuse and, if abused, can result in serious injustice to the victims. The only protection against such abuse is the judgment and responsibility of the members of Congress. As always, great power can be properly exercised only when controlled by great restraint. The record of members of Congress in this respect throughout the years has been good, but not perfect.

Special Prohibitions on Members of Congress

1]   No person may be a member of Congress and also hold any other federal office. This reflects a fundamental theory that runs through our Constitution, the theory of **separation of powers**. The powers to be kept as separate as is practical are the **Executive, Legislative,** and **Judicial.**

2]   Members of Congress cannot vote themselves a raise in pay. Any law increasing salaries does not apply to any member of Congress at the time the law is passed. The increase applies only to members elected after the law was passed. Hence, new members benefit immediately upon election, and so do the old ones after they have served out their terms and won reelection.

The Powers of Congress

Article I, Section 8 of the Constitution lists the powers of Congress. Congress has power:

*1]   to levy and collect taxes

2]   to borrow money

3]   to regulate foreign and interstate commerce

4]   to establish uniform rules of naturalization and uniform rules of bankruptcies

5]   to coin money and regulate a currency system

6]   to punish counterfeiters

7]   to establish post offices and post roads

8]   to issue patents and copyrights

9]   to constitute courts inferior to the Supreme Court

10]   to punish piracy

11]   to declare war

12]   to provide an army

13]   to provide a navy

14]   to make rules for the armed forces

15]   to call out the National Guard

16]   to organize and train the National Guard

17]   to govern the District of Columbia

18]   to make all laws necessary and proper for carrying into execution the provisions of this Constitution (a paraphrase of the **implied powers** or **elastic clause**).

* See further comment in the following paragraphs.

Brief Comment on Certain Powers of Congress

• To levy and collect taxes

The Constitution restricts this power to three purposes. Every tax must be levied in order to pay the public debt of the United States, to provide for the common defense, or to promote the general welfare. A tax levied for any other purpose would be illegal.

If there is resistance to the collection of taxes, Congress is empowered by the elastic clause to pass any laws necessary and proper to force the collection of taxes.

• To regulate foreign and interstate commerce

The Mount Vernon and Annapolis meetings were attempts to do something about the confused state of commerce due to interstate tariffs and the varying regulations of the several states in regard to foreign commerce. This weakness of the Articles of Confederation was the one that led to the Phildelphia Constitutional Convention. Granting Congress exclusive authority in regulating interstate and foreign commerce solved the problem.

• To declare war

Congress declares war only in response to a request by the President who makes such a request by speaking to a joint meeting of both houses held in the chamber of the House of Representatives. After the President has requested a declaration of war, the members of the Senate go back to their own quarters. Both the House and the Senate vote separately. A simple majority vote in each house is required. Modern warfare has made the declaration of war a rather empty procedure. In World War I and World War II the declaration was not a decision; it was merely a recognition of what had already happened. Any future war may be over before it occurs to the President or Congress to go through the motions of declaring war. Or the next war may be some "limited" action which will not be called a war, and for which there will be no declaration.

• "To make all laws which shall be necessary and proper for carrying into execution the foregoing powers, and all other powers vested by this Constitution in the government of the United States, or in any department or officer thereof."

Later we shall discuss the word *necessary* in this "implied powers" clause, but at this juncture there are two other points to notice.

1]   This provision is the last of the list of direct grants of powers to Congress. So listed, it appears as one more power added to those previously listed. Its purpose would then seem to be to assure Congress that it has ample power to carry out the provisions of the Constitution. Had this "implied powers" clause been placed in Section 9 of Article I, a different interpretation would be in order. Then the clause would appear to be a caution to Congress not to exceed its powers, to be careful to do only what was necessary and no more. This clause taken away from its context could be telling Congress to do whatever is necessary, or it could be warning Congress to do only that which is necessary. The first interpretation tends to increase the powers of Congress, while the second tends to restrict them.

2]   In Section 10 of Article I of the Constitution the following words occur, "...except what may be *absolutely necessary* for..." If in one part of the Constitution the words *absolutely necessary* are used, while in another the word *necessary* occurs, what difference is there, if any, in the meaning?

These small distinctions are helpful to a consideration of the formation of the first major parties under President Washington.

Miscellaneous Facts About Congress

1]   Except for the fact that the Vice-President is the presiding officer of the Senate, both the House and Senate choose their own officers and make their own rules.

2]   If a President or Vice-President has been impeached by the House, the trial before the Senate will be presided over by the Chief Justice of the Supreme Court. In all other cases the Vice-President will preside.

3]   Congress must meet at least once a year. This regular meeting begins on January 3 as provided by the Twentieth Amendment adopted in 1933.

4]   A quorum is a simple majority of each house. Fewer than a quorum may adjourn from day to day and may take measures to compel other members to attend in order to achieve a quorum.

5]   Each house must keep a journal containing a record of the proceedings. The record shall include all debates and speeches as well as a record of the voting. Anything which, in the judgment of Congress, requires secrecy may be omitted from the record. In accordance with this provision the Congress prints the *Congressional Record* in two sections, a Senate edition and a House edition.

6] A roll call vote with the yeas and nays of the members individually recorded can be demanded by a vote of one-fifth of those present.

7] A member of either house may be expelled by a two-thirds vote.

8] A member of either house may be refused his or her seat by a simple majority. Occasionally an election of a member to Congress comes under serious questioning due to irregularities during the campaign. A member of Congress elected under such circumstances may find himself or herself excluded.

9] A vote of censure in either house requires a simple majority. This is a way Congress has of severely reprimanding one of its members for conduct they consider extremely inappropriate but for which they do not wish to invoke expulsion.

10] Both houses must agree on the same time for the adjournment of a session of Congress. However, adjournments within a session of Congress can be for not more than three days, and in such cases the House and Senate may act independently.

Powers Forbidden to the United States

• The privilege of the **writ of habeas corpus** shall not be suspended, except in cases of rebellion or invasion when the public safety may require it.

A writ of habeas corpus could be translated into "thou shalt have the body." It is a strange legal way of saying that people who have been arrested have the right to be brought before a proper official to be told why they are being held, to be informed what law they are alleged to have broken. A person must be so informed within a reasonable time after arrest, usually within 48 to 72 hours. A prisoner gains three protections from a writ of habeas corpus.

1] It practically eliminates intentional false arrest. In early English history, kings sometimes put individuals in jail because they didn't like them, frequently because they had refused to lend money to them. Under a writ of habeas corpus a person arrested for no legal reason can be freed again so quickly that the arrest may make little sense. Of course, now there are severe legal penalties against any persons or officials guilty of causing a false arrest.

2] As soon as an accused person knows the precise charges, that individual can then prepare for a defense.

3] Being charged with breaking a particular law puts an accused person in a position where he or she can demand the right to be released on bail. In some extremely serious crimes, bail may be refused. Anyone released on bail is free until the trial. Bail is refunded when the trial begins, but if the defendant has "jumped bail" (not returned for trial), he or she forfeits the bail and is subject to arrest for the offense of jumping bail in addition to the original charge.

• No **bill of attainder** or **ex post facto law** shall be passed.

A bill of attainder is a special law made to apply in a particular instance. It treats this one case in a different manner than that prescribed by law. The unusual treatment contained in the bill of attainder denies trial by jury and other safeguards to a fair trial. The necessity for protection against a bill of attainder grew out of English history.

An ex post facto law is one that makes punishable an act that was legal when committed.

• There shall be no export taxes.

In the regulation of interstate and foreign commerce, there shall be no favoring of one state over another.

• No money shall be drawn from the United States Treasury unless an appropriation has been made by Congress.

• No title of nobility shall be granted by the United States.

• No direct tax shall be levied by the United States unless it is apportioned among the several states according to their population. While this prohibition is still in effect, there is one huge exception to it, the income tax, which became the Sixteenth Amendment in 1913.

Powers Forbidden to the States

States shall not make treaties, grant letters of marque and reprisal, coin money, issue paper money, make anything except gold and silver legal tender, pass a bill of attainder or an ex post facto law, pass a law impairing the obligation of a contract, or grant a title of nobility.

Qualifications for the President and Term of Office

The President must be at least **35 years old**, have lived in the United States for **14 years**, and be a **citizen** by birth. No President may be elected more than twice or serve for more than ten years. The term of office is **four years** and shall begin at noon on January 20. If a Vice-President becomes President after the middle of a presidential term, that individual serves out the last two years. He or she may then be elected for two full terms and, in this manner, achieve the maximum period of just under ten years. If a Vice President becomes President before the middle of the term of office, he or she is then eligible to be elected only once. In this case, the maximum period as President could be as little as just over six years.

How the President and Vice-President Are Elected by the Electoral College

The President is elected by a simple majority vote of the **Electoral College**. Each state has as many votes in the Electoral college as it has members in Congress. The District of Columbia has as many electoral votes as any state having the least number of such votes.

Election day is the first Tuesday after the first Monday in November. A presidential election occurs every fourth year, always falling on the years with a date evenly divisible by four. The political parties hold conventions in each state, usually in the spring, to nominate the members of the Electoral College. Whichever party polls the largest vote in the state has thereby elected its nominees to the Electoral College. The Electoral College members meet, usually in their state capitals, on the first Monday after the second Wednesday in December and cast their votes for President. By custom, not by Constitutional provision, the electors vote for the candidate of their party, which results in all the electoral votes of any state going to the candidate with the largest popular vote in that state. The list of votes is signed and sealed by the governor of the state and sent to the president of the United States Senate, the Vice-President. On January 6 a joint session of Congress is held at which the Vice-President presides and the ballots are counted. Technically, this is the election of the President. If January 6 is a Sunday, the election is held the following day.

The Electoral College members vote for President and Vice-President on separate ballots. The President and Vice-President must come from different states. The procedures for election of President and Vice-President are identical unless the Electoral College fails to give a majority vote to any candidate. In that case the procedures differ from that point on.

How the President and the Vice-President Are Elected When the Electoral College Fails to Reach a Decision

If no candidate for President gets a majority of the electoral votes, the election goes to the House of Representatives. There each state has one vote. The members of the House from each state have to **caucus**, hold a meeting, and decide how to cast their one vote.

Two-thirds of the total number of states must be present, and it takes a majority of all the states to elect the President. The House is restricted in its choice to the top three candidates who received the most votes in the Electoral College.

If no candidate for Vice-President gets a majority of the electoral vote, the election goes to the Senate. There each Senator has one vote. Two-thirds of the total number of Senators must be present, and it takes a majority of all the Senators to elect the Vice-President. The Senate is restricted in its choice to the top two candidates who received the most votes in the Electoral College.

No matter what the circumstances of the election, the President and the Vice-President must be from different states.

When circumstances arise during an election for which there is no provision in the Constitution or other law, it will be the duty of Congress to find a solution.

Oath of Office for the President

When the President takes office on January 20 at noon, the following oath is taken as prescribed in the Constitution: "I do solemnly swear (or affirm) that I will faithfully execute the office of President of the United States, and will, to the best of my ability, preserve, protect, and defend the Constitution of the United States."

There is a choice here between an oath, "I do solemnly swear," and an affirmation, "I do solemnly affirm." This may reflect the Quaker influence so strong in Pennsylvania at the time of the Constitutional Convention. It would be a violation of Quaker beliefs to "swear" to anything. It certainly reflects the concern shown by those who drew up the Constitution to avoid having in our framework of government anything that would set up a conflict between religious convictions and participation in government. Usually the oath or affirmation is administered by the Chief Justice of the Supreme Court.

Very similar oaths or affirmations are taken by members of state legislatures, by governors, by Congressmen, by judges and by many other office holders, both state and federal. Note that the oath or affirmation is not to support any person, such as a governor or a President, but is always to support laws: the state constitutions, the federal Constitution, the laws of the land. Loyalty is given to governments, not to officials as individuals.

Powers of the President (Article II, Section 2)

1] The President is Commander-in-Chief of the armed forces of the United States at all times. Any state militia automatically comes under the President's command whenever used in the service of the United States.

2] The President may require written reports from "the principal officer in each of the executive departments."

This is an example of the brevity and effectiveness of the wording of the Constitution. Nothing else is said about "executive departments" and "the principal office," but from these few words in conjunction with the implied powers clause, the Cabinet has been established. If the Constitution provides for the President's getting reports from heads of executive departments, Congress must pass laws "necessary and proper" in order to create such departments, each with a "principal officer." During the first year of Washington's presidency, Congress created the departments of State, Treasury, War, Justice, and Post Office. There are now (1990) 13 executive departments, each with a principal officer called a member of the President's Cabinet.†

3] The President can "grant reprieves and pardons" to federal prisoners, "except in cases of impeachment."

4] The President can make treaties which become effective only after ratification by a two-thirds vote of the Senate.

5] The President may make appointments with or without the approval of the Senate as specified by the Constitution and the laws of Congress.

6] The President may make recess appointments to executive positions. Such appointments will last through the recess and also to the end of the next session of Congress.

Duties of the President

1] He must, "from time to time," deliver to Congress a message on "the State of the Union."

This "State of the Union" message is given at the opening of each regular session of Congress. The President may read it to Congress or may send it to be read to Congress. With the greatly increased complexity and scope of federal affairs, the Congress has by law required the President to send two more messages to them each year. In 1921 Congress required a budget message each year from the President, and since then a third message, one on the economic state of the Union, has been added. The State of the Union message required by the Constitution is usually the Presi-

dent's own thoughts on what should occupy the attention of Congress for the coming session. The budget message and the economic message are more technical in content and are largely the work of advisors to the President who are specialists in these fields.

2] He may call special sessions of Congress.

3] If the two houses of Congress cannot agree on a date for adjournment, the President may set the date for them.

4] "He shall receive ambassadors and other public ministers."

5] He shall "commission all the officers of the United States."

6] "He shall take care that the laws be faithfully executed."

This, of course, is the chief responsibility of the President. It is so much the core of the office that the President is often called the **Chief Executive**.

The Judicial Power of the United States (Article III)

The Constitution directs Congress to establish "one Supreme Court" and "such inferior courts" as Congress sees fit.

In September 1789 Congress passed the **Federal Judiciary Act**, which established a **Supreme Court** with a **Chief Justice** and five **Associate Justices**. District and circuit courts were created. The pattern set by this law is still in effect. In February 1790 **John Jay** was appointed as the first Chief Justice.

Term of Office and Pay for Federal Judges

Judges shall serve during "good behavior." For all practical purposes this means for life or until voluntary retirement. Judges can be impeached for cause.

The pay of a judge cannot be reduced during the term of office. The appointment, the term of office, and the pay of federal judges combine to make them independent, that is, free from pressures that could threaten their status and possibly influence their judgment.

Jurisdiction of Federal Courts

Federal courts have jurisdiction in the following cases:

---

†As of 1990, the executive departments of Cabinets rank were State, Treasury, Defense, Justice, Interior, Agriculture, Commerce, Labor, Health and Human Services, Housing and Urban Development, Transportation, Energy, Education, Veterans

1] Arising under the Constitution and laws of Congress

2] "Affecting ambassadors, other public ministers, and consuls"

3] "Of admiralty and maritime jurisdiction"

4] "Of controversies to which the United States shall be a party"

5] "Between citizens of different States"

6] "Between a State, or a citizen thereof, and foreign states, citizens or subjects"

Original Jurisdiction of the Supreme Court

When a case is heard by the Supreme Court before it has been taken to any other court, it is said to be a case of **original jurisdiction**. Cases involving "ambassadors, other public ministers and consuls, and those in which a State shall be a party" are cases of original jurisdiction.

Ambassadors, ministers, and consuls on duty in the United States are most unlikely to become involved in court action. If such an official representative of another nation becomes entangled with the law in a manner that reflects unfavorably upon him or her, that person will be recalled. The point here is that troubles involving diplomats practically never get into our courts; they are handled in some other manner. Hence, cases of original jurisdiction before the Supreme Court involving foreign officials are extremely rare.

There are cases involving States that come under the original jurisdiction of the Supreme Court, but by far the greater number of cases before the Court are those that have been tried in lower courts and have been appealed. Whenever a case is retried, it must be by a court of higher jurisdiction than the court rendering the decision in question. All such cases are known as cases of **appellate jurisdiction**.

The appellate jurisdiction of the Supreme Court is subject to complete regulation by Congress. As the Constitution puts it, the Supreme Court's appellate jurisdiction may be modified "with such exceptions and under such regulations as the Congress shall make." (Article III, Section 2) If Congress and the Supreme Court ever develop a spirit of hostility toward one another resulting from decisions in which the Court has declared laws of Congress unconstitutional, the Congress could drastically modify the jurisdiction of the Court in all *appellate* cases. Many of the most important decisions in our history involving the constitutionality of laws of Congress have been made in cases of appellate jurisdiction. Congress has not used this grant of power in any such manner; there seems very little likelihood that it will, but the power is available.

The Congress has no authority over the original jurisdiction of the Supreme Court.

There is absolutely no way in which a decision of the Supreme Court can be altered in any particular case. The Supreme Court is the final authority at any given time. The Supreme Court has given a decision one way at one time and reversed itself, changed its mind some years later and given a very different answer to the same question. But each decision, when made, was final and authoritative. What the Supreme Court has declared illegal, such as an income tax law in 1894, may be made legal by a Constitutional amendment (the Sixteenth Amendment in 1913). But this does not qualify in the least the fact that, at any given time, the Supreme Court is the final authority.

Definition of Treason (Article III, Section 3)

"Treason against the United States shall consist only in levying war against them, or in adhering to their enemies, giving them aid and comfort." "No person shall be convicted of treason unless on the testimony of two witnesses to the same overt act, or on confession in open court."

States Should Recognize Each Other's Official Acts

Article IV states that "Full faith and credit shall be given in each State to the public acts, records, and judicial proceedings of every other State." It goes on to say that each state should aid other states in the recovery of fugitives from justice and of "persons held to service or labor in one State, under the laws thereof, escaping into another...."(slaves) This is one part of the Constitution that has been repeatedly broken. Sometimes states have refused to honor divorces granted in other states. Governors of states have refused to return fugitives from justice at the request of other states. In the years before the Civil War several states passed laws designed to prevent the recapture of fugitive slaves. When a state deliberately violates the Constitution in these respects, it does so with the solid backing of public opinion within its own borders, and probably the public opinion of a much larger area.

Admission of States of the Union

The Constitution gives Congress the power to admit states to the Union. This became a political issue of major importance at the close of the Civil War. President Lincoln usually referred to the war as a rebellion; that is, an unsuccessful four-year attempt to leave the Union. Restoring the ex-rebellious states to their normal status in Congress would, in this case, be under the authority of the President. On the other hand, if the eleven Confederate states had really left the Union, it then became the responsibility of Congress to readmit them on such terms and in such manner as Congress decided.

No state can be divided into more than one state without the consent of the states concerned and of Congress. No states can combine into one state without the consent of the states concerned and of Congress. In 1820 Massachusetts was divided into Massachusetts and Maine with the consent of both states and of Congress. This was part of the Missouri Compromise.

Every State in the Union Is Guaranteed a Republican Form of Government

The conditions that constitute a "republican form of government," as stated in the Constitution, are that each state must have a legislature elected by the people under broad suffrage privileges which allow a large part of the adult citizens to vote.

Supremacy of the Constitution

Article VI contains the famous "Supreme Law of the Land" clause. It is a part of the Constitution that deserves close attention. The following is an acceptable paraphrase of this clause.

This Constitution, the laws made in pursuance thereof, and treaties to which the United States is a party constitute the supreme law of the land; and the judges in every state shall be bound thereby. Any state laws and any provisions in any state constitution incompatible with the supreme law of the land are unconstitutional, null and void.

This makes three legal authorities supreme, the Constitution, the laws made in pursuance thereof, and treaties. There is no certain justification for assuming that there is any significance in the order in which these three legal authorities are listed. Plausible reasons can be advanced for placing the Constitution as first in importance; there are also plausible reasons for considering treaties first in importance.

The Constitution is our basic law, the very foundation of our government. Laws made in pursuance thereof are intended to carry out the provisions of the Constitution. Treaties are made and become binding upon the United States in accordance with procedures set forth in the Constitution. This may seem to support giving the Constitution precedence over a treaty in case there appears to be a conflict between them.

As federal laws are made only by Congress, why does the Constitution state, "laws made in pursuance thereof" rather than simply stating "laws of Congress"? It strongly suggests that the founders considered the possibility that Congress might pass a law that would not be in pursuance of the Constitution, and, if it did, such a law would not be part of the supreme law of the land. The Constitution still leaves a key question unanswered: namely, Who is to decide whether a law of Congress is, or is not, in pursuance of the Constitution? The Supreme Court has, over the years, assumed this responsibility; but its doing so is not based on any constitutional provision. This assumption of power by the Supreme Court to pass upon the constitutionality of laws of Congress is part of what is called **judicial review**. The other part of judicial review is a power specifically given to the courts by the "supreme law of the land" clause, that is, the power to pass upon the constitutionality of state laws and state constitutions.

The practice of judicial review over laws of Congress is by now well-established. This is a unique feature of our government, as no other nation grants its courts the authority to nullify the acts of its legislature.

The judicial review written into the Constitution over state laws and state constitutions is absolutely essential. Without it we would soon have as many interpretations of the Constitution as we have states. Federal laws and the interpretation of the Constitution must be uniform throughout the 50 states in order to prevent intolerable chaos.

No Religious Test

Article VI states, "....no religious test shall ever be required as a qualification to any office or public trust under the United States." This means that a person's religion should have no bearing upon his or her eligibility for public office.

Methods of Amending the Constitution

Article V set forth four methods. Amendments must first be proposed and then ratified; there are two ways of doing each.

Amendments may be proposed by:

1] a two-thirds vote of each house of Congress

2] a convention of the states called by Congress whenever the legislatures of two-thirds of the states request such a convention.

Amendments may be ratified by:

1] the legislatures of three-fourths of the states.

2] conventions in three-fourths of the states.

When an amendment is proposed, Congress shall tell the states which method of ratification is to be used. The same method of ratification must be used by all the states for any given amendment. The four possible combinations of proposing and ratifying an amendment are as follows:

```
  *    Proposal 1 and ratification 1
 **      "     1    "       "      2
***      "     2    "       "      1
***      "     2    "       "      2
```

  * Used for all amendments except the Twenty-first
 ** Used for the Twenty-first Amendment only. (repeal of prohibition)
*** Never used

Article V also reiterates that "...no state, without its consent, shall be deprived of its equal suffrage in the Senate."

The Reasons for Checks and Balances

Our federal government operates according to the provisions of the Constitution, to laws "made in pursuance thereof," to procedures so well-established that they have become "unwritten law," and to practices that have developed from a combination of circumstances and common sense.

When the Constitution was drawn up at Philadelphia, care was taken to achieve balance between the power of any one of the three major departments of government (Executive, Legislative, and Judicial), and the other two. No one department was to be able to dominate the others. The problem of balance was important *within* the Legislative department, between the House of Representatives and the Senate. The basic difference of approach among the delegates at the Constitutional Convention was a matter of balance. All wanted a government stronger than the Articles of Confederation. Some were intent upon creating a new government very much stronger in order to make sure that it would have effective authority; others were intent upon creating a government that would have no more authority than absolutely necessary to maintain the union of states. With a good deal of sense, one might look upon the Constitution as an intricate, intellectual balancing act: federal power v. states's rights; the inter-

play of Executive, Legislative, and Judicial departments; the granting of powers to officials, and the limiting of power of the officials. The ideal balance is one that grants to federal government effective power while reserving to the states and the people adequate freedom. Yet, everything that is written into law as a power of government is a restriction on the freedom of the individual; everything that guarantees freedom to the individual is a restriction on the power of government. Emphasize freedom for the individual to a ridiculous extent and anarchy develops; emphasize power for the government to an extreme degree and tyranny develops. The framers of the Constitution were struggling with an age-old problem in seeking safety for the states, safety for the people, and efficiency for the federal government, all in proper balance. They wrote certain devices into the Constitution to achieve this, and we have since developed political practices designed for the same end. We are throwing all of these laws and practices together and calling them "checks and balances."

The Executive Department Can Check the Legislative Department

1] The President may veto a bill passed by Congress.

2] The President may pocket-veto a bill passed by Congress.

3] The President may call special sessions of Congress.

4] The President may recommend legislation.

5] Direct appeals to the people enable the President to influence Congress. Radio and television have greatly enhanced the President's influence.

6] The President as head of his party has considerable influence with members of Congress in his party. He can always get legislation introduced. The leaders in the House of Representatives and the Senate of the President's party, whether they be majority or minority leaders, try to put through bills favored by the President. The Speaker of the House is often a member of this legislative team working for the President. The Vice-President, who presides over the Senate, can sometimes be used by the President in ways that build his importance and influence in the party and hence with the Senate. Through the party organization and the President's position as its head, the President of the United States is the most powerful lobby in Washington.

The Legislative Department, Congress, Can Check the Executive Department

1] Congress can refuse to pass bills favored by the President.

2] Congress can override a presidential veto by a two-thirds vote.

3] Congress can make executive departments, commissions, committees, and programs ineffective by refusing sufficient appropriations for their operation.

4] The House of Representatives may impeach the President, and the Senate may then try the President.

5] The Senate may refuse to ratify a treaty presented to it by the President.

6] The Senate may refuse to approve appointments.

Checks Upon the Supreme Court Exist

1] The President appoints the members to the Supreme Court with the approval of the Senate.

Usually the President appoints a member of his own political party. The President naturally appoints a person whose views are like his own, or at least with opinions on public issues that are acceptable to him. This gives the President much less influence on the Supreme Court than it would seem to. Experience has shown that appointees tend to be independent in thought and action.

2] If Congress dislikes a decision of the Supreme Court when it declares a federal law unconstitutional, it may propose an amendment to the Constitution that will permit such a law. For example, the Supreme Court in 1894 declared a federal income-tax law unconstitutional, and Congress proposed the Income Tax Amendment in 1913.

3] The House of Representatives can impeach and the Senate can try a member of the Supreme Court. Certainly the legal possibility of impeachment and dismissal from office does not influence the Supreme Court.

4] Congress may refuse to confirm judicial appointments.

Checks Exercised by the Supreme Court

The Court can declare a law of Congress unconstitutional and, in doing so, cancel the work of Congress.

The Court can declare an act of a President unconstitutional. In 1952, during the conflict in Korea, President Truman ordered government seizure of the steel companies in a strike situation, which he claimed to be a national emergency of major proportions. The Supreme Court invalidated the presidential order on the grounds that there are no such powers as *emergency powers* of a President, and that every power must originate in the Constitution itself, either by a clause therein or through a law of Congress made in pursuance thereof.

The Balance of Power Within the Legislative Department

The primary function of the Senate is to act as a check upon the House of Representatives. The colonial assemblies were bicameral, with a governor's council as the upper house to check the popularly elected lower house. The upper house was appointed by the king or governor, or elected by the lower house. When the colonies became states, they kept the bicameral legislature, with the upper house still being a check upon the lower. For many decades under the Constitution, the members of the Senate were elected by state legislatures. The direct, or popular, election of Senators did not become a Constitutional provision until the Seventeenth Amendment adopted in 1913.

The facts that the minimum age for the Senate is five years older than for the House of Representatives, that the term of a Senator is three times as long, and that at each congressional election only one-third of the Senate seats are subject to change, instead of all of them as in the House of Representatives, were all designed to make the Senate the more permanent and stronger branch of Congress.

It is difficult to pressure the Senate into action that it is reluctant to take. Popular opinion "back home" has little effect on a Senator with over two more years to serve. If the Senator plans to run for another term, the last eighteen months should be long enough for "mending political fences." As only one-third of the seats are open for election at any one time, only a slight change in the membership of the Senate can take place. The shift in the party strength in the Senate is apt to be somewhat less marked than the slight shift in personnel.

All of these factors combine to make it easy for Senators to vote their convictions with a minimum of modification due to any sort of pressure. As many Senators have served in the House of Representatives or in state legislatures or as governors, they represent a great deal of political experience. The Senate is admirably suited to give considered judgment to public issues; it need not be swayed by popular clamor nor be set off course by a wave of emotionalism. Wisdom has a chance to survive and prevail in the United States Senate.

The House of Representatives is very sensitive to the public opinion of the states, sometimes of the congressional districts within the states. These varying opinions find expression and votes in the House of Representatives and in combination are as good a reflection of the opinion of the nation as is obtainable in a legislative body. A two-year term is very short. Whenever there is an irreconcilable clash between the views of their constituents and their own judgment on a public issue, they must think more than twice before deciding which way to vote.

A Representative sometimes leans on the Senate for sound legislation. He or she may vote to include some unwise provision in a bill because the people back home favor it strongly. However, the Representative knows that the Senate will change the House bill by excluding the provision. When the improved legislation comes back to the House, he or she votes for it. The Representative can claim that he or she served the will of his or her constituents. The chances are good that this technique will serve the Representative's immediate goal, to stay in office, and also his or her long-term purpose, the good of the nation.

The Senate and the House of Representatives combine to form a balanced legislature. It is remarkable that a plan made in 1787 is still suitable. The most difficult problem before the Constitutional Convention was well resolved in the "Great Compromise."

AMENDMENTS TO THE CONSTITUTION

The Bill of Rights

The first ten amendments are called the Bill of Rights. During the campaign to ratify the Constitution, the most telling argument against ratification was the absence of a bill of rights. The state constitutions had their individual bills of rights. The Federalists, who were campaigning for ratification, explained that the federal government could do only those things provided for in the Constitution and that there was no need to list what it could not do or to list the rights reserved to the states or the people. But the argument was not convincing. Some states ratified only with the proviso that a bill of rights be added; they even submitted such a bill of rights with their ratification.

The first ten amendments were added to protect the states against possible encroachment by the federal government. The first amendment begins, "Congress shall make no law...." The next seven amendments were interpreted to be prohibitions on Congress even though Congress is not mentioned. This acceptance of the Bill of Rights as restrictions on the federal government persisted until the 1870s. With the Slaughter House Cases of 1873, the *minority* opinion in a five-to-four decision held that provisions in the Fourteenth Amendment protected the individual from any encroachment by a state on any of the privileges and immunities listed in the Bill of Rights. This minority decision has, over the years, become the majority decision in a series of cases, so that today it is true that the Bill of Rights does protect the individual from all governments, federal, state and subdivisions of states. It is through the instrumentality of the Fourteenth Amendment that individuals get the protection of the Bill of Rights. The sentence of the Fourteenth Amendment that gives this protection reads, "No State shall make or enforce any law which shall abridge the privileges or immunities of citizens of the United States; nor shall any State deprive any person of life, liberty, or property, without due process of law, nor deny to any person within its jurisdiction the equal protection of the laws."

The Fourteenth Amendment, adopted in 1868, was part of the settlement of the Civil War. The 1954 Supreme Court decision against segregation in public schools and the 1962 decision concerning apportionment of representatives in the lower house of state legislatures has brought the Fourteenth Amendment to the forefront in the protection of civil rights of the individual.

The Bill of Rights might be considered an integral part of the Constitution, not an addition. The agreement that there would be such provisions added was made a condition to be met in order to secure ratification by the states. All ten amendments were ratified by 1791.

Privileges and Immunities in the Bill of Rights (See actual wording of Amendments I to X, pages 429 to 436).

Freedom of religion (First Amendment)
Freedom of speech (First Amendment)
Freedom of press (First Amendment)
Freedom of assembly (First Amendment)
Freedom of petition (First Amendment)
Freedom of a state to have a militia and the people to bear arms (Amendment II)
Freedom from having soldiers quartered in private homes in time of peace; or even in time of war unless a special law to that effect has been passed (Amendment III)
Freedom from unreasonable searches and seizures (Amendment IV)
Freedom from being held for an alleged criminal act unless a grand jury has brought an indictment (Amendment V)
Freedom from being tried again for the same offense when one has already been tried and found innocent (Amendment V)
Freedom from being forced to testify against one's self (Amendment V)
Freedom from being deprived of life, liberty, or property without due process of law (Amendment V)
Freedom from having one's property taken for a public use without just compensation (Amendment V)
Freedom, in all criminal cases, to have a speedy, public trial by jury; to have counsel for one's defense, to compel witnesses in one's behalf to testify, and to be confronted by witnesses against one's self (Amendment VI)
Freedom to demand a jury trial in any case where the value in controversy exceeds $20 (Amendment VII)
Freedom from excessive bails, excessive fines, and cruel and unusual punishments (Amendment VIII)

The preceding list of freedoms is contained in the first eight Amendments. The Ninth Amendment gives a blanket protection for other individual rights: "The enumeration in the Constitution of certain rights shall not be construed to deny or disparage others retained by the people."

The Tenth Amendment state in all-inclusive specific terms the purpose and intent of the Bill of Rights. It explains why the Bill of Rights was accepted as a defense for the states against possible encroachment by the federal government. "The powers not delegated to the United States by the Constitution, nor prohibited by it to the States, are reserved to the States respectively, or to the people."

AMENDMENT XI   *Modification of the Original Jurisdiction of the Supreme Court.*

It cancels the right previously given of federal courts to have original jurisdiction in cases where a state is involved in a case with a citizen of another state or with a subject of a foreign nation.

AMENDMENT XII   *Election of President and Vice-President.*

AMENDMENT XIII   *Slavery Is Abolished.*

AMENDMENT XIV

This amendment contains several provisions.
1] It defines citizens as, "All persons born or naturalized in the United States, and subject to the jurisdiction thereof, are citizens of the United States and of the State wherein they reside."

2] "No State shall make or enforce any law which shall abridge the privileges or immunities of citizens of the United States; nor shall any State deprive any person of life, liberty, or property, without due process of law, nor deny to any person within its jurisdiction the equal protection of the laws."

3] Representation in the House of Representatives for each state shall be based upon the total population. If any state denies the right to vote to any adult male inhabitant, it shall have its representation in the House of Representatives reduced. All states deny suffrage to thousands of male citizens for a variety of reasons, mostly legitimate. No state has ever lost representation in Congress in accordance with this clause of the Fourteenth Amendment. It has never been enforced.

4] Any person who held a public office which required an oath of allegiance to the Constitution and later joined the armed forces of the Confederate States is prevented from holding any such office again. The theory is that a person who broke his oath once should not be allowed to take another oath.

5] The United States shall pay its Civil War debts, but the debts "incurred in aid of insurrection or rebellion against the United States...shall be held illegal and void.

AMENDMENT XV   *Black Americans Made Potential Voters.*

"The rights of citizens of the United States to vote shall not be denied or abridged by the United States, or by any State, on account of race, color, or previous condition of servitude."

This does not extend the right to vote to any person, although, of course, its intent was to make the ex-Confederate States extend suffrage to black Americans on the same basis as it did to whites. It does give three reasons that cannot serve as a legal basis for denying the right to vote. The Thirteenth Amendment failed to achieve its purpose. Intimidation of blacks and a variety of state laws prevented many black Americans from voting in the South until the passage of civil rights laws in the 1960s.

AMENDMENT XVI   *Income Tax.*

Congress may levy a *direct* tax on incomes *from whatever source derived* without apportionment among the several states according to population. This tax is our single largest source of income. It is the only direct tax the federal government can levy without apportionment among the states according to population.

AMENDMENT XVII   *Direct Election of Senators.*

The Constitutional provision that United States Senators be elected by state legislatures had been under popular attack for at least three decades. The direct election of Senators by the voters as granted by this amendment accomplished the demanded reform.

Notice that it is the states that determine who shall vote for a United States Senator. The state sets the qualifications required for voting for a member of the lower house of its own legislature; it is these same qualifications that must then allow one to vote for a United States Senator.

AMENDMENT XVII   *Prohibition of the Manufacture, Sale, and Transportation of Intoxicating Beverages.*

This proved an unsuccessful attempt to deal with the problem presented to the nation by the intemperate use of alcoholic beverages. It was in effect from 1920 to 1933.

AMENDMENT XIX   *Suffrage for Women.*

No citizen can be denied the right to vote "on account of sex." As in the Fifteenth Amendment, this does not guarantee to any individual the right to vote. It adds a fourth reason that cannot be used to deny the right to vote.

AMENDMENT XX   *Makes "Lame Duck" Sessions of Congress Most Unlikely.*

Before this amendment there were four months between election day in early November and inauguration day on March 4. Between these dates there was a short session of Congress. The "Lame Ducks" were those members of Congress who had failed to win reelection but, nevertheless, were still in office during this session. There are now only two months between election day and the convening of the new Congress on January 3. The Christmas recess occurs during this two-month period, so there isn't time for a session of Congress until the new Congress takes over. The date of the inauguration of the President is January 20. It is possible, but very unlikely, that a special session of Congress could be called between early November and January 3.

AMENDMENT XXI   *Repeal of Prohibition.*

This amendment repealed, or ended, the Eighteenth Amendment.

AMENDMENT XXII   *The President Restricted to Two Terms.*

This amendment was ratified in 1951 to make into written law what had been unbroken tradition (unwritten law) for about 150 years. It prevents anyone being elected President more than twice and prevents holding that office more than 10 years. When the death of a President brings a successor into office during the first two years of a term, this amendment limits the new President to one election; thus restricting the term to anywhere from six to eight years. If the President dies within the last two years of a term, the new President will be eligible to be elected twice and thus may serve as long as ten years. The election of Franklin Roosevelt in 1940 broke the only-two-terms tradition, which had been observed for about 150 years, and then he went on to win election for a fourth term in 1944. This amendment was a reaction to this situation.

AMENDMENT XXIII   *District of Columbia Given Votes in the Electoral College.*

The District of Columbia is governed by Congress. Its residents had no suffrage rights. This amendment gives them a vote for President and Vice-President by giving to the District as many votes in the Electoral College as those states having the smallest number of electoral votes.

AMENDMENT XXIV   *Nonpayment of taxes cannot be used as a reason for denying to any citizen the right to vote for President, Vice-President, or a member of Congress.*

This abolished the practice, common in some Southern states, of using a poll tax as a device to prevent black Americans from voting.

AMENDMENT XXV   *When and How the Vice-President Becomes Acting President.*

This amendment was ratified in 1967 and sets up procedures to determine when and how the Vice-President will become acting President in case the President is no longer able to carry out the duties of the office. It also provides for the return to the President of the full powers of the office when the President is again able to assume them. The major provisions are:

1] Upon the death of the Vice-President, the President may appoint, with the majority approval of each House of Congress, a successor.

2] When the President states in writing to the Speaker of the House and to the Temporary Chairman of the Senate that he is unable to discharge the duties of his office, the Vice-President becomes acting President and remains such until another written message from the President to the same officers of the House and Senate states that he is able to resume the duties of the office of President. This transfer of power will occur within four days unless the acting President (the Vice-President) and a majority of the Cabinet state in writing to the contrary to the Speaker of the House and to the Temporary Chairman of the Senate. In such case Congress will meet within 48 hours to decide the question within 21 days by a two-thirds majority vote of both the House and Senate.

3] When the Vice-President and a majority of the Cabinet heads state in writing to the Speaker of the House and the Temporary Chairman of the Senate that the President is not able to discharge the duties of office, the Vice-President becomes acting President. Congress may by law put this responsibility on some other group.

AMENDMENT XXVI *The right of citizens to vote at 18 is guaranteed.*

This amendment was ratified in 1971. Young citizens received the right to vote at age 18 in all elections—federal, state, and local. Previously, each state had its own minimum voting age, ranging from 18 to 21. Since young men were still being drafted into the military at age 18 to fight in the Korean War (1950-53) and Vietnam War (1965-1973), the popular motto had become: "Old enough to fight, old enough to vote."

AMENDMENT XXVII *Congressional pay increases.*

First proposed in the 19th century, this amendment went into effect after Michigan became the 38th state to ratify it in 1992. Congress is not allowed to increase its current pay. An increase in salary that Congress votes for itself cannot go into effect until after the next congressional election.

The Constitution and Statute Law

Statute law refers to laws passed by legislatures as distinguished from **fundamental law**, which is the Constitution itself. Good constitution writing is quite a different task from writing statutes. Statutes should be specific, so expressed as to be subject to only one reasonable interpretation, so clear as to leave no room for differing opinions as to its meaning. Constitutions, on the contrary, should make considerable use of general terms that defy exact interpretation. Our Constitution gives some splendid examples of the wise use of general terms and the wise avoidance of detail.

In the Bill of Rights we have such words as *excessive* bails, *cruel* and *unusual* punishments, and *unreasonable* searches. Had any attempt been made to write into the Constitution exactly what these words meant, the meanings suitable for 1800 would be unsuitable for 1900. As it is, each generation can, through its courts, give a reasonable, workable definition to such words. The phrase *due process of law* and the word *commerce* have been interpreted in importantly different ways to suit a changing environment with its shifting climate of public opinion. In 1789 the word *person* in the Fifth Amendment (no *person* shall be deprived of life, liberty, or property without *due process of law*) did not include slaves; in the Fourteenth Amendment it particularly meant ex-slaves, and since the middle 1880s it has come to mean all human beings plus corporations, now considered to be "legal persons."

The wisdom of not going into detail in writing a Constitution is shown in Article III. "The judicial power of the United States shall be vested in one Supreme Court, and in such inferior courts as the Congress may from time to time ordain and establish." Not a word more about the structure of our federal court system. Let Congress construct the court system by statute law; it will need adjustments from time to time, and it is easier to pass and repeal laws than to amend the Constitution.

The Constitution did not attempt to set up Executive departments. It says that the President may get reports from heads of executive departments. Only time would tell what departments are necessary, how they might best be set up, and what their duties should be.

This use of general terms and avoidance of detail was skillfully done in the right places so that our Constitution has adaptability; it is part of the reason it has lasted for over two centuries.

Knowing the Constitution

To know well all the information about the Constitution on the preceding pages is not equivalent to knowing the Constitution. It is a good start, and a start is all that can be expected short of intensive study in the field of constitutional law, a specialized field for lawyers. The following illustrations will show that knowing what the Constitution says is not the same as knowing the Constitution.

Article I opens with, "All legislative powers herein granted shall be vested in a Congress...." "All" is a difficult word to quibble about. It has only one meaning. Yet, it is common knowledge that the President arranges and puts into effect changes in tariffs. This is clearly a legislative power exercised by the President.

The Thirteenth Amendment states that there shall be no "involuntary servitude" except as a punishment for crime. For many years it was commonly believed that compulsory military service in time of peace was impossible in the United States because it would involve "involuntary servitude." Yet, in September 1940, over a year before we entered World War II, Congress passed the first peacetime draft in our history.

Just what freedom of religion, speech, and press mean are issues that repeatedly come before the courts. In several decisions before 1954, segregated schools did not violate the Fourteenth Amendment, but since then they do. Uneven representation of election districts in state legislatures had existed for many years, but in 1962 they were declared unconstitutional because they denied "equal protection of the laws." This is a reversal of previous Court decisions.

Obviously, then, to be able to read the Constitution and interpret it according to its literal sense is far from a safe guide to its legal interpretation. The Constitution is interwoven with the threads of our economic, political, and social history; it is interpreted in that complex context by the Supreme Court.

PART THREE

PRESIDENTS OF THE

UNITED STATES

George Washington 1789-1797

1732 -1799

Vice-President   JOHN ADAMS

Secretary of State   THOMAS JEFFERSON   Secretary of Treasury   ALEXANDER HAMILTON

WASHINGTON'S PUBLIC SERVICE BEFORE HE BECAME PRESIDENT

Lieutenant Colonel in the French and Indian War (1753-1756)
Virginia delegate to the First and Second Continental Congresses (1774 and 1775)
Head command of the Continental armies in the Revolution (1775-1783)
Virginia delegate to the Annapolis Convention (1786)
Chairman of the Constitutional Convention (1787)

MAJOR ITEMS OF WASHINGTON'S ADMINISTRATIONS

Judiciary Act (1789)   *Foreign Debt*
Tariff (1789)   *Assumption of State Debts*
Sale of Public Lands   *French Revolution (Citizen Genet)*
Whiskey Rebellion   *Jay Treaty with England (1795)*
First Bank of the United States   *Pinckney Treaty with Spain (1795)*
Domestic Debt   *Farewell Address*

Election

George Washington was elected by the unanimous vote of the Electoral College. He was inaugurated on April 30, 1789, at the Federal Hall in New York City. Before leaving Mount Vernon for the ceremonies, he had written a letter expressing doubts about both his suitability for the position and the success of the republic. But he did believe he possessed certain qualifications for the office, for he wrote, "Integrity and firmness are all I can promise."

Regardless of political affiliation, the Congress and the people had confidence in Washington. They had different ideas of what should be done, but there was no faction trying to wreck the republic. Those who had opposed ratification of the Constitution were now working to establish the government. They accepted the fact that the Constitution was the government and were willing to work for changes to make it more to their liking by peaceful, legal procedures. This sort of political maturity was remarkable.

Reelection

On December 5, 1792, the presidential electors, members of the Electoral College, gave Washington 132 votes. Three did not vote. No one else got a vote. John Adams was reelected to the vice presidency with a vote of 77. An Anti-federalist, George Clinton, received 50 votes.

Judiciary Act of 1789

1]   It established a **Supreme Court** of six Justices, a Chief Justice, and five Associate Justices. (**John Jay** was the first **Chief Justice.**)

2]   It provided for thirteen District Courts and three Circuit Courts.

3]   It established the office of **Attorney General.** (**Edmund Randolph** was the first Attorney General, head of the Justice department.)

This was a very complete and detailed law setting forth procedures which, for the most part, are still in effect. Part of this law became an important factor in the *Marbury* v. *Madison* case of 1803.

* Tariff (1789)

This tariff, passed on the 4th of July, has been called **Alexander Hamilton**'s 10 percent tariff. Duties on about 90 items ranged from 5 to 10 percent ad valorem (according to their invoiced value). Most of the rates were below 10 percent. Hamilton, as Secretary of the Treasury, was anxious to establish the tariff as a regular source of revenue, and he was just as anxious to establish the principle of protection of domestic manufacture by tariffs. The revenue was an immediate necessity; the protection was of minor immediate importance but was destined to develop into a persistent political issue throughout our history.

Sale of Public Lands

Under the Articles of Confederation, the Land Ordinance of 1785 and the Northwest Ordinance of 1787 set the pattern followed under the Constitution. In spite of minor adjustments such as raising the minimum price of land per acre to $2.00 and cutting the minimum acreage per purchase from 640 acres to 320 acres, a series of land laws encouraged purchase of huge areas by speculators rather than farms by settlers. It raised considerable revenue quickly and easily.

Excise Tax

An **excise tax** is one levied on something produced, sold, and used in the United States. Excise taxes were bound to cause trouble. To have to pay excise taxes was looked upon as a violation of the liberty for which the Revolution was fought. Hamilton recommended and Congress passed an excise tax on whiskey. This was especially unpopular with the corn farmers west of the Alleghenies because they had to change their corn into whiskey in order to transport it for miles without roads to market.

* Whiskey Rebellion (1794)

The western areas from Pennsylvania through North Carolina produced corn. Bulky loads of corn could not be hauled to markets in the East, but barrels of whiskey could be transported. If a farmer couldn't get the whiskey to market this year, it became more valuable as it aged in the wood. To corn farmers the whiskey tax was a tax on a large part of their year's labor and they felt picked upon.

Throughout the western counties in Pennsylvania, tax collectors were tarred and feathered. Along the Allegheny and Monongahela rivers, armed bands were formed to resist the tax. The Governor of Pennsylvania was reluctant to quell the uprisings, but this time (unlike Shays' Rebellion) the central government did not stand aside. Hamilton led between 15,000 and 16,000 soldiers into western Pennsylvania. President Washington rode with the troops for a few miles to give the prestige of his person and office to the enforcement of the tax laws. The troops under federal command overawed the rebellious farmers. Their resistance crumbled without a clash of arms and the tax was paid. This little rebellion was turned into a big victory for the United States government.

* An Appreciation of the Tax Problems Faced by Hamilton

From the Sugar Act of 1733 to the Treaty of Paris of 1763, non payment of taxes and smuggling were so commonplace as to be respectable. It was the period of "salutary neglect." From 1763 to 1775 it became increasingly patriotic for the American colonials to not pay taxes to England. From 1781 to 1789 the Congress under the Articles of Confederation could not collect taxes. After over half a century of largely successful resistance to taxation, there is little wonder that an excise tax would run into trouble. The tariff, the sale of public lands, and the excise tax were the three major sources of revenue. The first two were comparatively painless, but the excise tax was painful. The lesson of taxation had to be learned, and Hamilton taught it well.

** First Bank of the United States (1791-1811)

A **Bank of the United States** (B.U.S.) was proposed by Hamilton. President Washington received written statements from Hamilton and Jefferson on the constitutionality of such a bank. Hamilton developed the theory of **"loose" construction** of the Constitution in support of the bank, while Jefferson expounded the theory of **"strict" construction** in opposition to it. Washington accepted Hamilton's reasoning, and Congress passed the law establishing the bank.

Does the implied powers (elastic) clause give Congress the right to create a bank? Jefferson's answer was an emphatic "No!" "Congress shall have power to make all laws which shall be *necessary* and proper for carrying into execution for foregoing powers...." If *necessary* means something less than absolutely necessary, it begins to mean highly convenient, or merely convenient, or perhaps just a bit helpful. If the word *necessary* is to have its strict meaning modified at all, how can there be any particular point beyond which no further modification is permissible? Any such loose interpretation clears the way for the United States government to accumulate power and eventually overwhelm the states. "Loose" construction would destroy the protection the states believed they had in the Tenth Amendment. "The powers *not delegated* to the United States by the Constitution, or prohibited by it to the States, are reserved to the States respectively, or to the people." Thus reasoned Jefferson.

Hamilton insisted that a sovereign government must have ample authority to carry out any specific grant of power in the Constitution. He pointed out that navigation aids, such as lighthouses, had been authorized by laws of Congress under the right to regulate commerce. Nowhere did the Constitution state, or need to, that Congress could erect lighthouses. He expressed his reasoning so well in one sentence of his defense of "loose" construction that it is worth close consideration. "If the end be clearly comprehended within any of the specific powers, and if the measure have an obvious relation to that end, and is not forbidden by any particular provision of the Constitution, it may safely be deemed to come within the compass of the national authority." From this view it became apparent that the creation of a United States Bank would be a measure with an obvious relation to the following powers granted in the Constitution:

1] to collect taxes

2] to borrow money

3] to pay the public debt

4] to regulate commerce

With this Hamilton (loose construction) versus Jefferson (strict construction) debate, the people split into two groups, which soon became definite political parties. Loose constructionists were **Federalists**; strict constructionists were **Republicans**. (The Republicans were sometimes called Democratic Republicans.) The Federalists were pretty much the same people who had most ardently supported ratification of the Constitution. They were the more prominent business owners, the people whose property was closely associated with commerce and trade, and the professional people of the larger communities. The Republicans were those who had opposed ratification of the Constitution and those who had supported it with some misgivings. These people were small farmers living away from the towns and the more prosperous land owners of the coastal areas of the South; in short, the agrarian interests. While the differences that separated the two parties included education, wealth, and social position, the basic factor that outweighed all others was economic. How people made their living placed them in one party or the other; it was agriculture versus commerce and manufacturing. One important group of business people did oppose the bank, even though they were Federalists. This was the bankers. To them the Bank of the United States was unfair competition to all other banks. It was a private bank which enjoyed exclusive advantages from the government.

Some of the following facts explain why the Secretary of the Treasury considered the establishment of the Bank of the United States the key point of his financial program.

1] The bank was a private institution.
80 percent of its stock was owned by private individals.
20 percent of its stock was owned by the United States.

2] Total capitalization was $10 million.

3] The bank could issue paper money, that is, bank notes, so long as it was redeemable in gold.

4] Branches of the bank in major cities could transfer credit easily from city to city by bank drafts and thus greatly aid business.

5] Taxes could be paid to the bank.

6] The sale of United States bonds could be handled by the bank.

7] Short-term loans could be made by the bank to the United States.

As it turned out the B.U.S. aided the Treasury Department in several of its functions. It had a stabilizing effect on the currency system, and it tended to make other banks adopt sound banking practices. It was an asset to the economy. It was a very prosperous private business.

The Domestic and Foreign Debts

The people of the United States held government bonds totaling, with accumulated interest, almost $45 million. The foreign debt was almost $12 million. Hamilton advocated combining these two debts by issuing new bonds in exchange for the original bonds, which were greatly depreciated. This would form one new debt that had every prospect of being paid at the face value of the bonds, plus the interest. There was no organized opposition to paying the foreign debt, which was owed chiefly to France and Holland. But there was strong opposition to handling the domestic debt in this manner. This combining of the domestic and foreign debts and refinancing them by a new issue of bonds is often called *funding* the debt.

The opposition stemmed from the fact that those who originally bought the bonds were no longer the owners. This was more true of small bondholders than of others. Almost all of the thousands of people of modest means who had bought government bonds during the Revolution had long since sold them at a small fraction of their face value. The depression of the middle 1780s had forced them to sell. By the time Hamilton proposed funding the debts, the owners of the bonds were wealthy people in the larger cities. The Republicans again charged that this was another scheme of Hamilton's to enrich the rich at the expense of the poor.

Hamilton got his way with Congress by insisting that the credit of the United States must be established. The infant nation could never get respect or make favorable trade agreements with other countries until it had earned the reputation that it paid its bills and that its currency was sound. Hamilton also stated that a government bond was a contract with the bondholder, that part of the value of a bond was the fact that it could be sold whenever the owner could find a purchaser at a price acceptable to both parties. Establishing credit and the integrity of a government contract were of fundamental importance, not be set aside because some people gained and others lost.

* The Assumption of State Debts

The total debt of all the states was about $25 million. Of this over $21 million had been spent by the states in conducting the Revolutionary War. Left to themselves, some of the states would certainly have failed to pay off their bonds at face value. Again

Hamilton emphasized the necessity of establishing the credit of governments, state as well as federal. Congress passed the bill by which the United States assumed the debts contracted as part of their war effort, the $21 million. This money had been spent in a common cause.

It so happened that the Southern states had already paid off a much larger share of their bonds than had the New England states. So again, Hamilton's plan brought financial advantage to commercial interests at the expense of agrarian interests. The **Assumption Bill** meant that all of the states would pay off the total debt.

The Federalists needed some Republican support to get the Assumption Bill passed. Jefferson agreed to persuade a few Republicans to vote for the bill if Hamilton would persuade a few New Englanders to vote to have the permanent capital of the United States located on the Potomac River. Thus, the Assumption Bill was passed, and the capital was located on the Potomac. This sort of political deal whereby one bloc or party gives support for one measure in return for support for another is called *logrolling*.

* French Revolution and Citizen Genêt

In the early spring of 1793, France was at war with England and Spain. In April, Americans heard the news of the beheading of King Louis XVI the previous January. The Girondist party, the moderate revolutionary party, sent Citizen Genêt, who arrived April 8, to seek aid under the Treaty of Alliance of 1778. Washington issued a **Neutrality Proclamation**.

There was a good deal of enthusiasm for the French Revolution among the people of the United States. "Liberty, equality, fraternity" and Lafayette's "Declaration of the Rights of Man" had a good sound to American ears so recently tuned to their own Revolution. Intense dislike of England was widespread because of the recent war and because there were constant sources of irritation left over from the Treaty of Paris, 1783. Comparatively few people in the United States were pro-English. England bought well over half of our exports and paid an even larger part of the duties collected on imports. Friendship with England was important to private commercial interests because of trade, and to our government because of revenue. Again we have the same lineup. Those who were pro-French were the same people who opposed the B.U.S., opposed the payment of the domestic debt, and opposed the government's assumption of the states' debts. Those who had favored these policies were now the ones who favored England. It is difficult to say precisely when the Republicans and Federalists recognized themselves as political parties, but, when their differences included foreign policy as well as domestic fiscal policy, the division was well defined.

President Washington's Neutrality Proclamation set our official policy. Jefferson favored a sympathetic attitude toward France, but not to the extent of going to war as its ally. When Genêt realized he could get no help through our government, he appealed directly to the people by recruiting men and outfitting privateers. His aim was to raise troops to take Florida and Louisiana from Spain to become French possessions, and to take Canada as an addition to the United States. The privateers were to prey upon British merchant ships in the Caribbean. Jefferson, whose followers had held banquets and parades in Genêt's honor when he first arrived, agreed with the President that he must demand Genêt's recall. By this time, August of 1793, the Girondists had been overthrown by the Jacobins in France, and the new French minister had an order for Genêt's arrest. Return to France during the Reign of Terror probably meant the guillotine, President Washington allowed him to remain in the United States.

* Jay Treaty with England (1795)

In 1793 England made it clear that it would not leave the trading and military posts on our Great Lakes-Ohio River Valley area until British merchants had been paid the debts owed to them by American merchants. England also sought recompense for the Loyalists whose property had been seized during the Revolution.

In November 1793 the British began a campaign against neutral shipping in the West Indian waters. Any ship carrying products from French colonies to any destination was seized. Its cargo was confiscated, some of the crew impressed into the British Navy, and others put in jail. The enforcement of this policy was such that any American ship that the British could catch was seized, regardless of where it got its cargo or where it was going. This was a serious blow to Yankee shipping. The Federalists began to think war with England was the only answer.

In the spring of 1794 Washington sent Chief Justice Jay to attempt a settlement of these difficulties. Jay did not do well. The problems of British interference with our shipping, the debts owed to the British merchants, and the Maine-Canadian border were left for settlement by British-American commissioners.

The terms of the **Jay Treaty** were:

1]   The British would get out of the Northwest trading and military posts by June 1796.

2]   American ships displacing not over 70 tons could trade with the British West Indies, but their cargoes must not include cotton, molasses, or sugar.

The treaty was so unsatisfactory that the Senate considered it in a secret session, but the terms leaked out. Genuine and bitter protests greeted the treaty. Mr. Jay was burned in effigy at protest meetings and parades. President Washington also was not happy with the treaty. However, when Washington sent Jay to London, he sent him to make arrangements that would permit this nation to remain at peace. If Jay's mission was not one of "peace at any price," it was a "peace-at-almost-any-price" mission. Washington requested the Senate to ratify the treaty even though his Secretary of State, **Edmund Randolph**, opposed it. By a close vote the Senate gave the President the necessary two-thirds majority. Washington's acceptance of the treaty was an act that was unpopular, wise, and courageous. We could survive humiliation, but not war.

* Pinckney Treaty with Spain (1795)

This treaty is also known as the **San Lorenzo Treaty. Thomas Pinckney** got better terms than he hoped for, much better than we might have expected. Both Republicans and Federalists were pleased. The terms of the **Pinckney Treaty** were:

1]   The United States had free navigation of the Mississippi River.

2]   The 31st parallel was accepted as our southern boundary line.

3]   The United States had the right of deposit at New Orleans. This gave us the use of the port of New Orleans on the same basis as Spain. It permitted Americans to ship goods down the river on flat boats for transshipment by sailing vessels to foreign ports. New Orleans was the only exit for foreign trade by Americans living west of the Alleghenies.

** Washington's Farewell Address

This address was printed in the *American Daily Advertiser,* September 17, 1796. It was Washington's statement that he would not run for a third term. He had been formulating his ideas since the end of his first term. During that period he consulted with Madison, Hamilton, and Jay; but the address was Washington's. In his **Farewell Address** Washington warned Americans against the formation of political parties and to avoid "permanent alliances" with "any portion of the foreign world."

On Foreign Relations

"The great rule of conduct for us in regard to foreign nations is, in extending our commercial relations, to have with them as little political connection as possible. It is our true policy to steer clear of permanent alliances with any portion of the foreign world."

On Strife Between Political Parties

"I have already intimated to you the danger of parties in the State, with particular reference to the founding of them on geographical discriminations. Let me . . . warn you in the most solemn manner against the baneful effects of the spirit of party generally. . . . It serves always to distract the public councils and enfeeble the public administration. It agitates the community with ill-founded jealousies and false alarms; kindles the animosity of one part against another; foments occasionally riot and insurrection. It opens the door to foreign influence and corruption, which find a facilitated access to the government itself through the channels of party passion.

John Adams   1797-1801

1735-1826

F<small>EDERALIST</small>

Vice-President   THOMAS JEFFERSON

ADAMS' PUBLIC SERVICE BEFORE HE BECAME PRESIDENT

One of the most effective writers against the Stamp Act
Defended the British soldiers involved in the "Boston Massacre"
Massachusetts delegate to both the First and Second Continental Congresses
Helped to negotiate the Treaty of Paris, 1783
Vice-President under Washington

MAJOR ITEMS OF JOHN ADAMS' ADMINISTRATION

XYZ Affair	*"Midnight Judges"*
Alien Act	*Naturalization Act*
Sedition Act	*Kentucky and Virginia Resolutions*

Election 1796

John Adams received 71 electoral votes. **Thomas Jefferson**, leader of the Republican party, received 68 votes. This is the first presidential election under the Constitution determined along party lines. The issue of the campaign was the **Jay Treaty.** The election of the two rival candidates as President and Vice-President resulted from the original provisions of the Constitution. Members of the Electoral College voted for two persons with no designation as to whether they were intended as votes for President or for Vice-President. The votes were then totaled and the candidate receiving the most votes, provided it was a majority, became President; the candidate receiving the next largest vote became Vice-President. This unsatisfactory method was replaced in 1804 by the Twelfth Amendment.

* XYZ Affair (1797)

The American people were unhappy about the Jay Treaty; France was angry about it. France considered it a violation of the Treaty of Alliance of 1778. France also resented America's refusal to aid France, which was its obligation under the Treaty of 1778. So, in 1797, the French began attacking our shipping, much as England had done in 1793. The five-man **Directory** was in charge of France. **Talleyrand,** foreign minister Directory, sought to take advantage of the weakness of our new nation and the public sympathy in the United States for the French Revolution.

President Adams was anxious to avoid war. He appointed commissioners **Charles C. Pinckney, Elbridge G. Gerry,** and **John Marshall** to try to come to some acceptable terms with France. Three "unofficial" French envoys informed our commissioners that before formal talks could begin, they must be prepared to arrange a loan to France and pay a bribe of $240,000. This proposition was offered on October 18, 1797. The demand of bribe and a loan as conditions to arrange for the opening of official talks between governments was outrageous. Marshall refused to make any concessions. He and Pinckney returned to report to President Adams.

When the President reported this story to Congress on March 19, 1798, the "unofficial" French envoys

91

were referred to as "X Y, and Z". A wave of indignation swept through the United States. "Millions for defense, but not one cent for tribute," was the slogan of the day. President Adams enjoyed a brief spell of popularity. The Republican party lost many supporters.

The United States prepared for war. France was expected to declare war, but instead, Talleyrand pretended that the XYZ episode was all a misunderstanding. He claimed that the "unofficial" French envoys had no connection with the French government and acted without his knowledge. Obviously France did not want war with America, and this suited President Adams. Negotiations dragged on through most of 1800, when it was agreed that the Treaty of Alliance of 1778 was not in effect. During the approximately two years that negotiations were taking place, there was a full-fledged naval war, though undeclared, between France and the United States. Several engagements between warships occurred, and the Yankee privateers just about drove French commerce out of West Indian waters.

* Naturalization Act; Alien Act; Sedition Act; "Midnight Judges"

These items are listed together because they were all acts that contributed to the downfall of the Federalist party.

The Naturalization Act (June 18, 1798)

It provided that aliens could not become citizens until they had lived in the United States fourteen years. The previous residence requirement had been five years.

The Alien Act (June 25, 1798)

It gave the President the power to deport all aliens considered dangerous to our peace and safety or inclined to be engaged in treason. No alien was ever deported under this law.

The Sedition Act (July 14, 1798)

1] A fine of not more than $2,000 and imprisonment for not more than two years for publishing "any false, scandalous, and malicious writing" about the government of the United States, Congress, or the President.

2] A fine of not more than $5,000 and imprisonment for not more than five years for persons unlawfully conspiring to oppose any law or official of the government.

3] The truth of statements published shall be accepted as a defense thereof.

4] This act shall continue in force until March 3, 1801.

"Midnight Judges" (Feb. 27, 1801-March 3, 1801)

Less than a week before Jefferson's inauguration, the "lame duck" Federalist Congress and the rejected President Adams passed and signed the **Judiciary Act of 1801**. It changed the Supreme Court from six to five judges, created 16 additional circuit court judgeships, and provided jobs for several marshals, attorneys, and clerks. Some of the commissions for these judgeships and other jobs were signed the last night of Adams' term in an effort to maintain Federalist control over the judicial branch of the government. The new President and the new Republican Congress repealed the Judiciary Act of 1801 two months after it had been passed. But the "midnight judges" proved to many that the Federalist party had defied public opinion as clearly expressed in the election of 1800, and had used the establishment of federal courts for purely political purposes.

The Naturalization Act, the Alien Act, and the Sedition Act all purported to defend the United States from dangerous subversives. The Reign of Terror of the French Revolution was followed by the XYZ Affair and two years of undeclared war with France.

This made it easy for the Federalist party to pose as the defender of the United States from a foreign menace. However, the laws were also designed to weaken the Republican party. Most naturalized citizens became Republicans. Almost all immigrants were rather poor people who earned their living as hired help in the towns or as farmers on the more remote and poorer farms. The overwhelming majority of them would eventually vote Republican, if they voted at all. The Sedition Act didn't bother any French aliens, but it did put Republican newspaper editors in jail. As the scare over France subsided, the suspicion grew that the Naturalization, Alien, and Sedition laws were Federalist tricks to hurt the Republican party. The Sedition Act especially aroused antagonism. It seemed a denial of the restriction put upon Congress by the First Amendment: "Congress shall make no law...abridging the freedom of the press; of the right to...assemble, and to petition...." To assemble might be considered a conspiracy, or to petition the government for a redress of grievances might be considered a malicious criticism of the government or its officers according to the Sedition Act. These restrictive laws boomeranged against the Federalists.

* Kentucky and Virginia Resolutions (November and December 1798)

Jefferson wrote the Kentucky Resolutions, and Madison wrote the Virginia Resolutions. These men were sincerely alarmed at the growing power of the central government under "loose construction." They were sure that the Sedition Act and the Alien Act were unconstitutional.

The Kentucky Resolutions Made the Following Points

1] The state made a "compact," an agreement, known as the Constitution.

2] The Constitution set up a "general government," the federal government, for special purposes, gave it definite powers, and reserved to each state all other rights and powers.

3] Whenever the "general government assumes undelegated powers, its acts are unauthoritative, void, and of no force."

4] The government made by this compact,"...was not made the exclusive or final judge of the extent of the powers delegated to itself."

5] The limited power of the general government and the sovereignty of the states is made clear by the Tenth Amendment: "the powers not delegated to the United States by the Constitution, or prohibited by it to the States, are reserved to the States respectively, or to the people."

** Significance of the Kentucky and Virginia Resolutions

At the time these resolutions were adopted by Kentucky and Virginia, there was no intent to claim, much less act upon, the right of a state to withdraw from the Union. But it clearly followed, and this was noted at the time, that acceptance of the Jefferson and Madison reasoning would make both nullification of laws of Congress by states and the withdrawal of states from the Union obviously lawful steps for any state to take. The Constitution says nothing about the power to nullify acts of Congress, and it says nothing about a state withdrawing from the Union. It therefore follows that these powers or rights are residual, and thus belong to the states, or to the people. It is an interesting detail that the Articles of Confederation contained the words, "perpetual Union," but no such designation occurs in the Constitution.

Thomas Jefferson   1801-1809

1743-1826

REPUBLICAN

☆

Vice President   AARON BURR
GEORGE CLINTON

Secretary of State   JAMES MADISON

JEFFERSON'S PUBLIC SERVICES BEFORE HE BECAME PRESIDENT

Member of the Virginia House of Burgesses
Wrote "A Summary View of the Rights of British America" in 1774
Virginia delegate to the Second Continental Congress, 1775-1776
Wrote the Declaration of Independence
Governor of Virginia, 1779-1781
United States Minister to France, 1785-1789
Secretary of State, 1789-1793
Leader of the Republican party (Democratic Republican)
Vice-President under Adams
Wrote the Kentucky Resolutions

MAJOR ITEMS OF JEFFERSON'S ADMINISTRATIONS

Marbury v. Madison (1803)
Louisiana Purchase (1803)
Lewis and Clark Expedition
Twelfth Amendment (1804)
Embargo Act (1807)
Non-Intercourse Act (1809)

Election of 1800 and Reelection in 1804

In 1800 the campaign issues were the Alien and Sedition Acts and relations with France and England. Trade with France had almost vanished; we were officially at peace and actually at war. Impressment and the Jay Treaty still created anti-English sentiment, which hurt the Federalists.

President **John Adams** and **Alexander Hamilton** had split the Federalist party. Their disagreement over how to handle our relations with France grew into a bitter personal feud that had the party fighting within itself more vigorously than it fought the Republicans.

Thomas Jefferson and **Aaron Burr** both received 73 electoral votes to 65 for John Adams. It was the intention of the Republic electors to elect Jefferson as President and Burr as Vice-President. Legally, however, Burr had as good a claim to the office as did Jefferson. The election went to the House of Representatives, with each state having one vote. It took 36 ballots to elect Jefferson. The Federalist party had control of the House. They decided in a caucus to elect Burr, but Hamilton was able to persuade them to reverse this decision and vote for Jefferson.

The reelection of Jefferson in 1804 marked the first time the members of the Electoral College voted separately for President and Vice-President under the terms of the Twelfth Amendment. Jefferson got 162 electoral votes to 14 for the Federalist candidate, Charles C. Pinckney. Even the New England states, except for Connecticut, voted for Jefferson.

** *Marbury* v. *Madison* (1803)

President Adams had appointed **William Marbury** as a Justice of the Peace in the District of Columbia. The commission had been properly signed, but had not been delivered. When Jefferson took office, he instructed his Secretary of State, James Madison, not to deliver any of the commissions to the "midnight" appointees who hadn't yet received them. William Marbury asked for an order from the Supreme Court directing the Secretary of State to deliver his commission to him. Such an affirmative order, whereby the court tells someone to do something, is called a *mandamus*. President Jefferson instructed Madison to pay no attention to the mandamus. The Judiciary Act of 1789 provided that the Supreme Court could issue a writ of mandamus to any officer of the United States. The officer in this case was Secretary of State Madison. At this point we have a President refusing to do, through the Secretary of State, what a law of Congress empowers the Supreme Court to order done.

The pertinent points in the decision delivered by **Chief Justice Marshall,** were:

1] Marbury was entitled to his commission.

2] It was the duty of the President to see that the commission was delivered to Marbury.

3] The Supreme Court could not issue an order (mandamus) that the commission be delivered, because the clause in the Judiciary Act of 1789 authorizing the Court to do so was unconstitutional.

    a. This clause enlarged the *original* jurisdiction of the Supreme Court, a jurisdiction fixed by the Constitution and not subject to modification by Congress.

    b. This clause violated the fundamental principle of **separation of powers**. It provided that Congress reach over into the Judicial branch, the Supreme Court, to enlarge its powers beyond the limits defined in the Constitution.

This case is to be understood as a political contest between a Federalist Chief Justice and a Republican President. Had Marshall ordered Jefferson to deliver the commission to Marbury, Jefferson would not have done so. The Chief Justice could not made the President obey a Court order. The Supreme Court would then invite public ridicule, endanger its prestige and a popular President would be a bit more popular. Had Marshall ruled that the President didn't have to obey the Judiciary Act, it would have been an abject surrender by the Court to the President. So the Chief Justice ruled that Marbury should get his commission, that Jefferson was wrong in not giving it to him, and that the Court's hands were tied because the mandamus clause of the Judiciary Act was unconstitutional. This decision did more than get the Chief Justice out of a dilemma. It gave Jefferson a petty political victory by withholding commissions from Marbury and a few other "midnight" appointees. But it also established the principle of **judicial review** of laws of Congress. It was a tremendous victory for "loose construction" of the Constitution and the tendency toward a stronger federal government. It was not until 1857, the **Dred Scott** case, that the Supreme Court again ruled that a law of Congress was unconstitutional.

** Louisiana Purchase, 1803

The **Louisiana Territory** was bought from France for $15 million. The area totaled about 830,000 square miles and just about doubled the size of our nation. The boundaries were indefinite. The Mississippi River was the eastern border. On the south the territory extended to the Gulf of Mexico, on the west to the Rocky Mountains, and on the north to Canada.

Our minister to France, who handled most of the negotiations, was **Robert Livingston. James Monroe** was sent over by President Jefferson as a special minister to help bring about a favorable deal. The day before Monroe arrived in Paris, Napoleon's foreign minister, Talleyrand, still refused to sell only the New Orleans' area; but he did suggest that the United States buy the whole Louisiana Territory. Both Monroe and Livingston recognized this offer as not only too good to lose but one to be concluded as quickly as possible. The agreement was made on May 2, 1803.

Livingston and Monroe had not been authorized to buy any such vast area or to agree to a price over $10 million.

The Senate ratified this treaty with France by a vote of 24 to 7 on Oct. 20, 1803.

** President Jefferson Had Compelling Reasons for This Purchase

1] The Pinckney Treaty of 1795 gave the United States freedom to use the Mississippi River and the port of New Orleans. In May 1801, Jefferson learned that Napoleon had forced Spain to sign over Louisiana to France. This change caused Jefferson to write to Robert Livingston in Paris, "The day that France takes over New Orleans...we must marry ourselves to the British fleet and nation."

2]   The situation in the southwestern area of the United States made the use of the Mississippi River an urgent matter. The volume of trade down the Mississippi totaled about $1 million a year. The settlers of the Ohio Valley area (what is now Ohio, Indiana, Illinois, and Kentucky) could get cash for goods shipped to New Orleans. The whole western area including the Ohio Valley and what is now Tennessee, Mississippi, Louisiana, and Alabama were suspicious of Congress and the eastern seaboard. To President Jefferson, this was a serious problem. The climate of opinion in the south-western corner of the United States in 1803 was self-centered and strictly sectional. Their attitude toward the "original thirteen" ranged from indifference to unfriendliness. President Jefferson had reason for concern lest the Southwest fall away from the United States if it had to choose between loyalty and the use of the Mississippi River. The uncertainties in this area were emphasized a little later, in 1805 and 1806, when Aaron Burr and General Wilkinson were suspected of some sort of plot. We don't know what their plans were. Wilkinson betrayed Burr, who was tried for treason and acquitted in 1807. President Jefferson knew the situation was delicate and that loss of the use of the Mississippi could set off serious internal trouble.

3]   It was clear that the United States must get all of the Louisiana Territory if the opportunity arose. The Napoleonic Wars were on. If England won, it would take Louisiana. England had Canada and control of the seas. In short, a British victory meant that the United States would be surrounded by British Canada, British Louisiana, and British naval power. If Napoleon won, France would force England to give back Canada. Canada and Louisiana would then be French, and France would control the seas, for it could not win without first destroying British sea power. To President Jefferson the outlook was bleak indeed. Little wonder that Talleyrand's offer was eagerly accepted!

** The Purchase of Louisiana Posed a Special Problem for President Jefferson

We have seen how Jefferson changed his attitude toward England and France, as soon as France threatened our use of the Mississippi River. Strange as it may have seemed to him to be pro-English and anti-French, he could see clearly where our national inter-

est lay. Another problem bothered him deeply. He believed in the "strict" interpretation of the Constitution. No officer of the federal government, no department, had the right to exercise any power or do anything unless that power was expressly and clearly stated in the Constitution. But nowhere in the Constitution was there any provision about buying such a tremendous area of land. On the other hand, the Constitution did say, in the Tenth Amendment, that any power not given to the United States and not denied to the states did belong to the states or to the people. Jefferson saw that what must be done for reasons of national interest (the acquisition of Louisiana) would violate his basic principles. His inclination was to take the issue to Congress. Had he done so, it almost certainly would have become an interparty fight, during which Napoleon might have withdrawn the offer or England might have seized Louisiana. Consequently, President Jefferson put national necessity above all else; about the Constitution as he saw it, above the political convictions of a lifetime.

** Why Napoleon Was Willing to Sell the Louisiana Territory

Slave revolts on the island of Haiti (Santo Domingo) had been erupting intermittently since about 1795. To quell the disorder, Napoleon sent a sizable expedition of ships and soldiers to Haiti. When order had been restored to Haiti, this force was then to go to New Orleans and set up a military and naval garrison there. However, a native leader, **Toussaint L'Ouverture,** offered such effective leadership to the slaves of Haiti and such damaging resistance to the French that Napoleon's naval and land forces were depleted to the point of uselessness. Napoleon's chance to build a base for his empire in the Western Hemisphere was lost. His problem became one of selling Louisiana before the British took it. At the crucial moment, April 1803, Napoleon was as anxious to sell as Livingston and Monroe were to buy. Moreover, Napoleon needed all the cash he could get.

Lewis and Clark Expedition

Meriwether Lewis and **William Clark** were sent by President Jefferson to explore the Louisiana Territory. They started up the Missouri River in May 1804 and reached the Pacific Ocean in November 1805. They wrote reports on the plants, animals, Native Americans, soil, rivers, type of country, etc. It was a scientific as well as an exploring undertaking. On the return trip, completed in September 1806, Lewis and Clark separated for part of the journey to take different routes.

There were between 40 and 50 men in the party. All but one returned safely. They had been instructed to avoid trouble with the Native Americans and to find a pass over the Rockies; both instructions were carried out.

Apparently Jefferson was not bothered by the fact that he had ordered the expedition to go across the Rockies beyond our western border. Captain Robert Gray had sailed into the mouth of the Columbia River in 1792; in fact, the river got its name from his ship. The Lewis and Clark expedition came down the Columbia to the Pacific (1805), and half a dozen years later the permanent settlement at Astoria, established by John Jacob Astor, was a fur trading post near the mouth of the river. These facts combined to give the United States its claim to the Oregon Territory, which we acquired in 1846.

Twelfth Amendment (1804)

The amendment provides for the election of President and Vice-President.

Embargo Act (1807)

The Napoleonic War was raging in Europe and on the high seas. Recruiting in England for the British Navy was accomplished, in some instances, by direct action. Any sailor who was alone when he left a waterfront tavern a bit unsteadily might be kidnapped by a pair of recruiting officers. By the time the lone sailor recovered his wits, he might well be enlisted in the Royal Navy and already on board a British warship. Equally direct recruiting for the Royal Navy took place on the high seas. United States ships were stopped, boarded, and the crew lined up on deck. Any sailors who seemed physically fit and who spoke English were likely to be taken off as deserters from the British Navy. This was impressment. In June 1807 a flagrant violation of our rights occurred when the United States frigate *Chesapeake* was stopped off the Virginia coast by the British frigate *Leopard*. Three Americans were killed, eighteen were wounded, and four men were impressed into the British Navy. One of the four was a deserter; the other three had been impressed before and then escaped only to be impressed a second time. Jefferson's answer to the *Chesapeake* incident was not war but the Embargo Act.

The terms of the Embargo Act were:

1]   No American ship can leave an American port for a foreign port.

2]   No foreign vessel can load a cargo at an American port.

3]   Coastwise shipping must post a bond equal to twice the value of the ship and cargo before leaving port. On delivery of the cargo, the bond will be repaid.

Smuggling by ship and also over the Canadian border, especially through New York State, robbed the Embargo Act of whatever effect it might have had. Above all, Jefferson wished to avoid war. Both France and England were violating our rights as a neutral nation. The Embargo Act made no attempt to assert our rights; it was intended to keep our ships out of danger by keeping them home. Its adverse economic effects ruined the shipping business along the Atlantic Coast. It hit New England with special force. State officials refused to support the enforcement of the embargo. There were not enough federal officials to do the job without local support. A New England convention was seriously considered, but not called, to protest the Embargo Act as an unconstitutional exercise of federal authority. The Governor of Connecticut flatly branded the Embargo Act unconstitutional. The Northeast now advanced the nullification theories of Jefferson and Madison.

Non-Intercourse Act (1809)

The Non-Intercourse Act of 1809 was passed a few days before the end of Jefferson's second term. It allowed American ships to trade everywhere except in ports controlled by England or by France. There followed a slight increase in trade, but no increase in the respect paid to our rights as a neutral nation. England and France continued to interfere with our commerce.

* Jefferson's Administrations Illustrate a Basic Pattern in American Politics

Presidential campaigns are carried on as if the nation would be saved or ruined, depending on which party won. Yet, shifts from one party to the other have resulted in so little change in the direction of public affairs that a common criticism of our political set-up is that both parties are as alike as two peas in a pod. Jefferson's election and administrations illustrate this pattern.

During the campaign of 1800 dire prophecies were made. The Federalists claimed, and seemed to believe, that a Republican victory would be the beginning of a revolution.

Jefferson did not disturb the Bank of the United States, which he and his party had so bitterly opposed.

He, as Washington and Adams had done, conducted foreign affairs with avoidance of war as the key aim. In trying to avoid war, the Federalists accepted the unpopular Jay Treaty, much as Jefferson accepted the humiliation of continued violation of our rights on the high seas by France and England. Because the vital interest of this republic demanded it, Jefferson cast aside his political theories of strict construction and states' rights. It is difficult to see what President Adams and the Federalists would have done, had they won in 1800, that would have been importantly different from the program of the Republicans. This was so true that a faction of Jefferson's party opposed the "Federalist policies" of President Jefferson. Their leader was John Randolph of Virginia, and they were call Quids. Other Republicans who thought Jefferson had deserted Republican principles and measures called themselves "Old Republicans."

As Washington established the "no third term" precedent, Jefferson also rooted it into our political "unwritten law" by refusing to run for a third term. It was 144 years before this precedent was broken, whereupon the unwritten law was made into constitutional law by the Twenty-second Amendment.

James Madison   1809-1817

1751-1836

REPUBLICAN

☆

Vice-President   GEORGE CLINTON
ELBRIDGE GERRY

Secretary of State   JAMES MONROE

MADISON'S PUBLIC SERVICE BEFORE HE BECAME PRESIDENT

Member of the Second Continental Congress from Virginia, 1780-1783
A leading force in arranging the Mount Vernon, Annapolis, and Philadelphia Constitutional
*   Conventions*
Author of several issues of the Federalist Papers
Secretary of State under Jefferson

MAJOR ITEMS OF MADISON'S ADMINISTRATIONS

Macon Act—Berlin and Milan Decrees—Orders in Council
War Hawks
War of 1812
Hartford Convention (1814)
First Protective Tariff (1816)

Election in 1808 and Reelection in 1812

The electoral vote was 122 for **James Madison** and 47 for **Charles C. Pinckney,** the Federalist candidate. The loss of the shipping business and the continued violation of our neutral rights by France and England were the major points of attack on the Republicans. The Federalist party revived in New England to made considerable gains in the House of Representatives, but not enough to get control.

The reelection of Madison took place five months after the start of the War of 1812. Some antiwar Republicans joined with the Federalists of the northeastern seaboard to oppose his reelection. But the electoral vote was Madison, 128; Clinton, 89. The Federalists made heavy gains in Congress. The South and West supported Madison, but the only state of the Northeast that Madison carried was Vermont, a state without a seacoast.

* Macon Act—Berlin and Milan Decrees —Orders in Council

These three items complete the story begun by the **Embargo Act of 1807** and continued by the **Non-Intercourse Act of 1809**. Together they tell what our government did in its efforts to keep out of war and, at the same time, force belligerents to recognize our rights as neutrals.

The British Parliament by its **Orders in Council** and Napoleon by his **Berlin and Milan Decrees** had established the policy of seizing any neutral shipping headed for enemy ports. This had almost the same effect as making all neutral shipping bound for the British Isles or a European port subject to capture by either England or France. In enforcing their orders and decrees, neither England nor France was too careful about confining its attacks to ships carrying contraband or actually bound for an enemy port.

The **Macon Act of 1810** withdrew all restrictions on trade with England and France. It further provided that whichever nation ceased its attacks upon our commerce would be rewarded by having the United States cease trading with the other nation. The American hope was that both England and France would repeal the Orders in Council and Berlin and Milan Decrees respectively. Napoleon quickly announced the repeal of the Berlin and Milan Decrees but actually continued to harass American shipping. However, over a year went by before the British Parliament repealed the Orders in Council. Meanwhile, we had renewed the embargo against England in accordance with the Macon Act, and England, in retaliation, stepped up impressment of American sailors and other violations of our rights. The Macon Act had enabled Napoleon to maneuver the United States to the verge of war against England. In fact, some fighting occurred off the coast of Virginia. On May 16, 1811, the U.S. Frigate *President* attacked the British corvette *Little Belt*, killing 9 and wounding 23 of her crew. This attack was our reaction to the continuing impressment and other interference with our shipping.

The War Hawks

Henry Clay was leader of the **War Hawks.** He made the most of his position as Speaker of the House to fan the war spirit. **John C. Calhoun** of South Carolina, Felix Grundy of Tennessee, Richard Johnson of Kentucky, and Langdon Cheves of South Carolina were other leading War Hawks. They were motivated by hatred of England or by ambition for expansion, or both. Clay thought the Kentucky militia could capture Canada. There was talk of taking Florida and Mexico. The members of Congress clamoring for war represented the inland areas. They blamed the Indian wars on the Canadians. It was in this period that **William Henry Harrison**, Governor of Indiana Territory, defeated the Native American confederacy of **Tecumseh** in the battle of **Tippecanoe,** November 6, 1811.

** The War of 1812

This was a very strange war. Neither side wanted it to happen. The United States had a very small navy, yet we won our most brilliant successes on the seas and on the lakes against the "Mistress of the Seas."

The British burned Washington. Our failure to take Canada was about as complete as it could be. Peace was agreed even though no agreement on peace terms could be reached. The **Treaty of Ghent** was signed on December 24, 1814. It contained no indemnities, no penalties, no territorial adjustments. Everything was to be as it had been before the war started. The problems left unsolved were to be taken up later by commissioners from each nation. Fifteen days after peace had been arranged, but before the news had reached America, the **Battle of New Orleans** took place. **General Andrew Jackson's** artillery and riflemen mowed down close formations of British infantry. In less than half an hour, 2,000 British soldiers were killed or wounded. The Americans lost thirteen.

The results of the War of 1812 on the United States were tremendous. The American people believed we had won the war. No one complained of a peace without victory. Perhaps the enthusiasm over the victory at New Orleans created the feeling of triumph. But there were other factors.

1] Twice within 40 years the United States had been at war with the greatest power on earth. The first time we gained independence. The second time we suffered no penalties. This was not the usual pattern for the enemies of Great Britain.

2] The Treaty of Ghent convinced Europe that the United States had established itself as a permanent government. The financial responsibility built into our government by the Federalists, plus the demonstrated ability to maintain ourselves by force of arms, gave the United States standing among the nations of the world.

3] A wave of nationalism swept over America. Pride in the United States as a nation hit a very high point. Political leaders spoke of themselves as citizens of America. They urged the people to think in terms of the nation as a whole and not to confine their loyalties or narrow their interests to their state or even to their section of the country. The Federalist party committed its final act of self-destruction at the **Hartford Convention.** One political party, a great victory at New Orleans and a peace treaty combined to form a tidal wave of pride and patriotism. It ushered in the **Era of Good Feelings.**

A Chronology of Events in the War of 1812

Note the series of brilliant naval victories, but realize that they did not break the British blockade of our major Atlantic ports. News of these naval exploits were great morale boosters. American forces couldn't penetrate Canada. British forces couldn't effectively invade the United States.

1]   *June 18, 1812*   War was declared. The vote in the House of Representatives was 79 to 49 and the vote in the Senate was 19 to 13. The War of 1812 started with a dangerously divided Congress and people.

2]   *August 16, 1812*   General William Hull surrendered Detroit to the British without firing a shot. He was court-martialed and dismissed from the army.

3]   *August 19, 1812*   Captain Isaac Hull of the frigate *Constitution* destroyed the British frigate *Guerriere* off Nova Scotia.

4]   *October 17, 1812*   Captain John Jacobs of the sloop *Wasp* defeated the British brig *Frolic* off the Virginia coast.

5]   *October 25, 1812*   Captain Stephen Decatur of the frigate *United States* brought the British frigate *Macedonian* into New London after forcing her surrender off the coast of Morocco.

6]   *December 29, 1812*   Captain William Bainbridge of the frigate *Constitution* destroyed the British frigate *Java* off the coast of Brazil. This slugging match at close range earned the *Constitution* its popular name, "Old Ironsides."

7]   *April 27, 1813*   General Henry Dearborn and Captain Isaac Chauncey crossed Lake Ontario from Sackett's Harbor and took York, the capital of Ontario. York is now Toronto. The governor's house and the government buildings were burned. The British raid on Washington and the burning of government buildings was claimed to be retaliation for this event.

8]   *May 28-29, 1813*   General Jacob J. Brown repulsed a strong British attack on Sackett's Harbor in an attempt to invade the United States by force.

9]   *June 1, 1813*   The British frigate *Shannon* captured the American frigate *Chesapeake*, with **Captain James Lawrence** in command. Captain Lawrence died during the battle. His last order, "Don't give up the ship," became a slogan of the U.S. Navy.

10]   *September 10, 1813*   The battle of Lake Erie was fought near Put in Bay. **Captain Oliver H. Perry** commanded 10 ships mounting 55 guns. The British had 6 ships mounting 65 guns. Perry's flagship, the *Lawrence*, was cut to pieces and 80 percent of her crew were casualties. Perry announced his victory with the message, "we have met the enemy and they are ours."

11]   *October 5, 1813*   Perry's victory on Lake Erie persuaded the British to evacuate Detroit. Major General William H. Harrison reoccupied Detroit and pursued the British northward to Canada. At the Thames River, east of Lake St. Clair, he defeated the enemy. The great Native American leader **Tecumseh** was killed in this battle. His death brought an end to Native American support of the British.

12]   *July 25, 1814*   Lundy's Lane, a little west of Niagara Falls and a few miles into Canada, was the most evenly fought and hardest fought land battle of the war. Both sides claim to have won it. The Americans with 2,600 men under General Jacob Brown fought a British force of 3,000. After the battle was over, the Americans withdrew from the area.

13]   *August 24-25 1814*   The British entered Washington on August 24.   They left on the next day. The approaches to Washington were very weakly defended. When the British arrived, the city had been evacuated. The Secretary of the Navy had burned the navy yard to prevent supplies falling to the enemy. The British continued the burning by setting fire to the White House, several government offices, some private homes, and a newspaper office.

14]   *September 11, 1814*   Captain Thomas Macdonough drove the British off Lake Champlain. This victory by Macdonough's squadron stopped another British attempt to penetrate the United States.

15]   *September 13-14, 1814*   The British approached Baltimore by land and the sea. They found the defenses too well-guarded. The bombardment of **Fort McHenry** by British ships inspired **Francis Scott Key,** an eyewitness, to write the words of the first stanza of the *Star Spangled Banner* during the firing, which lasted, intermittently, over 24 hours. On March 3, 1931, Congress made the "Star Spangled Banner" our national anthem.

16]   *December 24, 1814*   The Treaty of Ghent (Belgium) was agreed on by representatives of the United States and England.

17]   *January 8, 1815*   Jackson defeated the British at New Orleans.

* The Hartford Convention (December 15, 1814-January 5, 1815)

The legislatures of Massachusetts, Connecticut, and Rhode Island elected delegates to this convention. New Hampshire and Vermont chose delegates by Federalist party conventions. Hence, the delegates from the first three states were official representatives of the states, while those from New Hampshire and Vermont represented the Federalist party only. The Massachusetts legislature sent out the call for such a convention in October. George Cabot of Massachusetts presided over the convention. It was his leadership that curbed the more extreme Federalists and kept the resolutions clearly within legal bounds. In view of the climate of opinion prevailing in southern New England, the **Hartford Convention** displayed self-restraint and moderation.

The extreme Federalists openly expressed pleasure over the burning of Washington. **Timothy Pickering,** who had been Secretary of State in President Washington's second term and also under President John Adams, proposed secession of New England from the Union. New England states refused to allow their militia to fight beyond the boundaries of their own states. An attack on Montreal was frustrated when units of state militia refused to cross the border into Canada. New York State militia joined with New England in this attitude. Smuggling goods to the British army and navy was a lucrative and widespread practice. It was "Madison's war." This was the atmosphere in which the Hartford Convention met.

The issue of secession was debated. The convention rejected secession as inexpedient, not as unconstitutional. The convention judged it to be inexpedient because the troubles of New England at the moment were due to a war (between France and England) in which the United States should play no part. The convention recognized these misfortunes as temporary. Secession was too drastic a cure for problems that time and a few adjustments to the Constitution could remedy.

The most significant resolutions adopted by the Hartford Convention were proposals for amendments to the Constitution. They were as follows:

1]   No embargoes shall last for more than 60 days.

2]   A two-thirds vote of each House of Congress shall be required to

  a. declare war. (This would have prevented the War of 1812.)

  b. place restrictions on foreign trade.

  c. admit new states to the Union. (New states would be western agricultural states and therefore Republican.)

3]   No naturalized citizen shall hold any federal office. (Almost all naturalized citizens would be Republicans.)

4]   Direct taxes and representation in the House of Representatives shall be apportioned among the states according to the number of free inhabitants therein. (This would abolish the counting of three-fifths of the slaves and thus reduce congressional delegations from the South where the states were Republican.)

5]   No President shall have more than one term. (The only President elected on the Federalist ticket, John Adams, served only one term. The other three Presidents had served two terms.)

6]   No two successive Presidents shall be from the same state. (Washington, Jefferson, and Madison were Virginians.) New England was fed up with the "Virginia dynasty."

A committee of three, who called themselves "ambassadors," headed by Harrison Otis of Massachusetts, set out for Washington to "negotiate" with the federal government. News of Jackson's victory at New Orleans and of the Treaty of Ghent hit Washington at the same time Otis and his colleagues reached Baltimore on their way from Hartford. The "ambassadors" went home. Public ridicule and contempt were heaped upon the Federalists and their proposals. Many labeled them traitors. While the Federalists party continued as an organization in local elections, the Hartford Convention may well be considered its last act as a major party.

* First Protective Tariff (1816)

The time had arrived when the ideas expressed by Hamilton in favor of protection became popular. From the Embargo Act of 1807 to the end of the War of 1812, the policies of our own government and the Napoleonic Wars combined to depress imports. Hostility toward England had created ill will toward British products. The spirit of unity and nationalism following the war smothered the sectionalism so characteristic of tariff legislation. The victory over the Native American at Tippecanoe in 1811, soon followed by the death of Tecumseh, greatly lessened their menace in the Northwest Territory.

People were moving west. Indiana became a state in 1816 and Illinois in 1818. The Southwest was also growing; Louisiana had become a state in 1812, and Mississippi and Alabama would become states in 1817 and 1819. Holding the spreading population together became a common concern. The **protective tariff** seemed a good start. American manufacturers would have the domestic market relatively free from British competition. Agricultural America could feed the towns and cities and supply many of the raw products for factories. If highways, turnpikes, and canals, extending east and west, could be combined with a protective tariff program, the outlook for prosperity and unity seemed promising.

There were sharper and more demanding factors that favored a protective tariff. At the end of the war, British merchants were ready to flood our markets with superior merchandise at prices the new and comparatively inefficient American manufacturers could not meet. Hundreds of small enterprises had been formed, especially in the North, to supply the demand created by the lack of imports. Every section of the nation either had enterprises to protect or believed it soon would have.

The average rates were about 25 percent ad valorum. The votes in Congress in favor of the bill came from all sections of the nation. **John Calhoun**, soon to be the great Southern leader against protective tariffs, was working hand in hand with **Henry Clay** in favor of this first protective tariff. Even Jefferson, who also changed his mind later, favored it.

James Monroe 1817-1825

1758-1831

REPUBLICAN

Vice-President   DANIEL D. TOMPKINS
Secretary of State   JOHN QUINCY ADAMS

MONROE'S PUBLIC SERVICE BEFORE HE BECAME PRESIDENT

Revolutionary War record
- *Fought at White Plains, Trenton (wounded), Brandywine, Germantown, and Monmouth*
- *Promoted to major during the winter at Valley Forge*
- *Member of the Virginia legislature*

United States Senator
United States Minister to France (1794-1796)
Governor of Virginia
Special envoy to France at the time of the Louisiana Purchase (1803)
United States Minister to England (1803-1806)
Secretary of State under Madison (1811-1817) and also Secretary of War (1814-1815)

MAJOR ITEMS OF MONROE'S ADMINISTRATIONS

Supreme Court Decisions under Chief Justice John Marshall
- McCulloch *v.* Maryland
- Dartmouth College Case
- Gibbons *v.* Ogden

Acquisition of Florida from Spain (1819)
Missouri Compromise (1820)
Monroe Doctrine (1823)
Sectional Tariff (1824)
Favorite Sons Election (Jackson, J.Q. Adams, Crawford, Clay) (1824)

Election and Reelection of Monroe (1816 and 1820)

The unpopularity of the Federalist party resulting from their opposition to the War of 1812 gave **James Monroe** an easy victory. The electoral vote was Monroe, 183; **Rufus King** (New York), 34.

The reelection of Monroe was unchallenged. He got 231 electoral votes. Three electors didn't vote, and one voted for John Quincy Adams. This reserved to Washington the distinction of being the only presidential candidate to receive a unanimous vote of the Electoral College.

* Marshall's Decisions

These decisions built prestige for the Supreme Court and set a pattern that was followed for many years. **Chief Justice John Marshall** thought the nation ought to be run by a strong central government, to which the states would play strictly second fiddle. The Federalist party was dead; but, with Marshall on the Supreme Court for 34 years, Federalists principles were being woven into the fabric of our financial, business, and commercial life.

McCulloch v. Maryland

The state of Maryland passed a law to serve the interests of the local banks chartered by the state. These state banks had always resented the favored position of the Bank of the United States. Seven other states passed similar restrictive laws to embarrass the B.U.S. and its branches. The test case came when the cashier, McCulloch, of the Baltimore branch of the B.U.S., refused to comply with the Maryland law. The law required that any bank in Maryland not chartered by the state must print its bank notes on special stamped paper at excessive costs. This was, in effect, a stamp tax. As an alternative, the "foreign" bank could pay an annual fee of $15,000. There was a fine of $500 for each note printed improperly.

The attorneys for Maryland challenged the constitutionality of the B.U.S. All of the Hamilton-Jefferson arguments were re-aired (p. 87). The Court accepted the "loose construction" reasoning of Hamilton and declared constitutional the law of Congress that had established the Second Bank of the United States.

The Maryland law with its restrictions, fees, and fines not only could have destroyed the Baltimore branch of the B. U.S. but was intended to do so. Here was a direct conflict between the state law of Maryland and the law of Congress, a state law that destroyed what a federal law had created. In such a conflict of legal authorities, the "Supreme Law of the Land" clause of the Constitution clearly directs that the state law shall be declared null and void. Chief Justice Marshall so declared, with the unanimous approval of the Associate Justices.

The Dartmouth College Case

The trustees of Dartmouth College split into two factions. One wanted to continue the college as a private institution; the other wanted the state of New Hampshire to take it over. The latter faction won support in the legislature which passed a law changing Dartmouth College to Dartmouth University, a state institution. The highest court of New Hampshire declared this action legal. An appeal was made to the Supreme Court.

Marshall accepted the contention of the lawyers opposing the state of New Hampshire, one of whom was **Daniel Webster,** that the original charter granted by the king to the trustees of Dartmouth College in 1769 was a **contract.** This charter remained in force after the Revolution as a contract between the state of New Hampshire and the Dartmouth trustees. Under powers denied to the states, the Constitution provides that no state shall "pass any law impairing the obligation of contracts." Thus, a direct conflict was established between a clause in the Constitution and a law of New Hampshire. The "Supreme Law of the Land" clause directs that state laws in conflict with the Constitution must be declared null and void. Dartmouth remained a private college.

Gibbons v. Ogden

The New York legislature granted a franchise to Fulton and Livingston allowing them a monopoly of steamboat transportation of New York waters. Under their franchise from New York State, Fulton and Livingston could sell a license to others to operate steamboats. Ogden had bought a license from them to operate between New York City and New Jersey. Gibbons had a license from the United States to operate steamboats along the coast. Ogden got a New York court to enjoin Gibbons from operating his boats, whereupon Gibbons appealed to the United States Supreme Court.

Marshall ruled that the New York franchise affected **interstate commerce** and was "repugnant to the Constitution" because it violated the clause that allows Congress to regulate commerce among the several states. Therefore, he declared the monopoly unconstitutional. Marshall also defined interstate commerce, claiming that it not only involved the exchange of goods but all forms of trade and business. This broad definition meant that what affected interstate commerce came under federal control. It enabled the federal government to control such interstate commerce as telegraph, telephone, radio, and television in the 1900s. Marshall also ruled that New York had violated the clause in the Constitution authorizing Congress to promote the progress of science and the useful arts.

Acquisition of Florida from Spain (1819)

During the War of 1812 a fort had been built at the mouth of the Apalachicola River on the Gulf coast of Florida. It had become a refuge for escaped slaves, border ruffians, and hostile Native Americans. In 1816 United States forces, acting under official orders, penetrated Spanish Florida and destroyed the fort. The next year **General Andrew Jackson** was put in command of the Georgia border patrol forces, with orders permitting him to penetrate Florida in pursuit of "hostile elements." Jackson wrote to President Monroe saying that if the United States desired Florida, he could take it in 60 days. There was no response and Jackson apparently assumed that silence meant consent. In the spring of 1818 he pursued hostile Native Americans into Florida for about 175 miles and took Pensacola. On the way, two English traders, Ambrister and Arbuthot, were captured and executed after Jackson had them court-martialed. They were charged with stirring up the Indians and "aiding the enemy." British newspapers expressed indignation, but the British ministry, after a formal inquiry, made no complaint. Public opinion in the United States, especially in the West, acclaimed Jackson a hero. Senate and House committees reported unfavorably on Jackson's action. Several members of the Cabinet urged disciplinary action against him. But President Monroe and Secretary of State John Quincy Adams realized that this strong action improved our position in pending negotiations with Spain. In February 1819, the United States and Spain reached agreement. Florida (East and West) was to belong to the United States. We gave up our claim to Texas and accepted responsibility for claims by people in Florida against Spain up to $5 million. The Spanish Step Line was established. It marked a definite western boundary to the Louisiana Territory from the mouth of the Sabine River in a series of steps to the 42nd parallel. As of 1819, the area south of the Step Line was Spanish and the area north of it was the Louisiana Territory and the Oregon Territory. Oregon was then in dispute between England and the United States.

* The Missouri Compromise (1820)

In 1820 there were eleven free and eleven slave states in the Union. Because of the greater population in the North, the 11 free states had 105 seats in the House to 81 seats for the slave states. The South was determined to maintain equal voting power in the Senate. The people of Maine petitioned Congress for admission as a state. Missouri also petitioned Congress for admission. Perhaps, as had happened several times in the past, a slave and a free state could have been admitted without any political explosions if Representative Tallmadge of New York had not introduced an amendment to the bill for the admission of Missouri.

The Tallmadge Amendment would have prohibited any additional slaves entering Missouri and would have declared free on their twenty-fifth birthday any slaves born in Missouri after it became a state. It passed the

House by a close vote but was easily defeated in the Senate. A furious political storm broke. The slave states held that Congress had no right to attach conditions a state applying for admission. It could admit or refuse to admit, but it could not dictate social and economic conditions. If Congress had any such power, it could create a class of inferior states and utterly destroy the sovereign equality of the states so essential to a federal union. But the free states pointed to the Northwest Ordinance, which had set a precedent by forbidding slavery in the territories, and states to be made therefrom, at the same time that it guaranteed their equality with the original states.

The compromise reached was that Maine should be admitted to the Union as a free state and Missouri as a slave state. The political balance in the Senate was maintained. A line was established to set the pattern for the rest of Louisiana Territory: South of the parallel 36° 36' within the Territory slavery would be legal; but north of this parallel, except in Missouri, slavery would be prohibited. The southern border of the new state of Missouri was on the 36°30' parallel.

The threat lurking in this controversy did not go unobserved. Jefferson wrote, "This momentous question, like a fire bell in the night, awakened and filled me with terror. I considered it at once as the knell of the Union." And John Quincy Adams wrote in his diary, "I take it for granted that the present question is a mere preamble—a title page to a great, tragic volume."

** Monroe Doctrine (1823)

After Napoleon's defeat, the Congress of Vienna, 1814 and 1815, rearranged Europe. Having undone the work of Napoleon on the continent, the next order of business was to straighten out the chaos that had resulted in the Spanish Empire from Mexico to the tip of South America. Able revolutionary leaders such as Simón Bolívar, José San Martín, and Bernardo O'Higgins led revolutions that changed the Spanish colonies into republics.

England had established a very lucrative trade with the new republics. English subjects had invested substantially in mining rights. There was great promise of expansion for English trade and investment.

Russia, Austria, and Prussia (the Holy Alliance) wanted England to join with them in a reconquest of the Spanish Empire in the Americas. England rejected the idea. Without the support of the British fleet, the Holy Alliance would be unable to carry through such a project.

The United States was negotiating the acquisition of Florida and the Step Line boundary was finally fixed in 1819. Until that was complete, Monroe and his Secretary of State, J.Q. Adams, made no move toward recognition of the new republics to the south. However, with ratification of the Spanish treaty, the United States promptly extended recognition to the new republics.

George Canning, the British Foreign Secretary, suggested to our ambassador, Richard Rush, that the United States join with England in telling the European nations to refrain from any attack upon the former Spanish Empire in the Western Hemisphere. President Monroe submitted this idea to Jefferson and Madison who both liked the idea. J. Q. Adams felt it would be wiser to act independently of England and deliver to Europe, including England, the message that the United States would look with displeasure at any interference by them with the independence of any republic in the Western Hemisphere. At the moment, England would favor such a policy even though it might be surprised that we made the declaration alone. There was really very little danger of any attack by the continental powers of Europe. If such an attack did occur, England could squelch it. In his annual message to Congress, December 2, 1823, President Monroe included the **Monroe Doctrine.** It became a guiding principle of our foreign policy.

"...the American continents, by the free and independent condition which they have assumed and maintain, are henceforth not to be considered as subjects for future colonization by any European powers..."

"In the wars of the European powers in matters relating to themselves we have never taken any part, nor does it comport with our policy so to do."

"We owe it, therefore, to candor and to the amicable relations existing between the United States and those powers to declare that we should consider any attempt on their part to extend their system to any portion of this hemisphere as dangerous to our peace and safety."

"With the existing colonies or dependencies of any European powers we have not interfered and shall not interfere."

"...we could not view any interposition for the purpose of oppressing them, or controlling in any other manner their destiny, by any European power in any other light than as the manifestation of an unfriendly disposition toward the United States."

"Our policy in regard to Europe is...not to interfere in the internal concerns of any of its powers."

"It is impossible that the allied powers should extend their political system to any portion of either continent without endangering our peace and happiness."

* Sectional Tariff (1824)

In the eight years separating the Tariff of 1816 from that of 1824, the South, especially South Carolina, had discovered that textile mills were not going to locate next to the cotton fields. Cotton was moving away from the Atlantic seaboard because repeated cultivation of the same soil without crop rotation or proper use of fertilizers greatly reduced the yield per acre. The few attempts to establish cotton mills had failed. In the South neither the investment capital to establish the cotton mills nor the capable managers to run them were readily available.

Only in combination with a system of highways linking the East, South, and West could the protective tariff be effective in building the nation as a whole. Only then could the products of each section find markets in the other two areas; the prosperity of one would then tend to be reflected in the others. The effect on business of the Tariff of 1816 was immediate, but no east-west highways could be built immediately. All the benefits of the tariff were felt in the Northeast. So, by 1824, Calhoun, who earlier had gone along with Clay's advocacy of protective tariffs and roads, had become opposed to both. Calhoun expressed the position of the South. He saw the protective tariff as a device that raised the cost of living by increasing the price of manufactured articles. A program of turnpikes built at federal expense would mean a tax burden on the South out of proportion to any benefits received by the South. Worst of all, vast building projects planned and paid for by the federal government would concentrate in Washington legal authority and political power that properly belonged to the individual states. At just about the same time that the South was turning against protective tariffs, Clay was advocating his three-point "American System": **internal improvements** at federal expense, the **Bank of the United States,** and **protective tariffs.** The harmonious note of national unity reflected by the Tariff of 1816 had changed to the discordant note of sectional strife reflected by the Tariff of 1824.

The Tariff of 1824 passed Congress with the vote clearly emphasizing the sectional interests of the Northeast and the South. The political balance of power was held by the West. If the South or the Northeast could gain the support of the West, it could control Congress and put its program into law.

* Favorite Sons' Elections (Jackson, J.Q. Adams, Crawford, Clay) (1824)

All the candidates were Republicans. William Crawford (Georgia) had been chosen in the usual manner, by congressional caucus. The other candidates represented sections of the country. Andrew Jackson (Tennessee) and Henry Clay (Kentucky) spoke for the West. John Quincy Adams (Massachusetts) represented the Northeast. Crawford was stricken with a serious illness during the campaign. Jackson was the hero of New Orleans and Florida. He was the man of action and the most popular candidate. Clay had a distinguished career in Congress and possessed more personal charm than any of the others. Adams had the most impressive record of public service. The election results were as follows:

	Popular Vote	Electoral Vote
Jackson	155,872	99
Adams	105,321	84
Crawford	44,282	41
Clay	46,587	37

No candidate had received the necessary majority of electoral votes. As provided in the Twelfth Amendment, the election went to the House of Representatives where each state had one vote. Each state delegation in Congress had to caucus to decide how to cast its one vote. Clay was out of the race, as only the top three candidates were eligible. However, Clay was Speaker of the House and had considerable influence. Upon his advice Adams was elected. Calhoun had considered being a fifth candidate for the presidency but had changed his mind and campaigned for the vice-presidency. He won easily with 182 electoral votes.

Under the best of circumstances this outcome would have been hard to accept. Many felt that there was a moral obligation on the part of the House of Representatives to elect Jackson because he had received the largest vote, both electoral and popular. When President Adams appointed Clay Secretary of State, the Era of Good Feelings came to an end and there were two political parties, National Republicans and Democratic Republicans. The Jackson supporters and many thousands of others believed that the charge of "corrupt bargain" was justified. The charge was that Adams and Clay had plotted to bring about the result. There was no evidence of such an understanding, and the verdict of history is that there was no bargain of any kind. Clay supported Adams instead of Jackson because the two men were in agreement on public policy. Adams was an ardent supporter of Clay's "American System." Clay felt Jackson was unsuited to be President. Adams asked Clay to be Secretary of State because he considered Clay best qualified for the post. John Q. Adams served one term as President, but the people were just biding their time until 1828. It was an open secret that Jackson would be the next President.

John Quincy Adams 1825-1829

1767-1848

NATIONAL REPUBLICAN

☆

Vice-President JOHN C. CALHOUN

Secretary of State HENRY CLAY

ADAMS' PUBLIC SERVICE BEFORE HE BECAME PRESIDENT

Minister to the Netherlands (1794-1796)
Minister to Prussia (1797-1801)
Minister to Russia (1809-1814)
Minister to Great Britain (1815-1817)
Secretary of State under President Monroe

MAJOR ITEMS OF ADAMS' ADMINISTRATION

New York State's Erie Canal
Tariff of Abominations (1828)
Calhoun's Exposition and Protest

New York State's Erie Canal

The first great east-west highway in the United States was the Erie Canal. Completed in 1825, it was wholly within the State of New York and was paid for by the state. Taxes and lotteries raised the $7 million it cost to make a 363 mile ditch 4 feet deep and 40 feet wide. It had 82 locks to raise boats a total of 571 feet between the Hudson River and Buffalo. It was by far the most comfortable and quickest way for passenger travel over such a distance. Costs for freight were cut as much as 90 percent. Passenger fares were about a cent and a half a mile. From New York City to Buffalo was a five-day trip, as the barges were pulled along the canal by horses on the tow paths.

A look at the map shows that the Mississippi River and its great tributaries form a splendid transportation system converging on New Orleans. Commerce and trade from the Great Lakes regions and the Ohio

Valley flowed southward before the Erie Canal. But with the new route from Buffalo to Albany, the traffic turned eastward. The population was to the east, the best markets were to the east, and the best approach to Europe was to the east. The Erie Canal bound the West to the Northeast much more effectively than the Mississippi River tied the West to the South. Before the Erie Canal, the port of New Orleans held promise of being the busiest port in the United States. After the Erie Canal, the city of New York was an easy winner. Boston, Philadelphia, Baltimore, Charleston, and New Orleans all grew more slowly as a result of Governor Clinton's ditch. But the economic pull of the Erie Canal was not the whole story. Commercial ties form political ties. The political struggle between the Northeast and the South for the support of the West in their increasingly bitter conflict over commercial versus agrarian interests, over increasing federal power versus states rights, over interpretation of the Constitution, and finally over slavery were also part of the Erie Canal story. The Northeast and the West were brought closer together while the South was slipping into isolation.

* Tariff of Abominations (1828)

The political lesson the South learned from the Tariff of 1824 was that the South would lose in both the House of Representatives and the Senate in any vote on the issue of protection. The pro-tariff members of Congress outnumbered the anti-tariff members in 1824 and 1828, and their number would continue to increase. The Northeast and the West were growing closer together economically, as compared with the South and the West. There was every prospect that several new states would be formed from the northern areas of the Northwest Territory and the Louisiana Territory. Michigan entered the Union in 1837, Iowa in 1846, and Minnesota in 1858. The political outlook for the South was bleak. Only Arkansas, and possibly Kansas, could have been recognized as potential new states to give political support to the Southern way of life.

There was one tactic that might bring victory to the South. To defeat a protective tariff, they must outsmart the opposition. Their attempt to do this resulted in the Tariff of Abominations of 1828. As the tariff bill was drawn up, Southern members of Congress supported ample protective rates for most manufactured products of the Northeast, and ridiculously high protective rates for raw products that were vital to manufacturing. The resulting high prices the manufacturers would have to pay for raw materials would rob them of the advantages they would receive from the protection afforded their own products. This tactic, the South hoped, would so disgust several members of Congress from the Northeast that they would vote against the bill. The southerners would also vote against it. Their combined vote might defeat this abominable tariff. However, the bill passed the House 105 to 94 and the Senate by 26 to 21. In South Carolina flags were flown at half-mast. There was talk of boycotts against New England's manufactured goods. Refusal to obey the new tariff law was seriously considered. Some even began to question the value of remaining in the Union. Calhoun sensed a deeper rift between North and South than tariff. In 1830 Calhoun said that the basic cause of the growing friction was "the *peculiar domestic institutions* of the Southern States."

** Calhoun's *Exposition and Protest* (1828) and South Carolina's Nullification Act (1832)

Calhoun claimed that protective tariffs were unconstitutional. The Kentucky and Virginia Resolutions framed by Jefferson and Madison gave him all the arguments he needed, although he did extend them a bit. The reasoning followed these lines.

1] The Constitution is a compact (an agreement) among several sovereign states.

2] The federal government has only those powers specifically delegated to it by the Constitution. (Tenth Amendment)

3] The power to regulate foreign commerce was clearly intended to be a means "of extending commerce, by coercing foreign nations to a fair reciprocity in their intercourse with us," and only "incidentally connected with the encouragement of agriculture and manufactures."

4] No mention is made in the Constitution about power to nullify a law of Congress, or about the right of a state to withdraw from the Union. All powers not denied to the states and not granted to the federal government belong to the states. (Tenth Amendment)

The above four points express the Calhoun, Hayne, Davis thinking on the nature of the Union. Calhoun's Exposition and Protest, Hayne's arguments in the Webster-Hayne debate, and South Carolina's Nullification Act were the vehicles that gave effective expression to them.

Calhoun's claim that a protective tariff was unconstitutional rests on the fact that a tariff is a tax. The Constitution says that taxes may be levied for only three purposes; to pay the public debt, to provide for the common defense, and to promote the general welfare. A protective tariff is intended to keep goods from entering the country. If it accomplishes this purpose, it raises no revenue, or does so only incidentally and in small amounts. Hence a protective tariff obviously is not a tax for raising money to pay debts or to build defenses. It is equally clear that a protective tariff promotes sectional division, that it seriously threatens the harmony of the Union, and therefore it can not promote the general welfare. Being a tax for a purpose not in the Constitution, it is therefore unconstitutional. Acting on this theory South Carolina passed the Nullification Act in November 1832.

** An Answer to Calhoun, Hayne, and Davis

1] The Constitution is not a compact of sovereign states. "We the people...do ordain and establish this Constitution."

2] Control over foreign commerce is granted in the

Constitution to Congress. The word *commerce* was given a very broad interpretation by the Supreme Court in the *Gibbons* v. *Ogden* case. It certainly included regulation of imports.

3] Acceptance of the right of a state to nullify a law of Congress would soon result in utter confusion. Federal laws recognized in one state would not be recognized in other states. Eventually there would be as many interpretations of the federal Constitution as there were states.

4] The right of a state to secede from the Union contradicts the very purpose of the Constitution. "To form a more perfect Union" was the historical reason for abandoning the Articles of Confederation and became the first aim of the Constitution as stated in the Preamble. The inevitable result of acting upon secession would be the destruction of the Union. As Webster put it, the Union would become "a rope of sand." With the possible exception of South Carolina, no Southern state in 1832 was willing to entertain any such extreme position.

Andrew Jackson   1829-1837

1767-1845

DEMOCRAT

Vice-President   JOHN C. CALHOUN
MARTIN VAN BUREN

JACKSON'S PUBLIC SERVICE BEFORE HE BECAME PRESIDENT

> *United States Senator from Tennessee (1797)*
> *Judge of the Tennessee Supreme Court*
> *Major General and hero at the Battle of New Orleans (1815)*
> *Led the conquest of Florida (1818)*
> *Military Governor of Florida (1823)*
> *United States Senator from Tennessee (1823-1825)*

MAJOR ITEMS OF JACKSON'S ADMINISTRATIONS

> *Jacksonian Democracy*
> *Tariffs of 1832 and 1833*
> *The Second Bank of the United States*
> *Indian Removals*
> *Formation of the Whig Party*

Jackson's Election (1828) and Reelection (1832)

The campaign of 1828 revived the "corrupt bargain" cry against President John Quincy Adams who was running for reelection. Adams simply didn't have a chance. Andrew Jackson, the hero of New Orleans and of Florida, was clearly the people's favorite. As they saw it, he had been cheated in 1824, and now it was time for him to become President. The popular vote for Jackson was 647,231, for Adams 509,097; the electoral vote, Jackson 178, Adams 83.

The reelection of Jackson in 1832 was an even more crushing defeat of the National Republican party led by Henry Clay. The popular vote for Jackson was 647,231, for Adams 509,097; the electoral vote, Jackson 178, Adams 83.

The reelection of Jackson in 1832 was an even more crushing defeat of the National Republican party led by Henry Clay. The popular vote for Jackson was 687,502, for Clay 530,189; the electoral vote, Jackson 219, Clay 49. The Second Bank of the United States was the great issue on which Jackson and Clay campaigned.

** Jacksonian Democracy

Andrew Jackson was the first President that the people could feel was one of them. His parents had been immigrants from northern Ireland who had settled in a backwoods area of South Carolina, where Jackson was born. At the age of fourteen, he had been a prisoner of the British during the Revolution. Story has it that at this fairly tender age, he defied a British officer when told to polish shoes and received a blow with a sword, which left a lifelong scar on his head. He also carried two bullets in his body, one in his chest and one in his left arm. These were mementoes from duels.

He was the victim of vicious slander because his marriage took place a few weeks before his wife obtained a divorce from her first husband, the result of a legal tangle. His climb to prominence in law, in war, and in politics brought wealth, but he was still a frontier settler in outlook. His integrity was as real and obvious as his courage. **"Old Hickory"** was the affectionate name given him by the soldiers at New Orleans. All preceding Presidents had been from what the voters of America considered the aristocracy of Virginia and Massachusetts. Now they had a President from west of the Alleghenies. The elevation of such a man to the White House gave a new spirit to the nation, which proved fertile soil for reform movements, political, economic, and social. These reforms of the 1820s and 1830s are known as **Jacksonian Democracy**.

1] The caucus was replaced by the **nominating convention**. Crawford was the last presidential candidate to be selected by a caucus of the leading members of his party in Congress. The nominating convention was organized by the political party. The change from caucus to convention brought into use a political device that shifted the selection of candidates from a few party leaders to a substantial segment of the party membership.

2] States that were still choosing their presidential electors by their legislatures changed to the democratic system of direct election by the voters.

3] The remnants of religious qualifications for voting, which still prevailed in some states, were dropped. In many states property qualifications were greatly reduced or eliminated.

4] The **spoils system** was favored by Jackson. He thought that the party that won the election should have its members appointed to government jobs. He believed that the demands made on public officials could be met adequately by almost any ordinary citizen. Jackson's contention was that rotation in office achieved a superior quality of democracy by developing more citizens versed in the arts of government. But the fact is that Jackson did not practice rotation in office to any unusual degree. Professors Morison and Commager point out that Jackson, during the eight years he was in office, removed only one employee out of every six, a record much the same as under President Jefferson.

5] Labor unions began to seek political power. The first labor group to organize as a political force was in Philadelphia. In the late 1820s they had representatives on the city council. Similar progress was made in Boston and New York. These early unions were in the Northern states in the larger cities. They worked for reforms such as the abolition of imprisonment for debt, free education for all, abolition of prison contract labor, laws against taking a craftperson's tools in payment of debt, and for a ten-hour day to replace the usual twelve-hour day. All of these labor activities were on the city and state levels. Laws varied widely from state to state. In 1842 a strike was illegal in New York State, but legal in Massachusetts. The **panic of 1837**, with its unemployment and severe wage cuts, put an abrupt end to organized labor. The real struggle of labor for recognition and rights did not get under way until after the Civil War.

6] Social reform was part of Jacksonian Democracy.

Dorothea Dix made people realize that the insane needed hospitalization rather than imprisonment. She also started the movement for prison reform.

Emma Willard founded the Troy Female Seminary at Troy, New York, in 1821. It was the first women's college in the United States. It is now the Emma Willard School.

Oberlin College became the first coeducational college in 1834.

Mary Lyon founded Mount Holyoke Seminary in 1837. It is now Mount Holyoke College.

The **American Temperance Union** held its first national convention in 1836.

The **Grimké sisters**, Sarah and Angelina, freed their slaves and left their homes in South Carolina to preach the cause of abolition. Both sisters were Quakers, a small sect that made a large contribution to the leadership of humanitarian reforms.

Frances (Fanny) Wright set up a colony of free blacks near Memphis, Tennessee. The pressure of public and official opinion forced its abandonment, and the blacks were sent to Haiti. Frances Wright lectured and wrote in support of women's rights, labor unions, free public education, and against slavery.

Lucretia Mott opposed slavery and supported equal rights for women. She, with **Elizabeth Cady Stanton** wrote a *Declaration of Sentiments*, which was closely modeled on the Declaration of Independence. It made as good a case for equal rights for women as Jefferson's masterpiece had done for independence of the colonies.

William Lloyd Garrison was the most effective voice against slavery. His paper, the *Liberator*, first appeared in Boston in 1831 and continued for 35 years with Garrison as its editor. Garrison was one of the new militant leaders of the abolition movement who demanded immediate emancipation. With the cause of abolition won by the Civil War, Garrison turned to temperance reform and votes for women.

7] Free Public Education was extended.

Horace Mann organized a public school system in Massachusetts in the late 1830s, and middle 1840s that greatly influenced public education throughout the United States. The first high school in the nation was in Boston (1821). In 1827 every town of 500 families or over had to have a high school. The first normal school, a training school for teachers, was established at Lexington in 1839. While Massachusetts took the lead in free public education under the guidance of Horace Mann, New York State was a rather close second. Worker's organizations in the cities of the Northeast were the most active groups supporting the creation and extension of free public schools.

William Ladd played a leading part in the forming of the *American Peace Society* in 1828, which called for a congress of nations and an international court. The idea that there must be some way other than war as a last resort for settling disputes among nations is an old one, much older than the American Peace Society.

* Tariffs of 1832 and 1833

After the Tariff of 1828 (the Tariff of Abominations) was passed, the South had one hope left. That was that the incoming President, Jackson, would reflect the tariff views common to most people of the South and Southwest. But President Jackson's position as President was that he would accept any tariff policy the Congress saw fit to enact into law, and he would see to it that the law was enforced. Congress passed the **Tariff of 1832**, which was an unimportant modification of the Tariff of Abominations. Calhoun resigned as Vice-President and entered the United States Senate. The split between Jackson and Calhoun fed upon both public and personal issues. Calhoun's *Exposition* and South Carolina's Nullification Act were flatly rejected by Jackson.

Mrs. Calhoun, the society leader among the wives of the President's official family, refused to accept Mrs. Eaton (Peggy O'Neal Eaton), wife of the Secretary of War. Mrs. Eaton had been a friend of the late Mrs. Jackson, who had died a short time before her husband's inauguration in 1829. This social tempest swirling around the White House caught Jackson's attention and didn't help Calhoun. The Jackson-Calhoun break was not only a political difference of opinion; it was a bitter personal feud.

The **Nullification Act** was a threat by South Carolina that it would not permit import duties to be collected within its borders in accordance with the tariff law. Jackson, determined to make South Carolina obey the law, asked Congress for a power he already possessed, the power to use whatever force might be necessary in order to carry out the laws of the United States. In passing this **Force Bill** in March 1833 by overwhelming majorities (Senate 32-1; House 149-47), the Congress was telling South Carolina and Calhoun that they had no sympathy with nullification and the states intention not to obey the tariff law. Passed at the same time was Clay's compromise Tariff of 1833. This provided for automatic annual reductions of tariff rates for ten years, so that at the end of this period the rates would be approximately at the moderate protective level of 1816. This "saved face" for Calhoun and South Carolina and was quite satisfactory to the President, whose whole point had been that the law would be enforced in South Carolina. The doctrine of nullification and the claim that protective tariffs were unconstitutional were dropped, at least for the time being.

* The Second Bank of the United States

This bank had been established in 1816. It had functioned well as a stabilizer for business as well as a conservative check upon less responsible banks. Ownership of its stock was held in about equal amounts by wealthy families in the South, in the Middle States, and by Europeans. Nicholas Biddle was president of the Second Bank of the United States when Clay opposed Jackson's reelection in 1832. Clay persuaded Biddle, a National Republican, to make the recharter of the B.U.S. the major issue of the campaign. As the bank's charter had over three years to run before it expired, there was no need to bring it up until many months after the election. However, Clay needed a sound issue in order to make any headway against the reelection of a popular President, and he believed that Jackson would oppose the recharter of the Second B.U.S. Clay led the political maneuvering in Congress that got the recharter bill passed in July 1832. President Jackson vetoed the bill.

Jackson's veto message contained the following points:

1] The Bank of the United States is unconstitutional.

2] It is a monopoly.

3] The shares of stock of the B.U.S. are owned by "opulent" citizens and foreigners who thereby benefit at the expense of the people.

4] The present stockholders have no right to special favors.

5]   The B.U.S. could influence foreign policy through the power of its foreign stockholders, and it is therefore dangerous.

6]   The B.U.S. had used its funds in an irregular manner to further the political views of its president, Nicholas Biddle, views shared by Clay and his National Republican party.

7]   The Supreme Court's decision that the B.U.S. is constitutional carries no authority. It is equally the right of the President and of Congress to make such a judgment.

So the campaign became a debate about the bank. Had the debate been a sober search for the truth, there could have been no other conclusion than that Clay was right and Jackson was wrong.

The result was what might easily have been predicted. Those who liked Jackson believed, at least during the campaign, that the bank was unconstitutional, was corrupt, and was a wicked device to enrich the rich by letting them use the taxpayers' funds supplied largely by the people. Those who liked Clay, and especially those who hated Jackson, saw the soundness of the bank and its great usefulness in the economy.

Jackson's reelection meant the destruction of the Second B.U.S. No more government funds were deposited, and as expenditures depleted the government's funds already in the bank, the B.U.S. limped to its death at the expiration of the charter in 1836. The government funds were deposited in about 80 state banks. Those that were chosen were called Jackson's "pet banks."

Indian Removals

Jackson and others saw Native Americans as competitors for ownership of the land of the Southeast. These included the Seminoles of Florida; the Creeks and Cherokees in the Carolinas, Georgia, and Alabama; and the Chickasaw and Choctaw largely in Mississippi. Although those "Civilized Tribes" lived in villages and farmed extensively, the white settlers claimed a greater right to the land. Those tribes (and others in the old Northwest Territory) were forced to move to Indian Territory, mostly in present-day Oklahoma, well west of the Mississippi River. The tragic 800-mile journey of the Cherokees during the winter of 1838 along that "Trail of Tears" was especially bitter. Indian tribes lost thousands of people during those forced removals as a result of disease and starvation. The plight of the American Indian would worsen still after the Civil War.

Formation of the Whig party

After his defeat in 1832, Clay pondered on how to beat Jackson's Democratic party. There was a growing number of Democrats who thoroughly disliked Jackson's appeal to the "people" and his tendency to view unkindly the people of both wealth and social prestige. The eastern seaboard states of the South contained many families who held the political power of the area and who were unhappy with the fact that a Westerner of humble origin led their party. Add to these the anger of the extremists in the South who could never forgive Jackson's firm stand against nullification, and also the much larger number of Southerners who were bitterly disappointed that Jackson had not taken a definite stand against protective tariffs. Clay saw that these anti-Jackson people had no political home. It was too much to expect them to join the National Republican party because that was, to them, the traditional opposition party. The device of dropping the name *National Republican* and adopting the name *Whig party* was the magnet that drew thousands of anti-Jackson Southerners into the same political fold as the National Republicans. There was one basic weakness in the Whig party. It was founded on the dislike of Jackson. Jackson and his influence could not last very long, so the cement that at first held them firmly together would gradually disintegrate and lose its adhesive strength. The Southern wing of the Whig party did not believe in Clay's American System as did most of the old National Republicans. The attitude of the Northern wing of the Whig party on tariff and slavery was incompatible with the views of the Southern members. As long as the Whig party lasted, it had to avoid major political issues because any major issue would split the party.

Martin Van Buren   1837-1841

1782-1862

DEMOCRAT

Vice-President   RICHARD M. JOHNSON

VAN BUREN'S PUBLIC SERVICE BEFORE HE BECAME PRESIDENT

United States Senator from New York (1821-1828)
Governor of New York (1829)
Secretary of State under Jackson (1829-1832)
Vice-President under Jackson (1833-1837)

MAJOR ITEMS OF VAN BUREN'S ADMINISTRATION

Panic of 1837
Independent Treasury or Sub-Treasuries (1840)
Gag Resolution (1836-1844)

Election of Van Buren (1836)

The Democratic convention nominated **Martin Van Buren** by a unanimous vote. Because Jackson's influence in the party and his popularity with the people was still at a high level, his preference for Van Buren assured Van Buren of the candidacy. Sometimes Van Buren was referred to as the "Crown Prince" because he "inherited" the presidency from his predecessor.

The Whig party nominated two candidates, **Daniel Webster** of Massachusetts to represent the Northern faction, and **Hugh L. White** of Tennessee to appeal to the anti-Jackson Southerners. A third group, the **Anti-Masons**, nominated **William Henry Harrison** of Ohio.

All three of these candidates knew they had no chance to win a majority of the electoral vote, but they did hope to split the vote enough to throw the election into the House of Representatives. The election returns were as follows:

	Popular Vote	Electoral Vote
Van Buren	762,678	170
Harrison	548,007	73
White	145,396	26
Webster	41,287	14

(South Carolina's 11 votes went to W. Mangum, who was not a candidate.) (Vice-President Richard Johnson was elected by the Senate.)

Panic of 1837

The panic resulted from a combination of factors: overspeculation in land, unsound financing by state governments, the disturbing effects of the absence of the Bank of the United States, and the Specie Circular. The Specie Circular was issued in midsummer of 1836 by President Jackson. This prevented payment for public lands in any other money than gold and silver and certain paper money that was as sound as the gold and silver specie. As almost all sales had been paid for in bank notes of questionable soundness, this order from Jackson brought a sharp decline in the number of sales. Fraud and speculation in public lands had become a grave public issue. Something had to be done. The **Specie Circular** was Jackson's method of protecting the United States Treasury from accumulating vast amounts of greatly depreciated paper money. The Specie Circular did precipitate the **Panic of 1837**, but it did not cause it.

A depression set in that lasted throughout Van Buren's term of office. This alone would have made his administration unpopular, but there were other factors that further aggravated an already hopeless situation. Van Buren was a city man of considerable polish and wealth. He had aristocratic tastes and was without the "common touch" of Andrew Jackson.

Independent Treasury System or Sub-Treasuries (1840)

Jackson had always favored a safety deposit vault for federal funds. He didn't like the government's being in the banking business. With the expiration of the charter of the Second Bank of the United States in 1836 and the depositing of government monies in state banks, Van Buren pressed for the creation of **sub-treasuries** in a few cities for the safekeeping of federal funds. When the panic and depression witnessed many bank failures and some loss of government funds, Congress went along with the President and established the **Independent Treasury System**; that is, independent of any banking system. As the law provided places

in different cities for the safekeeping of government funds, these safety deposit vaults were sometimes called **sub-treasuries**. This system had a major virtue; it kept government funds safe from loss through fraud and mismanagement, both of which had taken heavy toll in the past. The law that was passed in 1840 was repealed in 1841 but passed again in 1846, to remain in effect until the Federal Reserve System replaced it in 1913.

* Gag Resolutions (1836-44)

Debate over slavery was time-consuming, temper-provoking, and useless. Opinions in Congress would not be swayed by more discussion. Consequently, in 1836 the House passed a **Gag Resolution** which read as follows:

"...all petitions, memorials, resolutions, propositions or papers relating in any way or to any extent whatever to the subject of slavery or the abolition of slavery shall, without being printed or referred, be laid upon the table and that no further action whatever shall be had thereon."

Ex-President John Quincy Adams served in the House of Representatives from 1831 to 1848. When it came his time to vote on a roll call, he refused to cast a vote on the Gag Resolution. Instead, he said, "I hold the resolution to be a direct violation of the Constitution of the United States, of the rules of this House, and of the rights of my constituents." What good was the right of petition guaranteed in the First Amendment if the House or the Senate operated under a Gag Resolution? Each year John Quincy Adams spoke vigorously against it, and by 1844 he won his fight. Gag Resolutions were discontinued.

William Henry Harrison   1841

1773-1841

WHIG

Vice-President   JOHN TYLER

Secretary of State   DANIEL WEBSTER

HARRISON'S PUBLIC SERVICE BEFORE HE BECAME PRESIDENT

Governor of the Indiana Territory (1801-1812)
In command at the Battle of Tippecanoe (1811)
Defeated the British in Canada (Thomas River, 1813)
United States Senator from Ohio (1825-1828)

Election of Harrison (1840)

Martin Van Buren was nominated by the Democrats to run for reelection. The party platform called for opposition to Clay's American System, favored strict construction of the Constitution, and opposed interference by Congress in the slavery issue. The Whigs nominated **William Henry Harrison** who had no known convictions on any of the public issues of the day. Clay, who had organized the Whig party, was obviously a man of real stature and capacity; but his nomination would almost certainly have split the Whigs into Northern and Southern factions. Clay recognized this political fact and stepped into the background. The Whig party avoided taking a position on the issues of banking, tariff, internal improvements at federal expense, slavery, and loose v. strict construction of the Constitution. Harrison had taken no position on these issues and therefore had made no enemies. He could be presented to the voters as a great Indian fighter and as a hero of the War of 1812. To insure unity between the Northern and Southern Whigs, **John Tyler** of Virginia was put on the ticket as Harrison's running mate. "Tippecanoe and Tyler too" and "Van, Van, is a used-up man" were slogans of the campaign.

	Popular Vote	Electoral Vote
Harrison	1,275,017	234
Van Buren	1,128,702	60

On April 4, 1841, just one month after his inauguration, Harrison died.

118

John Tyler 1841-1845

1790 -1862

ANTI-JACKSON DEMOCRAT RAN AS VICE-PRESIDENT ON THE WHIG TICKET

☆

Secretary of State   DANIEL WEBSTER

TYLER'S PUBLIC SERVICE BEFORE HE BECAME PRESIDENT

> *Governor of Virginia (1825-1836)*
> *United States Senator from Virginia (1827-1836)*

MAJOR ITEMS OF TYLER'S ADMINISTRATION

> *Veto of Clay's Bill for a Third Bank of the United States*
> *Webster-Ashburton Treaty (1842)*

Veto of Clay's Bill for a Third Bank of the United States

President Harrison's sudden death changed the Whig victory into a defeat. Senator Clay took the lead in forming a legislative program that abolished the Independent Treasury and passed a bill to establish a Third Bank of the United States. President Tyler vetoed the bank bill and thereby started a political war between the President and Congress. The Whig Cabinet members resigned, with the exception of Secretary of State Daniel Webster.

* Webster-Ashburton Treaty (1842)

Webster did not resign because he was in the midst of negotiations with Lord Ashburton over the Maine-Canadian border. This boundary dispute had been long and, at times, bitter. In 1838 and 1839 lumberjacks of Maine and New Brunswick had threatened to "shoot it out." The situation was so tense during this winter that it was called the **"Aroostook War,"** even though no lives were lost. By 1842 the **Webster-Ashburton Treaty** line was fixed. It followed the St. Croix River to its source, then went straight north to the St. John's River, along the St. John's River westward in an irregular horseshoe bend toward the south. The line left the St. John's River and proceeded in an irregular southward line to the 45th parallel at a point almost on the Connecticut river. At the 45th parallel the boundary extended west on the parallel to the St. Lawrence River and along the St. Lawrence to Lake Ontario. At the same time the border between the Lake of the Woods and Lake Superior was fixed along the Rainy River and a chain of lakes. This settlement left the Mesabi iron deposits within the United States.

James K. Polk   1845-1849

1795-1849

DEMOCRAT

Vice-President   GEORGE M. DALLAS

Secretary of State   JAMES BUCHANAN

POLK'S PUBLIC SERVICE BEFORE HE BECAME PRESIDENT

Member of the House of Representatives from Tennessee (1825-1839)
Speaker of the House (1835-1839)
Governor of Tennessee (1839-1841)

MAJOR ITEMS OF POLK'S ADMINISTRATION

Texas Became a State (1845)
Oregon Boundary Settled (1846)
Mexican War (1846-1848)
Guadalupe Hidalgo Treaty (1848)
Wilmot Proviso v. Calhoun-Davis Theory

* Election of Polk (1844)

In this campaign the organizer of the Whig party, **Henry Clay**, became its candidate. The Whigs did write a platform, but it said as little as possible. On the crucial issues of Texas and slavery, it said nothing; it even avoided saying anything about a national bank. In 1832 Clay had lost to Andrew Jackson because Jackson had overshadowed him in prominence and popularity; now Clay had his opportunity to win the presidency because he overshadowed all prospective opponents. It seemed to be Clay's year to become President.

Martin Van Buren was expected to get the nomination of the Democratic party. However, on the ninth ballot **James K. Polk** was nominated and the news was carried over the new invention, the telegraph. This news was greeted with one question, "Who is Polk?" This was the first surprise nomination, the first **"dark horse"** selection, in our history.

Van Buren and Clay had discussed privately the issue of Texas and found that they agreed that Texas should not be annexed. This was when they both expected to be presidential candidates, but before the nominating conventions. In letters to the newspapers they made their views known. They agreed that admitting Texas would offend Mexico and almost certainly result in war because the United States would then inherit the boundary dispute that Texas was still having with Mexico. Admission of Texas would also necessarily stir up the slave controversy between the North and South. But Andrew Jackson, who was still alive, said the Democrats needed a candidate in favor of expansion, preferably a man from the Southwest. Polk, who won the ninth ballot, was an expansionist from the Southwest. He not only favored annexing Texas, he wanted Oregon too. "Reannexation of Texas and Reoccupation of Oregon" became an effective slogan; even better was the **"Fifty-four forty or fight"** claim to Oregon.

Clay was thus put in a difficult situation. Should he continue to oppose the annexation of Texas and repudiate the extreme demands for Oregon? If he did, he would be right again, as he had been about the bank issue in 1832, but he would probably lose. Clay decided to shift his ground on the issues. Clay said that he didn't object to annexing Texas if it didn't cause war with Mexico, that he didn't think the question of slavery should be confused with the annexation of Texas, and that he would be quite willing to do whatever the people of the United States wished about expansion. Clay would still have won on this slippery approach had it not been for a new minor party that entered the field for the first time. The **Liberty party** ran **James G. Birney** for President. They favored abolition of slavery and almost all of their members were Whigs who would have voted for Clay if the Liberty party had not been organized. The Liberty party took enough votes away from Clay in Michigan and New York to give both states to Polk.

	Popular Vote	Electoral Vote
Polk	1,337,243	170
Clay	1,299,068	105
Birney	62,300	0

(New York State had 36 electoral votes)

Texas Became a State (1845)

On March 1, three days before Polk was inaugurated, Texas became a territory of the United States. The Americans who had lived almost ten years in the Lone Star Republic saw their cherished ambition realized when Texas became a state on December 29, 1845.

Oregon Boundary Settled (1846)

"Fifty-four forty or fight" and "All of Oregon or none" were emotionally satisfying slogans, especially during a presidential campaign; but going to war against England over 54°40' was quite a different matter from going to war with Mexico over the Rio Grande. In December of 1845, when England suggested that it would give consideration to the extension of the 49th parallel to the Pacific Coast, a peaceful settlement was assured. On June 15, 1846, the Senate ratified the Oregon settlement, which made the boundary an extension of the 49th parallel from the Rocky Mountains to the Pacific Ocean.

* The Mexican War (1846-1848)

Both Clay and Van Buren had said before the 1844 presidential campaign got under way that the annexation of Texas would involve the United States in a boundary dispute with Mexico, which might bring on a war. It did. When Texas was a state within Mexico, its boundary was the Nueces River, not the Rio Grande. But when Texans under **Sam Houston** defeated the Mexican general, **Santa Anna**, at the San Jacinto River in April 1836, it declared itself an independent republic. This new Republic of Texas claimed the Rio Grande River as its southwestern border. General Santa Anna had signed a "treaty" after his defeat at San Jacinto, which accepted the Rio Grande as the boundary. The Mexican Congress had rejected this agreement as having no legal status because it was made under force by a person unauthorized to conclude a treaty.

Almost as soon as the United States annexed Texas, Mexico broke off diplomatic relations. On June 15, 1845, General **Zachary Taylor** was ordered to defend the "territory of Texas" along the Rio Grande. Sizeable United States forces were in the disputed area by late summer. Several months before fighting broke out, the United States tried to buy from Mexico the area we were soon to take by force of arms. Mexico refused to sell. In April 1846 an American force of 63 men was captured. In the accompanying skirmish eleven Americans were killed. The war was on. President Polk appeared before Congress on May 11 to ask for a declaration of war because Mexico had "shed blood upon American soil." War was declared on May 13.

The states south of the Ohio River and west of the Alleghenies were enthusiastically in favor of this war. To the Northeast, the Mexican War was a plot to acquire more slave states.

Fighting during this war was often severe, but there was never any doubt about the final outcome. **John C. Fremont**, the "Pathfinder," took a leading part in the conquest of California. General **Stephen Kearny** carried the war into New Mexico from Fort Leavenworth on the Missouri River to Santa Fe, then westward along the Gila River and on to San Diego and Los Angeles. General Zachary Taylor's victory at Buena Vista ended the war in northern Mexico. General **Winfield Scott's** campaign from Vera Cruz to Mexico City brought the war to a close. On September 14, 1847, the Marines took control of the Mexican capital, Mexico City.

* Guadalupe Hidalgo Treaty (1848)

The United States added New Mexico and California to its territory. Mexico recognized the Rio Grande River as the southwest border of Texas. Including Texas, this area was over one million square miles. the United States paid $15 million to Mexico and assumed claims amounting to about $3.25 million.

There was considerable objection to this treaty among the people of the United States. In the Senate 14 votes were cast against it (38-14). The **Gadsden Purchase** in 1853 for the very generous price of $10 million may well be considered part of the peace settlement. The United States wanted this relatively small additional territory because it contained a pass through the mountains suitable for a railroad.

The Wilmot Proviso v. the Calhoun-Davis Theory

David Wilmot was a Democrat from Pennsylvania in the House of Representatives. He, along with the rest of Congress, took it for granted that the United States would acquire a large area of land from Mexico. While the war was going on, he introduced a resolution that said, "...neither slavery nor involuntary servitude shall ever exist in any part of said territory." The Wilmot Proviso passed the House by a comfortable margin, but had no chance to get by in the Senate. The raising of this question started a political storm. Wilmot's supporters claimed that Congress had a right to legislate about slavery in the territories, while his opponents called the Proviso an attack on states' rights. Calhoun reiterated the arguments for nullification, the compact theory, secession, and what is sometimes called interposition (the theory that a state may reject a federal mandate it considers an encroachment on its rights). This political war was to prove much more difficult to bring to a conclusion than the Mexican War.

Zachary Taylor 1849-1850

1784-1850

WHIG

☆

Vice-President MILLARD FILLMORE

TAYLOR'S PUBLIC SERVICE BEFORE HE BECAME PRESIDENT

Forty Years in the United States Army (1808-1848)
Defeated Santa Anna at Buena Vista (1847)

Election of Taylor (1848)

Both the Democrats and the Whigs were beginning to fall apart over the slavery issue. Northern Democrats who supported the Wilmot Proviso were called **Barnburners.** The name indicated that they were willing to destroy the Democratic party over the single issue of slavery; that is, to burn the barn down in order to kill one rat. They withdrew from the Democratic Nominating Convention. Many Northern Whigs were fed up with their party's careful avoidance of major issues, and they left the Whig party. The **Liberty party** was a third organized group against slavery. These three groups united to form the **Free Soil party** with **Martin Van Buren** as their candidate. "Free soil, free speech, free labor, and free men" was its campaign slogan. The Free Soil party opposed the extension of slavery into any new areas but would tolerate slavery in the states where it already existed. This view had a strong appeal for those people who opposed slavery, but also recognized the difficulties inherent in any attempt at abolition.

The Democrats nominated **General Lewis Cass.** Polk did not seek renomination. Cass had favored expansion and hence was popular in the West. The Democratic Platform denied the right of Congress to interfere with slavery in the states but said nothing about the real question of the day. Did Congress have the right to legislate about slavery in the territories?

The Whigs nominated **Zachary Taylor** because he had been a recent hero at the battle of Buena Vista. As Taylor had taken no strong position on any real public issue, he had no enemies.

The new Free Soil party got enough support in New York State to throw its 36 electoral votes into the Whig column and the election to Taylor.

	Popular Vote	*Electoral Vote*
Taylor	1,360,101	163
Cass	1,220,544	127
Van Buren	291,263	0

(In New York State, Van Buren received more votes than Cass.)

President Taylor died on July 9, 1850. The great issue before the nation was the problem of slavery in the land taken from Mexico. The **Compromise of 1850,** which was in the making, was completed under President Millard Fillmore.

1800 -1874

WHIG

Secretary of State DANIEL WEBSTER

FILLMORE'S PUBLIC SERVICE BEFORE HE BECAME PRESIDENT

> *Member of the House of Representatives for Eight Years*
> *Vice-President under Taylor*

MAJOR ITEMS OF FILLMORE'S ADMINISTRATION

> *Compromise of 1850 (the Omnibus Bill)*
> *Clayton-Bulwer Treaty (1850)*
> Uncle Tom's Cabin

** Compromise of 1850 (Omnibus Bill)

A solution to the question of slavery in our newly acquired territories had to be found. Clay was the man with a plan and with the political stature to command attention. There had to be a Northerner to give the plan national status. **Daniel Webster** from Massachusetts filled this necessary role. The debates on these measures rank among the best that have occurred in Congress.

The following provisions were finally passed by Congress after months of consideration:

1] California was admitted into the Union as a free state.

The **Gold Rush of 1849** had brought to California thousands of settlers from all over the United States and from all over the world.

2] Slavery was already established in Texas, and nothing was done to disturb it.

3] The areas taken from Mexico between Texas and California were divided at the 37th parallel. South of the parallel was the Territory of New Mexico and north of it was the Territory of Utah. In these two territories there were no restrictions on slavery. But when either territory or any part of either territory became a state, the people living there could then decide by popular vote (squatter sovereignty) whether they wanted a slave or a free state.

4] A **Fugitive Slave Law** was passed that contained provisions to make recovery of fugitive slaves as certain as a law could make it.

a. All law enforcement officials who failed to cooperate in the apprehension of fugitive slaves were made liable up to the value of the slave, if the slave was not captured or escaped while being held in custody.

b. All "good citizens are hereby commanded to aid and assist in the prompt execution of this law."

c. No alleged fugitive was allowed to testify in his or her own behalf, and no trial by jury was allowed.

d. Any person who hindered the recovery of a fugitive slave was subject to $1,000 fine, imprisonment for six months, and the payment of $1,000 to the owner.

e. If mob violence threatened to rescue a recovered fugitive from a master's custody, it was the duty of local officials to provide for the delivery of the slave to the place from which he or she had escaped.

5] The buying and selling of slaves was prohibited within the District of Columbia. Otherwise the institution of slavery within the District was not affected.

The South was willing to live with the Compromise. But many Northerners resented the fugitive slave law. They were beginning to share the view of **William H. Seward** of New York, who had said during the debates in Congress that there was "a higher law" than laws of Congress and the Constitution. But a period of quiet set in as the early 1850s witnessed prosperity throughout the nation. Calhoun foresaw what was to happen more clearly than other leaders. He died in March 1850, but he had already said that the Compromise could settle nothing, that it could merely postpone a settlement, and that such postponement could help only the North. Clay died in June and Webster in October of 1852. These two men had postponed the Civil War for ten years by their Compromise.

* Clayton-Bulwer Treaty (1850)

Our acquisition of California in 1848 and the Gold Rush in 1849 increased United States' interest in the possibility of a canal across Central America. During the Mexican War we had made a treaty with Colombia, then called New Granada, giving us exclusive transit rights across the Isthmus of Panama. This was the most practical crossing from ocean to ocean. For about a decade, Great Britain and the United States considered each other as rivals seeking special influence in Cen-

tral America, especially in the areas where a canal seemed feasible. Hostility was increasing. The **Clayton-Bulwer Treaty** cleared the air. The terms agreed upon were as follows:

1] Neither Great Britain nor the United States will seek or acquire control over Central America or any special privilege therein.

2] If any canal through Central America is built, it must be open to the ships of all nations on the same terms in both peace and war. The approaches to each end of the canal shall be similarly open to the use of all nations.

3] If such a canal is built, it must be with the free consent of the nation through whose territory it passes. Both Great Britain and the United States guarantee its neutrality by protecting it and the areas adjacent to it, both during its construction and thereafter.

Uncle Tom's Cabin

This novel by **Harriet Beecher Stowe** had a profound effect. As Tom Paine's *Common Sense* crystallized public opinion in support of revolution, so *Uncle Tom's Cabin,* published in March 1852, changed the abolitionists from a small group of fanatics to a great company of righteous crusaders. Her book convinced thousands that slavery was a moral wrong. When Harriet Beecher Stowe was introduced to President Lincoln, his response was, "So, you're the little lady who caused the Civil War." It took the North and most of the world by storm. Letters of appreciation and praise came to Mrs. Stowe from England, Germany, Switzerland, Sweden, Italy, and from many prominent persons.

Franklin Pierce   1853-1857

1804 -1869

DEMOCRAT

Vice President   WILLIAM R. KING

Secretary of War   JEFFERSON DAVIS

PIERCE'S PUBLIC SERVICE BEFORE HE BECAME PRESIDENT

Brigadier General under General Scott in the Mexican War

MAJOR ITEMS OF PIERCE'S ADMINISTRATION

Japan Opened to World Trade (1853)
Kansas-Nebraska Bill (1854)
Underground Railroad and Personal Liberty Laws
Strife in Kansas
Ostend Manifesto (1854)

Pierce's Election (1852)

This is certainly one of the campaigns where the two major parties were as alike as two peas in a pod. **Franklin Pierce**, Democrat, and **Winfield Scott**, Whig, got the nomination at their party conventions on the 49th and 53rd ballots respectively. Both party platforms pledged adherence to the Compromise of 1850 and both condemned any further agitation about slavery. The Whig party began to break up because it had originated as an anti-Jackson party and had never been able to take a stand on an important public issue. The Southern members of the Whig party were going back to the Democrats. The result of this shift was a landslide victory for Pierce in 1852.

	Popular Vote	*Electoral Vote*
Pierce	1,601,474	254
Scott	1,386,578	42

Japan Opened to World Trade (1853)

Commodore **Matthew C. Perry** sailed into Tokyo Bay in July 1853. His mission was to make a trade treaty with Japan. A miniature railroad and a telegraph, displayed by Perry, convinced the Japanese emperor that our civilization might have some merit. A trade treaty was concluded. The historical significance of Perry's visit was that Japan moved away from its policy of isolation. It soon began a program of modernization. Japan began to copy Western ways, which were destined to make Japan the dominant Asiatic power in the Far East.

** Kansas-Nebraska Bill (1854)

Stephen A. Douglas reopened the slavery issue in January. From then to late in May, an increasingly bitter debate over this bill split the major parties and reorganized the people of the United States into a dangerous political pattern. The breakup of the Whig party became complete as the Southerners still in the party now left it to join the Southern Democrats. Political alignment was dictated by one issue, slavery. The Republican party was born during the debate over the Kansas-Nebraska Bill. By the late 1850s political lines had been drawn to coincide with geographical areas. No longer were there two *national* parties; there were two *sectional* parties.

The provisions of the bill divided the Nebraska Territory at the 40th parallel into the Territory of Kansas south of the line, and the Territory of Nebraska north of the line. The settlers in each territory were to decide the issue of slavery by popular vote as soon as they had organized a territorial government. All of this area was in the Louisiana Territory north of 36°30' that had been made free by the Missouri Compromise of 1820, which the Kansas-Nebraska Bill specifically repealed. The repeal of the Missouri Compromise and the introduction of squatter sovereignty (popular vote) was a victory for the South because it took the decision away from Congress and gave it to the people who lived in the area.

When Douglas introduced the Kansas-Nebraska Bill, he did not intend to stir up sectional controversy. His plan was to encourage the rapid settlement of the region west of Missouri and the building of a transcontinental railroad westward from Chicago. However, the result of the bill was to end the political truce over slavery and to create disaster.

* Underground Railroad and Personal Liberty Laws

By 1830 an organized **Underground Railroad** existed in fourteen Northern states. Fugitive slaves were hidden in houses and barns, called stations, along escape routes extending into Canada. About 50,000 slaves traveled this route to freedom over the 30 years before the Civil War. During the 1850s it is estimated that the total slave population was somewhat in excess of 3.5 million. These statistics show clearly that fugitive slaves did not constitute a serious problem to slave owners, nor did the Underground Railroad threaten slavery as an institution.

The **Personal Liberty Laws** were direct violations of the fugitive slave provisions of the **Compromise of 1850.** As state laws clearly incompatible with a law of Congress, they were unconstitutional. The South saw these Personal Liberty Laws a denial by the North of the one provision in the Compromise of 1850 that was the most important. To the North, these laws were a justified defiance of the federal law that ought not to be obeyed. Ralph Waldo Emerson expressed the Northern view of the federal fugitive slave law when he wrote, "I will not obey it." The state Personal Liberty Laws varied, but provisions common to many were: jury trial for alleged fugitives, local jails not be used to detain suspected fugitives, and alleged fugitives allowed to testify in their own behalf. In the face of these laws, the recovery of fugitive slaves was extremely difficult. In the Northern states the apprehension of a fugitive slave was likely to result in mob violence against the owner.

* Strife in Kansas

After the passage of the Kansas-Nebraska Bill both Northerners and Southerners rushed into the area to win it for their cause. Kansas was not suited for cotton and slavery, but, with feelings aroused, this made no difference. Neither side was in any mood to be reasonable. Massachusetts organized the New England Emigrant Aid Company to finance young men willing to settle in Kansas in order to make it a free territory. In Missouri, the slave state adjacent to Kansas, organizations were formed to recruit settlers bent upon establishing slavery in Kansas. By 1856 two rival governments claimed authority in Kansas. Congress, accepting the popular sovereignty principle, looked on but did nothing. President Pierce warned both factions to stop fighting, but the frequent armed clashes between proslavery and antislavery forces continued and people began to refer to **"bleeding Kansas."** "Border Ruffians" from Missouri and Northerners armed with "Beecher Bibles" (rifles) raided each others' settlements. About 200 were killed and property damage ran into the millions of dollars. One of the most senseless acts of violence was **John Brown's raid** at Pottawatomie Creek, where he and his four sons murdered five proslavery settlers.

In Congress Senator Charles Sumner of Massachusetts gave a speech in 1856 which was a bitter and coarse attack not only on slavery but on individual Southern Senators. Senator Butler of South Carolina, who was not present at the time, was the target of much of Sumner's vituperation. Two days later, Representative Brooks of South Carolina, a nephew of Senator Butler, entered Sumner's office and beat him over the head with a cane. Several months later Sumner was able to resume his seat in the Senate. Brooks resigned his seat in the House and was quickly reelected by South Carolina. In his own state he was a hero.

Constitutional conventions and elections were held in Kansas amid violence, trickery, and corruption. During this chaos President Pierce's term ended and **James Buchanan** became President. Buchanan's strategy, if it can be called one, was to avoid trouble. His decisions seemed motivated by a desire to preserve party harmony in a situation that clearly made such an outcome impossible.

In 1857 the **Lecompton Constitution** was submitted to the people of Kansas. The original agreement was to allow a vote on the Constitution as a whole. It became evident that a proslavery constitution would be rejected. The Lecompton convention was controlled by proslavery delegates who refused to submit the constitution to a vote but, instead, submitted two propositions. One would accept the constitution with slavery. The other would accept it without slavery, but "without slavery" meant forbidding any more slaves to enter Kansas but permitting all those already there to remain slaves. No matter which way the vote went, there would be slavery in Kansas. Naturally, the antislavery voters refused to take part in any such fraudulent election, and the proslavery voters won by a landslide. This "Lecompton Fraud" was sent to Washington, and President Buchanan advised Congress to approve it. Congress refused. Douglas who had started all this trouble with his Kansas-Nebraska Bill, opposed Buchanan on this issue and thus created a split in the Democratic party, which made John Breckenridge the leader of many Southern Democrats. This split was to put the Republicans into the presidency in 1860.

* Ostend Manifesto (1854)

This document was the culmination of the strong desire of certain Southerners for Cuba. In 1848 under President Polk, the United States had offered Spain $100 million for Cuba. Although Spain refused, some Southerners still hoped to obtain Cuba. In 1854 after a crisis when Spain seized an American ship, the **Black Warrior**, for violation of customs regulations, the American ministers to Great Britain, France, and Spain met in Ostend, Belgium to plan American action. They drew up an unofficial statement known as the **Ostend Manifesto.** In this document they declared that if Spain refused to sell Cuba, the United States would be justified in seizing it by force. President Pierce repudiated the document, which provoked strong protest in the North and in Europe. It showed how far the South would go to add more slave territory.

James Buchanan   1856-1861

1791-1868

DEMOCRAT

Vice-President   JOHN C. BRECKINRIDGE

BUCHANAN'S PUBLIC SERVICE BEFORE HE BECAME PRESIDENT

> *United States Minister to Russia*
> *Secretary of State under Polk*
> *Minister to Great Britain*

MAJOR ITEMS OF BUCHANAN'S ADMINISTRATION

> * *Taney's* Dred Scott *Decision (1857)*
> * *Lincoln-Douglas Debates (1858)*
>   *Moving Toward War*

Buchanan's Election (1856)

A third party, with ex-President **Millard Fillmore** at its head, entered this campaign. It was a combination of the American party (**Know Nothings**) and the remnants of the Whig party. The Know Nothings began their deservedly short life under the name of the "Order of the Star-Spangled Banner." **James Buchanan** was chosen to lead the Democrats because he had gained favor with the South through his association with the **Ostend Manifesto**, and he was expected to appeal to the North because he came from Pennsylvania. **John Breckinridge** of Kentucky was his running mate on the ticket. The new Republican party put its first candidate for President into the race, **John Fremont** of California.

The Democrats supported the Compromise of 1850 and the Kansas-Nebraska Bill. The Republicans claimed that Congress had the right to legislate on slavery in the territories, attacked the Ostend Manifesto, and favored the admission of Kansas as a free state. For a new party, the Republicans showed surprising strength.

	Popular Vote	*Electoral Vote*
Buchanan	1,838,169	174
Frémont	1,335,264	114
Fillmore	874,534	8

Only five free states voted for Buchanan. The Democratic party was becoming a slave-state party. The Republicans were so elated with winning eleven states that they set to work building the party for the election of 1860.

** Taney's *Dred Scott* Decision (1857)

When President Buchanan was sworn into office, the **Dred Scott** case was before the Supreme Court. The decision came two days later. Chief Justice **Roger B. Taney**, who had succeeded John Marshall in 1836, gave the seven to two decision of the Court. In view of the extended period of controversy over the Kansas-Nebraska Bill and "Bleeding Kansas," many Northerners were convinced that the decision rendered was influenced by the fact that five Justices were Southerners and seven of them were Democrats.

Dred Scott had been taken by his master from the slave state of Missouri into the free state of Illinois, then into the free territory of Wisconsin, and back to Missouri. Scott claimed his freedom on the basis of his residence in Illinois and Wisconsin where he had lived for a considerable period of time. The Court reached the following decisions.

1] Dred Scott was not a citizen and, therefore had no right to sue in a federal court.

His parents had been brought to the United States from Africa as slaves. The fact that Dred Scott was born in the United States did not make him a *citizen* within the meaning of that word as used in the Constitution. Any state could make him a citizen of the state, but such citizenship would not extend beyond the borders of that state and would not include citizenship of the United States.

2] The Missouri Compromise was unconstitutional.

The Territory of Wisconsin had no right to exclude slavery. Property in the form of slaves was precisely the same as any other property and Congress had no right to restrict its ownership. Hence, the action taken by Congress in 1820, when it declared the Louisiana Territory north of 36°30' free, was illegal.

3] Only a state had the right to forbid slavery.

There was no legal way to exclude slavery from the territories.

Dred Scott was not fighting for his freedom; he had already been assured of that. His owner, Sandford, was opposed to slavery and was using Scott as a test case to get a decision from the Supreme Court on the legal status of slavery in the territories. As we have noted, the first opinion given was that Dred Scott was not a citizen and couldn't bring suit in a federal court. Here the case could have ended; but the Court chose to go on to determine the legal status of slavery in the territories. This gave opponents of the decision a chance to claim that the case was actually closed as soon as the Court denied citizenship to Scott. In this view, all additional points made by the Court were unnecessary and uncalled for, that is, unofficial statements suggested by, but not part of, the case. Such a meandering of judicial opinion is called an *obiter dictum*. Public opinion in the North refused to accept Taney's pronouncements as anything other than *obiter dictum*.

* Lincoln-Douglas Debates (1858)

During the summer and early fall of the midterm elections, Lincoln and Douglas met in a series of debates throughout Illinois. Douglas was seeking reelection to the United States Senate. Lincoln believed slavery was wrong, the Republican party believed slavery was wrong, and slavery, being wrong, should be prevented from spreading. There was a legal obligation to recognize the rights of slave states. But Lincoln and the Republican party rejected the Supreme Court's *Dred Scott* decision. Douglas held to the view that whether slavery was right or wrong was a matter to be decided in each state separately. Douglas, a bit obtuse about the moral force that was gathering strength in the North, saw no reason why the Union could not go on indefinitely part free and part slave. Lincoln had said, "I believe this government cannot endure permanently half slave and half free. I do not expect the Union to be dissolved ... but I do expect it will cease to be divided. It will become all one thing, or all the other."

In the **Freeport debate**, Lincoln tried to force Douglas to make a choice between the Kansas-Nebraska principle of squatter sovereignty and the Dred Scott case. The Supreme Court had said that slavery could not be kept out of the territories, yet the Kansas-Nebraska Bill permitted the settlers to make a choice. It seemed that Douglas must either repudiate the Supreme Court decision, which would ruin him in the eyes of Southern Democrats, or he must admit the error of the Kansas-Nebraska Bill, which was his work. Douglas refused to make a direct choice, but he did give an answer satisfactory to the Illinois voters. He said, "Slavery cannot exist a day or an hour anywhere, unless it is supported by local police regulations." This answer, known as the **Freeport Doctrine**, pointed out that slavery, while legal in all territories, could not exist in Northern areas. Everyone knew that no Northern territory would pass laws to sustain slavery, let alone enforce them. So the good people of Illinois could go home and sleep peacefully in full confidence that slavery was not going to spread northward. Douglas won reelection to the Senate, but he drove many more Southern Democrats into the Breckinridge camp. To please them, Douglas would have had to urge strict adherence and support for the *Dred Scott* decision, regardless of one's personal views about slavery. Any such firm stand in support of the Supreme Court would have lost Douglas his Senate seat. He had to win in the Senate race in 1858 to be in a position in 1860 to get the Democratic presidential nomination. Lincoln had put Douglas in a political dilemma. The tactics Douglas had to use to win his Senate seat cost him the presidency.

Moving Toward War

Since the Fugitive Slave Law of 1850, the North had increasingly accepted Seward's statement that there was a "higher law" than the laws of Congress and the

Constitution of the United States. In 1859, at **Harpers Ferry** in Virginia, **John Brown** and eighteen followers seized a federal arsenal. After two days they surrendered to Colonel Robert E. Lee. Two of Brown's sons and eight others of his small band were dead or dying. About six weeks later, John Brown was hanged, and, soon afterward, six others went to the gallows. The audacity of John Brown's plan to organize a slave revolt and the fanaticism of the leader created concern throughout the South. Thousands of Northerners accepted Brown as a hero, a martyr in a righteous cause. Many Southerners came to believe that the North was going to try to end slavery and with it the Southern way of life.

Early in 1860, Senator **Jefferson Davis** of Mississippi offered a series of resolutions that were adopted. They pushed the political alignment a bit closer to war.

1] No state has the right to interfere with the domestic institutions of the other states.

2] The federal government must extend all needful protection to slavery in the territories.

3] All state laws interfering with the recovery of fugitive slaves are unconstitutional.

The political result of these resolutions was the increased concentration of Northern Democrats in the Douglas camp, and the Southern Democrats in the Breckinridge faction. This solidifying of the sectional division of Democrats broke up the presidential nominating convention soon to be held.

Abraham Lincoln　　1861-1865

1809-1865

REPUBLICAN

☆

Vice-President　ANDREW JOHNSON

Secretary of State　WILLIAM H. SEWARD　　　　　　　Secretary of Treasury　SALMON P. CHASE

LINCOLN'S PUBLIC SERVICE BEFORE HE BECAME PRESIDENT

Member of Illinois State Legislature (Whig)
Member of United States House of Representatives (1846-1848)

MAJOR ITEMS DURING LINCOLN'S ADMINISTRATION

The Union and the Confederacy Compared　　*A Few Major Military Engagements of the War*
The Problems Facing Each Side　　　　　　　*Lincoln v. Congress at the End of the Civil War*
Raising Men and Money　　　　　　　　　　*Homestead Act*
Relations with Foreign Nations　　　　　　　*Lincoln's Assassination*

* Election and Reelection of Lincoln (1860 and 1864)

After 10 days and 57 ballots the Democrats adjourned their nominating convention at Charleston, South Carolina, without selecting a candidate. The following month they held two separate conventions in Baltimore, Maryland, where one faction nominated **Stephen Douglas** and the other, **John C. Breckinridge**. The two platforms were similar, with Breckinridge's making a more aggressively stated demand for federal protection of slavery in the territories. President Buchanan had broken with Douglas over the Lecompton Constitution and used his influence in favor of his Vice-President, Breckinridge. After his Freeport Doctrine, the Southern Democrats did not trust Douglas.

The Republican nominating convention met in Chicago. Lincoln won the nomination on the third ballot. **Abraham Lincoln** was chosen because he could carry Illinois and probably Indiana, and he had won quite a national reputation by the Lincoln-Douglas debates of 1858. The Republican platform rejected the *Dred Scott* decision, asserted the right of Congress to exclude slavery in the territories, condemned the Lecompton

Constitution, and advocated a protective tariff.

The Constitutional Union party nominated **John Bell** of Tennessee. The Constitutional Unionists feared a war was coming, they earnestly hoped it wouldn't, and they had no idea what to do about it.

	Popular Vote		Electoral Vote
Lincoln	1,866,352	180	(18 free states)
Douglas	1,375,157	12	(1 slave state—Mo.)
Breckinridge	847,953	72	(13 slave states)
Bell	589,581	39	(3 slave states)

Between election day in November 1860 and inauguration day the following March 4, seven states seceded from the Union: South Carolina, Mississippi, Florida, Alabama, Georgia, Louisiana, and Texas. President Buchanan took the position that these states had no right to secede but that he had no right to prevent secession. Before Lincoln's inauguration the **Confederate States of America** had been organized. **Jefferson**

Davis had been elected its president; Montgomery, Alabama, had become its capital; the Stars and Bars had been adopted as its flag; it had sent agents abroad to seek aid, and President Davis had been authorized to raise 100,000 troops. In view of these preparations, Lincoln's first inaugural address was temperate as well as firm; it invited reconsideration by the secessionists.

> "I have no purpose, directly or indirectly,...to interfere with the institution of slavery in the states where it exists. I believe I have no lawful right to do so, and I have no inclination to do so."

> "I...consider...the Union is unbroken...I shall take care...that the laws of the Union be faithfully executed in all States."

> "...there need be no bloodshed or violence; and there shall be none, unless it be forced upon the national authority."

> "The government will not assail you. You can have no conflict without yourselves being the aggressors. You have no oath registered in heaven to destroy the government, while I shall have the most solemn one to preserve, protect, and defend it."

Lincoln's Reelection in 1864

This campaign was a struggle between the "Copperheads" and the fortunes of war. **Copperheads** were Northerners who opposed the Civil War. Lincoln supporters gave them the name, referring to the poisonous snake. The mayor of New York, Fernando Wood, published the *Daily News*, which advocated that the city secede from the Union. Agitation by Confederate spies, genuine labor unrest, and anger over the unfairness of the draft were whipped into a flame by the *Daily News* and resulted in four terrible days, July 13-16, 1863, of rioting, stealing, burning, and killing. The national leader of the Copperheads was Representative Clement L. Vallandigham of Ohio. The anti-war Democrats nominated General **George B. McClellan** on a platform calling for immediate cessation of hostilities and the preservation of the Federal Union of States. The terrific casualty lists and over three long years of fighting had brought the morale of the North close to the breaking point. The Confederacy had banked heavily on their ability to outlast the North, and this calculation missed by a narrow margin. From July to October, General Philip Sheridan drove Jubal Early out of the Shenandoah Valley, and in September **Sherman** took Atlanta. The lift to Northern morale from these victories turned the tide toward Lincoln. Because thousands of "war Democrats" supported Lincoln, the Republican party changed its name, for this election, to the Union party.

	Popular Vote	*Electoral Vote*
Lincoln	2,216,067	212
McClellan	1,808,725	21

* The Union and the Confederacy Compared at the Beginning of the Civil War

Counting West Virginia, there were 24 Union states with a population of about 22 million. They contained most of the industry, most of the banks, and most of the railroad mileage. Their farms supplied a diversity of products, including ample foodstuffs. Almost all of the merchant marine was owned by Northerners. The federal government was their government with its army and navy and the organization to prosecute a war.

The Confederacy contained 11 states with a population of about 5.5 million free persons and 3.5 million slaves. Its industrial development and financial resources were less than one-third that of the Union. Much of its agricultural wealth was in cotton, tobacco, sugar, and naval stores, all of which could aid in the war effort only if sold and delivered by ship to foreign ports. It could raise foodstuffs, but with grossly inadequate railroad mileage and water transport, it could not deliver them where needed. The Southerners had to organize a government, a task made doubly difficult because they were fighting for state sovereignty and were extremely reluctant to grant power to a central government, even their own Confederacy in time of war.

The Confederate States were fully aware of the political, economic, financial, and manpower advantages of the Union, but they thought other factors made military success for their side well within the bounds of probability:

1] Great Britain wanted Southern products. A tariff-free exchange of British manufactured products for the agricultural raw materials of the South made such an attractive trade picture that the Confederacy fully expected an early alliance with England.

2] For the same reasons, but to a less compelling extent, France might materially aid the Confederacy.

3] Southerners knew firearms, horses, and the outdoor life. They believed that one Southern soldier would be worth four or five Northern clerks, shopkeepers, farmers, artisans, and mill hands.

4] The South had a military tradition. Many of its men were professional soldiers and officers. Southerners had taken a major part in the Mexican War.

5] The Confederacy could fight a defensive war. It had

no need to conquer the Union but had simply only to resist stoutly enough to make the North war-weary.

6] The Confederacy more than half believed that the Union would not fight, and, if it did, they expected the North would be divided and half-hearted about it.

* The Problems Facing Each Side in the Civil War

The Union believed that the defeat of the Confederacy required four major objectives: capture Richmond, the nerve center and capital; blockade Confederate ports; control the Mississippi River and thus divide the Confederacy as well as cut off its meat supply from Texas; and cut the Confederacy into sections and then round up its armies. Clearly, this was a large order.

The Confederacy faced a seemingly much less formidable task. It had no military conquests that it must make. Its four tactics were: fight a basically defensive war; keep the Union off balance by threatening or making stabs at its nerve center, Washington; create dissension in the North; and outlast the Union by a resistance so spirited that Northern morale would break.

* Raising Troops and Money

Raising Troops

Although troops were drafted from April 1863 to the end of the war, the great bulk of the Union army was always made up of volunteers. The states had their quotas to raise, and each state assigned quotas to cities, towns, and counties within its borders. So much pressure was created by local opinion and the desire of each community to meet its quota that many "volunteered" with something less than enthusiasm. The effort to keep enlistments up led to the offering of **bounties** by local governments to all who volunteered. This encouraged "bounty jumping," a practice that consisted of enlisting to collect the bounty and then deserting in order to enlist again at another place to collect another bounty. Some bounty jumpers made 20 to 30 jumps. In March 1863, the draft was started and was very poorly organized. A drafted man could pay the government $300 and thus avoid service, or he could provide a substitute. Providing a substitute meant paying something less than $300 to another person willing to take one's place, and this meant that sons of well-to-do families could stay home while the young men who couldn't raise the money were drafted. The obvious injustice of the situation led to the saying that the conflict was a "rich man's war but a poor man's fight." Some made money by war profiteering. Boots made of

cheap substitute materials were sold at prices paid for fine quality leather. Bribing government purchasing agents was common.

The Confederacy started drafting men into the service in April 1862, but it was the volunteers who kept the ranks filled throughout the war. There were no bounties in the Confederacy, but there was some disaffection over the draft which, like that of the Union, permitted a drafted man to buy a substitute.

Raising Money

The Union financed the war by a tariff, an income tax, the National Banking System, excise taxes, and **greenbacks** (government paper money). The Morrill Tariff had high rates, which were intended to encourage American manufacturing. The income tax took about 5 percent on incomes between $600 and $5,000 and 10 percent on higher incomes.

The National Banking System was established in 1863 and was aimed to attract large amounts of money quickly. Banks bought United States bonds to the amount of $30,000 or more and, to belong to the system, had to invest at least one-third of their capital in such bonds. The banks could issue bank notes up to 90 percent of the face value of the bonds they purchased and then lend these notes at interest. Interest on their bank notes and interest on the bonds they purchased gave the banks almost double interest on their money, a circumstance that created much criticism. As it took some time to get this National Banking System under way, its effect on Civil War financing was not great; but it remained the mainstay of our banking system until replaced by the Federal Reserve System in 1913.

Excise taxes, taxes on goods originating in this country, were placed on a great number of items, even including some food products. Greenbacks were issued to the amount of about $400 million. This "printing press" money had no material backing and was therefore completely inflationary. It was made legal tender for all private debts, but its value fluctuated during the war between 35 cents and 78 cents on the dollar. While the printing of such fiat money is always a dangerous type of financing, the federal government restricted the amount issued to less that 15 percent of the cost of the war. By 1879 Congress had passed legislation that provided for the redemption of greenbacks in specie (coins) at face value.

The Confederacy levied excise taxes, sold bonds to its people, borrowed from foreign bankers, and printed fiat money. Loans from abroad were far smaller than the Confederacy had expected and totaled not more than $15 million. Income from excise taxes and from the sale of bonds amounted to no more than 15 percent of the total cost of the war to the South. The printing presses made most of the money, and with the fortunes of war against it, the Confederate paper dollar was worth about 1.5 cents after the defeats at Vicksburg and Gettysburg in July 1863.

** Relations with Foreign Nations During the Civil War

England

1] On May 13, 1861, just one month after the surrender of Fort Sumter, Queen Victoria recognized the belligerency of the Confederacy. Recognition of the Confederacy did not mean that England acknowledged the independence of the South, but only that it was ready to treat the Confederacy according to international laws usually observed between belligerents and neutrals. It was common knowledge that official England favored the Confederacy, and this alone made the United States look with suspicion on any move England made. Lincoln was insisting that the Southern states could not, under our Constitution, secede; that they were rebelling, and that he was using the power of the federal government to quell the rebellion. Queen Victoria's quick recognition of "certain states styling themselves the Confederate States of America" was hardly in harmony with Lincoln's view of the nature of the Civil War and caused strong resentment throughout the Union.

2] When Captain Wilkes of the U.S.S. *San Jacinto* stopped the British mail steamer *Trent* on the high seas and seized two Confederate agents, Mason and Slidell, the American press and people hailed the incident with joy, while the English press demanded an apology and reparations. Mason and Slidell were on their way to England and France, respectively, to raise money on cotton and tobacco and to urge whatever support for the Confederacy they could persuade these nations to give. They had evaded the Union blockade and had reached Cuba, where they boarded the *Trent* at Havana. Secretary of State Seward advised President Lincoln that Captain Wilkes' action was legally indefensible, and Lincoln very wisely accepted this view of the affair and not only released Mason and Slidell but had Seward apologize to the British minister.

3] Lincoln's announcement in September 1862, that the following New Year's Day the **Emancipation Proclamation** would become operative was far more important for its reception in England than for any effect it had within the Union or on the Confederacy.

Lincoln announced the Emancipation Proclamation because he was convinced that such a proclamation would help preserve the Union. And he was right. As long as the people of Europe believed that the war was over the legal right of states to secede from the Union,

they were inclined to favor the seceding states. Why should states be forced to remain in a government against their will? Our minister to Spain, Carl Schurz, informed President Lincoln that Europe would be sympathetic to the Union only when they realized that a Union victory meant the end of slavery, and a Southern victory meant the continuance of slavery. Lincoln's Emancipation Proclamation was a political master-stroke for the preservation of the Union. Mass meetings in England demanded that their government stop the construction of ships for the Confederacy; unemployed mill hands in English towns demonstrated in favor of the Union, even though their loss of jobs was due to the Union blockade; and the Russian czar, who had recently freed the serfs, sent some of his warships to American waters in readiness to help the Union if England entered the war on the side of the Confederacy. The Emancipation Proclamation certainly had something to do with the presence of well over 50,000 black troops in the Union forces and the aid given by an even larger number of black laborers who worked with the army.

4] In 1862 and 1863 several commerce raiders were built in English shipyards for the Confederacy. English law, as well as international law, forbade the building and equipping of fighting ships in a neutral nation for a belligerent. But a Confederate agent persuaded English shipbuilders that it was legal to build such ships if only they didn't quite complete them and sent them to a foreign yard for the finishing touches. This they did. The *Alabama*, *Florida*, and *Shenandoah* were such vessels. They destroyed over 250 Union ships. These commerce raiders, built in English shipyards and finished in France or elsewhere, became the subject of arbitration at Geneva in 1872.

France

1] The French government made a substantial loan to the Confederacy.

2] Emperor **Napoleon III** of France permitted commerce raiders to be built in French shipyards, and he had, in July 1862, suggested to the British government that the time was ripe for the recognition of the independence of the Confederacy. Slidell was then in Paris, thousands of bales of cotton in the Confederacy were ready for shipment, the shortages of cotton for the mills of France and England had become acute, and McClellan had been driven back in his attempt to take Richmond. This combination of factors convinced Napoleon III that the time was approaching when open assistance to the Confederacy might be good policy for France. Suddenly in mid-September of 1862, the picture changed. The repulse of Lee by McClellan at Antietam was followed by Lincoln's announcement of the Emancipation Proclamation, a combination of events that put an end to any plans Napoleon had for more active support of the Confederacy.

3] The most ambitious action of Napoleon III against the United States was his challenge to the Monroe Doctrine. In 1861 England, Spain, and France sent warships to Mexico in a move to collect debts owed to them. Mexico was able to negotiate a settlement with England and Spain, but France used the situation as a pretext for colonization. Napoleon III sent troops into Mexico and took Mexico City. He then invited the Austrian archduke, **Maximillian**, to accept the position of Emperor of Mexico. Maximillian, with the support of French troops, maintained control of Mexico throughout the Civil War. But soon after Appomattox, Lincoln ordered General Sheridan to proceed to Mexico with 50,000 Union soldiers. Napoleon promptly ordered the withdrawal of the French forces supporting Maximillian, who unwisely stayed after losing French aid and was executed by the Mexican government.

A Few Major Military Engagements of the Civil War

Fort Sumter (Surrendered April 14, 1861)

Union Major Anderson surrendered to Confederate General **P.G.T. Beauregard**.

The battle of **Fort Sumter** was really more a political maneuver than an armed conflict. The Southern view of federal forts was that the forts went with the states, that is, if a state seceded, the forts automatically belonged to the states. Of course, Lincoln could not accept any such view. Lincoln's Cabinet, including Secretary of State Seward, advised against any attempt to send supplies to Fort Sumter, but, after several days' delay, Lincoln notified South Carolina, on April 6, 1861, that an expedition "with provisions only" was being dispatched to relieve Major Anderson and his garrison. On April 11, South Carolina ordered Major Anderson to surrender; this he was willing to do after his supplies ran out and he then could surrender with honor. But the next day, April 12, Confederate General **Beauregard** opened fire on Fort Sumter and, after a bombardment of about 34 hours, forced the surrender of the Union garrison. There were no casualties.

On April 15, the day after Major Anderson's surrender, President Lincoln called for 75,000 volunteers. On April 17 Virginia seceded, and within a month Arkansas, Tennessee, and North Carolina had joined the Confederacy. Perhaps the greatest blow to follow from Fort Sumter was General **Robert E. Lee's** resignation from the United States Army because, as he put it, "I

have been unable to raise my hand against my native state, my relatives, my children, and my home."

First Bull Run (Manassas Junction) July 21, 1861

Union forces under General McDowell were routed by Generals Thomas J. ("**Stonewall**") **Jackson**, Beauregard, and Joseph E. Johnston.

This battle was fought by Union recruits with not more than three months' training. With cries of "On to Richmond" 30,000 men and boys marched south to Manassas, where they attacked before dawn on July 21. Until midafternoon the Union seemed to be winning, but when Confederate reinforcements arrived, the battle turned into a disorderly rout of the undisciplined raw recruits under McDowell. For over 24 hours Union soldiers straggled back to Washington and, in their retreat, passed civilians driving south in their carriages to see the "fun." The spirit of expectant celebration of any easy victory changed to fear for the safety of Washington.

The Peninsular Campaign (March to July 1862)

McClellan had 110,000 well-trained, well-equipped soldiers ready for battle. By mid-May this Army of the Potomac was within 20 miles of Richmond, and then McClellan waited for reenforcement, which he didn't need. He won battles but failed to press his advantage. On June 26 McClellan found his army seriously threatened by a trap set by General Lee. There followed the Seven Days' Battles in which the Union forces fought superbly and accomplished a retreat from a disadvantageous position. McClellan had saved the Army of the Potomac from capture, a substantial achievement, but hardly the task he had set out to do, namely, capture Richmond. Lincoln was impatient, perhaps disgusted, with McClellan's over-cautious tactics, and McClellan was deeply dissatisfied with Lincoln's withholding reenforcement he though he should have had.

Second Bull Run (Manassas Junction) August 29-30, 1862

Union General John Pope was defeated by Generals Lee and "Stonewall" Jackson.

This was a bad setback for the Union. It cancelled what success the Union had so far in Virginia and posed a serious threat to Washington. Lincoln, without consulting his cabinet, put McClellan back in command on the theory that, in spite of his faults he could win battles.

Antietam (Sharpsburg) September 17, 1862

Union General McClellan defeated Lee.

Had the Confederates won this battle, its forces under Lee would have been in a good position to advance on Washington or Philadelphia. Napoleon III of France was conferring with England about recognizing the independence of the Confederate States of America and proposing an end to the war. Had Lee been the victor and the peace feelers by England and France been rejected, the active intervention by England on behalf of the Confederacy would have been a distinct possibility. In the bloodiest single day's fighting of the war, McClellan's men fought Lee to a draw. The Union forces could have poured in fresh troops to change the result into a decisive victory, but McClellan allowed Lee to withdraw his forces. Casualties were about even, over 2,000 killed and over 9,000 wounded on each side. The fact that McClellan had forced Lee to retreat was overshadowed by the fact that he had failed to capture or to defeat the enemy when the opportunity to do so was excellent. Nevertheless, the stopping of Lee at **Antietam** checked all immediate intention by France and England to propose a peace or to make any official moves toward support of the Confederacy. This repulse of Lee's army gave Lincoln the situation he needed to announce the Emancipation Proclamation, which was to become effective on January 1, 1863. This announcement, made on September 22, 1862, greatly lessened the likelihood of foreign intervention.

Vicksburg (July 4, 1863)

With the surrender of **Vicksburg** to General **Ulysses S. Grant** by the Confederate General, Pemberton, the Union had complete control of the Mississippi River.

Commodore Foote and General Grant started this campaign in the west by taking **Fort Henry** and **Fort Donelson** on the Tennessee and Cumberland rivers respectively. The Union occupied Cairo at the junction of the Ohio and Mississippi rivers, and from there General Pope and Commodore Foote went down the Mississippi and captured Island No. 10. Grant marched south from Fort Donelson to **Shiloh** (Pittsburg Landing), where, in a tough two-day battle on April 6-7,1862, he turned a near defeat into a victory. Union forces held Memphis, Tennessee. From there Grant marched south along the Mississippi, which he crossed to the west bank in order to get south of **Vicksburg**. He then recrossed the Mississippi to the east bank on April 30, 1863, and went northeast until he could approach the Confederate fortress from the rear. The march to Vicksburg from the land side entailed a series of battles over a period of three weeks. Grant's army of 20,000 outfought larger Confederate forces over a distance of about 200 miles in enemy territory, and, on May 22, 1863, the seige of Vicksburg began. The Confederate garrison under Pemberton held out under a brutal bombardment and two major assaults until July 4, when he surrendered with his 30,000 troops who were on the point of mutiny through lack of food. Aside from prisoners, the casualties were about equal, between 9,000 and 10,000. Lincoln had found a general who could win and stick at it until he ran the enemy right into the ground.

While Grant, Foote, and Pope were securing the upper Mississippi River, Admiral Farragut had successfully forced his way by Forts St. Philip and Jackson, which guarded the approach to New Orleans. The next obstacle up the Mississippi, Port Hudson at the northern border of Louisiana, fell to the Union on July 9, 1863, after about a seven weeks' seige. Between Port Hudson and Vicksburg there were no defenses, and the Mississippi was wholly under Union control. The Confederacy was cut in half.

Gettysburg (July 1-4, 1863)

Union General Meade defeated General Lee.

Lee's advance into Pennsylvania was a stab into a Northern state to break the morale of the Union. A victory on Northern soil could greatly increase the influence of the Copperheads and multiply the dissension already breaking out in draft riots. A victory in Pennsylvania could revive the probability of foreign aid for the Confederacy; it could make the task of winning the war appear to the North to be too tough and too long delayed to be worth the sacrifice required. A Confederate victory at **Gettysburg** might have achieved these ends, but it was not to be. Meade took favorable positions and awaited attack. The battles raged for three days, for Gettysburg was a series of engagements on a large battlefield. On July 3, Confederate General Pickett led a massive charge up Cemetery Ridge and failed. Lee maintained his positions until the next day and then withdrew. Confederate soldiers killed totaled about 4,000, and the Union totaled about 3,000.

From Chattanooga to Savannah (May 7 to December 22, 1864)

General **William Sherman** took **Atlanta** and cut a 60-mile-wide swath to Savannah.

In the march from Chattanooga to Atlanta, Sherman's army of about 60,000 was delayed by a series of skirmishes and some real battles, but it was evident that the Union forces were too strong to be stopped. On July 17 Sherman came within eight miles of Atlanta and, after a seige of six weeks, took the city on September 2. After destroying everything of use to the enemy, Sherman left Atlanta for his famous march to the sea. For 300 miles his troops cut a path 60 miles wide in which railroads, bridges, warehouses, many homes, factories, crops, livestock, and any other property that was useful, or took the fancy of the Union troops, was confiscated or destroyed. On December 10, Sherman reached **Savannah**, which he captured on December 22 in time to present to President Lincoln for Christmas.

The Wilderness Campaign and Drive on Richmond (May and June 1864)

Grant forced Lee to surrender at **Appomattox**.

At Culpeper, about 70 miles southwest of Washington and 80 miles northwest of Richmond, Grant had the Army of the Potomac ready to hammer its way, foot by foot, to the Confederate capital. Lee picked the battle sites along his route of retreat. He picked them well and forced Grant to pay dearly, but in numbers and equipment the Union was greatly superior. The gruelling campaign lasted from early May until the middle of June in 1864. Some of the major battles were: The Wilderness (May 4-6), Spotsylvania (May 8-12), Cold Harbor (June 1-3), and the unsuccessful assault on Petersburg (June 15-18). Union losses were twice those of the Confederacy, but the Union could still go on while the Confederacy had spent its strength.

For nine more months Petersburg was under siege. On April 2, 1865, Lee evacuated Petersburg in an attempt to go to Lynchburg, a few miles to the west, but Grant forced his surrender at Appomattox on April 9, 1865.

** Lincoln v. Congress at the End of the Civil War

Lincoln insisted that the Southern states were in rebellion, that they had attempted to secede from the Union, and that they had been prevented from doing so. In December 1863, when it was evident that the question was no longer which side would win but only how long the war could last, Lincoln announced his **reconstruction** plan. The rebelling states must adopt constitutions that forbade slavery, and, in addition, the voters in these states must take an oath of allegiance to the United States. The number of voters required to take the oath of allegiance was to be not less that 10 percent of the number of persons who voted in each state in the election of 1860. This was called Lincoln's **Ten Percent Plan**. Months before the war ended, Tennessee, Arkansas, and Louisiana conformed to this presidential plan, but Congress refused to seat their representatives. To take the view that the Confederate states had seceded would be to give Congress authority to set the pattern for their re-admission, for the Constitution gives to Congress the power to admit states to the Union. But quelling any civil disorder, even a four-year rebellion, is an executive function and, when peace is restored, it is the Chief Executive's proper function to set things in order again. This Lincoln hoped to do.

Lincoln's prestige might have been enough, coupled with his persuasiveness and the inherent wisdom of his program, to have won the political battle. But to stifle the desire for revenge after such a grievous conflict, especially when the spirit of revenge was the obvious method to sustain power for the Republican party, may well have been too great a task for any leader. However, we will never know, for an assassin's bullet killed Lincoln less than a week after Appomattox.

* Homestead Act (1862)

Westward expansion of our population continued during the Civil War. Prospectors were seeking gold and silver, California and Oregon were attracting new settlers, and many were going west to escape the draft. The **Homestead Act** stimulated this westward movement by offering 160 acres to any head of a family. The land was free if it was lived on for five years, or it could be bought at $1.25 an acre after it was lived on for six months. The purpose of the act was frustrated to a degree by land companies and other speculators buying the better lands at $1.25 an acre for resale.

Lincoln's Assassination (April 14, 1865)

On the morning of April 14, five days after Appomattox, there was a Cabinet meeting at which talk turned to the treatment of the rebels. Lincoln opposed any attempt to designate certain rebels as criminals to be hanged. As he put it, "Enough lives have been sacrificed." That evening he went to Ford's Theater with his wife. It was common knowledge in Washington where he would be and what box at the theater the presidential party would occupy. A Washington police officer was on duty to stand guard at the entrance of the presidential box during the play, but he left his post long enough to permit the assassin to enter unnoticed, stand directly behind the President, and fire at very close range into the back of Lincoln's head. This murder was the act of **John Wilkes Booth**, an actor, whose compelling motive seems to have been an intense hatred for Lincoln. After firing the shot, Booth stepped onto the front rail of the box and jumped, but, as he jumped, one foot caught in a flag and he fell to the stage. As he got up he yelled, "Sic semper tyrannis—Virginia is avenged."

On July 7, 1865, three men and a woman were hanged. Mrs. Mary Surratt kept the boarding house where Booth and the other men had frequently met to plot the assassination of Lincoln, Secretary of State Seward, and Vice-President Johnson. Seward was attacked at his home but recovered from a slashed throat, and the attack on Johnson never occurred. It may be that Lincoln would have lost the battle with the Radical Republicans in Congress over the policy of Reconstruction; but, with Andrew Johnson in the White House, there was neither the prestige nor the tact required if the presidential Ten Percent Plan was to prevail.

Andrew Johnson   1865-1869

1808-1875

REPUBLICAN

☆

Secretary of State   W.H. SEWARD

JOHNSON'S PUBLIC SERVICE BEFORE HE BECAME PRESIDENT

Democratic Representative from Tennessee (1843-1853)
Democratic Senator from Tennessee (1857-1862)
Military Governor of Tennessee (1862-1864)
Vice-President in Lincoln's second term (43 days)

MAJOR ITEMS OF JOHNSON'S ADMINISTRATION

Thirteenth Amendment (1865)   *Ku Klux Klan*
Fourteenth Amendment (1868)   *Purchase of Alaska*
Fifteenth Amendment (1870)   *Tenure of Office Act (1867)*
Black Codes   *Johnson's Trial*
Reconstruction Act (1867)

* Unfortunate Political Facts about President Johnson

Andrew Johnson had always been a Democrat, but as a "war Democrat" who had been the only United States Senator from a Confederate state to remain loyal to the Union, he had been put on the "National Union" (Republican) ticket with Lincoln in 1864 to give the party a national flavor. He had separated himself from the Democratic party and was never accepted by the Republican party. Lincoln's Cabinet and the experienced Republican leaders in Congress looked on Johnson as an outsider who was merely the *nominal* head of the party and a President by accident. Congress was determined to reconstruct the South and to run the country, and no one, especially Andrew Johnson, who wasn't really a Republican, was going to stop them. Unfortunately, one of Johnson's few weaknesses was an inability to win people to his views or to work well with others. It was a time that demanded in great abundance the very characteristics that Johnson lacked.

Thirteenth Amendment (1865)

This amendment was necessary to abolish slavery. The **Emancipation Proclamation** of January 1, 1863, applied only to "all persons held as slaves within a state or designated part of a state....in rebellion against the United States..." This left slavery unaffected in the four loyal slave states: Delaware, Maryland, Kentucky, and Missouri. It applied only to rebellious areas that were still beyond the control of the federal government. Only as Union armies occupied Confederate territory were slaves freed under the Emancipation Proclamation. Missouri and Maryland freed their slaves by state law before the Thirteenth Amendment was adopted, but individual state action could not guarantee abolition throughout the nation.

"Neither slavery nor involuntary servitude, except as a punishment for crime whereof the party shall have been duly convicted, shall exist within the United States, or any place subject to their jurisdiction."

Fourteenth Amendment (1868)

This amendment marks the end of the presidential Reconstruction plan and the beginning of congressional control. Its major purpose was to force the South to give equal civil rights to blacks.

1] A citizen was defined so as to include black Americans. "All persons born or naturalized in the United States, and subject to the jurisdiction thereof, are citizens of the United States and of the State wherein they reside."

2] "No State shall make or enforce any law which shall abridge the privileges or immunities of citizens of the United States;..."

3] "Nor shall any State deprive any person of life, liberty, or property, without due process of law;..."

4] "...nor (shall any state) deny to any person within its jurisdiction the equal protection of the laws."

5] If males over twenty-one were not allowed to vote, the state would lose representation in the House in the same proportion it had denied suffrage. This was to punish any state that withheld the vote from its black adults.

6] Any persons who had held a public office requiring an oath of allegiance to the Constitution and then had "broken" that oath by joining the confederate armed forces were not permitted to hold any such public office again.

7] The Confederate debts shall not be paid.

President Johnson was opposed to this Fourteenth Amendment and advised the ex-Confederate states not to ratify it. Only Tennessee quickly ratified it and thus escaped the worst effects of Reconstruction. The legislatures set up in the other ten ex-Confederate states during the summer of 1865 under the presidential Ten Percent Plan rejected the amendment. The Radical Republicans refused recognition to these reorganized state governments and proceeded to draw up the **Reconstruction Act of 1867**. This act stated that there was no legal government in any ex-Confederate state except Tennessee. It then went on to set up the congressional plan of Reconstruction.

Fifteenth Amendment (1870)

"The right of citizens of the United States to vote shall not be denied or abridged by the United States or by any State on account of race, color, or previous condition of servitude."

This amendment was intended to force the states to permit black suffrage.

* Black Codes

After the war, the Southern states tried to restore their former way of life. Southern legislatures passed laws called **black codes** to regulate the lives of the freed slaves. Similar to the "slave codes" in existence before the war, these black codes were not as harsh. They permitted black Southerners a few basic rights, including the right to own property, to marry members of their own race, and to sue and be sued in court. However, they were not allowed to vote, to serve on juries, to assemble unless white Southerners were present, to be on the streets past sunset, or to travel without permits. Moreover, the black codes established white control over black labor by requiring that black Southerners make long-term work contracts with employers, which included apprenticeship regulations that included a provision for harsh punishment if broken. Those without jobs could be arrested and forced to work for the highest bidder. They also prevented black Southerners from starting their own business. The black codes showed that white Southerners intended to keep the newly freed slaves in a subordinate status.

* Reconstruction Act (1867)

The first Reconstruction Act was passed over President Johnson's veto on March 2, 1867. It required each of ten ex-Confederate states to replace its already functioning government, established under the Ten Percent Plan, with another government to be established through a state constitutional convention to which delegates were to be chosen by universal manhood suffrage, except for those leading white citizens who would be disqualified by the terms of the Fourteenth Amendment. When elections were held in accordance with these new state constitutions and representatives were elected to the federal legislature, Congress could then decide whether each candidate was to be allowed to take his seat. Because the state governments believed, as did President Johnson, the Reconstruction Act to be unconstitutional, they stalled and resisted by all means short of violence. The answer of Congress was a series of supplements to the original Reconstruction Act, which were passed in March and July 1867 and July 1868. This was true in the North as well as the South. In fact, this was a period of corruption and poor government throughout the United States.

The ten states (not including Tennessee) were divided into five military districts, with a general in charge of each district. Martial law prevailed.

The state legislatures elected under these new constitutions were led by **scalawags** and **carpetbaggers**. Scalawags were white Southerners who cooperated fully with the Radical Republicans. Carpetbaggers were Northerners who came to the South to become political leaders. Many black legislators were elected to the Reconstruction governments. The state constitutions were well drafted and, in many cases, improvements on the previous ones; but many of these governments were marked by corruption.

It is sometimes pointed out that many carpetbaggers were sincere reformers who went South to try to help in its orderly recovery. There were undoubtedly some scalawags with similar motives. But three factors made their work largely ineffective and certain to be resented by the South. One was the overthrow of the Ten Percent Plan state governments, which were organized and in operation by the fall of 1866. A second factor was the presence of thousands of federal troops in the South. And the third factor was the liberal sprinkling of rogues among the carpetbaggers and scalawags. From the Southern view it was the "crime of Reconstruction" and not the Civil War that was the basis of the long-sustained ill feeling between the North and South.

Ku Klux Klan

The Klan started almost immediately after Appomattox. In the two years between Appomattox and the Reconstruction Acts, its activities were primarily restricted to frightening freedmen away from political activity or any conduct considered a threat to white supremacy. The Klan was only one of the secret societies organized to control blacks in the South. Others were the Knights of the White Camelia and the Order of the White Rose. In the 1860s and 1870s, these secret terrorist societies tried to frighten carpetbaggers, scalawags, and politically active black Southerns out of politics. When warnings failed, they used violence, including whippings and murder.

Purchase of Alaska (1867)

Throughout the early 1800s, the Russians and British competed vigorously in fur hunting and trading in the Bering Sea area. The remoteness of Alaska from European Russia, the difficulties of administering and defending it, and the declining revenue from the fur trade made Russia willing to sell. In 1854, during the Crimean War, and again in 1856 Russia suggested that the United States buy Alaska. In 1867 Secretary of State William H. Seward urged that the purchase be made and Alaska was purchased for $7.2 million. "Seward's Icebox" and "Seward's Folly," like the Louisiana Territory purchased over half a century before, turned out to be another great real estate deal.

** Tenure of Office Act (1867)

By the middle of 1866 it had become clear that President Johnson was very obstinate, even though not skillful, in his fight to maintain the Ten Percent Plan of Reconstruction. Many agreed with him and spoke for his program, but they did not organize any group to put up congressional candidates pledged to their program. The result was that the voters had no real choice in the election of 1866. They could vote for a Democrat or for a Radical Republican. The Democrats were easily pictured as too closely associated with the late rebellion and the black codes were used effectively against them. The Radical Republicans advocated the measures soon to be the Fourteenth and Fifteenth Amendments. With no choice but a Democrat v. a Radical Republican, the result was that the new Congress was overwhelmingly Radical Republican. This Congress overrode Johnson's vetoes, and **Thaddeus Stevens**, chairman of the House delegation on the Joint Committee on Reconstruction, became more powerful than the President. The **Tenure of Office Act** was a deliberate attempt to get rid of Johnson and make the Executive department of the government subservient to the Congress.

The Tenure of Office Act provided that all officials appointed by the President with the advice and consent of the Senate were subject to dismissal only with the consent of the Senate. President Johnson consulted with his Cabinet, all of whom, including Secretary of War Stanton, considered the Tenure of Office Act to be unconstitutional. Johnson accepted this challenge by Congress by dismissing Stanton, who was a staunch supporter of the Radical Republican program. In spite of his own view that the Tenure of Office Act was unconstitutional, Stanton refused to resign as Secretary of War. Johnson, nevertheless, appointed General Lorenzo Thomas to this cabinet post. Now Congress thought they had a case against President Johnson. He had deliberately violated a law of Congress. They drew up eleven charges against him and easily got the required simple majority vote in the House to bring him to trial before the Senate. Thus Johnson was impeached.

Johnson's Trial

By no stretch of the imagination had President Johnson been guilty of any "high Crimes and Misdemeanors," in the phraseology of the Constitution. The whole episode was recognized at the time as a political plot to unseat the President; nevertheless it almost succeeded. At the trial before the Senate the vote was 35 to 19 against Johnson, just one vote shy of the required two-thirds majority. Seven Republican Senators refused to vote against Johnson. The trial had kept the country on edge from March 30 to May 26, 1868. During the last ten months of Johnson's term, the feuding between Congress and the President subsided and the campaign to elect Grant began.

Ulysses S. Grant 1869-1877

1822 -1885

REPUBLICAN

Vice-President SCHUYLER COLFAX
HENRY WILSON

Secretary of State   HAMILTON FISH

GRANT'S PUBLIC SERVICE BEFORE HE BECAME PRESIDENT

Captain in the Mexican War
"Unconditional Surrender" Grant at Forts Henry and Donelson
After Vicksburg and Chattanooga, in supreme command of the Union Army
Forced Lee's surrender at Appomattox

MAJOR ITEMS OF GRANT'S ADMINISTRATIONS

First Transcontinental Railroad (1869)   *Tweed Ring*
Crédit Mobilier   *Panic of 1873*
Whiskey Ring   *"Alabama" Claims (Geneva Tribunal)*

Grant's Elections in 1868 and 1872

During the last week of Johnson's trial before the Senate, the Republican party held its nominating convention in Chicago. The Radical Republicans were in full control and nominated **Ulysses S. Grant** by unanimous vote. The Democrats nominated a colorless candidate, **Horatio Seymour,** who had been governor of New York. Grant won 26 states out of 34. Three states, Virginia, Mississippi, and Texas, had no vote, as they had not yet been readmitted to the Union.

Grant's reelection in 1872 was assured by the vitality still left in the "bloody shirt" attacks by the Republicans, which created the feeling that the Democratic party was to blame for the Civil War. That was still a powerful political handicap for the Democrats. The weakness of the Democrats, rather than the strength of Grant and the Republicans, decided the election.

Anti-Grant Republicans organized as Liberal Republicans and nominated **Horace Greeley,** who was also nominated several weeks later by the Democrats. The only chance the Democrats had of winning was to cut deeply into the Republican vote. The one common factor Greeley shared with the Democrats was his opposition to Grant on the basis of Grant's unsuitability for the presidency and the corruption of his associates. On the tariff issue, Greeley was an extreme protectionist. He had been a Republican from the birth of that party; he had, in fact, named it. He had supported the Civil War as a crusade against slavery rather than as a struggle to preserve the Union. Thus, Greeley had little appeal to Democrats other than that anyone would be better than Grant.

	Popular Vote	*Electoral Vote*
Grant	3,597,070	286
Greeley	2,834,079	66*

*Greeley died Nov. 29, 1872, before the electoral votes were cast, so the six states that had supported him divided their votes among public figures who had not been candidates.

First Transcontinental Railroad 1869

Railroad building was big in many ways. The laying of tracks and building of bridges was a big job; the recruiting of a labor force from all over the United States, from western Europe, and from China was a big job; the feeding and housing of the labor force was a big job; the bringing in of supplies and construction materials was a big job; the difficulties presented by weather, mountains, rivers, deserts, and Native Americans were big; the grants of land and money by the government were big; and the bribery and stealing that marred the railroad building were big.

In 1865 a race began between the **Central Pacific Railroad** (cutting the Pacific coastal area about at the center) and the **Union Pacific Railroad** (forming a union with roads east of the Missouri River and the new road being built from the Pacific Coast). The Central Pacific, building from Sacramento, used thousands of Chinese workers to cut the path through the Rockies and go out across the desert to the Great Salt Lake. This was a tough job with extremes of temperature from far below zero to well over 100 degrees. Blasting through mountains would sometimes keep daily progress measured in yards, while laying track over the prairie or on the salt flats went along at several miles a day. The Union Pacific, employing hordes of Irish laborers, began at Council Bluffs, Iowa, on the east side of the Missouri River directly across from Omaha, Nebraska. On May 10, 1869, the Central Pacific and the Union Pacific met at **Promontory Point, Utah**, and the occasion was marked by driving a gold spike with a silver sledge hammer as the finishing touch to a tremendous achievement.

The building of this first **transcontinental railroad** was early in the period of great industrial expansion that dominated our history between the Civil War and World War I. In the 1860s and 1870s the maximum of individual freedom and the minimum of government control was the ideal generally accepted as the natural and proper way of life. It was called *laissez faire*.

The railroads received aid from the government in the form of subsidies and gifts. Even before the Civil War, considerable land had been given for turnpikes, canals, and railroads. Any transportation routes that aid commerce are also actual or potential assets for postal and military uses. In the case of the Union Pacific and Central Pacific, the land grants totaled about 44 million acres and the loans about $64 million. In the desire to attract railroads to build through their states, legislatures offered tax concessions, land and funds in an effort to outbid neighboring states. The simple fact is that railroads could not have been built without very substantial government aid. In the United States, railroads were extended through vast areas of almost uninhabited land. There could be no profits from freight rates and pas-

senger fares until towns and farm communities developed along the railroads, and that would take years. The early income for these pioneering railroads came from the sale of land at attractive rates to settlers. The early railroads were in the real estate business, the cattle business, the grain business, and they either controlled or sought to control the federal Congress, state legislatures, and city councils.

* Crédit Mobilier (krā de mō blē ā)

In 1864 some of the larger stockholders of the Union Pacific Railroad formed the **Crédit Mobilier**, a corporation to finance and construct the Union Pacific. The Crédit Mobilier sold supplies and construction materials at exorbitant prices to the Union Pacific. It took on contracts for a multitude of individual jobs as part of building the Union Pacific and received outrageously high fees. The graft, in a variety of forms, resulted in the Union Pacific's paying fraudulently excessive prices and fees, while the profits rolled into the coffers of the Crédit Mobilier. Congressman Oakes Ames of Massachusetts was the agent for Crédit Mobilier who sold, or gave, its lucrative stock to key Senators and Representatives who would use their influence to see that Congress extended favors to the Union Pacific. Ames's double duty was to get all he could from the government and to prevent any investigation of Crédit Mobilier. But investigation did begin after the New York *Sun* reported the scandal on September 4, 1872, and it continued through February of the next year. Vice-President Colfax resigned and Representative Ames received a vote of censure from the House.

* Whiskey Ring

The **Whiskey Ring** started in St. Louis and spread to other cities. General John McDonald, supervisor of the Internal Revenue Department in St. Louis, headed the conspiracy to defraud the government. The scheme was simple. Revenue officials allowed distillers to sell a portion of their output without paying the tax thereon. For example, a distiller was allowed to pay $5,000 less in taxes than the law required if he would pay $3,000 to the revenue officials. The distiller saved $2,000 while the tax collectors got $3,000; the United States Treasury lost $5,000. Those business owners who were reluctant to enter into such a conspiracy were pressured into it by threats of harassment by revenue officials. The result was that, between the desire to dodge taxes and to avoid harassment, the whiskey fraud was widespread and involved huge sums of money. Some officials of the Treasury Department were part of the conspiracy and sought protection for their "racket" by contributing handsomely to campaign funds for the reelection of Grant in 1872. Grant's private secretary, General O. E. Babcock, supervised the ring's activities from Washington, and the chief clerk of the Treasury Department was on the payroll of the gang to warn of any moves that might be made toward investigation. In April 1875 the Secretary of the Treasury, Benjamin H. Bristow, sent agents secretly to St. Louis. Distillery records were seized, which exposed the whole mess.

* Tweed Ring

"Boss" **William M. Tweed** was the Grand Sachem of Tammany Hall, the Democratic Club of New York City. Since his day, any political organization referred to as a *machine* controlled by a *boss* brings forth a picture of corruption. That Tweed so affected the public mind is explained by two factors: the effectiveness of the Tammany organization with the gigantic stealing it accomplished, and the cartoons drawn by **Thomas Nast** in *Harper's Weekly* picturing Tammany Hall as a tiger. The loot collected by Tweed and his ring came from contracts for goods and services purchased by the city and from all types of organized vice and illegal activities by which money could be made. Companies selling goods or services to the city were told to add from 10 to 100 percent, and sometimes much more, to the legitimate price when they presented their bills. The companies would get a fair price, and the ring would get the extra 10 to 100 percent or much more. The Tweed Ring flourished in the late 1860s and the early 1870s. It was Nast's cartoons that made the general public resent the Ring's activities.

The total stolen by the Tweed Ring from New York City in about six years has been estimated at about $200 million. After the Tweed Ring was exposed by the *Times* and Nast, William M. Tweed fled to Spain, where he was apprehended and returned for trial to New York City. The onetime millionaire was without friends or funds and died in a city jail in 1878.

Panic of 1873

The Panic was precipitated by the failure in September 1873, of Jay Cooke & Company of Philadelphia, the most famous and presumably the strongest financial institution in the United States. It had put too much of its funds in the development of the Northern Pacific Railroad. Overextension of credit, the prevalence of fraud in both government and private business, and thousands of investors using money for speculative ventures rather than productive purposes combined to create an economic situation destined to collapse. Western agriculture had overextended to supply a European market, which faded away with the end of the Franco-Prussian War. European business was in the doldrums and increased the severity of the depression in the United States. From 20,000 to 25,000 enterprises failed in the three years following the bankruptcy of Jay Cooke & Co. Hundreds of thousands of workers were unemployed and roamed the country in search of nonexistent jobs. Farmers and factory workers bore the brunt of the hardships. Under the pressure of the depression, organized labor fell from a membership of about 300,000 to about 50,000. The most violent event of the depression was the railroad strike of 1877 which tied up the main northern roads from the Atlantic seaboard to the Mississippi River. The scene of greatest violence was Chicago. This strike started when four railroads in the east cut wages at the same time. In about six years, the depression had run its course and economic recovery set in.

* "Alabama" Claims (Geneva Tribunal) (1869-1872)

One of the last acts of Secretary of State William H. Seward was to start negotiations with England in an attempt to recover damages caused during the Civil War by the commerce raiders *Alabama, Florida,* and *Shenandoah.* By 1871, Secretary of State Hamilton Fish was able to reach an agreement with England to submit the issue to any international tribunal for arbitration. The tribunal consisted of representatives from Brazil, Italy, and Switzerland. The findings of the tribunal were that England had clearly violated international law by permitting the construction of the commerce raiders in British shipyards, even though they were sent elsewhere to be completed. The United States was awarded $15 million, a sum somewhat in excess of the actual property damage caused by the raiders. The most significant result of the diplomacy of Secretary of State Hamilton Fish was the signing of the Treaty of Washington in 1871, by which England and the United States agreed to settle disputes over fisheries, boundaries, and the *Alabama* by arbitration.

Rutherford B. Hayes   1877-1881

1822-1893

REPUBLICAN

☆

Vice-President   WILLIAM A. WHEELER

HAYES' PUBLIC SERVICE BEFORE HE BECAME PRESIDENT

Governor of Ohio for Three Terms

MAJOR ITEMS OF HAYES' ADMINISTRATION

Bland-Allison Act (1878)
Indian Wars

** Election of Hayes (1876)

By 1876 the "bloody shirt" technique had lost most of its effectiveness, and the corruption prevalent during the past ten years made Republican prospects seem dim. Their party was split between the Liberal Republicans who had supported Greeley in 1872 and the regulars who had reelected Grant. Those who had backed Grant now wanted **James G. Blaine. Rutherford B. Hayes**, three times governor of Ohio, got the nomination on the seventh ballot.

The Democrats nominated **Samuel J. Tilden** of New York, who had won a reputation as a reform Democrat. As state chairman he forced the removal from office of corrupt judges in New York City, and later, when elected governor of New York in 1874, he played a major role in destroying the Tweed Ring. Tilden was a strong candidate well calculated to carry the Democratic party into the presidency for the first time since the Civil War. But it was not to be.

Tilden carried the Northern states of New York, New Jersey, Connecticut, and Indiana. Having made this inroad into Republican territory, it was assumed that he had the election. But three Southern states — Florida, Louisiana, and South Carolina—sent in two sets of electoral votes, one favoring the Democrats and the other favoring the Republicans. Widespread fraud by both parties was apparent in these states. Not counting the electoral votes of these states, Tilden had 184 votes, one short of the simple majority required for election—185. There were no constitutional provisions for handling this situation, so Congress had to improvise a solution.

An Electoral Commission of fifteen members was created. It was composed of five Senators (three Republicans and two Democrats), five Representatives (three Democrats and two Republicans), and five judges of the Supreme Court (two Republicans and two Democrats, with a fifth judge to be chosen by these four). The Electoral Commission was thus formed of eight Republicans and seven Democrats, and right down the line of the disputed states, that is the way they voted. Hayes won by 185 to 184. In popular vote, Tilden won by over 250,000. That this vote by the Electoral Commission was tolerated is explained by the bargain the Southern Democrats were willing to make. They were more anxious to get rid of federal troops stationed in their states than they were concerned about the presidency. In return for accepting the findings of the Electoral Commission, pledges were made and kept to withdraw federal troops from the South, to make substantial federal appropriations for railroads in the South, and to appoint a Southerner to a Cabinet post. The decision of the Electoral Commission was not made until March 2, 1877, only two days before Hayes took office.

This election marked the end of the Reconstruction. With federal troops out of the South, the black Southerners were soon frightened out of public affairs. The Fourteenth and Fifteenth Amendments were largely ignored, and black Americans in the South were disenfranchised.

	Popular Vote	Electoral Vote
Hayes	4,033,950	185
Tilden	4,284,757	184

Bland-Allison Act (1878)

Ever since the Civil War, the demand had been for more greenbacks. The farmers as a class, and especially those of the South and West, were for cheap money because it raised the prices of farm products, resulted in easy credit, and favored debtors. During the early 1870s several European nations went off the bimetallic (gold and silver) standard onto the gold standard. The United States, by the Coinage Act of 1873, stopped coining silver dollars and thus went on the gold standard. During the 1860s and early 1870s, no one wished to sell silver to the government because the market price was higher than the 16-to-1 ratio the government paid for silver. But when the new deposits of silver found in Nevada, Colorado, and Utah hit the market in the middle 1870s, the increased supply drove the market price down, and there was a rush to sell silver to the government at 16 to 1. Then the knowledge that the United States was no longer buying silver for coinage purposes resulted in an angry cry of "The crime of 73."

With silver now a political issue, it made sense for the Greenbackers to shift their support to a demand for the unlimited coinage of silver at the ratio of 16 to 1. By doing so, the farmers and laborers would join with the silver-mine interests and greatly increase their political power; they would add some numbers to their cause and a great deal of money to promote lobbying. It was much less frightening to the conservatives to contemplate free coinage of silver than the unlimited printing of greenbacks, for silver did have obvious substance and value and was more convincing than a government promise that might be broken. Richard Bland of Missouri introduced a bill in the House providing for unlimited (free) coinage of silver at the ratio of 16 to 1. In the Senate the bill was amended by Allison of Iowa to limit the government's purchase of silver at the market price to not less than $2 million or more than $4 million worth per month. The bill passed over President Hayes' veto. The government purchased the minimum amount each month, and the inflationary effect was unnoticeable. Agitation continued for more cheap money until a second silver purchase act was passed in 1890.

Indian Wars

Ever since Congress enacted the "Indian Removal Bill" in 1830, and forced Native Americans off their prosperous farmlands in the Southeast (p. 115), white/Indian relations worsened. As white settlers moved relentlessly westward after the Civil War, Indians living in one place were driven to another. Each new location provided them with less land than the previous one. Railroaders, cattle ranchers, miners, and eventually farmers swarmed over land that had been given to the Indians by treaty "so long as the grass shall grow and the rivers shall flow." Statistics reveal one aspect of Indian extermination: of the millions of Indians who had lived there when Columbus arrived, only some 250,000 remained in the United States by 1860.

In desperation, the western Indians fought back, starting with an 1862 Sioux uprising in Minnesota. The U.S. cavalry and the buffalo hunters helped destroy the Indians' way of life. In 1890 the last resisting tribe, the Dakotas, fought their last battle at Wounded Knee. The survivors of all tribes were herded onto Indian reservations where many remain today, mostly in poverty.

James A. Garfield

1881
Mar. 4 to Sept. 19

1831-1881

REPUBLICAN

☆

Vice-President   CHESTER A. ARTHUR

Secretary of State   JAMES G. BLAINE

GARFIELD'S PUBLIC SERVICE BEFORE HE BECAME PRESIDENT

> *Member of the Ohio Senate*
> *General in the Civil War*
> *Distinguished Service at Shiloh and Chickamauga*
> *United States Senator from Ohio (1880)*

Garfield's Election (1880)

The wing of the party known as Radical Republicans during the Reconstruction era was pretty much the same group now known as "Stalwarts." In 1880 they wished to nominate former President Grant. But on the 36th ballot, the reform faction won out at the convention and nominated **James A. Garfield**, a Civil War General with a good military record. To keep party unity during the election, Chester Arthur, a Stalwart choice, was accepted as the vice-presidential candidate. The Democrats nominated **General Winfield Hancock** of Pennsylvania, whose Civil War record was excellent, and the **Greenback Labor party** put up **General James Weaver**. Aside from the fact that the Republicans advocated a protective tariff and the Democrats favored a revenue tariff, there was no significant difference between the two major parties. It was a close election in the popular vote, but a comfortable margin of victory for Garfield in the electoral vote.

	Popular Vote	Electoral Vote
Garfield	4,449,053	214
Hancock	4,442,030	155
Weaver	308,578	0

On July 2, 1881, Garfield was shot by C. Julius Guiteau, a mentally unstable and disappointed government job seeker. The attack occurred at the Washington railway station. President Garfield died on September 19. The assassination aroused the public and made them aware of the problem of the spoils system.

Chester A. Arthur   1881-1885

1830-1886

REPUBLICAN

ARTHUR'S PUBLIC SERVICE BEFORE HE BECAME PRESIDENT

Quartermaster General of New York during the Civil War
Collector of Customs Duties at the Port of New York

MAJOR ITEMS OF ARTHUR'S ADMINISTRATION

* *Pendleton Act (1883)*
A Steel Navy Started

* Pendleton Act (1883)

After Chester Arthur took office he proved to be an able administrator with a constructive program. Perhaps it was the responsibility of the presidency and the shock of Garfield's assassination that persuaded Arthur to sponsor civil service reform. For years a Civil Service Reform League had advocated a **merit system** for the selection of public employees, and when Senator George Pendleton of Ohio introduced a bill including this principle, it received full support from the President. Congress passed the **Pendleton Act,** which set up a three person **Civil Service Commission** to implement the act. Some of the provisions were:

1] Competitive examinations must be given to determine which candidates merit the government positions.

2] Federal officeholders cannot be forced to contribute to campaign funds or dismissed from office for refusing to contribute.

3] A list of federal positions was drawn up to which the law would apply, and the President was empowered to add to this list at his discretion.

4] In the granting of government jobs, attention was to be given to apportioning them among the several states according to their population.

The Pendleton Act covered about 15,000 jobs, or about 12 percent of the civilian employees of the federal government. It was a good beginning, even though it made only a small dent in the total spoils system. States were encouraged to create merit systems of their own, and the lists of jobs under the merit systems, both state and federal, have been growing ever since.

A Steel Navy Started

The engagement of the *Monitor* and the ironclad *Merrimac* (Virginia) had clearly announced that all wooden navies were obsolete. Yet this historic Civil War naval battle of 1862 had not stirred Congress, or any President, to rebuild our Navy. In 1882 we had a puny Navy, which ranked twelfth among the nations. President Arthur pushed for a steel Navy, and Congress went along to the extent of starting construction on the steel cruisers *Chicago* and *Boston*. The first step had been made toward bringing the United States into the position as a leading naval power.

Grover Cleveland   1885-1889

1837-1908

DEMOCRAT

☆

Vice-President   THOMAS A. HENDRICKS

CLEVELAND'S PUBLIC SERVICE BEFORE HE BECAME PRESIDENT

Assistant District Attorney of Erie County, New York
Sheriff of Erie County, New York
Mayor of Buffalo, New York
Governor of New York

MAJOR ITEMS OF CLEVELAND'S FIRST ADMINISTRATION

Mills Bill and the Surplus
Major Social Changes
Labor Unions
Knights of Labor

Haymarket Riot
Granges and Granger Laws
Interstate Commerce Act (1887)

* Cleveland's Election (1884)

This campaign was a noisy, nasty contest in personal abuse. One could say that Civil Service reform, tariff, and monopolies were the issues of the day; but the oratory of the campaign and the interest of the voters were directed at the two candidates, **James G. Blaine** ("The Plumed Knight") and Grover Cleveland ("Grover the Good"). They were the real issue. Blaine personified loyalty to the Republican party organization. He had been one of the first supporters of Lincoln. As early as 1854, he edited the Kennebunk (Maine) *Journal*, which was the first paper in the East to declare itself to be Republican. He had been Speaker of the House, and for over a dozen years his "bloody shirt" orations had served his party well. Under Garfield he had served a brief term as Secretary of State. But there were thoughtful Republicans among the leaders of the party and the nation who would not accept Blaine's leadership. They would not overlook scandals associated with his Speakership in the House. They included James Russell Lowell, the New England poet, Henry

Ward Beecher, the noted Brooklyn preacher, Charles Francis Adams, our able ambassador to England during the Civil War, and Carl Schurz, who had persuaded Lincoln of the necessity of an emancipation proclamation. In derision, the Stalwart Republicans backing Blaine called the reform Republicans "Mugwumps." The Democrats nominated Grover Cleveland on the second ballot. He was fully acceptable to the Mugwumps, and with the split in the Republican party, the Democrats were headed for the presidency. Cleveland's public life as district attorney of Erie County, as sheriff, as mayor of Buffalo, and as Governor of New York had been marked by economy, honesty, courage, and common sense.

	Popular Vote	Electoral Vote
Cleveland	4,911,017	219
Blaine	4,848,334	182

The returns showed clearly that the Mugwumps had put Cleveland in office. The New York State vote was

151

so close that Cleveland won by less than 1,200 votes out of a total of about 1.25 million. This close victory in a key state was bought about late in the campaign by a prejudice-loaded remark at an interview Blaine held with a group of Republican clergy. The Reverend Dr. Samuel Burchard described the Democratic party as one "whose antecedents have been rum, Romanism, and rebellion." Blaine was convinced that Burchar's three "R's" had cost him the election.

* Mills Bill and the Surplus

Tariff reform was the one message in Cleveland's "State of the Union" speech to Congress in 1887. He pointed out that the government had been collecting more in taxes than was required to meet government expenses and that the largest single source of revenue was the tariff. An annual surplus of about $100 million had piled up in the Treasury for about seven years and was still growing. This Cleveland considered intolerable. As he expressed it, "Our present tariff laws, the vicious, inequitable, and illogical source of unnecessary taxation, ought to be at once revised and amended."

Cleveland was not a theorist on tariff; he merely used his common sense. The result of this approach, as he saw it, was that protective tariffs were good in some instances, and the rates should then be only as high as needed. He felt that there was a strong tendency for manufacturers to exaggerate their need for protection and to combine to maintain excessive prices and profits. Both parties agreed that a tax cut was called for in view of the surplus in the Treasury; their point of disagreement was how to do it. Cleveland took the position that lowering the tariff and putting some goods on the "free" list was the method that would best serve the nation, while the Republicans took the position that tariff revision was the one approach that they would not accept. The **Mills Bill,** incorporating Cleveland's ideas on tariff revision, passed the House but could not get through the Senate. While most Republicans opposed the Mills Bill and most Democrats favored it, the two parties were split on the issue. The Mills Bill failed to become law, and the surplus was larger than ever as Cleveland's first administration ended.

Major Social Changes

From the Civil War to the beginning of the 20th century, the United States changed from a basically agricultural to a largely industrial nation. The population more than doubled between 1860 and 1900, from 32 million to 76 million. During that time, the size of the working class soared; they were engaged in railroad building, mining, construction, and manufacturing. People who had been raised on family farms or in small towns became indus-

trial workers performing the same monotonous tasks for many hours at a stretch. Wages for unskilled labor were as low as two to three dollars a week, and child labor was common in all industrialized countries. Coal mines and textile factories were dangerous places to work, and accidents on the job were frequent.

Labor Unions

As factories in the cities grew in size, and the owners and managers grew in wealth, the distance between employers and employees also grew. The workers' problems of low wages, long hours (often ten hours a day, six days a week), unsafe working conditions, and seasonal unemployment were no longer of personal concern to the "bosses" as they had been in a smaller and earlier workshop setting.

Workers sought to improve their ability to bargain for better wages and working conditions by forming labor unions. The first successful national labor organization was the Knights of Labor, organized by **Uriah P. Stephens.** Members were recruited in secret because employers usually fired anyone suspected of being in a union.

* Knights of Labor

The **Knights of Labor** reached their peak of power in 1886. In the previous year they had won a strike against the Southwest Railroad System when their Grand Master, **Terence V. Powderly,** met with the financier Jay Gould and arranged terms of settlement favorable to the Knights. This marked labor's first collective bargaining. The prestige from this first instance of the representative of a union meeting with a representative of industry resulted in a mushroom growth in the membership of the Knights of Labor to a peak of about 700,000. This union tried to bring all workers together in one big union. It included skilled and unskilled workers, blacks and whites, men and women, white-collar workers and manual laborers. The program of the Knights of Labor was political as well as economic. Their demands included a graduated income tax, abolition of child labor, temperance, consumers' and producers' cooperatives, and an eight-hour day. To gain their aims they favored boycotts and arbitration in preference to strikes.

* Haymarket Riot

A general strike was planned for May 1, 1886, in which all workers were urged to quit their jobs and hold meetings demanding an eight-hour day. Over 300,000 workers attended meetings throughout the

United States, but after the first day the protest fizzled out. The revolutionary character of a general strike aroused fear and hostility, which hurt labor's cause. At the time there was a prolonged strike going on at the McCormick Harvester Company in Chicago. On May 3, police fired into a group of strikers assembled for picket duty. One striker was killed and others were wounded. The next day, May 4, a meeting was held at **Haymarket Square** to protest the police brutality of the previous day. Anarchists, socialists, strikers, indignant citizens, and the simply curious formed a crowd of about 3,000. The meeting was orderly and uninteresting at first. Later, speakers were violent in their opposition to "law and order," which they claimed was loaded against them. The police decided to disperse the meeting. As they moved in from the fringe of the crowd, someone threw a dynamite bomb that killed 7 and wounded 66 police officers. The police charged the crowd with police revolvers taking an even larger toll then the bomb. Public opinion went violently against the unions.

A roundup of anarchists, socialists, and labor leaders followed. Eight men were convicted. Judge Joseph E. Gary of the Cook County Criminal Court of Chicago informed the jury that anyone who had said or written anything that might incite the throwing of a bomb was equally guilty with the person who actually threw it. The eight men found guilty were anarchists and labor organizers. Some of them had not been at the Haymarket meeting, but under the judge's ruling, that made no difference. On appeal to higher courts, this strange procedure was confirmed and four men were hanged. One committed suicide in jail, and the other three had the death sentence commuted to life imprisonment. Six years later the newly elected governor of Illinois, John P. Altgeld, pardoned these three men on the ground that their trail had been unfair because of the "malicious ferocity" with which Judge Gary had conducted the case.

Although the Knights of Labor as an organization played no part in the May Day general strike, and its president, Powderly, called those responsible for the bomb throwing at Haymarket Square "cowardly murderers," the first week in May of 1886 was a sorry one for organized labor. In the public mind, union members were anarchists, as view encouraged by the press and used by management to fight the organization of labor. The Knights of Labor declined rapidly, and before 1890 had, for all practical purposes, ceased to exist.

It would be slowly replaced by the American Federation of Labor, started in 1886.

** Granges and Granger Laws

The big post-Civil War depression hit in 1873, but the distress of the farmers was real as early as 1867. In President Johnson's administration the Agriculture Department, following the advice of **Oliver H. Kelley**, helped the farmers organized the **Patrons of Husbandry.** The local units were called **Granges** and their program was social and economic. Women were encouraged to be members, and monthly meetings at which food, entertainment, lectures, and general sociability prevailed, helped mightily to dispel the effects of the loneliness and hard work of farm life. Of course, both farm women and farm men talked shop and shared their experiences concerning home and farm problems. Outside speakers would inform the Granges on handling mortgages, credit, crop rotation, seed selection, fertilizers, livestock, and hundreds of other practical matters.

With the Granges well-established, it was inevitable that local officeholders, especially the elected ones, would cultivate the Granges, and that the Granges would invite members of the state legislatures to address their meetings. In short, the Granges became political as well as social and economic clubs. The way to get elected to office in a farm community was to be well-known and well-liked by the Grangers; they had the votes.

In the economic field the Granges organized cooperatives. The Grangers sometimes bought livestock, fertilizer, farm tools and machines, and supplies collectively, which saved substantial amounts for the individual farmers. They formed insurance companies, creameries, general stores, warehouses, and even factories to build farm machinery. Most of the more specialized businesses, such as the factories, succeeded for a short time only, as inexpert management and inadequate financing often led to failure.

The political activity of the Granges in the 1870s and 1880s was concerned with railroads. While cities such as Chicago and New York were served by more than one railroad, almost all rural areas were completely dependent on one railroad. This monopoly situation led to many abuses. Railroad rate-fixing followed the principle of charging "all the traffic will bear." Where railroads competed, rates were low; where a railroad had a monopoly, rates were high. Rather than not market their crops farmers would pay exorbitant freight rates. Railroads built storage bins, or grain elevators, at the side of the tracks, and the farmers could store their grain as they harvested it. The charges for the use of these elevators were often very high. These problems were taken to the state legislatures through the Granges. The Illinois legislature passed laws regulating rates and other charges made by the railroads. Several other states did the same during the 1870s. These state laws were challenged in the courts.

The first test case was *Munn* v. *Illinois* in 1876. The state law fixed a maximum rate for the storage of grain in warehouses and elevators. The law was challenged on the basis that it violated the clause in the Fourteenth

Amendment that reads, "...no State shall deprive any person of life, liberty, or property, without the due process of law..." the Supreme Court ruled that whenever private property was used in a manner that clothed it with a public interest, it ceased to be only private property and was therefore subject to regulation by government. The use of storage warehouses and elevators where hundreds of farmers store grain in order to market it clothed such storage facilities with an obvious public interest and brought them within the regulatory powers of the state. The Illinois law fixing a maximum charge for the storage of grain was constitutional and valid. A second ruling in this case took notice of the fact that grain was sometimes part of interstate commerce and that the state law would, in some instances, have an indirect effect on interstate commerce. But as the effect was *indirect* and the federal government *was not exercising* its right to regulate interstate commerce, there was not interference with or encroachment on federal authority. This ruling by the Supreme Court was soon substantially modified by the *Wabash* v. *Illinois* decision in 1886.

In the Wabash case the Illinois law had fixed freight rates within the state for the purpose of preventing a common abuse that set higher rates for short hauls than for much longer hauls. The Supreme Court ruled that to regulate railroad rates within a state did in fact regulate rates throughout the continuous journey through the several states. If individual states could fix rates within their borders, they could create confusion that would make it utterly impossible to operate railroads. If they could regulate rates, they could regulate safety devices, size of railroad crews, construction of cars, and an infinite number of other matters that come under the police powers of any state dealing with purely *intrastate* commerce. The Supreme Court declared unconstitutional and void the rate-fixing laws of Illinois. This decision did not actually contradict the *Munn* v. *Illinois* case, but it did make it impossible for states to deal effectively with many real railroad abuses. This decision took the steam out of the political activities of the Granges. By the late 1880s, the Granges had decreased substantially in membership and had settled back into social activities and mutual self-help.

** The Interstate Commerce Act (1887)

After several futile attempts to pass legislation dealing with the railroads, Congress passed the **Interstate Commerce Act.**

Its passage was demanded by public resentment over railroad abuses and by the Wabash decision that made state laws unable to cope with the situation. The act set up an **Interstate Commerce Commission** (ICC) to enforce the terms of the law.

1] The Interstate Commerce Commission would have five members appointed by the President with the advise and consent of the Senate. Each commissioner would serve six years with the terms so arranged that only one commissioner's term expired in any one year. No more than three commissioners could belong to the same political party, and they could have no other employment while serving on the commission.

2] All charges by the railroads had to be reasonable and just.

3] No special preference or advantage could be extended by the railroads to any one using their services. Secret rebates, drawbacks, or other devices extending such special advantages were illegal.

4] Pooling was forbidden.

5] No more could be charged for a short haul than for a long haul over the same road in the same direction.

6] Schedules of rates, fares, and charges had to be published and posted. No changes could be made without ten days' notice.

7] Railroads had to use an accounting system that was uniform and met with the approval of the I.C.C.

Pooling was usually an agreement among two or more railroads to charge the same rates in an area, such as New York or Chicago, to avoid competition in passenger, freight, and other charges. Business would then go to the railroad on the basis of convenience to the passengers or shippers rather than on the basis of the cost of the service. Every month, or some other agreed-upon interval, the railroads involved would divide among themselves the revenue taken during the period. The division would be in accordance with the terms of the pooling arrangement and would be based on the volume of traffic each road had carried in that area in the past. Of course, the common rates set for such pools would be high. Such pooling schemes did prevent "cut-throat" competition among railroads, that is, selling services below cost in order to drive another road into bankruptcy. If the rate set by a pooling agreement was "fair and just," much could be said in its favor. But the almost certain result of pooling was excessive rates; hence the legal provision against it.

The ICC was not a success. Its ineffectiveness was due to the commission's lack of power to make the railroads obey its orders. Railroads could challenge the orders of the ICC in the courts and, in the meantime, continue the abuses the ICC was trying to correct. The burden of proof was on the ICC: it had to show that its orders were just and reasonable. After almost 20 years of ineffectiveness, the ICC had life breathed into it by the Hepburn Bill of 1906.

The very real significance of the Interstate Commerce Act lies in the fact that it was the first federal law to regulate a major private business. It marked a shift from the conviction that government must not interfere with private business to the reluctant admission that some private business was unavoidably an important factor in the public welfare and that government must therefore exercise substantial regulation over it. The Interstate Commerce Act of 1887 was the first big step in this new direction. Three years later the Sherman Antitrust Act was the second step.

Benjamin Harrison   1889-1893

1833-1901

REPUBLICAN

Vice-President   LEVI P. MORTON
Secretary of State   JAMES G. BLAINE

HARRISON'S PUBLIC SERVICE BEFORE HE BECAME PRESIDENT

Officer in the Civil War (Indiana Regiment)
United State Senator from Indiana 1881-1887

MAJOR ITEMS OF HARRISON'S ADMINISTRATION

Foreign Policy Under Blaine   *McKinley Tariff and Sherman Silver Act*
Six States Enter the Union   *Navy and Coast Defenses*
Sherman Antitrust Act (1890)   *Populist Party Platform of 1892*

Harrison's Election (1888)

The Democrats nominated **President Grover Cleveland** for a second term. The Republicans nominated **Benjamin Harrison**, grandson of President William Henry Harrison. The major issue of the campaign was the tariff. The Republicans advocated a high protective tariff, and Cleveland continued his fight for a tariff such as the Mills Bill he had tried to put through during the previous two years. Harrison carried his home state of Indiana, which, with New York, was a key state in this election.

	Popular Vote	Electoral Vote
Harrison	5,444,337	233
Cleveland	5,540,050	168

Without winning the popular vote, Harrison had won the election by 65 electoral votes.

** Foreign Policy under Secretary of State Blaine

Blaine was an aggressive Secretary of State in his attitude toward other nations and, perhaps because of this, popular with the American people. With some unnecessary blustering and, at times, extreme demands, Blaine achieved satisfactory results for the United States in his handling of incidents with Germany, England, Italy, and Chile.

Samoan Islands

In the early 1870s the United States made an agreement with the native government of the Samoan Islands, which gave us control of the harbor of Pago Pago on the island of Tutuila. Here we had a naval base and a coaling station. Germany and England had similar agreements in this island group. American whalers had stopped frequently at the Samoan Islands as early as the 1830s, and American missionaries had established themselves there. The three powers, the United States, England, and Germany, suspected each other of seeking favor with the native government to the detriment of the other two. Finally, in 1889 Germany made a move to push the United States and England off the islands, and a tense situation developed when warships of the three powers were anchored in the harbor at Apia at the island of Upolu. A hurricane settled the issue by wrecking all the ships in the harbor. After talking the problem over, England agreed to withdraw from the Samoan Islands in exchange for German territory in Africa, and the United States and Germany made a peaceful division of the islands between them. This was our first venture into international agreements about a place far from our shores involving a people of quite different culture.

Bering Sea

The Bering Sea dispute between the United States and Great Britain began soon after we purchased Alaska from Russia in 1867. When Russia owned both Siberia and Alaska, the Bering Sea was considered a closed sea belonging to Russia. But when the Bering Sea had Russian Siberia on one side and American Alaska on the other, the status of the Bering Sea was less clear. We had made laws restricting the killing of seals along the Alaskan coast and had established the months of June to October as the only time of the year when hunting seals was legal. We maintained that the Bering Sea was still a *mare clausum* and that it belonged to us. Great Britain ignored our claims to the Bering Sea, and Canadian sealers were depleting the seals to a point threatening extermination. Blaine took decisive action by having several Canadian ships seized by our revenue cutters. Britain complained and we continued to seize Canadian ships. In 1891 it was agreed that the dispute would be submitted to arbitration. As a result, the Bering Sea was declared an open sea with the usual three-mile limit for territorial waters adjacent to Alaska, including the Aleutian Islands. But, more important, an international agreement accepted the regulation of hunting seals so that the severe threat of their extermination was removed.

Reciprocity with Latin America

Blaine achieved a high degree of statesmanship when he initiated and worked for closer trade relations between the United States and the nations of Central and South America. Blaine's purpose was to expand the volume of trade between the United States and the nations to the south of us. Their products were, for the most part, foodstuffs and other raw materials unavail-

able in the United States. Latin American nations were buying almost all of their imports from European countries. We levied tariffs on a few of their products, but most of their noncompetitive items came into the United States duty-free. Blaine proposed that we tell them that we would levy tariffs on their products unless they removed the tariffs against our exports to them. While Blaine was a protective tariff advocate for the east-west trade in competitive items between the United States and Europe, he wanted free trade, or an approximation to it, for the north-south trade in noncompetitive items between the United States and Latin America. Blaine did not call his program free trade; he called it reciprocity in tariffs. If Latin America would let United States' exports in with very low duties, or no duty at all, we would do the same for their products. It was Blaine's hope that the United States would replace Europe as the chief supplier of manufactured goods for Latin America; he thought geography invited such an economic community of interests and that our position as a great power demanded it. When Blaine again became Secretary of State under President Benjamin Harrison, 1889-93, he got his first Pan-American Congress at Washington. Eighteen nations had delegates at the conference, but little progress was made. The United States was so big and so advanced economically, compared to the Latin American republics, that they shied away from commitments.

Six States Enter the Union

North Dakota, South Dakota, Montana, and Washington entered the Union in 1889 and Idaho and Wyoming in 1890. These "omnibus states" with twelve Senators and six Representatives made a political prize worth a political price. The Republican party paid the price; it gave support for silver legislation in return for support for the McKinley Tariff.

** Sherman Antitrust Act 1890

Several states had passed anti-monopoly legislation, and public opinion was aroused to the need for some controls far more effective than any yet available. Even though Harrison's administration was extremely friendly to business, it was crystal clear that the voters demanded antitrust legislation. So, with more reluctance than enthusiasm, the Republican Congress formulated the **Sherman Antitrust Act**. It was passed by an almost unanimous vote, for, in the election of 1888, both parties had promised some sort of federal action on the trust problem.

The key provision of the Sherman Act stated, "Every contract, combination in the form of trust or otherwise, or conspiracy, in restraint of trade or commerce among the several states, or with foreign nations, is hereby declared to be illegal." The key weakness of the law was the prevalence of "weasel" words that were not only ambiguous but may have been intended to be so. What was a "trust"? Just when was an understanding an agreement, and when was it a "conspiracy"? The situation was so confusing that the law was interpreted as though it meant almost nothing. The sugar "trust", which controlled over 95 percent of the refining process, was declared not a trust because refining was manufacturing, not interstate trade (*U.S.* v. *E.C. Knight & Co.* 1895). The government lost cases so consistently under the Sherman Act that the Attorney General's office was reluctant to start cases. One Attorney General, Olney, thought the law impossible to enforce and saw no point in "prosecuting under a law I believe to be no good." The ten years after the Sherman Act was passed saw over seven times as many business combinations as there had been in the decade before the law. Not until the Northern Securities Case of 1904 was the government able to break up a trust. It was this case which breathed a spark of life into a Sherman Antitrust Act, which for fourteen years had been considered dead.

In spite of its shortcomings as an effective weapon against monopoly power in business, the Sherman Antitrust Act was a very significant law. Since its passage it has been supplemented by further antitrust legislation really intended to curb the power of business combinations exercising monopoly power against the public interest. Today, the view that government has the right to protect the public welfare from abuses by aggregates of private economic power is accepted.

* McKinley Tariff and Sherman Silver Act (1890)

The Republicans may have taken no joy in the passage of the Sherman Antitrust Act, but they did enthusiastically support the McKinley Tariff. The average ad valorum (according to value) rate was 49.5 percent, about every American manufacturer who wanted protection got it. For the first time, farmers' products, wheat, corn, and potatoes were on the protective list. This was a bit silly as the United States had great surpluses of wheat and corn, which were exported. No one was trying to send these products into this country. American sugar growers were encouraged by a bounty of 2 cents per pound for their raw sugar, and the American sugar refiners were favored by duty-free raw sugar from abroad. The principle of reciprocity was written into the bill at the insistence of Secretary of State Blaine.

There was more political maneuvering than usual in getting this tariff through Congress. The western states, including the new "omnibus states" had to be promised support for silver legislation. To keep the South from combining with the West to defeat the bill, it was necessary for the Republican party to promise to discontinue all efforts to enforce the Fourteenth and Fifteenth Amendments in efforts to improve the civil rights of black Americans. In 1890 the Republican House had passed the Federal Election Bill which would have had federal inspectors supervising, under certain conditions, elections in Southern states involving federal offices. With the assurance that the North would drop efforts to interfere with the South's own system of handling its race problem, the Southern Democrats made no serious attempt to block the McKinley Tariff.

The Sherman Silver Act of 1890 provided that the government buy 4.5 million ounces each month at the market price. This silver would be paid for in Treasury notes that would be legal tender and redeemable in gold or silver at the discretion of the government. The 4.5 million ounces was about the total output of the silver mines in the United States. The eastern Republicans disliked this law, but they voted for it in order to get the western members of Congress to vote for the McKinley Tariff. The Westerners supported the McKinley Tariff only to get the support of the Easterners for the Sherman Silver Act. The farmers demanded the Bland-Allison Act and the Sherman Silver Act because they expected the increased amount of money to result in higher prices for farm products and an easier way to pay off mortgages. The silver mining industry favored these laws because it wanted a guaranteed market for silver. Yet, neither of these groups achieved their aims. Farm prices continued downward, a fact which meant that, instead of getting cheaper, money was increasing in purchasing power. The silver mines were producing so much more silver that, in spite of the extensive government purchases, the surplus silver increased and the price fell. The value of the bullion in a silver dollar fell, but as the Treasury redeemed all money in gold, the silver and paper money were as good as gold. The farmers and the mining interests were still unhappy; their answer to the situation was free coinage of silver at the ratio of 16 to 1. The big struggle to apply this remedy was to come in the presidential campaign of 1896.

Navy and Coast Defenses

We have seen that President Arthur began the construction of a modern navy. President Cleveland continued work by starting the building of about 30 steel ships. In 1890 **Captain Alfred Mahan's** monumental book, *Influence of Sea Power Upon History*, was acclaimed throughout the western world. Captain Mahan's writings made him unofficial spokesman for imperialism and aroused enthusiasm about the United States' becoming a great naval power, perhaps one day the leading naval power of the world. The use of domestic steel for the new ships placed the business community solidly in favor of a large navy. The historical evidence compiled by Mahan in his nine-volume treatise was supported by the academic world of the universities. With a sense of pride, the American citizens embraced the idea of a powerful United States Navy. Congress appropriated the money. Late in Harrison's administration we had climbed to fifth place among the navies of the world, and less than ten years later our navy held third place, with only Great Britain and France ahead of us. In addition to the stepped-up expenditures for the new ships, large sums were spent for defenses along our coasts and for the improvement of rivers and harbors. The total appropriated by the first Congress under Harrison hit a new high at over a billion dollars. The Democrats raised the cry of extravagance, but the Republicans brushed it aside with the boast that the United States was a "billion dollar country."

* Populist Party Platform of 1892

Western farmers were not happy in the Republican party; neither were the people in the silvermining towns. Both were suffering from overproduction. Wheat was at the ruinous low price of 50 cents a bushel, and corn was being used by the farmers for fuel because it didn't pay to cart it to the market. The silver mines had produced more than could be sold. The farmers of the South were, if anything, worse off with cotton too low in price to cover costs of production.

The fundamental problem was overproduction; too much wheat, too much corn, too much silver, too much cotton, etc. But while there was "too much" of so many things, there was a widespread poverty throughout the United States and the other advanced nations of the world. The Populist party (the People's party) was formed to protest this suffering amidst plenty and to offer a corrective program. At Omaha, Nebraska, they nominated **James B. Weaver** for President and wrote a famous platform. Appropriately, they opened their nomination convention on July 4, 1892.

From the Omaha Platform's Preamble

"...we meet in the midst of a nation brought to the verge of moral, political, and material ruin. Corruption dominates the ballot-box, the Legislatures, the Congress, and touches even the ermine of the bench...The newspapers are largely subsidized or muzzled, public opinion silenced, business prostrated, homes covered with mortgages, labor impoverished, and the land concentrating in the hands of capitalists...The fruits of the toil of millions are boldly stolen to build up colossal fortunes for the few...From the same prolific womb of governmental injustice we breed the two great classes—tramps and millionaires...We have witnessed far more than a quarter of a century the struggles of the two great political parties for power and plunder, while grievous wrongs have been inflicted upon the suffering people...They propose to sacrifice our homes, lives, and children on the alter of mammon..."

Demands of the Omaha Platform

1] Graduated income tax

2] Direct election of Senators

3] Australian (secret) ballot

4] Extension of the merit system in Civil Service

5] Restriction of immigration

6] Initiative and referendum

7] Eight-hour day for labor

8] Postal savings banks

9] Government ownership of railroads

10] Government ownership of telegraph and telephone

11] Return to the government of lands granted to railroads and corporations in excess of their actual needs

12] Free coinage of silver at the ratio of 16 to 1

Two of these "radical" demands are now the Sixteenth and Seventeenth Amendments of the Constitution. Most of the others have been substantially fulfilled or become accepted practice. The Populists did a superb job, far better than they knew, in setting up a substantial part of the agenda for Congress for a generation or two.

Grover Cleveland   1893-1897

Second Administration

DEMOCRAT

Vice-President   ADLAI E. STEVENSON

MAJOR ITEMS OF CLEVELAND'S SECOND ADMINISTRATION

Panic of 1893
Hawaiian Incident (1893)
Venezuelan Boundary Affair (1895)
Problem of the Gold Reserve

Wilson-Gorman Tariff (1894)
Pullman Strike (1894)
American Federation of Labor

Cleveland's Election (1892)

The Republicans nominated **Harrison** for a second term, and the Democrats nominated **Cleveland** for the third consecutive time and a second term. The tariff was again the main issue, with the Democratic platform restating Calhoun's position by asserting that "the federal government has no Constitutional power to impose and collect tariff duties, except for the purposes of revenue only." Cleveland took a firm stand for the gold standard and sound money, a position that won votes for him in the East and lost them in the West. The McKinley Tariff was still hurting the Republican party. In July the "massacre" (seven persons killed) at Homestead, Pennsylvania occurred as Pinkerton's 300 private police shot it out with strikers of the Carnegie Steel Company. That a "private army" was hired by Henry Frick, general manager of Carnegie Steel, plus the fact that protection given steel by the McKinley Tariff failed to provide high wages, made the violence at Homestead an embarrassment to the Republicans. The presence of an articulate third party in the field, the Populists which took Colorado, Idaho, Kansas, and Nevada with a total of 22 electoral votes, did not affect the outcome of the struggle between the two major parties.

	Popular Vote	Electoral Vote
Cleveland	5,554,414	277
Harrison	5,190,802	145
Weaver	1,027,329	22

The Democrats gained majorities in both the House and the Senate.

Panic of 1893

Cleveland's second term was four years of depression. In the spring of 1893 the National Cordage Company and the Philadelphia & Reading Railroad failed. Before the year was over, almost 500 banks and more than 15,000 businesses had failed. About 4 million unemployed were roaming the streets looking for jobs that did not exist. Several factors seemed to contribute to this depression: the farmers had experienced no real prosperity since the early 1870s, and their purchasing power had been low; strikes had cut the purchasing power of industrial and railroad workers; hard times in Europe stifled our export trade; the silver purchase acts had persuaded foreign holders of American securities to sell them while they could still get a good price; the McKinley Tariff had dried up the revenue usually received from imports; the "billion dollar" expenditures under Harrison had depleted the surplus and created a deficit; and the gold reserve to support our currency system had sunk some $20 million below the legal minimum of $100 million. Cleveland did not create the depression, but he did get blamed for it.

* Hawaiian Incident (1893)

Queen Liliuokalani came to the throne in 1891. At this time the McKinley Tariff with its bounty of 2 cents

160

per pound for all the sugar grown in the United States had hit the Hawaiian sugar plantations with full force. The encouragement to American sugar growers was such a blow to Hawaii that the whole economy of the islands had been seriously threatened. The queen decided to meet the situation by establishing a dictatorship and shifting Hawaiian economic dependence away from the United States. Her attempt to set aside the native constitution met with a native revolt, and the policy of orienting the Hawaiian economy away from the United States alienated the American citizens who had invested heavily in the island sugar plantations. The obvious move for the American sugar planters on the islands was to have Hawaii become a possession of the United States with free entry for its products to the mainland markets. John Stevens, our minister at Honolulu, was fully in sympathy with the American sugar planters on the islands and used his influence to aid the native revolt. The Queen was deposed, and a provisional government with Sanford B. Dole as president was set up. This government petitioned the United States to annex the Hawaiian Islands. President Harrison approved the request and submitted it to the Senate as a treaty. It was mid-February with only three weeks left in his term, and before the Senate acted upon the treaty, Cleveland had been inaugurated. Cleveland thought it strange that the government of Hawaii would be asking to be annexed to the United States, and upon investigation, he found that the revolution had been largely an American accomplishment. He withdrew the treaty, asked the queen to pardon the revolutionists, and suggested that the provisional government step down in favor of Liliuokalani. But the queen would not forgive; instead she made angry comments about the United States while threatening to behead the revolutionists. With little difficulty the provisional government continued to rule the islands and wish for annexation. After the Spanish-American War, the urge to annex Hawaii was irresistible and no one in Washington wanted to resist it. On July 7, 1898, Hawaii was annexed by a joint resolution of Congress, and in 1900 all the inhabitants of the Hawaiian Islands became citizens of the United States in the Territory of Hawaii.

* Venezuelan Boundary Dispute (1895)

British Guiana and Venezuela had a boundary dispute of some 50 years standing. Twice Cleveland had suggested arbitration, once in 1887 and again in 1894. The dispute flared up again after the discovery of gold deposits in the border areas. There was danger that either side might precipitate hostilities and thus involve the United States, for any loss of territory by Venezuela to Great Britain would involve the Monroe Doctrine. A European power would be colonizing at the expense of a republic in the Western Hemisphere. Secretary of State **Richard Olney** sent a message to the British Foreign Minister, Lord Salisbury, expressing the American view with great clarity and greater bluntness. Olney said that the United States "is practically sovereign on this continent." He went on to state that when the United States chose to enter into any situation in the Western Hemisphere, its word then became law. It contained the boast that the United States could take this position because it had the power to do so. "Its (the United States) infinite resources combined with its isolated position render it master of the situation and practically invulnerable against any and all other powers." The communication ended with an appeal for arbitration. After four months, Lord Salisbury replied with a refusal to arbitrate and an assertion that the Monroe Doctrine had no standing in international law and, in any case, did not apply to this situation. England sent troops to British Guiana. President Cleveland asked Congress to appropriate the necessary funds to send a commission to determine the proper boundary line which, if necessary, the United States would maintain against any attempt Great Britain might make to violate it. Fortunately, both sides calmed down. Neither really wanted war. The **Venezuelan boundary dispute** was arbitrated with the stipulation that any area actually occupied by either party for 50 years would belong to that party. The Monroe Doctrine had been respected; England got most of the land: and Venezuela no longer needed to fear encroachments by Britain.

Problem of the Gold Reserve

As the price of silver fell, the value of the silver acquired by the Treasury under the terms of the Sherman Silver Purchase Act depreciated. Silver dollars and silver certificates were cheaper money than gold coins and gold certificates. It was true that all money could be redeemed in gold, but this was due to government policy, which could be changed at short notice. The mere fact that one kind of money was more valuable than another resulted in people's using the cheaper and saving the sounder money. Foreign traders would stipulate that their bills must be paid in gold. As long as the government exchanged gold for all legal tender, it was inevitable that gold would be drawn out of the Treasury while silver accumulated there. The minimum gold reserve required by law was $100 million but it had fallen much below this limit and was inadequate to redeem the greenbacks and silver certificates then in circulation. Cleveland moved to correct this situation by calling a special session of Congress, which repealed the Sherman Silver Purchase Act. This stopped the steady flow of new silver into the Treasury. The next problem was to get gold to come into the Treasury and stay there. Two issues of government bonds totaling $100 million were sold for gold, but the purchasers then presented greenbacks or silver certificates to be redeemed in gold. There was a steady flow of gold through the Treasury, but no buildup of the gold reserve, which had fallen to $41 million. At this point John Pierpont Morgan and a group of associates proposed to pay gold for bonds to the total of $62 million. Half of this gold was to come from abroad, and the bankers pledged not to withdraw gold from the Treasury by redeeming legal-tender paper. Cleveland accepted this plan. The gold reserve recovered, confidence in the currency system returned, the nation remained on the gold standard, and the credit of the United States had been preserved. But this transaction was political poison for a Democrat. The rank and file of the Democratic party could neither understand nor forgive Cleveland for the Morgan "deal" which not only served the government but gave handsome profits to the bankers.

* Wilson-Gorman Tariff (1894)

During his second administration, Cleveland was as determined to achieve tariff reform as he had been when he fought unsuccessfully for the Mills Bill in his first term. Representative William Wilson of West Virginia introduced the bill Cleveland wanted. It put some raw materials on the free list (coal, copper, iron ore, sugar, wool), and some manufactured products had their rates cut to a moderate revenue level (china, cotton and woolen goods, glass, silk). The bill passed the House easily, but when Gorman of Maryland piloted it through the Senate, it was amended over 600 times. Democrats from Alabama, Louisiana, and West Virginia wanted protection for iron ore, sugar, and coal. When the **Wilson-Gorman Tariff** passed, it was protective with rates averaging about 40 percent as compared with the McKinley average of about 50 percent. Again Cleveland had been defeated on his tariff program.

* Pullman Strike (1894)

The Pullman Company dismissed their employees and then hired about a third of them back with wage cuts of 20 to 25 percent. A few of the Pullman employees were members of the American Railway Union, which had just won a restoration of a wage cut from the Great Northern Railway System of James J. Hill. They appealed to **Eugene V. Debs**, president of the American Railway Union for help. The Pullman workers lived in a company town where the houses were owned by George M. Pullman and rents, gas and

water rates were from 10 to 25 percent higher than in nearby areas. Because a few employees formed a committee to discuss the situation with Mr. Pullman, he fired them. Debs suggested arbitration; Pullman said, "We have nothing to arbitrate." More ill feeling was generated by the knowledge that the company had just paid its usual dividends totaling over $2.5 million and had a surplus of some $25 million.

Debs ordered a boycott, and within a week 100,000 workers refused to work on any train with a Pullman car. Debs warned them not to interfere with mail trains and not to try to prevent others from taking their jobs. He was confident that the railroads could not replace 100,000 skilled and semiskilled employees and that running the roads with incompetent help would prove intolerably dangerous and expensive. The strike was beaten by the United States government through the use of injunctions issued by federal courts. (An injunction is a negative court order directing someone not to do something or to stop doing what is already under way.)

A court order was issued telling Debs not to interfere with the mails and defended as a proper procedure for stopping a violation of the Sherman Antitrust Act. Was not the strike a conspiracy that restrained interstate commerce? Thus the Sherman Antitrust Act was used to deny to labor the right to strike.

Federal troops were sent to Illinois to protect the trains. Mayor Hopkins of Chicago and Governor Altgeld of Illinois bitterly protested the entrance of federal troops into their city and state. The strike was orderly and controlled by a local authorities. There was no appreciable disorder until July 3 when federal troops were ordered to Chicago; then extensive property damage occurred and twelve men were killed.

The injunction issued against Debs ordered him not to obstruct the mail, not to damage railroad property, and not to communicate with the strikers to direct their actions. Debs agreed with the first two prohibitions. But there was no way to escape the third. Newspapers that opposed the strike were highly critical of this "government by injunction." After violence flared up, Debs issued the following instructions to the strikers and thus violated the injunction. "I appeal to you to be men, orderly and law-abiding. Our cause is just....Let it be borne in mind that if the railroads can secure men to handle their trains, they have that right. Our men have the right to quit, but their right ends there. Other men have the right to take their places....Keep away from railway yards, or rights-of-way, or those places where large crowds congregate....Respect the law, conduct yourselves as becomes men and our cause shall be crowned with success." Debs was arrested. When tried for violating the Sherman Antitrust Act, the jury voted eleven to one for acquittal. One of the jurors became too ill to continue serving so the judge dismissed them, and no further action was taken on the conspiracy charge. Debs served a six months' sentence. The **Pullman Strike** was a severe blow to unions.

* The American Federation of Labor

In the 1870s **Samuel Gompers** organized a small craft, the cigar makers, into a union in New York City's lower East Side. He organized other unions in other crafts. In 1886 the **American Federation of Labor (AFL)** was born. The several groups forming the Federation were national organizations made up of local craft unions. The national organization advised and often aided their locals. The federation advised the national organizations, aided in drives for membership, tried to prevent the formation of rival labor groups, and set the policy of keeping the union aims restricted to very practical and immediate goals, such as collective bargaining, better pay, shorter hours, etc. The AFL avoided reform movements and political parties. The AFL touched but a small fraction of the wage earners because it limited itself to organizing skilled workers. By the outbreak of World War I, the AFL had about two million members. With Gompers as its president for 37 years, the AFL dominated the labor field for about forty years.

1899 TO PRESENT
William McKinley   1897-1901

1843-1901

REPUBLICAN

Vice-President   THEODORE ROOSEVELT

Secretary of State   JOHN HAY

MCKINLEY'S PUBLIC SERVICE BEFORE HE BECAME PRESIDENT

Officer in the Union Army at Antietam and other battles
Member of the House of Representatives from Ohio
Governor of Ohio

MAJOR ITEMS OF MCKINLEY'S ADMINISTRATIONS

Spanish-American War (April 1898-February 1899)
Governing Our New Possessions
Open Door Policy and the Boxer Rebellion
McKinley Assassinated by Czolgosz

* McKinley's Election in 1896 and 1900

The Republican convention met at St. Louis to adopt a platform advocating the gold standard, protective tariff, and the control of the Hawaiian Islands. They were confident of victory and boasted that any Republican could win. **Marcus Hanna**, an extremely wealthy merchant, industrialist, and financier who had great capacity for organization and a zest for power dropped his business interests to groom **William McKinley** for the presidency. His preconvention plans worked out perfectly with his candidate winning the nomination on the first ballot.

The Democratic party was in a sad state in 1896: it was blamed for the 1893 panic and the ensuing depression years; the congressional elections of 1894 had put the Republicans in control of both House and Senate; and President Cleveland had managed to offend several blocs of voters. His vigorous support of the injunction against Debs in the pullman strike had alienated labor; his insistence that the Sherman Silver Purchase Act be repealed had offended cheap-money advocates; and his battles for revenue tariff had divided his party.

At the Democratic convention in Chicago, eastern leaders made speeches in support of the gold standard. Finally the last of a long list of speakers was a much younger man of 36, **William Jennings Bryan**, who made a rousing speech in favor of free silver. "The humblest citizen in all the land, when clad in the armor of a righteous cause, is stronger than all the hosts of error. I come to speak to you in defense of a cause as holy as the cause of liberty—the cause of humanity." Almost every sentence brought applause and cheers. He concluded,"...we will answer their demand for a gold standard by saying to them: You shall not press down upon the brow of labor this crown of thorn, you shall not crucify mankind upon a cross of gold." Bryan had organized his supporters before the convention; he was thoroughly confident he would win the nomination. Perhaps his speech alone would have done it. On the fifth ballot he got the necessary two-thirds majority of the delegates, and the "Boy Orator of the Platte" was the Democratic nominee. The "gold standard" Democrats withdrew from the convention.

The early days of the campaign found the Republicans complacent and confident, but by late summer

164

they were running scared. Twenty-two states went to Bryan and twenty-three to McKinley.

	Popular Vote	Electoral Vote
McKinley	7,035,638	271
Bryan	6,467,946	176

"Big Business" had won over the agrarian interests. The "boy orator of the Platte" had made a gallant fight in support of the common people, but he made that fight on an unsound economic doctrine of free silver at 16 to 1. Bryan seemed destined to devote his life to unfortunate causes, but his uprightness and his devotion to the "little man" attracted the affection of thousands and won him his title, "The Great Commoner."

McKinley Reelected in 1900

The campaign of 1900 was an easy victory for the Republicans. Prosperity had returned early in McKinley's first term, and the **Klondike gold rush,** begun in 1896, had reached peak production in 1900, thus taking the life out of the demand for free coinage of silver. **Theodore Roosevelt** was a popular figure and he was induced to accept the nomination as Vice-President. The party bosses were anxious to put him safely out of the way on the vice-presidential "shelf," where his name would attract support to the ticket. The platform called for a continuation of the protective tariff, the gold standard, and an Isthmian canal under United States control across Panama. It also claimed credit for prosperity which, with their "full dinner pail" slogan, made the main issue of the campaign.

The Democrats nominated Bryan, who again chose to hammer away at an issue that was bound to lose, anti-imperialism. The Spanish-American War had been an easy victory and, perhaps for that reason, a popular one. Bryan also continued to demand free silver at 16 to 1.

** Spanish-American War

The formal declaration of war was on April 25, 1898, and the ratification of the **Treaty of Paris** restored peace on February 6, 1899. The fighting began at Manila Bay in the Philippines on May 1 and ended with the surrender of Santiago, Cuba, on July 17—an eleven weeks' fight.

The United States had shown from time to time an interest in Cuba. President John Quincy Adams had written that it seemed in the nature of things to come that Cuba would one day belong to the United States. Buchanan, when Secretary of State under President Polk, had tried to purchase Cuba from Spain; and under President Pierce the Ostend Manifesto had embarrassed us. Spanish rule in Cuba was usually cruel and always inefficient. During most of the 1870s rebellion was rampant throughout the island and atrocities by Spanish authorities against the rebels were frequent. The late 1890s saw similar widespread rebellion with accompanying atrocities. But by this time the sugar crop of Cuba was more important to the United States, the American investments in Cuba were more extensive, and the United States Navy was new and ranked second only to the navies of Great Britain and France. Our government and people found it easier to think in terms of worldwide interests. But all of these factors combined would not have precipitated the war with Spain had it not been for the blatant jingoism and calculated fake-atrocity stories and pictures by the press. The Spanish-American War was an accomplishment of the sensationalist **yellow press;** the most influential newspapers of this stripe were Hearst's *New York Journal* and Pulitzer's *New York World.*

Early in 1896 concentration camps established by General ("Butcher") Weyler in Cuba imprisoned men, women, and children. Disease, semi-starvation, cruelty, and lack of sanitation gave the *Journal* and the *World* good copy for atrocity stories. A change in the Spanish ministry in November 1897 resulted in the recall of "Butcher" Weyler, a plan for local autonomy for Cuba, and the release of United States' citizens from Cuban jails. But these concessions came too late to satisfy the rebels. The following month McKinley urged that Spain be given a reasonable opportunity to carry out its new policy. The "Old Guard" of the Republican party and most of the business leaders approved McKinley's purpose to avoid war.

On the evening of February 15, 1898, in Havana harbor an explosion killed 260 men on the American battleship *Maine.* McKinley asked the people to reserve judgment, but the newspapers had a field day. The *New York Journal* of February 17 displayed a front page picture (artist's drawing) showing the Maine with a submerged mine under it. Its biggest headline was, "DESTRUCTION OF THE WAR SHIP MAINE WAS THE WORK OF AN ENEMY." The *Journal* and the *World* struck the popular note. McKinley allowed himself to be swept away by the hysteria of the moment.

On March 27, 1898, McKinley advised Spain that we had no territorial ambitions in Cuba; but we did desire that an armistice be arranged between the rebels and Spanish forces in Cuba, and that the concentration-camp policy be discontinued. On April 10 McKinley received news that both conditions he had requested had been accepted by Spain. But before the President got this message, he had reversed his antiwar policy and had decided to go along with the irresistible pressure of public opinion. He sent his war message to Congress on April 11 with the full knowledge that Congress would declare war.

The response of Congress to this war message contained four points: (1) The United States recognizes the independence of Cuba; (2) Spain must withdraw its armed forces from Cuba; (3) The President of the United States is to use whatever armed force is necessary to carry out the first two resolutions; and (4) the United States does not intend to annex Cuba and will leave its government to its own people. This fourth point was known as the **Teller Resolution**.

The Navy's Part in the War

Two months before Congress sent its declaration of war to Spain, **Theodore Roosevelt**, Assistant Secretary of the Navy, sent orders to **Commodore Dewey** in the Far East to be ready for an attack on the Philippines. Dewey's four cruisers and two gunboats steamed into Manila Bay early in the morning of May 1 and opened fire on the Spanish squadron of ten ships. After several hours of bombardment the Spanish ships were sunk, silenced, or captured. The American casualties totaled eight wounded and one man dead (from heat prostration); Spanish casualties were 381 killed and many more wounded. No damage was suffered by the American ships. Dewey did not have the force needed for an assault upon Manila until reinforcements arrived late in July. In the meantime he occupied Manila Bay.

The Spanish fleet in the Caribbean took a position in Santiago harbor under the protection of land batteries. By June 1 both Commodore Schley and Rear Admiral Sampson had their squadrons blocking the harbor. The Spanish admiral, Cervera, had four cruisers and three destroyers, while the United States blockading force had five battleships and two cruisers. Among the American ships was the *Oregon,* which had steamed 14,000 miles from the north Pacific Coast around South America to Cuba and was still in good fighting trim. Cervera attempted to escape on July 3 and in a running fight along the coast, the Spanish ships were totally destroyed.

The United States Navy was modern, well-built, and well-trained. It was thoroughly prepared and effectively officered. Quite the opposite was true of the Spanish ships. Their equipment was in poor condition and the navy poorly trained.

The Army's Part in the War

President McKinley called for 200,000 volunteers. But there were neither uniforms nor modern rifles for them. Lack of lightweight khaki cloth resulted in troops being sent to the tropics in heavy blue winter uniforms; contaminated meat proved a more effective enemy than the Spanish; the volunteers were unbelievably undertrained; and the inexperience of the soldiers combined with poor organization resulted in dangerously unsanitary encampments. Between June 20 and 25, 1896 about 16,000 American troops landed at Daiquiri, less than 20 miles from Santiago, Cuba. On July 1 a sharp battle was fought at El Caney, a few miles inland from Daiquiri, and on the following day another battle occurred at **San Juan Hill**. These encounters were severe. Casualties (killed and wounded) for the Americans reached 1,600. Santiago was now open to bombardment from high ground north and east of the city. **Theodore Roosevelt** had resigned as Assistant Secretary of the Navy to serve under General Leonard Wood with the rank of Lieutenant Colonel of the "**Rough Riders**," a cavalry unit. This unit played a prominent part in the charge on foot, up San Juan Hill, an engagement that gave a good boost to Roosevelt's public career. News of the naval victory over Admiral Cervera and the victories at El Caney and San Juan Hill gave the United States a noisy, exuberant Fourth of July celebration. Two weeks later the city of Santiago, next to Havana in importance, surrendered, and on July 26 Spain asked for peace terms. It had been a short war full of victories for the United States and, as wars go, at minor costs.

WAR COSTS

Killed in action	a few less than 400
Died from other causes	a few more than 5,000
Expense of conducting the war	about $250 million

* Treaty of Paris

(Accepted by Spain December 10, 1898) (Ratified by the Senate February 6, 1899)

1] Spain gave up all claims to Cuba.

2] The United States got the Philippines for $20 million.

3] Spain ceded Puerto Rico and Guam to the United States.

It was not easy to get the Senate to ratify the treaty. The vote was 57 to 27, just one vote more than the required two-thirds majority. The closeness of the vote reflected the anti-imperialist views held by many who disliked the acquisition by the United States of distant islands inhabited by people of an alien culture. Pushing Spain out of Cuba was popular, but acquiring Puerto Rico, the Philippines, and Guam was quite another matter. While most of the anti-imperialists were Democrats, the division cut across party lines. We had a few spokesmen for the "superior race" nonsense, and many more who defended empire building on the basis that the United States needed Pacific Ocean outposts if we were to develop and protect our trading opportunities with the Far East. William Allen White, editor of the *Emporia Gazette* (Kansas) wrote, "It is the Anglo-Saxon's manifest destiny to go forth as a world conqueror....This is what fate holds for the chosen people." Senator Albert Beveridge of Indiana told the Senate, "He (God) has made us master organizers of the world to establish system where chaos reigns....He has made us adept in government that we may administer government among savage and senile peoples....He has marked the American people as His chosen nation to finally lead in the regeneration of the world." The debate raged in magazines and newspapers with a very articulate minority condemning the decision to govern alien and distant peoples. The United States was not really comfortable with its foray into imperialism and almost immediately began plans to lead the subject people toward self-government—a long-range program far more consistent with our own national origin and republican principles.

* Governing Our New Possessions

The Philippines

Before leaving Hong Kong for Manila Bay, Dewey had arranged to have **Emilio Aguinaldo**, a Filipino insurrectionist leader in exile at Singapore, go to the Philippines to lead the Filipinos against the Spanish. Dewey promised to supply them with the necessary arms. The United States' minister at Singapore and Dewey made some arrangements, which Aguinaldo claimed was a promise to turn the Philippines over to the Filipinos under his leadership as soon as the Spanish had been driven out. Of course, neither Dewey nor the United States' minister at Singapore had the authority to make any such arrangement. Just what agreements were made we don't know. The United States was expelling Spain from Cuba with the promise to turn the island over to native rule, so it is not surprising that Aguinaldo and the Filipinos sought and expected similar treatment. As soon as it was clear to Aguinaldo, whose troops had helped Dewey take Manila, that the United States had replaced Spain as master of the islands, he took to guerrilla warfare. From February 1899 to April 1902 a cruel war raged, with too many atrocities on both sides. Over 4,000 American soldiers were killed and about 600,000 Filipinos lost their lives. The Manila area was pacified long before the rebellion was over. In April 1900,

William H. Taft was appointed with five commissioners to set up a civilian government at Manila. In July 1902, Congress provided for a native assembly to act with Governor-General Taft and his commission. By 1907 a native assembly had been elected and Taft's commission served as an upper house. In 1916 the Jones Act allowed all male adults to vote if they could read and write in English, Spanish, or a native dialect. The Governor-general's commission was replaced by a native upper house (Senate). The Governor-General was still appointed by the President of the United States and still had veto power over acts of the native legislature. In 1934 the Tydings-McDuffie Act provided that the native legislature draw up a constitution. President Franklin Roosevelt approved this constitution and in 1935, the first president of the Philippine Commonwealth, **Manuel Quezon**, was elected. A ten-year trial run of this native government was to culminate with complete independence. World War II brought a delay of one year, but on July 4, 1946, **Manuel Roxas** became the first President of the new Philippine Republic. The United States granted $600 million to help restore damage from World War II and gave the Philippines an eight-year guarantee of free trade with the United States to steady the economy.

Puerto Rico

In general, Puerto Rico followed similar steps toward self-government as had the Philippines. The **Foraker Act of 1900** set up a Governor-General and a council appointed by the President of the United States. A native assembly was elected, and the council became the senate. In 1917 Puerto Rico became a territory and its people became citizens of the United States. In 1952 the people of Puerto Rico drafted a constitution, which President Truman approved. This gave the island the status of a free commonwealth voluntarily associated with the United States.

Cuba

True to the promise of the Teller Resolution, Cuba was granted independence. In November 1900, General Leonard Wood arranged a convention where a constitution for Cuba was drawn up. It was similar to that of the United States. In March 1901, the United States Congress made certain additions, which the Cubans accepted, as an unamendable part of their constitution. These changes are known as the **Platt Amendment.**

1] Cuba shall make no treaty that endangers its independence.

2] Cuba shall borrow no money beyond its capacity to repay.

3] The United States may intervene in Cuba when necessary to preserve order.

4] Cuba will sell or lease coaling and naval stations to the United States.

In 1934 the terms of the Platt Amendment were abolished by treaty except for the naval base that the United States maintains at Guantanamo.

Insular Cases

During 1901 cases involving Puerto Rico and the Philippines came before the Supreme Court. These cases involved several important questions: Were the people in the territories entitled to the rights guaranteed by the Constitution to citizens of the United States? Could a tariff be levied on goods coming from these possessions into the United States? Were Puerto Rico and the Philippines part of the United States? Would every child born in these islands after the United States took possession of them automatically be citizens? In general, these questions involved one basic question: Does the Constitution follow one flag? The Supreme Court said that the question of what to do about the island possessions and the Constitution might be considered a political question to be decided by Congress rather than a legal one for the courts. On the specific point raised, concerning the legality of a tariff on goods entering the United States from Puerto Rico, the Court ruled that Congress could levy tariffs on goods from Puerto Rico. Except for this decision on the revenue clauses, the Supreme Court tossed the problem into the lap of Congress. In the **Insular Cases** the court agreed in general that the new territories were under almost complete control of Congress rather than having the same rights under the Constitution as citizens of the states. Thus, it was decided that the Constitution does not necessarily follow the flag.

* Open Door Policy and the Boxer Rebellion

As early as 1844 Caleb Cushing had gained for the United States the right of extraterritoriality in China. Missionaries had been in China continuously since then, but after the era of the clipper ships, trade with China had lagged. Throughout the period, American ships had traded in Chinese ports under the same terms as ships of other nations. But in the 1890s China was being carved into spheres of influence by the European powers. With the acquisition of the Philippines, the United States had a quickened interest in China and looked with displeasure on its dismemberment. For the moment, British and American interests in Far Eastern trade made them share a common desire to check the setting up of spheres of influence.

Our Secretary of State, **John Hay** wrote in September 1899 to the several nations with spheres of influence in China and expressed the hope that the areas recently acquired by them were open to the trade of all nations on equal terms; that ports and railroads would be available to all; and that tariffs would be collected by the Chinese government. All of the nations except Russia replied with noncommittal generalities, which seemed to say that each would be willing to comply with the ideas expressed by the Hay if all the other nations would do the same. In March 1900 Secretary Hay sent another letter to London, Paris, Berlin, St. Petersburg, Rome, and Tokyo informing them that their replies indicated a common willingness to permit equal trading rights for all nations within their respective spheres of influence. That being the case, the United States would "consider the assent given" ... "as final and definitive." On paper, at least, it seemed that John Hay had won over the European nations and Japan to the acceptance of the **Open Door Policy.**

In 1900 serious trouble developed in the Peking area. A Chinese nationalist organization, the Order of the Patriotic and Harmonious Fists (**Boxers**), was intent upon driving the "foreign devils" out of their country. Missionaries and foreign traders were murdered, and hundreds sought protection at the foreign legations in Peking. The dowager empress was secretly aiding the Boxers. An international force with about 2,500 American troops from the Philippines arrived at Peking on August 14, 1900 and rescued the besieged foreigners. However, the German ambassador had been murdered and a total of about 200 foreigners had been killed during the disorders. The attack on Peking lasted seven weeks. While the Boxers were besieging Peking, John Hay firmly opposed seizing any more of China's territory. He made it clear that the United States was interested in restoring order in Peking; "permanent safety and peace in China"; the preservation of China as an independent nation; and the safeguarding to "friendly powers...equal and impartial trade with all parts of the Chinese Empire." Japan and the European powers gave up any immediate designs they may have had for partitioning China.

John Hay gave prestige to the United States; expressed the desire of the American people to develop trade with the Far East on as favorable terms as any other nation; and reflected the opposition of Americans to the partitioning of China. The final settlement for the **Boxer Rebellion** was an indemnity against China of $333 million of which the United States got $24 million. Because we thought it excessive, we returned half this amount, which the Chinese government set aside to finance Chinese students in American colleges.

McKinley Assassinated by Czolgosz

On September 6, 1901, President McKinley was shot by Leon Czolgosz, an American citizen, at the Pan-American Exposition in Buffalo, New York. He was an anarchist who thought he had a mission to kill "Czar McKinley." The President died eight days later. Czolgosz was electrocuted. Marcus Hanna, then United States Senator from Ohio and who was largely responsible for McKinley's public career, said of Vice-President Theodore Roosevelt, "I told William McKinley it was a mistake to nominate that wild man at Philadelphia....Now look, that damned cowboy is President of the United States!"

Theodore Roosevelt

1901-1909

1858-1919

REPUBLICAN

☆

Vice-President CHARLES W. FAIRBANKS

Secretary of State JOHN HAY
ELIHU ROOT

THEODORE ROOSEVELT'S PUBLIC SERVICE BEFORE HE BECAME PRESIDENT

Assemblyman in the New York State Legislature
United States Civil Service Commissioner
New York City Police Commissioner
Assistant Secretary of the Navy
Organized and led the Rough Riders in the Spanish-American War
Governor of New York
Vice-President during the six months of McKinley's second term

MAJOR ITEMS OF THEODORE ROOSEVELT'S ADMINISTRATIONS

Panama Canal
Trust Problem
Coal Strike (1902)
Conservation Program
Venezuelan Debt Controversy and the Drago Doctrine
Corollary to the Monroe Doctrine
Receivership of the Dominican Republic
Portsmouth Treaty (1905)

Agreements with Japan (Gentlemen's and Root-Takahira)
Algeciras Conference (1906)
Hague Conferences (1899 and 1907)
Hepburn Act (1906)
Pure Food and Drug Act and Meat Inspection Act and Muckrakers
Political Reforms of the Roosevelt Era

Theodore Roosevelt's Election in 1904

By 1904 the people had adopted "T.R." as their hero. In the popular mind he stood for what was fair and good. They liked his concern for the public during the coal strike; they liked his success in fighting the trusts; they liked his vigorous speeches extolling patriotism, displaying a warmth of feeling for people, and denouncing what was fraudulent and false; they liked his family life; and they liked him. The nominating convention at Chicago didn't bother to take a vote; they nominated Roosevelt by acclamation.

The Democrats passed by Bryan to nominate a very conservative candidate, **Judge Alton B. Parker** of New York. There was nothing the Democratic party stood for in 1904 that didn't seem more likely of accomplishment under Teddy Roosevelt than under Judge Parker.

The Socialists nominated **Eugene V. Debs.**

	Popular Vote	Electoral Vote
Theodore Roosevelt	7,628,834	336
Judge Alton Parker	5,084,401	140
Eugene V. Debs (Socialist)	402,460	0

Roosevelt acknowledged the tribute the people had paid him by announcing to the press that, as he had served all but six months of McKinley's second term, he would "under no circumstances be a candidate for or accept another nomination."

* Panama Canal

The 71-day trip of the U.S.S. *Oregon* from the northwest coast of the United States around South America to Cuba had dramatically called attention to the strategic value of a canal to link the Atlantic and Pacific Oceans. Our acquisitions in the Pacific of the Philippines, Guam, and the Hawaiian Islands, and of Puerto Rico in the Atlantic gave the United States possessions stretching about half the distance around the globe. Great Britain and the United States had put the world on notice that the area through which such a canal was built, no matter who built it, would be policed by British and American forces, and the canal itself must be open to the use of ships of all nations on identical terms (Clayton-Bulwer Treaty, 1850). French interests had purchased the right from Colombia to build a canal and had spent $260 million on the project before they gave up in 1889. Malaria, yellow fever, engineering difficulties, mismanagement, and financial corruption had forced the French Panama Company headed by De Lesseps, builder of the Suez Canal, into bankruptcy.

President Roosevelt, some of the army engineers, and many members of Congress favored cutting the canal through Panama; but there was considerable support for a sea level canal through Nicaragua. Congress approved expenditure of $40 million for the purchase of the rights and machinery from the French Panama Company. But, above all, it was the Spanish-American War and an aggressive President that really got the project under way. In 1901 Secretary of State **John Hay** was able to reach an agreement with foreign minister Pauncefote of England. With the assurance by the United States that ships of all nations would be allowed to use the canal on equal terms, England readily gave up its right to share in the policing of the canal area. This **Hay-Pauncefote Treaty** cleared the way for negotiations with Colombia. Hay reached an agreement with Herran, the Colombian representative, which would have given the United States a six-mile-wide strip of land across Panama and a renewable ninety-nine-year lease. The United States would have paid $10 million and an annual rental of $250,000.

President Roosevelt and the Senate were pleased with these terms, but the Colombian Senate refused to approve because it considered the $10 million too small a fee. Roosevelt was angry and the Colombian state of Panama was dismayed. Dr. Guerrero from Panama and **Philippe Bunau-Varilla**, who had been associated with the French attempt to build the canal, planned a revolution by Panama from Colombia. President Roosevelt had no direct dealings with them, but on November 3, 1903, the day before the revolution, the U.S.S. *Nashville* arrived off the Caribbean coast of Panama. Other United States warships hovered off the Isthmus, and Colombia was unable to interfere with the revolution. Within a week Panama declared itself independent, and the United States immediately extended official recognition to the new republic. By November 18 the **Hay-Bunau Varilla Treaty** had been drawn up, granting the United States a ten-mile-wide strip across the Isthmus for $10 million and a perpetual lease at $250,000 per year.

The medical work and splendid organization accomplished under the army doctor, **Colonel Gorgas**, changed a tropical jungle pest hole into a livable zone in which blasting through the mountains could proceed under the direction of army engineer **Colonel Goethals**. It took about ten years to dig the big ditch. The first ship went through August 15, 1914, but huge landslides soon closed it again. The canal was intermittently in service but not officially declared finished until 1921.

** Trust Problem

The Sherman Antitrust Act of 1890 had failed to check the merging of businesses into huge aggregations of capital, which were called "trusts." President Roosevelt considered that the ineffectiveness of the law denied a "square deal" to the people and to business in general. Unable to persuade Congress to pass new antitrust legislation with teeth in it, he ordered his Attorney General to bring suit against the Northern Securities Company. This company combined under one management the railroads of the northwest, an area roughly one-fourth of the United States. The Supreme Court by a five-to-four decision ordered the merger dissolved and thus gave the government its first substantial victory over a business combination.

The majority of the Court held that if a holding company could be formed to control the railroads in one section of the nation, then, "...the entire railway systems of the country may be absorbed, merged and consolidated, thus placing the public at the absolute mercy of the holding corporation." The Court also said, "...it need not be shown that the combination, in fact, results or will result in a total suppression of trade or in a complete monopoly, but it is only essential to show that...it tends to restrain interstate commerce...and to deprive the public of the advantages that flow from free competition."

Roosevelt was intent on bringing, as he put it, an end to the "immunity from government control" that big business had enjoyed in spite of the Interstate Commerce Act of 1887 and the Sherman Antitrust Act of 1890. The trust-busting program continued with successful suits against the Standard Oil Company of New Jersey, the American Tobacco Company, the beef trust, and the fertilizer trust. Although about forty antitrust cases were prosecuted while Roosevelt was in office, the problem still remained unsolved.

One should not think of President Roosevelt as opponent of "big business." His position was that large-scale business operations were the strength of the American economy and accounted for the tremendous strides the United States was making in the world of manufacture and commerce. He appreciated the lower prices, the variety of products, and the constant introduction of new products that resulted from adequate capitalization and size of industrial units. His opposition was reserved for those business combinations that refused to operate within the law, or whose practices were so obviously against the public welfare that he would consider them morally wrong—incompatible with a square deal.

* Coal Strike (1902)

In May 1902, about 140,000 miners went out on strike in the anthracite coal fields of northeastern Pennsylvania. For months the miners had protested working conditions, and the president of the United Mine Workers of America, John Mitchell, tried in vain to meet with the mine operators to talk over the situation. The grievances of the miners were many and real.

1] Their average annual wage was about $300.

2] The houses in the mining towns were owned by the company; they were usually miserable shacks.

3] The miners were sometimes paid per ton of coal dug, but the "ton" was measured at 3,000 pounds.

4] On certain jobs, miners were paid by the number of cars they filled, but a "full" car was one topped nine inches above the edge.

5] Miners who needed dynamite, blasting power or other essential items for their jobs had to buy their own supplies from a company store at prices far above normal.

6] Some mines paid in token money, good only at company stores where prices were high.

Bad as the above grievances may seem, the basic demand of the miners was the recognition of their union. They wanted the mine owners to talk to their president who would represent them in collective bargaining. By October a coal shortage had set in and winter was very close. President Roosevelt called John Mitchell and George Baer, the spokesperson for the mine owners, to the White House. His view of the controversy was that the public was the victim. Coal had risen from $5 per ton to $30, and householders were waiting in lines at coal yards to buy a few pounds at a time. Hard coal was the only fuel used in almost all the city homes of the Northeast. To prevent widespread suffering, sickness, and death, the differences between miners and management must be settled quickly. With this purpose in mind the President brought the two leaders together. He made a strong plea for arbitration. Mitchell accepted but Baer scolded Roosevelt for "negotiating with the fomenters of anarchy" and left the White House in a huff. J. P. Morgan was the financial power behind the coal mines, so the President informed him that United States troops would seize and operate the mines unless arbitration began. Morgan told Baer to arbitrate and the miners got a 10 percent raise and a few other improvements.

When Roosevelt threatened to seize the mines, he knew that there was nothing in the Constitution that gave him any such power. But his theory about presidential powers was that the President could do anything he thought necessary so long as there was nothing in the Constitution or laws that said he couldn't. Of course, quite the contrary is true. Our government is one of limited powers; no officer of the government can legally do anything unless the right to do so is in the Constitution or implied therein. In case of dispute over whether a power is implied, the issue may be settled in the courts.

** Conservation Program

The first step indicating that the government realized that our natural resources were not inexhaustible was the **Forest Reserve Act of 1891**, which permitted the President to close timber areas to settlers and declare them national parks. Harrison, Cleveland, and McKinley had reserved a total of 45 million acres, and Roosevelt added another 150 million. In addition, he set aside 85 million acres of mineral lands in Alaska. In June 1902, the **Newlands Act (Reclamation Act)** provided that the money received from the sale of public lands in sixteen western states would be used for the construction and maintenance of irrigation projects.

The irrigated land was to be sold to settlers on a ten-year payment plan, with the income therefrom used to create more irrigation projects. Semiarid land blossomed into valuable fruit, sugar beet, and vegetable farms. The first great project was the Roosevelt Dam on the Salt River in Arizona.

In 1905 the supervision of public lands was put under the care of **Gifford Pinchot**, the first Chief Forester of the United States. Pinchot had studied forestry in Europe and had been an influence in stimulating Roosevelt's interest in conservation. He brought knowledge, enthusiasm, vision, integrity, and administrative ability into the federal program while his close friend and boss, the President, made speeches and held conferences, which won popular support and set in motion conservation programs in the several states.

In May 1908, Roosevelt held a conference at the White House on conservation. The delegates included governors of 34 states and 5 territories, representatives from 68 national societies devoted to the preservation of natural resources, members of the Supreme Court and the Cabinet, several members of Congress and individuals who were prominent in conservation or allied fields. Pinchot and Roosevelt apparently succeeded in their efforts, for soon after this conference, 40 states established conservation commissions. A National Conservation Committee with Pinchot as its chairman was set up to make the first inventory of the natural resources of the United States. The total effect of the conservation program of the United States and the several states was by far Roosevelt's greatest achievement.

The conservation program and the coal strike illustrate the great use Roosevelt made of the influence of the office of President. He had no right to order the governors, judges, and others to the White House Conference; but an invitation by the President is not refused. In the coal strike he could not order Mitchell and Baer to meet at the White House nor could he order J.P. Morgan to arrange for arbitration; but the invitations, requests, and suggestions of the President can wield a great deal of influence. Roosevelt was a master of this political skill, and his use of it served as an example for others to follow. He had built greater prestige into the office of the President.

Venezuelan Debt Controversy and the Drago Doctrine

Cipriano Castro, dictator of Venezuela, made no effort to meet debt payments due investors in England, Germany, Italy, and the United States. The European powers let it be known that they were considering the use of force even though they were aware of the Monroe Doctrine. Our government had been consulted by Germany and Great Britain before they established a blockade of Venezuelan ports in December 1902. Italian ships soon joined in the blockade. This much was done with the consent of the United States and with a definite understanding that the European powers were not to seize any Venezuelan territory. But when the blockade resulted in the sinking of Venezuelan gunboats and the lobbing of shells into their ports, Castro asked President Roosevelt to urge arbitration of the dispute. The European powers accepted Secretary of State Hay's proposal to submit the controversy to the Hague Tribunal. It cut the European claims from $40 million to $8 million and the United States claims from about $4 million to $81,000. The episode was a clear recognition by European powers of the Monroe Doctrine; they had brought pressure by force against Venezuela only after consulting with the United States, and they had stopped the use of force when we asked for arbitration.

Dr. **Luis M. Drago**, foreign minister of Argentina, formulated a doctrine during the Venezuelan debt dispute of 1902 that declared that any attempt by European powers to collect debts by force from American nations would be contrary to international law. This proposal was placed before the Hague Peace Conference of 1907 and adopted by the 46 nations there.

** Corollary to the Monroe Doctrine (1904)

President Roosevelt seemed to think the **Drago Doctrine** needed an answer from the United States. In his annual message of December 1904, he said of the Latin-American nations, "Chronic wrongdoing, or an impotence which results in a general loosening of the ties of civilized society...may force the United States, however reluctantly, in flagrant cases of wrongdoing or impotence, to the exercise of an international police power....We would interfere with them only in the last resort, and then only if it became evident that their inability or unwillingness to do justice at home and abroad...had invited foreign aggression...." Thus the United States became the debt collector in Latin America for its European creditors. This **Roosevelt Corollary** led to our intervention in the Dominican Republic (Santo Domingo), Haiti, Nicaragua, and Cuba. The United States was known as the "Colossus of the North," and we entered upon an era of about twenty years of bad relations with our southern neighbors.

Receivership of the Dominican Republic

For about two years, 1903 to 1905, European creditors were seeking through their respective governments to receive payment from the Dominican Republic, but political instability and financial chaos in the island nation presented a hopeless situation. When, in 1904, some American creditors were paid, the demands from European creditors grew louder. The Dominican Republic was under the shadow of President Roosevelt's "big stick" ("Speak softly and carry a big stick"). An agreement was reached between the President and the Dominican Republic whereby the United States could collect the customs duties at Dominican ports and administer the payment of its foreign debts. About 55 percent of the duties were turned over to creditors and 45 percent went to the running of the Dominican government. In two years the debts were paid and the finances of the island republic were in good shape. This was the first time the Roosevelt Corollary was put into operation.

Portsmouth Treaty (1905)

When the **Russo-Japanese War** broke out in 1904, Roosevelt was interested in an outcome that would best preserve the balance of power in the Far East. President Roosevelt learned of the desire each belligerent had for peace, so he quickly invited them to send representatives to Portsmouth, New Hampshire, for a conference. It was Roosevelt's influence that persuaded Japan to give up its demands for a huge cash indemnity and induced Russia to give Japan the southern half of the island of Sakhalin. For bringing this war to an early conclusion, President Roosevelt was awarded the Nobel Peace Prize in 1906.

* Agreements with Japan (Gentlemen's and Root-Takahira)

The Peace of Portsmouth seemed to usher in a period of ill feeling between Japan and the United States. When the Japanese learned that Roosevelt had opposed the cash indemnity demanded from Russia, there were anti-American demonstrations in Japanese cities. This state of mind was further inflamed when they learned that San Francisco made Japanese children attend segregated schools. Newspapers in both nations stirred racial hatreds. The San Francisco school situation and the marked increase in the number of Japanese immigrants entering California after 1900 did pose problems of international importance. Of course, Roosevelt had no legal right to interfere with the San Francisco public school system, but he called the mayor and other anti-Japanese leaders of California to Washington for a talk. The result of the Washington talks was the "Gentlemen's Agreement" of 1907 by which segregation in California schools was discontinued and the Japanese government agreed not to allow any more laborers to come to the United States.

In 1908 Secretary of State, **Elihu Root** (John Hay had died) concluded the **Root-Takahira** executive agreement at Washington. The United States recognized Japan's dominance in Manghuria and Korea, and Japan recognized American sovereignty in the Philippines. Both nations reiterated their support of the Open Door Policy in China.

Algeciras Conference (1906)

By 1904 the Fashoda Affair (1898) and the Boer War (1899-1902) had led to British-French collaboration against Germany, the dominant partner in the **Triple Alliance** of Germany, Austria, and Italy. Russia was allied to France, but in 1904 to 1905 it was suffering a humiliating defeat in the Russo-Japanese War and was in no position to play European power politics. The British-French combination, called the Entente Cordiale, and the Triple Alliance formed a hostile lineup that constituted a balance of power where neither side was expected to risk war with the other. England had extended its colonial control in Africa southward from the Sudan and northward from the Union of South Africa—with French approval. France had colonized Algeria and Tunisia in northern Africa and was in the process of annexing Morocco—with British approval. In 1905 Kaiser Wilhelm II visited the Sultan of Morocco publically to announce that Germany recognized the independence of Morocco.

Wilhelm II called for a conference and asked President Roosevelt to arrange it. The conference met at Algeciras, Spain, where Roosevelt's influence and the good work of Henry White, our representative there, accomplished a settlement that avoided an immediate war. Moroccan independence was recognized, but in 1912 it became a French protectorate and in 1914 World War I began. Roosevelt had entered world politics in the Open Door policy, the Boxer Rebellion, the Root-Takahira Agreement, and the **Algeciras Conference.** It was a new role for an American President, and the Senate expressed its discomfort with a resolution that its ratification of the Algeciras agreement was not to be interpreted as a departure from "the traditional American foreign policy," which forbade our participation in purely European affairs.

* Hague Conferences (1899 and 1907)

In 1898 Czar Nicholas II of Russia called for an international conference to seek ways and means of stopping the wasteful use of wealth in an "armed peace" that could lead only to cataclysmic horror. His immediate reason for calling a halt to the armament race was his plan to spend huge sums on a program of modernizing Russian agriculture and industry. But if his unfriendly neighbor, Germany, continued its rapid buildup of armaments, there was nothing Russia could do but follow suit. The conference was held at The Hague in Holland (Netherlands) in 1899 with 26 nations represented. Every move toward disarmament was blocked because several nations, especially Germany, still hoped their status might be improved some day by the use of armed force. Due largely to the efforts of the American delegation, an international court of arbitration, the Hague Tribunal, was established. There was no force behind the decision of the Hague Tribunal, and no nation had to submit the disputes to it. The court was used for minor differences that were no real threat to the peace.

In 1904 President Roosevelt suggested a second Hague Conference, but the Russo-Japanese War broke out and the meeting got under way at the call of Russia in 1907. The United States again stressed arbitration of international disputes and use of the Hague Tribunal. As in 1899, the arbitration was not compulsory. Our Senate made the provision that no dispute to which the United States was a party could be submitted to arbitration without its approval. The Drago Doctrine (prohibiting international debt collection by force) was accepted by the conference. Both Hague conferences show the realization by nations of the necessity for abolishing war and also the inability of nations to submit to any plan that would limit their freedom of action.

* The Hepburn Act (1906)

For nineteen years the Interstate Commerce Act had been ineffective. "T.R." was fed up with "the immunity from government control" that the railroads still enjoyed. To breathe some life into the Interstate Commerce Commission, Roosevelt sponsored the **Hepburn Bill**, which Congress passed in June 1906.

Its provisions were as follows:

1] The number of commissioners was increased from five to seven.

2] The commission's authority was extended to cover sleeping cars, oil pipelines, ferries, terminals, bridges, and express companies.

3] Reasonable maximum rates could be fixed for railroad services.

4] Rebates were forbidden.

5] With a few unimportant exceptions, free passes were prohibited.

6] Uniform accounting methods prescribed by the commission must be used.

7] The order of the commission were to go into effect even though an appeal might be made to the courts.

The teeth of the act are to be found in the provision that made the railroads and others obey the orders of the commission even though there was court action contesting them. Before the Hepburn Act, the railroads frequently protested rate changes ordered by the commission, no matter how reasonable.

* Pure Food and Drug Act and Meat Inspection Act and Muckrakers

President Roosevelt remembered that the canned meat was much more fatal to the troops in Cuba than Spanish bullets. When he read **Upton Sinclair's** book *The Jungle*, he couldn't believe it; and when word from investigators proved Sinclair's work to be substantially true, he demanded legislation.

The U.S. Department of Agriculture, the American Medical Association, and several *muckraking* magazine articles and books supported the President's efforts to get corrective legislation, while the meatpackers, patent medicine producers, and the Liquor Dealers' Association pooh-poohed the necessity for reform. *The Jungle* overwhelmed the opposition by arousing a public demand that literally drove the laws through Congress within a year. After the laws went into effect (1906), the United States had the best supervision of food, drugs, and meat of any nation.

The muckrakers uncovered corruption in many fields.

THE LEADING MUCKRAKERS

Lincoln Steffens	*Autobiography*
Lincoln Steffens	*The Shame of the Cities*
Upton Sinclair	*The Jungle*
Ida Tarbell	*History of the Standard Oil Company*
Frank Norris	*Octopus*
Winston Churchill (American novelist)	*Coniston*

LEADING MUCKRAKING MAGAZINES

Cosmopolitan David Phillips *The Treason of the Senate*
McClure's carried *History of the Standard Oil Company* and *Shame of the Cities*
Collier's Series of articles on patent medicines
Ladies Home Journal Series of articles on patent medicines
Everybody's Thomas Lawson *Frenzied Finance*

Political Reforms of the Roosevelt Era

There is a school of thought that looks upon "T.R." as having shown more bluster than action in the field of reform. But the job of reform is rarely accomplished in one grand attack with a single remedy; it is usually a long-time process that is never really finished. If the disappointment with Roosevelt as a reformer arises from the fact that there was so much to be done that was left undone, there is still a substantial defense to be made for him. Cleveland said Roosevelt was the ablest politician to occupy the White House. The art of the politician is to know when not to fight, when to compromise, and when to fight to a finish; to know when to let the loaf alone, when to accept half a loaf, and when to grab for the whole loaf. What Roosevelt accomplished he did in spite of his party, and he had to lead the party in a direction it was reluctant to take. He received the affection of the people who were stimulated to demand and achieve reforms on their own so that political democracy was increased in state governments through the initiative, referendum, recall, and the direct primary.

Initiative

A petition containing a draft of a proposed law must be signed by a designated percent of the voters (five to eight). This petition is then filed with the proper state official to be submitted to the state legislature, which must act upon it. There are variations of this procedure. Some states permit the legislature to amend the draft submitted on the petition or to propose a rival bill. Where amendments or rival bills are proposed, they must appear on the ballot at the next general election.

Referendum

The Protest Referendum—A petition signed by a designated percent of the voters (five to eight) asks that a law already passed by the legislature be submitted to the voters of the state so that they may have a chance to defeat it at the next general election. Sometimes the presentation of the petition suspends the law until after the election. This referendum gives the voters veto power.

The Ordinary Referendum—Many state constitutions require that certain laws can be passed only by being referred to the voters. This is often true of bond issues and amendments to state constitutions. Some states require consitutional amendments to be referred to the voters at two or three successive elections and to become law only when approved each time.

Recall

This is a device whereby the voters may start the machinery for the dismissal of an elected or appointed official. A petition requiring a designated percent (25 or more) of the voters results in a special election to determine whether the official will retain his or her position. Some states arrange for another candidate to be on the ballot so that the one getting the greater number of votes fills the office. This device is seldom used.

Direct Primary

Anyone who wishes to run for office may circulate a petition and get the required number of signatures. The total number varies widely, and usually there is a minimum needed in each county of the state. At the primary elections the registered party members elect the nominees from these candidates.

All of these devices—initiative, referendum, recall, and direct primary—give the voters a more direct role in government. To a degree they substitute democracy for republicanism, direct participation for representation.

William H. Taft   1909-1913

1857-1930

REPUBLICAN

Vice-President   JAMES S. SHERMAN

TAFT'S PUBLIC SERVICE BEFORE HE BECAME PRESIDENT

United States Solicitor General under Harrison
Judge of Federal Circuit Court
Head of commission to organize government of Philippines
First Governor-General of the Philippines
Secretary of War under Theodore T. Roosevelt

MAJOR ITEMS OF TAFT'S ADMINISTRATION

* Tariff (Paine-Aldrich, 1909)
Conservation (Pinchot-Ballinger)
Midterm Elections (1910)

Taft's Election in 1908

There was no contest at the Republican convention at Chicago. The Republicans were glad to take advantage of Roosevelt's popularity by nominating his choice of successor. "T.R." campaigned for **William Howard Taft** on a platform pledging continuation of conservation policies, enforcement of antitrust laws, and a downward revision of the tariff. The Democrats nominated William Jennings Bryan for the third time. Their platform was similar to that of the Republicans, but was more vigorous in its stand against monopolies and promised a sharper reduction in the tariff to revenue levels.

	Popular Vote	*Electoral Vote*
Taft	7,679,006	321
Bryan	6,409,106	162

The Republicans retained majorities in both Houses of Congress.

Tariff (Payne-Aldrich, 1909)

* Payne-Aldrich Tariff

Taft had pledged a tariff that would reduce rates appreciably without abandoning protection. This was a feasible plan because the Dingley Tariff of 1897 was extravagantly overprotective. Representative Payne introduced a bill to carry out Taft's pledge. When it got to the Senate, Aldrich of Rhode Island managed to have some 600 rates increased and some 250 other changes made. Several progressive Republicans, among them La Follette and Norris, joined the Democrats in the Senate in angry opposition to the bill. But it passed, and Taft, instead of vetoing it, signed it. A few weeks later he made a speech in Minnesota praising the **Payne-Aldrich Tariff** as the best the Republican party had ever passed. This set the stage for a serious split in the party and a lively midterm election.

* Conservation (Pinchot-Ballinger)

President Roosevelt frequently did what he thought was good for the country with little concern about his legal right to do it. Taft was much more aware of and sensitive to the consitutional limits of his office. Under Roosevelt, according to Taft, some water power sites had been set aside for public development without proper legal authority. These sites were opened to private enterprise. Coal deposits in Alaska, which Chief Forester Pinchot considered set aside as government reserves, were released for private use. Pinchot's superior, Secretary of the Interior Balliner, defended this Alaskan deal, which was investigated and approved by a committee of Congress. Pinchot was then dismissed. but the fat was in the fire. The members of Congress were not impressed with the findings of their own investigating committee; neither were the people, for Pinchot had the support of his old friend and colleague, Roosevelt. The insurgent Republicans and the Democrats combined to oppose Taft. This attack on Taft over **conservation** really made no sense. His program of conservation as a whole was excellent. He retraced "T.R's" steps in setting aside natural resources of water power, forests, and minerals to plug legal gaps and thus make these reserves secure for the government. He persuaded Congress to set up a Bureau of Mines to watch over the government mineral sites; his new chief forester added tremendous tracts of timber in the Appalachians to the national preserves, and set aside oil lands for government use, and was thus the first President to give practical recognition to the importance of this natural resource. Yet, in spite of the facts, his contemporaries judged Taft to be either the betrayer of Roosevelt's conservation policies or, at best, a very weak supporter thereof.

Midterm Elections (1910)

Taft's acceptance of the Payne-Aldrich tariff lost him much of the support of Republican voters, who still looked on Roosevelt as their political hero. The Pinchot-Ballinger tiff over conservation was interpreted by the public and the insurgent Republicans in Congress as proof that Taft had turned his back on Roosevelt's program. While this was grossly unfair to Taft, it was a political factor of importance. Then there was the Speaker of the House, "Uncle Joe" Cannon of Illinois. Joseph Cannon had used the powers of the Speakership to the limit. He appointed the members to the several House committees, he was chairman of the Rules Committee and, as such, could get bills on or keep them off. He made himself a one-man bottleneck through which he had control. Taft had avoided clashing with Cannon in an attempt to avert a party split. When, in the spring of 1910, a combination of insurgents and Democrats voted a change in the rules of the House which deprived the Speaker of membership on the Rules Committee, "Uncle Joe" Cannon could not longer control the flow of bills through the House. This defeat of the Old Guard by a coalition foreshadowed the Republican defeat at the polls in 1910.

In the summer of 1910 Roosevelt returned from his hunting trip in Africa and his visits with the heads of governments in Europe. He had taken a position against Taft on the tariff and conservation. He was heartily in sympathy with the views of the insurgents and reiterated his square deal slogan with appeals to the people, such as "the power of the national government extends to the protection of the whole people against the special interests."

While Roosevelt was reestablishing his political leadership, Taft was losing the confidence of the people. But at that very time (June 1910) he was strengthening the Interstate Commerce Commission by supporting the passage of the **Mann-Elkins Act**, which gave it the right to prevent new rates if challenged in the courts. The act also placed telephone, telegraph, cable, and wireless companies under the authority of the Interstate Commerce Commission. Taft also got Congress to set up Postal Savings banks, as had been advocated in the Populist Platform of 1892. Certain post offices were designated as depositories for savings. But the insurgents and Roosevelt caught public attention, while the deeds of Taft went unnoticed. For the first time in sixteen years, the Democrats gained control of the House and made large gains in the Senate. The nominal majority still held in the Senate by the Republicans lost control to the coalition of insurgents and Democrats. The Democrats also elected 26 governors, one of whom was Woodrow Wilson of New Jersey.

A midterm defeat of such proportions was a defeat for the President. For the balance of his term, Taft continued quietly at work. Before he left office he had initiated 90 antitrust suits, 36 more than the record set by Roosevelt. Taft was to serve in two capacities better suited to his temperament and in which his specialized knowledge and keen intellect could achieve full effectiveness. During 1913 to 1921, he taught law at Yale University, and from 1921 until his death in 1930, he was Chief Justice of the U.S. Supreme Court.

Woodrow Wilson   1913-1921

1856-1924

DEMOCRAT

Vice-President THOMAS R. MARSHALL
Secretary of State WILLIAM J. BRYAN
      ROBERT LANSING

WILSON'S PUBLIC SERVICE BEFORE HE BECAME PRESIDENT

Governor of New Jersey (1911-1912)

MAJOR ITEMS OF WILSON'S ADMINISTRATIONS

*Sixteenth, Seventeenth, Eighteenth
  and Nineteenth Amendments
Underwood Tariff (1913)
Federal Reserve System
  (Glass-Owen Act) (1913)
Federal Trade Commission (1914)
Clayton Antitrust Act (1914)
United States in the Caribbean
  Nicaragua—Dominican Republic—
  Haiti—Virgin Islands
United States and Mexico*

*The Lusitania (May 1915)
Sussex Pledge Broken (February 1917)
Organizing for War
  Liberty Loans and War Revenue Acts—
  Railroads and Ships—War Industries
  Board—Lever Food and
  Fuel Acts—Overman Act
"Fourteen Points" (January 1918)
American Expeditionary Force in France
Treaty of Versailles
The War Record*

* Wilson's Election in 1912 and Reelection in 1916

The first story of the 1912 campaign is that of Roosevelt's unsuccessful attempt to get the Republican nomination away from Taft and his success at replacing La Follette as the leader of the Progressives. The Republican National Convention met at Chicago in mid-June. While Roosevelt had a large following among Progressive Republicans and independent voters, he did not have the support of the Conservative Republicans. The Republican insurgents under the leadership of Senator Robert M. La Follette of Wisconsin had organized a National Republican Progressive League in January 1911. In the autumn of 1911 they had issued a statement that "the logical candidate for the presidency of the United States" was La Follette. But as election day approached, the Progressive wing of the Republican Party realized that Roosevelt, if he would line up with the Progressives, could pull more votes than La Follette. However, Roosevelt was unwilling to commit himself to the Progressives until he had made an attempt to get the regular Republican nomination at the Chicago convention in June. But at the convention the machinery was controlled by the Taft forces. On the first ballot Taft won the nomination with 561 votes to 107 for Roosevelt and 41 for La Follette. In August the Progressives had their convention in Chicago and nominated Roosevelt by acclamation. The man who had been a master politician in the White House had committed a major political blunder. Forming a separate political party could do nothing but split the Republican vote and hand the election to the Democrats. But at the convention all was enthusiasm, almost reaching religious fervor with the singing of "Onward Christian Soldiers." The popular leader declared himself "feeling like a bull moose" and ready for the fray.

The second story of the 1912 campaign is that of

how a college professor with only three years of political experience won the Democratic nomination and the presidency. **Thomas Woodrow Wilson** taught history at Bryn Mawr and Wesleyan, and political economy at Princeton, where he became president in 1902. By 1910 Wilson's books and magazine articles had made him the foremost American scholar in the field of government. George Harvey, editor of *Harper's Weekly*, was seeking a replacement for Bryan as the spokesman for the Democratic party and aspirant for the presidency. The first political move was to get Wilson the nomination for the governorship of New Jersey. Wilson won the election for Governor and within a little over a year had the eyes of the nation focused on Trenton. He accomplished an unbelievable number of reforms: worker's compensation law, direct primary, corrupt practices act, utility control act, and election reforms. In 1911 he visited the Western states on an extensive speaking tour, which enabled him to return to New Jersey as a truly national figure. The next contest would be at the Democratic National Convention at Baltimore in June 1912.

Bryan was still the most influential man in the Democratic party. He was at the convention, not to get the nomination but to see that the liberal faction of the party prevailed. Champ Clark of Missouri led in the early balloting. On the tenth ballot Bryan made a dramatic plea to other states to follow the lead of Nebraska (which had voted for Clark) by changing their support from Clark to Woodrow Wilson, a true liberal. In ballot after ballot one or two states left Clark and went to Wilson, until the New Jersey Governor got the nomination on the 46th ballot. The Democrats and many Independents voted for Wilson, and the Republicans split their votes between Taft and Roosevelt.

	Popular Vote	Electoral Vote
Wilson	6,286,214	435
Roosevelt	4,126,020	88
Taft	3,483,922	8
Debs	897,011	0

The Democrats gained control of both House and Senate.

The election of 1916 was one of the closest in American history. The Republicans nominated **Charles Evans Hughes**, who resigned from the Supreme Court to run. The Progressive party nominated Roosevelt, but he refused and advised them to follow him back into the regular Republican fold. This caused disintegration of the Progressive party and repaired the rift in the Republican party.

The Democrats renominated Wilson, whose greatest campaign asset was the slogan, "He kept us out of war." When the states with the largest blocs of electoral votes, New York, Pennsylvania and Illinois, had voted for Hughes, many newspapers conceded Wilson's defeat. But the next morning, returns from Western states began to change the picture until the final result depended on California. California had gone for Wilson by the narrow margin of 3,773 votes. The Democratic party did not fare as well as its leader. Their majorities in both House and Senate fell almost to the vanishing point, and they lost many governorships to the Republicans. The election was a personal, not a party, victory.

	Popular Vote	Electoral Vote
Wilson	9,129,606	277
Hughes	8,538,221	254

Sixteenth, Seventeenth, Eighteenth, and Nineteenth Amendments

The **Sixteenth Amendment** was proposed in 1909 and ratified in February 1913. (It is considered here, instead of under Taft, for the convenience of having these four amendments together.) It gave Congress the power to establish a federal income tax. This amendment is more evidence supporting the judgment that Taft's alleged conservatism was an illusion fostered by his appearance and personality, but belied by his thinking and the accomplishments of his administration.

The **Seventeenth Amendment** was proposed in 1912 and ratified in May 1913. Both Taft and Wilson approved. It provided for direct election of Senators by the people, a reform long supported by popular opinion.

The **Eighteenth Amendment** was proposed in late 1917, ratified in 1919, and put into effect on January 16, 1920. It outlawed the "manufacture, sale, or transportation of intoxicating liquors." For decades the Anti-Saloon League and the Women's Christian Temperance Union had been agitating for **Prohibition**. Several factors combined to make 1917 to 1920 a favorable time for the adoption of this amendment. Many people thought it a crime to use vast quantities of grain in the production of beer and liquor when food was needed for the Allies in World War I and armed forces on the Western Front. The period of about two years when the amendment was before the states was the time when hundreds of thousands of American men were in Europe and elsewhere in the armed forces and were unable to exert political influence on the issue. The **Volstead Act**, passed over President Wilson's veto, defined "intoxicating" (as used in the amendment) as any beverage containing over one-half of 1 percent alcohol. From the beginning opposition to prohibition was too strong and widespread to permit enforcement. Corruption between federal agents and "bootleggers" reached serious proportions. Making "homebrew" became a fad throughout the land, and the "speakeasies" were a far more dangerous social hazard than the saloons they had replaced. In many "wet" areas the local police refused to cooperate with, and often worked against, federal agents. Supplying illicit alcoholic beverages was large-scale business, and the competition between suppliers resulted in a crime wave.

The **Nineteenth Amendment** granted the vote to women. **Susan B. Anthony** started the campaign for women's suffrage in 1869. That same year the territory of Wyoming permitted women to vote. In the 1890s the states of Wyoming, Colorado, Idaho, and Utah granted **women's suffrage**, as had over a dozen states before World War I. The way many thousands of women did "men's work" in war industries and drove trucks and buses helped their cause with many voters. Congress proposed the amendment in 1919, and it was ratified in August 1920 in time for the women to take part in the presidential election in November.

* Underwood Tariff (1913)

On the day of his inauguration, Wilson called a special session of Congress to meet April 7 to consider downward revision of tariff. Cleveland had failed twice (Mills Bill and the Wilson-Gorman Tariff) and Taft once (Payne-Aldrich Tariff) to achieve this result. For the first time since Jefferson, the President appeared in person to address both Houses in joint session. The chairman of the Ways and Means Committee, Oscar Underwood of Alabama, got the bill through the House as Wilson wanted it. Rates were reduced on over 950 items, mostly necessities, while rates on luxuries were increased. Some 300 items were put on the free list. Altogether it was a reduction of from 25 to 30 percent from the Payne-Aldrich level. The **Underwood Tariff** was the first substantial reduction in 56 years.

Part of the tariff was an income tax (made legal by the Sixteenth Amendment) with rates of 1 percent on single persons with incomes from $3,000 to $20,000 and on married couples with incomes from $4,000 to $20,000. The rate rose to 2 percent on incomes from $20,000 to $50,000 and was graduated until it reached the top limit of 6 percent on incomes above $500,000. In 1913 a foreman in an industrial plant or a highly skilled craftworker made about $1,300 to $1,800 a year.

For years the major parties had been arguing about tariffs. The Republicans had pictured tariff protection as a primary reason for the great industrial growth and prosperity of the United States, the protector of the "full dinner pail" of the workers. The Democrats had claimed that the protective tariff poured profits into the pockets of the rich squeezed from everybody by high prices. Now, for the first time since the United States had become industrialized, we had a tariff for revenue instead of protection.

Less than a year after the passage of the Underwood

Tariff, war broke out in Europe (late July 1914). It started with Austria and Serbia, but within a few days Germany, Russia, France, and England were involved. With Europe shifting to a war economy, imports to the United States dropped and the demand for American products rose. The tariff, no matter what its provisions, shriveled to a point of insignificance as a factor in international trade. Even for revenue purposes the tariff lost out to the much more productive income tax, which soon took the lead as a source of government funds.

* Federal Reserve System (Glass-Owen Act) (1913)

In 1894 Henry Lloyd in his "Wealth Against Commonwealth" charged that a very small group controlled American industry, transportation, and credit. The muckrakers of the following decade uncovered evidence that there was truth in this charge. The Pujo Committee, set up by Congress, investigated. Its report in 1913 served as an excellent background for Wilson's financial and antitrust legislation.

As Wilson put it to Congress when he appeared before them to suggest a new banking system, "...the control of this system...must be public, not private...so that the banks may be the instruments, not the masters of business and of individual enterprise and initiative." Carter Glass of Virginia had been working on a plan for months in collaboration with several bankers and members of Congress. It became the **Federal Reserve Act**. The major provisions were as follows:

1] The nation was divided into twelve Federal Reserve districts with a Federal Reserve bank in each district.

1	Boston	7	Chicago
2	New York	8	St. Louis
3	Philadelphia	9	Minneapolis
4	Cleveland	10	Kansas City
5	Richmond	11	Dallas
6	Atlanta	12	San Francisco

2] All national banks (under the National Banking Act of 1863) had to join the system and deposit 6 percent of their capital and surplus with the Federal Reserve bank in their district. Other banks could join. These member banks thus supplied funds for the twelve Federal Reserve banks. Only banks can do business with the Federal Reserve banks; they are strictly banks for banks.

3] A **Federal Reserve Board** of eight members appointed by the President supervises the system. One of the key powers of this board is to regulate the rediscount rate charged the member banks for loans. This power exercises a major control over the credit available to business.

4] Money can be transferred from any Federal Reserve bank to any other. The supply of money and credit can flow easily to any part of the nation as required by business conditions. The thousands of member banks can obtain funds for sound loans by applying to the Federal Reserve bank of their district. Whether business conditions are sound is a decision made by the Federal Reserve Board and reflected in the rediscount rate.

5] Federal Reserve notes, paper money, can be issued by the Federal Reserve banks with commercial paper as security and the backing of a 40 percent gold reserve.

* Federal Trade Commission (1914)

When Wilson gave the title "New Freedom" to his program, he was talking about freedom for consumers and workers from unfair practices commonly, but by no means exclusively, associated with monopoly power. In his address to Congress in January 1914, he made several specific recommendations, which were, in large part, carried out by the establishment of the Federal Trade Commission and the passage of the Clayton Antitrust Act.

The Federal Trade Commission consisted of five members appointed by the President. Both parties were to be represented on the commission, whose members served a seven year term. Except for banking and transportation, they had jurisdiction over large corporations. Their powers included the right to demand annual and special reports to assist them in fact finding; to publish their findings if such publicity served the public interest; and to issue cease and desist orders, which were subject to review by the courts. The unfair practices most frequently encountered were deceptive and false labeling, adulteration of products, conspiracies to maintain prices, and false claims to patents. The commission was set up to warn and advise corporations in order to prevent violations of law. It proved very useful in advising the government of situations that invited prosecution under the antitrust laws and supplying facts to support antitrust suits.

** Clayton Antitrust Act (1914)

This law was made to correct weaknesses in the Sherman Antitrust Act, add new provisions, and remove labor unions from liability under antitrust laws. To prevent monopoly by preserving competition, it forbade

1] interlocking directorates that would lessen competition among large corporations;

2] ownership of stock by one corporation in a competing corporation;

3] tying contracts, which restricted the retailer to handling only the product of one supplier (for example, an agreement by which a grocer must sell only one brand of soft drink);

4] price cutting below cost in an effort to eliminate a competitor.

The provisions especially favorable to labor provided that

1] antitrust laws do not apply to labor unions, farm organizations, or other nonprofit mutual help associations;

2] injunctions shall not be issued in labor disputes unless there is a threat of irreparable damage to property (This grew out of the injunction against Debs in the Pullman strike of 1894.);

3] boycotts, peaceful strikes, and peaceful picketing are legal;

4] "The labor of a human being is not a commodity or article of commerce."

Interpretation by the courts robbed the labor provisions of the vitality Wilson, and probably Congress, intended. From the Sherman Antitrust Act of 1890 until after the financial crash of 1929, court decisions leaned heavily in favor of the views of business leaders.

United States in the Caribbean

The Roosevelt Corollary initiated a relationship between the United States and Latin America, termed "dollar diplomacy." This means that the diplomacy of our government toward the republics to the south had as its main consideration the protection of investments made by American citizens in those countries. Wherever there were large-scale American businesses in Latin America, such as the United Fruit Company and oil companies, they dominated the economy of the area and sometimes the government of the republic.

Nicaragua

In 1911 President Taft approved a loan by New York bankers of $1.5 million to Nicaragua. To make sure the terms of repayment were fulfilled, Americans operated the National Bank of Nicaragua and United States Marines were stationed there until 1933.

Dominican Republic

Under Theodore Roosevelt, the finances of the Dominican Republic had been put in good order in 1907 but from 1912 to 1915 revolution and general irresponsibility brought the Dominican finances to a chaotic state. President Wilson sent in troops, which established a military government in November 1916. By 1922 the finances were in good order. The next two years settled the political disorders as authority was gradually transferred to the Dominicans. With the election of a president in July 1924, the United States forces were withdrawn.

Haiti

Haiti had two revolutions within six months early in 1915. Because it was unable to meet its financial obligations, President Wilson sent in United States troops and took over the island, which we governed until 1934. During this time the United States held Haiti in receivership; that is, the people of Haiti elected their own officials, whose decisions, especially in the field of finances, were subject to our approval.

Virgin Islands

In 1917 both Denmark and the United States feared Germany might take the Virgin Islands, an eastern outpost of the Caribbean Sea. President Wilson arranged the purchase of the islands for $25 million. In 1927 the inhabitants were made citizens of the United States; in 1936 the islands were organized as a territory; and in 1938 universal suffrage was adopted.

* United States and Mexico

By 1910 **Porfirio Diaz** had been dictator of Mexico for over 30 years. During his regime, foreign investments, mostly American, totaled about $2 billion, with the biggest single investment in oil. Diaz had maintained order and granted liberal concessions to foreign companies. In 1911 Diaz was forced by the liberal revolutionary leader, **Francisco Madero**, to resign, but not until there had been considerable destruction of property and some Americans had lost their lives. President Taft recognized the Madero government and made no move toward military occupation. In February

1913, Madero was assassinated by an agent of **General Huerta**. American business interests strongly urged the recognition of Huerta, but Taft refused. Within two weeks President Wilson was inaugurated. He expressed disapproval of dictators who attained their position by assassination, declared that he would not pursue a policy of dollar diplomacy, refused to recognize Huerta as president, and announced a policy of "watchful waiting." Wilson soon told Huerta that the United States would use its influence to force him from power. An embargo was put on arms shipments to Huerta. In addition, a naval blockade off Veracruz was established to prevent military supplies getting to Huerta from other countries.

On April 9, 1914, unarmed Marines from the U.S.S. *Dolphin* went ashore for supplies at Tampico. They were arrested but released. Huerta refused to apologize for the incident, and Wilson ordered the occupation of Veracruz, Mexico's greatest port. The real reason for the seizure of the port was the shipment from Germany to Veracruz of arms to Huerta. On April 21, 1914, United States ships bombarded Veracruz, and the Marines occupied the city. Wilson was determined on two points: not to permit Huerta to retain power and not to allow this incident to develop into war. When Argentina, Brazil, and Chile (sometimes called the "ABC powers") suggested arbitration, Wilson quickly agreed. These three nations met with the United States and Mexico at the ABC Conference at Niagara Falls, Canada, during late May and all of June 1914. The result was that Huerta went into exile (to Long Island, New York); Carranza, favored by Wilson, was recognized as president of Mexico, and late in 1914 the Marines left Veracruz.

The **Zimmermann note** was an interesting bit of news that broke on March 1, 1917. The British Navy had intercepted and decoded a message sent by the German foreign minister to the German ambassador at Mexico City. It contained instructions to be carried out by the ambassador if and when the United States entered the war against Germany. Mexico was to be promised its "lost territory in New Mexico, Texas, and Arizona" in return for entering the war as an ally of Germany.

* The *Lusitania* (May 1915)

A few days before the *Lusitania* left New York on her last voyage, a notice signed by the Imperial German embassy was printed in *The New York Times* and some other papers. It stated that ships flying the British flag and traveling in the war zone adjacent to the British Isles were liable to destruction. The *Lusitania* was sunk off the coast of Ireland in 1915. (Total aboard—1,924; total lost—1,198; Americans killed—128.) Part of the *Lusitania's* cargo, over 4,000 cases of rifle cartridges, was contraband. International law made such a ship a legal target for enemy action, but it also provided that a warning shot be fired across her bow to stop her and, if she then stopped, there must be reasonable provision made for the safety of the passengers and crew.

Reactions differed sharply throughout America. Congress talked of passing laws forbidding American citizens to travel on ships of belligerents. Wilson favored protests and insistence on our rights as a neutral. But Secretary of State Bryan resigned because he thought such a course would lead to war.

* Sussex Pledge Broken (February 1917)

On August 19, 1915, two American lives were lost when the British passenger ship *Arabic* was torpedoed. The German ambassador assured our government that "liners will not be sunk by our submarines without warning and without safety of the lives of noncombatants, provided that the liners do not try to escape or offer resistance." A month later the German government offered an indemnity for the loss of American lives on the *Arabic*. Wilson's insistence on our rights as a neutral seemed to be bringing results, although this pledge referred only to passenger ships.

On March 24, 1916, the French passenger liner *Sussex* was sunk in the English channel, with the loss of several lives and injury to some Americans. President Wilson threatened to break off diplomatic relations unless there was an immediate end to Germany's "present method of submarine warfare." In the so-called **Sussex Pledge** Germany pledged that it would abide by Wilson's demands on condition that the United States would compel the Allies to respect international law in their naval warfare. From the spring of 1916 to February 1917, there was a lull in submarine activity.

On January 31, 1917, the German ambassador informed the United States that it was returning to unrestricted submarine warfare. The United States was to be allowed one ship a week to the British Isles and three a week to Mediterranean ports. This was both an insult and a breaking of the Sussex Pledge. On February 3 an American ship was torpedoed, and that same day President Wilson announced that the relations between Germany and the United States were severed. He made it clear that additional "actual overt acts" would result in war. On March 16 three American vessels were sunk by submarines. On April 2 Wilson asked Congress for a declaration of war, which the Senate approved by a vote of 82 to 6 on April 4 and the House approved by 373 to 50 on April 6. The United States was at war.

* Organizing for War

Liberty Loans and War Revenue Acts

The government's policy was to raise about two-thirds of the war's cost by borrowing (selling bonds) and the other one third by taxes. During the war there were four **Liberty Loans** (bond issues) and after the war in 1919, a Victory Loan. Instead of borrowing in large sums from banks, as was the case in the Civil War, the government borrowed as little as $50 from individuals. One could buy war stamps at any post office for 25 cents and stick them in a booklet provided for the purpose; when the book was full, it could be turned in for a $50 Liberty bond. These five bond issues raised over $21 billion.

The most important special war tax was the increased levies on incomes, with a graduated rate beginning at 4 percent and reaching a maximum at 65 percent. Corporations were taxed from 20 percent to 60 percent on excess profits, "excess" meaning profits above the level the corporation earned before the war in 1911 to 1913. Railroad tickets, telephone and telegraph messages, theater tickets, liquor, gasoline, and whatever else Congress could think of bore a special war tax. Income from taxes totaled about $11.25 billion.

Railroads and Ships

In the summer of 1916 the railroad workers' unions were demanding more pay and shorter hours. A strike was set for September 8. President Wilson pointed out that the nation was mobilizing its strength under the threat of war; under no conditions could a stoppage of the railroads be permitted. At the last minute Congress passed the **Adamson Act**, which gave railroad workers an eight-hour day with the same pay they had received for a ten-hour day, plus time and a half for overtime. It also gave the President power to take over the railroads if, for military reasons, he thought it necessary.

On December 12, 1917, President Wilson took over the railroads. William G. McAdoo became Railroad Administrator. He enforced a system of priorities, discouraged unnecessary passenger traffic, placed embargoes on nonessential freight, and coordinated all roads into serving the war effort.

The **Esch-Cummins Act of 1920** (Transportation Act of 1920) returned the railroads to private operation. In running all the roads as one coordinated system, the government had become convinced of the efficiency and economy consolidation promoted. The main features of the act were as follows:

1] The Interstate Commerce Commission can evaluate railroad property and fix rates that will yield a fair return.

2] The commission was to work out a plan for consolidating the railroads into fewer systems in order to improve service.

3] A railroad labor board was set up to settle disputes between labor and management.

The end of World War I just about marks the beginning of the decline of railroads. Automobiles, trucks, busses, and finally planes became stronger competitors year by year. The depression of the 1930s hit railroads hard.

In September 1916, Congress set up a shipping board of five members empowered to build, lease, requisition, and purchase ships; that is, to get ships any way they could. This was done effectively through the Emergency Fleet Corporation created ten days after we declared war. Neutral ships were bought, private ships were requisitioned, shipyards, some newly built, performed miracles of construction in wooden, steel, prefabricated, and even concrete ships. By such means the Emergency Fleet Corporation supplied ten million tons of shipping, which meant that we were increasing our tonnage about twice as fast as the submarines were sinking it.

War Industries Board

In late July 1916, the **War Industries Board** was created to supervise all war industries. **Bernard Baruch** was its chairman for most of the war. He had authority to convert factories to war work, to allocate fuel and materials, to fix prices and purchase supplies. He was truly a czar of industry. Our industrial production during the war was so great that it amazed ourselves, our allies, and our enemies.

Lever Food and Fuel Act

Herbert Hoover headed the Food Administration. He had already won a worldwide reputation by his work in Belgian War Relief. As Food Administrator he could fix prices on staple foods and do whatever seemed effective to "stimulate and conserve the production and control the distribution of foods." The law prevented the use of grain for the manufacture of alcoholic beverages. A very effective program worked well because the public cooperated wholeheartedly; it included wheatless Mondays, meatless Tuesdays, and porkless Thursdays. The farmers expanded acreage and stepped up production until they were feeding America,

much of war-torn Europe, and the Allied armed forces.

Harry Garfield was Fuel Administrator. His powers and responsibilities paralleled those of Hoover for food. Monday was fuelless day when householders kept the temperature no higher than 65 degrees. Sunday was gasless day when anyone driving a private car other than in a funeral procession felt embarrassed. Nonessential factories often were shut down so that their fuel supply could be transferred to a war plant. Electric advertising signs remained unlighted, and daylight saving was instituted.

Overman Act

In May 1918, President Wilson was given unprecedented powers by the **Overman Act**, which was to be in effect only during the war. It allowed him to create or abolish Executive bureaus, agencies, and offices; to shift personnel from one to another; to reallocate funds from one to another; in short, to do as he thought best for the conduct of the war.

** Fourteen Points (January 1918)

On January 8 President Wilson addressed Congress to state the war aims and peace terms of the United States. He called it the "only possible" program that could maintain world peace. Some points dealt with territorial adjustments of immediate concern, and others stated principles that Wilson thought should guide and permeate international relationships. We are concerned with the latter only.

1] Open covenants (treaties) openly arrived at.

2] Absolute freedom of the seas in peace and war.

3] Removal of barriers to international trade.
   This referred to tariffs, quota systems, and any artificial hindrances to commerce.

4] Reduction of armaments to the point where each nation has only a police force to keep domestic order.

5] Self-determination of peoples.
   Throughout the world any area that has the extent and resources to be a nation should be governed according to the free choice of its people.

6] A general association of nations must be formed. Wilson states this to be the most important of the **Fourteen Points.** It could be a continuing force working to achieve a better world.

The American Expeditionary Forces In France

The month the United States entered the war was the peak of the submarine offensive. That April over 880,000 tons of shipping went to the bottom. The average monthly loss was 200,000 tons. The last six months of 1917 found the Allies at their lowest point. They were maintaining a desperate defense, with no capacity to mount an attack. The arrival of the first American troops in France on June 26 was a boost to Allied morale, but little else. These troops took positions in the fighting front in late October. But there was bad news. In October the Italian army in the Caporetto campaign began to crumble; by December it had collapsed and left northeastern Italy to the Germans. The November revolution in Russia released huge German forces for use in France. American troops arrived at an accelerating rate, to reach a total in one month, April 1918, of over 313,000. Before the war ended, American troops in France totaled 2,084,000. **General John J. Pershing** was in command of the **Allied Expeditionary Forces, (AEF)**.

Chronology of Major Actions Involving Substantial American Forces

June 3-4 1918	Chateau-Thierry (defensive)
June 6-July 1	Belleau Wood—27,500 U.S. Troops with the French. Successful counterattack.
July 18-Aug. 6	Second Battle of the Marne (defensive) 85,000 U.S. Troops. The German offensive begun in March was stopped here.
Aug. 8-Nov. 11	The Somme (offensive) 54,000 U.S. troops with the British.
Aug. 19-Nov. 11	Ypres (offensive) 108,000 U.S. troops with the British.
Sept. 12-16	St. Mihiel (offensive) 550,000 U.S. Troops wiped out a dangerous salient south of Verdun
Sept. 26-Nov. 11	Meuse-Argonne (offensive) 1,200,000 U.S. troops.

The armistice terms with Germany were agreed to on November 11, 1918.

WAR COST	
Dead	112,432 Americans (over half from disease, chiefly influenza)
Money Spent	$21,850,000,000
Money loaned to Allies	$10,350,000,000

Treaty of Versailles

On October 24, 1918, President Wilson asked to elect Democratic majorities in both Houses of Congress, not because "any political party is paramount in matters of patriotism, " but because the times demand a "unified leadership, and that a Republican Congress would divide the leadership....The return of a Republican majority to either House of Congress would, moreover, be interpreted on the other side of the water as a repudiation of my leadership." This was a most unfortunate and impolitic message. Unfortunate because the opportunity for successful compromise with Republicans on plans for the peace should have been obvious to the President. Whatever the outcome of the congressional elections, bipartisan participation in the task of building the peace held the greatest promise. Impolitic because Wilson must have known that his message to the people might be resented by them as an attempt to wield undue influence in state affairs. His appeal for a Democratic Congress backfired. The Republicans won the House by 50 seats and the Senate by 2. Two weeks after the election he announced that he was going to Paris for the Peace Conference. A substantial objection to his trip was that, among the four advisors he had selected to go with him, only one was a Republican and none were Senators. If he came back with a treaty, it would be the Senate that would either ratify it, or refuse to!

Wilson negotiated with **Georges Clemenceau** of France, **David Lloyd George** of Great Britain, and **Vittorio Orlando** of Italy. These men, the **Big Four**, made most of the decisions. In order to get the **League of Nations** written into the treaty, Wilson gave in on some terms neither he nor the United States approved. He made the point that some inequities and mistakes, as we saw them, could be corrected later through the League of Nations as time proved them to be unwise.

The bulk of the **Versailles Treaty** was the **Covenant of the League of Nations**. Other terms included the forced admission of guilt by Germany for the war and the return of Alsace-Lorraine to France. The Saar Basin (rich in iron and coal) was put under the League of Nations for fifteen years, after which the people could vote to go with either France or Germany. Danzig was made a free city (to give Poland a seaport). The German Rhineland was demilitarized and German colonies were mandated under the League of Nations. The ratification of this treaty, with the Covenant of the League of Nations as the heart of it, became the great debate of the campaign of 1920.

* The War Record

A brief look back over World War I shows a job remarkably well-done. The President, Congress, industry, agriculture, shipping, labor, the armed forces, and the people became an effective team. General Pershing proved to be a more than capable head of the AEF. About 4.5 million men were in the armed forces. Liberty bonds and the **Selective Service Act** raised money and men wisely, effectively, and fairly.

There was one blot on the picture, the almost hysterical behavior of too many people encouraged by Attorney General Palmer, the Espionage Act, and the Sedition Act. Some schools dropped German and some libraries removed German books from the shelves, and some colleges revoked honorary degrees they had given to distinguished Germans.

Warren G. Harding   1921-1923

1865-1923

REPUBLICAN

☆

Vice-President   CALVIN COOLIDGE

Secretary of State   CHARLES E. HUGHES

HARDING'S PUBLIC SERVICE BEFORE HE BECAME PRESIDENT

Senator in the Ohio Legislature
United States Senator from Ohio (1915-1921)

MAJOR ITEMS OF HARDING'S ADMINISTRATION

Washington Conference (1921-1922)
Fordney-McCumber Tariff (1922)

Election of Harding (1920)

Ohio's **Senator Warren G. Harding** was nominated at the Republican Convention, with Governor **Calvin Coolidge** of Massachusetts as his running mate. Harding was a "dark horse" selection made after more prominent candidates had fought to a deadlock through nine ballots. The Old Guard picked him. His qualifications included a pleasing personality, party regularity, handsome appearance, and no enemies. Harding seemed sometimes to be flatly against the League of Nations and at others to favor it with a few modifications. This strategy resulted from differences within the party. Those who were strongly opposed to the League would certainly support Harding; but, on the other hand, such Republican leaders of caliber as Elihu Root, Charles E. Hughes, and Herbert Hoover said that a vote for Harding was the best way to get the United States into the League with some reservations to safeguard American interests.

James M. Cox, also from Ohio, was nominated at the Democratic Convention with **Franklin Roosevelt** as his running mate. The platform advocated ratification of the Versailles Treaty, which contained the Covenant of the League of Nations. The Democrats were intent on

making the League of Nations the one issue of the campaign, but the real debate on the League was over. It had begun in September 1919 when Wilson decided to take his cause to the people. He had started on a western tour speaking to large, enthusiastic audiences. He had been followed a few days later by Republican Senator Lodge, who spoke against the League. On September 26 Wilson had started back east from Colorado, when he collapsed and was incapacitated for the rest of his term. With the loss of his eloquence and crusading zeal, the vitality had gone out of the debate.

Harding advocated a "return to normalcy." It suggested a return to the days when we were not entangled in foreign problems, pestered by demands for reforms, and annoyed by government regulations. During the war the people had responded to the idealism of Wilson, they had accepted government controls, they had sacrificed individual freedoms for a cause bigger than themselves—and now they were weary. Let's "return to normalcy" were welcome words.

When the ballots were counted, the overwhelming Republican victory was "explained" in terms of a protest against government regulation, high taxes, the high cost of living, weariness from the war, and perhaps the League of Nations.

	Popular Vote	Electoral Vote
Harding	16,152,200	404
Cox	9,147,353	127
Debs	919,799	0

This was the first presidential election in which women voted.

Debs had been convicted of sedition and ran his campaign from the federal penitentiary in Atlanta.

* Washington Conference (November 12, 1921-February 6, 1922)

This conference was called to ease tensions that existed over the situation in the Far East and to reduce naval armaments. The nations represented were Belgium, China, France, Great Britain, Italy, Japan, Netherlands, Portugal, and the United States. Secretary of State Hughes was chairman of the conference.

The **Washington Conference** resulted in a series of treaties.

1] The Five Power Pact (United States, Great Britain, Japan, France, and Italy) provided for the limitation of naval armaments. The ratio of capital ships (over 10,000 tons displacement) was to be United States—5; Great Britain—5; Japan—3; France—1.75; and Italy—1.75. For a period of ten years, no new capital ships were to be built. The United States and Great Britain already had more than their quota of capital ships, so both destroyed some and cancelled their plans for others. The United States, Great Britain and Japan agreed to maintain the "status quo" of their "fortifications and naval bases" in the Far East. Japan returned Shantung with its port of Kiao-chow to China. The fact that smaller cruisers, submarines, destroyers, etc., were not limited made the treaty meaningless as far as maintaining any ratio of strength of one navy to another. But the treaty reduced naval appropriations for a while

and gave hope (which turned out to be false) for the future.

2] A Four Power Pact (United States, Great Britain, France, and Japan) agreed to respect each others rights in the Pacific Ocean region and to settle by peaceful means disagreements that might arise. This replaced an Anglo-Japanese Alliance of 1905 which had worried Australia, New Zealand, Canada, and the United States.

3] A Nine Power Pact (including all nations at the conference) provided that China's political and territorial sovereignty would be respected. It was also agreed that submarines should be used only in accordance with the recognized rules of war. The use of asphyxiating gases in warfare was outlawed.

* Fordney-McCumber Tariff (1922)

The Republicans were anxious to get back to protective tariff policies. Fearing Europe's efforts to sell in the American market, Congress passed the **Fordney-McCumber Tariff**. It was the highest yet. Apparently Congress was not attracted to Wilson's idea that lowering trade barriers was essential to international peace. There were no immediate ill effects from the tariff. The twenties were to be known as the "gilded twenties" because we experienced a frothy prosperity as we headed for the 1929 crash. The real harm in the Fordney-McCumber Tariff was the example it set. Other nations were bound to retaliate. As tariff walls went up, many American manufacturers established plants in foreign countries. Some leading industrialists and bankers retreated from their support of protection as they awoke to the fact that foreign trade has to be a two-way street. This economic truth did not penetrate quickly or easily. It was after the depression of the 1930s that more and more nations turned to reciprocal trade agreements as a method of chipping away at the tariff walls.

Calvin Coolidge 1923-1929

1872-1933

REPUBLICAN

☆

Vice-President CHARLES G. DAWES
Secretary of State FRANK B. KELLOGG

COOLIDGE'S PUBLIC SERVICE BEFORE HE BECAME PRESIDENT

Mayor of Northampton, Massachusetts
Lieutenant Governor of Massachusetts
Governor of Massachusetts
Vice-President of the United States

MAJOR ITEMS OF COOLIDGE'S ADMINISTRATION

Oil in the Cabinet
Oil in Mexico
Kellogg-Briand Peace Pact (Pact of Paris) (1928)

Election of Coolidge (1924)

While returning from a trip to Alaska, President Harding died in San Francisco on August 2, 1923. He had found the responsibilities of the office of President too great for his capacities. Under the most favorable circumstances, Harding would probably have been miserable under the strain, and conditions were far from favorable. He had brought too many "friends" with him from Ohio, some of whom had helped him up the political ladder. He had not been President long before he realized that several important appointments made on the basis of political spoils had gone sour. Harding lacked the moral courage to attack corruption when those involved were his friends.

Vice-President Coolidge (who became President), was quite unlike Harding; he was neither handsome nor congenial; no one could lead him where he didn't want to go; he was thrifty and honest. The end of Harding's term was a sordid story of scandal. Nothing could have been better for the Republicans than the presence of

Calvin Coolidge in the White House.

The Republican Convention met in Cleveland and nominated Coolidge by an almost unanimous vote. The platform called for a continuation of the Fordney-McCumber Tariff, membership in the World Court, international cooperation to prevent war, and limitation of armaments. Our attitude toward the League of Nations was still one of confusion. We wouldn't join it, but we favored its purposes and frequently worked with it.

The Democrats tore their party apart at the Democratic Convention in New York. William G. McAdoo of Tennessee and Alfred E. Smith of New York battled for 101 ballots. Finally both candidates withdrew, and on the 103rd ballot **John W. Davis**, a conservative, was nominated. In a listless election, the Republicans won almost without a contest.

	Popular Vote	*Electoral Vote*
Coolidge	15,725,016	382
Davis	8,385,586	136

* Oil in the Cabinet

Before Harding had gone on his Alaska trip, there were rumors of graft in the President's official family. About two months after his death, a Senate committee under Thomas Walsh of Montana was formed to investigate oil leases made to private companies from government reserves in Wyoming (**Teapot Dome**) and California (**Elk Hills**). These reserves of oil had been set aside under Taft and Wilson for the use of the navy. In its essentials, the story uncovered was as follows. Soon after his inauguration, President Harding transferred the Teapot Dome and Elk Hills oil reserves from the Navy Department (Secretary Denby) to the Interior Department (Secretary Fall). Fall then entered into a secret, illegal, and corrupt deal with two oil men, Harry Sinclair and Edward Doheny. Without competitive bidding and at a bargain price, Teapot Dome was leased to Sinclair, who had made a large contribution to the Republican campaign in 1920; and the Elk Hills reserve was leased to Doheny, a close friend of Fall. In March 1923, Fall resigned from the Cabinet much richer than before he entered it.

The investigating committee discovered that Fall had received a "loan" of $100,000 from Doheny on which he was charged no interest, for which he put up no security, and for which no arrangements had been made for repayment. Fall also received a "loan" of about $300,000 from Sinclair. Fall went to jail for accepting a bribe from Doheny. Doheny and Sinclair were tried on charges of "conspiracy to defraud the government" and were acquitted; but the Supreme Court declared the leases cancelled because they were a "conspiracy" involving "fraud" and "corruption." Secretary of the Navy Denby resigned during the Senate investigations.

Attorney General Daugherty should have been aware of the oil deal before the Senate started to investigate. He was one of Harding's appointees known as the "Ohio gang". The apparent ignorance of the Justice Department of what was going on suggested, at the very best, incompetence. Investigation brought out gross irregularities. Daugherty had been bribed by Prohibition law violators, and he had known of graft in the Veterans' Bureau but had done nothing about it. He was tried for conspiracy and acquitted. President Coolidge forced him to resign.

Colonel Forbes, head of the Veterans' Bureau, went to jail for conspiring to sell narcotics, liquor, and other government property. Colonel Thomas Miller, Custodian of Alien Property, sold German chemical patents for such small sums that bribery seemed the only explanation. He went to prison for "conspiring to defraud the government."

** Oil in Mexico

Under Coolidge a long and difficult controversy with Mexico was finally put on the right road to a settlement. The trouble started with the new Mexican constitution of 1917. Article 27 stated that all mineral wealth (including oil) in Mexico belonged to the government, and concessions to develop mineral resources could be granted only to Mexican nationals. This was not a necessary source of friction unless Article 27 was made retroactive. The United States was ready to accept the view that Mexico could do what it wished with its natural resources, provided property rights already acquired by Americans were not disturbed. Americans had about $300 million in such investments by 1919. In 1919 **Obregon** became President and would give no such assurance. We increased our border patrol to proportions suggesting intervention, but tension was relieved when the Mexican Supreme Court declared that Article 27 did not apply to properties acquired before the adoption of the constitution of 1917. In 1925 President Calles embarked on a revolutionary reform program to redistribute land, to break the power of the Roman Catholic Church, and to confiscate foreign holdings of mineral wealth under Article 27. President Coolidge sent Dwight W. Morrow as ambassador to Mexico. Painstakingly and patiently Morrow persuaded President Calles that the United States basically approved of his revolutionary aims and that it was only the confiscation of lawful property to which we objected. Morrow made himself a very welcome ambassador in Mexico City and set the pattern for the eventual solution of American investments in Mexican land and minerals.

* Kellogg-Briand Treaty (Pact of Paris) (1928)

Ten years after the end of World War I, Secretary of State Frank Kellogg decided to give the anniversary suitable recognition. Briand, the French foreign minister, had suggested a bilateral agreement to outlaw war. Kellogg suggested a multilateral agreement. Eventually 62 nations signed it.

The "outlawry of war" was a pledge to reject war as an instrument of international policy. Up until this time, war had been a legally respectable, though drastic, procedure by which nations sought to accomplish their purposes. The Kellogg-Briand Treaty made war a criminal act on the part of any nation signing the agreement. There was no force to back it up except the moral influence of world opinion, and war was restricted to mean only offensive war.

Herbert Hoover   1929-1933

1874 -1964

REPUBLICAN

☆

Vice President   CHARLES CURTIS
Secretary of State   HENRY L. STIMSON

HOOVER'S PUBLIC SERVICE BEFORE HE BECAME PRESIDENT

Headed war relief in Belgium
Food Administrator in World War I
Secretary of Commerce under Harding and Coolidge

MAJOR ITEMS OF HOOVER'S ADMINISTRATION

National Origins Immigration Act (1929)
Panic and Depression
Hawley-Smoot Tariff (1930)

* Hoover's Election (1928)

President Coolidge could have had the nomination, but he had said several months before the convention, "I do not choose to run." At the convention in Kansas City, Missouri, the Republicans nominated **Herbert Hoover.** He had shown great capacity as an administrator in Belgian Relief and as Food Administrator; he had become very wealthy as a mining engineer and consultant. He was looked upon by the people as a humanitarian and a business person, one who combined a sympathetic understanding of great human needs with the practical ability to administer a program with businesslike efficiency. The platform favored the continuance of Prohibition and protective tariffs. In his "rugged individualism" speech at the close of the campaign, Hoover expressed his philosophy of government.

At the Nominating Convention at Houston, Texas, the Democrats nominated **Alfred E. Smith,** four-time governor of New York. The platform advocated the enforcement of Prohibition, regulation of water resources, independence of the Philippines, and better enforcement of the anti-injunction provision of the Clayton Antitrust Act. In the campaign, Smith advocated

repeal of Prohibition. Al Smith was very popular in the cities of the Northeast, but his reception in the West and South was less than friendly. That he favored repeal of Prohibition, was the first Roman Catholic to run for presidency, and had ties to the Tammany Hall political machine made him unpopular with voters in the West and South.

	Popular Vote	Electoral Vote
Hoover	21,392,190	444
Smith	15,016,443	87

** National Origins Immigration Act (1929)

This act established a policy of immigration control. Earlier, laws and international agreements had excluded the Chinese, the Japanese, and most other Asians. However, it was not until the 1920s that total immigration was restricted and the doors to America closed.

The census of 1890 showed a new trend in immigration. In the preceding decade a great increase of people from eastern and southern Europe occurred. In 1914 almost 75 percent of all immigrants came from eastern and southern Europe.

In 1921 the first quota law allowed 3 percent based on the census of 1910. For example: if the census showed 10,000 persons in the United States who had been born in X nation, this law would give the nation a quota of 300. In 1924 a new law provided for 2 percent based on the census of 1890. The earlier the census date, the smaller the proportion of eastern and southern Europeans to the total population. This is so because they didn't begin to come here until 1880 and didn't reach their highest yearly peak until 1914. The 1924 law not only cut the number by 1 percent, but also held back the eastern and southern Europeans, while making comparatively little difference to quotas for western and northern Europe. On July 1, 1929, the **National Origins Formula** became law. This was the most drastic in its discrimination on the basis of nationality.

THE FORMULA

$$\frac{X}{150,000} = \frac{\text{Number of persons who trace their origin to X nation according to the census of 1890}}{120,000,000 \text{ (approximate population in 1920)}}$$

Asians were excluded.

Quotas did not apply to Latin America and Canada or to a few individuals such as college students, professors, and ministers.

If a quota was less than 100, that nation could send in 100 provided the total of 150,000 had not been reached.

Immigration policy was one subject on which Hoover and Smith agreed in the campaign of 1928. Both opposed the National Origin Formula, which was before Congress. They considered it unfair and arbitrary.

In 1952 the **McCarran-Walter Act** modified the 1929 law by including Asians in the formula. Some provisions were also added to keep out "subversives" and to expel immigrants belonging to "Communist or Communist-front" organizations.

The **Immigration Act of 1965** abolished the system of national quotas. Instead it provided for a "global quota" with the annual admission of 120,000 immigrants from the Western Hemisphere and 170,000 from all other nations. Those who were relatives of American citizens and those who had special skills were given preference. This law resulted in an increase in the number of Asians and Hispanics entering the United States.

** Panic and Depression

Some of the Causes

For a week before October 29, 1929, stock prices slumped, but on that date the bottom fell out of the market. From October 21 to November 13, total prices of securities declined about $30 billion and by June about $75 billion. Why? Several factors contributed, but the one most often given is overspeculation in securities (shares of stock of all kinds of enterprises). During the "gilded prosperity" of the 1920s, the middle-income group, which had rarely bought stock before, entered the market. Tens of thousands of these new purchasers of stocks bought stock on 10 percent which meant that they could purchase securities priced at $500 by putting down $50, plus a small brokerage fee. A few years of almost steadily rising stock prices meant that the price of securities had risen far beyond the value behind them. If a share of stock in 1922 representing $100 actually invested in a corporation were sold many times at a higher price each time, it might reach a market price in 1929 of $500; but only its price would have risen, not its value. How long can this sort of "bull market" (rising prices) last and how high can it go? "What goes up must come down" applies to such a stock market situation as prevailed throughout the 1920s. Overspeculation was only part of the story, however; other factors also contributed.

During the 1920s a substantial part of the goods we sold to Europe were purchased with money loaned by American investors. No business can prosper by lending money to its customers so that they can buy its products. While not quite as simple as this, it was essentially the explanation of the apparently healthy export trade the United States enjoyed. When the loans were not repaid and no more were made, business stopped. Form 1929 to 1931 foreign trade fell over 55 percent.

A war-impoverished Europe was a strong force pulling the American economy down. By the late 1920s there was some suspicion that was debts might not be paid. By June 1931 President Hoover declared a **moratorium** on a $250 million war-debt installment then due. Moratorium followed moratorium until it was recognized that the debts wouldn't be paid. Finland was the only nation that paid its war debt in full to the United States, and almost surely the only nation that could do so.

The farmers of America had been in a depression since about 1920. Rural America was still a large enough segment of the population to affect the economy as a whole. When farm families slow down on their purchases over a period of years, the farm machinery companies and the merchants in the smaller towns feel the pinch, and eventually the factories that supply the rural retailers become idle.

Wages rose slowly, about 12 percent, during the 1920s before the crash. Those whose chief income was the form of dividends, profits, and rents fared much better. This is another was of saying that a maldistribution of wealth developed until it became marked enough to adversely affect the economy. It was estimated that one twentieth of the people had one-third of the purchasing power. Our foreign trade had fallen away, and most of our own people were unable to buy the products of our own factories. When too many have too little and too few have too much, business stagnates.

Installment buying went to great extremes during the 1920s. Although the installment system has its proper place, it can be a serious deterrent to business. For example, if a family buys several items (house, car, furniture, vacuum cleaner, refrigerator) on the installment plan, the purchasing power of that family is curtailed. If the family overextends itself and is unable to meet all these payments, it will have some purchases reclaimed by the merchant and thus lose the money already paid and the item. If the family is hard-pressed to meet all payments, it will curtail expenditures for food, medical care, fuel, and other essentials that are more important to the family welfare that the installment purchases. Multiply this unsound family financing by a few million and the result is an unsound economy.

A Few Immediate Results

1] About 15 million unemployed.

2] About one-third of the railroad mileage bankrupt.

3] About $132 billion loss in national income from 1930 to 1938.

4] Over 5,500 banks closed between the stock market crash in 1929 and the bank "holidays" proclaimed by several governors and the President in 1933.

5] Pitiful shacks made from whatever materials the city dumps supplied grew into sizeable communities ("**Hoovervilles**") at the dump sites.

6] About one-fourth of the farms were lost through nonpayment of taxes or mortgages.

7] The "**bonus marchers**" converged on Washington from as far away as Portland, Oregon. Most of them had a $1,000 bonus payable in 20 years. Over President Hoover's veto, Congress passed a law in February 1931

to pay them half their bonus immediately. In July 1932, 10,000 veterans were at the capitol building demanding the other half. They encamped at several places in Washington, the largest being at Anacosta Flats. These unemployed veterans, some with their families, made a sorry spectacle in the capital city. Many left after the Senate refused to pass the second bonus bill, but those who stayed in the tumble-down encampments because they had no jobs and no reason to go anywhere else were finally driven off by tanks, tear gas, and some gunfire. Two soldiers, later to become famous, were officers in charge of this very distasteful job, Douglas MacArthur and Dwight Eisenhower.

8] Cities and towns all over the United States and private charitable organizations did what they could for relief; but the bread lines were long and the need for shelter too great.

Some Things Hoover Did

1] Business owners were urged to maintain their payrolls at normal levels.

2] To keep prices up, the **Federal Farm Board** attempted, with little success, to stabilize prices in cotton, grain, wool, and some other commodities by purchasing them on the open market.

3] The federal government supplied leadership at state and local levels in organizing voluntary relief agencies.

4] In December 1930, a small program of public works called for expenditures up to $150 million.

5] In February 1932 the **Reconstruction Finance Corporation** (RFC) was formed. It was empowered to lend up to $2 billion to railroads, insurance companies, banks, farm mortgage associations, and building and loan associations. This was a "pump priming" measure. If such a corporation was threatened with bankruptcy, the RFC could decide whether a loan might save it; if a loan restored the business to a sound economic footing, the benefits would spread to the shareholders, the employees, and thousands of persons doing business with the corporation. In such a case the loan would be repaid. In some cases the corporations failed and the loans were lost.

6] In July 1932, when unemployment had climbed to about 10 million, the Relief and Construction Act was passed, making available $3 billion for public works of a "self-liquidating" type (something that, once completed, would bring in revenue to pay for itself). States and cities could become part of this program. About

$300 million was set aside for loans to states that were unable to finance their relief burdens.

President Hoover suffered two injustices. One was that he was blamed for the depression. The other injustice was the charge that he did nothing to relieve the depression. As we have noted, he did do several things; but they were woefully small in scope until early 1932 (the RFC), and then it seemed to the people that the government would make but the feeblest moves for relief of individuals, but had billions to help bail out distressed corporations. The President's approach to the problem of the depression was consistent with the ideas he had many times expressed. Handing out relief for multitudes of individuals, imperative as it was, should he thought, be done by private charity and at the local levels of government. The RFC, however, was a constructive relief that sought to put corporations in a position to prosper and thus maintain productive employment; it was reviving economic life to a self-sustaining status.

It should be remembered that the depression of the 1930s was the first one that produced planning by governments—city, state, and federal. Our procedure in all previous depressions was to wait it out. This explains Hoover's early, and too long continued, assertions that the country was "fundamentally sound," that "all we need is confidence," and that "prosperity is just around the corner." This was no cheap attempt to fool the people and stall for time; it was a conviction based on his economic philosophy and apparently backed by America's experience.

* Hawley-Smoot Tariff (1930)

Hoover had asked for a slight revision of the tariff; what he got was a very considerable revision that pushed protection to a new high and brought protests from importers, some bankers and a few industrialists. Foreign reaction to the **Hawley-Smoot Tariff** was marked and fast; 25 nations put up tariff barriers against American goods, and our foreign trade, both exports and imports, fell off over 50 percent within 18 months. Of course the depression must have been an important factor, but some of the decline in trade can be put at the door of the Hawley-Smoot Tariff. More American manufacturers built factories in European countries.

Franklin D. Roosevelt 1933-1945

1882-1945

DEMOCRAT

☆

Vice-President   JOHN N. GARNER
HENRY A. WALLACE
HARRY S TRUMAN

Secretary of State   CORDELL HULL

FRANKLIN ROOSEVELT'S PUBLIC SERVICE BEFORE HE BECAME PRESIDENT

State Senator in New York
Assistant Secretary of the Navy
Governor of New York (1928-1932)

MAJOR ITEMS OF FRANKLIN ROOSEVELT'S ADMINISTRATION

Twentieth and Twenty-First Amendments
("Lame Duck" and Repeal of
Prohibition)
New Deal
   Major Financial Measures—
   Unemployment—Housing—
   Agriculture—Labor—Business

and Industry—Youth—Tennessee Valley
Authority—Social Security—Supreme
   Court Fight
Approaching World War II
Fighting World War II
Building the Peace
Eleanor Roosevelt

Franklin Roosevelt's Election in 1932, 1936, 1940, and 1944

Hoover was nominated at the Republican Convention in Chicago on the first ballot; no one else made any effort to get the nomination. The Democratic Convention met in the same hall a few days later and nominated Franklin D. Roosevelt, the Governor of New York State on the fourth ballot. Al Smith made a try for the nomination, but the party feared a revival of the religious issue. Besides, Roosevelt had shown great vote-getting ability in New York by winning the governorship in 1928 and 1930. **John Nance Garner** of Texas (Speaker of the House) was nominated as the Democratic vice-presidential candidate.

During the campaign, Roosevelt not only used radio effectively, he made a tour of the country. He wished to demonstrate his physical vigor in spite of the paralysis in his legs (polio) and to take full advantage of per-

sonal appearances which he had found such an effective vote-getter. He pictured the depression as an emergency every bit as real as war and a situation demanding "action." He promised a **"New Deal,"** especially in behalf of "the forgotten man at the bottom of the economic pyramid." He asserted it to be the proper concern of the federal government to see that no American citizen starved. President Hoover blamed the depression on world conditions and claimed his administration had prevented the situation from becoming worse. The Republican platform pledged continued protective tariffs, revision of Prohibition, decrease in public spending, and a balanced budget. The Democratic platform pledged a revenue tariff, a balanced budget, decreased public spending, repeal of Prohibition, aid to farmers to bring farm prices above costs, banking and stock-exchange reforms to prevent fraud, and regulation of holding companies to prevent a repetition of the Insull public utilities abuses.

	Popular Vote	Electoral Vote
F. D. Roosevelt	22,809,638	472
Hoover	15,758,901	59

Hoover won Maine, Vermont, New Hampshire, Connecticut, Pennsylvania, and Delaware.

The Democrats swept the Congress—60 to 35 in the Senate and 310 to 117 in the House.

Election of 1936

This campaign presented the voters with a chance to pass judgment on the New Deal. Recovery, though far from complete, had restored the will and the strength to the opposition to unite their forces.

The Republicans nominated **Governor Alfred (Alf) Landon** of Kansas, who had been among the very few Republicans strong enough to win during the Democratic landslide of 1932. He attracted further attention by maintaining a balanced budget in his state. Two former Democratic presidential candidates, Al Smith and John W. Davis, broke with the New Deal and came out for Landon. The Republicans waged a spirited attack on the idealogy of the New Deal but did not urge the repeal of any major New Deal legislation.

The Democrats nominated Roosevelt and Garner by acclamation. Their platform was a recital of their record and a promise to continue along the same lines. Because the campaign was waged on a clash of ideas rather than the approval or rejection of separate laws or measures, feeling ran high and the campaign was bitterly fought even through the result was extremely one-sided.

	Popular Vote	Electoral Vote
F. D. Roosevelt	27,751,612	523
Landon	16,681,913	8

Landon got Maine and Vermont. The Democrats won control of the Senate by 76 to 16 and of the House by 331 to 89.

Election of 1940

In 1940 the attention of America was focused on the war in Europe. In September, Congress passed the first peacetime draft in our history, and a few days later Great Britain gave us a lease on several air bases in exchange for 50 destroyers. There was a nationwide committee, "Defend America by Aiding the Allies," and another to keep us isolated, "America First." The pro-Ally and the pro-isolation groups cut across party lines.

The Republicans met at Philadelphia where Taft (Ohio), Vandenberg (Michigan), and the New York Attorney General, Dewey, were considered the leading candidates. But a group of nonprofessional Republicans had organized to present the name of **Wendell Willkie** before the convention. Willkie had fought the establishment of TVA and had been a leading critic of the New Deal (its performance rather than its program). His charm, youthful vigor, and lively good sense enabled the amateur politicians to put him over the sixth ballot. "Win with Willkie" became the Republican cry.

The Democrats met at Chicago faced with a third-term problem. The two-terms-only tradition had never been broken. The convention broke the third-term tradition by nominating Roosevelt, who replied by radio that "in the face of the danger which confronts our times" he felt that he could not refuse. There seems little doubt that F.D.R. was anxious to stay in power to see the European situation to a conclusion.

In the campaign there was not much of an issue except the third term. Willkie approved most of the New Deal but deplored what he termed its inefficiencies and wastefulness. He had supported the Defend America by Aiding the Allies committee, so there was no important issue in foreign policy. The Democrats warned against "changing horses in midstream."

	Popular Vote	Electoral Vote
F. D. Roosevelt	27,244,160	449
Willkie	22,305,198	82

Election of 1944

The Republicans nominated **Governor Thomas E. Dewey** of New York, who had become nationally famous as the courageous and clever Attorney General of New York State in the successful prosecution of some of gangland's most notorious criminals. The Democrats nominated Roosevelt, who selected **Harry Truman** of Missouri as his running mate. In the campaign Dewey advised the replacement of "tired old men" by a new and vigorous administration. "It's time for a change" was the gist of his campaign message. Both parties favored an international organization to preserve the peace. For the first time, organized labor set up a **Political Action Committee** (PAC) to campaign for individual candidates whose records or promises they approved.

	Popular Vote	Electoral Vote
F. D. Roosevelt	25,602,505	432
Dewey	12,006,278	99

Twentieth and Twenty-First Amendments

The Twentieth Amendment to the U.S. Constitution (1933) moved the date of the inauguration of a president from March 4th to January 20th, shortening the period during which his predecessor would be a "lame duck." The Twenty-First Amendment (1933) *repealed* the Eighteenth Amendment (1919), ending the unsuccessful attempt to prohibit the manufacture, transportation, or sale of beer, wine, or liquor in the entire United States.

NEW DEAL

Its Point of View

When Franklin Roosevelt took office on March 4, 1933, business owners, bankers, organized labor, the general public, and Congress were ready to accept positive, confident leadership. "F.D.R." supplied the leadership. Under his direction the government began to plan, to pass laws, to spend money, and to assume the burden of lifting the nation out of the depression. Altogether the vast program of legislation constituted the **New Deal**.

Major Financial Measures

1] **Emergency Banking Relief Act** (1933).

The day after his inauguration the President called Congress into a special session to begin on March 9 and declared a four-day bank holiday, which stopped all activities of the Federal Reserve System and other banks, loan associations, and credit unions. Most such financial institutions had been closed a day or two earlier through the action of the several governors. The first day of its special session Congress passed the Emergency Banking Relief Act, which confirmed the bank holiday and provided for the reopening of the banks as soon as examiners had found them sound. A rapid inspection resulted in an end to the bank panic as over 5,000 banks opened within three days. March 9 was the beginning of the **Hundred Days** which resulted in an unprecedented number of laws—the first New Deal. Legislation passed under Roosevelt after this first hundred day session is sometimes called the second New Deal.

2] **Federal Securities Act** (1933 and 1934).

This law made sweeping reforms in the selling of securities. Securities offered for sale had to be accompanied with full and true information concerning the properties represented. Misleading information or the absence of pertinent information could result in prosecution. The Federal Trade Commission supervised the stock market for about a year and then a separate body, the **Securities and Exchange Commission,** took over the police job in 1934.

3] **Gold standard** abandoned, and gold dollar devalued (1933).

In April 1933, all gold and gold certificates were called in and all debts were made payable in legal tender. Any contract calling for payment only in gold was made void, as well as the promise of the United States on gold certificates to pay gold on demand to the bearer.

In June 1933, President Roosevelt, in order to "make possible the payment of debts at more nearly the price level at which they were incurred," lowered the gold content of the dollar to 59.06 percent of its former content. Other reasons for going off the gold standard and lowering the gold content of the dollar were to raise commodity prices and increase the funds in the Treasury.

4] **Banking Acts of 1933 (Steagall Act) and of 1935.**

The more important terms of these two acts were

a. The Federal Reserve Board was given tighter control of the investment practices of member banks.

b. The Federal Deposit Insurance Corporation was set up to insure all deposits in Federal Reserve member banks up to $5,000 (currently $100,000.)

c. Investment banking was separated from commercial banking so that a commercial bank with an investment department would no longer be under any temptation to unload its own bad investments on its customers.

d. Savings banks and industrial banks were permitted to join the Federal Reserve System.

e. The Federal Reserve Board was changed to the Board of Governors. There were seven members, but the treasurer and comptroller of the currency no longer serve.

Unemployment

Works Progress Administration (WPA) 1935.

This huge undertaking was directed by **Harry Hopkins**. There were subdivisions, such as the CCC and the NYA, which we will take up separately, as plans to help young Americans just out of school or still in college. Another subdivision was the **Public Works Administration** (PWA) under **Harold Ickes,** Secretary of the Interior.

The WPA was intended to put wages into the possession of as many unemployed as possible. By early spring in 1936 about 3.5 million persons were on WPA. Laborers, writers, musicians, actors and clerks were given work in their own fields. Writers went to work compiling state histories; musicians formed orchestras and gave concerts; actors formed companies and put on dramas and other entertainment. Critics of the program thought much of the employment useless work and called it "boondoggling."

The PWA under Secretary of the Interior Harold Ickes went in for construction jobs, such as schools, hospitals, post offices, roads, and even the Grand Coulee Dam on the Columbia River. WPA also built roads and public buildings. The total number employed was about 8.5 million persons at a cost of about $11 billion.

Housing

1] **Home Owners Loan Act 1934**.

By refinancing mortgages at lower rates of interest over longer periods of time, this act was aimed at preventing the foreclosure of home mortgages.

2] **National Housing Act, 1934 (FHA)**.

This law set up the Federal Housing Authority (FHA), which encouraged banks, building and loan associations, etc., to make loans for building homes, small business establishments, and farm buildings.

3] **National Housing Act, 1937 (USHA)**.

This act set up the United States Housing Authority to encourage slum clearance. It made 60-year loans at low interest to local governments, which would put up 10 percent of the cost of the slum-clearance project. Rents in these apartment-house blocks were fixed and available only to low-income families.

Agriculture

Agricultural Adjustment Act (AAA), 1933 and 1938.

Whatever the faults of this legislation, it struck at the heart of the farm problem, overproduction. The AAA paid farmers not to raise crops and livestock; it paid them to destroy acreage under production. The money to pay the farmers for cutting back production by about 30 percent was raised by a tax on companies that bought the farm products and processed them into food or clothing. It was called a processing tax. In 1932, farm income was about $5.5 billion, and in 1935 it was $8.5 billion. Not all of this increased farm income was due to the AAA; nature took a cruel hand in the situation in 1933 to 1935 when severe drought and heavy winds created dust storms that lifted topsoil in such huge amounts off western farms that the air along the eastern seaboard was hazy. The removal of farms and farmers, along with the AAA, cut production.

By a six-to-three decision (*U.S.* v. *Butler*) in 1936, the Supreme Court declared the AAA unconstitutional. The majority ruled that it was illegal to levy a tax on one group (the processors) in order to pay it to another (the farmers). They ruled that farming was not interstate commerce and hence not subject to federal regulation. In 1938, another AAA was passed without the processing tax. It was financed out of the general tax funds and thus met one of the objections of the Court. In 1939 (*Mulford* v. *Smith*) and again in 1942 (*Wickard* v. *Filburn*) the Supreme Court completely reversed the 1936 decision that farming was not interstate commerce. It accepted the fact that the crops commonly became part of interstate trade as justifying Congress in the regulation of these crops. In both the 1933 and the 1938 Agricultural Adjustment Acts, the farmers were free to join the program or to operate independently.

Labor

Wagner-Connery Act, 1935.

This law was the beginning of what was to be referred to a "big labor." For many years labor had the right to organize and to strike, but employers had the right to fire employees because they joined unions or went on strike. The result was that the pressures employers could bring to bear on employees were far more real than any bargaining power held by the employees. Under these conditions, organized labor embraced about 10 percent of the workers and was concentrated among those who were highly skilled.

The **Wagner Act** guaranteed labor's right to organize and bargain collectively. A National Labor Relations Board (NLRB) was set up to make truly effective labor's right to organize. At the request of the workers, the NLRB would conduct an election to determine whether the employees wanted a union. If two groups of employees disagreed on which should be the official union in a plant, the NLRB would settle the question by a supervised election. It would hear complaints by employees of unfair labor practices on the part of the employer. Some of the practices the Wagner Act declared unfair were attempts by the employer to dominate a union; to attempt by word-of-mouth, pamphlets, posters, notices, etc., to discourage union membership; to fire anyone for union activity; to adopt a hiring policy intended to discourage union activity; and to refuse to bargain with accredited representatives of the unions. In 1937 the Supreme Court, Chief Justice Hughes giving the decision, declared the Wagner Act constitutional.

Business and Industry

National Industrial Recovery Act, 1933 (NIRA and NRA).

Its purpose was to restore prosperity by organizing thousands of businesses under **fair trade codes** drawn up by trade associations and industries. Most of the several hundred codes were prepared by prominent business leaders. When the codes were ready, all business owners were urged to operate under them in a huge national effort to pull out of the depression. Great emphasis was placed on holding prices down, at least until signs of substantial recovery, and keeping employment up. The blue eagle, adopted as the symbol of the NRA, appeared everywhere. The task the NRA attempted was too large and too complex; it was bound to fall of its own weight, to become entangled in its own regulations. The codes actually encouraged monopoly by setting regulations impossible for small companies to follow and by being immune from antitrust laws. Before this gigantic scheme collapsed from its own unwieldiness, the Supreme Court declared it unconstitutional in 1935 (*Schechter Poultry Corp.* v. *U.S.*). The reasons given were that many codes were an illegal delegation of legislative authority; that the federal government had invaded fields reserved to the states; and that the NRA stretched the commerce clause of the Constitution beyond all reason.

Youth

1] Civilian Conservation Corps (CCC), 1933.

This program tackled the problem of the unemployed young men eighteen to twenty-five years old. CCC camps were set up all over the United States, most of them in the forests convenient to conservation work. At its peak the program had about 500,000 enrolled, and the total served throughout its existence (1933-1941) was almost 3 million. The pay was $30 a month, with $22 of it being sent home to dependents or family. The young men planted billions of trees, built thousands of miles of fire lanes and fire breaks in the forests, built public parks and camp sites, drained swamps to fight malaria, worked on flood control projects, helped control forest pests and diseases, restocked streams with fish, and did anything and everything to preserve and improve "the great outdoors." This useful work helped to build their bodies and renew their spirit and sent many CCC boys back into private employment with new skills and selfconfidence.

2] National Youth Administration (NYA) 1935.

This program helped those who were between the ages of sixteen to twenty-five and wanted to continue with their education by providing them with part-time jobs. They performed useful work such as typing at their schools. More than 700,000 enrolled in this program.

Tennessee Valley Authority (TVA), (1933)

During World War I at Muscle Shoals, Alabama, on the Tennessee River, a $145 million hydroelectric plant and two munitions factories had been built. Under Franklin Roosevelt, the **Tennessee Valley Authority** was established. The munitions factories became chemical plants for the manufacture of fertilizer and the hydroelectric plant generated power for distribution throughout parts of seven states (Virginia, North Carolina, Georgia, Tennessee, Kentucky, Alabama, Mississippi). The TVA, which is government owned and operated, was a multipurpose project of tremendous scope, which changed the economy of a large section of the United States. The several purposes of TVA included flood control, reforestation, improved use of land, irrigation, navigation, preservation of wildlife, recreation, production of fertilizer, and the development of electric power. While the socialistic nature of the program was a reason for opposition, the most spirited fight against it developed because TVA competed with private utility companies in the production and distribution of electric power. TVA power was sold at much lower rates than those charged by private utilities and gave the government what some call a "yardstick" by which to judge the fairness of private utility rates. The 34 dams on the Tennessee and Cumberland rivers and their tributaries not only play a part in the production of electric power, but also are part of flood control, irrigation, and navigation. Many once-isolated and backward areas soon had telephones, libraries and electricity. The standard of living in TVA land has risen appreciably. During World War II the Muscle Shoals plants produced munitions, and TVA power was a key factor in producing aluminum and the atomic bomb at Oak Ridge, Tennessee.

Social Security Act (1935)

A key measure of the New Deal was the **Social Security Act, (1935)**. This law made the federal government responsible for the social problems of caring for the elderly, the handicapped and the unemployed through a national plan of compulsory insurance. The Social Security Act provided 1) a federal program of old-age insurance beginning at the age of 65 for retired persons and benefits for dependent survivors of workers who died; these benefits were financed by a payroll tax on both employers and employees. 2) The same law established a system of federal aid to the states for forms of assistance to several types of indigent persons: pensions for the aged, maternal and child health services, and aid for crippled children and the blind. 3) The law also established a system of unemployment benefits administered by the states but financed by payroll taxes. The Federal Social Security Board administered all these benefits.

The Social Security Administration in time issued Social Security numbers to almost all persons; probably no measure of the New Deal affected so many individuals. Amendments have repeatedly extend the coverages to more persons, have increased the taxes to support it, and the benefits and amounts paid. The system created a workable means by which individuals made compulsory contributions to provide security for themselves and their dependents.

* Supreme Court Fight (1937)

Early in February, President Roosevelt sent Congress a plan for reorganizing the Supreme Court and making several changes in federal court procedures. He had just won reelection by a margin of over 10 million votes, a political victory that seemed to him to mean that the people wanted the New Deal continued. The Supreme Court when it struck down the NRA and the AAA, as well as some less important New Deal laws, was the only effective opposition to his program.

Six of the judges on the Court were over seventy, and Roosevelt had said that they were still living in the horse-and-buggy days. A popular book referred to them as *The Nine Old Men*.

The Roosevelt Court Reorganization plan called for an additional judge for every justice still on the Court at age seventy, until the number of judges reached fifteen. If none of the six Justices over seventy then on the Court would retire with full pay, the President would be allowed to appoint six additional judges. The debate over the bill lasted about six months, and it soon became clear that this was one political fight F.D.R. would lose. His own party in Congress failed to go along with him, and public opinion seemed to consider the move too drastic. From late March through May, the Supreme Court declared constitutional the Social Security Act and the Wagner-Connery Labor Act as well as a few lesser New Deal laws. One Justice announced he would resign, and with the prospects good for further retirements and the more friendly view of the Court toward the New Deal, there seemed no necessity for reorganization. On July 22 the Senate killed the Court Reorganization Bill. During the next four years, Roosevelt appointed seven judges, and the Supreme Court was then called the **"Roosevelt Court."**

* Approaching World War II

Europe Blunders Toward War

With the close of World War I, even though we were reluctant to accept the fact, the United States had replaced Great Britain as the leading power of the world. Events anywhere in the world had significance for us. In the 1930s this was particularly true of events in Europe. This makes a chronology of events in the 1930s in Europe an integral part of our story.

1933—**Hitler** became Chancellor of Germany.

1934—Hitler took Germany out of the League of Nations.

1935—Hitler renounced the Versailles Treaty by rearming Germany in direct violation of its terms. Nothing was done to stop him.

1935—**Mussolini** attacked Ethiopia. Nothing was done.

1936—Hitler sent German troops into the demilitarized Rhineland in direct violation of the Versailles Treaty. The French army was overwhelmingly superior to the German forces, but the French government seemed incapable of making positive decisions.

1936—Germany, Italy, and Japan formed the "**Axis**," an alliance of aggressive dictatorships.

1936-1939—A vicious civil war in Spain ended in the defeat of a republican government and the re-establishment of a dictatorship under **General Franco**. Germany and Italy, adjacent to Spain, supported the rightist dictatorship, while distant U.S.S.R. gave air support to the leftist "United Front" Loyalists.

1938—Hitler took Austria.

1938—Hitler took the Sudeten district of Czechoslovakia. This was arranged at Munich with the consent of England and France in violation of their pledge to Czechoslovakia. It is this Munich betrayal that made "appeasement" an indecent word in the jargon of diplomacy. Prime Minister **Neville Chamberlain** hailed the sellout as a guarantee of "peace in our time." In less than a year, World War II had begun.

1939—Hitler took the rest of Czechoslovakia.

1939—Mussolini took Albania.

1939—Russia and Germany made a pact that startled the world. They made an agreement that neither would attack the other, and that if a third party attacked one of them, the other would remain neutral.

1939—On September 1 the "**blitzkrieg**" began as Warsaw became the first city to be wiped off the map by massive air attack. This act by Hitler brought a declaration of war from England and France. World War II was on. By September 28 Poland had disappeared, split between Germany and Russia.

1939 (October) to 1940 (March)—Russia invaded Finland to take a slice of it and then annexed the small Baltic nations, Estonia, Latvia, and Lithuania.

The United States' Steps Toward War

1932—The **Stimson Doctrine** made a formal protest against Japan's aggression in Manchuria. The doctrine stated that the United States would not recognize any change in sovereignty brought about by external aggression; in short, we would not recognize Manchukuo. The situation that brought forth this doctrine was as follows. In the fall of 1931, Japan invaded Manchuria and about a year later recognized a new nation, Manchukuo. It was our contention that Japan had violated the Nine Power Pact of the Washington Conference of 1921, the Kellogg-Briand Treaty of 1928, and the Covenant of the League of Nations. The League sent a commission under Lord Lytton to Manchuria to get the facts. The Lyton report confirmed the United States' claims, and Japan withdrew from the League of Nations in February 1933.

1935—**Neutrality Act** This was a reaction to Italy's attack upon Ethiopia. It provided that after the President formally recognized that a war was in progress, American citizens could not sell arms to belligerents. Such embargoes were to last six months and were renewable. The law also stated that American citizens traveling on ships of belligerents did so at their own risk.

1936—**Neutrality Act** This law merely renewed the Act of 1935 and forbade loans or credits to belligerents.

1937—**Neutrality Acts** The Spanish conflict broke out in July 1936, but the previous neutrality laws did not apply to civil wars. So in January 1937 Congress placed an embargo on munitions to either side. This embargo kept munitions from the Loyalists, while the rebels got massive help from Germany and Italy. In May, another Neutrality Act gave the President discretion in the use of embargoes and forbade travel by United States citizens on ships of belligerents. This act was aimed at the renewed Sino-Japanese conflict. The President forbade any U.S. government vessels to carry munitions to belligerents but allowed any private ships to do so at their own risk.

1937—**The "Quarantine" Speech** In October, President Roosevelt said that, more often than not, our neutrality laws had aided the aggressors (the rebels in Spain and the Japanese in Asia). He urged a "worldwide quarantine" against aggressors and by these remarks clearly took a partisan position, which created quite a bit of criticism. However, he proved to be just a step or two ahead of public opinion, which soon caught up with him.

1937—**Panay Incident (December 12)** Japanese planes bombed the U.S. Gunboat *Panay* in the Yangtze River. The attack, which killed two Americans and wounded several, was deliberate on the part of the Japanese pilots, although their government called it an accident and agreed to our demands for an apology and reparations. As Asia seemed very remote, public opinion in the United States was strongly opposed to war with Japan.

1938—Japan denounced the Five Power Pact of the Washington Conference of 1921 because it was no longer willing to accept a ratio of capital ships inferior to that of Great Britain and the United States. The reaction of our Congress was the appropriation of over $1 billion to start building a two-ocean navy.

1939—**Neutrality Act** This was a **"cash and carry"** plan. All arms embargoes were lifted so that any ships could come to our ports, pay cash, and carry away anything they could buy. Here, finally, was a "neutrality" law that served our purposes. The British and French had control of the seas, and their merchant marine could have almost a monopoly of this "cash and carry" trade. This was our first step toward becoming the "arsenal of democracy."

1940 (January)—President Roosevelt called for 50,000 planes a year and $18 billion for national defense-and got them both. Four months later he got another $1.3 billion.

1940 (April to June)—Hitler took Norway.

1940 (May to June)—Hitler took the Netherlands and Belgium.

1940 (May 28 to June 4)—British and French troops totaling about 340,000 were rescued from the beaches at Dunkirk.

1940 (June)—Prime Minister **Churchill** appealed for war supplies, "Give us the tools and we'll do the job." The United States responded so wholeheartedly that we were soon extending "all aid short of war."

1940 (June)—President Roosevelt appointed two Republicans to Cabinet posts: Henry L. Stimson as Secretary of War and Frank Knox as Secretary of the Navy.

1940 (July)—France fell.

1940 (August to October)—**Battle of Britain** The RAF (Royal Air Force) beat off the German Luftwaffe and prevented an invasion of the British Isles.

1940 (September)—The United States transferred to

England 50 "overage" destroyers in return for air bases on Newfoundland, Bermuda, Jamaica, Trinidad, and several smaller islands in the Caribbean area.

1940 (September)—**Selective Service Act** This was the first peacetime draft in our history. All men between the ages of twenty-one and thirty-five were registered.

1941 (March)—**Lend-Lease** Britain had spent all its money and exhausted all its credits, so Congress passed the Lend-Lease Act to permit the President to "sell, transfer, exchange, lease, or otherwise dispose of" war equipment to any nation for use in the interests of the United States.

1941 (April)—The United States agreed to defend Greenland for Denmark in return for the use of the island during the war.

1941 (June 22)—Hitler astounded the world, and probably defeated himself, by attacking the U.S.S.R. The reason for this break with Russia was the refusal of the Soviet Union to give up its ambition to control the Dardanelles. Both F.D.R. and Churchill immediately welcomed the U.S.S.R. as a partner in war and hoped it could keep Hitler occupied on the eastern front for as long as six months. Lend-Lease was extended to Russia.

1941 (July)—Iceland agreed to U.S. occupation for the duration of the war.

1941 (August)—**The Atlantic Charter** A conference between Roosevelt and Churchill on British and American warships off Newfoundland brought forth a statement of war aims. Some of them were:

1] No territorial gains are sought by the United States or Britain.

2] Readjustment of territories must be in accord with the wishes of the inhabitants.

3] People have the right to choose their own form of government.

4] Trade barriers should be lowered.

5] There must be disarmament, first of the aggressors and then of all other nations.

6] There must be freedom from fear and want. (With speech and religion, these are the "four freedoms.")

7] Freedom of the seas must be established for all.

8] An association of nations must be formed.

1941 (September to October)—"Shoot on sight" German submarines had attacked U.S. naval vessels: the *Greer* and the *Kearny* were attacked but not sunk; the *Reuben James* was sunk with about 100 lives lost. Roosevelt gave orders for U.S. naval craft to "shoot on sight" any submarines in the North Atlantic.

1941 (December 7)—**Pearl Harbor** At 7:55 A.M. Hawaiian time (1:20 P.M., Washington time) the surprise attack sunk or damaged 19 naval vessels, destroyed 150 planes, killed 2,335 soldiers and sailors and 68 civilians.

1941 (December 8)—Germany and Italy declared war on the United States.

Fighting World War II

In the Pacific

1941 (December)—Japan took the islands of Guam and Wake.

1942 (April 18)—Major General **"Jimmy" Doolittle's** squadron of B-25's carried the war to Japan by bombing Tokyo.

1942 (May 6)—General **Douglas MacArthur** was forced to evacuate Corregidor and surrender the Philippines. Upon leaving, after a severe and heroic struggle, MacArthur said, "I shall return."

1942 (May 7-8)—In the Coral Sea off the northeast coast of Australia, a carrier-based air battle took place. None of the ships got near enough to engage each other, but the planes sank one carrier on each side and, in addition, U.S. planes damaged other Japanese naval vessels.

1942 (June 3-6)—An air-naval battle off Midway Island was the first major U.S. victory over Japan. Japan's attempt to take Midway was repulsed, with losses to the enemy of 4 carriers and about 275 planes.

1942 (August 7, 1942 to February 9, 1943)—United States started its island-hopping offensive toward Japan with a landing at Guadalcanal in the Solomon Islands.

1943 (November)—Landings on Tarawa and Makin gave the United States control of the Gilbert Islands.

1944 (February)—Landings on Kwajalein and Eniwetok gave the United States control of the Marshall Islands.

1944 (July)—Landings on Saipan and Guam gave the United States control of the Mariana Islands.

1944 (October)—The battle in Leyte Gulf in the southern Philippines broke the back of the Japanese fleet. Their losses included 2 battleships, 4 carriers, 9 cruisers, and 9 destroyers. Japan lacked the reserve strength to replace or to sustain such losses.

1944 (December)—MacArthur's "I shall return" promise was fulfilled when he led a landing force onto the island of Mindoro.

1945 (February)—Tokyo suffered its first heavy bombing raid by 90 B-29's.

1945 (February)—The island of Iwo Jima was taken at the cost of 4,000 marines killed and over 15,000 wounded.

1945 (March to June)—The island of Okinawa was taken at the cost of over 11,000 killed and about 34,000 wounded. The United States had fought its way to within 360 miles of Japan.

1945 (August 6)—The first **atomic bomb** dropped on Hiroshima. The death toll was about 160,000.

1945 (August 9)—The second atomic bomb was dropped on Nagasaki

1945 (August 15)—"**V. J. Day.**"

In Africa and Europe

1942 (November)—General **Dwight D. Eisenhower,** in cooperation with the British, made landings in Africa and took Casablanca, Oran, and Algiers.

1943 (February to May)—On February 14 General Eisenhower took command of the Allied forces in North Africa. Aided by General **George S. Patton** and British General **Bernard Montgomery,** he forced the surrender on May 13 of 250,000 troops and brought the African campaign to a close.

1943 (September)—General **Mark Clark** led an American invasion of Italy at Salerno, south of Naples.

1944 (January)—General Eisenhower was made Supreme Commander of the Allied Expeditionary Forces. His headquarters (SHAEF) were in London.

1944 (June 6)—"**D-Day**" Invasion by Allied forces of western Europe was the start of "**Operation Overlord,**" the greatest naval military assault of all time. The first few hours of Operation Overlord included heavy air bombardment all along the French and Belgian coasts; 4,000 troop ships crossing the English Channel; 176,000 troops; air cover by 11,000 planes; glider planes with parachute troops being dropped behind enemy lines; and about 600 fighting ships escorting the troops and bombarding the enemy batteries that defended the landing areas. This mammoth operation was under the command of General Eisenhower. By July a million troops had crossed into France, and by September the number had reached more than

two million.

1944 (September 12)—United States troops entered Germany.

1944 (December 16 to 26)—The **Battle of the Bulge** was Germany's last counter offensive. It took place near the French-Belgian border in the Ardennes sector along the Meuse River and cost the Americans 8,000 killed and 21,000 wounded.

1945 (May 1)—Hitler's death was reported. Berlin was occupied on May 2.

1945 (May 8)—"**V.E. Day**" Unconditional surrender.

STATISTICS
(to the nearest 1,000)

Total U.S. forces	12,466,000
Dead	322,000
Wounded	676,000
Captured	124,000
Captives returned	111,000

** Building the Peace

Apparently the experience of World War I taught the necessity of preparing for peace while still fighting the war. At many conferences called primarily to plan the next moves and objectives of the war, there was also serious attention given to preparing the peace. The following list gives a skeletal account in chronological order of peace moves leading to the formation of the **United Nations.**

1943 (September)—Representative James W. Fulbright introduced a resolution favoring United States' participation in an international organization with power enough to establish and maintain "a just and lasting peace." The House resolution passed by a vote of 360 to 29.

1943 (October)—The **Moscow Conference** was the first meeting during the war of the United States, Great Britain, and the U.S.S.R. The heads of foreign affairs, Cordell Hull, Anthony Eden, and Vyacheslav Molotov recognized the "necessity of establishing at the earliest practicable date a general international organization based on the principle of the sovereign equality of all peace-loving states, and open to membership by all states, large and small, for the maintenance of international peace and security."

1943 (October)—Senator Tom Connally, chairman of the Foreign Relations Committee, introduced a resolution that quoted the above Moscow declaration. It was adopted in the Senate by 85 to 5. This was significant as an assurance to other nations that the United States would ratify a treaty making us a member of whatever peace machinery was set up.

1943 (November)—**Roosevelt, Churchill,** and **Stalin** met at **Teheran,** the capital of Iran, marking the first meeting of the heads of state for the "Big Three." Some tentative plans were made to start the international organization for peace that the Moscow Conference had recently declared to be necessary.

1944 (July)—The **Bretton Woods Conference** met in the White Mountains of New Hampshire with the representatives of 44 nations present. An **International Monetary Fund** was established to help stabilize the currencies of western Europe and hence promote trade. An **International Bank for Reconstruction and Development** was created to aid devastated nations. The United States contributed about 25 percent the $8.8 billion for the Monetary Fund and about 35 percent of the $9.1 billion for the bank. The U.S.S.R. had been invited but did not attend.

1944 (August to October)—The **Dumbarton Oaks Conference** was held in Washington D.C. The United States, Great Britain, the U.S.S.R. and China drew up a charter that was to serve as a starting point from which to work at the San Francisco Conference to be held later.

1945 (February)—The **Yalta Conference** in the Crimea found Roosevelt, Churchill, and Stalin considering plans to attempt a quick end to the war they were obviously winning. Russia promised to set up a front against Japan, a pledge which Roosevelt thought, by having Russia share the burden of attack, would save a great many American lives. The three powers agreed to see that the liberated states had representative governments chosen by free elections. The date was set for the San Francisco Conference on April 25, 1945.

The Yalta Conference has long been a controversial issue in America. The Russians did set up a front in Manchuria and occupy northern Korea as agreed at Yalta, but the atomic bomb made the presence of Russian forces unnecessary for victory. Stalin broke his promise to promote, or at least allow, free elections and representative government in the nations adjacent to the Soviet Union. At the time, Roosevelt was especially pleased with the Yalta meeting because he had a definite pledge of help against Japan and a definite assurance that Russia would attend the San Francisco meeting to help form the United Nations.

1945 (April to June)—The **San Francisco Conference,** which drew up the **United Nations charter**, was attended by delegates from 50 nations The main organs of the United Nations were: a **Council** of eleven members, with five of them permanent and having veto power, while the other six members served two-year terms; a **General Assembly**, where every member nation had one vote; an **Economic and Social Council** of 18 members chosen by the General Assembly to deal with a great variety of problems other than military; an **International Court of Justice** composed of 15 judges selected by the Assembly, and the **Security Council**; a **Trusteeship Council** consisting of members from all nations administering trust areas and an equal number of nations without such trusteeships; and a **Secretariat**, presided over by the chief officer of the UN, the Secretary General, to do the administrative work of the UN.

1945 (July 28)—By a vote of 89 to 2 the United States Senate ratified the treaty, making us members of the United Nations.

Eleanor Roosevelt

One of Roosevelt's greatest assets was his wife, Eleanor. She was a champion of the poor and the weak, truly the heart of the Roosevelt administration. She supported organized labor before her husband did and became a spokesperson for American blacks when F.D.R. was still seeking segregationist support for the New Deal. She helped Robert Weaver to become the first black appointed to a cabinet position. After F.D.R.'s death in office in 1945, Eleanor continued to serve the nation in important ways. She was a member of the first U.S. delegation to the United Nations General Assembly, and served from 1945 to 1952. As chair of the Commission on Human Rights, she led in the adoption by the United Nations of the International Declaration of Human Rights (1948).

Harry S Truman 1945-1953

1884 -1972

DEMOCRAT

☆

Vice-President   ALBEN W. BARKLEY
Secretary of State   GEORGE C. MARSHALL
                     DEAN ACHESON

TRUMAN'S PUBLIC SERVICE BEFORE HE BECAME PRESIDENT

Captain in the Field Artillery in World War I
Judge of Jackson County Court in Missouri
United States Senator from Missouri
Vice-President of the United States

MAJOR ITEMS OF TRUMAN'S ADMINISTRATION

World War II Ends (V. E. Day; Atomic   *Truman Doctrine (1947)*
*   Bombs; V. J. Day)—See p. 204*   *Marshall Plan (1947)*
Taft-Hartley Act (1947)   *Germany and Berlin*
Presidential Succession Act   *North Atlantic Treaty Organization (NATO)*
Trials of War Criminals   *Korea (1950-1953)*
The Cold War Begins   *Cold War, Loyalty, and McCarthyism*

After having served less than three months of his fourth term, President Franklin D. Roosevelt died on April 12 of a cerebral hemorrhage. Vice-President **Harry Truman** assumed office faced with a war to be finished and the difficult problems of a postwar period.

Truman's Election In 1948

The Democrats had approached General **Dwight D. Eisenhower** to see if he would accept the nomination, but he had already refused a similar offer from the Republicans on the ground that a civilian would more suitably occupy the office. It was a bit awkward for Truman when, after having been President for almost four years, his party nominated him only after trying to get someone else to run. The seventy-year-old Senator **Alben W. Barkley** of Kentucky was persuaded to help the party by accepting the second spot on the ticket. Truman had offended the deep South by a strong stand in favor of civil rights, and it was hoped that the Kentucky Senator would hold the South in the Democratic column. Nevertheless, several delegates from Southern states (Louisiana, Mississippi, Alabama, Florida, Georgia, South Carolina) walked out of the convention and formed the **States' Rights party (Dixiecrats)** with **Governor Strom Thurmond** of South Carolina as their candidate. The Democratic party was still further weakened when **Henry Wallace,** Secretary of Agriculture, organized and headed a **Progressive party,** which promised to expand the New Deal more vigorously and to accomplish good relations with the

U.S.S.R. Both Thurmond and Wallace cut into the regular Democratic vote. But President Truman made an aggressive campaign. He lambasted the "do-nothing" 80th Congress.

After General Eisenhower had refused the nomination, the Republicans, for the second time, nominated **Governor Dewey** of New York. Dewey expected to win, and most newspapers and public opinion polls predicted he would win since the Democratic party was divided.

	Popular Vote	*Electoral Vote*
Truman	24,105,812	303
Dewey	21,970,065	189
Thurmond	1,169,063	39
Wallace	1,157,172	0

The Democrats regained control of both houses of Congress and won 20 of the 33 gubernatorial contests. President Truman had won a campaign while his own party practically sat on the sidelines and watched; he had fought his way to the undisputed leadership of the party.

* Taft-Hartley Act (1947)

This act reflected the views of the Congress elected in 1946, which had Republican majorities in both Houses for the first time since Hoover's administration. Congress felt the Wagner-Connery Labor Act had tipped the advantage heavily in favor of labor, and so it passed the **Taft-Hartley Act** to restore the balance. It passed over President Truman's veto.

Major Provisions

1] Unions, as well as employers, were subject to being sued for breach of contract.

2] The closed shop was declared illegal. (A closed shop is one that requires a worker to belong to the union at the time he is hired.)

3] Unions must submit financial reports to public authorities.

4] The "check-off" system of paying union dues was made illegal. (The check-off was a deduction from the worker's pay to be given to the union and thus made the employer collect dues for the union.)

5] Union officers had to take an oath that they were not members of the Communist party.

6] The National Labor Relations Board could issue an injunction to delay a strike for 80 days if the strike threatened "irreparable damage" to the public interest.

7] Secondary boycotts and jurisdictional disputes were outlawed. (A jurisdictional dispute is one between two unions over which one has the right (jurisdiction) to perform a certain job.)

Organized labor bitterly attacked the Taft-Hartley Act, calling it a "slave-labor" law.

Presidential Succession Act[†]

At President Truman's request, Congress passed a **Presidential Succession Act**, which provided for the Vice-President to be followed in order by the Speaker of the House, the President pro-tempore of the Senate, the Secretary of State, and down the Cabinet according to rank. This replaced the order in effect since 1885, which had gone right from Vice-President to the Cabinet officials.

Trials of War Criminals

An **International Military Tribunal** was established under the direction of Supreme Court Justice Robert Jackson, who also served as chief counsel for the prosecution. The crimes were classified as against "peace," "humanity," and "international law."

The Cold War Begins

During World War II, a common interest in destroying Nazi aggression brought together a Communist dictatorship in the U.S.S.R. (now Russia) with western democracies led by Great Britain and the United States. The Russians appreciated the massive American aid that helped them stop the Germans. People in the West admired the courage and determination of the Soviet population. After the war, former feelings of mutual mistrust returned, fueled by political disagreements about eastern Europe, which the U.S.S.R. would soon control. In March 1946, former British prime minister Winston Churchill spoke of an "iron curtain" having descended between eastern and western Europe. He called on the western democracies to take action to halt the expansion of Communism, a policy of **containment.** The increased tension and hostile relations between the western allies and the Soviet Union from 1946 to about 1988 were known as the **Cold War.**

[†]Superseded by Twenty-fifth Amendment.

** Truman Doctrine (1947)

Late in 1946 about 13,000 Communist-led guerrillas entered northern Greece from Albania, Yugoslavia, and Bulgaria. The U.S.S.R. claimed that there was a genuine revolt of the Greek people against the government, but the fact was that the guerrillas were Communist invaders. The situation in Greece reached a climax at this time because UNRRA (United Nations Relief & Rehabilitation Administration) was closing up shop on March 31, 1947, and, in addition, British troops, which had helped to discourage Communist aggression, were being pulled out of Greece because England couldn't afford to maintain them any longer.

At the same time, Turkey was being pressured by Russia. In 1945 Russia refused to renew a twenty-year-old friendship pact, which placed control of the Dardanelles under a commission of nine nations. Russia was insisting that the nine-nation control be changed to a two-nation control, Russia and Turkey.

This was the setting for the **Truman Doctrine**. President Truman said he would base the policy of this country on "the frank recognition that totalitarian regimes imposed on free peoples, by direct or indirect aggression, undermine the foundations of international peace and hence the security of the United States." On March 12, 1947, he began aid to both Greece and Turkey. For Greece there were relief supplies as well as military equipment and military personnel to help organize anti-guerrilla forces. For Turkey the aid was almost completely military. This unilateral action stopped the penetration of the U.S.S.R. toward the Mediterranean. Three years after the Truman Doctrine, the guerrillas were no longer in Greece.

The Truman Doctrine was often said to be a policy of opposing Communism all over the world. A more accurate statement would be that it advocated opposing *aggressive* Communism all over the world.

** The Marshall Plan (1947)

About three months after the President announced the Truman Doctrine, Secretary of State General **George C. Marshall** announced a gigantic plan for European recovery (ERP), usually called the **Marshall Plan.** As Marshall said in his speech at Harvard University on June 5, 1947, it was aimed against "hunger, poverty, desperation, and chaos"; which European nations were invited to join. They were asked to form plans for putting their transportation systems, their industrial plants, their agriculture, etc., into good working condition. The United States agreed to provide money and machinery for war-devastated Europe.

Twenty-two nations met in Paris in late June to consider the Marshall Plan, and although foreign minister Molotov of the U.S.S.R. called it an "imperialist plot" to enslave Europe, sixteen nations continued the conference until a four-year plan had been formulated that would cost from $16 to $24 billion. The debate in this country, in and out of Congress, went on for months. Some said the United States called the ERP "operation rat-hole." Others believed that an economically prostrate Europe was fertile soil for Communist idealogy and that Russia would roll over western Europe. Russia helped measurably to decide the issue by its attach on Czechoslovakia in March 1948. Czechoslovakia's loss of freedom through Communist infiltration and Moscow-directed coup was answered in the United States Congress by an overwhelming vote for the Marshall Plan, which became law on April 3, 1948. Congress appropriated $5.8 billion for the first 15 months and contemplated further expenditures over four years totaling $17 billion. As a very feeble counterbalance to the Marshall Plan, Russia formed the **Council of Mutual Economic Assistance** (U.S.S.R., Poland, Czechoslovakia, Bulgaria, Hungary, and Rumania).

* Germany and Berlin

In order to bring the war to a close, it was necessary to arrange treaties with several nations. From the outset, Russia used tactics of delay. For instance, it was not until February 1947 that treaties were concluded with Bulgaria, Finland, Hungary, Italy, and Rumania. The Russians continued to stall over the settlement about Germany. Over two months before V.E. Day, a temporary plan for the occupation of Germany had been agreed upon. Some of eastern Germany was added to Poland and some to Russia. Then Germany was divided into an eastern zone occupied by Russia, and a somewhat larger western zone divided among Britain, France, and the United States. Berlin was 100 miles within the Russian zone and was itself divided into **East Berlin** as the Russian area and **West Berlin** for the British, French, and American sectors (see map that follows). By late 1946 Russia's delaying tactics had convinced the Allies that Stalin would accept no agreement unless it made Germany a communist nation under Soviet control. The Allied answer was the unification of the British, French, and American zones into West Germany, called the **German Federal Republic,** which became a vigorous commercial and industrial economy. Under Allied direction a constitution was drawn up for a federal government with a bicameral legislature. A president had duties that were more ceremonial than important; a chancellor was the real chief executive. These political and economic buildups made substantial progress in 1947 and brought from Russia the charge that the western Allies had violated the Potsdam Agreement. The Allies suggested the extension of the Bonn government to include East

Germany and Berlin—Divided

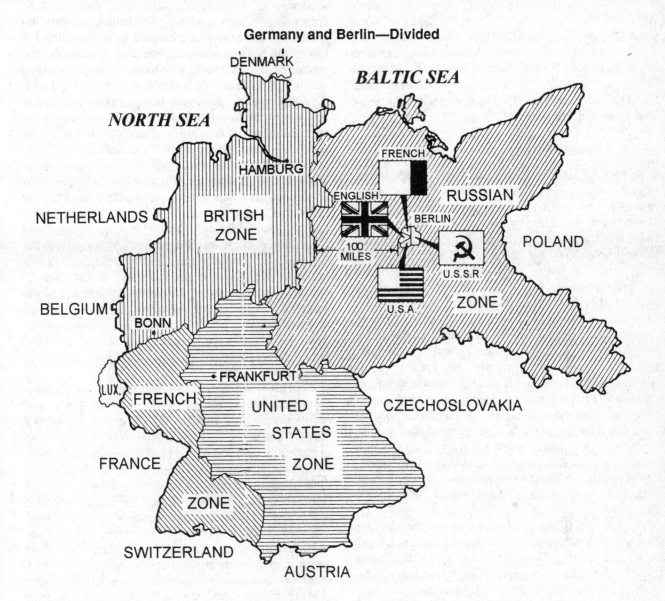

Germany as it was a people's government established through free elections; but the U.S.S.R. set up a militarized puppet state in East Germany, which they called the **People's Republic of Germany**.

In an attempt to force the Western Allies out of Berlin, the Russians created a crisis in June 1948. Russia placed barriers on highways, waterways, and railways and allowed no traffic between Berlin and West Germany. The Americans, with some British help, organized the **"Berlin air lift"**. The apparently impossible was achieved. From June 24, 1948, through May 17, 1949, a population of 2.25 million was supplied by planes with food, fuel, and other necessities. This remarkable display of organizational skill and air power brought a settlement and resumption of normal transportation facilities.

** North Atlantic Treaty Organization (NATO) (1949)

On April 4, 1949, in Washington, twelve nations signed the **North Atlantic Treaty Organization (NATO)**. On July 21 the Senate ratified the treaty, which stated in part that "the parties agree that an armed attack on one or more of them in Europe or North America shall be considered an attack against them all ... and agree that if such an attack occurs, each of them will assist the party or parties so attacked by taking such action as it deems necessary, including the use of armed force, to restore and maintain the security of the North Atlantic area." It was a purely military defensive alliance. Turkey, Greece, and West Germany joined to make a total membership of fifteen nations. (Belgium, Britain, Canada, Denmark, Netherlands (Holland), Norway, Portugal, Turkey, West Germany, and the United States.)

The Truman Doctrine turned back a serious threat of Soviet expansion to the Mediterranean, The Marshall Plan (ERP) started recovery in western Europe, and NATO started a military defense against Soviet expansion westward into Europe.

** Korea (1950-1953)

At both Cairo in 1943 and Potsdam in 1945, it was agreed by the major powers that Korea would "in due course" be free and independent. Russia reaffirmed this pledge when it declared war on Japan on August 8, 1945. When Japan accepted surrender terms, the United States proposed that the Japanese in Korea north of the 38th parallel surrender to Russian troops, and those south of the parallel surrender to U.S. forces. While it was not the intention of the United States that the division of Korea would be permanent, it soon became clear that the Soviet Union had assumed otherwise. In November 1947 a United Nations Temporary Commission was formed to supervise the drafting of a constitution for a national Korean government. Russia claimed that the UN had no jurisdiction and refused to allow their commission to enter North Korea. So the UN formed a representative government chosen by free elections, and thus the Republic of Korea (South Korea only) was officially established on August 15, 1948. Russia set up the People's Republic of Korea, a militarized Communist dictatorship, north of the 38th parallel.

On June 25, 1950, the North Koreans crossed the 38th parallel in force. At the request of the United States, the Security Council met and by a vote of nine to zero adopted a resolution calling for withdrawal of North Korean forces to the 38th parallel and cessation of hostilities. It also called on "all Members to render every assistance to the United Nations in the execution of this resolution and to refrain from giving assistance to North Korean authorities." A few hours later, President Truman ordered United States' forces to Korea. This fast action by the UN was made possible by the absence of the Soviet delegate on the Security Council. On January 13, 1950, he had walked out of the Security Council because Communist China was not recognized as the official China, given membership in the United Nations, or made a permanent member of the Council. Russia was without a member on the Council until August 1, 1950.

President Truman appointed General **Douglas MacArthur** as a commanding general of United Nations forces. Somewhat over half of the troops opposing the North Korean Communists were South Koreans; the bulk of the remainder were Americans, with a scattering of soldiers and equipment from about a dozen other UN members. By mid-September the buildup of UN troops and superior air and sea support turned the North Koreans who had been pushed to the southern tip of the peninsula, back up the peninsula so that by the last week of September, the fighting was at the 38th parallel. A month later, General MacArthur had taken the North Korean capital, Pyongyang, and gone on to within five miles of the Yalu River, which separated North Korea from Manchuria.

President Truman and General MacArthur met on Wake Island on October 14 to discuss the advisability of pressing the attack north of the 38th parallel. On October 11 Mao Tse-tung said that his government "cannot stand idly by" while UN forces penetrated North Korea; but it was MacArthur's judgment that the Chinese would not interfere and that the best way to settle the Korean problem, once and for all, was to launch an "end-the-war" offensive. President Truman accepted this judgment. However, on November 26 thousands of Red Chinese troops came down from the Yalu River and forced a bitterly contested and very costly retreat down the peninsula and back across the 38th parallel.

General MacArthur called this a new war that called for a new policy. His new policy included bombing enemy supply lines and depots in Manchuria, bombing major Chinese cities, blockading Chinese ports, and mounting an invasion of the Chinese mainland, with the Nationalist Chinese army under General Chiang Kaishek. President Truman flatly rejected this plan, and General Omar Bradley, Chief of Staff, opposed MacArthur's policy because it would get the United States into "the wrong war, at the wrong time, in the wrong place, with the wrong enemy." MacArthur made public statements in support of his ideas and in opposition to those of the President. He was clearly guilty of insubordination and had tried to *make* policy instead of just carry it out. There was nothing for President Truman to do except fire him.

As the UN forces were pushed south below Seoul, the capital of South Korea, they faced a winter to remember (January through March 1951). In late March, General MacArthur threatened to launch an air and naval attack on Red China. As such an action would be a gross violation of the policy of President Truman, MacArthur was removed from command and replaced by General Matthew Rideway. In April the UN forces started a spring offensive, which, by June, took them back to the 38th parallel and just a bit beyond it. Here the fighting stopped after it had lasted almost exactly a year. North Koreans and Red Chinese suffered 1.5 million casualties, the South Koreans about 400,000, and the Americans 33,000 dead and 103,000 wounded.

The Cold War, Loyalty, and McCarthyism

The Cold War, which was on in earnest when the Truman Doctrine counteracted the Russian push toward the Mediterranean, brought with it a fear of Communist infiltration into labor unions, government, education, scientific research, and even the clergy. That such dangers existed was obvious, but to what extent the Moscow-directed Communists had infiltrated such areas was difficult, if not impossible, to know.

Attempts to screen government employees through "loyalty boards" produced very questionable results. Even the courts had their troubles with the **Smith Act of 1940** (Alien Registration Act), which tried to control Communists by making it a crime to advocate the overthrow of the United States by force and violence.

Senator Joseph McCarthy of Wisconsin, seeking reelection in 1952, used the issue that had made Richard Nixon a national figure—Communist infiltration of government. He claimed to have lists of Communists working in the U.S. Army, the State Department, and the Hollywood film industry. He conducted Congressional hearings that often denied witnesses civil rights that would be accorded them in a court trial. In 1954, televised hearings of the Army-McCarthy controversy exposed McCarthy as a man with no information who was destroying the reputations of innocent people. The Senate censured his actions as unbecoming his office. **McCarthyism** meant accusing as a traitor anyone who dissented from approved ideas, or who was thought to have done so.

Dwight D. Eisenhower   1953-1961

1890-1969

REPUBLICAN

☆

Vice-President   RICHARD M. NIXON

Secretary of State   JOHN FOSTER DULLES

EISENHOWER'S PUBLIC SERVICE BEFORE HE BECAME PRESIDENT

Assistant Military Advisor to the Philippines (1935-1939)
Chief of War Plans Division in Office of Chief of Staff
Chief of Operations Division in Office of Chief of Staff
Commander of Invasion of North Africa (1942)
Commander of Invasion of Europe—SHAEF (1944)
Chief of Staff (1945)
Supreme Commander of Allied Powers in Europe—SHAPE (1951)

MAJOR ITEMS OF EISENHOWER'S ADMINISTRATIONS

Twenty-Second Amendment
Brown v. Board of Education of
*   Topeka, Kansas*
More Suburbs and Highways
French Indochina
Southeast Asia Treaty Organization
*   (SEATO)*

Taiwan—Quemoy—Matsu
Suez Crisis (1956)
Eisenhower Doctrine
St. Lawrence Seaway
Alaska and Hawaii Become States
*   (1959)*
Summit Conference and the U2

Eisenhower's Election in 1952 and Reelection in 1956

The Republican National Convention at Chicago witnesses a divided party with **Senator Robert A. Taft** ("Mr. Republican") leading the conservative (right wing) faction in opposition to liberal Republicans. But the liberal Republicans offered **Dwight D. Eisenhower** as their candidate. Eisenhower was nominated on the first ballot. **Senator Richard M. Nixon** of California shared the ticket with him.

The Democrats met in Chicago with no candidate having a distinct advantage. Four months earlier, President Truman had made it clear that he would not run again. **Governor Adlai Stevenson** of Illinois was nominated on the third ballot.

Stevenson supported New Deal-Fair Deal foreign and domestic policies and advocated the repeal of the Taft-Hartley Labor Law. General Eisenhower was a great military hero; and his career had demonstrated strength and ability. He promised to go to Korea and get the long drawn out arguments over the exchange of prisoners settled quickly. He promised a housecleaning in Washington which, the people were convinced, needed some attention.

	Popular Vote	*Electoral Vote*
Eisenhower	33,936,252	442
Stevenson	27,314,922	89

Stevenson carried only nine states, but the Republican party did not fare well. It won a majority of only eight in the House and broke even in the Senate. The election was a tremendous Eisenhower victory; the man, not the party, had won.

The reelection of Eisenhower in 1956 was a foregone conclusion. At the Republican Nominating Convention in San Francisco, "Ike" was nominated by acclamation. Vice-President Nixon was again to be his running mate.

The Democrats met at Chicago and nominated **Adlai Stevenson** on the first ballot. The campaign was not very interesting as the issues and the candidates were the same as in 1952, with the similarities between the parties being more real than the differences.

	Popular Vote	*Electoral Vote*
Eisenhower	35,585,316	457
Stevenson	26,031,322	74

While Eisenhower was winning all but seven states and a plurality of about 9.5 million votes, the Republican party lost ground in the House and made no gain in the Senate. Again it was a personal victory.

In September 1955, President Eisenhower had a heart attack; in June 1957, he underwent a major operation, and in November 1957 he suffered a slight stroke; but Congress had not yet passed any legislation to deal with the circumstance of a President who is unable to carry the responsibilities of the office. Fortunately, except for very brief periods of time, President Eisenhower's illnesses did not incapacitate him.

** Brown v. Board of Education of Topeka, Kansas

The Fourteenth Amendment was adopted in 1868 and was part of the terms imposed on the South by a victorious North after the Civil War. The amendment begins with a definition of a citizen, which included the recently freed blacks, and then goes on to guarantee to all citizens equal rights and equal treatment under the law. During the Reconstruction years, black Americans did vote and hold office as every effort was made to enforce the letter of the Fourteenth and Fifteenth Amendments. After the election of Hayes in 1876 and the withdrawal of federal troops from the South, southern whites regained control of the state governments. After 1877 a pattern of segregation developed in the Southern states. The *Plessy* v. *Ferguson* case of 1896 gave legal support to segregation and was the legal reasoning until **Brown** v. **Topeka Board of Education** in 1954.

In *Plessy* v. *Ferguson* the case involved one-eighth black man, Plessy, who had been fined $25 for riding in the white section of a railroad coach. Some of the key statements of the Court follow.

"Laws permitting, and even requiring, their (blacks and whites) separation in places where they are liable to be brought into contact do not necessarily imply the inferiority of either race to the other, and have been generally, if not universally, recognized as within the competency of the state legislatures in the exercise of their police power. The most common instance of this is connected with the establishment of separate schools for white and colored children, which has been held to be a valid exercise of the legislative power even by courts of states where the political rights of the colored race have been longest and most earnestly enforced." This so called "separate but equal" argument was the law until 1954.

Brown v. *Topeka Board of Education* involved suits by citizens from Kansas, South Carolina, Virginia, and Delaware. They all protested segregated schools and were essentially the same, so the Court considered them as part of this case. Black parents claimed that the refusal to permit their children to attend schools with white children deprived them of the equal protection of the laws under the Fourteenth Amendment. Chief Justice Warren, in delivering the unanimous decision of the Court, made the following statements.

"In these days, it is doubtful that any child may reasonably be expected to succeed in life if he is denied the opportunity of an education. Such an opportunity, where the state has undertaken to provide it, is a right which must be made available to all on equal terms."

"Does segregation of children in public schools solely on the basis of race, even though the physical facilities and other 'tangible' factors may be equal, deprive the children of the minority group of equal educational opportunities? We believe that it does."

"Separate educational facilities are inherently unequal. Therefore, we hold that the plaintiffs and others similarly situated for whom the actions have been brought are, by reason of the segregation complained of, deprived of the equal protection of the laws guaranteed by the Fourteenth Amendment. This disposition makes unnecessary any discussion whether such segregation also violates the Due Process Clause of the Fourteenth Amendment."

A separate case, *Bolling* v. *Sharpe*, in 1954 applied to the District of Columbia, and the Court gave the same ruling but based it on the due process of law guaranteed by the Fifth Amendment.

More Suburbs and Highways

The Eisenhower years saw the rapid growth of suburban housing, often mass-produced homes built on former farmland on the outskirts of cities. As an example, Levittown, New York, was transformed from potato farms into a city of 17,000 homes on Long Island. Traffic jams of commuters driving between suburban homes and city workplaces caused a demand for roads. In 1956, Congress passed the **Interstate Highway Act,** authorizing the federal government to pay up to 90 percent of the cost of a national road network. This has been named the Eisenhower Interstate Highway system. The construction of a transcontinental transport system for cars, trucks, and buses has been good for the automotive and petroleum industries but has led to the further decline of American railroads for both passenger and freight use.

French Indochina

In 1953 Communist guerrillas, called **Vietminh,** had occupied the northern part of Vietnam in Indochina. Laos, the adjacent state in Indochina was in imminent danger and, if Laos collapsed, the whole of Southeast Asia could fall to the Communists, who were backed by Red China. The United States had no desire to bolster up the French colonial Indochina, but we had every interest in preventing the spread of communist influence throughout Southeast Asia. The United States had paid about 75 percent of the expense of the French fighting in Indochina, but President Eisenhower would not commit troops in the struggle. When the Vietminh captured the French fortress of **Dienbienphu** on May 7, 1954, the French had been thrown out of Indochina. At a conference in Geneva in July, a settlement was made. Vietnam was split at the 17th parallel, much as Korea had been divided at the 38th. North of the 17th parallel was to be a Communist state, and south of it was to be independent. Laos and Cambodia were to be independent. To resist further Communist successes, President Eisenhower and Secretary of State Dulles organized the **Southeast Asia Treaty Organization (SEATO).**

* Southeast Asia Treaty Organization (SEATO)

In November 1954, SEATO was formed. Eight nations combined under a pledge to meet any threat of armed aggression by united action. They would "meet in order to agree on the measures which should be taken for common defense." The members of SEATO were the United States, Great Britain, France, Australia, New Zealand, Thailand, Pakistan, and the Philippines. The Alliance was disrupted by the Vietnam War, its last joint exercises were held in 1976, and it was formally dissolved in 1977.

Taiwan-Quemoy-Matsu

In February 1953, President Eisenhower lifted the blockade of Taiwan (Formosa), which had prevented any move by Chiang Kai-shek against the mainland of China. This released Taiwan naval forces for hit-and-run bombardments of Amoy or other points on the coast of Communist China opposite Taiwan. The Chinese declared their intention of taking Taiwan, and President Eisenhower said that it could be done only after the Seventh Fleet had been driven off the sea or sunk. Communist China threatened to take Quemoy and Matsu islands which, although very close to the shore of mainland China, were occupied by Nationalist China. In September 1954, Eisenhower rejected proposals that direct action be taken against Communist China. In December 1954, the President assured Nationalist China that the United States would come to their aid if they were attacked, but this promise did not include the small islands of Quemoy and Matsu. As to those two islands so near the Red China shore, the President asked Congress to leave to his judgment what to do in case an attack was made against them. If he considered such an attack part of a move against Taiwan, he would repel it; if he did not so interpret the attack, he might not take action. The Pescadores Islands, much nearer to Taiwan than to Communist China, would be protected by the Seventh Fleet. This statement of policy was made early in 1955, and the uneasy peace was maintained quietly until 1958 when Communist China began bombardments of Quemoy and Matsu islands. The Seventh Fleet convoyed Nationalist Chinese supply ships to these islands and carefully avoided entering waters within three miles of Communist China's coast. Both Communist China and the United States were being careful not to provoke the other into large-scale attack. It was an uneasy situation. The islands have remained Taiwanese.

* Suez Crisis (1956)

The Suez crisis resulted when **Colonel Gamal Abdel Nasser** of Egypt used the power-politics maneuvers of the Soviet Union and the United States to advance his position as leader of the Arab states of the Middle East. While getting arms from the Communist bloc, Nasser asked both the U.S.S.R. and the United

States to finance the building of the **Aswan Dam** on the upper Nile, a project that could tremendously improve irrigation and produce vast hydroelectric power. The plans called for construction of the largest dam in the world. In December 1955, the United States and Great Britain, in cooperation with the International Bank of the United Nations, agreed to finance the Aswan Dam. Later, the United States withdrew its offer, as did Great Britain and the International Bank. The enthusiasm of the United States for the project had been cooling during the eighteen months since the offer was first made. Egypt had leaned more and more toward Russia and it was obvious that Nasser's chief interest was in becoming head of an Arab league in order to reopen the war against Israel.

In 1869 the French had finished construction of the Suez Canal and shared its ownership with the khedive (ruler) of Egypt, who later, in 1875, sold his canal shares to England. This link in Britain's "lifeline" to the Far East was so important to the empire that British troops occupied the canal area from 1882 until June 1956, when they were finally withdrawn after continued pressure from Nasser to get foreign troops off Egyptian soil. All the time France and England managed the canal, there was an international agreement to allow ships of all nations the use of the canal on equal terms. After the British troops left, Nasser announced he was going to nationalize it, that is, take it over and run it as Egyptian property. Nasser refused to permit international supervision of the canal's operation or, at least, to observe previous international rules concerning its use. Nasser closed the canal to Israeli shipping, justifying his action on the ground that they were still legally at war.

The takeover of the canal by Nasser was a severe blow to Britain and France as well as a crippling action against Israeli commerce. On October 25, 1956, Israeli forces drove into the Sinai Peninsula and fought their way to the Suez Canal by October 29. On October 31 French and British forces arrived by air to cooperate with Israel in the seizure and control of the area. Nasser had blocked the canal by sinking ships at strategic points. The day France and England made their attack, President Eisenhower expressed strong disapproval of the use of force as an instrument of international policy. Russia threatened to intervene. Under pressure of the Russian threat, the world opinion expressed through the UN, and United States' disapproval, France and England announced a cease-fire agreement for November 6. UN forces took over supervision of the canal area and cleared the canal for traffic by the middle of April. The Suez crisis greatly strengthened Nasser's prestige in the Middle East and, temporarily at least, put a severe strain on Anglo-American relations. The United States gained stature in the eyes of the many new and small nations of the world for opposing aggression, even when committed by our friends.

* Eisenhower Doctrine (1957)

The Suez crisis had lessened British and French prestige in the Middle East and put a rift in Anglo-American relationships. As the Western Allies' position was made weaker, so the Communist's was enhanced. President Eisenhower recovered some ground by proclaiming the **Eisenhower Doctrine**. After requesting and receiving the approval of Congress, he offered economic and financial aid to any Middle Eastern nation asking for it (a tiny $200 million Marshall Plan) plus the support of American armed force to resist aggression, or threatened aggression, by any Communist nation. During much of 1957 and 1958, the Sixth Fleet was in the Mediterranean ready to give quick assistance on call. When in May 1958, Syria and Egypt stirred up a rebellion in pro-Western Lebanon, President Eisenhower sent in 14,000 marines, who restored order in Lebanon, re-established Lebanese authority, and got an agreement from the offending Arab states to leave Lebanon alone.

Alaska and Hawaii Become States (1959)

Alaska was admitted on January 3 and Hawaii on August 21, becoming the 49th and 50th states.

St. Lawrence Seaway

A 1954 agreement between the United States and Canada established a St. Lawrence Seaway Authority to construct and maintain a deep-water passage between Montreal and Lake Erie, in order to carry large freighters from the Atlantic Ocean to Chicago and Great Lakes ports. Also included were joint hydroelectric power stations. The seaway was officially opened for traffic in June 1959 by President Eisenhower and Queen Elizabeth II. It is used from April to September as a major route for world trade.

Summit Conference and the U2

President Eisenhower, in order to discuss nuclear testing and disarmament, wished to arrange with **Krushchev** for a meeting of the heads of states sometime in the spring of 1960. With all arrangements completed and the summit conference only days away, the **U2 incident** occurred. On May 1, 1960, a U2 high-altitude spy plane was shot down over central Russia (near Sverdlovsk). At first the United States said that it must be a meteorological plane that had drifted off course. This story wouldn't hold, as the Russians had the plane's equipment practically intact and the pilot, Francis Powers, was alive. It was admitted that the U2 was an espionage plane on a routine picture-taking mission. On May 9 the United States said that the U2 espionage flights would continue; but on May 16, the opening day of the summit conference, President Eisenhower said that he had ordered such flights stopped. Khrushchev demanded an apology and a statement condemning the violation of Russian territory; Eisenhower refused both demands. The conference broke up before it got under way.

John F. Kennedy 1961-1963

1917-1963

DEMOCRAT

Vice-President LYNDON B. JOHNSON

Secretary of State DEAN RUSK
Attorney General ROBERT KENNEDY
Secretary of Defense ROBERT McNAMARA

KENNEDY'S PUBLIC SERVICE BEFORE HE BECAME PRESIDENT

Distinguished record in Pacific theater of World War II
Member of the House of Representatives from Massachusetts
Member of the Senate from Massachusetts

MAJOR ITEMS OF KENNEDY'S ADMINISTRATION

Twenty-Third Amendment
Alliance for Progress
Peace Corps
Cuba, Castro, and the United States

Nuclear Test-Ban Treaty
Kennedy Assassinated at Dallas, Texas
(November 22, 1963)

Kennedy's Election in 1960

President Eisenhower was ineligible for another term (Amendment 22), but he left no doubt that he favored his Vice-President, **Richard Nixon**, as his successor. Nixon won the nomination at the Chicago Convention on the first ballot. Henry Cabot Lodge of Massachusetts was his running mate.

Senator John F. Kennedy entered seven state primaries and won them all as he made himself known in widely scattered parts of the United States. He was nominated at the Los Angeles Convention on the first ballot. Senator Lyndon Johnson of Texas was his running mate.

The platforms of both parties had strong civil rights planks and favored federal aid in financing a national health program (two different programs). There was no substantial difference in foreign affairs.

	Popular Vote	Electoral Vote
Kennedy	34,226,925	303
Nixon	34,108,662	219

Kennedy's margin of victory was less than one-fifth of 1 percent of the popular vote. He was the youngest President to be elected (forty-three years old), although Theodore Roosevelt was only forty-two when McKin-

ley was shot. Kennedy was the first Roman Catholic to be elected.

Alliance for Progress

Because of the Communist government in Cuba, President Kennedy proposed a long-term program called the **Alliance for Progress** to improve the living standards in the nations of Latin America. The United States and nineteen Latin American countries were members of the alliance by 1961. They agreed to a ten-year program to improve social and economic conditions through projects for better schools, for housing and public health, and for fairer taxes and land redistribution. Funds for the program were to come from private and government sources in the United States, Latin America, Japan, western Europe and international agencies such as the World Bank. Although some progress was made, generally the results of the program were disappointing. Although reform was made in some nations, much of the money was used to aid big business and the military.

Peace Corps

In March 1961, Congress approved President Kennedy's **Peace Corps**, which put American citizens to work side by side with those they helped. The first year, about 3,000 volunteers served abroad. The program sent volunteers to nations in Africa, Asia, and Latin America. Peace Corps members learned the native language and lived in local communities in the same style as the inhabitants. Peace Corps workers were sent only to those nations that requested them. The term of service for a Corps member was two years, and the age limit was from eighteen up. Some members have been over sixty, but the great majority were in their twenties or early thirties. The Peace Corps was a great success.

Cuba, Castro, and the United States

On January 1, 1959, Fidel Castro overthrew the corrupt dictatorship of Juan Batista. Within three years he publicly declared himself a Marxist-Leninist and ended representative democracy as well as all opposition political activity. He established close ties with the Soviet Union, receiving economic and military assistance until the 1991 demise of the U.S.S.R. American relations with Castro were further soured by two events. On April 17, 1961, an invading force of Cuban refugees trained by the United States landed at the **Bay of Pigs** on the south shore of Cuba. Without air cover, their supply ships were sunk by Cuba's air force, and the abortive attack was soon smothered, with 400 killed and some 1,200 taken prisoner. Fidel Castro blamed the United States for the invasion attempt.

In October 1962, President Kennedy announced that the U.S.S.R. had placed ballistic missiles and jet bombers in Cuba, about 100 miles from Florida. The president demanded the removal of the offensive weapons and the jet bombers. He established an air-sea blockade of Cuba until the removal. Within five days, Soviet premier Khrushchev promised to withdraw the missiles and planes on condition that the U.S. would pledge not to invade Cuba. The president agreed, provided that the United States be permitted to verify the removal by an on-site inspection. The missiles and planes were removed. During the first few days of the air-sea blockade of Cuba, the U.S. and the U.S.S.R. stood toe to toe on the brink of war. That confrontation was known as the **Cuban Missile Crisis.**

The major obstacle to improved U.S.-Cuban relations in the 1990s was Cuban resistance to democratic reforms, such as freedom of expression, and free and fair elections under international supervision.

Nuclear Test-Ban Treaty (1963)

This treaty prohibits nuclear testing in the atmosphere, in space, and under water. Underground tests were not banned as there was no way to detect them without an inspection system. The U.S. and the U.S.S.R. were unable to agree on a method of inspection.

France and Communist China were the only nuclear powers not signing the treaty. Over 100 nations signed the treaty very soon after the U.S. and the U.S.S.R. had reached an agreement.

Kennedy Assassinated in Dallas, Texas (November 22, 1963)

President Kennedy and Mrs. Kennedy were seated in the rear seat of an automobile with the top down. Texas Governor Connally and Mrs. Connally were seated directly in front of them. The presidential motorcade, formed at the city airport, was nearing downtown Dallas. Happily enthusiastic crowds lined the street. At 12:30 P.M. two shots were fired; both hit the President, wounding him in the head and neck and causing death within half an hour. The second shot also seriously wounded Governor Connally who recovered several weeks later. The bullets were fired from an upper window in the Texas Book Depository Building used for storage space by the Dallas school department.

About an hour and a half after the assassination a suspect, **Lee Harvey Oswald,** was arrested. But within that 90 minutes Oswald had shot and killed a police officer who approached him for questioning. Throughout the 30 hours Oswald was under close examination by the police, he stuck to his story that he was innocent of the assassination of President Kennedy. On November 24 the Dallas police were escorting Oswald from the city to the county jail. A bystander, Jack Rubenstein (Jack Ruby), stepped forward directly in front of Oswald and fired at point-blank range. Oswald died 40 minutes later with no opportunity for further questioning. The nation was truly grief-stricken. Television had brought the young and vital presidential family close to the American people.

Shortly after 2:30 P.M. **Lyndon B. Johnson** took the oath of office as President of the United States. The ceremony took place in the cabin of the plane at Dallas, which was about to take off for Washington with the body of the slain President.

President Johnson appointed a national commission headed by Chief Justice Earl Warren to investigate the circumstances of the assassination and to issue a report of its findings. After a careful investigation, the **Warren Commission** released its report in September 1964. It concluded that Lee Harvey Oswald was the assassin, that he acted alone, and that there was no evidence of a conspiracy. Nonetheless, the report still left questions unanswered. In 1979 a committee of the House of Representatives held its own investigation and examined new evidence. It did not come to any new conclusions. Various theories about a conspiracy to assassinate Kennedy have been offered but none have ever been proven.

Lyndon B. Johnson   1963-1969

1908 -1973

DEMOCRAT

Vice-President   HUBERT H. HUMPHREY

JOHNSON'S PUBLIC SERVICE BEFORE HE BECAME PRESIDENT

Member of the House of Representatives from Texas (1937-1949, except wartime service)
Commander in Navy—Distinguished War Record (1941-1945)
Member of the Senate from Texas (1949-1961)
Minority Leader (1953-1955) Majority Leader (1955-1961)
Vice-President (1961-1963)

MAJOR ITEMS OF JOHNSON'S ADMINISTRATION

Cuban Policy
Income Tax Cut (1964)
Supreme Court Decisions
Martin Luther King and the
  Civil Rights Movement
Civil Rights Act (1964)
Anti-Poverty Act (1964)
Immigration Act (1965)

Medicare (1965)
Urban Riots (National Advisory Commission on
  Civil Disorders)
War in Middle East (1967)
The Vietnam War Begins
LBJ and the Vietnam War
The Tragedy of Lyndon Johnson

Johnson's Election in 1964

Lyndon B. Johnson received 61 percent of the popular vote, an even greater popular endorsement than Franklin Roosevelt won in 1936. The Republican candidate, **Senator Barry Goldwater,** took only six states (South Carolina, Georgia, Mississippi, Alabama, Louisiana, and his home state, Arizona).

	Popular Vote	**Electoral Vote*
Johnson	42,328,350	486
Goldwater	26,640,178	52

* First election in which the District of Columbia had an electoral vote (Twenty-Third Amendment).

The transition from President Kennedy to President Johnson was accomplished with a smoothness and lack of confusion that gave great emphasis to the stability of the federal government. Both the personnel and the policies in the field of foreign affairs established under Kennedy were satisfactory to President Johnson who, as Vice-President, had been well-informed about and active in the making of foreign policy. The **Nuclear Test-Ban Treaty** (1965) did point toward co-existence rather than increased tension between the East and the West.

* Cuban Policy

Cuba shut off the fresh-water supply to the United States naval base at Guantanamo. President Johnson's response was to supply fresh water by tankers while setting up a huge converter at the base to transform salt water to fresh in ample quantities. This not only made

219

Guantanamo independent of Cuba for its fresh water but deprived Cuba of revenue it had been getting.

President Johnson announced that American U2 spy planes would continue to fly inspection missions over Cuba. **Castro** said he would shoot them down, and Johnson made it clear that attacks on U2s would be met with severe action. The President's policy toward Cuba sought to avoid war while refusing to negotiate. He hoped to restrict trade with Cuba enough to force Castro from power. Cuba's major threat to the United States was that it could serve as a base for Communist infiltration into other Latin American republics.

Income Tax Cut (1964)

Late in February the income tax was reduced to some extent all across the board. Most people were affected by the cuts in the income brackets up to $8,000 per year. Based on a family of four, an income of $5,000 was taxed $290 instead of $420; an income of $8,000 was taxed $772 instead of $972. Along with the tax cut and part of the same financial policy, cuts were made in government spending. Several armed forces installations were shut down.

** Supreme Court Decisions

The *Wesberry* v. *Sanders* (1964) case originated in Georgia as a test case to find out whether grossly unequal congressional districts within a state were constitutional. Such districts gave one voter a very different amount of influence as a voter than another in a different district. The decision of the Supreme Court was that all congressional districts within any state must "as nearly as practicable" have the same number of voters. It required states to equalize representation in elections, working toward "one person, one vote." As population shifts took place over the years, many states neglected to readjust their congressional districts. The result was that urban areas were often very much under-represented and rural areas very much over-represented. This situation existed throughout the United States.

In a previous case, *Baker* v. *Carr* (1962) the Court had ruled that election districts within each state, from which members of the lower house of the state legislature are sent, must be of approximately equal population. There are many more such election districts in each state than there are congressional districts. Compliance with this decision required changes in 40 states or more.

Both of these decisions were based on the clause of the Fourteenth Amendment stating, "...nor shall any State deprive any person within its jurisdiction the equal protection of the laws." Any person's vote for a representative in the federal Congress or in a state legislature should have approximately as much weight as the vote of any other resident of the state.

Martin Luther King and the Civil Rights Movement

In 1955, the civil rights movement was energized when Rosa Parks, a black woman, refused to give up her bus seat to a white man in Montgomery, Alabama. Her arrest led to a protest boycott of the city's segregated buses by the black community, which was led by a young minister, the **Reverend Dr. Martin Luther King, Jr.** (1929-1968). The boycott ended successfully when the U.S. Supreme Court ruled that the city's bus segregation laws were unconstitutional. As head of the Southern Christian Leadership Conference, Dr. King led black voter registration drives, organized sit-ins at segregated lunch counters, and backed "freedom riders" trying to end racial segregation in southern bus station facilities.

A southern white backlash against the growing civil rights movement included killings and burning buses. Dr. King, an admirer of Thoreau and Gandhi, insisted on a nonviolent response, convinced that blacks could achieve equality only through peaceful civil disobedience to immoral laws. The desegregation of Central High School in Little Rock, Arkansas, was achieved when President Eisenhower sent federal troops in 1957 to protect the first black students. Attorney General **Robert F. Kennedy** sent U.S. marshalls to protect the right of qualified blacks to enroll at the all-white Universities of Mississippi (1962) and Alabama (1963).

In August 1963, Dr. King was an organizer of the March on Washington on behalf of civil rights laws then pending in Congress. At this largest civil rights demonstration in American history, 250,000 people heard Dr. King give his memorable "I Have a Dream" address. Congress would later pass a key **Civil Rights Act** (1964) and a **Voting Rights Act** (1965). In April 1968, Dr. King went to Memphis, Tennessee, for a demonstration, despite threats to his life. That night he was shot by an assassin. An eloquent champion of peace and nonviolence had been lost.

** Civil Rights Act (1964)

After a three-month filibuster by Southern Senators was ended by cloture, the **Civil Rights Act** was passed. Its most important provisions were the following.

1] Uniform standards must prevail for establishing the right to vote. Schooling through the sixth grade constitutes legal proof of literacy. Literacy tests must be in writing, and copies of the applicants' answers must be supplied on request. The attorney general may institute legal proceedings if he or she finds a pattern of discrimination in any voting district. The **Voting Rights Act of 1965** also provided that the attorney general could send officials to investigate charges of racial discrimination at the polls.

2] A public accommodations' provision makes establishments offering food, lodging, gasoline, or entertainment available to all persons without discrimination based on race, color, religion, or national origin. Private clubs and proprietor-occupied houses with five rooms or less for rent are exempt. Any complainant may have the service of an attorney without cost. The attorney general may initiate legal action in any area where there is a pattern of resistance to the law.

3] When the attorney general receives a complaint in writing which charges segregation in public schools, parks, playgrounds, swimming pools, libraries, or similar public facilities, he or she may bring suit on behalf of the complainant.

4] Projects involving federal funds will have such funds cut off if there is discrimination based on race, color, or national origin.

5] An employment agency, a union, or an employer may not discriminate in the hiring, firing, or promotion of persons on the basis of race, color, or national origin. Racial quotas shall not be used, nor will merit or seniority systems be disturbed.

6] The attorney general may intervene in any civil rights case under the Fourteenth Amendment if the case is of general public significance.

It is to be noted that throughout the Civil Rights Act, the repeated reference to the attorney general clearly recognized that resistance to the enforcement of its several provisions was likely and that the federal government was determined to enforce them.

Anti-Poverty Act (1964)

This was the first major law that was wholly a Johnson measure, one not initiated by President Kennedy. President Johnson called it the opening gun in his total war on poverty. The act aimed to help people to climb out of poverty and stay out. The $947 million appropriation provided for:

    job-training centers
    conservation camps
    basic education
    aid to needy college students
    loans to low-income farmers
    loans to low-income business people
    a domestic peace corps

** Immigration Act (1965)

This law discontinued quotas based on national origin. The basic factor of selection was made the occupation of the applicant. The United States will welcome a stated number of immigrants each year divided among several occupational categories. Preference will be given to those who have relatives already in the United States. Race, religion, color, and national origin are no part of the selective process.

** Medicare (1965)

Effective July 1, 1966, this provided payment of hospital and doctor expenses to a substantial degree for persons 65 and over. It does not apply to aliens or to certain civil employees who are already covered by government insurance.

War in Middle East (1967)

In June 1967 in the **Six Days War,** Israel won a quick and impressive military victory over Egypt, Syria, and Jordan. Israel struck at its three neighbors because it believed the Arab nations were massing large military forces to destroy Israel. After the war, Israel kept areas of land in these three Arab states that it had captured during the war. Bitter at their defeat, the Arab states began guerrilla attacks against Israel and the Israelis continued to strike back. Several days after the war, except for some sniping and minor sorties, the UN Assembly and Security Council arranged for UN inspection patrols along both sides of the Suez Canal and at other points where hostile forces confronted one another. A cease-fire had been accomplished with no assurance that negotiations would proceed to arrange a peace.

** Urban Riots (National Advisory Commission on Civil Disorders)

The summers of 1966 and 1967 brought large scale rioting ("a long, hot summer") in Brooklyn, Buffalo, and Rochester in New York State; in Los Angeles, California; in Chicago, Illinois; in Cleveland and Toledo in Ohio; and in Detroit, Michigan. By far the most serious destruction of life and property was in Los Angeles and Detroit. The life and property cost in Los Angeles was 35 killed and many millions of dollars' loss by fire; in Detroit 40 killed and even greater property damage than in Los Angeles. Detroit's terror flared for five nights, July 23 to 27, 1967.

On July 28, 1967, President Johnson appointed a National Advisory Commission on Civil Disorders, which seven months later submitted a report widely acclaimed as comprehensive, wise, and highly accurate. The sense and spirit of this report is reflected by the following quotations from the report. "Our nation is moving toward two societies, one black, one white—separate and unequal." To prevent two "separate and unequal" societies "will require from every American new attitudes, new understanding, and above all, new will." "It is time to make good the promises of American democracy to all citizens—urban or rural, white or black, Spanish-sur-name, American Indian, and every minority group." "...There can be no higher priority for national action and no higher claim on the nation's conscience."

In order of priority, the commission listed twelve areas where improvement should be started immedi-ately, with adequate financing by both the federal and local governments. The first four were "police prac-tices, unemployment and underemployment, inadequate housing, and inadequate education."

The Vietnam War Begins

After World War II, France tried to keep control of her southeast Asian colony of Indochina. (See p. 214.) The spirit of nationalism was strong in all the former European colonies in Africa and Asia. The French were defeated by the anticolonial Vietminh (1954), led by a Communist, **Ho Chi Minh.** Vietnam, part of former French Indochina, was partitioned as Korea had been, with the Vietminh governing North Vietnam, and an anti-Communist government in South Vietnam. By 1956, the United States was sending substantial aid, including military advisers, to South Vietnam.

LBJ and the Vietnam War

American involvement in Vietnam grew from 1954 on, during the presidencies of **Dwight Eisenhower** and **John Kennedy.** In 1964, Congress authorized President Lyndon Johnson to take all steps necessary to protect American troops and "prevent further aggression in Southeast Asia." That **Gulf of Tonkin Resolution** enabled President Johnson to escalate rapidly during 1964 and 1965 the American commitment to the war in Vietnam. By 1967, about 500,000 U.S. troops were in Vietnam, and continuing the war became one of the most divisive issues in American politics. In 1968, the Communist **Tet Offensive** was a massive attack on South Vietnamese and American forces. U.S. losses raised the level of antiwar sentiment in the United States, as did nightly television coverage of the destruc-tion of Vietnamese villages by American firepower.

The first two months of 1968 found public opinion and the leading spokespersons of both major parties advocating policies aimed at withdrawal from **Vietnam.** Our involvement began in the early 1950s under President Truman with heavy financial aid to France in its futile attempt to keep French Indochina as a colony. In the middle 1950s, the SEATO agreements under Eisenhower based U.S. policy on the domino theory. In 1961 to 1962, President Kennedy greatly stepped up the material support to South Vietnam and Thailand. American military advisors already in South Vietnam were joined by a few thousand U.S. troops. Under President Johnson a massive buildup of U.S. ground forces occurred, supplemented by impressive air and naval power. Even with well over 500,000 U.S. troops supported by ships and planes, the prospects for a conclusion of the war seemed no better than they had been when the U.S. took over from France in 1954. The war had become costly and unpopular, both at home and abroad. Many Americans became convinced that the South Vietnamese government could not have been established or maintained without U.S. support; that corruption, both financial and political, was rampant; and that the great mass of people who suffered the hard-ships and horrors of war wanted it to end. Such a cli-mate of opinion made a successful attempt for Johnson's reelection questionable. But in addition to the decision to avoid what seemed probable defeat at the polls, Johnson wished to end his more than five years as President by attaining peace in Vietnam or at least mak-ing substantial progress toward it.

The move toward this end was his announcement on March 31, 1968, that he was not a candidate for reelec-tion. This placed him in a position where he could negotiate for peace free from charges that his moves were merely partisan party politics in an election year. Nevertheless, negotiations resulted in no perceptible progress toward ending the fighting in Vietnam. So the 1968 presidential campaign had both major parties agreeing on bringing peace, but differing on the manner of accomplishing it.

The Tragedy of Lyndon Johnson

Johnson came to the presidency with a strong desire to complete Franklin Roosevelt's **New Deal** program. His **"War on Poverty"** would never receive the funding levels necessary for its success, because of the escalat-ing costs of the Vietnam War. There simply was not enough revenue available for both "guns and butter."

Richard Nixon   1969-1974

1913-1994

REPUBLICAN

☆

Vice-President   SPIRO T. AGNEW
GERALD R. FORD
Secretary of State   HENRY KISSINGER

NIXON'S PUBLIC SERVICE BEFORE HE BECAME PRESIDENT

Officer in the Navy 1942-1946
Member of the House of Representatives from California 1947-1951
Member of the Senate from California from 1951-1953
Vice-President 1953-1961

MAJOR ITEMS OF NIXON'S ADMINISTRATION

The Moon Landing
Postal Service Reorganized
Individual Rights Extended
(Twenty-Sixth and Proposed
Twenty-Seventh Amendments)
The Aftermath of the Vietnam War
Amtrak
Nixon's War on Inflation
The Pentagon Papers

Consumer Groups
Ecology
Cold War Events (Summit Talks in China
and the Soviet Union)
Watergate
Vice-President Spiro T. Agnew Resigns
Yom Kippur War (October War)
Energy Crisis

Election of 1968

This election year was marked by senseless tragedy, by a concerned population split into unfriendly groups, and by both major parties lacking unity. Martin Luther King, Jr., was assassinated in April and Senator Robert F. Kennedy (New York) in June. Senator Kennedy was campaigning in state primaries to win support as a presidential candidate on the Democratic ticket.

In a television address on March 31 President Johnson announced that he would not be a candidate for reelection. During his administration the U.S. commitment in Vietnam had mushroomed, yet victory seemed no closer. The people were divided and discouraged concerning our involvement and the likelihood of eventual victory. By clearly taking himself out of the presidential race, Johnson more effectively could devote his energies to gain a negotiated settlement. Senators **Eugene McCarthy** (Minnesota) and **Robert F. Kennedy** (New York), both Democrats, were leaders with substantial following. They advocated an orderly but rapid withdrawal from Vietnam.

The Democratic Nominating Convention met in Chicago. There was rioting in the city and turbulence in the convention. Vice-President **Hubert H. Humphrey** won the nomination on the first ballot. Senator **Edmund S. Muskie** (Maine) was nominated for Vice-President. Humphrey was handicapped by having been part of the Johnson team. He differed with Johnson's Vietnam policy but still had to be loyal to the President. The result was that his position on Vietnam was fuzzy and his campaigning ineffective.

Two weeks earlier the Republicans had nominated **Richard M. Nixon** at their convention at Miami. A surprise choice for Vice-President was **Spiro T. Agnew** of Maryland. Nixon's campaign message called for a negotiated settlement in Vietnam such as would fulfill our treaty obligations and maintain our national honor. On the domestic front he decried riotous demonstrations, crime in the streets, and promised a rule of law and order.

George C. Wallace of Alabama led a third party, the **American Independent party.** His program favored resistance to desegregation in the public schools, military victory in Vietnam by whatever means required, and less interference from Washington in state affairs. He hoped to gain enough votes to throw the election into the House of Representatives.

	Popular Vote	*Electoral Vote*
Richard Nixon	31,770,237	301
Hubert H. Humphrey	31,270,533	191
George C. Wallace	9,906,141	46 [†]

Reelection of Richard Nixon, 1972

Senator **George McGovern,** a liberal Democrat, won victory in the primaries and so control of the Democratic convention where he won the nomination. But the Democratic party was splintered. Senator Thomas Eagleton of Missouri, McGovern's choice, was nominated as Vice-President. But only a few weeks later, McGovern felt compelled to ask him to step down. Tom Eagleton had a record of severe mental depression, which twice required extended hospitalization. McGovern chose **Sargent Shriver,** who had headed the Peace Corps under President Kennedy as the vice-presidential nominee.

At the Republican Nominating Convention, President Nixon, with his running mate Spiro Agnew, were nominated without opposition.

The polls and the press predicted victory by large majorities. Nixon won by even larger ones. However, only 55 percent of those eligible voted. Nixon got 61 percent of the approximately 75 million votes. Only Massachusetts and the District of Columbia gave their electoral votes to McGovern. But Nixon had no coat-tails. Both houses of Congress remained in Democratic hands. In the Senate a gain of 2 for the Democrats gave them a 57 to 43 advantage. In the House a loss of 12 for the Democrats left them with 243 seats to 190 for the Republicans.

[†] One elector in North Carolina voted for Wallace even though Nixon carried the state.

	Popular Vote	*Electoral Vote*
Nixon	46,631,189	521
McGovern	28,422,015	17

** The Moon Landing

The race for space began in 1957 when the Soviet Union orbited the first earth satellite, named *Sputnik.* The next year the United States launched its own first satellite, *Explorer I,* which discovered the Van Allen radiation belts around the earth. The major goal of the American space program was to land a man on the moon.

During the next decade, great strides were made in space exploration. Astronauts, multiple orbitings of the earth, photos of Mars and the moon, space dockings, and space walks seemed almost commonplace.

On July 20, 1969, **Neil Armstrong** and Colonel **Edwin E. Aldrin, Jr.,** landed on the moon in *Apollo 11's* four-legged module, the "Eagle." Neil Armstrong descended a short ladder, took the first cautious step, and said, "That's one small step for a man, one giant leap for mankind." Television images were relayed throughout the world of two men walking about collecting samples of the moon's surface, setting up apparatus to report scientific data to the earth, planting the American flag, and finally taking off for the return trip. **Michael Collins** guided *Apollo 11's* command module, the "Columbia," in orbits around the moon.

During the next eight years as the crash program to send a man to the moon was proceeding, a feeling of uneasiness developed and increased. Vietnam, urban riots, the drug problem, inflation and unemployment at the same time, skyrocketing medical costs, and increase in violent crime all caused some Americans to suggest that attention might better be focused elsewhere than on space exploration. The Apollo space program was curtailed as a result of reconsideration of priorities and phased out by the end of 1972. During that period, fantastically successful moon flights were made.

Postal Service Reorganized (Cabinet Department Was Abolished)

The main objectives of this change were to establish a postal service that was efficient and self supporting. Another purpose was to greatly lessen political interference. The postmaster general is no longer a member of the Cabinet. On August 12, 1970, President Nixon signed into a law a long-overdue reform. Heavy annual deficits stretching back for sixteen years, deteriorating service, and pressure from the President brought about the transformation of the Post Office Department into a quasi-independent corporation, the United States Postal Service. This corporation is directed by an eleven-person Board of Governors appointed by the President. The board appoints a postmaster general and a deputy postmaster general to operate the system. Postal rates are no longer decided by Congress but by a Rates Commision of five members appointed by the postmaster general with the approval of the Board of Governors.

* Individual Rights Extended (Twenty-Sixth and Proposed Twenty-Seventh Amendment)

Legislation by Congress set the voting age at eighteen, banned literacy tests for voting, and restricted residency requirements for voting to no more than thirty days. By a five-to-four decision, the Supreme Court declared these laws constitutional if applied to the election of federal officials only. For the first time, eighteen-year-olds were entitled to vote in 1972 for President, Vice-President, and members of Congress. Eight states had already permitted under-twenty-one voting: Hawaii, Maine, and Nebraska at twenty; Massachusetts and Montana at nineteen; and Alaska, Georgia, and Kentucky at eighteen. The **Twenty-Sixth Amendment** was proposed March 23, 1971, and ratified by June 30. It stated, "The right of citizens of the United States, who are eighteen years of age or older, to vote shall not be denied or abridged by the United States or any state on account of age."

In March 1972 Congress proposed the **Twenty-Seventh Amendment** to make unmistakably clear that "the equal protection of the laws" clause of the Fourteenth Amendment applies to females as well as males. The amendment states, "Equality of rights under the law shall not be denied or abridged by the United States or by any state on account of sex." Twice between 1972 and 1988 the proposed **Equal Rights Amendment** (ERA) failed to gain ratification by the necessary 38 states.

The Aftermath of the Vietnam War

President Nixon worked to replace American forces with those from South Vietnam, and the last U.S. troops left Vietnam in 1973, their mission unaccomplished. Those who had warned against U.S. involvement in a land war in Asia had been proven right. After the American withdrawal, hostilities continued between North and South Vietnam until the latter's defeat in 1975. Following a general election for a National Assembly to represent the whole country, all of Vietnam was unified as the Socialist Republic of Vietnam in July 1976.

In 1975 the United States imposed a trade embargo on Vietnam, which remained in effect for almost 20 years, until 1994. Normalization of relations would be linked to withdrawal of Vietnamese military forces from Cambodia, a western neighbor, and to providing information about Americans still missing from the war. A general political settlement was achieved in Southeast Asia in 1992, and improved cooperation with the Hanoi government reduced the number of U.S. service personnel still listed as missing in action. A January 1994 Senate resolution urged President Clinton to lift the trade embargo, giving him political cover. He did so, and in July 1995 he announced the normalization of diplomatic ties with Vietnam. American companies were already entering the Vietnamese market, and American investments there grew quickly.

Amtrak

Setting **Amtrak** into operation was the first major attempt to reestablish adequate railroad passenger service. The Department of Transportation, organized in 1966, had the plan in operation on May 1, 1971. The new system cut the number of trains by about 50 percent; the number of cities served by passenger trains was reduced. The cities served were along 21 basic routes. New equipment, revised services, and speed ranging close to 100 miles an hour could make trains a superior method of mass transportation.

Nixon's War on Inflation (a Temporary NEP)

In 1971 President Nixon declared war on inflation. For about three decades, economists and millions of victims of rising prices had looked upon inflation as public enemy No. 1 in the economy. Savings accounts, insurance policies, and pension plans were yielding less and less year by year. President Nixon judged the situation so intolerable and dangerous that he reversed his longheld position against government controls. The President's plan brought about the following:

Prices, wages, and rents were immediately frozen.

The U.S. dollar was no longer valued at any stated amount of gold; it was allowed to fluctuate in value compared with foreign currencies; it had become a floating dollar.

Pay raises for federal employees were postponed.

The number of federal jobs was to be cut by 5 percent.

A 10 percent surcharge was added to all import duties.

The 7 percent excise tax on automobiles was repealed.

New investments would entitle the investor to a 10 percent tax credit.

The higher allowances for dependents on income taxes scheduled for 1973 were to become effective January 1, 1972.

Where necessary Congress took quick action to implement Nixon's temporary **New Economic Policy** (NEP). Phase 1 of the program was to last at least 90 days, when a reevaluation would be made.

The President announced Phase 2 of his NEP in October 1971. He expressed satisfaction with the wage-and-price controls, which would continue for the balance of the 90-day period and probably be extended beyond that. Phase 2 had as its main goal getting the rate of inflation within a yearly increase of 2 percent to 3 percent by 1973. A Cost of Living Council, headed by Secretary of the Treasury, John B. Connally, was to work closely with a Price Commission and a Pay Board. The Pay Board of fifteen members (five from labor, five from business, five from the public) ran into trouble. Wage gains already agreed on through collective bargaining were cut over the objections of labor members, who argued it was unfair because there were no provisions for cutting profits. Four of the labor members resigned. The Pay Board was immediately reorganized by the President by reducing its size to one labor member, one business member, and five public members. To avoid a top-heavy bureaucracy, the government checked only prices charged by large businesses, whose combined sales accounted for about 75 percent of the total.

The *Pentagon Papers*

On June 13, 14, and 15, 1971, *The New York Times* published excerpts from the secret government documents prepared by the Pentagon under the direction of Defense Secretary **Robert McNamara.** The documents filled 47 volumes and gave a detailed account of the history of United States involvement in Indochina. **Daniel Ellsberg,** a member of the faculty at Massachusetts Institute of Technology, had been a member of McNamara's staff when the *Pentagon Papers* were compiled. He was charged with turning over the secret papers to *The New York Times.* Ellsberg said he learned from these records that "There has never been a year when there would have been a war in Indochina without American money." Fighting started there with the revolt of Indochina against France, a revolt that succeeded in 1954 and for which the United States paid about 75 percent of the costs.

On June 15 the Justice Department got a restraining order, which stopped the publication of the *Pentagon Papers.* Federal appellate courts in Washington, D.C. and in New York City, both ruled that it was constitutional for newspapers (*Washington Post* and *The New York Times*) to print the *Pentagon Papers.* The newspapers argued that it was their "fundamental responsibility" to print such material; the government argued that such publication of documents classified as "secret" would cause "irreparable injury" to the national defense. The Supreme Court heard the case on June 30, 1971,

and by six-to-three vote declared that the First Amendment permitted such publications. The fact that the *Pentagon Papers* did not contain present-day, current material but records going back to Eisenhower's administration counted heavily against the government's claim of "irreparable injury." Justice Black said, "The press was to serve the governed, not the government."

Consumer Groups

In the 1960s, consumer groups came alive. President Kennedy listed four rights of consumers: the rights to safety, to be informed, to choose, and to be heard. The basic aim of the consumer movement is to insure that the buyer is effectively protected from fraud and deceit through law, enforced by government agencies.

Ralph Nader, a lawyer, stood out in the 1970s as the champion of the consumer. He attracted many young lawyers and other college people to the cause. His influence was largely responsible for legislation passed by Congress in 1971 establishing a **Consumer Protection Agency.**

* Ecology

Early in 1970 President Nixon offered strong leadership in the "war on pollution" in the United States. He promised an attack to reclaim "the purity of its air and waters." By the 1960s and 1970s it had become clear that serious damage was being done to the earth's resources, especially its air and water. Emissions from motor vehicles, industries, power plants, and homes were polluting the air and causing smog in the nation's cities. Human and industrial wastes poured into America's rivers and lakes. Hazardous wastes from chemical plants, nuclear reactors, and industries were piling up. Public concern about such problems was first aroused by **Rachel Carson** in her 1962 book *Silent Spring.* In 1970 Congress passed a **Clean Air Act** that set limits on exhaust emissions from new automobiles and on factories, power plants, and incinerators. Also, in 1970 President Nixon established the **Environmental Protection Agency** (EPA).

Cold War Events

* Summit Conference in China

For about a quarter century, the United States had opposed entrance to the United Nations of Mao Tse-Tung's Communist People's Republic of China and had refused it official recognition. The China the United States did recognize was Chiang Kai-shek's Nationalist China on the island of Taiwan.

President Nixon made the first moves to change our foreign policy toward China. Early in 1971 the United States relaxed restrictions on visitors from Communist China. China invited the United States to send a table-tennis team to compete with their teams. Both nations relaxed trade restrictions. In July 1971 President Nixon announced that he had been invited by Premier Chou En-lai to visit China and would go. The President also stated that in the coming fall session of the United Nations, the United States would support the admission of the People's Republic to the UN but would oppose any attempt to expel Nationalist China. On October 25, 1971 the General Assembly admitted the People's Republic but at the same time expelled Nationalist China (Taiwan) from the U.N.

That 1972 visit ended 22 years of openly hostile relations between the United States and China. As President Nixon put it, "The primary goal of this trip was to reestablish communication with the People's Republic of China. We achieved this goal."

In May 1972, after the President returned from the China trip, Okinawa Island was returned to Japan, but the United States retained its military base there.

Summit Conference in the U.S.S.R.

On May 22, 1972, President Nixon arrived in Moscow to begin a week of conferences with the leadership of the Soviet Union. His two top advisors were his chief advisor on foreign affairs, Henry Kissinger, and our ambassador at Moscow, Gerard Smith. The Soviet's team of three top men was Leonid I. Brezhnev, Communist Party Secretary; Alexei N. Kosygin, Premier; and Nikolai V. Podgorney, Chairman of the Presidium and President of the U.S.S.R. The U.S. and the U.S.S.R. were ready to:

conduct joint space teams to develop spaceships by 1975 to serve as bases for rescue attempts in aid of space missions of either nation;

have scientists of both nations work together for cures of cancer and heart diseases;

cease from any further incidents of U.S. and U.S.S.R. warships maneuvering to taunt or dare one another;

cooperate in solving the problems of air and water pollution;

increase cooperation in scientific and technological fields.

These five areas of agreement had been reached during the previous two and a half years.

The main hope of the conference was to reach meaningful agreements developed in **Strategic Arms Limitation Talks** (SALT). By strategic arms was meant nuclear weapons, both defensive and offensive. Two agreements of some substance were reached.

1] A treaty was drawn up, subject to ratification by the United States Senate. It limited the United States and Soviet Union to 100 defensive missiles (ABMs) at each of two sites: one site the nation's capital and the other wherever selected.

2] A rather complex agreement on numbers of land-based and submarine-borne nuclear missiles allotted to each nation gives approximate equality of firepower. This is an executive agreement, not subject to Senate approval.

** Watergate 1972

On June 17, 1972, at 2:30 A.M. five men were arrested in the Washington, D.C., Watergate Hotel complex. They had broken into the national headquarters of the Democratic party. These burglars brought with them walkie-talkies adjusted to frequencies used by the Republican National Committee. Linking of this burglary with the White House set off the **Watergate Affair.** However, Watergate soon became a reference not only to this burglary but also to all the crimes, other illegal acts, and "dirty tricks" of the 1972 presidential campaign traceable to the White House staff or to the Committee to Reelect the President.

The committee formed to investigate the Watergate Affair was a Senate Committee of seven members. The four Democrats were **Sam Ervin** (chairman) of North Carolina, Herman Talmadge of Georgia, Joseph Montoya of New Mexico, and Daniel Inouye of Hawaii; the three Republicans were **Howard H. Baker** (vice-chairman) of Tennessee, Edward J. Gurney of Florida, and Lowell Weicker of Connecticut. The committee's purpose was to gather as complete and accurate a picture of presidential campaigns as possible so that Congress would have the knowledge required to formulate legislation well-calculated to prevent further abuses. The committee hearings began May 17, 1973, and by August 9 had taken over 7,000 pages of testimony. Most of these hearings were televised. By granting limited immunity to several witnesses, many perpetrators of crimes, other illegal acts, and dirty tricks were exposed. By October 1973, the White House Staff had been decimated with resignations followed by grand jury indictments and court convictions. The President, the White House Staff, and the Committee to Reelect the President were under the cloud of:

influencing the IRS (Internal Revenue Service) to give special attention to tax returns of listed "enemies" of President Nixon, "enemies" being political opponents or their supporters;

burglarizing, bugging, wiretapping, and spying against dissenting demonstrators, news reports, and government employees;

invoking a principle or theory of "inherent" power of the President to override laws and the Constitution whenever, in his view, such action is necessary to protect or advance national interests.

One fact brought out by the Ervin Committee was that electronic equipment had been installed in the President's office to secretly record and tape conversations. Senator Ervin asked the President to make these tapes available to the Committee. The President refused.

The volume of court cases growing out of the several investigations was too great for the attorney general and his Department of Justice to handle. So a special prosecutor, **Archibald Cox,** was appointed by President Nixon with a promise of full authority to prosecute cases without interference. But Cox soon found that conflicting testimony in several cases could not be resolved without access to the tapes that President Nixon would not release.

The major concern of the news media, the Congress, and the people focused not on any particular crime, other illegal act, or dirty trick but on the question of the president's part therein. Did he play any part in authorizing, planning, or carrying out such activities? Did he order or acquiesce in any cover-ups? There were tapes and other records which presumably had the answers but which the President would not release. On June 20, 1972, only three days after the Watergate burglary, the President and members of his staff, Ehrlichman, Haldeman, Dean, and Mitchell, had conversations with one another. Other consultations involving Nixon, the two top men of his White House staff, and the chairman of the Committee to Reelect the President followed. It was the tape recordings of these meetings that Special Prosecutor Cox demanded. Nixon refused them on the grounds of executive privilege and national security.

On October 12, 1973, the Court of Appeals ordered the President to deliver the tapes to Judge Sirica. The President could have five days' grace in which to decide whether to appeal the case to the Supreme Court. During the five-day period Cox was fired, Attorney General Richardson resigned, Deputy Attorney General Ruckelshaus was fired, and Solicitor General Bork was appointed Acting Attorney General. Instead of taking his case to the Supreme Court, the President announced he would deliver nine of the most wanted tapes to Judge Sirica. One tape, which was expected to clear up the question of the President's knowledge of the Watergate burglary and its cover-up, had an eighteen-minute gap. Six experts examined the tapes and agreed that at least five erasures, and possibly nine, had been made. They agreed that those erasures could not have been accidental.

During the first two months of 1974, speculation about the possibility of the President's resignation or impeachment was widespread. The new special prosecutor, **Leon Jaworski,** continued to try to get more tapes and other White House records. Publicly, at least, the President seemed to believe that the prolonged investigations of the tactics used during the election campaign of 1972 had become fishing expeditions to "get" the President.

The Judiciary Committee of the House of Representatives was formed to examine evidence collected by Special Prosecutor Leon Jaworski and to advise the House whether or not to impeach the President. While the House Judiciary Committee was being set up, Jaworski was requesting many more tapes from President Nixon. In response, Nixon sent him edited transcripts of tapes, which he also offered for general publication.

Judge Sirica issued a subpoena to President Nixon demanding that the specified tapes be delivered to Jaworski. Nixon refused to obey the subpoena. Special Prosecutor Leon Jaworski requested the Supreme Court to resolve the conflicting views concerning the power of subpoena and "executive privilege." On June 24, 1974, a unanimous vote of the Supreme Court decided that President Nixon was legally obligated to deliver the requested tapes to Special Prosecutor Jaworski. Only six days later, the House Judiciary Committee voted to recommend that the House impeach Nixon on three charges: (1) obstruction of justice, (2) abusing his authority and violating his oath of office, and (3) subverting the Constitution by defying eight subpoenas for tapes in order to block impeachment. After the House Judiciary Committee had advised impeachment, the tapes were sent to Jaworski and examined. They revealed direct evidence that six days after the Watergate burglary, Nixon had taken part in and directed moves to cover up evidence connecting the White House with Watergate.

As support for the President weakened, Republican leaders in Congress advised Nixon to resign. He was told the House would impeach him by an overwhelming vote and the Senate would probably find him guilty by a wide margin over the two-thirds vote required. In a televised address, President Nixon announced his resignation to take effect the following day, August 9, 1974. He said he could no longer continue to justify an effort to finish his term because, "In the past few days, it has become evident to me that I no longer have a strong enough base in Congress to justify continuing that effort." Vice-President **Gerald Ford** became the new President.

* Vice-President Spiro T. Agnew Resigns (Succeeded by Gerald R. Ford)

While President Nixon was still fighting Watergate charges, Vice-President Agnew pleaded *nolo contendere* (no contest) to charges of income-tax evasion. A plea of *nolo contendere,* as a matter of law, carries with it the same penalties as a plea of guilty. However, the defendant does not formally acknowledge guilt; expense and publicity of the procedure are kept at a minimum; and there is a presumption that penalties applied will be something less than the maximum. As previously arranged, Agnew stated before Judge Hoffman, Attorney General Richardson, and a few other witnesses, "I hereby resign the office of Vice-President of the United States." The law requires that the resignation be sent in writing to the Secretary of State. Agnew sent a formal letter to Secretary Henry Kissinger.

The major charges against Agnew were bribery and extortion while Governor of Maryland and Vice-President of the United States. These more serious charges were dropped, and Agnew was allowed to plead guilty to the lesser charge of income-tax evasion. Another agreement reached with the court was that the sworn evidence against Agnew and the bribery and extortion charges would be made part of the public record. Although not part of any legally binding agreement, the attorney general of Maryland, Francis Burch, said there would be no state criminal prosecution of Agnew. The penalty imposed by the court was a fine of $10,000 and three years' probation with no requirement that Agnew report periodically to any probation officer.

The resignation brought the Twenty-Fifth Amendment into operation. President Nixon submitted the name of **Gerald R. Ford**, a member of the House of Representatives from Michigan for 25 years, as the new Vice-President. Ford was sixty years old, a conservative Republican, and considered by members of both houses of Congress as a suitable choice. He took the oath of office December 6, 1973.

Yom Kippur War or October War (October 6-22, 1973)

On October 6, 1973, a massive Egyptian attack across the Suez Canal pushed the Israeli forces from the East Bank into the Sinai Peninsula. The surprised Israelis no longer had air supremacy as in the Six-Day War of 1967. The Syrians attacked at the Golan Heights, so Israel faced a two-front war. This surprise attack came while the Israelis were observing Yom Kippur, a holy day, and thus their armed forces were not fully mobilized.

Israel gave immediate attention to the Syrian border. By the end of a week, the Syrians were driven from the Golan Heights, and by October 21 Israeli forces had outposts at points 60 to 20 miles from Damascus. By October 21 the Egyptians had been forced back to the canal, where they continued to hold the East Bank. At the southern end of the canal, about nine miles north of Suez City, Israeli tanks crossed to the East Bank and swung around, entrapping the Egyptian Third Army.

On October 22, 1973, the United States and the Soviet Union joined together to introduce a cease-fire resolution in the Security Council of the UN. It was adopted unanimously. A UN force was formed to police the cease-fire. There were many violations, but the war sputtered down to minor outbreaks.

However, there was no cease-fire on the Israeli-Syrian border along the Golan Heights. There was constant fighting, including artillery exchanges, tank forays, and air attacks. Diplomatic efforts in Washington, Moscow, Cairo, and especially in Jerusalem and Damascus finally produced a cease-fire by May 31, 1974. Throughout the month of May, Secretary of State Henry Kissinger shuttled between Jerusalem and Damascus to achieve a separation of forces. A border line (the "Kissinger Line") was established along the entire length of the Golan Heights; a United Nations force of 1,250 soldiers (UN Disengagement Observer Force) was to occupy a strip one to four miles wide along the new border; and Israeli and Syrian forces could occupy a strip 12 miles wide, each on its own side of the UN buffer zone. During the next 30 years, there was no improvement in relations between Syria and Israel.

* Energy Crisis

United States' production of crude oil had earlier been more than ample to supply domestic needs, but by 1972 it was clear that this was no longer true. In fact, domestic production was declining while domestic consumption was rising rapidly.

After the October 1973 Arab-Israeli War, several oil-rich Arab states of the Middle East decided to cut off shipments of oil to the United States and other countries that supported Israel.

Within the United States this cutoff of oil created an energy crisis. Many independent oil refineries failed, hundreds of independent service stations failed, and motorists formed long lines waiting their turns at the pump. Congress was startled into action and in a semipanic atmosphere authorized the construction of the Alaskan pipeline connecting the oil fields with the port of Valdez. President Nixon proposed that Congress join with him in setting 1980 as the date when the United States would never again be dependent on any other nation for energy. However, by the mid 1990s, the United States was again importing larger amounts of foreign oil, and car manufacturers were building lots of gas-guzzling sport utility vehicles. (See also pg. 235.)

Gerald R. Ford 1974-1977

1913-

REPUBLICAN

Vice-President NELSON ROCKEFELLER
Secretary of State HENRY KISSINGER

FORD'S PUBLIC SERVICE BEFORE HE BECAME PRESIDENT

Lieutenant Commander in the Navy during World War II
Member of the House of Representatives from Michigan 1949-1974
Republican Leader of the House of Representatives, 1966-1974
Member of the Warren Commission investigating Assassination of President Kennedy
Appointed Vice-President after resignation of Spiro Agnew 1973-1974

MAJOR ITEMS OF FORD'S ADMINISTRATION

Ford Pardons Nixon
Ford's Asian Trip
Congressional Reform
Ford and Congress
Supreme Court Decisions

International Events
Federal Campaign Finance Law
Conrail
Presidential Nominating Conventions

* Ford Pardons Nixon

Gerald Ford became President on August 9, 1974, after Nixon's resignation. He nominated and Congress approved Nelson Rockefeller, former Governor of New York, as his Vice-President. The nation now had its first nonelected President and Vice-President.

There was immediate interest in what President Ford would do about former President Nixon, who had named him to be his Vice-President. On his thirty-first day in office, September 8, President Ford granted Richard Nixon a "full, free, and absolute pardon." Shock and dismay were reactions from many members of Congress. An eventual pardon had been considered likely, but not until guilt had been legally established.

Ford's Asian Trip

In November 1974 President Ford and Leonid Brezhnev met at a health resort near Vladivostok in the eastern U.S.S.R. They reached tentative decisions

presumably to be confirmed at a future conference. A ceiling was placed on the number of ICBMs, of missiles launched from submarines, of multiple war heads (MIRVs), and bombers. The limits were higher than either the United States or the Soviet Union had yet reached. The conference indicated that the policy of "detente" was still alive; that is, the U.S. and the U.S.S.R. would seek agreements to prevent a nuclear third world war.

From Vladivostok, President Ford went to Japan and then to South Korea. His four-day stay in Japan was a goodwill gesture. His one-day stop at Seoul was to remind North Korea that the United States was still a staunch friend of South Korea. This Asian trip also served to give status to President Ford's experience in conducting foreign policy.

* Congressional Reform

The Senate and the House make their own rules on how they organize, and the rules may be changed from session to session.

Early in December 1974, some inroads were made on the congressional **seniority system** of appointing chairpersons of committees. House Democrats met in closed session to reorganize the Ways and Means Committee. For sixty-three years this committee had chosen the members to serve on the other House committees. Wilbur Mills, Democrat of Arkansas, as chairman of the Ways and Means Committee over a period of several years, had become one of the most influential men in Congress, largely through his exercise of this power of appointment. The Democratic caucus increased the size of the Ways and Means Committee from 25 to 37 members, transferred the authority to appoint members to other committees to the Steering and Policy Committee, and ruled that no member of the House could be chairperson of two major committees at the same time. Three major committee chairmen, all Democrats, were voted out of their seniority-held positions and replaced by other Democrats.

Ford and Congress

The fact that Gerald Ford had become Vice-President and President without having been elected gave him less prestige with Congress than is usually accorded a President. The misuse by President Nixon of the FBI, the CIA, and the IRS, and Nixon's assertion of "executive privilege" as justification for denying "top secret" documents to the Ervin Senate committee, the Rodino House committee, and Special Prosecutor Jaworski had put Congress in a less than cooperative mood toward the Executive branch. Then President Ford granted Nixon a "full, free, and absolute pardon" before there had been any legal determination of guilt or innocence. Whatever cooperative intent had existed between Ford and Congress soon dissolved. The mid-term elections of 1974 had given the Democrats 24 more seats than the Republicans in the Senate and 147 more seats in the House. With the presidential election approaching, both the Democratic Congress and the Republican President blamed each other for the nation's ills.

Supreme Court Decisions (all in 1975)

School pupils cannot be suspended without being told of charges against them and without having a chance to tell their side of the story. (Five-to-four decision.)

The President of the United States has no right to "freeze" funds appropriated by Congress. (Nixon had refused to release $9 billion for state and local water-pollution control.) (Unanimous decision.)

The United States has title to oil and gas found in the Atlantic Continental Shelf beyond the three-mile limit. (Unanimous decision.)

Declared unconstitutional a Utah law declaring girls adults at eighteen, but boys at twenty-one.

Let stand a Georgia court's decision allowing a Georgia official to be liable for damages for refusing to accept a job application from a white man because he was married to a black woman.

International Events

Two major events affecting American foreign policy occurred in 1975 during the Ford presidency.

1] The Vietnam War ended on April 30, 1975, when North Vietnamese troops entered Saigon, and the South Vietnamese government formally surrendered. Saigon was then renamed Ho Chi Minh City. (See also pg. 225.)

2] The first of the Helsinki Accords was signed by Canada, the United States, the Soviet Union and 32 other members of the Organization for Security and Cooperation in Europe. Meeting in the capital of Finland, they pledged increased cooperation between the nations of Eastern and Western Europe. The main goal of these accords was to reduce international tensions associated with the Cold War. Western countries finally recognized Eastern European boundaries that had been set up after World War II ended in 1945. All signers promised to respect human rights, which led to increased popular demand for the exercise of human rights in Eastern Europe and the Soviet Union. This demand became one cause of the democratic revolutions that toppled communist governments in Eastern Europe from 1989 on, and led to the fall from power of the Soviet Communist Party in August, 1991. These developments contributed to a sharp improvement in Western countries' relations with Eastern European nations, and with the former Soviet Union.

** Federal Campaign Finance Law (passed in 1974; revised in 1976)

This law set up a six-member **Federal Election Commission** with power to investigate alleged violations of the law as well as to carry out its many provisions. It became operative in time to apply to the presidential primaries beginning in April 1976.

A few of the provisions of the **Federal Campaign Finance Law** follow:

1] The Federal Election Commission may impose fines up to $10,000 for each violation of the law in a civil case. Any criminal violations will be handled by the Justice Department.

2] Political Action Committees formed by unions, corporations, and other membership organizations may contribute no more than $5,000 per candidate. If a union, corporation, or other membership organization has several Political Action Committees, the total from all of them must not exceed $5,000.

3] An individual may contribute any amount to support a candidate, but if the amount is over $100, the donor must certify under penalty of perjury that no cooperation, communication, or consultation about the donation occurred between the donor and the candidate or the campaign organization.

4] Whenever a union, corporation, or other membership organization spends more than $2,000 on political communication in support of a party or candidate, the amount must be disclosed.

The presidential primaries and the presidential election expenses were financed by many small contributions and the $95 million from the $1 check-off people made on their income-tax returns.

The intent of the above reforms was to be severely challenged in later presidential and congressional elections.

** Conrail (1976)

The **Consolidated Rail Corporation** combined seven railroads in the northeastern United States in an attempt to revitalize service. The railroads combined were the Penn Central, Lehigh Valley, Central of New Jersey, Reading, Lehigh Valley & Hudson River, Erie Lackawanna, and Ann Arbor. All were actually bankrupt or nearly so. This quasi-governmental merger was a last-ditch attempt to avoid outright government ownership and operation. This combination of roads serves an area with 17,000 miles of track, includes over half the manufacturing plants in the United States, and contains about 100 million people. Conrail handles about one-fourth of the nation's freight. The $2.1 billion of government money used to improve roadbeds and equipment was a loan to be repaid. Amtrak, organized in 1971, was heavily subsidized by the government. Conrail is primarily a freight service system, while Amtrak is a passenger service system.

Presidential Nominating Conventions (1976)

The Democrats held their convention in New York City in July. There were 31 states holding presidential primaries, with New Hampshire the first. **James Earl Carter, Jr.**, former Governor of Georgia who was not known nationally, entered more primaries than any other Democratic hopeful and won in nineteen of them. He finished with enough pledged delegate votes to win the nomination on the first ballot. The Party Platform was a Carter platform; and the choice of Senator Walter F. Mondale of Minnesota as the Vice-Presidential candidate was a Carter selection.

The Republicans held their convention in Kansas City, Missouri, in August. Before the state presidential primaries began, the assumption was that President Ford would be unopposed as a nominee. However, former Governor of California Ronald Reagan entered several state presidential primaries and picked up substantial delegate support. He represented the more conservative wing of the party, while Ford occupied a middle position. Ford was chosen. The convention accepted Ford's choice of Senator Robert J. Dole of Kansas to run on the ticket as Vice-President.

James E. Carter 1977-1981

1924-

DEMOCRAT

Vice President   WALTER F. MONDALE
Secretary of State   CYRUS R. VANCE

CARTER'S PUBLIC SERVICE BEFORE HE BECAME PRESIDENT

Graduated from Annapolis Naval Academy
Aide to Admiral Rickover (Nuclear Submarine Program)
Member of the Georgia Senate
Governor of Georgia (1971-1975)

MAJOR ITEMS DURING CARTER'S ADMINISTRATION

Panama Canal Treaties (1978)
United States Promotes Peace Efforts in the Middle East
SALT II Agreement, 1979
Three-Mile Island Nuclear Power Plant (March 29, 1979)
The Energy Problem as of 1979
President Carter's Energy Plan
U.S. Embassy at Tehran, Iran, Seized and Held 444 Days
Alaska National Interest Lands Conservation Act (1980)
After the White House

Carter's Election in 1976

The "Who is Jimmy Carter?" question asked so often in the early presidential primary days of April 1976 was answered the following November. He was the President-elect of the United States.

Ford supporters seemed to feel that the President was considerably less than great, but certainly acceptable and definitely a better choice than Carter. Many Carter supporters were in some doubt about how effective a President he might be but judged that he would be better than Ford. Neither candidate had caught on as a great leader of his party. About 53 percent of those qualified to vote did so. In several states a few thousand votes could have changed the results, so that in a statistical sense the decision made was done by about 25 percent of the total who could have voted.

	Popular Vote	Electoral Vote
Carter	40,276,040	297
Ford	38,532,630	241

(Ronald Reagan received one electoral vote from the state of Washington.)

	Senate	House of Representatives
Democrats	61	291
Republicans	38	144
Independents	1	

Panama Canal Treaties

The 99-year renewable lease period of the **Hay-Bunau-Varilla Treaty** had been in effect for 75 years. The original annual fee of $250,000, paid by the United States to Panama, had been readjusted upward several times, sometimes on the initiative of the United States and at other times on the urging of Panama. By 1955 the annual fee was $2.3 million. The 1970s was an appropriate time for a decision on whether the Hay-Bunau-Varilla Treaty should be extended for a considerable period or terminated.

President Carter favored termination, as had the previous three Presidents, Johnson, Nixon, and Ford. There was plenty of time for a gradual turnover of technical and administrative functions to Panama.

Two treaties were drawn up: one to return control of the **Panama Canal Zone** and the operation of the canal to Panama; the other to provide for the defense of the canal by Panama and the United States. Both treaties were signed September 7, 1977, by representatives of both nations. Ratification by Panama was quick and enthusiastic. On October 23, 1977, a national plebiscite brought out a massive vote resulting in a two-to-one majority favoring the treaties. In the United States, ratification was delayed by vigorous opposition in the Senate but did squeak through with the required two-thirds majority. Clauses in the treaty concerning the defense of the Panama Canal give the United States rather complete freedom of action.

There were basically important reasons for terminating the Hay-Bunau-Varilla Treaty. Refusal to do so would activate bitterness against the United States throughout the republics of Central and South America. They could accept no reason as justifying another 99-year lease extending complete control to the United States of a strip of land and a canal through the center of the Republic of Panama.

United States Promotes Peace Efforts in Middle East

In November 1977 **President Anwar Sadat** of Egypt announced to his parliament, "I am ready to go to the Israeli parliament itself to discuss peace." A few days later **Prime Minister Menachem Begin** invited Sadat to address the Israeli Knesset. On November 20 both statesmen spoke at length not only to the Knesset but, through television, to much of the world. Both emphatically rejected war as a means to settle Middle East problems, no matter how difficult a negotiated settlement may be or how long it might take. Sadat suggested that such negotiations might well be furthered by the United States, the United Nations, and the Soviet Union.

Sadat arranged a conference at Cairo in mid-December 1977. The U.S.S.R., the P.L.O. (**Palestine Liberation Organization**), Lebanon, and Jordan were invited but did not attend. Only Egypt, Israel, the United States, and the United Nations were represented. Both Sadat and Begin presented proposals as a basis for an eventual treaty, but no binding agreements were made.

In early August 1978, President Carter invited Begin and Sadat to Camp David, the presidential retreat in Maryland, for Middle East talks. A comprehensive series of tentative agreements was drawn up concerning Israeli occupation of the Sinai Peninsula, oil in the Sinai, the West Bank of the Jordan, the Gaza Strip, the status of the P.L.O., and the status of Jerusalem. While there was considerable agreement on these issues, there were important unsolved points at issue. But the dominant note was still the determination to achieve a negotiated settlement. The work accomplished was called the **Camp David Accord**. Within three months it was to become the basis of a treaty of peace between Israel and Egypt.

Israel agreed to return all of the Sinai Peninsula to Egypt within three years. Both agreed to end the state of war, and after the return of at least two-thirds of the Sinai to Egypt, "normal and friendly" relations would be in effect. "Normal" referred to diplomatic exchanges of ambassadors, ministers, consuls, and other official personnel, while "friendly" referred to a great variety of economic and cultural relationships common among nations.

President Carter invited Sadat and Begin to have the treaty signed in Washington. The ceremony was held on the White House lawn the afternoon of March 26, 1979. A "cold peace" followed. (See also pg. 254.)

SALT II Agreement, 1979

The Nixon-Kosygin **Strategic Arms Limitation Talks** of 1972 became SALT I when ratified a few months later by the United States Senate. Its expiration date was December 31, 1977. The Carter-Brezhnev SALT agreements were signed in Vienna in June 1979. This **SALT II** treaty was a highly complicated and technical agreement limiting strategic nuclear-delivery vehicles to 2,250 for each nation. These included intercontinental ballistic missiles, submarine-launched ballistic missiles, heavy bombers, and air-to-surface ballistic missiles with a range of over 375 miles. It also set limits on the number of warheads on each missile and missile weights. Ratification of the SALT II treaty ran into trouble in the Senate because many Senators feared the treaty gave the Soviets nuclear superiority.

After the Soviet invasion of Afghanistan, the treaty was never ratified. However, Presidents Carter and Reagan honored its terms.

Three Mile Island Nuclear Power Plant (March 29, 1979)

In Middletown, Pennsylvania, a reactor in a nuclear power plant overheated and allowed the release of low-level radioactive gases. Some metal parts had been melted and thus presented the reality that unless a cooling-off could be induced, the hydrogen bubble formed in the reactor would explode. Government officials urged the evacuation of preschool children and pregnant women living within five miles of **Three Mile Island**.

Before the overheated hydrogen bubble threat, nuclear power plants held first place as an answer to our shortage of electric power. After the malfunction of this reactor, nuclear power plants held first place as a major threat to public safety. The television drama and the millions of words on the air and in print created overwhelming support for a second look at nuclear power plants before making a deeper commitment to them. The following list contains some of the ideas, facts, and opinions that brought about such a quick reversal in public opinion.

1] Workers exposed to "tolerable" amounts of radioactive radiation during the 1950s had a higher-than-usual incidence of cancer.

2] Nuclear wastes remain active for thousands of years.

3] Nuclear power plants have a life of about 35 years. If torn down, means of disposing of nuclear wastes must be found. If the plants are not dismantled, they must be sealed. In either case the problem of the thousand years or more of radioactive radiation remains.

4] Regulations concerning the operation of nuclear power plants were inadequate, and largely unenforced.

5] Many employees in nuclear power plants are not competent to perform the duties demanded by their position.

6] Some nuclear power plants are poorly located. They are too near densely populated areas. Not enough attention is given to the prevailing winds that would carry the radiation.

7] Faulty design was part of the cause of the Three Mile Island malfunction, and there are other plants of the same design. During the next 20 years few new nuclear power plants were built in the United States, and many older ones were closed. Concerns about safety were a major reason.

The Energy Problem, as of 1979

OPEC (Organization of Petroleum Exporting Countries), Three Mile Island, and long lines of automobiles ending at service stations combined to persuade the people of the United States that there was a genuine energy problem.

In 1979 a revolution in Iran ended its oil shipments and disrupted the world oil supply. Americans were affected by an energy crisis in the spring of 1979. The gasoline shortage soon led to long lines of cars at service stations. The oil-producing nations raised prices, and the cost of gas and oil rose rapidly.

President Carter's Energy Plan (July 15, 1979)

President Carter set forth an ambitious energy program to cut down on foreign oil imports and on American reliance on petroleum. It called for developing alternative energy sources such as solar power and synthetic gasoline (gasohol). Congress was asked to:

1] Commit funds and resources to develop alternative energy sources. ("Windfall profits" taxes were to be a major source of financing.)

2] Require the nation's utilities to reduce their use of oil by 50 percent.

3] Spend an additional $10 billion in the next 10 years on public mass transportation.

None of these things happened. Oil imports rose again, commuter rail and bus lines faced increased competition from personal autos, and the development of alternative energy sources received no significant national boost. President Carter attacked the oil lobby in 1979. Its power in Congress remained evident for more than the next 30 years.

United States Embassy at Teheran, Iran, Seized November 4, 1979

Mohammed Reza Pahlavi inherited the throne of Iran in 1941 from his father, who had accomplished a military coup d'état in 1921. The World War II events of 1940-1941 determined the acceptance of Mohammed Reza Pahlavi as Shah. In this tumultuous period the overriding need of Iran was a stable government. The Soviet Union, England, and the United States favored Mohammed Reza Pahlavi as most likely to achieve such stability. Over three decades later, **Ayatollah Khomeini** was to claim that the United States had played the leading role in establishing the shah in office and referred to the shah as "the United States' boy."

In 1953 the shah proclaimed a "White Revolution," which meant westernization. From 1953 to about 1970, the "White Revolution" made several significant changes.

1] Many factories were built. Profit-sharing with the workers was introduced.

2] Tremendous land reform took place. Fifteen million people were given land on which to settle. This was more than half the population. The shah's own lands were used. The thousand wealthiest families had much of their land distributed by this program.

3] Compulsory education was established. This was an attack on the prevailing fifty percent illiteracy.

4] Women's suffrage was granted in 1963.

5] Enormous military buildup in armament, especially air force, occurred. Most of it was bought from the United States.

6] Major dams were built in the 1960s to supply hydroelectric power.

7] In 1972 a grand celebration of Iran's 2,500th anniversary was observed in Teheran. President Nixon was a guest.

But the White Revolution alienated many wealthy Iranians. The ayatollahs, the most prestigious religious leaders, were less than happy with the increasing Western, chiefly American, influence stemming from the presence of many Americans aiding in the buildup of Iran's military strength and from the number of students attending American colleges. Women's suffrage and modifications in dress were disturbing factors.

In the early 1970s the shah's secret police arrested thousands and executed hundreds. Torture was routine treatment. By the middle 1970s strikes, rioting, and general disorder prevailed. By 1978 twelve cities were under martial law. The ayatollahs had joined the people, and a full-fledged revolution was under way. The Ayatollah Khomeini was exiled by the shah and went to Paris. From there he was an important factor both in the inspiration and direction of the revolutionary forces.

The shah left Iran January 16, 1979. He may have been seeking safety from the revolution, but he was certainly seeking medical and surgical care not available in Iran. On February 11, 1979, the shah's Imperial Guard was put to rout. The revolution was over. Ayatollah Khomeini directed that an Islamic republic be set up. Khomeini's power became apparent on November 4, 1979, when a mob formed and led by militant students attacked and occupied the United States embassy at Teheran, taking 52 hostages. On November 1 Khomeini had addressed a student mass meeting. The students reiterated Khomeini's decision that "the hostages at the embassy would be released only when the United States returned the shah to Iran."

All of President Carter's efforts to free the hostages failed. Immediately after the seizure of the embassy, President Carter froze all Iranian assets in the United States federal bank and Iranian funds in United States' banks in foreign countries. The United States would make them available to Iran on the release of the hostages. The length of time it took to free the hostages—one year and seventy-nine days—also illustrated the difficulty of negotiating with Iran.

In April 1980 President Carter authorized a rescue attempt to free the hostages. Eight helicopters took off from the USS *Nimitz* in the Gulf of Oman for a rendezvous in the Great Salt Desert about two hundred miles from Teheran. At the same time six army transport planes carrying equipment, extra fuel for the helicopters, and ninety commandos left from Egypt. However, one helicopter had mechanical trouble, so only five were available to use. The commander and the officers decided not to attempt a rescue. They were in communication with President Carter, who agreed with their decision. On taking off to return, a helicopter collided with a transport plane. The desert winds were very high. Eight men were killed, five were injured.

There were two events that gave some impetus to the negotiations. On September 22, 1980, Iran was the victim of a surprise attack by its neighbor Iraq. It was an outbreak of a long-standing quarrel over oil lands along their border and over control of the Tigris and Euphrates rivers where they enter the Persian Gulf. Both nations did considerable damage by air raids against each other's airport and oil refineries.

The second event to add impetus to the haggling was the election of Ronald Reagan on November 4, 1980. Candidate Reagan had deliberately talked tough on the Iranian situation. The Iranians knew Reagan advocated a much tougher foreign policy than President Carter. Reagan also insisted on a greatly increased buildup of military power for the United States. In the period between Reagan's election

(November 4) and his inauguration (January 20) agreement was reached. On January 20, 1981, at nine o'clock at night in Teheran, twelve-thirty in the afternoon in Washington, D.C., the 52 hostages left the Teheran airport in two planes heading for Algeria. Reagan had been President for half an hour.

TERMS OF THE SETTLEMENT

At the suggestion of the United States, the frozen funds of Iran were brought together into an escrow account in Algeria's central bank. These funds totaled about $5.5 billion, and there was another $1.8 billion probably available. Court action already started by Americans against Iran totaled about $2.2 billion.

It was agreed that the Americans would drop their court proceedings and submit their claims to settlement by international arbitration.

It was agreed that the assets of the late Shah Mohammed Reza Pahlavi and 53 of his relatives and associates were the property of Iran. The United States would not hinder Iran from locating and recovering such assets.

It was agreed that any claims that the United States might have against Iran or Iran against the United States would be submitted to international arbitration.

Alaska National Interest Lands Conservation Act (1980)

This legislation was passed by Congress and signed by President Carter on December 2. The total area of our national parks was doubled, adding about 158,000 square miles, an area about the size of California. There are four types of restricted areas: National Park System, National Wildlife Refuge System, National Conservation and Recreation Area, and the National Forest System.

The political problem of getting such legislation through Congress was solved by compromise. Some oil, mining, and timber resources are designated available for development. Nevertheless, the National Resources Defense Council was pleased, as was Secretary of the Interior Cecil Andrus, who called the law "the single most important conservation legislation ever passed in the United States." He referred to the Alaskan lands as the "crown jewels" of America's natural heritage.

After the White House

For more than 10 years after he was defeated for reelection, Mr. Carter taught at Emory University in Atlanta, Georgia. He also established the Carter Center at Emory, which is dedicated to eradicating disease and to promoting cooperation among diplomats, scholars, and others of different viewpoints. Mr. Carter and his wife Rosalynn donated their time and labor for one week each year to Habitat for Humanity, which builds housing for low-income families in rural hollows and in urban slums such as some of those found in New York City's Lower East Side. In 2002, Mr. Carter was awarded the Nobel Peace Prize.

Ronald Reagan 1981-1989

1911-

REPUBLICAN

Vice-President   GEORGE BUSH
Secretary of State   ALEXANDER HAIG
GEORGE SHULTZ

REAGAN'S PUBLIC SERVICE BEFORE HE BECAME PRESIDENT

Captain in United States Army (1942-1945)
Governor of California (1967-1974)

MAJOR ITEMS OF REAGAN'S ADMINISTRATIONS

A Conservative Mandate
Reaganomics
Federal Budget Deficits
The Budget, the National Debt,
and the Overvalued Dollar
Taxation
Economic Growth and Deregulation
Social Issues
The Cold War Renewed
Problems in Central America
and the Caribbean
Problems in the Middle East

Problems in Africa
A Controversial Visit (1985)
Economic Events of Reagan's Second Term
Tax Reform Act of 1986
Stock Market Crash, 1987
Organized Labor
Economic Legacy
Changes in the Eighties
Iran-Contra Affair
Intermediate Nuclear Forces Treaty (INF)
Was the Cold War Over?

A Conservative Mandate

Ronald Reagan and his Republican advisors viewed the overwhelming 1980 victory as a mandate for conservative economic policies.

	Popular Vote	Electoral Vote
Reagan	43,899,248	489
Carter	35,481,435	49
Anderson	5,719,437	0
(Independent)		

Enough new conservative Republicans then replaced Democratic liberals in the United States Senate to give the Republicans control of the upper house of Congress for the first time in thirty years.

While the Democrats maintained a reduced majority in the House of Representatives, conservative Democrats, or "boll weevils," often voted for the President's policies, erasing the Democratic majority in the House. (The boll weevil is an insect that attacks the boll of the growing cotton plant, where the fiber is maturing. Cotton is an important staple crop of the South, and conservative Democrats are often Southerners.)

Reagan's Reelection in 1984

President Ronald Reagan sought and won his party's nomination without challenge, while eight Democratic challengers competed for their party's

238

call. Former Vice-President **Walter Mondale** gained that nomination, with Senator Gary Hart of Colorado and the Reverend Jesse Jackson of Chicago as close contenders. Jackson had gained prominence as a civil rights leader and was the first black presidential candidate. As part of his campaign, Jackson worked to increase black voter registration throughout the country.

Mondale chose New York Congresswoman **Geraldine Ferraro** as his Vice-Presidential running mate, the first woman on a major party ticket. The Mondale-Ferraro campaign effort was marred by a financial scandal involving Ferraro's husband. Most voters were convinced that the nation was better off economically in 1984 than it had been in 1980, and they reelected Reagan by a landslide. The incumbent received 525 of the 538 electoral votes cast, and about 58 percent of the popular vote.

	Popular vote	Electoral vote
Ronald Reagan	53,354,037	525
Walter Mondale	36,884,260	13

Mondale carried only his home state of Minnesota and the District of Columbia.

* Reaganomics

During the 1980 election campaign, Reagan had attacked the large government expenditures and the resulting federal budget deficits that he claimed were responsible for double-digit inflation. The annual rate of inflation was more than 11 percent when Reagan took office in January 1981. He promised, if elected, to reduce the deficit.

Once in office, Reagan convinced Congress to cut $35 billion from the budgets of social welfare programs like Medicare, food stamps, college-student loans, mass transit, disability benefits, and school-lunch programs. The President believed that state and local governments as well as voluntary efforts should take over much of the responsibility of the federal government in these areas. While critics of the President's program predicted that it would deprive needy people of the sources of food, shelter, and medical care on which they depended, Reagan denied that, declaring that there would always be a "safety net" of government aid for the truly needy.

President Reagan endorsed the theory of **supply-side economics**, which held that cuts in income taxes, especially for Americans with higher incomes, would stimulate new investments in business. Similarly, cuts in corporate taxes would spur businesses to expand production, produce more goods, and hire more workers. Thus, the national economy would be revived by increasing the supply of goods rather than the demand: a painless way to cure inflation. Through tax cuts and tax incentives, industry rather than the government would take the lead in restoring jobs and prosperity. Spending cuts in the federal government would help balance the budget and reduce federal deficits. Restraints on government spending, along with high interest rates, would put a brake on inflation.

Inflation did abate because of government spending cuts and continued high interest rates, but the "cure" accelerated the business recession under way since 1979, leading to the worst downturn in the economy since the 1930s. Factories closed, businesses went bankrupt, and farm mortgages were foreclosed at an increasing rate. By the end of 1982, more than 12 million Americans were out of work, more than 10 percent of the labor force. Double-digit inflation had been ended at the cost of double-digit unemployment.

The President urged the nation to "stay the course," and by the beginning of 1983 the economy had begun to revive. The Federal Reserve Board permitted interest rates to drop, making it easier for businesses and individuals to borrow money. With inflation down, the cost of living remained relatively stable. Meanwhile, a 25 percent across-the-board cut in personal income taxes put more money in the hands of consumers. Feeling new confidence in the economy, consumers purchased more goods and services. Manufacturers of autos, computers, furniture, clothing, and other items rehired workers laid off during the recession. More than two million unemployed people went back to work in 1983. By 1984, with inflation, unemployment, and interest rates declining steadily, the stage was set for the reelection of a popular President. While the Republicans gained fifteen seats in the House of Representatives, the Democrats retained their majority in the House and gained two seats in the Senate.

* Federal Budget Deficits

When he first took office, Reagan had promised to work for a balanced budget by 1984. However, Congress refused to make the deeper cuts in domestic spending requested by the President, fearing a loss of votes back home. The President's attack on "big government" and his policy of cutting taxes were offset by his increasing defense spending. He was convinced that the Soviet Union posed an increasingly serious threat to the United States that only greater military preparedness could counter. The annual rise of about 8.3 percent in military spending included such expensive and controversial programs as the MX missile and the Strategic Defense Initiative, or "Star Wars."

The result was the most unbalanced federal budget in American history. From 1983 through 1985, the federal deficit, or the difference between what the government took in and what it spent, was almost $200 billion a year.

Sticking to his campaign promises, Reagan refused to support tax increases, which would lower business investment and consumer spending, and could lead to unemployment and recession. He refused to lower Social Security benefits, an act that would make him seem uncaring.

The Budget, the National Debt, and the Overvalued Dollar

The problem of the federal budget deficit was largely responsible for turning the United States into a debtor nation by 1985. To close the gap between its income (mostly taxes) and its growing (military) expenditures, the government had to borrow huge amounts of money by selling government bonds. The national debt, or the amount of money owed by the national government, doubled in four years, rising from $930 billion in January 1981, when President Reagan was inaugurated, to over $1 trillion in 1982, and to $1,680 billion by April 1985. These statistics were provided by Senator Daniel Patrick Moynihan (New York).

A large portion of this borrowed money was lent to the United States government by foreign investors, an interest rates were kept high enough to persuade them to do so. The result was that for the first time in three generations, the United States came to owe more money abroad than it was owed. The nation was first out of debt to foreigners in 1914, when European nations liquidated their assets to pay for World War I. Now, the richest and most powerful country on earth had become a debtor to its poorer neighbors.

Foreigners wanted to lend money to the United States because its interest rates were high, but the Treasury would accept only dollars—not pesos, marks, or yen—for its bonds. So foreign investors had to buy dollars with their currencies. Because so many wanted to, the price of the dollar in foreign currencies was bid up. Between 1980 and 1984, the price of the dollar increased 60 percent against the currencies of ten major trading partners. While a "strong dollar" sounds good, an overvalued dollar can bring severe economic problems. It makes American exports like wheat, soybeans, and Kodak cameras more expensive for others to buy. It makes Canadian onions and Japanese cars a better buy than their domestic competition. It can cost Americans their jobs and their farms. How to deal with the overpriced dollar without resorting to protectionism—tariffs, quotas,

closed trading systems—is a major challenge to the government.

Taxation

Reagan resisted a tax increase except as a "last resort." He wanted to reform taxes, not raise them. Starting in November 1984, the Treasury announced a plan to lower individual federal income-tax rates in return for eliminating many tax loopholes, such as deductions for charitable contributions and for business lunches. Special interests sent up a howl. The next May, the President called for an income tax system that would be "clear, simple, and fair for all." The tax law that Congress enacted in 1986 brought about the most thorough revision of the tax system since World War II, when wage withholding began and most Americans became subject to income taxes for the first time.

* Economic Growth and Deregulation

Economic expansion was Reagan's sweeping solution to the federal deficit. His key to growth was a free-enterprise system loosed from government red tape, which would pour revenue into the pockets of taxpayers and hence the Treasury. Reagan's Task Force on Regulatory Relief scrutinized federal regulations and recommended eliminating burdensome rules that they claimed wasted billions for business and consumers.

The President's economic initiatives were aimed at dismantling government programs. However, there was a public outcry at attempts to weaken the Clean Air and Clean Water Acts, and to dismantle the Occupational Safety and Health Administration. Environmental deregulation was halted after a national scandal in which Environmental Protection Agency officials were accused of making "sweetheart" deals with industry. The administration later expanded efforts to clean up toxic waste sites.

Social Issues

As a conservative, Reagan aligned with the New Right's push for organized prayer in public schools and a ban on abortion. By 1985, the Justice Department, led by Attorney General **Edwin Meese**, reversed its long commitment to affirmative action programs for hiring and promoting minority workers. Although opposed to the Equal Rights Amendment that would give women equal legal and economic protection with men, Reagan cited his appointment of the first female Justice of the Supreme Court, **Sandra Day O'Connor**, as a practical example of his helping women break down old barriers.

* The Cold War Renewed

A critic of detente, Reagan believed that the SALT II treaty had granted too many concessions to the Soviets, and he used his influence in the Senate to block ratification of the treaty. Nevertheless, the treaty terms were basically observed by both sides. The relaxation of East-West tensions seemed ended, as Reagan in 1983 described the Soviet Union as "the focus of evil in the modern world." Death removed Soviet leaders Leonid Brezhnev, Yuri Andropov, and Konstantin Chernenko, raising **Mikhail Gorbachev** at age fifty-three to party leadership, and **Andrei Gromyko** at seventy-five to the ceremonial presidency. Each change of leadership occasioned further testing of the other side.

Reagan's anti-Soviet rhetoric caused anxieties among America's Western European allies. Antinuclear demonstrations expressed the fear that the installation of new American nuclear missiles in Europe might precipitate a nuclear war in which our allies there would be the first Soviet targets. Yuri Andropov proposed several plans for arms reduction that he knew Reagan would not accept. The purpose was to split the NATO Alliance and to have the Soviets appear more friendly to Europe than to the United States. When European leaders, including Prime Minister **Margaret Thatcher** of Great Britain, Chancellor **Helmut Kohl** of West Germany, and President **Francois Mitterand** of France, remained firmly loyal to the alliance, Reagan had made the point that he would not back down from a difficult confrontation but would negotiate from strength. Arms talks resumed in the spring of 1985, and Reagan and Gorbachev agreed to meet in Geneva in November 1985 to explore better relations.

Problems in Central America and the Caribbean

* Nicaragua

In 1979 Nicaraguans, aided by Cuban "volunteers," ousted the repressive military regime of Anastasio Somoza. The victorious Sandinistas (named after a national hero, General Sandino, who led a liberal uprising in 1926) were viewed by the Reagan administration as a group of Soviet-allied Marxists whose hold on Nicaragua would pose a danger of leftist revolution spreading to neighboring Central American countries and even to Mexico. Washington's strategy to prevent that was to sponsor the anti-Sandinista **Contras** and to send them arms with which to overthrow the Sandinistas. By June 1984 Congress refused to continue financing such arms shipments, recalling the Vietnam debacle that resulted from a prior United States involvement in a foreign civil war, and fearing the effect of further United States involvement in Nicaragua on our relations with the rest of Latin America.

The United States was also seen as partly responsible for the impasse with Nicaragua. Historically, the United States had helped keep the dictatorial Somoza family in power for decades, supporting them until the very end, and thus allowing the relatively radical Sandinistas to triumph over the other groups that participated in the revolution. Portraying themselves as "David challenging Goliath" won sympathy for the Sandinistas in Latin America. Seeming lack of United States appreciation for the peacemaking efforts of the **Contadora** countries—Mexico, Venezuela, Colombia, and Panama—also hurt the United States position, because a negotiated settlement pushed by the Contadora group with the total support of the region could make a major difference in Nicaraguan politics. Nicaragua would be exposed as a totalitarian state and would have none of the moral and political support it enjoyed in the Americas.

The Contadora process was an effort by four Caribbean sponsors to mediate among five Central American nations where much national and international tension existed: Nicaragua, El Salvador, Costa Rica, Honduras, and Guatamala. In July 1983 the presidents of the four Contadora states (the name taken from the island where they met) stated that their aims included effective control of the regional arms race, the withdrawal of all foreign advisers, and the prohibition of the use of the territory of one state to plan military or political activities that would cause instability in other states.

Unfortunately, there was no clear United States course in Central America. Administration policy seemed to waver between moves toward negotiation and statements of support for the Contadoras, on the one hand, and increasing military involvement in the region, on the other. When the Sandinistas accepted the treaty in supposedly final form in September 1984, Washington called the document unsatisfactory because it was "unverifiable." The Untied States government also influenced its clients, the governments of El Salvador, Honduras, and Costa Rice, to raise new objections.

In April 1984 it was revealed that the United States government had been involved in mining Nicaraguan harbors as part of a larger plan to cripple Nicaragua's economy and hamper claimed Nicaraguan aid to

Salvadoran guerrillas. Critics of the mining operation expressed concern that it might provoke an incident with the Soviet Union and that it risked angering United States allies in Europe by endangering international shipping. It was argued that such a CIA-directed operation had been undertaken without congressional consultation and that it violated international law. Both houses of Congress voted to condemn United Sates participation in the operation and later cut off funds for military aid to the Contras.

Nicaragua asked the International Court of Justice in The Hague to order the United States to halt mining and to cease aiding attacks on its territory. It asked the World Court for reparations for a claimed loss of life and property and for economic disruption.

In anticipation of the Nicaraguan move, the Reagan administration had announced that, for a two-year period, it would not accept the Court's jurisdiction in United States disputes involving Central America. The State Department described the move as an attempt to head off a "propaganda spectacular" by Nicaragua, not as a sign of disrespect for the Court.

El Salvador

Civil War devastated El Salvador from 1979 to 1990. It pitted a Untied States-backed army and a popularly elected leader, President **Jose Napoleon Duarte**, against leftist insurgents. The election of March 1984 resulted in the defeat of right-wing leader Roberto D'Aubisson, accused of involvement with the nation's notorious death squads. Since 1979, when a Marxist-rebel threat emerged, Salvadoran death squads had taken the law into their own hands, self-appointed crusaders against anyone they considered a leftist. They were financed by former landowners and by ransoms extorted from kidnap victims.

The two main problems in El Salvador were the military stalemate between the government and the guerrillas and the behavior of the extreme right, which supported the government only to a limited degree, that is, in its struggle against guerrillas, but not in most other policy areas. This extreme right controlled the national economy, concentrated in the hands of a few dozen powerful families long accustomed to unchallenged political power, and used that power to delay and obstruct reforms in agriculture, in labor, and in measures to increase control over the antiquated laissez-faire economy.

Guerrilla attacks on economic targets ended in 1992, and improved investor confidence led to increased investment. U.S. investors put money into El Salvador's newly privatized electrical and telecommunications markets. Loans from international financial institutions like the World Bank and the

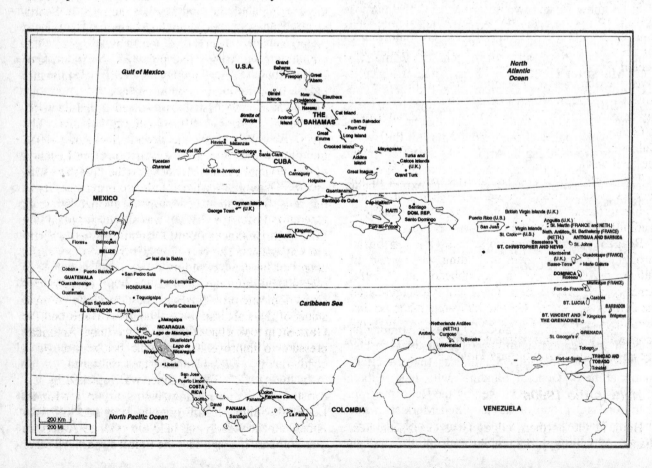

Inter-American Development Bank were used for agricultural reform, the alleviation of poverty, and road repair. Rich soil, moderate climate, and a hard-working and enterprising labor pool comprised El Salvador's greatest assets.

Grenada

Determined to resist communist pressure throughout the Americas, Reagan startled the world in October 1983 when he announced that United States Marines and paratroopers had invaded the tiny eastern Caribbean island nation of Grenada. A March 1979 coup had installed a leftist government there that cemented strong ties to Cuba and the Soviet Union, including building a landing strip which the United States saw as long enough to serve as a forward base for Cuban MIG fighters and for refueling transport planes ferrying Soviet arms and supplies to Central America. In 1983 a brief civil war in Grenada was won by more radical rebel forces supported by Cuban soldiers. This was seen as another example of Fidel Castro promoting revolution in the Americas. The governments of neighboring islands became alarmed, and the Organization of Eastern Caribbean States, along with Jamaica and Barbados, asked for United States intervention.

Communists were endangering the lives and liberties of seven hundred American medical students residing in Grenada. Here also was an opportunity for the kind of clear military victory that eluded the United States in Nicaragua or El Salvador. United States action would communicate to the Soviets America's determination to honor its collective security responsibilities. The six thousand American troops in Grenada remained only long enough to remove the Cuban-supported government from power and to stop the civil war.

The United States operation was seen as a major success, vindicating a tough approach, countering Cuban influence in the region, and restoring American credibility throughout the Caribbean Basin.

Reagan administration policies in the Caribbean through 1985 succeeded in halting the spread of radical revolutions in the Caribbean and Central America and placed the Cubans and Nicaraguans on the defensive. Yet, the United States had made no discernible progress in dealing with the region's massive economic, social, and political problems that provided the impetus for revolutionary violence.

Haiti in the 1990s

Haiti, at the northern edge of the Caribbean Sea, shares the island of Hispaniola with the Dominican Republic. In 1986 the 30-year dictatorship of the Duvalier family ended there. In early 1991 Haiti's constitutionally elected president, **Jean-Bertrand Aristide**, was overthrown by a military coup. The coup created a large-scale exodus of refugees fleeing repression, assassination, torture, and rape. The United Nations imposed an oil and arms embargo, which brought the Haitian military to the bargaining table, after ruling illegally for three years.

In 1994 the United States led 31 UN members in forming a multinational force (MNF) to carry out a UN mandate to restore constitutional rule and Aristide's presidency. By 1996 the MNF and its U.S. troops were replaced by a smaller UN mission in Haiti. The mission ended in February 2001 with the return to power of Aristide, but the country remains gravely impoverished.

* Problems in the Middle East

On the same day that United States Marines invaded Grenada, American Marines stationed in Lebanon in order to help bring peace to that war-ravaged country suffered the loss of 241 of their number killed in a suicide terrorist attack on their barracks at Beirut airport. Muslim groups in Lebanon regarded American troops as allied with the Israeli enemy. The Marines were too few in number to affect the warring Christian and Muslim factions. In February 1984 Reagan evacuated the Marines to the fleet of American ships anchored off the Lebanese coast. The withdrawal was widely interpreted as an admission of United States inability to play a significant diplomatic role in Lebanon in the near future.

In January 1985 Israel announced a phased withdrawal of its troops from southern Lebanon. The Jerusalem government conceded in effect that its 1982 invasion, while forcing the evacuation from Lebanon of one of Israel's principal enemies (the **Palestine Liberation Organization**), had failed to bring stability to the area. The announced purpose of that invasion, Operation Peace for Galilee, was successful in ending PLO terrorist attacks from Lebanon on Israel's northern settlements. The cost of war had added to Israel's economic burdens, including an annual inflation rate of over 400 percent (at mid-1985). As Israel concentrated on its domestic problems, the question of the political status of the **Palestinians** on the **West Bank** and the **Gaza Strip** took a back seat. Israel was under American pressure to improve its economic performance as a condition of continued Untied States assistance.

In June 1985 a TWA jetliner was hijacked by terrorists shortly after leaving Athens airport for Rome. Lebanese Shiite Muslim gunmen beat and killed an American Navy diver and held the other 39 American men on board hostage near the Beirut airport. All other passengers were released. The principal demand was that Israel immediately release over seven hundred Lebanese Muslims under detention, although Israel had already announced plans to free them all. President Reagan, whose 1980 election campaign included attacks on Jimmy Carter for failing to free by force the American hostages held in Iran for 444 days faced the frustration of being unable to use force to effect the release of the American hostages held for 18 days in 1985 by Amal militiamen and Party of God Islamic fundamentalists. Successful negotiations involving Nabih Berri, leader of the mainstream Lebanese Shiite movement, and Syrian President Hafez al-Assad enabled both the United States and Israel to appear not to give in to terrorist demands.

Problems in Africa

A change of climate in a wide swath of Africa south of the Sahara plagued many developing nations with drought and famine in the 1980s. The United States, through both governmental and private organizations, provided more than half the emergency aid needed to feed Africa's hungry millions. By such humanitarian gestures, the United States gained friendship in such devastated countries as Chad, Niger, and even Marxist Ethiopia.

In the Republic of South Africa and at home, the Reagan administration's policy of "constructive engagement" with that government touched off bitter and growing controversy. The policy aimed to encourage the South African regime to ease its oppressive racial system of apartheid (or racial segregation of nonwhites in a nation that is 80 percent nonwhite) by diplomatic pressure rather than public denunciation. Reagan also doubted the effectiveness of an alternative policy—the limited economic sanctions favored by Congress.

During the year ending in November 1985, South Africa was wracked by black protests and violent official reactions, in which thousands of blacks died. Many Americans demonstrated against both apartheid and the Reagan policy, charging that such a policy supported a racist regime. Growing domestic unrest and the world's economic and political pressure led to major changes in South Africa.

In 1990, President **F. W. de Klerk** released **Nelson Mandela** from prison, where he had served 27 years for opposing apartheid. In 1992, white South Africans voted two to one to end apartheid. In 1993 President de Klerk and Mandela, president of the African National Congress (the black majority political party), shared the Nobel Peace Prize. In 1994 a government of national unity was established, with Mandela and de Klerk sharing power until Mandela became president.

A Controversial Visit

In May 1985 President Reagan visited the German military cemetery at Bitburg, West Germany, at the invitation of Chancellor Helmut Kohl. This was part of Reagan's visit to commemorate the fortieth anniversary of the end of World War II in Europe and to attend an economic summit in Bonn. The cemetery chosen contained the graves of members of the Waffen S.S., Hitler's elite troops who oversaw the death camps where millions of victims of the Nazis were killed. The Waffen S.S. also committed atrocities against American prisoners of war during the Battle of the Bulge.

Although the facts became public, Reagan refused to change his itinerary because that might embarrass his host, Mr. Kohl. Reagan's visit was seen by many as a major error in judgment.

Economic Events of Reagan's Second Term

Tax Reform Act of 1986

Collection of a federal income tax, first permitted by the Sixteenth Amendment (1913), was generally accepted because it was a *progressive* tax. That means that as the taxpayer's earnings increase, his or her *rate* of taxation also increases. Before the second round of Reagan tax changes were enacted by the **Tax Reform Act of 1986**, the range of progressive tax rates on personal income extended from 14 percent up to 70 percent. The 1986 law promised to reduce and simplify tax rates. Only three rates would be in use: 15 percent for those taxpayers with lower incomes, 28 percent for middle income taxpayers, and 33 percent for those whose taxable income was between $75,000 and $175,000. The tax money lost because of lower rates was to be made up by closing previous tax loopholes.

However, the richest still did not necessarily pay the most in taxes. Because of changes in the act, persons with taxable incomes above $175,000 were to pay at 28 percent, not 33 percent. That was a blow at the basic concept of the progressive nature of the personal income tax. Also, various tax loopholes were not closed by the 1986 tax law.

Stock Market Crash, 1987

On October 19, 1987, the stockmarket crashed in its worst price collapse since 1929. The Brady Commission report of January 1988 said that an immediate cause of the fall in prices was the use of computerized program trading in stocks and stock-index futures by a few large institutional investors. By the spring of 1988, the United States economy was showing continued, steady growth, but 15,000 jobs were lost in the financial community, and small investors were staying away from the stock market, turning to safer forms of investment. Yet, within a year of the fall, the average stock prices were higher than before the event.

Organized Labor

The 1980s saw a continued decline in the membership and power of the large industrial unions as the nature of work and the workplaces of Americans changed. There were fewer factory workers and more service industry personnel, and miners can be organized into a labor union far more easily than the workers at McDonald's or a self-service gas station/convenience store. Members of the United Auto Workers and United Mine Workers, previously militant, accepted diminished contracts during the late 1980s. They gave up wages and benefits in exchange for greater job security.

The industrial workers and their families had also changed. From the 1950s to the 1980s there had been a tripling of American per capita income. Those families had become members of the middle class and more and more they voted their economic concerns.

** Economic Legacy

Ronald Reagan was able to hand over to his successor a healthy economy in the midst of a long period of expansion in which 16 million new jobs had been created without the inflationary excesses of the past. **Reaganomics** had cut taxes and civilian spending; it had established a stable money policy to reduce inflation. Deregulation of industry (such as reduced government interference with airline ticket pricing) was another part of the *new populism*. Whereas the old populism had enlisted the aid of the government, the new populism made the government itself the villain.

While elected on promises to reduce the budget, Reagan seems to have been right to set aside the deficit problem once in office and to concentrate on the stable growth of the supply of cash and credit circulating in the economy at any one time. The Federal Reserve System, under able chairman Paul Volcker, kept the money supply from growing too fast and helped to reduce inflation from 13 percent to 4 percent in two years.

While cutting taxes and increasing defense budget requests did lead to increased short-term deficits, increased cost of the interest on the widening debt crowded out other civilian spending. Borrowing it-self created self-reinforcing pressures for additional spending cuts and deficit reduction. These were objectives clearly favored by the Reagan administration. At just the time that Reagan decided to tolerate more borrowing, West Germany, Japan, and other export-based economies in Europe and Asia were experiencing huge trade surpluses (partly because Americans were such good customers for their products). Those trade surpluses generated large government and private savings that were invested in U.S. Treasury bills, stocks, and real estate. Reagan's faith in "the magic of the markets," in this case world capital markets, was justified. So long as there was no runaway U.S. inflation to ruin the dollar as a sound investment, foreigners would continue to invest their surplus here.

The most unpleasant part of the Reagan domestic legacy was the continuation of unbalanced budgets. The average deficit from 1982 to 1988 was $180 billion. The national debt of the United States had risen by 1988 to over $2.6 trillion, representing borrowed money that the U.S. government has faithfully promised to repay. The interest alone on this huge sum amounted to tens of billions of dollars that must be paid from the U.S. Treasury each year. Until the budget deficit is substantially reduced—and the Gramm-Rudman Act forced some reduction—we and even future generations could be saddled with this heavy burden.

** Changes in the Eighties

During the Carter years, Americans still suffered guilt from our Vietnam War involvement (1964-1973). Reagan, the "great communicator," used his oratory to rally the American public to embrace his version of a reborn American spirit steeped in patriotism, old-fashioned values, and pride.

His new kind of American populism saw the government as the problem. Reaganism included a determined, systematic effort to reduce the domestic functions of government by choking off its revenue.

The Reagan administration slashed $45 billion from health, housing, and social service programs designed to transfer income to the poorest Americans. It weakened civil rights enforcement. It was unaware of a terrible scandal brewing at HUD (Department of Housing and Urban Development) which will be discussed later. Despite an announced attempt to eliminate the Department of Education, its Secretary, **William Benson**, focused national attention on educational reform. By the end of Reagan's administration, 40 states had passed laws mandating improved educational results.

By that time also, the share of the national income of the wealthiest 20 percent of the population had become greater than at any time since the end of World War II (1945). By contrast, the share of the poorest 40 percent had fallen to its lowest level since 1945. The income of the top one percent of earners rose from 9.2 percent to 12.5 percent. Critics said Reagan's fiscal policy was to blame for polarizing American society, with the rich getting richer and the poor, poorer.

Some groups fared much better than others in the 1980s. Women's earnings grew faster than men's, narrowing the income gap between the sexes. The Census Bureau reported that the main reason was an increasing number of women finding work in such traditionally male-dominated and high-paying fields as engineering and law. The elderly generally fared well. Rising benefits from Social Security—one of the few social programs to be spared the budget ax in the Reagan 1980s—improved the income of the elderly compared with workers, whose income did not rise as fast.

Children as a group fared worse in the 1980s. Families with children whose parents were under thirty suffered a 25.5 percent fall in median income from 1973 to 1986, according to the Children's Defense Fund. Many of the young parents found only part-time or temporary work, often with few or no benefits like health insurance. In this group, even families with two workers were less likely to have health insurance and more likely to need child care.

Some geographic areas did well. The New England and North Atlantic states benefited from the rise of the computer industry and service industries such as banking. The Southeast and Rust Belt states of the Midwest continued to suffer from a decline in manufacturing. Although there were more jobs created, there was a decline in median wages.

During his eight years in office, Mr. Reagan was able to appoint for life conservative replacements for over 50 percent of the nation's federal judges. One result is that laws and prior Supreme Court decisions that were considered settled will in the future be challenged by those who seek a more conservative interpretation. One such area is that of abortion rights.

* The Iran-Contra Affair

The Reagan administration was frustrated by two foreign policy issues and resorted to unfortunate measures in attempting to deal with them. In 1984 Congress ended and forbade further government aid to the **Contras**, the guerrilla opponents of the Nicaraguan Sandinista government in Nicaragua. Starting at about that time, a number of American citizens were kidnapped in Beirut, Lebanon, by Shiite Moslem supporters of the government of Iran. *Candidate* Reagan's

criticism of President Carter's inability to free 52 American hostages seized at the American embassy in Teheran by the Iranians had helped to elect him in 1980. In the mid-1980s, *President* Reagan was also plagued by problems with terrorists.

Nationally televised congressional hearings revealed that the Reagan administration had authorized the sale of arms to Iran in exchange for help in freeing United States hostages in Lebanon. It was also revealed that the money gained from the arms sale to Iran was illegally diverted to aid the Contras. The congressional report criticized Reagan for his detached, hands-off management style. Singled out were National Security Adviser **John Poindexter** and National Security Council aide **Colonel Oliver North**, who were indicted by a federal grand jury. The national feeling, however, was that the President either knew or should have known that there had been an arms-for-hostages deal. Also rebuked by Congress were Attorney General Edwin Meese, CIA director William Casey (who died in office), White House Chief of Staff Donald Regan, and National Security Adviser Robert McFarlane. The first to be convicted of charges stemming from the scandal, including lying to Congress, was Colonel North. He was, however, not sentenced to prison, an indication that higher-ups in the Reagan administration were really responsible for defying the will of Congress.

Intermediate Nuclear Forces Treaty (INF)

An important treaty to eliminate Soviet and American medium-range nuclear missiles was signed by President Reagan and Soviet General Secretary Mikhail Gorbachev in 1987. This marked a major change in the attitude of both leaders. Gorbachev was responding to the need for the faltering Soviet economy to cut back on military expenditures. Reagan no longer spoke of the Soviet Union as "the evil empire," as in his first term.

The deployment of American missiles in Europe had been undertaken more for political than military reasons. NATO then felt it should make a clear response to the threat of political intimidation that could weaken Atlantic ties. That was achieved. The treaty was a political gain for the West, won by steadfastness in the NATO Alliance. The elements that influenced a Soviet turnaround included the Reagan administration's military buildup and Mikhail Gorbachev's sense of need for lessened East-West tensions to promote his domestic reform plans. Soviet failure to split the alliance was crucial.

Progress on the above issues also sparked new efforts on more critical problems: the big long-range missiles, the balance of conventional forces, nuclear testing. Of symbolic importance was this first *joint reduction* of one part of the arsenals, instead of only partial limits on expansion, as before. Here was official recognition of the futility of the arms race. Missiles would be physically destroyed. On-site inspection was agreed to for the first time.

* Was the Cold War Over?

Reversing his previous anti-Soviet ("evil empire") stance, Reagan declared in December 1987 that the Soviet Union had abandoned the goal of "one-world Marxist domination." Had Mr. Reagan not rejected Cold War doctrine, his administration could never have signed an arms-control treaty or actively pursued detente during his last year in office. How had Mikhail Gorbachev and the Soviet Union earned such praise? In his first four years in office (1985 through 1988), Mr. Gorbachev pushed Yasir Arafat toward renouncing terrorism and accepting Israel, supported political settlements in Angola and Cambodia, pulled Soviet troops out of Afghanistan, agreed to large and unequal cuts in medium-range land-based missiles, and pledged considerable unilateral reductions in Soviet forces in eastern Europe.

On the domestic side, the Soviet leader undertook steps that gave hope for a more open Soviet society and government. He introduced economic decentralization (part of *perestroika*, or restructuring), encouraged freer speech, and experimented with freer elections (part of *glasnost*, or openness). He also allowed some Soviet nationalities to assert their separate identities (as opposed to a long-standing policy of Russification).

President Bush began by cautiously exploring Moscow's willingness to compromise on cutting troops in Europe, and otherwise reducing the costs and risks of security.

Pressures for maintaining high levels of military spending were reduced by 1988, as the Cold War seemed to be ending. Over Reagan's eight years, there had been a $2.4 trillion defense buildup that raised military spending 35 percent above the 1980 level. Two very expensive items in the above were the Strategic Defense Initiative, or Star Wars program to develop a defense against nuclear missiles, and development of a radar-evading bomber (the Stealth, or B-2).

The Bush administration later ran into strong Congressional opposition to full funding for these particular programs. The SDI was widely perceived as unlikely to provide the defense shield it promised. The B-2 bomber faced both design and production problems, with huge cost overruns. Congress also weighed military requests against the Reagan and Bush budget deficits and the warming of the Cold War.

George Herbert Walker Bush   1989-1993

1924-

REPUBLICAN

☆

Vice-President   J. DANFORTH (DAN) QUAYLE
Secretary of State   JAMES A. BAKER, III

BUSH'S PUBLIC SERVICE BEFORE HE BECAME PRESIDENT

United States Navy carrier pilot (1942-1945)
United States House of Representatives (1967-1971)
Ambassador to the United Nations (1971-1972)
Chairman, Republican National Committee (1973-1974)
Head, United States Liaison Office, Beijing (1974-1975)
Director, Central Intelligence Agency (1976-1977)
Vice-President of the United States (1981-1989)

MAJOR ITEMS OF BUSH'S ADMINISTRATION

Election of 1988   *Hurricane Andrew*
The Bush Team   *Los Angeles Riots*
Ethics in Government   *Peace in Nicaragua*
The Environment Fights Back   *Panama and Noriega*
EPA Unleashed   *End of the Cold War*
Health Care Coverage   *Iraq, Kuwait, and Persian Gulf War*
Scandal at HUD   *Arab-Israeli Peace Talks*
Saving the Savings and Loans   *Aid to Somalia*
The War on Drugs   *America: What Went Wrong?*
Supreme Court Appointments   *1992 Election Campaign*

* Election of 1988

George Herbert Walker Bush was elected the 41st President of the United States on November 8, 1988. He entered the White House expecting to continue the policies of his predecessor, Ronald Reagan. Bush, the Republican, defeated the Democratic nominee, **Governor Michael Dukakis** of Massachusetts by a wide margin (54 percent to 46 percent) and won the electoral votes of 40 states!

	Popular Vote	Electoral Vote
Bush	47,946,422	426
Dukakis	41,016,429	112

Senator J. Danforth Quayle of Indiana was the successful, if controversial, vice-presidential nominee. Senator Lloyd Bentsen of Texas was the Democratic nominee for Vice-President. The Democrats continued to hold strong control in both houses of the 101st Congress.

	Senate	House of Representatives
Democrats	55	261
Republicans	45	176

The Bush campaign used short, hard-hitting television commercials that showed the little-known Dukakis as soft on crime and not strong on patriotism.

These charges defined the agenda for much of the campaign. Dukakis did not seem to appreciate the emotional impact of those charges, and failed to respond quickly enough. Bush pointed to the nation's peace and prosperity. Unemployment was at a fourteen-year-low of 5.2 percent. He hailed progress in arms talks with the Soviet Union, which Bush attributed to Reagan's massive military buildup and steadfastness at the bargaining table. The start of the Soviet military withdrawal from Afghanistan also represented an important victory for U.S. policy. Bush pledged not to raise taxes and to create thirty million jobs in the next eight years.

The Bush Team

Even before he took office, George Bush sought to distance himself from the scandals of the Reagan regime (e.g., Iran-Contra). Bush's Cabinet appointments included two Hispanics—Lauro Cavazos, Secretary of Education, and Manuel Lujan, Secretary of the Interior; another woman—Elizabeth Dole, Secretary of Labor; and a black—Dr. Louis Sullivan, dean of the Morehouse College School of Medicine, as Secretary of Health and Human Services.

Two important government agencies in the limelight also received new and energetic leaders. Former Congressman from New York **Jack Kemp** took over leadership at scandal-ridden HUD (Department of Housing and Urban Development). Promising a new "war on poverty" from his position, he claimed to recognize that "you cannot balance the budget off the backs of the poor." **William Reilly**, president of the World Wildlife Fund, was Bush's choice for the Environmental Protection Agency.

Ethics in Government

Early in 1989, the Senate refused to confirm President Bush's nomination of former Texas Senator John Tower to be Secretary of Defense. Senate critics claimed that close ties to the military-industrial complex, and evidence of drinking and womanizing, made him an unsuitable appointee. The House of Representatives, meanwhile, was weighing evidence of wrongdoing by its Speaker, Jim Wright, who resigned from Congress.

The main ethical issues, however, still needed to be confronted. One of those concerned former legislators and government agency officials who were reaping large fees for lobbying their recent colleagues on behalf of special interests. Another dealt with the weak laws governing campaign spending for the presidency and for Congress. Four years later, those problems still remained.

** The Environment Fights Back

The earth fought back in 1988, protesting loudly against environmental pollution:

1] In March 1988 scientists reported that the natural **ozone shield** protecting living things from the sun's ultraviolet radiation had declined significantly over the past two decades. Human-made chemicals were responsible. The ozone loss was linked to damage to many plant and animal species, including skin cancer and eye damage in humans.

2] A dramatic summer drought helped focus attention on the **greenhouse effect**, a general warming of temperatures on earth, accompanied by drier conditions. This is caused by an increase in atmospheric carbon dioxide released by burning fossil fuels like coal, gasoline products, and natural gas, and by rapid deforestation. If allowed to continue, this global heat trap could cut down the world's food supply and flood our low-lying coastlines. A 1997 international agreement in Kyoto, Japan, was the first to address the problem.

3] In 1988 an area of the Amazon rain forest equal in size to the state of Nebraska was purposely burned. Rain forests, such as those in Brazil and Southeast Asia, absorb carbon dioxide and release oxygen. (They also contain two-thirds of the known species of plants and animals on earth, whose habitats are being destroyed. Some of the plants there may be the key to humans' future survival.)

4] The hot, dry summer became even more uncomfortable for many Americans when beaches were closed after hospital waste floated ashore along the East Coast, Lake Michigan, and Lake Erie. Hazardous waste included hypodermic needles, catheter bags, and blood—some infected with the AIDS virus.

5] Pollution of coastal waters, including those near Boston and New York, was concentrating pollutants as they traveled up the food chain, making fish inedible.

6] **Acid rain** caused by sulfur dioxide from mid-West power plants, and by nitrogen oxides from auto exhausts, continued to destroy forests, lakes, and buildings in the northeast United States and in southeast Canada.

7] Abuse of the environment led to an increase in the number and force of natural disasters. In 1988, hurricane Gilbert was the world's worst. It packed winds of 175 miles an hour in the Caribbean. It left 750,000 people homeless, killed 109, and caused $10 billion in damage. A monsoon flood in Bangladesh left 28 million homeless and destroyed much of 17 years of economic development. About 80 percent of the nation was under water.

8] In the Soviet bloc, large stretches of ecological wasteland were created by the crash industrialization drives of state socialism, as in the early 1980s.

9] Some of the world's worst environmental offenders have been developing countries that came of age in a world grown far less forgiving of pollution of land, air, and water. In the 1990s, leaders of Third World countries increasingly began to accept that development cannot be sustained without protecting natural resources. (See also pg. 264.)

The EPA Unleashed

An important early action of President Bush was to appoint William K. Reilly as EPA administrator. The **Environmental Protection Agency** is the non-Cabinet regulatory body that enforces antipollution laws, including the Clean Air Act, the Clean Water Act, and the Superfund for the cleanup of toxic wastes.

After eight years of environmental neglect by the administration, President Bush announced in June 1989 his proposals to fight air pollution, especially to act on the long-delayed devastation of acid rain. He asked to cut ten million tons of sulfur dioxide a year, as well as two million tons of nitrous oxide, another cause of acid rain, by the year 2000. To fight *urban smog*, he asked Congress to tighten standards for automobile emissions and to require alternative-fueled vehicles for up to 30 percent of the market in the nation's dirtiest cities. He promised to reduce auto tailpipe emissions of hydrocarbons and nitrogen oxides, which are "cooked" by the sun to produce ozone. (Ozone is good in the stratosphere, but it is poisonous to humans.) A tough clean-air bill mattered at home and abroad, where it sent a clear signal about Americans' willingness to tackle an expensive, controversial issue, as environmentalists increasingly asked for world cooperation to fight pollution—the host of ills threatening earth's life-sustaining capacity.

The EPA announced a gradual ban on cancer-causing asbestos, which the Office of Management and Budget had prevented for years. Reilly also moved against toxic material in crop sprays, which upset people engaged in agribusiness. He fought the Energy Department's request to exempt the nation's largest nuclear-weapons plant from federal water-pollution standards. (See also pg. 264.)

Health Care Coverage

President-elect Bush and congressional leaders had pledged to address the problem of 37 million Americans without health care insurance in 1989, and another 53 million underinsured. Fully half of those were people living in poverty, according to the government statistics. Six million people had family incomes of under $5,000 a year and 12.5 million had family incomes of under $10,000 in 1988. The 1987 poverty line was drawn at $11,612 for a family of four. The cost of providing the additional required health care coverage was then estimated at $24 to $27 *billion*.

At issue was the extent to which that cost should be borne by government, business, and those uninsured who were able to pay something. Unfortunately, as with many other campaign promises and political pledges, nothing was done, and during the next four years the cost of health care kept rising, as did the number of Americans without health care coverage. (See also pg. 263.)

The Scandal at HUD

Early in the Bush administration, it became apparent that former top officials at the **Department of Housing and Urban Development**, Reagan appointees, had been involved in unethical if not illegal activities there. Those officials and well-connected Republicans had "milked" a low-income housing rehabilitation program by selling their services as "consultants" to developers seeking valuable contracts. In fact, they had influenced Samuel Pierce, then Housing Secretary, and key aides like his executive assistant, Deborah Gore Dean. The HUD Inspector General reported that more than $5.7 million had been paid in "consulting fees" to just twenty recipients who lobbied officials of HUD to approve low-income housing projects. His warnings were ignored during the Reagan administration. President Bush appointed former New York Congressman Jack Kemp as his Housing Secretary and he began to uncover the facts.

* Saving the Savings and Loans

At one point in the history of American banking, there was a need for a group of banks, in addition to regular savings banks, to finance mortgages. Thus, savings and loan associations (S&Ls) were created. During the 1980s, over 400 of the nation's S&Ls became insolvent. Those thrift institutions had plunged into high-risk investments with poor security. Many suffered from hard times in the Southwest, especially Texas. Others had incompetent or dishonest managers and owners.

In August 1989 President Bush signed a monumental bailout bill for the savings and loan industry. The legislation called for spending $159 *billion* over ten years to close or find buyers for those 400 or more insolvent S&Ls and any additional ones expected to fail. Investors are now required to put up more of their own money in order to receive deposit insurance. Until now, that insurance was provided by the Federal Savings and Loan Insurance Corporation, up to $100,000 per account. The new regulators are the Treasury Department and the Federal Deposit Insurance Corporation (which continues to insure savings bank deposits). Also required is that 70 percent of an S&L's loans go toward housing and housing-related investments.

The Resolution Trust Corporation was set up to manage the assets and liabilities of institutions that became insolvent between 1989 and 1992. The FDIC would handle any S&L failures after August 1992. The total cost of the program over 30 years was estimated at over $300 billion, with taxpayers picking up 75 percent of the tab.

The War on Drugs

In September 1989 President Bush announced his new anti-drug strategy, to be implemented by William Bennett, Bush's drug-law coordinator and a former Reagan Secretary of Education. Bennett's report depicted the devastating impact of drug abuse and recognized that inner-city crack cocaine is the nation's biggest and most immediate narcotics problem. The report acknowledged that many different approaches are needed and that overreliance on any single element would fail, such as the enormous concentration on drug-law enforcement of the previous eight years, which had minimal impact on drug abuse and drug trafficking. Critics of the report called for more support for prevention, education, and treatment. Studies have suggested that half the estimated 6 million Americans with serious drug problems might benefit from treatment, yet programs in 1989 enrolled fewer than one million. Mr. Bennett wanted to make a special effort to enroll more female addicts who were pregnant. The success of the plan will ultimately be measured in terms of reductions in the destructive effects of drug dealing and drug abuse: the number of babies born drug-addicted, the rate of transmission of the AIDS virus by intravenous drug users, the numbers of drug-related crimes and children arrested for drug dealing.

Also in the Bush plan was a swift response to Colombia's cry for help in its war against the drug cartels. His decision to dispatch helicopters, arms, and other equipment to Bogota met an urgent need.

Supreme Court Appointments

President Bush had two opportunities to fill Supreme Court vacancies. In 1990 he nominated David H. Souter, a federal judge from New Hampshire, who easily won Senate confirmation. In 1991 Justice Thurgood Marshall, the only African-American on the Court, retired after nearly a quarter century.

Marshall, great-grandson of a slave, had one of the most distinguished legal careers in the 20th century. As head of the NAACP Legal Defense and Educational Fund for over 20 years, he had persuaded the Supreme Court to strike down segregation in voting, housing, public accommodations, buses, railroads, public schools, and state universities. His most crucial victory, *Brown* v. *Board of Education* in 1954, established the right of children to attend desegregated public elementary and secondary schools. He also served on the United States Circuit Court of Appeals and as Solicitor General of the United States, the third ranking post in the Justice Department.

Bush then nominated another black, Clarence Thomas, a federal Court of Appeals judge with strong conservative views. Allegations of sexual harassment against Thomas by a former staff assistant, Anita Hill, were followed by three days of nationally televised hearings during which Thomas denied any wrongdoing. The Senate narrowly voted for confirmation, and Professor Hill was widely regarded as a martyr. The backlash against perceived injustice to her helped send four additional women to the U.S. Senate in 1992.

Hurricane Andrew

In August 1992 Hurricane Andrew ripped through the southeastern United States, killing at least 22 people and causing $20 billion worth of damage by wind and water. The storm left hundreds of thousands of people homeless and dependent upon federal aid for food, water, and shelter. Andrew was a *Force 5* hurricane, which occurs only once or twice every century. It carried wind gusts of up to 170 miles per hour, leaving a trail of destruction from Florida to Louisiana. Particularly hard-hit was an area of South Florida where mushrooming development had brought shoddy home construction and a large number of mobile homes.

Despite preparations a week in advance—the military had moved in 63 million "meals ready to eat"—

there were delays in delivering aid to the storm victims. That led to criticism of the Federal Emergency Management Agency (FEMA). That agency had been created in 1979 to provide a single point of accountability for the federal government's disaster response. FEMA faced another major challenge a year later, in assisting victims of flooding in the Midwest.

Los Angeles Riots

Race relations continued to play an emotional role in American life in the 1990s. In March 1991 Los Angeles police officers arrested Rodney G. King after a high-speed car chase. An amateur videotape showed King being beaten by four policemen after he was stopped for speeding. At their state trial, the issue was whether the more-than-50 baton blows recorded were necessary to subdue King, or were an example of white police brutality against a black man.

In April 1992 the four officers were acquitted of assaulting King. That verdict set off widespread riots that caused $1 billion in damages and took more than 50 lives. Many victims in South Central Los Angeles were Korean merchants along with their property. A second federal trial found that two of the police officers had deprived Mr. King of his civil rights (a federal offense) and they were sentenced to two-and-a-half years in prison (well below the ten-year maximum).

Across the nation in New York City, Mayor David Dinkins earned high praise for helping keep the Big Apple calm at that time. However, he was later blamed for inaction when the Brooklyn neighborhood of Crown Heights was the scene of three days of uncontrolled rioting by blacks, which followed the accidental auto death of a black child and the retaliatory stabbing to death of a Hasidic Jewish scholar.

Peace in Nicaragua

United States involvement in Nicaragua after World War II was nothing to be proud of. Our government had long supported the dictatorship of the Somoza family. The Reagan administration later aided the Contra rebels illegally. (See pg. 246, The Iran-Contra Affair.)

In August 1989 the presidents of five Central American countries agreed on a workable plan to demobilize the Contras, the American-supported Nicaraguan rebels, and to end the civil war that had racked Nicaragua for eight years. They called for disbanding rebel camps in southern Honduras by December, three months after stationing international monitors from the United Nations and the Organization of American States in the jungle to oversee compliance and deter cross-border raiding.

Violeta Chamorro helped to heal the wounds of civil war. In 1990 she won a stunning election victory over the Sandinistas. As the new president of Nicaragua, she worked together with a Sandinista head of the nation's military to disarm the Contras by promising them free land to farm. Her enemies were economic problems like severe inflation, serious strikes, and land-hungry groups taking over properties. It seemed that sheer national exhaustion and fear of renewed war were all that kept her government together.

Panama and Noriega

The United States' interests in Panama are centered on the strategic importance of the Panama Canal, which has connected the Atlantic Ocean's Caribbean Sea with the Pacific Ocean since 1914. Two treaties signed in 1977 with the United States recognized Panama's sovereignty over the canal, created a system of bilateral management, and agreed to Panama assuming full ownership by 1999. Panama's share of canal profits was increased, and so were its responsibilities for canal operation and defense. The canal's neutrality after 1999 was also guaranteed.

Omar Torrijos, the military commander who had assumed sole political power in 1969, governed as a dictator, and dismantled the civil political system that had evolved since Panama was created in 1903. After his death in 1988, Panama's president could not remove the Defense Forces leader, General Manuel Noriega, who had been indicted in the United States for drug trafficking, and who then had the National Assembly replace President Del Valle.

When U.S. sanctions against Panama and an attempted military coup in October 1989 failed to bring down Noriega, U.S. troops invaded Panama that very month. Dubbed Operation Just Cause, this was the largest United States military operation since the Vietnam War. Some 12,000 Army, Navy, Air Force, and Marine troops were sent from the United States to join another 12,000 American military personnel already stationed in Panama. (American troops have been stationed in Panama since 1903, when that country obtained its freedom from Colombia and President Theodore Roosevelt was able to continue his plans to build the Panama Canal.)

Noriega fled to the Vatican embassy there, and surrendered to U.S. military authorities on January 3, 1990. He was tried in the United States, convicted of various charges, including drug trafficking, and sent to jail.

End of the Cold War

The Cold War, the extended conflict between the communist states led by the Soviet Union and the Western states led by the United States, lasted from the end of World War II in 1945 (during which the two leaders had been allies against Nazi Germany) until 1990.

During that period, the United States fought in two major wars against communist forces. In Korea (1950-1953) American troops fought under the UN flag to resist an invasion of South Korea by North Korea. The war in Vietnam (1965-1975) failed to prevent North Vietnam from bringing South Vietnam under communist rule.

A major change in Soviet-American relations took place during the administration of Soviet General Secretary Mikhail Gorbachev. He presided over the dissolution of the communist system in the USSR, brought freedom to hundreds of millions of oppressed peoples, and lifted the threat of a cataclysmic nuclear war. He began these reforms in 1985, and was forced to resign from office in December 1991.

One of the unexpected by-products of Gorbachev's policies was the collapse of the communist regimes in Europe in 1989 and 1990. A series of spontaneous popular upheavals spread from Poland to East Germany and Eastern Europe, leading to the establishment of noncommunist political parties, free elections, and the first genuinely democratic governments in the region in more than four decades. By not interfering in those revolutions, Gorbachev abandoned the Brezhnev Doctrine, which asserted Moscow's right to use military force to keep communist governments in power. In October 1990 the German Democratic Republic (East Germany) was abolished, and East and West Germany became one democratic state. The Berlin Wall was torn down. It had been built by communist East Germany to prevent contact between East Berlin, which was under communist control, and democratically run West Berlin. For 40 years the wall had been a symbol of communist oppression.

In 1991 the Warsaw Pact was disbanded. Both Bush and Gorbachev proclaimed the end of the Cold War and the birth of a "new world order." The Cold War ended because the Soviet Union ceased to be a superpower, and the bipolar organization of the international power system gave way to a complex, multipolar world in which the United States was the dominant global power.

Only weeks after Bush and Gorbachev had signed a strategic arms reduction treaty in Moscow, the Soviet leader was nearly ousted in an attempted coup. Thanks to Boris Yeltsin's resistance to the coup, Gorbachev returned to power, briefly. In December 1991 the Soviet Union dissolved into a loose confederation of independent republics (the Commonwealth of Independent States) and President Bush granted recognition to the new nations, most important of which were Russia, Ukraine, and Belarus. The remnants of Soviet government were taken over by Russia, the successor state to the USSR. In the spring of 1992 Bush and Russian President Yeltsin agreed to substantial cuts in nuclear weapons. In exchange, Russia was to receive a bilateral investment treaty, removal of Cold War trade barriers, and quick congressional approval of a Russian economic aid package. Additional agreements on control and disposal of nuclear weapons also included Belarus, Kazakhstan, and Ukraine, where many of the strategic nuclear weapons of the former Soviet Union were located. In May 1994 the United States and Russia stopped targeting their nuclear missiles at each other. (See also pg. 266.)

Iraq, Kuwait, and the Persian Gulf War

Both Iraq (ancient Mesopotamia) and Kuwait (a small sheikdom on the Persian Gulf) had been part of the Ottoman Empire, or Turkey, until World War I. The Treaty of Versailles (1919) made both mandates of Britain under the League of Nations. They became independent states in 1961, and both produce large amounts of petroleum. Saddam Hussein became the military dictator of Iraq, and in 1980 he invaded neighboring Iran (Persia), weakened by a recent revolution.

Saddam achieved an expensive and incomplete victory in an eight-year-long war (1980-1988) that he had begun. The war caused a million casualties, created a million refugees, reintroduced the horror of poison gas, and led to the kidnapping of civilians for use as human shields—all in the attempt to extend Saddam's power.

In August 1990 Iraq invaded and occupied neighboring Kuwait. Saddam sought to insure his recovery from the Iran-Iraq war and elevate himself to leadership of the Arab world. By this step he would cancel his multi-billion dollar debt to Kuwait, and be in a position to dominate OPEC oil policy. Saddam expected his seizure of Kuwait to be popular at home because the belief that Kuwait was a lost Iraqi territory (which it was NOT) was a dogma of Iraqi nationalism.

World reaction was rapid and critical. The UN Security Council passed Resolution 660 the night of the invasion, calling for immediate and unconditional Iraqi withdrawal and threatening the use of economic and military sanctions. This set the pattern of subsequent UN actions.

The crisis provided George Bush with his finest hour as President. First, he led a worldwide, UN-approved trade embargo against Iraq to force its withdrawal from defenseless Kuwait and to block Iraq's attempt to control a larger portion of the world's oil reserves. Next, Bush sent a military contingent to Saudi Arabia, Iraq's large southern neighbor, to safeguard that nation against Iraqi pressure. Then he skillfully built up a coalition of Western European and Arab states against Iraq. Over the objections of those who favored giving the embargo more time to be effective, he increased U.S. military pressure in the Persian Gulf region to about 500,000 troops within a few months. Those actions were called Operation Desert Shield. Meanwhile, Iraq was looting Kuwait and terrorizing its population.

In January 1991 Bush received approval from Congress to use force. Iraq ignored a UN-backed ultimatum to withdraw from Kuwait by January 15, and Bush authorized a devastating U.S.-led air offensive against strategic sites in Iraq. The ensuing Persian Gulf War, or Operation Desert Storm, culminated in an Allied ground offensive in late February that decimated Iraq's armies and restored Kuwait to independence.

Retreating Iraqi troops dynamited Kuwaiti oil wells and set fire to Kuwait's oil fields. Those fires took months to extinguish, during which time the oily smoke drifted over large areas of the western Persian Gulf. The additional pollution caused by spilled oil was devastating to bird and sea life. These disasters and the Gulf War itself were the subjects of nonstop media coverage, broadcast worldwide via satellite television.

During the conflict, Iraq fired Scud missiles into civilian areas of Israel and into Saudi Arabia. The ground war lasted only 100 hours, and caused few American casualties. Bush's popularity rose to historic highs; however, he was criticized for ordering a ceasefire before Saddam Hussein could be ousted. Saddam Hussein not only retained power, but suppressed revolts by Shiites in the south, and Kurds in the north of Iraq. U.S. troops were replaced by a United Nations observer force. However, Iraq continually obstructed UN attempts to implement the peace terms, including UN inspection of Iraqi military sites.

During the Clinton presidency, United Nations inspections of suspected Iraqi sites for building chemical, biological, and nuclear weapons of mass destruction were suspended. President George W. Bush would later call for a return to inspections and for the ouster of Saddam Hussein.

In June 1993 it was revealed that Saddam Hussein had ordered the (thwarted) assassination of former President George H. W. Bush during the latter's April visit to Kuwait. In retaliation, U.S. armed forces, on orders of President Bill Clinton, bombed Iraqi military intelligence headquarters in Baghdad.

Arab-Israeli Peace Talks

During Operation Desert Storm, Iraq launched missile attacks using Scuds, an inaccurate terror weapon, against Israel. At the urging of the United States, Israel did not retaliate, and Saddam Hussein was prevented from linking his attack against Kuwait to the Arab-Israeli conflict. Most Arab nations were opposed to Saddam's expansionism, and following the Persian Gulf War were receptive to American calls for a general Middle East settlement. President Bush was able to initiate the first face-to-face peace talks between Israel and its Arab neighbors: Lebanon, Jordan, Syria, and the Palestinians. The first conference took place in Madrid in November 1991, and several later ones were held in Washington. Progress was very slow.

In 1993 secret meetings in Oslo, Norway, between Israeli officials and representatives of the Palestine Liberation Organization (PLO) led to a proposed peace process during which Israel would negotiate directly with the PLO. In return for the PLO promise of peace and recognition of Israel's right to exist, Prime Minister Yitzhak Rabin was ready to offer Yasir Arafat much of the West Bank (of the Jordan River). In that area and in Gaza a Palestinian state could be created.

The following conditions made Oslo possible:

1] the collapse of Soviet patronage of Arab intransigence,

2] the demonstration of the United States' capacity for leadership in the Persian Gulf War,

3] the isolation resulting from Yasir Arafat's commitment to the losing side in the Gulf War.

Extremists on both sides opposed peace. For making peace with Israel in 1977, President Anwar el-Sadat had been assassinated by a fellow Egyptian. For working for peace with the PLO, Prime Minister Rabin was killed by a fellow Israeli in 1995. (See also Clinton as Mid-East Peacemaker, pg. 267.)

* Aid to Somalia

Somalia is a coastal nation of easternmost Africa between the Gulf of Aden and the Indian Ocean. In December 1990 a civil war began, waged largely in Somalia's small but productive agricultural region. Rival factions practiced scorched-earth tactics, burning farm villages, looting seed supplies, and destroying water systems. As the country descended into

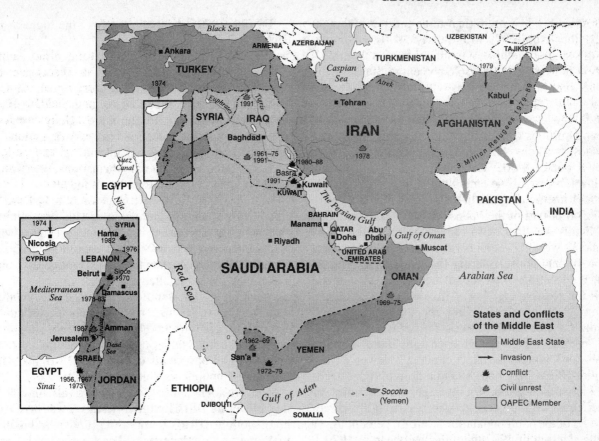

States and Conflicts
of the Middle East

- Middle East State
- → Invasion
- Conflict
- Civil unrest
- OAPEC Member

chaos, agricultural production dropped 90 percent, and Somalia, which already imported one-third of its staple foods, became totally dependent on outside aid. Many died of disease or starvation. The United Nations authorized a peacekeeping mission to enable relief supplies to reach the people of Somalia. In December 1992 U.S. forces swept into Somalia on a limited humanitarian operation to feed a stricken country, open corridors for emergency food shipments, and contain, if not end, a civil war. The Bush administration rejected pleas to disarm warring factions and pressed instead for negotiations among rival warlords. Five months later U.S. forces turned over control of the relief effort to the United Nations.

In October 1993, 18 U.S. soldiers were killed in Somalia during a mission to capture a local warlord. That incident had a disabling effect on American foreign policy and on President Clinton's willingness to commit troops abroad. Unfortunately, rival Somali clans returned to their feuding following the United Nations pullout in March 1995.

* America: What Went Wrong?

In 1992 two investigative journalists for *The Philadelphia Inquirer* researched and wrote a series of articles with the above title, and soon expanded their story into a best-selling book. It explored the plight of the American middle class and drew the following conclusions:

1] During the past generation, Congress and the presidents have been changing the rules of the American economy, by design or by default, "to favor the privileged, the powerful, and the influential. At the expense of everyone else."

2] As a result, say the authors, those with a middle-class taxable income of $20,000 to $50,000 are likely to see a drop in their standard of living in the coming years. For a growing number of individuals and families, this "means the end of the American dream."

3] The factors that created this revolution range from a tolerant view of inflated expense accounts to a tolerant view of the soaring national debt. They include junk bonds, lenient regulations and industry deregulation, and favorable tax and bankruptcy laws. The real beneficiaries are not people who want to start new businesses and thereby create jobs, but the corporate raiders who want to buy up, loot, and close companies, or do their manufacturing abroad.

4] Our valuable manufacturing jobs have been systematically exported, particularly to the Far East. The

U.S. economy lost more than three million manufacturing jobs from 1979 to the early 1990s. Manufacturing's share of total U.S. employment fell from 23.4 percent in March 1979 to 16.6 percent in March 1993. Those were high-paying jobs.

While takeover sharks and their attorneys were reaping millions from the frenzy of mergers and bankruptcies, millions of middle-class employees were thrown out of work. They were forced into lower-paying jobs, part-time employment, premature retirement, or unemployment. In the process they also were losing all or part of their pensions and health benefits.

All this was bad news for our society. Black and Hispanic workers were hardest hit in finding new employment. Those entering the work force without higher education often found themselves in demand only for low-paying, low-skill jobs. The results: a declining standard of living for the working and middle classes; fewer or weaker benefits; less disposable income for consumer spending; more working wives and more "latchkey children"; fewer young couples able to buy homes; and a drop in those seeking higher education. On average, the incomes of Americans without college degrees (roughly three-quarters of the adult population) were 16 percent lower by the election of 1992 than they had been in 1970.

The 1980s in particular was seen as a decade of extreme greed and selfishness, with little sense of community. Many Americans were looking for a change when they voted in November 1992.

* 1992 Presidential Election Campaign

At first Bush's reelection prospects seemed good. He had earned strong support from the public for his handling of foreign affairs, including his leadership role in bringing together a broad coalition of UN member nations to expel Iraq from Kuwait with the loss of few American lives. He had promoted face-to-face peace talks between Arabs and Israelis. The last remaining American hostages in Lebanon had been freed in 1991. He proposed economic aid to the successor states of the former Soviet Union and reaped the political benefits of the end of the Cold War. An economic recession cost Bush the election.

By mid-1992 unemployment was the highest since 1984, and the Census Bureau reported that 14.2 percent of all Americans were living in poverty, the highest proportion since 1983. Voters increasingly began to focus on their fears about those domestic issues that Bush seemed to have neglected. From the beginning of Ronald Reagan's presidency to the end of George Bush's, the federal budget deficit grew from $40 billion a year to $340 billion—an 850 percent increase. Interest payment on the national debt became largest single item in the national budget.

In June 1990 Bush had abandoned his "Read my lips. No new taxes" campaign pledge and admitted that new or increased taxes were needed. Many Republican conservatives were especially critical of that shift. Patrick Buchanan, a conservative newspaper columnist, even challenged Bush for the G.O.P. nomination on that issue. While Buchanan eventually endorsed Bush, Buchanan's televised speech and the Republican platform tied Bush to the right wing of the party, including religious fundamentalists, foes of abortion, and opponents of homosexual rights. Many moderate Republicans felt abandoned.

The president faced two major rivals on election day. Governor Bill Clinton of Arkansas was the Democratic nominee. Ross Perot, a wealthy Texas businessman, ran as an independent. Perot earned great credit (and 19 percent of the popular vote) for forcing the nation to concentrate on the budget deficit, and also for his consistent call for campaign finance reform and stricter control on lobbyists. However, he was unable to turn his convictions into a coherent program of action. In July, following the Democratic National Convention, Perot suddenly withdrew as a candidate, shocking his millions of eager followers. Many of them, along with other white conservatives, walked away from Bush's "status quo" presidency and turned to Bill Clinton as the only remaining agent of change. Clinton's vice-presidential running mate, Senator Albert Gore of Tennessee, ran on his own record as a strong environmentalist, while Vice-President Dan Quayle was perceived as an uninformed liability to the Republican effort.

Despite Perot's late and unexpected return to the race, Clinton won the popular vote in November and was elected by a 43 percent to 38 percent margin over President Bush. Perot formed a new political group, United We Stand America, to further his ideas.

William Jefferson Clinton   1993-2001

1946-

DEMOCRAT

☆

Vice-President   ALBERT GORE, JR.
Secretary of State   WARREN CHRISTOPHER
MADELEINE K. ALBRIGHT

CLINTON'S PUBLIC SERVICE BEFORE HE BECAME PRESIDENT

Arkansas Attorney General (1976-1978)
Governor of Arkansas (1978-1980, 1982-1992)

MAJOR ITEMS OF CLINTON'S ADMINISTRATION

Election of 1992	*The Environmental Agenda*
Election of 1996	*Global Warming*
The Clinton Team	*The Political Climate During the Clinton Presidency*
Family and Medical Leave Act of 1993	*The Monica Lewinsky Scandal*
Abortion Policy Changes	*The Election of 2000*
Handgun Control	*Farewell, Clintons*
Budget Priorities	*Steps to End Nuclear Testing*
Campaign Finance Reform	*International Trade Agreements*
The Campaign Money Mess	*NAFTA*
Supreme Court Appointments	*Trade Policy and Relations with China*
Military Base Closings	*Aftermath of the Persian Gulf War*
Gays in the Military	*The Gulf War Syndrome*
Midwest Flooding	*Clinton as Peacemaker*
Terrorist Plots	*Rwanda*
National Service Trust Act	*Civil War in Yugoslavia*
Contract with America	*Land Mines*
Welfare Reform	*The United Nations at 50*
Taxpayer Relief Act of 1997	*G.I. Bill Echoes*
Changes in Health Care	*The Marshall Plan Turns 50*
Tobacco, Health, and the Law	*NATO Expansion*

Election of 1992

William Jefferson Clinton received a first-ballot Democratic Party nomination for president after more prominent party leaders chose not to run. They were sure President Bush would win reelection. However, the country was mired in a recession, and Bush's popularity plummeted because he lacked an effective domestic program. Clinton called for a more activist reform government, proposing higher taxes on the wealthy, cuts in defense, and job-training programs. He pledged to cut the federal budget deficit of $290 billion in half in four years. On social issues Clinton supported freedom of choice on abortion, welfare payments limited to those who could not find work, and universal health care. Clinton's strategy of focusing on the economy and the high unemployment rate proved successful, and voters elected him over George Bush and Ross Perot.

	1992 Popular Vote	Electoral Vote
Clinton	43,682,624 (43%)	370
Bush	38,117,331 (38%)	168
Perot	19,217,213 (19%)	0

Election of 1996

In the most expensive presidential year campaign to date, the Democratic incumbents, Bill Clinton and Albert Gore, defeated their Republican rivals, former Senate Majority Leader **Robert Dole** and Jack Kemp. Clinton was the first Democratic President to be reelected since Franklin Roosevelt in 1936. At age 50, he was also the youngest President to be reelected. 1996 marked the first time that a Democrat was sent to the White House when both houses of Congress were controlled by the opposition. This was the first Republican Congress reelected since 1930.

Three factors contributed to Clinton's victory:

1] a robust economy, with high employment and low inflation;

2] acceptance of Republican ideas like cutting taxes, balancing the budget, and restricting welfare;

3] Senator Dole's failed strategy of assailing Clinton's character and ethical standards.

The electorate returned a moderate Democratic President to carry out a moderate Republican agenda. Yet the issues not discussed by the candidates were the ones the voters took most seriously: spending cuts, campaign finance reform, and keeping the Social Security and Medicare Systems healthy.

	1996 Popular Vote	Electoral Vote
Clinton	45,628,667 (50%)	379 (31 states)
Dole	37,869,435 (41%)	159 (19 states)
Perot	7,874,283 (9%)	0 (no states)

In 1996 Clinton gained increased support among females, Asian-Americans, and Hispanics. Environmental groups and most labor unions also supported the Democrats. Sadly, 10 million fewer voters went to the polls in 1996 than in 1992. The U.S. Chamber of Commerce and other business groups, plus antiabortion and gun-rights lobbyists, supported Republicans.

* The Clinton Team

Bill Clinton, the 42nd President of the United States, was the first born after World War II and the first to govern in the post-Cold War era. Clinton at 46 and Gore at 44 were the youngest team to occupy the White House.

Clinton was the first president in American history to entrust the top power positions in the administration to the First Lady and the Vice-President. Hillary Rodham Clinton was charged with producing a health care reform package that would cover all Americans at a manageable cost. Vice-President Albert Gore's expertise in environmental areas was important to the new administration.

* Family and Medical Leave Act of 1993

This bill, previously vetoed by Presidents Reagan and Bush, was one of the first items of legislation signed by Clinton. It requires companies with more than 50 employees to allow workers to take up to 12 weeks unpaid leave, with health benefits, during any 12-month period for: the birth of a child or an adoption; the need to care for a child, spouse, or parent with a serious health condition; or their own serious health condition that makes them unable to perform their job. Only workers who have already been employed at the company for at least one year and worked at least 25 hours a week are covered. Workers must then be allowed to return to their old job or an equivalent position.

Some say the big question is not whether employers can afford to grant family leave, but whether employees can afford to take it.

* Abortion Policy Changes

On the 20th anniversary of *Roe* v. *Wade*, the Supreme Court decision that established a constitutional right to abortion, President Clinton signed a group of abortion-related memoranda that revoked a decade of bans imposed by Republican administrations. He also repeated the careful posture on abortion that he had taken throughout his campaign, calling for "an America where abortion is safe and legal, but rare."

1] He repealed the "gag rule" against abortion counseling at federally financed clinics.

2] He directed federal regulators to reassess the Bush administration's prohibition on importing a French abortion pill, RU486, for personal use.

3] Another memo permitted abortions in military hospitals overseas for women who would pay for the procedure.

4] Reversing a policy set by President Reagan in 1984, Clinton promised to restore American financing of international family planning programs that provide abortion-related activities, if Congress supplied the money.

5] Clinton lifted restrictions on federal financing of fetal tissue research, which offered promising results for millions suffering from Alzheimer's and Parkinson's disease.

Handgun Control

In November 1993, Congress passed the Brady Bill, named after White House Press Secretary James S. Brady who was severely wounded in an assassination attempt on the life of President Ronald Reagan. The law required people to wait five working days between the time they purchased a handgun and when they could take possession. That interval provided time for a computer check to keep new weapons out of the hands of known criminals. An anticrime law also outlawed the sale of certain types of assault weapons, but handgun sales without background checks were still permitted at gun shows.

Budget Priorities

The first budget presented to Congress by the Clinton administration was in marked contrast to those of his Republican predecessors. While proposing, like Reagan and Bush, to cut the federal deficit, he sought to increase national investments in public works, job training (and retraining for workers who lose their jobs because of military cuts and factory closings), early education for poor children (like Operation Head Start), childhood immunization, women's health, and drug abuse treatment. Clinton asked for an increase in energy taxes (as on gasoline) and income taxes on upper-income families, while making major cuts in agricultural payments and defense spending, as for unnecessary military bases.

Despite the budget cutting, Clinton insisted on expanding the earned income tax credit for the working poor. This fulfilled a campaign promise: No one should have to work 40 hours a week and raise a family in poverty. In the next five years, this credit increased the incomes of 15 million families earning less than $27,000 a year. Included were many service industry workers—waitresses, hospital orderlies, and janitors.

The minimum wage was again raised in 1996. Americorps, the national service program, was expanded. Funding for Operation Head Start, which provides preschool education for at-risk four-year-olds, almost doubled between 1993 and 2000.

Congress did not act on Clinton's plan for sweeping reform of the nation's health care system. However, in August 1996 Congress did approve the Kennedy-Kassebaum bill, which included two important parts of Clinton's 1993 plan. The bill provided (1) that workers can change jobs without losing their medical insurance coverage, and (2) that workers cannot be denied medical insurance because of a pre-existing condition.

The budget agreement finally approved by the narrowest of margins in Congress in August 1993 gave Clinton only half a loaf. Despite its focus on reducing the annual budget deficit and the national debt, this detailed plan for government spending and taxing did little to hasten economic growth and provide better jobs.

The new budget raised income taxes on the rich from 31 percent to 36 percent, with a 10 percent surcharge on those earning more than $250,000, lifting their top rate to 39.6 percent. The taxable portion of Social Security benefits for couples earning more than $44,000 rose from 50 percent to 85 percent. Taxes on gasoline and diesel fuel were raised, and some business deductions were lowered. Earned income tax credit for the working poor was expanded, as were some incentives for business investment in urban areas and in research.

Campaign Finance Reform

In 1992 Congress passed a comprehensive campaign finance reform bill that would have made significant progress toward cleaning up the scandalous way congressional elections are financed. President Bush vetoed the legislation, but President Clinton promised early action. In 1993 a majority of both houses of the 103rd Congress were publicly on record in support of reform, so long as passage of a real reform bill remained unlikely. Such a law was finally passed in 2002.

The cost of House campaigns skyrocketed during the 1980s. For example, in 1988 the average House candidate spent $312,000, about twice the amount spent in 1980. During this same time period, contributions from PACs—the special-interest political action committees that came to supply half the campaign money raised by House incumbents—grew by 175 percent from $40,000 to $110,000 on average for House campaigns.

These high levels of PAC contributions resulted in a dangerous distortion of the American political system, giving those groups a predominance of political influence disproportionate to their real numbers. Another distorting influence was the flow of *soft money*—contributions to political parties in order to circumvent the legal limits on contributions to candidates.

The Campaign Money Mess

Together, the two parties spent over a half billion dollars to get their 1996 message out. The Democrats spent $250 million and the Republicans spent $400 million, totaling twice as much as in 1992. Both parties were accused of unethical and illegal practices. These charges, the subject of extensive Senate hearings in 1997, included violating laws about:

1] allowing foreign influence in U.S. national elections,

2] using Federal property (including the White House) to raise campaign funds,

3] distinguishing between limited contributions to candidates and unlimited gifts to political parties.

Hard money, or campaign gifts to individual candidates, must be reported to the Federal Election Commission (FEC) and comply with certain limits. (See pg. 231.) *Soft money* was raised outside FEC limits and was supposed to go to "party-building" activities. It was not to be used to promote individual candidates. In practice, the spirit of that restriction was often ignored until soft money was outlawed in 2002.

Supreme Court Appointments

United States Court of Appeals Judge Ruth Bader Ginsburg was the first person in 26 years to be nominated for a Supreme Court seat by a Democratic president. She easily won Senate confirmation and became the second woman on that bench, along with Sandra Day O'Connor, and the first Jewish Supreme Court justice since 1969. Her previous professional life was one committed to equality for women. Her appointment stood in stark contrast with many of the less-qualified men chosen during the Reagan and Bush years for their ideology or with sparse credentials.

A second Clinton appointee to the United States Supreme Court was Stephen Breyer, in 1994. Justice Breyer, also from the Court of Appeals, brought expertise in government regulation, especially in antitrust enforcement.

Military Base Closings

In 1993 a nonpartisan commission appointed by Congress recommended a list of 70 major military bases to be closed. That was the third time in five years that the post-Cold War reduction in defense installations around the country had been kept out of the hands of the politicians. (With the state of California scheduled to lose five naval facilities and many jobs in the San Francisco Bay area alone, one can still hear the howl of their elected officials.) By approving the list, President Clinton helped save the nation billions of dollars.

The success of such nonpolitical decision-making led to proposals in Congress to test this approach on spending in nondefense agencies of the government.

Gays in the Military

A heated controversy arose both during the presidential campaign and afterward over Clinton's promise to end the ban on homosexuals in the military. As *The New York Times* said editorially, "the old ban on gay soldiers was unfair to dedicated individuals and deprived the services of valuable talent. Homosexuals were screened out by recruiters; if they slipped through the screen they were hunted down by investigators and discharged no matter how long and distinguished their service."

In July 1993 a compromise plan was endorsed by the President and the Joint Chiefs of Staff. It permitted homosexuals to serve in the military if they did not engage openly in homosexual behavior and remained quiet about their sexual identity. By making it more difficult for commanders to initiate investigations without clear evidence of homosexual behavior, a zone of privacy was created for gay members of the military.

The compromise was criticized both by those who insisted on complete exclusion of homosexuals from military service on moral grounds, and others who felt that a "don't ask, don't tell" policy gave insufficient backing to the constitutional guarantees of free speech and equal protection against discrimination.

Midwest Flooding

In June and July 1993 the upper Mississippi River and its tributaries, swollen by unusually heavy rains, overflowed their banks to flood farms and towns along a 400-mile stretch from southern Minnesota through Wisconsin, Iowa, Illinois, Nebraska, Kansas, and Missouri. Losses amounted to over $10 billion, including the destruction of more than 8,000 homes and businesses, the displacement of at least 30,000 people, and the inundation of hundreds of thousands of acres of some of the world's most productive farm bottomland. More than 30 people died.

The Federal Emergency Management Agency had agents and crews throughout the affected area working with state and local authorities and with legions of local people. They struggled day and night to ward off the water's advance. A large public and private relief effort was soon mounted. No less needed was a thorough review of measures to limit the threat of flooding in the future.

Over the previous 65 years, the United States government had spent billions of dollars to build some 300 dams and reservoirs, construct thousands of miles of levees and flood walls, and operate countless pumping stations to regulate water draining from parts of 35 states, in an area covering more than one-third of the nation. However, experts have been losing trust in levees, and many now favor more natural flood controls.

By cutting off the flood plain's waters, levees and diversion channels have destroyed and degraded stream-side habitats that contain some of the country's richest biological resources. They have also prevented the flood plain from performing one of its most important natural functions: flood control. By storing and slowing flood waters, the plain reduces their force and height. Containing this water in a narrowly corseted channel to protect farms and urban settlements can have the opposite effect. It raises both the velocity and height of the flood, making it even more destructive when it breaks through the defenses, as it has repeatedly done in the Midwest.

Flood-plain managers have now taken a new approach: cooperating with nature rather than trying to subdue it. The emphasis is on keeping new development away from the flood plain, preserving or restoring its ecosystems and letting water flow as freely as possible so that natural flood-control mechanisms can work.

Terrorist Plots

In late February 1993 a massive explosion in an underground parking garage rocked the foundation of the Twin Towers of Manhattan's World Trade Center, the second tallest building in the world and a center for one million workers and visitors daily. The blast killed six persons and injured more than 1,000 in the most destructive terrorist attack up to that time on U.S. soil. Evidence found in the seven-story-deep crater made by the explosion led to identification of the rented van used in the car bombing, and to the arrest of Moslem fundamentalist fanatics. They were followers of Sheikh Omar Abdel-Rahman, a blind cleric from Egypt, who was also arrested for fomenting violence.

Early the following summer, a team of F.B.I. agents and New York City police captured a group of five men preparing explosives in a Queens garage in New York City. These Moslem (Muslim) fundamentalists were charged with conspiracy to carry out bombings of United Nations headquarters and New York City tunnels.

As the world's sole superpower, this country had become a focus of many of the world's resentments. Home-grown terrorists also took a toll in the 1990s. On April 19, 1995, the Murrah Federal Building in Oklahoma City was destroyed by a bomb blast that killed 168 persons. Two men, Timothy McVeigh and Terry Nichols, were tried and convicted. Serious bombing plots involving militia cells in Oklahoma and Michigan were foiled in midstream by arrests. In 1996, there was an unsolved bombing in the Olympic stadium in Atlanta, Georgia. Women's health centers where abortions were performed were struck by arson and bombings; some doctors were killed. The preaching of hatred became a recipe for disaster.

National Service Trust Act

A central promise of the Clinton 1992 campaign, which had great appeal to middle-class voters, was a program of national service that would "revive America's commitment to community and make affordable the cost of a college education for every American." Clinton claimed that his National Service Trust Act would be to the 1990s what the G.I. Bill was for the 1950s and the Peace Corps was for the 1960s—the place "where higher learning goes hand in hand with the higher purpose of addressing our unmet needs."

High school graduates who volunteer for a year or two of community service would earn the minimum wage and also receive awards of up to $10,000 toward vocational training or a college education. Affordable student loans for college would also be provided directly by the government to students who do not volunteer for community service. Students would have the option to tie repayment of the loan to their future income.

President Bush previously enhanced volunteerism and community service when he signed the National Community Service Act of 1990. A key provision set up a youth corps to encourage teenagers who had dropped out or graduated from school to perform community service, with an education stipend of up to $5,000 after one year of full-time service. Participants who were not college bound and needed remedial instruction were to receive it. Unfortunately, little money was provided by Congress to carry out these worthwhile programs.

Contract with America

For the first time in half a century, Republicans took control of Congress in the November 1994 midterm elections. House Speaker Newt Gingrich promised that a "Contract with America" would be voted on in the House of Representatives in the first hundred days of the 104th Congress. Discussion of the controversial items of this proposal had already enlivened the 1994 Congressional election campaign. Let's examine their legislative fate.

1] A balanced budget amendment to the United States Constitution passed in the House but failed by one vote in the Senate. Had it succeeded, 38 state legislatures would still have taken years to ratify it. In 1997, President Clinton and a Republican Congress agreed to a balanced budget by 2002, with most of the pain of reduced spending to come in the later years, when Clinton and many members of the current Congress would no longer be in office. (See the Taxpayer Relief Act, next column.)

2] A line item veto allowing the President to delete specific spending items was passed by Congress and used by President Clinton in 1997. In 1998, the Supreme Court rejected the line item veto as a departure from the basic constitutional requirement that a President accept or reject bills in their entirety. He may not "rewrite" legislation passed by Congress.

3] A reduced capital gains tax was also included in the budget agreement in 1997.

4] A proposed constitutional amendment to limit the term of office for members of Congress (e.g., Senators to 12 years) was ignored by the Congress in power.

5] The President signed a bill ending the practice of imposing federal mandates on states without providing the money to carry them out. An example might be a requirement for states to conduct an educational or environmental survey for Congress.

Welfare Reform

In his 1992 campaign, candidate Clinton pledged to "end welfare as we know it." He was referring to the cycle of welfare dependency among some poor, often single-parent, families. In 1996, President Clinton approved a Republican-sponsored reversal of federal welfare policy.

1] It turned over most of the control of the welfare system to the states, shifting large amounts of money and decision-making power to devise ways of moving poor people from welfare to work.

2] It ended six decades of guaranteed help to the nation's poorest children, the program of Aid to Families with Dependent Children.

3] It limited welfare payments to families to a maximum of five years.

4] It required welfare recipients to be engaged in work within two years. *Workfare* refers to state and local programs requiring them to work for their cash benefits and food stamps (e.g., by feeding the elderly at community centers, sweeping the parks, or answering phones in city or state offices). Welfare recipients who take state jobs must be paid the minimum wage.

5] Benefits to teenage single mothers and to *legal* immigrants were limited, e.g., food stamps.

During the economic boom in the second half of the 1990s welfare rolls dropped by almost 50 percent. There was a remarkable expansion of employment opportunities for those on the lowest rungs of the economic ladder, including women, blacks, and Hispanics. Yet critics of welfare reform worried about how an economic recession would affect those whose welfare eligibility had run out. Such a recession became a reality by 2001.

The Taxpayer Relief Act of 1997

After nearly two years of debate, President Clinton and Republican leaders of Congress achieved an agreement to balance the federal budget by the year 2002, after years of deficit spending, and to provide the first federal tax cut in 16 years. Compromises reached in the agreement included:

1] Tax credits of $500 per child ($400 in 1998) up to age 17. It is estimated that 45 million children will benefit from this provision, which also fulfills a Republican commitment in the 1994 Contract with America.

2] Expanded health care coverage for uninsured children. Over five years, $24 billion was to be allocated to extend coverage to half the nation's ten million uninsured children.

3] College scholarships of $1,500 (tuition credit) during each of the first two years of college, falling to $1,000 every year thereafter.

4] Reduction in long-term capital gains tax rate from 28 percent to 20 percent for most investors. Capital gains are the profits made on the sale of stocks, bonds, property, and other investments or assets.

5] Exemption from tax of profits on sale of a primary home, up to $500,000 for married couples.

6] Exemption from inheritance tax to rise from $600,000 to $1,000,000 in ten years; family-owned farms and businesses exempt to $1.3 million in 1999.

By 1998, a strong economy helped lead to an unexpected $70 billion federal budget surplus, the first since 1969. By 2000, the budget surplus had grown to $230 billion, but the benefits were short-lived. Congress had failed to deal with the problems of long-term funding for Social Security and Medicare, and of health care coverage for the uninsured.

Changes in Health Care

Mrs. Clinton's complex proposed health-care reforms never got to first base. Large insurance companies and for-profit hospital chains lobbied Congress against further government involvement. Meanwhile, managed care expanded rapidly, largely through health maintenance organizations (HMOs). HMOs provide health care in return for pre-set monthly payments. Most HMOs provide care through a network of doctors and hospitals that their members must use in order to be covered. Large businesses and government units use HMOs to limit their health insurance costs.

By 1996, 50 million workers, some 70 percent of the nation's eligible employees, had health coverage through managed care—twice as many as those who still paid for each medical visit. Meanwhile, almost one in five adults at that time, or 40 million Americans, were without health insurance during the previous year. Of the uninsured, 45 percent had trouble getting health care when they needed it, and more than a third had difficulty paying their medical bills.

Managed care proponents asserted that the system would improve under its cost-conscious custody because the industry has a financial stake in early intervention and in making sure patients get better, not sicker. Critics worried that costs would drive medical decisions in huge, for-profit firms like Columbia Health Care. Seriously ill patients, the most expensive ones to treat, would lose out in the process.

The most serious failure of the Clinton legislative program was its inability to reform the nation's health care system. (See also pg. 250.)

Tobacco, Health, and the Law

The interests of the public and the interests of the tobacco industry are in conflict. The tobacco companies want to sell cigarettes and make as much money as possible. However, when the industry is doing well, the result is that enormous numbers of people fall ill with lung cancer, throat cancer, emphysema, and heart disease. For 40 years the industry got away with denying any connection to ill health, until 1996 when several tobacco officials began to admit that lethal link. Industry documents came to light proving that the tobacco companies manipulated nicotine levels to produce addiction, and targeted teenagers in their cigarette advertising. By then, many states and localities had filed suit against the major tobacco companies to recover billions of dollars spent on medical care for smoke-related illnesses. All told, 400,000 Americans die each year from such diseases, while 6,000 teenagers *each day* light up their first cigarette.

In August 1997 tobacco companies agreed to pay Florida $11.3 billion in a settlement that avoided a risky, televised trial over liability for Medicaid costs resulting from tobacco-related illnesses. The industry also flinched on the eve of a trial in Mississippi and agreed to a $3.6 billion settlement. More trials loomed. A New York City suit contended that tobacco use, promoted by the industry through a campaign of deceit and misrepresentation, had jacked up the city's costs for Medicaid, care for the indigent in public hospitals, and health insurance premiums for public workers.

Under such tremendous pressure, the major tobacco companies settled with the attorneys general of all the states to pay $246 billion over the next 25 years for the Medicaid costs arising from smoking-related diseases. Those settlements did not deal with the potential claims of millions of individual smokers, which may be far more expensive to resolve. In addition to the health costs of tobacco use to individuals and to state governments, the federal government was spending more than $20 billion a year treating people with smoking-related diseases under federal health programs. Congress, beholden to campaign contributions from the tobacco industry, refused in 1998 to give the Food and Drug Administration authority to regulate tobacco and nicotine. President Clinton's Justice Department sued to force the industry to stop marketing cigarettes to children and to accept greater federal regulation. There is a Catch 22—the Justice Department depends on Congress to provide the $20 million it needs to pursue the case. (See also pg. 277.)

The Environmental Agenda

The first **Earth Day**, April 22, 1970, was the beginning of a generation or more of environmental activism. In that year, President Nixon established the Environmental Protection Agency. The **Clean Air Act of 1970** set emission standards for many pollutants. Factories and power plants were required to install special smokestack filters, known as scrubbers, to cut down on dustlike particles called particulates. In 1997 the EPA proposed rules to require 22 states east of the Mississippi River to make deep cuts in their emissions of nitrogen oxides, the main source of the ozone in smog. That would require big investments in cleaner power plants, fuels, and cars. One important result would be improved public health.

The **1972 Clean Water Act** required industries, utilities, and sewage treatment plants to curb discharge of toxic wastes. The law eliminated dumping raw sewage into most U.S. lakes and rivers.

The **1973 Endangered Species Act** made it illegal to kill creatures listed as endangered or threatened. That followed the 1972 ban on agricultural or household use of DDT, a potent pesticide that can cause cancer and birth defects in humans and drive bird species to extinction. The return of the bald eagle and other cherished species once on the endangered list testifies to the Act's impact.

The environmental agenda pitted landowners and industries against environmentalists by limiting development in targeted species' habitats (e.g., logging, especially of public lands). That includes 650 million acres of national parks and wilderness areas, mostly in the West.

Before 1970, Americans gave little thought to the amount of garbage they generated. Aided by a booming plastics industry, the United States had become the world's leading throw-away society as styrofoam hamburger containers, plastic dishes, and disposable diapers replaced more durable, multiple-use consumer items. Concern over solid waste mounted as municipal landfills began to overflow. The result was a widespread grass-roots campaign to reduce the volume of household trash by composting vegetable matter and recycling plastics, metals, and paper. Growing demand for used newspapers, plastic bottles, and aluminum cans has made it increasingly cost-effective for manufacturers to incorporate recycled materials into their products.

Despite popular support of recycling programs, the United States, as the world's leading consumer society, also remains the leading throw-away society.

By 1990, each American produced 4.3 pounds of trash daily, up from 2.7 pounds in 1960. Wastes from manufacturing, mining, and oil and gas refining generate more than 100 times the volume of residential waste. Although burning trash reduces the strain on landfills and can be a relatively cheap source of electric power, it poses serious threats to the environment and human health. Industrial wastes containing toxic materials can release hazardous substances into the atmosphere, such as dioxin, a cancer-causing by-product of chlorine production and waste combustion. A related problem is cleaning up contaminated soil and water at toxic waste sites and making those who dumped the waste pay for it. For example, the General Electric Corporation was ordered by the federal government to dredge the Hudson River to remove PCBs (toxic chemicals).

A brighter note was the 1997 congressional pledge to provide funds to protect several very vulnerable pieces of the American landscape. The Interior Department's **Everglades Restoration Fund** would carry forward the largest environmental rescue operation ever—the restoration of Florida's Everglades. Located in southern Florida, the Everglades are a subtropical wetlands area occupying over 1700 square miles, and reserved to protect the abundant wildlife and tropical plants. The program would create buffer zones between the Everglades, (a "Sea of Grass"), and two of its greatest threats, the agricultural regions to the north and the exploding urban populations to the east.

Also included were the purchase of a potentially ruinous gold mining operation near Yellowstone National Park and the acquisition of California's Headwaters Redwood Grove from a private lumber company.

Global Warming

One hundred years ago the Swedish chemist Svante Arrhenius discovered the greenhouse effect. Burning fossil fuels and other industrial activities release carbon dioxide and other gases that trap solar heat in the earth's atmosphere. Predictions about the increasing pace of global warming caused by human activity alarmed policymakers and led to the signing of a landmark environmental accord by 160 nations in Kyoto, Japan, in December 1997.

The **Kyoto Accord** would require the industrialized nations to reduce their emissions of carbon dioxide and five other heat-trapping gases on an average of 5.2 percent below these of 1990. The United States would be required to cut emissions 7 percent below 1990 levels by the year 2012. Per capita emissions of carbon dioxide in the United States and Europe in 1995 are shown in the chart.

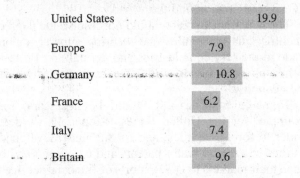

Per Capita Emissions of Carbon Dioxide In the United States and Europe in 1995

United States	19.9
Europe	7.9
Germany	10.8
France	6.2
Italy	7.4
Britain	9.6

Source: International Energy Agency

In July 2001, 178 nations endorsed the Kyoto Protocol, including all of the world's industrialized nations except the United States. Scientific research leading up to the agreement established two main points: Human activity is changing the atmosphere in unprecedented ways, and the earth is warming up.

The Political Climate During the Clinton Presidency

Clinton faced some of the fiercest partisan opposition of any U.S. Chief Executive.

1] An independent counsel, Kenneth Starr, appointed to investigate possible White House ("Whitewater") illegalities, spent three years and more than $30 million with virtually no result, seemingly driven by political compulsion to humiliate or financially bankrupt the President. (*Whitewater* referred to certain questionable loans made by some Arkansas banks while Mr. Clinton was governor.) In 1998, Starr expanded his investigation to include charges of sexual harassment against the President.

2] Meanwhile, a Senate Governmental Affairs Committee probe of 1996 campaign finance abuses also became an attempt to discredit the President and the Democrats, although the Republicans (in the majority in both houses of Congress) continued to receive and to spend far larger sums than their opponents.

3] In late 1995, the Republican-led Congress twice shut down the federal government as a tactic to prod President Clinton into accepting its version of a balanced budget. Congress refused to pay for most federal agencies until the public signaled its strong opposition to the loss of government services (for example, issuing passports). The result was that the Republicans lost some of their popular support.

4] Two 1997 foreign policy actions could have long-term consequences. Congress refused the President the ability to conduct "fast track" tariff negotiations without the need for Senate ratification. Previous presidents had not been limited this way. Congress also failed in 1997 to pay the arrears of over $1 billion owed to the United Nations by the United States. That diminished the ability of the American government to act as a UN leader (e.g., to rally the Gulf War UN allies against the challenges of Saddam Hussein of Iraq to UN inspectors entitled to search for and destroy his hidden weapons of mass destruction).

The Monica Lewinsky Scandal

In January 1998, Judge Kenneth Starr asked Attorney General Janet Reno to expand his investigation to include charges of sexual misconduct against the President. That probe revealed an improper relationship between Clinton and a young White House intern, Monica Lewinsky.

President Clinton's actions were seen as self-indulgent and self-destructive. Most members of Congress and much of the public favored a vote of censure by Congress, but some Republican leaders there intensely wished to punish Clinton. In December 1998, the U.S. House of Representatives *impeached* (brought charges against) Clinton for perjury and obstruction of justice as he had tried to conceal his relationship with Miss Lewinsky. The House sent its findings to the Senate, which conducted an impeachment trial, and found Clinton not guilty. He remained in office, but his reputation, his presidency, and his political party all suffered. The sordid affair and the media attention it generated had diverted public attention from more serious matters for a full year.

The Election of 2000

Vice-President Al Gore's campaign for the presidency was marred by Bill Clinton's scandal and impeachment. The Republican Governor of Texas, George W. Bush, son of President George Bush (1989-1993), promised "compassionate conservatism," spoke of "family values," and urged a change to clean up Washington.

This closest presidential race in our history was not decided for more than a month past Election Day. The candidate who would win in Florida (where George W.'s brother Jeb Bush was Governor) would receive a majority of the Electoral College votes. There were various election problems in Florida, including the design of the ballots, recounts in only some counties, and the denial of the ballot to many African-

Americans. The U.S. Supreme Court entered this political battle—a first—and narrowly ruled in a way that gave Bush his victory.

Farewell, Clintons

Election Day 2000 saw Hillary Rodham Clinton selected as the Democratic junior U.S. Senator from New York, the first wife of a U.S. President to win elected office. Shortly before leaving office, Bill Clinton issued a series of controversial presidential pardons, including one to Marc Rich, the fugitive former husband of a major Democratic party contributor. Clinton's critics fumed, and his supporters were again disappointed in his judgment.

Steps to End Nuclear Testing

Ever since World War II, our planet has lived with the threat of nuclear war. In 1963 the Limited Test Ban Treaty drove United States, Soviet, and British nuclear testing underground; however, a total ban on nuclear tests eluded the world's grasp. In 1993 President Clinton took steps to help achieve that goal.

He extended for at least 15 months the moratorium on U.S. tests mandated by Congress (that was due to expire). He declared that the United States would not test unless another nation does so first, making it easier for leaders in Russia and France to extend the moratoriums they were observing. He also declared his support for negotiating a total ban on nuclear testing.

In 1993 President Clinton extended an expiring moratorium on atomic testing mandated by Congress. He declared that the United States would not test unless another nation did so first. That made it easier for leaders in Russia and France to extend the moratoriums they were observing. In 1968 the United States and many other nations signed a 25-year nuclear nonproliferation treaty, a key to efforts to stop the spread of nuclear arms. In 1995 it was agreed to make that treaty permanent and to tighten controls on exports of materials that could be used to make atomic bombs.

* International Trade Agreements

In mid-1993 U.S. Trade Representative Mickey Kantor helped to reach an important trade agreement in Tokyo, Japan, among the seven major industrialized nations. They acted to eliminate tariffs on pharmaceuticals, medical equipment, construction equipment, paper products, beer, and other manufactured goods.

A major purpose of those across-the-board tariff cuts was to reduce consumer prices and therefore raise living standards around the world.

The new trade agreement did not resolve the degree of tariff cuts on textiles and wearing apparel, or on trade in the service industries and agriculture. Protectionist opposition was still fierce in those sectors of the economy.

To achieve success, it would be necessary, for example, for the United States to open its borders wider to foreign textiles, and for the underdeveloped nations to agree to honor patents and copyrights, or to open their markets to U.S. exports of financial services and movies. At stake was the addition of trillions of dollars worth of goods and services to world output during the following decade.

NAFTA

NAFTA, the **North American Free Trade Agreement**, was approved by Congress in November 1993. It is a program for the freer flow of capital, labor, and products among Canada, the United States, and Mexico. Canada and the United States, already linked by their own 1989 trade pact, hoped to be enriched by the opening of Mexico's economy. Mexico would rise on a flood of trade with and investment from its wealthy northern neighbors.

Within three and a half years, there were clear economic benefits. Mexican exports of cars and trucks to the north doubled, to one million units. Big textile and clothing firms in the southern United States and in Mexico set up joint ventures in Mexico, using local materials, labor, and management. These could now compete with Asian products.

Big American retailers, like Wal-Mart and Sears, expanded their presence in Mexico and began to buy their branded clothes from Mexican plants. They turned those factories from export-only *maquiladoras* (duty-free assembly plants that sit along the U.S.-Mexican borders) into contract suppliers for the Mexican market. They started promoting Mexican-made goods in their northern retail stores.

Trade Policy and Relations with China

During the 1990s China, with one-fifth of the world's consumers, was the fastest-growing emerging market in the world. U.S. businessmen anticipated large returns on their trade and investments; and Chinese imports of shoes, textiles, toys, and tools began to flood American stores. Many Americans were disappointed when the Clinton Administration caved in to China in 1994, and it agreed not to link the two countries' trade relations to Beijing's violations of human rights.

In June 1989, the Communist government massacred pro-democracy demonstrators in Beijing's Tiananmen Square. It persecuted and arrested dissidents, sentenced political opponents to forced labor, and denied freedom of speech and of worship. China had previously invaded Tibet and was destroying Tibetan culture. China was the top supplier of technology and materials for ballistic, nuclear, and chemical weapons—powerful weapons banned by international agreement—to countries like Iran, Syria, and Pakistan.

Advocates of Washington's policy of "engagement" with China argued that maintaining good relations with the world's fastest-growing economy is a necessity, not a luxury. They say that, by dealing with China, the United States can encourage it to play by civilized rules of international law (i.e., stop selling weapons to rogue regimes). They believe that sustained development of China's economy will lead to greater political freedom. Accordingly, the United States backed China's joining the WTO (World Trade Organization) in 2001.

Aftermath of the Persian Gulf War

Part of the armistice terms that ended the Persian Gulf War of 1991 required Saddam Hussein to agree to UN inspections of Iraqi military sites to find and destroy his hidden weapons of mass destruction. Until then, UN-imposed economic sanctions against Iraq were to remain, including severe restrictions on the sale of Iraqi oil. For six years Saddam constantly blocked UN efforts to locate and eliminate his nuclear, chemical and biological weapons.

Late in 1997, France, China, and Russia announced that they would use their UN Security Council veto power to prevent even a mild tightening of the sanctions against Iraq for sabotaging UN inspections. The reason? All three were signing big contracts with Iraq and campaigning to get sanctions lifted so that the deals could go into effect. Saddam took advantage of the split among the Security Council members. The United Kingdom and the United States insisted that before the Security Council could consider ending sanctions, the inspection commission would have to certify that Iraq's biological, chemical, and nuclear weapons program had been completely shut down and their stocks destroyed and that all missiles capable of flying farther than 95 miles had been destroyed.

In November 1997 Saddam ordered American UN inspectors out of Iraq, leading to a three-week crisis period of no inspections, and the opportunity for Iraq to disable inspection machinery and to relocate weapons the inspectors had come too close to. In 1998, an Iraqi-United Nations agreement for some weapons inspection also failed, and the Clinton administration took no effective action.

The Gulf War Syndrome

Some 70,000 U.S. troops of almost 700,000 who served in the Middle East during the Persian Gulf War have complained to either the Pentagon or the Department of Veterans Affairs that they suffer from one or more of these symptoms: chronic fatigue, headaches, joint pain, digestive problems, and difficulty concentrating. Pentagon officials believed that up to 20,000 U.S. troops may have been exposed to poison gas when they destroyed chemical weapons at a huge depot in southern Iraq. A Senate study in 1993 concluded that soldiers became ill because of widespread allied attacks on Iraq's chemical weapons factories and depots during the 39 day air war that began on January 16, 1991, before allied ground troops were sent in.

Clinton as Peacemaker—Northern Ireland

President Clinton made several trips to Ireland and Northern Ireland. In Northern Ireland, he helped bring Sinn Fein (an important organization of the minority Catholic group) into the peace process with the Protestant majority. He appointed former Maine Senator George Mitchell to chair the talks on power sharing between the two groups. That enabled Britain to establish an interim legislature in Northern Ireland to represent both groups, and help end many years of violence between them. The question of disarming paramilitary groups proved difficult.

Clinton as Mid-East Peacemaker

A Clinton priority was to achieve peace in the Middle East. In the last summer of his presidency, he invited Palestinian Authority Chairman Yasir Arafat and Israel Prime Minister Ehud Barak to Camp David to break the long-stalemated negotiations. Arafat refused a generous land for peace offer by Clinton and the Israelis, without any counterproposal. Arafat failed to inform his people that they were offered statehood on almost all of the territory they purported to seek. What followed was an escalation of anti-Israeli violence permitted by Arafat, Israeli military retaliation, and the collapse of any hope for an early peace. Arafat seemed to have lost control over the more violent groups he was allied with, namely Hamas and Islamic

Jihad. Their hatred of Israel would accept no compromise, making Arafat appear irrelevant as a negotiating partner.

Rwanda: A Tragic History of Ethnic Conflict

Rwanda is a country in east central Africa and is about the size of Maryland. It became independent from Belgium in 1962 (as did Burundi, its neighbor to the south). It has a long history of ethnic conflict between the Hutu and Tutsi people that led to genocidal warfare in 1994. Some two million refugees fled, more than a million others were murdered, and another million or more were displaced internally. The international community responded with one of the largest humanitarian relief efforts ever mounted. The United States was one of the largest contributors. A UN peacekeeping operation remained in Rwanda until 1996. Because of its experience in Somalia in 1993, the United States refused to intervene militarily to curb Rwandan genocide.

Civil War in Yugoslavia

Another instance of the violent eruption of ethnic hatreds occurred in the former Yugoslavia. Yugoslavia was a southeast European nation, created in 1918 at the end of World War I to give a national voice to various ethnic groups, most of which were previously ruled by the Austro-Hungarian Empire. These groups included Serbs, Croats, Slovenes, and Bosnians. Civil War broke out in Bosnia in the spring of 1992 after Muslims and Croats there voted to secede from Serb-dominated Yugoslavia. Serbia and Montenegro formed a new Yugoslavia.

This was a conflict in which civilians were the prime targets, and every method to terrorize, displace, or even kill them was part of the arsenal of each side. Two and a half million refugees were driven from their homes by August 1993 in an orgy of "ethnic cleansing." The worst offenders were Serbian soldiers and irregulars, armed and supported by the Serbian government in Belgrade. They swept through large swaths of Bosnian territory to expel Muslims and Croats so that Serbs could move in. More than 200,000 people were declared dead or missing. Charges of *genocide* were leveled at the Serbian leader, Slobodan Milosevic. (Genocide is the systematic killing of a whole people or nation. It is an international war crime, and the term was first applied to the mass murder of Jews during World War II by Nazi Germany.)

The warfare and its civilian casualties brought sympathy but no effective action from the European Community, the United Nations, nor the United States government (whose parachuted relief supplies in March 1993 fell mostly into the wrong hands).

At the end of 1997, about 8,000 American troops were serving in Bosnia, as part of a NATO-led international peacekeeping force of over 30,000.

In 1995, peace came to Croatia, and representatives of Bosnia, Croatia, and Serbia signed a peace plan for Bosnia. This was based on the Dayton Accords sponsored by U.S. President Bill Clinton. Milosevic, the former President of Serbia, was appointed President of Yugoslavia (Serbia and Montenegro only) in 1997.

The next year relations between Serbs and ethnic Albanians in the Yugoslav province of Kosovo broke down into armed conflict. Early in 1999, the Yugoslav army moved in. Alarmed by reports of ethnic cleansing, and unable to reach a peace plan with Serbian delegates, NATO retaliated with a U.S.-led bombing campaign against Yugoslav military targets to force acceptance of the peace plan. Hundreds of thousands of people fled continued Serb attacks on Kosovo. Serb military forces withdrew in June, and NATO sent an international peacekeeping force to Kosovo.

As details of Serb atrocities became known, prosecutors for the World Court at the Hague indicted Milosevic for war crimes as commander of the Yugoslav armed forces. Defeated in his bid for reelection in 2000, Slobodan Milosevic was arrested by the Yugoslav government in 2001, and turned over to the World Court. He was tried at the Hague, in Holland, in 2002. Other Yugoslav leaders accused of war crimes were also arrested and sent to the World Court for trial.

Land Mines

The 1997 Nobel Peace Prize was awarded to the International Campaign to Bar Land Mines. There are 110 million active land mines hidden in more than 80 countries, claiming 26,000 victims, mostly civilians, each year. The poorest people, including many children, have suffered savage injuries such as loss of limbs and bone infections. Most victims in the 1980s and 1990s were in Africa (Somalia), Asia (Vietnam), Central America (El Salvador and Nicaragua), and Europe (Bosnia). After the fighting stops, the deadly land mines remain in place. Some 55 nations manufacture antipersonnel mines, with the United States being the biggest producer.

A 1997 Oslo Treaty to prohibit the production and use of antipersonnel mines was ratified by more than 100 countries. The United States failed to sign, demanding exceptions to the total ban imposed by the treaty.

The United Nations at 50

During World War II, Allied leaders took steps to establish a system for permanent world peace after the war. The 1945 Charter of the United Nations was adopted unanimously by its 50 charter members in San Francisco. Its purposes are to maintain international peace and security, to develop friendly relations among nations, and to further international cooperation in solving economic, social, cultural and humanitarian problems. By 1995 the UN had 185 member states, from small Pacific island atolls to China, with 20 percent of the world's population.

The term **peacekeeping** does not appear in the UN charter, but resolution of disputes has always held a high priority. Its member states contribute troops for individual missions of collective security. During its first half-century, the United Nations has dispatched more than 750,000 peacekeepers on almost 40 missions around the world, at a cost of $14 billion. In 1995, 67,000 peacekeepers were deployed in such areas as Bosnia, Cyprus, Haiti, Israel and Lebanon, Iraq and Kuwait, India and Pakistan, and Rwanda. Although some UN peacekeeping missions have been more successful than others, some Americans fear that ineffectual intervention in a place like Bosnia (in the former Yugoslavia) could involve the United States in a very bloody and useless conflict.

Less controversial has been the work of UN specialized agencies like the World Health Organization (WHO), which helped to eliminate smallpox worldwide by 1980, and the United Nations Children's Fund (UNICEF).

UNICEF programs have brought the most basic, life-saving health care to the world's poorest children for very little money. An example is producing oral rehydration sachets—packets of salt and sugar for mixing with water, at a cost of 10 cents apiece—in 60 different nations. Adding the right amount of glucose and salt allows water to stay in the digestive tract long enough to be absorbed. UNICEF has trained armies of local women who monitor the weight of babies, provide oral rehydration therapy, promote breast feeding, and vaccinate children against measles and other diseases such as yaws and tuberculosis. By the year 2000 the agency hoped to eradicate polio worldwide. For the most part, the world's children today are dramatically healthier, better fed, better educated, and more likely to survive to adulthood than 50 years ago, before the work of UNICEF and WHO.

In addition to the obvious problems of peacekeeping, the United Nations faced two other serious issues in the late 1990s: the failure of the United States to pay over $1 billion in overdue dues and the need to reform the inefficient UN bureaucracy. Some members of Congress blamed the second problem for their failure to deal with the first.

Fifty Years Later—Echoes of the G.I. Bill

In 1944 Congress passed the G.I. Bill to subsidize education and home buying for returning World War II veterans. This law profoundly helped shape modern America by building a middle class. In 1940, only one in nine Americans was a high school graduate. There were fewer than 1.5 million college students, and only one in 20 had a college degree. All the veterans were back to civilian life by 1946, and a year later the 1.6 million veterans enrolled in college were 49 percent of all registered students. Sixty percent of the veterans enrolled in science and engineering programs. By the time the program ended in 1956, 2.2 million veterans had gone to college, 3.5 million had gone to technical school, and 700,000 had received off-campus agricultural instruction. By 1990 there were 14 million Americans in college and one in five Americans had a degree. The G.I. Bill contributed mightily to making college a middle-class expectation.

In 1940 two-thirds of Americans were renters. By 1949, partly because of subsidized loans for veterans, 60 percent of Americans were homeowners. In places like Levittown, Long Island, a basic tract house could then be bought for $8,000, a bargain at a time when the average family income was about $2,500.

The Marshall Plan Turns 50

The Marshall Plan has been a foreign policy triumph for the United States. From 1948 to 1952, this country contributed billions of dollars to rebuild western Europe after World War II. U.S. actions were based on those nations pledging their own resources to the effort as well as international cooperation. The result is an economically integrated European Union and political cooperation through the Parliament of Europe. France and Germany, once bitter enemies, are at the center of this growing organization which has torn down internal trade barriers. The cooperation that started with the Marshall Plan now extends to the free movement throughout the European Union of persons, goods, and capital.

NATO Expansion (1949–2002)

NATO was successful in promoting military cooperation among its members during the Cold War and in preventing further Soviet expansion in Europe. Although the Soviet Union collapsed by 1990, President Clinton led the NATO alliance to extend membership invitations in 1997 to the Czech Republic, Poland, and Hungary. NATO expansion is a response to three strategic challenges:

1] to enhance the relationship between the United States and a Europe becoming more democratic, including countries that had been in the Soviet sphere (e.g., the Czech Republic, Poland, and Hungary).

2] to engage the new Russia in a cooperative relationship with that Europe. (In July 1997 a NATO-Russia Founding Act was signed, providing a joint council for regular consultations regarding security matters of mutual concern.) NATO's expansion placed the alliance and the United States at the center of a wider regional security system to which Russia is related.

3] to reinforce the habits of democracy and the practices of peace in Central Europe. The very possibility of membership has already encouraged a number of countries to step up their internal reforms and improve relations with one another. Romania and Slovenia are among them.

Critics of NATO expansion point to Russian resentment of this military alliance on its borders. Even though Russia can consult with a growing NATO, Russia is still not a member. (See pg. 277.)

At the 2002 NATO meeting in Prague, capital of the Czech Republic, seven new members in Central and Eastern Europe were invited to join the 19 existing ones. All the invitees had been behind the former Iron Curtain as communist states or satellites of the Soviet Union. These nations include the Baltic states of Lithuania, Latvia, and Estonia, as well as Bulgaria, Romania, Slovakia, and Slovenia.

A unanimous statement committed the alliance to taking "effective action to assist and support" the United Nations' efforts to disarm Iraq of its remaining weapons of mass destruction (See also pg. 277.)

George Walker Bush 2001-

1946-

REPUBLICAN

Vice-President   RICHARD CHENEY
Secretary of State   COLIN POWELL

BUSH'S PUBLIC SERVICE BEFORE HE BECAME PRESIDENT

Governor of Texas (1995-2000)

MAJOR ITEMS DURING BUSH'S ADMINISTRATION

The Election of 2000
The Bush Team
The Bush Tax Cut
A Difficult Economy
Senate Power Shift
The Bush-Cheney Energy Plan
Corporate Scandals
Bush and the Environment
Terrorist Acts Against Americans
September 11, 2001
Afghanistan and the Taliban

The Roots of Muslim Rage
Bush, Israel, and the Palestinians
An Anthrax Mystery
Free Trade or Protectionism?
The Election of 2002
Department of Homeland Security
Iraq, the United States, and the United Nations
The United States, Russia, and NATO
The Roads Not Taken
Pending Issues

The Election of 2000

Heavily financed by big business, Texas Governor **George W. Bush** had no serious opposition for the Republican nomination for President. He campaigned with a slogan of "compassionate conservatism," appearing to lean away from his right-wing support. The extreme right wing of the party was represented by the candidacy of Patrick Buchanan, a journalist, media commentator, and former Nixon aide.

Bush was helped by the independent candidacy of consumer advocate Ralph Nader, who claimed there was no difference between Gore and Bush. Nader took enough votes away from Gore in Florida alone to help elect Bush, who carried that state by just over 500 votes.

In this extremely close election, **Al Gore** had a national plurality of half a million popular votes cast and counted. However, when the U.S. Supreme Court acted to stop all vote recounts in Florida, it effectively gave the electoral votes of Florida, and the presidency, to Mr. Bush.

	2000 Popular Vote	Electoral Vote
George W. Bush	50,459,211	271
Albert Gore	51,003,894	267
Ralph Nader	2,834,410	0
Patrick Buchanan	446,743	0

In the presidential election of 2000, voter turnout as a percentage of those eligible inched up 2.2 percent from 1996. That meant that 105,399,000 people voted in 2000, 51.2 percent of the eligible electorate, compared with 96,278,000 in 1996, 49 percent of eligible voters. Half of eligible Americans decided not to vote, even though spending on the presidential election had set a record, and control of the House and the Senate was hanging in the balance. Voter turnout remains at levels 25 percent below the turnout in the 1960s, and each generation of young potential citizens is voting at an even lower rate.

The Bush Team

George W. Bush leaned heavily on leaders of his father's administration (1989–1993) in choosing **Richard Cheney** as Vice-President, **Colin Powell** as Secretary of State, and **Donald Rumsfeld** as Secretary of Defense. From Texas he brought Karl Rove as his chief political advisor, and Condoleeza Rice as National Security Advisor. **John Ashcroft** had to overcome Senate opposition to his right-wing history to be confirmed as Attorney General. Governor Bush had campaigned as a moderate, but once elected, he chose mostly conservative advisors with big business ties; for example, Army Secretary Thomas White had been a major Enron executive and Cheney had been CEO of the Halliburton Company.

The Bush Tax Cut

A major campaign promise became President Bush's first legislative success. Early in 2001, Congress passed his ten-year $1.35 trillion tax cut, based on overly optimistic predictions of continued economic growth and increasing tax revenues. Critics claimed that the tax cuts were unfair, with 60 percent going to the best-off 10 percent of Americans. The wealthiest one percent of Americans alone would receive 45 percent of the Bush tax cut benefits—more than three times as much as the total for the poorest 60 percent of taxpayers. People making $1.1 million a year—the average income for the best-off one percent—would get an annual tax cut of $54,400 each, while the typical taxpayer would get only $550. However, the economy did not cooperate, having begun to contract during the second half of 2000. Unemployment rose with the collapse of high-flying technology and "dot.com" companies. In July 2001, the Treasury Department announced that it would borrow the money (by selling Treasury securities) to pay for the $38 billion in income tax rebates—up to $600 a couple or $300 for individuals—to be given to taxpayers later that year as part of President Bush's tax cut. Large federal budget surpluses of the previous few years were then replaced with looming budget deficits for years to come, brought on by the tax cuts, the recession, and the effects of the terrorist attacks of September 2001. (See pg. 275.)

A Difficult Economy

Early in the new Bush administration, the U.S. economy began to look weak after ten years of growth. The Federal Reserve System lowered short-term interest rates eleven times in 2001 to help maintain consumer spending, especially for automobiles and housing. However, businesses had overbuilt in the boom times of the late 1990s, and companies were stuck with too much capacity. For one technology example, only 25 percent of the Boston area's fiber-optic capacity was then being used.

After the terrorist attacks, the financial markets plummeted. Back in October of 1987, the stock market dropped more than 20 percent in one day, but only 20 percent of U.S. households directly held stocks or stock funds. In 2001, more than 50 percent did, so when the stock market fell, more people were poorer than a year earlier. Consumer confidence dropped, and fewer people were eager to make major purchases.

In the spring of 2002, statistical indicators pointed to an end of the recession, but unemployment figures were still at a high 6 percent—a jobless recovery?

Senate Power Shift

The 107th Congress convened in January 2001, with the Republicans controlling both houses. In the House of Representatives, the GOP held a majority over Democrats of 222 to 211. While the Senate was equally divided 50-50, the Republican Vice-President, presiding over the Senate, held the tie-breaking vote. The President seemed to have a green light to move his conservative agenda, including a reversal of Clinton conservation measures, and increasing domestic fossil fuel production.

In May 2001, U.S. Senator James Jeffords of Vermont bolted the Republican Party and became an independent aligned with the Democrats, giving them a 51-49 Senate majority. Before that, moving legislation in Congress was a deal made within the Republican party. Afterward, legislation could move forward only if both sides showed a willingness to compromise.

The Bush-Cheney Energy Plan

In the spring of 2001, Vice-President Richard Cheney gathered an energy task force to draw up an energy policy for the nation. Their plan proposed increasing energy production by expanding exploration and drilling for fossil fuels, and streamlining power plant approval. Conspicuously missing were calls for energy conservation (as by increasing auto gas mileage efficiency), and environmental concerns. In clear defiance of the law, Mr. Cheney at first refused to turn over to Congress information about the members of his energy task force. Those members were representatives of the energy industry, which strongly supported the 2000 Bush-Cheney ticket. The plan looked as if it were written by and for the companies that advised Cheney's task force.

Corporate Scandals

Enron

Enron, an energy company started in 1985, had become the seventh largest U.S. corporation when it imploded late in 2001 in the largest bankruptcy filing until then. Government investigation revealed various problems:

- Enron's top leaders were the heaviest contributors to the election of Texas Governor and then U.S. President George W. Bush.

- Enron contributed to the election campaigns of a majority of the members of the 107th Congress (2001-2002)—250 members, both Republican and Democratic.

- The story of Enron's collapse is about the abuse of corporate power. Top executives were allowed to sell off hundreds of millions of dollars of the company's stock before it became worthless. At that point, employees and most shareholders took devastating losses.

- During the fall of 2001, Enron employees whose 401(k) retirement accounts were filled with company stock watched helplessly as constant bad news wiped out their value. A company bookkeeping rule barred them from cashing out. Within a year, Enron's stock price had plummeted from $80 to $.67. Enron's failure eliminated $67 billion in shareholder value.

- In December 2000, Texas Senator Phil Gramm helped engineer stealth-like approval of a bill that exempted energy commodity trading from government regulation, and from public disclosure and scrutiny. Gramm's wife, Wendy, a former government official, became a member of Enron's board of directors, and earned well over a million dollars from Enron from 1993 to 2001.

- After California deregulated energy sales, Enron suddenly and enormously inflated the price of its electricity, deliberately creating the illusion of power shortages to gouge consumers.

- Arthur Andersen, one of the nation's five largest accounting firms, was Enron's auditor. Rather than acting as the public's policeman, Andersen signed off on dubious Enron accounting practices, including hundreds of secret offshore partnerships that did not show up as debt on the company books. Enron paid no federal income tax for four of the five last years before its collapse.

- When it became known that the government was investigating Enron, Andersen employees shredded documents related to their dealings with the troubled firm. This led to the government indicting Arthur Andersen for obstruction of justice. Andersen was convicted, and was ruined.

The Enron scandal was the catalyst for Congress to finally pass a campaign finance reform bill to eliminate unregulated soft money contributions by corporations, unions, and wealthy individuals. However, legal challenges to the new law promptly appeared.

WorldCom

Accounting mischief at other major corporations soon surfaced. In 2002, WorldCom, the largest handler of Internet data and the second-largest long-distance telephone company (including MCI), admitted that it had misreported $7 billion in expenses to reduce costs and increase earnings. For several years WorldCom reported profits when it was actually losing money. The imaginary profits led to large bonuses for executives, and to stockbrokers promoting the company. Hurt by its accounting scandal and huge real debt, WorldCom submitted the largest bankruptcy filing in U.S. history—more than twice the size of Enron's—in July 2002. Several company executives pleaded guilty to charges of fraud and conspiracy, while 17,000 WorldCom employees lost their jobs. Shareholders are expected to be virtually wiped out.

Congress reacted to this crisis in corporate ethics and government regulation by passing the Sarbanes-Oxley Act of 2002, which:

1] established an accounting oversight board to monitor accountants and firms that audit public companies. That replaced a system of self-regulation under which no major accounting firm ever failed a routine inspection.

2] banned accounting firms from offering consulting services to the companies they audit. That is to minimize the conflicts of interest that occur when firms depend on their audit clients for the more lucrative consulting fees.

The Fallout

With investors uneasy about corporate accounting scandals, economic weakness, the falling dollar, and the possibility of future terrorist attacks (see pg. 275), stock prices slid throughout the first three quarters of 2002. The domestic financial scandals shook the faith of investors in the honesty of Wall Street and corporate America, and led some foreign investors to reduce their holdings of United States stocks.

Bush and the Environment

The new President reversed course on many of Bill Clinton's environmental regulations:

- He quashed higher standards for arsenic in drinking water.

- He rolled back new energy-efficiency rules for air conditioners.

- He removed protection for millions of "roadless" acres in national forests.

- His first budget cut funds for renewable energy research by 50 percent.

- Conservation spending was cut by 25 percent.

- He rolled back Clinton rules for wetlands and streams in the interest of developers and mining companies, helping them avoid public scrutiny and possibly jeopardizing ecologically sensitive areas.

- He opposed mandatory reductions on carbon dioxide emissions from electric power plants—the core element in confronting the climate-change disorders addressed by the Kyoto Protocol. (See pg. 264, Global Warming.) Coal-using power plants include some of the biggest single sources of air pollution in the country, including smog-causing nitrogen oxides.

- He rejected U.S. participation in the 1997 Kyoto Protocol, in which 160 nations pledged to reduce their emissions of heat-trapping gases into the atmosphere. (See also pg. 264, Global Warming.)

- The Bush administration permitted Appalachia's coal companies to mine the tops off mountains, and to dump the debris down the mountainside into adjacent valleys and the streams that run through them.

Terrorist Acts Against Americans

During the 1980s and 1990s, the U.S. government failed to protect its citizens from foreign terrorist harm despite warnings from allies and a steady beat of major, organized terrorist incidents over 18 years!

- In 1983, there was a car-bombing of the U.S. Embassy in Beirut, Lebanon. In addition, a U.S. Marine base in Beirut was bombed by Arab terrorists, killing 241 Americans. Washington's response was to pull U.S. troops out of Lebanon. They had been stationed there after the United States demanded that Israeli troops leave Lebanon.

- In 1988, a Pan-American passenger jet blew up over Lockerbie, Scotland, killing all 270 aboard. The United States determined that Libya was responsible, but it took more than ten years to bring two alleged Libyan intelligence agents to trial by a Scottish court in Holland.

- In 1993, a truck bomb destroyed several stories of an underground garage in the World Trade Center in New York City, killing six and injuring 200. (See also pg. 261.) Key leaders were captured, brought to trial, and convicted. The name of **Osama bin Laden** turned up on a list of donors to an Islamic charity that helped finance the bombing.

- In November 1995, five Americans were murdered at an army base in Riyadh, Saudi Arabia, with no American military response.

- In June 1996, 19 Americans were murdered at another army base in Saudi Arabia. The Saudis were more of a hindrance than a help, killing suspects before they could be questioned by U.S. investigators.

- In August 1998, the U.S. embassies in the African nations of Kenya and Tanzania were bombed, killing 257 people, including 12 Americans. Faced with appearing impotent, and fearful if it did not react quickly, Washington chose to respond with cruise missile attacks against targets in the Sudan and in Afghanistan. Five defendants were convicted in the case. Despite the connection shown between **al-Qaeda** and anti-American terrorism, the State Department did not then list al-Qaeda as a terrorist organization.

• In October 2000, a U.S. destroyer, the *Cole*, was fueling up off the coast of Yemen (near the southern tip of the Arabian peninsula) when a small boat motored alongside. The two men in the boat waved, then blew themselves and their explosives-filled vessel to bits. The explosion blew a 40 by 40-foot hole in the port side of the destroyer. Seventeen American sailors died, and 39 were seriously wounded.

September 11, 2001

The New York Times wrote: "On a crystalline morning, four jetliners commandeered by 19 hijackers took deadly aim. The quarter-mile high towers of the World Trade Center exploded in an all-consuming fire. By the time the twin towers collapsed, more than 2,900 people were dead, lower Manhattan was covered in ash-laden debris and the lot where two of the world's tallest buildings had stood for more than a generation had a new name, ground zero. Then another hijacked airplane plowed deep into the side of the Pentagon [U.S. military defense headquarters], killing 189. The fourth plane crashed in western Pennsylvania, killing 44 people [on board], after some of the passengers apparently fought with the hijackers." That plane's target may have been the White House or the Capitol. Americans and their friends abroad admired the selfless courage of the firemen, policemen, rescue workers, and "ordinary" citizens who risked (and gave) their lives for others in New York, Washington, and in the air space over Pennsylvania.

The United States was attacked because it is the world leader in promoting democratic government and modern society. We are at war with religious fundamentalism and autocratic governments that sponsor terrorism against the West, whose power and values threaten the dictators' hold on their people. The external enemy is used to unite their subjects behind the vicious leaders, and to blind those subjects to their lack of economic opportunity and freedom.

In his finest speech, President George W. Bush identified the major terrorist suspects, Osama bin Laden and his al-Qaeda group of Islamic fundamentalists. Their leaders have distorted Moslem teachings

about martyrdom, and encourage young men to wage holy war (jihad) against their enemies as suicide bombers. The President called for an international coalition against both terrorists and those nations that support terrorism. The United States and Great Britain led in striking at al-Qaeda fighters and hideouts in Afghanistan, where the Taliban government had encouraged and protected them.

A major goal of bin Laden, often stated publicly, was to force the United States to disengage completely from the Middle East by inducing fear in the general public, which would turn into pressure on the government. How many of the terrorist acts listed above would fit that pattern?

Afghanistan and the Taliban

Afghanistan has a long history of fierce resistance to attempts at foreign rule. A Russian invasion in 1979 was met with determined opposition by guerrilla warriors. With American assistance and training, the Afghan mountain tribesmen defeated the Russians in what was a cold war battle against the spread of communism. After the defeat of the Soviets, the Taliban seized control of Afghanistan in 1990 and imposed a strict Islamic regime. They welcomed Osama bin Laden, providing a safe haven and training camps for his al-Qaeda terrorists. Munitions were stored in the mountain caves used earlier by anti-Russian fighters.

By the end of 2000, the Taliban regime was ousted by American, Afghan, and allied forces. An interim Afghan government was installed pending elections. However, al-Qaeda remained a challenging adversary. Their members were organized in cells, dispersed throughout Moslem (Muslim) areas of the world. They had a fanatical desire to harm the United States, and a willingness to die in the attempt.

The Roots of Muslim Rage

To understand the core of Muslim anger at the West, we must look at the history of Islam, their religion. Followers of Islam enjoyed a millennium of glory from the 7th to the 17th centuries, including hundreds of years when Western Europe was in the Dark Ages. That faith conquered much of the Eastern world, dominated the global economy through trade, and brought civilization to high flower in science, medicine, and classical learning. In recent centuries, the Muslim world has lost almost all of the above, as Western (Christian) societies leaped ahead. Many Muslims have a self-perception as the inheritors of a great civilization. This is in strong contrast to the present Islamic world, impoverished in almost everything but terrorism and despotism, causing the resentment against the success of America.

Many Muslims appear unable or unwilling to confront the evidence of what has happened to Islam in Arab lands. The Arab defeat by Israel in 1967 marked the transformation of Arabic Islam. The new radical Islam found in Israel an excuse for its own failures to battle overpopulation, poverty, and illiteracy in the Muslim world.

Autocratic governments in the Middle East have been unable or unwilling to liberalize their economies and societies in the way that developing East Asia has done. Singapore, Hong Kong, and South Korea have made extraordinary economic achievements since the end of World War II, but conservative rulers and their Muslim followers see such modernization as uncontrollable Westernization. This fear of becoming "Americanized" has paralyzed Arab civilization. Their people see the TV shows and fast food shops, but neither increased opportunities nor increased openness in their societies. Islamic fundamentalism is a path away from the West, and permits the old order to remain in power.

Bush, Israel, and the Palestinians

A wave of Palestinian homicide and suicide bombings against Israelis began as soon as the Camp David talks collapsed during the summer of 2000. (See also pg. 266.) At first, President Bush took a hands-off approach to the Arab-Israeli problem, but the escalating violence of the "**intifada**" and Israeli retaliation brought the United States back into the picture. Bush then demanded that Arafat dismantle the terrorist network, denounce suicide bombings, and tell his people in Arabic that the violence must end. Shown evidence of Arafat's direct complicity in terror operations, President Bush, in July 2002, called for the removal of Arafat from power, the remaking of the corrupt Palestinian Authority, and Israeli cooperation with a developing P.A. or its alternative.

An Anthrax Mystery

Anthrax is a highly infectious, usually fatal disease of cattle and sheep, which can also be transmitted to humans. In recent years, anthrax has been produced and stored as a possible weapon of biological warfare. It has also been studied to find an antidote.

In October 2001, within weeks of the terrorist attacks on the Pentagon and New York's World Trade Center, anthrax spores were discovered in mail sent to public officials and to others. Anthrax contaminated postal facilities in the areas of Washington, D.C., and New Jersey, and caused at least eight cases of lung disease. Five of those were fatal.

A year later, the source of those anthrax attacks was still a mystery. What was learned was that the Defense Department—without consulting the White House—had secretly produced anthrax, and had possibly put the United States in violation of the international Biological Weapons Convention.

Free Trade or Protectionism?

Tariffs on Steel

In March 2002, President Bush imposed hefty import tariffs of up to 30 percent on a range of foreign steel products in order to aid the ailing United States steel industry. While the protective tariffs do not apply to Canada or Mexico, our NAFTA free trade partners, other foreign steel producers from Europe to South Korea resent them. The 15-member European Union filed a complaint challenging the tariffs as violating our international trade treaties. The World Trade Organization has international authority as a court in such trade disputes among its 144 member nations. Other complaints would follow.

At a time when the United States was working hard to maintain international cohesion in the fight against terrorism, any action that frayed the ties among allies, and seemed to violate the spirit of international agreements could create major problems.

Agricultural Subsidies

In May 2002, President Bush reversed a six-year Republican effort to cut farm subsidies. He signed a congressional bill that raised such subsidies by at least $83 billion. With Mr. Bush pressing other countries to knock down their trade barriers and expand open markets, his approval of an 80 percent increase in U.S. government farm subsidies was widely viewed as a move in the opposite direction. These subsidies were portrayed by their supporters as a necessary safety net for American farmers. Critics called the action an election-year welfare program to win midwestern votes.

The large increase in subsidies became a magnet for international complaints against the United States. The European Union's foreign policy chief declared that the new American agricultural policy had created the most profound division between Europe and the United States, worse than disputes over steel tariffs, the Kyoto environmental treaty, or the international criminal court. At a June 2002 United Nations conference on hunger, developing countries pointed to the huge new subsidies to American farmers as one of the biggest obstacles to creating vital opportunities for their own farmers to climb out of poverty.

The heart of the dispute is that by underwriting its largest farmers, the United States will flood the world market with inexpensive corn, wheat, rice, and soybeans, which are sold at half the cost to produce the grain. That leads to artificially low world prices, which in turn undercuts grain produced in countries that do not give subsidies. Domestic markets are ruined for producers overseas and their chances of making inroads into foreign markets are reduced. American farm exports drive down prices paid to local farmers in developing countries, reduce rural family income around the world, and push farmers off the land and into overcrowded cities.

The Election of 2002

In November 2002, the Republican Party of President Bush regained control of the U.S. Senate, and expanded its control of the House of Representatives. No other president since Franklin D. Roosevelt in 1934 had seen his party gain ground in both houses of Congress two years into his first term. President Bush had campaigned vigorously for Republican candidates in close races, stressing the war on terrorism rather than a faltering economy.

Department of Homeland Security

President Bush proposed creation of a national Department of Homeland Security to bring together all the major domestic security agencies into a single department and under effective leadership. The new department would include border protection by such agencies as the Coast Guard, the Customs Service, and the Immigration and Naturalization Service. Previously, the Coast Guard was in the Transportation Department, the Customs Service came under the Treasury Department, and the I.N.S. belonged to the Department of Justice. Disaster response offices such as the Federal Emergency Management Agency would also be included. The head of the Department of Homeland Security would be a member of the President's Cabinet.

Congress passed the necessary legislation within a month of the 2002 elections providing for the largest reorganization of the federal government since World War II. It collected in a single department tasks previously spread over more than twenty federal agencies, involving 170,000 employees.

Iraq, the United States, and the United Nations

It had been more than four years since the last U.N. weapons inspectors had been able to search for Iraqi weapons of mass destruction. President Bush, prior to the U.S. midterm elections in 2002, demanded a resumption of the U.N. search for Iraq's remaining nuclear, chemical, and biological weapons, and threatened the use of military force should Iraq refuse to cooperate. In November 2002, all 15 members of the U.N. Security Council, including Syria, approved a new resolution that Iraq submit to unrestricted inspections of its weapons arsenal or face "serious consequences." Iraq's dictator, Saddam Hussein, seemed to agree to the Security Council demands, and U.N. weapons inspectors were again dispatched to Iraq.

The United States, Russia, and NATO

In May 2002, the United States and Russia ended a long period of confrontation that had lasted since the end of World War II in 1945. During that war we were allies against Nazi Germany. President Bush and Russian President Vladimir Putin signed the biggest nuclear reduction treaty in history, a postscript to their nations' Cold War rivalry. Over ten years, each would reduce its arsenal of strategic nuclear warheads from some 6,000 to about 2,000, a two-thirds cut.

The agreement seemed to accept the U.S. intention to withdraw from the 1972 Anti-Ballistic Missile Treaty in order to be free to develop a national missile defense system. Remaining issues included Russia's nuclear ties to Iran, and the protection and safe storage of dismantled nuclear warheads.

The day after Russia signed the 2002 nuclear reduction treaty with the United States, the North Atlantic Treaty Organization welcomed Russia into a new partnership, signaling a constructive new era in relations between Russia and the West. Russia would become an equal partner for discussions and actions with the 19 NATO members on issues including terrorism, arms control, and handling international crises. Russia was not (yet) a NATO member. The alliance remained free to add new members and decide about combat operations.

Considering that NATO was created in 1949 to defend war-weakened Western Europe against potential Soviet attack, and served throughout the Cold War as a symbol of opposition to Moscow, this agreement showed how much closer Russia had moved toward Europe and the United States since the disintegration of the Soviet Union in 1991.

The Roads Not Taken

Tobacco

Neither the Bill Clinton nor George W. Bush administration pursued court cases against major tobacco companies to recoup the government costs of smoke-related illnesses. Some 42 states did so, and they collected. (See also pg. 263.)

In 2002, the World Health Organization drew up a draft of an international treaty that would phase in bans on cigarette advertising and sports sponsorships by tobacco companies. The health agency says tobacco use is a serious threat to global health, with more than four million people dying from smoking-related diseases each year.

Stem Cell Research

Human stem cells have the ability to grow into various kinds of body tissue, and are potentially important in treating such diseases as Parkinson's and Alzheimer's. The Bush administration has limited government aid for stem cell research because antiabortionists oppose the use of fetal stem cells. Meanwhile, other countries are proceeding with such study.

Security vs. Civil Liberties

After the attacks of 9/11/01, the Justice Department detained an estimated 1,200 people. It refused to release their names and locations and insisted on conducting hearings in secret. It argued in court that an American-born detainee should not be allowed to talk to a lawyer. Making public the names of detainees, holding open immigration proceedings, and providing access to counsel are fundamental parts of our system of justice, not legal niceties. It is difficult to find a proper balance between security and civil rights.

Cuban Boycott

In 2002, former President Jimmy Carter visited Cuba and met with its communist President, Fidel Castro. Castro and his followers had ousted former Cuban dictator Juan Batista in 1959, and he has ruled that Caribbean island ever since. Carter urged an end to the U.S. boycott of trade with Cuba that was first imposed in the early 1960s. Bowing to the political pressure of an anti-Castro Cuban community in the Miami, Florida area, President Bush refused.

This recalls our long isolation from Communist China (1949-1971), until President Nixon's visit there. Today, we have close economic ties with China, and helped China join the World Trade Organization in 2001. Greater commerce with the West may bring political reform in China. It certainly can help build the foundations for change, including a growing middle class.

Family Planning

In July 2002, the Bush administration reversed course and withheld a previously approved $34 million in aid to the United Nations Population Fund. The money was to have been used for family planning and reproductive health services. The government said it would not contribute to a UN agency that it contends provides aid to Chinese agencies that force women to have abortions. However, by law, that United Nations program is already barred from using United States money in China.

Instead, the money was to be distributed by the State Department's own Agency for International Development, which operates in about 80 countries, compared with 142 for the United Nations group. The decision, which came shortly before the 2002 elections, drew warm praise from antiabortion groups. Critics of withholding the money said it would unfairly punish scores of other countries where funds for family planning were needed.

Pending Issues

Affordable Health Care

More than a year and a half into the younger Bush's administration, it had not yet articulated a program of affordable health care for all Americans, despite campaign promises of action.

- More than 40 million people still lacked any health insurance.

- There was no prescription drug coverage for needy senior citizens under Medicare.

- Congress had not yet acted on a patients' bill of rights enabling persons to sue insurance companies that refused them coverage for medically prescribed procedures.

Welfare Reform Renewal

Required renewal of the six-year old welfare reform bill was bogged down by how to provide for day care in order to meet the tough new work requirements that most legislators favored. By mid-2002, government funds for social programs had become scarce.

PART FOUR
SEVEN PRACTICE ACHIEVEMENT TESTS

To make effective use of these tests, consider the following:

The SAT II: United States History test consists of 95-100 multiple-choice questions in which you must select the best answer from the five choices given.

1] The forms used for the questions on this test are similar to those on the College Board SATs and PSATs. There is a danger in becoming accustomed to any form of questioning; it encourages careless reading of the questions so that deviations from the familiar pattern go undetected.
Therefore:

- Always read every question with deliberate care. If you must hurry, make up your mind quickly about the answer, but be sure you have the question accurately in mind.

- For questions based on graphs, pictures, and cartoons, first read the question, then read the title, and only then study the graphics. Use your common sense.

- Do not consult answer keys while working on the questions.

- Where you have a wrong answer (or merely a lucky right one), use the Contents and Index to search the text for the correct answer. The tests and answer explanations include time periods, names of people, places, events, etc., which can lead you to the answer in its meaningful setting. Then you not only know—you also understand. You may also pick up additional useful information along the way.

2] Learning why an answer is incorrect is a valuable learning technique. Approach the tests as teaching, as well as measuring, devices.

3] Some answers must be judgmental rather than factual responses. Differences of opinion as to the best choice for an answer will occur. In such cases, try to see why the choice you make may be considered a weaker one than the response designated as the answer.

4] Some questions demand knowledge in depth about a particular topic or circumstance. Such questions can serve as an effective starting point for a full discussion of facts and evaluations. Using questions can be much more beneficial than merely going over them to compile a score.

5] Review Test-Taking Techniques on page (XII).

ANSWER SHEET: TEST 1

1. Ⓐ Ⓑ Ⓒ Ⓓ Ⓔ	16. Ⓐ Ⓑ Ⓒ Ⓓ Ⓔ	31. Ⓐ Ⓑ Ⓒ Ⓓ Ⓔ
2. Ⓐ Ⓑ Ⓒ Ⓓ Ⓔ	17. Ⓐ Ⓑ Ⓒ Ⓓ Ⓔ	32. Ⓐ Ⓑ Ⓒ Ⓓ Ⓔ
3. Ⓐ Ⓑ Ⓒ Ⓓ Ⓔ	18. Ⓐ Ⓑ Ⓒ Ⓓ Ⓔ	33. Ⓐ Ⓑ Ⓒ Ⓓ Ⓔ
4. Ⓐ Ⓑ Ⓒ Ⓓ Ⓔ	19. Ⓐ Ⓑ Ⓒ Ⓓ Ⓔ	34. Ⓐ Ⓑ Ⓒ Ⓓ Ⓔ
5. Ⓐ Ⓑ Ⓒ Ⓓ Ⓔ	20. Ⓐ Ⓑ Ⓒ Ⓓ Ⓔ	35. Ⓐ Ⓑ Ⓒ Ⓓ Ⓔ
6. Ⓐ Ⓑ Ⓒ Ⓓ Ⓔ	21. Ⓐ Ⓑ Ⓒ Ⓓ Ⓔ	36. Ⓐ Ⓑ Ⓒ Ⓓ Ⓔ
7. Ⓐ Ⓑ Ⓒ Ⓓ Ⓔ	22. Ⓐ Ⓑ Ⓒ Ⓓ Ⓔ	37. Ⓐ Ⓑ Ⓒ Ⓓ Ⓔ
8. Ⓐ Ⓑ Ⓒ Ⓓ Ⓔ	23. Ⓐ Ⓑ Ⓒ Ⓓ Ⓔ	38. Ⓐ Ⓑ Ⓒ Ⓓ Ⓔ
9. Ⓐ Ⓑ Ⓒ Ⓓ Ⓔ	24. Ⓐ Ⓑ Ⓒ Ⓓ Ⓔ	39. Ⓐ Ⓑ Ⓒ Ⓓ Ⓔ
10. Ⓐ Ⓑ Ⓒ Ⓓ Ⓔ	25. Ⓐ Ⓑ Ⓒ Ⓓ Ⓔ	40. Ⓐ Ⓑ Ⓒ Ⓓ Ⓔ
11. Ⓐ Ⓑ Ⓒ Ⓓ Ⓔ	26. Ⓐ Ⓑ Ⓒ Ⓓ Ⓔ	41. Ⓐ Ⓑ Ⓒ Ⓓ Ⓔ
12. Ⓐ Ⓑ Ⓒ Ⓓ Ⓔ	27. Ⓐ Ⓑ Ⓒ Ⓓ Ⓔ	42. Ⓐ Ⓑ Ⓒ Ⓓ Ⓔ
13. Ⓐ Ⓑ Ⓒ Ⓓ Ⓔ	28. Ⓐ Ⓑ Ⓒ Ⓓ Ⓔ	43. Ⓐ Ⓑ Ⓒ Ⓓ Ⓔ
14. Ⓐ Ⓑ Ⓒ Ⓓ Ⓔ	29. Ⓐ Ⓑ Ⓒ Ⓓ Ⓔ	44. Ⓐ Ⓑ Ⓒ Ⓓ Ⓔ
15. Ⓐ Ⓑ Ⓒ Ⓓ Ⓔ	30. Ⓐ Ⓑ Ⓒ Ⓓ Ⓔ	45. Ⓐ Ⓑ Ⓒ Ⓓ Ⓔ

46. Ⓐ Ⓑ Ⓒ Ⓓ Ⓔ	61. Ⓐ Ⓑ Ⓒ Ⓓ Ⓔ	76. Ⓐ Ⓑ Ⓒ Ⓓ Ⓔ
47. Ⓐ Ⓑ Ⓒ Ⓓ Ⓔ	62. Ⓐ Ⓑ Ⓒ Ⓓ Ⓔ	77. Ⓐ Ⓑ Ⓒ Ⓓ Ⓔ
48. Ⓐ Ⓑ Ⓒ Ⓓ Ⓔ	63. Ⓐ Ⓑ Ⓒ Ⓓ Ⓔ	78. Ⓐ Ⓑ Ⓒ Ⓓ Ⓔ
49. Ⓐ Ⓑ Ⓒ Ⓓ Ⓔ	64. Ⓐ Ⓑ Ⓒ Ⓓ Ⓔ	79. Ⓐ Ⓑ Ⓒ Ⓓ Ⓔ
50. Ⓐ Ⓑ Ⓒ Ⓓ Ⓔ	65. Ⓐ Ⓑ Ⓒ Ⓓ Ⓔ	80. Ⓐ Ⓑ Ⓒ Ⓓ Ⓔ
51. Ⓐ Ⓑ Ⓒ Ⓓ Ⓔ	66. Ⓐ Ⓑ Ⓒ Ⓓ Ⓔ	81. Ⓐ Ⓑ Ⓒ Ⓓ Ⓔ
52. Ⓐ Ⓑ Ⓒ Ⓓ Ⓔ	67. Ⓐ Ⓑ Ⓒ Ⓓ Ⓔ	82. Ⓐ Ⓑ Ⓒ Ⓓ Ⓔ
53. Ⓐ Ⓑ Ⓒ Ⓓ Ⓔ	68. Ⓐ Ⓑ Ⓒ Ⓓ Ⓔ	83. Ⓐ Ⓑ Ⓒ Ⓓ Ⓔ
54. Ⓐ Ⓑ Ⓒ Ⓓ Ⓔ	69. Ⓐ Ⓑ Ⓒ Ⓓ Ⓔ	84. Ⓐ Ⓑ Ⓒ Ⓓ Ⓔ
55. Ⓐ Ⓑ Ⓒ Ⓓ Ⓔ	70. Ⓐ Ⓑ Ⓒ Ⓓ Ⓔ	85. Ⓐ Ⓑ Ⓒ Ⓓ Ⓔ
56. Ⓐ Ⓑ Ⓒ Ⓓ Ⓔ	71. Ⓐ Ⓑ Ⓒ Ⓓ Ⓔ	86. Ⓐ Ⓑ Ⓒ Ⓓ Ⓔ
57. Ⓐ Ⓑ Ⓒ Ⓓ Ⓔ	72. Ⓐ Ⓑ Ⓒ Ⓓ Ⓔ	87. Ⓐ Ⓑ Ⓒ Ⓓ Ⓔ
58. Ⓐ Ⓑ Ⓒ Ⓓ Ⓔ	73. Ⓐ Ⓑ Ⓒ Ⓓ Ⓔ	88. Ⓐ Ⓑ Ⓒ Ⓓ Ⓔ
59. Ⓐ Ⓑ Ⓒ Ⓓ Ⓔ	74. Ⓐ Ⓑ Ⓒ Ⓓ Ⓔ	89. Ⓐ Ⓑ Ⓒ Ⓓ Ⓔ
60. Ⓐ Ⓑ Ⓒ Ⓓ Ⓔ	75. Ⓐ Ⓑ Ⓒ Ⓓ Ⓔ	90. Ⓐ Ⓑ Ⓒ Ⓓ Ⓔ

91. Ⓐ Ⓑ Ⓒ Ⓓ Ⓔ
92. Ⓐ Ⓑ Ⓒ Ⓓ Ⓔ
93. Ⓐ Ⓑ Ⓒ Ⓓ Ⓔ
94. Ⓐ Ⓑ Ⓒ Ⓓ Ⓔ
95. Ⓐ Ⓑ Ⓒ Ⓓ Ⓔ
96. Ⓐ Ⓑ Ⓒ Ⓓ Ⓔ
97. Ⓐ Ⓑ Ⓒ Ⓓ Ⓔ
98. Ⓐ Ⓑ Ⓒ Ⓓ Ⓔ

Test 1

___

Directions: Each of the questions or incomplete statements is followed by five suggested answers or completions. Select the one that is best in each case and then blacken the corresponding space on the answer sheet.

Questions 1-2 refer to the following graph.

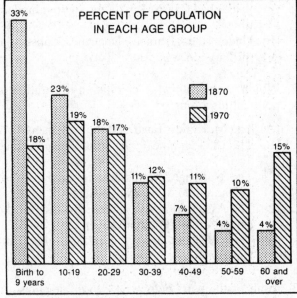

Copyright © 1977 by The New York Times Company.
Reprinted by permission.

1. From 1930 to 1970, the greatest change in the percentage of population occurred within which age group?

    (A) Birth to 9 years   (D) 50-59
    (B) 10-19   (E) 60 and over
    (C) 40-49

2. The information in the graph would be immediately useful to United States government officials concerned with

    (A) finding alternative energy resources
    (B) financing the Social Security system
    (C) planning defense projects
    (D) developing public works programs
    (E) identifying business trends

3. Where does the sole power lie to bring impeachment charges against the President?

    (A) House of Representatives
    (B) Senate
    (C) State legislatures
    (D) Supreme Court
    (E) The two houses of Congress

4. Which of the following statements does NOT represent a typical Federalist viewpoint (1789-1800)?

    (A) If "necessary" in the "implied powers" clause can be interpreted to mean anything less than absolutely necessary, there is then no point at which a line can be drawn, and thus "necessary' may mean anything Congress wants it to mean. Congress can become powerful beyond all intention.
    (B) A bank of the United States would obviously help in carrying into execution such powers of Congress as the collection of taxes, the borrowing of money, and the payment of the public debt.
    (C) We have no obligation to help the French. The situation is so changed by the French Revolution that the Treaty of Alliance made in 1778 no longer holds.
    (D) It is true that the Bank of the United States is proving a good investment for its stockholders, but, more important, it is having a steadying influence on other banks.
    (E) Treaty or no treaty, the important fact is that this new government is too uncertain and too weak to follow any policy other than that of neutrality.

Questions 5-8: Each of these slogans or quotations is associated with a specific individual. Select the name of the correct person.

5. "I am as strong as a bull moose."

    (A) Douglas MacArthur
    (B) Andrew Jackson
    (C) Abraham Lincoln
    (D) Theodore Roosevelt
    (E) Harry S Truman

6. "Liberty and Union, now and forever, one and inseparable."

   (A) Andrew Jackson   (D) James Monroe
   (B) Henry Clay   (E) Daniel Webster
   (C) John Calhoun

7. "In public education the 'separate but equal' doctrine has no place."

   (A) Louis Brandeis   (D) John Sirica
   (B) Felix Frankfurter   (E) Earl Warren
   (C) John Marshall

8. "Speak softly and carry a big stick; you will go far."

   (A) Andrew Jackson
   (B) Abraham Lincoln
   (C) Franklin D. Roosevelt
   (D) Theodore Roosevelt
   (B) Harry S Truman

9. Which of the following is the best expression of the meaning of "dollar diplomacy"?

   (A) Foreign affairs carried out with a sharp eye to curtailing expense.
   (B) Foreign affairs carried out without regard to expense.
   (C) Use of money for bribing foreign agents or for other methods that usually would be considered unethical-except in diplomacy.
   (D) Conducting foreign policy with protection of American investments abroad as its main objective
   (E) A term used to emphasize the inadequate pay received by those who make a career of serving the United States as consuls, ministers, and ambassadors

10. All of the following statements are true about the conflict between President Franklin D. Roosevelt and the Supreme Court that had declared unconstitutional the Agricultural Adjustment Act and the National Industrial Recovery Act EXCEPT

   (A) The extreme complexity of the President's plan was one of the factors that led to its defeat.
   (B) From the beginning, Roosevelt got little support for his plan.
   (C) While Roosevelt was promoting his plan to Congress and the nation, the Supreme Court declared some important New Deal laws to be constitutional.
   (D) Congress refused to pass any law changing the number of Justices on the Supreme Court.

   (E) While Roosevelt was President, he had the opportunity to make so many appointments to the Supreme Court that it was called, by those who didn't like it, a "Roosevelt Court."

11. All of the following statements are true about the Truman Doctrine and the circumstances to which it was directed EXCEPT

   (A) The Truman Doctrine was a unilateral action by the United States.
   (B) Greece and Spain were the principal beneficiaries of the Truman Doctrine.
   (C) Greece had appealed to the UN for help.
   (D) The Soviet Union was pushing toward an outlet and control on the Mediterranean Sea just as had Czarist Russia throughout modern times.
   (E) Under the Truman Doctrine, substantial military aid was sent to Turkey.

12. Which of the following pairs is an illustration of political logrolling?

   (A) The McKinley Tariff and the Adamson Act
   (B) The 1894 Income Tax and the Payne-Aldrich Tariff
   (C) The National Origins Immigration Law of 1929 and the McCarran-Walter Act
   (D) The Assumption Act and the location of the capitol on the Potomac River
   (E) The Wagner-Connery Act and the Taft-Hartley Act

13. In all of the pairs below, the words or phrase in parentheses helps to bring into effect, to support, or to make more effective the item with which it is paired EXCEPT

   (A) The desirability of the acquisition by the United States of the Louisiana Territory (France took Louisiana Territory from Spain)
   (B) Manufacturing in America (Tariff of 1816)
   (C) War between Mexico and Texas (Battle of San Jacinto)
   (D) The Democratic party split between Douglas and Breckinridge (Lecompton Constitution)
   (E) Acceptance of the decision of the Electoral Commission in 1876 (Democratic states of the South)

14. Which of the following events occurred FIRST?

   (A) Admission of California as a state
   (B) First law of Congress outlawing the importation of slaves
   (C) Lincoln's Cooper Union speech

(D) First slaves brought to Virginia
(E) First issue of Garrison's *Liberator*

15. Which of the items in question 14 occurred LAST?

16. Which of the following occurred FIRST?

(A) Missouri Compromise
(B) Lincoln-Douglas debates
(C) Admission of Texas as a state
(D) Emancipation Proclamation went into effect
(E) Firing on Fort Sumter

17. Which of the items in question 16 occurred LAST?

18. Which of the following occurred FIRST?

(A) The beginning of sharecropping
(B) The emergence of tobacco as a commercially important crop
(C) The Agricultural Adjustment Act (AAA)
(D) The emergence of cotton as a commercially important crop
(E) The use of the cotton-picking machine

19. Which of the items in question 18 occurred LAST?

20. Which of the following statements is NOT true concerning the railroad situation during World War I?

(A) The government took over the railroads before the war began.
(B) Under private management, grain was not moved to ships or coal to factories fast enough.
(C) Wilson called a conference of railroad presidents, who then coordinated the efforts of many railroad systems to improve service.
(D) The Adamson Act and the Esch-Cummins Act both dealt with railroads.
(E) The total war record of American railroads was excellent in terms of getting freight moved to the places where it was most needed.

21. One of President Wilson's "Fourteen Points" was reduction of armaments. Which of the following is closest to his stated goal in this respect?

(A) All nations should reduce their armaments by 25 percent three times at five-year intervals. Then they should hold a conference to decide how further to reduce them.

(B) The defeated nations should disarm immediately. The Allies should maintain their armaments until the stability of the postwar period was assured.
(C) Armaments should be reduced to the point where nations had only sufficient forces to maintain police protection against smuggling, piracy, etc., and to maintain domestic tranquility within their borders.
(D) The United States should make the first substantial move toward disarmament as an encouragement for other nations to follow suit.
(E) The United States and Great Britain should pledge sharp reductions in their naval power as an inducement to other nations to move in the same direction.

22. Which of the following statements comes closest to Franklin D. Roosevelt's meaning of the "New Deal"?

(A) These times call for policies that will bring a decent standard of living to the forgotten people at the bottom of the economic pyramid.
(B) It is time for a change, a change that will call forth abundant capital to turn the wheels of industry and activate the channels of trade.
(C) Our policy calls for a full dinner pail for every worker. It can be best accomplished by a moderate protective tariff.
(D) The farmer has too long been aided by federal laws. We need a new deal that favors no segment of our people but assures opportunity for all.
(E) Capital and labor should be treated equally by government.

23. During World War II in Europe, the head of SHAEF was General

(A) Clark
(B) Doolittle
(C) Eisenhower
(D) MacArthur
(E) Montgomery

24. In World War II, the leader who said, "I shall return," was

(A) Prime Minister Chamberlain
(B) Prime Minister Churchill
(C) General Eisenhower
(D) General MacArthur
(E) General Montgomery

25. The 20th-century political leader who promised "peace in our time" was

    (A) Prime Minister Chamberlain
    (B) Prime Minister Churchill
    (C) President Theodore Roosevelt
    (D) President Franklin D. Roosevelt
    (E) President Johnson

26. The last German counteroffensive of World War II occurred at

    (A) the Battle of the Bulge
    (B) Berlin
    (C) Corregidor
    (D) Dunkirk
    (E) Operation Overlord

27. Which of the following items was LEAST involved with the Cold War?

    (A) Berlin airlift
    (B) Truman Doctrine
    (C) NATO
    (D) Marshall Plan
    (E) Potsdam Conference

Questions 28-33 are based on the map of the Caribbean below.

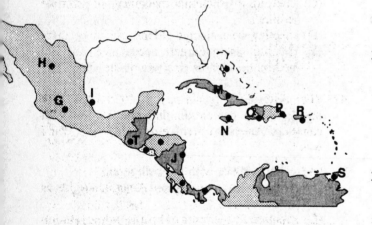

28. A protectorate of the United States from 1901 to 1934, this area was involved in a major crisis between the United States and the Soviet Union in 1962 over offensive missile bases located there.

    (A) G   (D) R
    (B) L   (E) T
    (C) M

29. Acquired by the United States as a result of the Spanish-American War, this island is a free "commonwealth," whose people are United States citizens.

    (A) M   (D) R
    (B) N   (E) S
    (C) P

30. This French-speaking nation, a poorhouse of the Caribbean, was long ruled by the dictatorial Duvalier family.

    (A) M   (D) R
    (B) O   (E) T
    (C) P

31. The capital of the Latin American nation with which the United States does most trade is located at

    (A) G   (D) J
    (B) H   (E) L
    (C) I

32. The country whose contra rebels had United States military support during the 1980s is located at

    (A) J   (D) N
    (B) K   (E) T
    (C) L

33. The United States favored the overthrow of dictator Manuel Noriega in this nation.

    (A) G   (D) L
    (B) J   (E) T
    (C) K

34. According to the United States Constitution, each of the following may be accomplished by a simple majority vote EXCEPT

    (A) Congress declares war.
    (B) The Senate approves the appointment of a Supreme Court Justice.
    (C) The Senate ratifies a treaty.
    (D) Congress passes an immigration law.
    (E) The electoral college must select a President.

35. In all of the pairs below, the words or phrase in parentheses helps to bring into effect, to support, or to make more effective the item with which it is paired EXCEPT

(A) Calhoun's *Exposition and Protest* (Kentucky Resolutions)
(B) Slavery controversy (Mexican War)
(C) Douglas's election to the United States Senate in 1858 (John Brown's raid on Harper's Ferry)
(D) Bland-Allison Act increased production of the silver mines)
(E) A strong demand for war against Spain in 1898 (*New York Journal* and *New York World*)

36. During the period immediately following the American Revolution, a factor that played an important part in the decline of European immigration to the United States was the

(A) instability of the government under the Articles of Confederation
(B) breakdown of the indenture system
(C) refusal of the British to transport Europeans to the United States
(D) economic distress in the United States after the Revolution
(E) Continental System of Napoleon Bonaparte

37. French, Spanish, and English colonies in North America were most similar in that they all

(A) were founded and developed by private enterprise
(B) were permitted representative legislative assemblies
(C) were subjected to mercantilist policies
(D) provided a haven for victims of religious persecution
(E) discouraged the introduction of feudalistic landholding systems

38. The Boston Tea Party was a demonstration of the opposition of colonial merchants to

(A) the high tax on tea
(B) the importation of tea from England
(C) the high tariffs imposed by England on the colonists
(D) high prices charged by the British East India Company
(E) British restrictions on the sale of tea

39. The British Navigation and Trade Laws permitted the American colonists which of the following activities?

I. They could use American-built ships to trade within the empire.
II. They could ship fish from America to southern Europe.
III. They could import sugar and molasses from the British West Indies tax-free.
IV. They could manufacture certain products not manufactured in England.

(A) I only
(B) II only
(C) III only
(D) IV only
(E) All of the above

40. The power of the press to influence American foreign policy is best shown in our relations with

(A) Britain in 1812
(B) Mexico in 1845
(C) France in 1867
(D) Spain in 1898
(E) Korea in 1950

41. During the period 1900-1914, a major concern that influenced our foreign policy was

(A) preventing the outbreak of war in Europe
(B) defending the approaches to the Panama Canal
(C) creating international machinery to arbitrate disputes
(D) meeting the challenge of Japanese imperialism
(E) gaining international acceptance of the neutral concept of freedom of the seas

42. The neutrality legislation of 1935-1937 was based on the contention that one of the chief causes of American involvement in World War I was

(A) economic ties with the belligerent
(B) Wilson's failure to uphold American rights as a neutral
(C) creation by the press of hostile public opinion toward the Central Powers
(D) failure of the Executive and Legislative branches of the government to agree on foreign policy
(E) lack of public support for a policy of collective security

43. Secretary of State George C. Marshall was credited with stemming the spread of communism by his proposal to

(A) create economic conditions favorable to the development of free institutions

(B) unite the free nations in western Europe against Russian attack
(C) give military assistance to nations opposing communism
(D) dispatch technical assistance to the world's underdeveloped nations
(E) impose a trade embargo on the Soviet Union and its satellites.

Questions 44-48 refer to the following cartoon.

The Other Road

HERBLOCK
©1960 THE WASHINGTON POST CO.

from STRAIGHT HERBLOCK (Simon & Schuster, 1964)

44. The umbrella in this cartoon is a symbol of

(A) an act of war
(B) an unsuccessful policy
(C) resistance to Italy
(D) hostility to the Nazis
(E) none of the above

45. Which statement is most clearly implied by the cartoon?

(A) World War II could have been prevented by further appeasement.

(B) Peaceful nations have usually been exploited.
(C) Appeasement has not prevented war.
(D) Humankind progresses despite wars.
(E) Use the United Nations more.

46. The cartoon refers to United States' action at the time of

(A) the construction of missile bases in Cuba
(B) the capture of a U-2 pilot by the Soviet Union
(C) Russia's insistence on the admission of Communist China to the United Nations
(D) the construction of the Berlin Wall
(E) all of the above

47. Which conclusion is supported by the cartoon?

(A) War is inevitable.
(B) Failure to compromise led to World War II.
(C) United States' policy from 1933-1939 was the chief cause of World War II.
(D) Compromise does not guarantee peace.
(E) The road to peace is a rocky one.

48. Which statement best supports the cartoonist's conclusions?

(A) History can be a valuable teacher.
(B) History always repeats itself.
(C) History is merely a record of past events.
(D) History shows that past policies should be continued.
(E) History is bunk.

49. The isolationist policies of the United States in the 1930s was broken down by the danger of

(A) a united Europe under the leadership of Soviet Russia
(B) a united Asia under the leadership of the Chinese People's Republic
(C) a simultaneous two-ocean war against a united Europe and a united Asia
(D) the growth of British trade in Latin America and Canada
(E) German imperialism in the middle East

50. Which statement relative to land in the West following the passage of the Homestead Act is correct?

(A) Since land was available without cost from the government, land speculators were forced out of business.
(B) The best lands were held back by the government for national parks.
(C) Most pioneers still had to purchase their farms.

(D) Preemption rights to land could no longer be claimed by early settlers.

(E) The railroads held their land grants until after the free land was gone in order to secure higher prices.

51. William Seward's chief motivation in his desire to purchase Alaska was

(A) fear that Alaska would develop into a Russian military base

(B) documented reports of Alaska's mineral wealth

(C) rumors of Britain's negotiation for the purchase of this territory

(D) repayment of Russia for its support of the North during the Civil War

(E) a vision of our "manifest destiny" ultimately including all the territory in the north

52. Which settlement best illustrates the thesis that people moved West because of political dissatisfaction?

(A) Stephen Austin—the Brazos and Colorado Rivers

(B) Jacob Astor—the Columbia River

(C) Brigham Young—the Valley of the Great Salt Lake

(D) Jason Lee—the Willamette Valley

(E) Thomas Hooker—the Connecticut River

53. These topics—efforts of the War Hawks, the Fenian raids, filibustering in Central America, and the Ostend Manifesto—might all be cited in an essay dealing with

(A) our relations with Great Britain

(B) wars in which the United States has been involved

(C) influences on our foreign policy prior to the Mexican War

(D) attempts to extend the boundaries of the United States

(E) incidents ultimately settled by arbitration

54. Which delayed the annexation of Hawaii by the United States?

(A) The growth of Japan as a world power.

(B) An impartial investigation of the Hawaiian revolt of 1893.

(C) The prospective annexation of the Philippines.

(D) Economic interests of American planters in the Islands.

(E) The decline of United States' naval power after the Spanish-American War.

55. Which statement best describes the status of America's literary nationalism in the first two decades of the 19th century?

(A) The writings of American political theorists of the late 18th century were just gaining recognition in other countries.

(B) The popularity of the essays of Emerson and Thoreau and the novels of Hawthorne and Melville had gained for the United States the reputation of having a national literature.

(C) Printers were eagerly seeking the writings of Americans in preference to reprinting those of English authors because they realized that American writers of the late 18th century were becoming world-famous.

(D) The "Hartford wits" had assured America of enduring literary fame.

(E) The United States was not as yet known for the richness of its literature, but rather for the lack of it.

56. Which of these factors best accounts for the shift of population westward in the 1940s?

(A) The depression after World War II

(B) Influx of new immigrants

(C) New irrigation projects

(D) Expansion of the aircraft industry

(E) Decline of the steel industry

57. Historians have disagreed concerning Congressional intent in respect to the provision of the Fourteenth Amendment dealing with

(A) reduction of representation in the House of Representatives

(B) repudiation of governmental debts

(C) denial of the right to hold office

(D) the due-process clause

(E) dual citizenship

58. Which answer choice pairs two aspects of United States' foreign policy having generally similar purposes?

(A) Platt Amendment—Teller Resolution

(B) Fourteen Points—Atlantic Charter

(C) Open Door Policy—Theodore Roosevelt Corollary

(D) Truman Doctrine—Johnson Act

(E) Washington Conference (1921-1922)—London Conference (1933)

59. The chief reason some workers in the United States are NOT subject to the Fair Labor Standards Act is that

(A) Congress exempted specific industries from the provisions of the act
(B) provisions of the law allow for local conditions that would make payment of the wage specified uneconomical
(C) enforcement of the act depends on enabling state legislation
(D) the act does not apply to workers covered by collective bargaining agreements
(E) the law is based on the commerce clause of the Constitution.

60. "...the discretion of the President in approving or prescribing codes, and thus enacting laws for the government of trade and industry throughout the country, is virtually unfettered. We think that the code-making authority thus conferred is an unconstitutional delegation of legislative power."

This quotation from a Supreme Court decision was in reference to the

(A) destruction of the Bank of the United States by Andrew Jackson
(B) determination of a Reconstruction policy by Andrew Johnson
(C) opposition to the extension of slavery by Abraham Lincoln
(D) prosecution of the trusts by Theodore Roosevelt
(E) continuance of a New Deal reform by Franklin D. Roosevelt

61. Which two Presidents were charged with trying to use the federal courts for political advantage?

(A) Andrew Jackson and Abraham Lincoln
(B) Grover Cleveland and William McKinley
(C) Herbert Hoover and Theodore Roosevelt
(D) John Adams and Franklin D. Roosevelt
(E) Ulysses S. Grant and William H. Taft

62. A major force promoting the development of a more aggressive, nationalistic United States' foreign policy at the end of the 19th century was the

(A) Populist demand for new markets to drain off agricultural surpluses
(B) religious revival and Christian missionary activity
(C) desire of the leaders of the Republican party to divert attention from the domestic ills of monopoly and concentration of wealth
(D) rapid economic development and industrial growth of the United States
(E) urgency for strengthening the Monroe Doctrine in protection of the newly completed Panama Canal

63. United States' policy toward the People's Republic of China during the 1950s was most like our policy toward

(A) Panama after its revolt from Colombia
(B) France after the overthrow of Louis XVI
(C) Great Britain during the Civil War
(D) Spain at the time of the DeLôme letter
(E) Mexico in 1913-1914

64. Herbert Hoover's victory in 1928 is best accounted for by the

(A) split in the Democratic party
(B) personal attacks on his Democratic opponent
(C) prosperous economic state of the union
(D) strong presidential leadership shown in his previous term
(E) Republican party's stand and record on the Prohibition issue

65. The appointments of Henry L. Stimson and Frank Knox to Franklin D. Roosevelt's Cabinet were unusual because both were

(A) career men
(B) isolationists
(C) Republicans
(D) inexperienced in government
(E) corporation lawyers

66. Why did so few of the immigrants who came to the United States from 1820 to 1860 settle in the South?

(A) There were fewer job opportunities for immigrants in the South than in the North and West.
(B) Anti-alien work laws in some Southern states discouraged new immigrants.
(C) Immigrants lacked the skills necessary for farming in the South.
(D) Travel from Northern ports of entry presented too many difficulties.
(E) Federal land policies were more liberal in the Northwest than in the Southwest.

67. The McCarran-Walter Act of 1952 changed our previous immigration policy by

(A) increasing the Japanese quota
(B) removing the formula that discriminated against southeastern Europeans
(C) doubling the previous 154,000 quota
(D) eliminating political screening of immigrants
(E) establishing special quotas for political refugees

68. Which contributed most to the growth of "big business" in the United States?

(A) Reconstruction Finance Corporation
(B) Fourteenth Amendment
(C) Federal Trade Commission
(D) National Industrial Recovery Act
(E) Tennessee Valley Authority

69. During the last quarter of the 19th century, the federal government's policies on trade, immigration, and business regulation were most favorable to

(A) small-business managers
(B) trade-union leaders
(C) "big business" organizers
(D) agricultural cooperatives
(E) the debtor class

70. In 1896 a business entrepreneur engaged in the manufacture of steel would probably NOT share a banker's point of view on

(A) the gold standard
(B) the protective tariff
(C) the Republican party
(D) interest rates
(E) the Populist party

71. The Federal Reserve System has improved on the earlier national banking system by providing for

(A) a national bank under the direct control of the federal government
(B) complete control over all United States banks
(C) a system for control of consumer credit
(D) greater elasticity of credit and currency
(E) insurance of bank deposits

72. The principal function of the Federal Reserve System is to

(A) facilitate the clearance and collection of checks
(B) provide fiscal agents, custodians, and depositories for the United States Treasury
(C) collect and interpret information bearing on the economic and credit structure of the nation
(D) examine and supervise state member banks
(E) regulate the flow of credit and money

73. Of the approximately eight million white people in the fifteen slave states in 1860, about what percentage were members of families holding one or more slaves?

(A) 85 percent   (D) 25 percent
(B) 65 percent   (E) 5 percent
(C) 45 percent

74. On the basis of a study of the Knights of Labor, a labor leader today would most likely conclude that at the time of the Knights of Labor,

(A) labor leaders were encouraged to run for public office
(B) unions organized on a local basis were more beneficial to the individual worker
(C) unions had to combine with farm organizations to influence the federal legislature
(D) organizing skilled and unskilled workers together lessened the union's effectiveness
(E) unions looked to legislation rather than to strikes to achieve their goals

75. Which statement most accurately describes the traditional attitude of the American Federation of Labor toward political action?

(A) A labor bloc will prove our strongest weapon.
(B) We will reward our friends and punish our enemies.
(C) We will drive a wedge between the two major political parties.
(D) The interests of labor are distinct and separate from politics.
(E) Direct political action through candidates chosen by the labor unions will strengthen our cause.

76. A long-range influence of Samuel Gompers on the American labor movement was his advocacy of

(A) unrestricted immigration
(B) industrial unionism
(C) noninvolvement in party politics
(D) compulsory arbitration of industrial disputes
(E) government regulation of hours and wages

77. The Clayton Antitrust Act was regarded as an important gain by labor because it declared illegal the

(A) method used by President Rutherford B. Hayes to help end the railroad strike of 1877
(B) method used by President Theodore Roosevelt to settle the Anthracite Coal Strike of 1902
(C) method used by the Governor of Pennsylvania to end the Homestead Strike
(D) kind of judicial action used in the Danbury Hatters' case
(E) kind of judicial action used against those accused in the Haymarket affair

78. During the 1920s, labor was most successful in achieving

(A) federal legislation to reduce the number of immigrants to the United States
(B) state legislation outlawing the open shop
(C) United States Supreme Court approval of minimum-wage laws

    (D) congressional action to guarantee the right of collective bargaining

    (E) exemption from the terms of the antitrust laws

79. The right of workers legally to combine into unions to promote their economic interests was established by the

    (A) application of the English common law to cases involving unions in American courts

    (B) decision of Chief Justice Shaw of Massachusetts in the case of *Commonwealth* v. *Hunt* (1942)

    (C) decision of the United States Supreme Court in the *Danbury Hatters'* case

    (D) actions of the Workingmen's party organized in Philadelphia in 1825

    (E) labor provisions of the Clayton Antitrust Act

80. During the period of the New Deal, the program of organized labor was most successful in

    (A) unifying the labor movement

    (B) restoring full employment to the economy

    (C) removing obstacles to unionization

    (D) securing a nationwide system of workers' compensation

    (E) safeguarding unions from authoritarian control

81. United States farmers have been reluctant to unite with the workers in a powerful farmer-labor political party because farmers

    (A) fear that the ultimate aim of the workers' program is collectivization

    (B) resent organized labor's great social and economic gains

    (C) tend to regard themselves as business persons whose economic security can be destroyed by labor

    (D) have little faith in seeking to solve their problems through politics

    (E) are opposed to third-party movements

82. Over the years, farmers have found it more difficult to promote their economic interests than have manufacturers because

    (A) farmers have been unsuccessful in organizing a political party to represent their interests

    (B) farmers sell in a free, competitive market

    (C) the protective tariff has not been extended to agricultural products

    (D) farm labor is more costly than industrial labor

    (E) mechanization has not been applied to agriculture

83. Which trend in farming during the first part of the 20th century has REVERSED itself since World War II?

    (A) Gradual increase in farm tenancy

    (B) Gradual decrease in the number of farms

    (C) Increase in the size of farms

    (D) Growth of regional specialization in farming

    (E) Increased efficiency of the American farmer

84. In the 1920s the farmers demanded a change in the government's farm program in order to obtain

    (A) a higher tariff barrier on agricultural goods

    (B) a legislative program that would limit farm production and reduce farm indebtedness

    (C) a federal program that would reduce surpluses rather than acreage

    (D) a farm program that included direct farm supports

    (E) agricultural prices designed to give the farmer an equitable share of national income

85. Free-trade advocates believe that the levying of a protective tariff

    (A) prevents a nation from becoming self-sufficient

    (B) encourages inefficiency in production

    (C) makes a balanced budget impractical

    (D) is deflationary

    (E) depresses wages

86. The need for universal health coverage became a political issue in the 1990s because

    (A) it was a prior political campaign pledge which had to be kept

    (B) Congress wanted the government to pay for national health insurance

    (C) half the people with inadequate health care coverage were living in poverty

    (D) such coverage required only small expenditures

    (E) both political parties wanted national health insurance

87. In which pair is the second item an example of the first?

    (A) tariff—excise tax

    (B) gold standard—inflation

    (C) laissez-faire—lend-lease

    (D) tenant farming—sharecropping

    (E) closed shop—lockout

88. Which was designed to have a deflationary effect on the economy of the United States?

(A) Sherman Silver Purchase Act
(B) Federal Reserve Act
(C) Gold Standard Act
(D) Abandonment of specie payment
(E) Reduction in gold content of the dollar

89. Andrew Jackson's program and Franklin D. Roosevelt's program differed sharply on the issue of

(A) tariff reduction
(B) protection of the working classes against the financial interests
(C) use of executive power
(D) sound money
(E) the sanctity of decisions of the Supreme Court

90. The Progressive movement of the early 20th century was LEAST successful in

(A) calling attention to slum conditions
(B) reforming municipal governments
(C) exposing practices of "big business"
(D) introducing election reforms
(E) achieving a federal law prohibiting child labor

91. During the Progressive era (1900-1915), which state was most prominent in the adoption of progressive reforms?

(A) Delaware   (D) Wisconsin
(B) Michigan   (E) Nevada
(C) Minnesota

92. Which internal reform passed in the Wilson administration was most acceptable to "big business"?

(A) Adamson Act
(B) Clayton Antitrust Act
(C) Underwood Tariff
(D) Federal Trade Commission Act
(E) Federal Reserve Act

93. The work of the Pujo Committee (1912-1913) paved the way for the passage of laws dealing with

(A) conservation   (D) labor
(B) banking   (E) the armed services
(C) federal courts

94. "The history of mankind is a history of repeated injuries and usurpations on the part of man toward woman, having in direct object the establishment of an absolute tyranny over her. To prove this, let facts be submitted to a candid world,"

This quotation is from which document?

(A) The Seneca Falls Declaration (1848)
(B) Resolutions of the Nashville Convention (1850)
(C) Ostend Manifesto (1854)
(D) Populist party platform (1892)
(E) Progressive party platform (1912)

95. The principal method used by the United States during the first two decades of the 20th century to make the Caribbean an "American lake" was the

(A) granting of low-interest loans to underdeveloped countries
(B) negotiation of reciprocal trade agreements
(C) annexation of Caribbean countries to the United States
(D) sponsorship of several Pan American conferences
(E) use of United States Marines to support American-sponsored governments

96. Woodrow Wilson's doctrine of "strict accountability" had specific application to

(A) submarine warfare
(B) war indemnities
(C) loans to belligerents
(D) investments in foreign countries
(E) treatment of prisoners of war

97. A President and his Secretary of State who had sharp differences of opinion with regard to the conduct of foreign affairs were

(A) Thomas Jefferson and James Madison
(B) Andrew Jackson and Martin Van Buren
(C) James Monroe and John Quincy Adams
(D) Theodore Roosevelt and John Hay
(E) Woodrow Wilson and William J. Bryan

98. In November 1916, Woodrow Wilson was reelected President, partly because "he kept us out of war." Less than six months later he asked for a declaration of war. A major influence in bringing about this change was

(A) a widespread belief that the Allies were in grave danger of losing the war
(B) effective British propaganda about the Hun menace
(C) the revelation in the Kruger telegram of an attempted German plot against the United States
(D) Germany's repudiation and violation of the Sussex Pledge
(E) the sinking of the Lusitania

ANSWER KEY: TEST 1

1. A	21. C	41. B	61. D	81. C
2. B	22. A	42. A	62. D	82. B
3. A	23. C	43. A	63. E	83. A
4. A	24. D	44. B	64. C	84. E
5. D	25. A	45. C	65. C	85. B
6. E	26. A	46. A	66. A	86. C
7. E	27. D	47. D	67. A	87. D
8. D	28. C	48. A	68. B	88. C
9. D	29. D	49. C	69. C	89. A
10. A	30. B	50. C	70. D	90. E
11. B	31. A	51. E	71. D	91. D
12. D	32. A	52. E	72. E	92. E
13. C	33. D	53. D	73. D	93. B
14. D	34. C	54. B	74. D	94. A
15. C	35. C	55. E	75. B	95. E
16. A	36. B	56. D	76. C	96. A
17. D	37. C	57. D	77. D	97. E
18. B	38. E	58. B	78. A	98. D
19. C	39. E	59. E	79. B	
20. A	40. D	60. E	80. C	

ANALYSIS CHART: TEST 1

Era	Number of Questions	Number Right	Number Wrong	Number Unanswered
Pre-Columbian to 1789: questions 36-39	4			
1790 to 1898: questions 4, 6, 13-17, 29, 40, 50-55, 57, 62, 66, 69, 70, 73, 74, 76, 94	24			
1899 to present: questions 5, 7-11, 20-28, 35, 41-47, 49, 56, 58-60, 63-65, 67, 71, 72, 77, 78, 80, 83, 84, 90-93, 95, 96, 98	46			
Cross period: questions 1, 18, 19, 30-33, 61, 68 75, 79, 81, 82, 88, 89, 97	16			
Nonchronological: questions 2, 3, 12, 34, 48, 85-87	8			

FINDING THE REASONS FOR INCORRECT ANSWERS

Be sure to check the answer explanations before completing the following chart.

Era	Number Wrong	Lack of Knowledge	Misunderstand Problem	Careless Error	Not Answered
Pre-Columbian to 1789					
1790 to 1898					
1899 to present					
Cross period					
Nonchronological					

ANSWER EXPLANATIONS: TEST 1

1. **A**   The 17 percent drop in the percentage of children below nine years of age in the total population is the largest percentage change shown. It represents a decrease in average family size as well as an increase in the life span of the population.

2. **B**   For example, the Social Security officials have to know how much active workers must pay in Social Security taxes to provide for the old-age benefits of an increasing number of retirees over a longer span of years.

3. **A**   Article I, Section 2 of the Constitution states, "The House of Representatives...shall have the sole Power of Impeachment [the bringing of charges against a government official]."

4. **A**   The Federalists favored loose construction of the Constitution, added power for Congress, and a strong central government.

5. **D**   Because of that statement, Theodore Roosevelt's Progressive party, organized for his 1912 presidential election campaign, was also called the Bull Moose party.

6. **E**   These words concluded Webster's reply to Senator Hayne of South Carolina during their 1830 debate of the nature of the federal union. Webster's main point was that if states could nullify acts of Con-gress, the Union would become a mere "rope of sand" and would soon dissolve.

7. **E**   Chief Justice Earl Warren led the United States Supreme Court in issuing the 1854 decision in *Brown* v. *Board of Education of Topeka, Kansas*, which declared unconstitutional the principle of racially segregated (separate but equal) facilities in public schools. The decision reversed the "separate but equal" doctrine established in *Plessy* v. *Ferguson* (1895).

8. **D**   In foreign affairs, Theodore Roosevelt's "big stick" was the United States Navy, which had been modernized and enlarged at his behest. The Big Stick policy was used especially in the Caribbean area.

9. **D**   Under President Taft (1909-1913), "dollar diplomacy" helped expand United States influence abroad. United States bankers were encouraged to invest in foreign areas of strategic importance to the United States, particularly in the Far East and in the Panama Canal area. In return, the bankers were assured that their investments would be protected by American diplomacy.

10. **A**   Roosevelt's 1937 plan to "pack" the Supreme Court was quite simple. He asked Congress to permit him to appoint one extra member to the Supreme Court for every Justice over the age of seventy. Six of

the nine justices were then over seventy and were the (conservative) appointees of Republican Presidents.

11. **B**   Turkey, not Spain, was the second benefici-ary. In March 1947, President Truman asked Congress to provide military and economic aid to nations threat-ened by Communist expansion, particularly Greece and Turkey. As a result of our aid, Greece was able to end a Communist menace and restore order. Turkey resisted Russian influence and demands for naval bases on the Dardanelles.

12. **D**   The Assumption Act of 1790 was the federal takeover of state debts. Those debts, argued Hamilton, resulted from state efforts to help the nation as a whole in the Revolution. To win over Virginia, which had paid off its own debt, Hamilton offered to round up Northern support for a Southern site for the national capital if Jefferson would persuade some Virginia members of Congress to stop opposing the Assump-tion Act.

13. **C**   In Texas's short but hard-fought struggle for independence from Mexico in 1835, the main battle took place at San Jacinto. That battle helped to end rather than bring about the war.

14. **D**   African slaves were first brought to Virginia in 1619. The other events all took place in the 1800s.

15. **C**   Congress first forbade the importation of slaves in 1808. Garrison's *Liberator* appeared in 1830. Congress admitted California to the Union as a free state as part of the Compromise of 1850. Lincoln's Cooper Union address in New York City in February 1860 was a compactly reasoned argument that nothing in the federal Constitution forbade the federal govern-ment from controlling slavery in the federal territories.

16. **A**   The Missouri Compromise of 1820, the work of Henry Clay, admitted Maine as a free state and Missouri as a slave state. It also excluded slavery from the Louisiana Purchase north of the 36°30′ line (the southern boundary of Missouri). Texas joined the Union as a slave state in 1848, after the Mexican War. The issue of the continued expansion of slavery con-tinued in the Lincoln-Douglas debates for the Senate seat for Illinois in 1858. Lincoln's election as Presi-dent in 1860 resulted in the secession of South Carolina and the firing on the United States' installa-tion at Fort Sumter in Charleston harbor in April 1861.

17. **D**   By the Emancipation Proclamation, which went into effect on January 1, 1863, Lincoln indicated that Northerners considered themselves to be fighting a war to end human bondage.

18. **B**   In 1612 John Rolfe secured and planted some West Indies tobacco seeds in the Virginia Colony, and tobacco was soon being exported to England. From 20,000 pounds in 1618, exports reached half a million pounds by 1630.

19. **C**   Most recent of the items listed was passage of the AAA of 1933 (and also of 1938). The govern-ment attempted to stop the creation of further farm surpluses (which depressed farm prices) by paying farmers to take land out of cultivation.

20. **A**   After the United States entered World War I in April 1917, the Railroad Administration took over the nation's railroads and ran them as a single system.

21. **C**   Wilson called for the reduction of national armaments "to the lowest point consistent with domes-tic safety."

22. **A**   The three aims of the New Deal were *relief* for the victims of the depression, national *recovery* from the depression, and *reform* of the economy.

23. **C**   General Dwight Eisenhower was head of SHAEF, the Supreme Headquarters of the head of Allied Expeditionary Forces in Europe.

24. **D**   When the Japanese conquered the Philippines in April 1942, General Douglas MacArthur vowed that he would return. Two years later, he was able to keep his promise.

25. **A**   British Prime Minister Neville Chamberlain became a worldwide symbol of the folly of appease-ment in September 1938, when he and French Premier Edward Daladier allowed Germany to annex part of Czechoslovakia, in return for Hitler's promise to make no further demands for territory. Their Munich Conference failed to bring "peace in our time," and their own nations had to oppose Hitler's Germany in war within one year.

26. **A**   A German counteroffensive in December 1944 in Belgium resulted in fierce fighting near Bastogne and in heavy losses on both sides.

27. **D**   In 1947 Secretary of State George Marshall offered American economic assistance to all European nations (including the Soviet Union and its satellites) to enable them to recover from the destruction of World War II.

28. **C**   President John Kennedy disclosed that the Soviet Union was secretly bringing offensive bombers and missiles into Cuba and building Cuban missile

bases. He ordered a *quarantine* by United States naval and air forces to prevent shipments of offensive arms from reaching Cuba. The Soviets backed down and removed their weapons, which were a threat to the security of the Western Hemisphere.

29. **D** The people of Puerto Rico will again be able to choose their future status from among commonwealth, independence, and statehood.

30. **B** Francois ("Papa Doc") Duvalier was president and dictator of Haiti from 1957 to 1971. His son, "Baby Doc," followed in his father's footsteps. Both were aided by the dreaded secret police, or "Ton Ton Macoutes."

31. **A** The capital of Mexico, our largest Latin trade partner, is at *G*, Mexico City. *H* represents Monterrey, and *I* locates Vera Cruz.

32. **A** Nicaragua is the country torn by civil war whose contra rebels were aided by the United States.

33. **D** Panama Whoever controls this isthmus controls access to the Panama Canal, the international waterway that connects commerce between the Atlantic and Pacific oceans.

34. **C** A two-thirds majority vote is required for Senate ratification of a treaty.

35. **C** Stephen Douglas was reelected to the Senate in 1858; John Brown's raid on the federal arsenal at Harper's Ferry, Virginia, took place the following year.

36. **B** Indentured servants traded passage money to cross the Atlantic from Europe for a fixed period of service, after which they were free. By the 1750s there were slaves in all the American colonies, often replacing indentured servants.

37. **C** In each case, the colonies existed to benefit the mother country.

38. **E** The monopoly given to the British East India Company took from American merchants their former tea profits.

39. **E** All of these were consistent with mercantilist theory and practice.

40. **D** William Randolph Hearst's *New York Journal* and Joseph Pulitzer's *New York World* were among the newspapers that engaged in "yellow journalism," exaggerating the 1890s atrocities of the Spanish and the suffering of the Cubans. Those papers whipped public opinion into supporting war against Spain in 1898 against President McKinley's better judgment.

41. **B** American foreign-policy interests during that period were basically concerned with the Caribbean basin and the building of the Panama Canal (completed in 1914). We were still isolationist toward Europe and Asia, seeking only an Open Door for Chinese trade.

42. **A** These laws barred the sale or transportation of arms to warring nations, refused loans to nations at war outside the Western Hemisphere, and ordered all Americans to stay out of war zones and not to travel on ships belonging to warring nations.

43. **A** In June 1947 Secretary of State Marshall proposed that the United States finance a massive recovery plan to restore the economies of the European nations devastated by World War II (1939-1945). Under the Marshall Plan, American money, supplies, and machinery would help end Europe's "hunger, poverty, desperation, and chaos." The $31 billion in American loans and grants (1948-1952) revived Western Europe economically and politically, and countered Communist strength in France and Italy.

44. **B** Associated with British Prime Minister Neville Chamberlain at the 1938 Munich Conference, the black umbrella became the symbol of appeasement. (See also the explanation of question 25.)

45. **C** President John F. Kennedy is shown in 1962 avoiding the "downhill" road of appeasement, or peace at any price.

46. **A** In October 1962 President Kennedy announced that the Soviet Union had secretly placed in Cuba long range missiles capable of carrying nuclear weapons and threatening the United States. Kennedy ordered a naval blockade to prevent the Russians from delivering any more missiles to Cuba, and demanded that the Cubans dismantle all their missile sites. The possibility of war seemed very real until the Russian ships turned back from the blockade and Soviet missiles were withdrawn from Cuba.

47. **D** Kennedy rejected Khrushchev's added demand during negotiations that the United States remove its own missiles from Turkey, on the Soviet border. That would have weakened the NATO Alliance.

48. **A** President Kennedy learned from the Munich conference that appeasement of aggressors did not bring about peace.

49. **C** The United States government could no longer ignore the threat to our security of a Europe increasingly dominated by Nazi and fascist governments (in Germany, Austria, Italy, and Spain), and of the rim of Asia increasingly dominated by the spread of Japan's "Greater East Asia Co-Prosperity Sphere." By 1937, Japan had absorbed Korea, Formosa, and Manchuria, and had invaded China proper.

50. **C** The Homestead Act of 1862 offered free up to 160 acres of western land to anyone who would occupy and improve the land for five years. However, much of the land ended up in the bands of speculators, railroads, and mining companies, who often used fraudulent means to obtain title.

51. **E** Seward, President Andrew Johnson's Secretary of State, wanted the United States to expand by annexing Canada, Hawaii, and several Caribbean islands. When purchased from Russia in 1867, Alaska was considered almost worthless.

52. **E** In 1636 the Reverend Thomas Hooker, a Puritan minister, led his congregation in search of richer farmland and a freer system of government. They started a settlement at Hartford, in the fertile Connecticut River Valley.

53. **D** The War Hawks of 1812 wanted to acquire Canada. The Ostend Manifesto of 1854 was an unofficial document drawn up by three United States diplomats, declaring that if Spain would not sell Cuba to the United States, we should take it by force. (The Secretary of State repudiated the document.) Filibusterers were armed adventurers who attempted to gain territory for the United States (as in Cuba and Nicaragua).

54. **B** The investigation convinced President Cleveland that the 1893 use of American sailors by Americans living in Hawaii to overturn the Hawaiian government was a violation of "national honesty." Cleveland opposed annexation, withdrew American soldiers from Hawaii, and tried to restore the Hawaiian queen to her throne.

55. **E** However, between 1825 and 1860, American authors wrote books that are still read on both sides of the Atlantic. Washington Irving dealt with the life and legends of the Hudson River Valley, James Fenimore Cooper wrote about wilderness scouts and Indians on the New York frontier, Nathaniel Hawthorne described the Puritan tradition of New England, and Herman Melville wrote about New England whalers in *Moby Dick*.

56. **D** During World War II, aircraft plants produced large numbers of fighters and bombers. Many of these plants were located on the West Coast (as were naval shipyards).

57. **D** In the late 19th and early 20th centuries, the due process clause was invoked by large corporations to protect them against government regulation. By the 1950s, a Supreme Court ruling used the "due process" clause to protect individuals against certain state actions and to protect civil liberties.

58. **B** The "Fourteen Points' was Woodrow Wilson's statement of America's aims in World War I. The Atlantic charter of August 1941, issued by President Franklin D. Roosevelt and British Prime Minister Winston Churchill (while the United States was still at peace), was a statement of common principles "for a better future for the world." Like the "Fourteen Points," the Atlantic Charter included a world without aggression, in which people could choose their form of government, in which resources would be shared, and weapons removed.

59. **E** Covered workers are those engaged in interstate commerce. Article I, Section 8 of the Constitution grants Congress power "...to regulate Commerce...among the several States...."

60. **E** The Supreme Court declared unconstitutional in May 1935 the National Industrial Recovery Act of 1933 in the case of *Schechter* v. *United States*. However, many of the act's features, such as workers' rights to collective bargaining, were carried on by later legislation.

61. **D** John Adams appointed "midnight judges," and Franklin D. Roosevelt tried to pack the Supreme Court in order to have key New Deal laws declared constitutional.

62. **D** In the explosive growth of American industry from the 1860s to 1900, the following factors played a major part: vast natural resources, new inventions, abundant capital, railroad building a large, mobile labor supply, a huge home market, formation of business corporations, the Protestant ethic.

63. **E** In both cases, the American President refused to recognize the new government, passing judgment on how the new government had come to power. In 1913 in Mexico, Victoriano Huerta seized power, and the former president, Francisco Madero, was murdered. In 1949 in China, the Communists overthrew the Nationalists. In both cases, American investors suffered losses.

64. **C**   As in 1924, the American people voted for prosperity. The Republicans were promising "two cars in every garage."

65. **C**   Previous presidents tended to appoint only members of their own political party to their Cabinet.

66. **A**   Slave labor performed the household tasks and heavy manual labor that could provide jobs to immigrants in the North.

67. **A**   The McCarran-Walter Act ended the earlier immigration policy of excluding Chinese, Japanese, and many other Asians.

68. **B**   Meant to protect the newly freed blacks, the Fourteenth Amendment read, "...nor shall any State deprive any person of life, liberty, or property, without due process of law." This "due process" clause was invoked by corporations to protect them against government regulation. This amendment was adopted in 1868, during the period of rapid business expansion.

69. **C**   The United States government practiced "laissez-faire," or hands-off business regulation, while permitting large-scale immigration to provide farm and factory labor.

70. **D**   Low interest rates would encourage business people to buy steel to build with borrowed money, and encourage steel makers to borrow from bankers to increase their capacity. Low rates would mean low profits for bankers; high interest rates could provide higher profit margins.

71. **D**   The Federal Reserve System can regulate the amount of credit available to business people and consumers by changing bank reserve requirements, changing the discount rate to member banks, and either buying or selling government securities.

72. **E**   This refers to monetary policy, or to the actions taken by the Fed to control the supply of money and credit in order to influence the level of economic activity. (See also the explanation of question 71.)

73. **D**   Yet this vocal minority was the opinion-making group in the South on political, social, and economic issues.

74. **D**   In case of a strike, unskilled workers could be fired and easily replaced by management. Wage rates also differed widely between skilled and unskilled workers. The unions of the 1870s and 1880s could far more easily gain economic benefits and better working conditions for skilled artisans.

75. **B**   The AFL avoided siding with any one political party, hoping that both Republicans and Democrats might woo labor.

76. **C**   Gompers was the founder of the AFL in 1881. (See the explanation of question 75.)

77. **D**   The Sherman Antitrust Act (1890), by barring conspiracies in restraint of trade, had done more harm to labor unions than to business monopolies. The Danbury Hatters' union was broken in 1912 when the court ordered it to pay triple damages to a hat manufacturer whose products it had ordered boycotted. The Clayton Act (1914) specifically exempted labor unions from such treatment.

78. **A**   With the frontier effectively closed by 1890, labor unions claimed their members suffered unfair competition from low-wage immigrants now living in great numbers in the big cities.

79. **B**   In that decision, the court ruled that a peaceful attempt by a "trade society" (labor union) to improve the lot of its members through organized pressure, such as a strike or a boycott, might be legal if the methods used were peaceful.

80. **C**   The Wagner-Connery (National Labor Relations) Act of 1935 granted labor unions the right to collective bargaining with employers. It was hailed as the Magna Carta of labor.

81. **C**   American farmers are employers of farm labor, whether full-time or part-time, and do not see their interests as being similar to the interests of labor (minimum wage, fringe benefits).

82. **B**   Farmers cannot influence the prices they receive for corn, wheat, tomatoes, milk, or hogs.

83. **A**   The collapse of cotton prices during the depression of the 1930s drove many southern rural farmers off the land. The Farm Security Administration created by the New Deal has given loans to help tenants purchase land. Farm tenancy was seen as a "dead end" to be avoided.

84. **E**   During World War I, farmers experienced very high demand for their products for domestic, military, and export sale. They enjoyed high prices and purchased more land and more farm machinery in order to increase output. When, after the war, demand for produce fell and prices declined, farmers

continued to produce large surpluses, which drove farm prices down further. Congress passed the Agricultural Marketing Act of 1929, which created a Federal Farm Board to lend money to farm organizations by purchasing and storing surplus crops until the surpluses could be resold in time of scarcity. Because the act made no attempt to limit production, it failed, and the Federal Farm Board soon exhausted its funds.

85. **B** Free traders believe in the principle of comparative advantage: that a nation should specialize in the production of those goods and services in which it is most efficient, and trade its surplus for whatever else it needs.

86. **C** Government statistics in 1989 showed 37 million persons without health care coverage, and 18.5 million with family incomes of under $10,000.

87. **D** In this case the tenant pays the landowner in an agreed-upon portion of the crop (say cotton), rather than in cash.

88. **C** The Gold Standard Act of 1900 declared that the United States was on the gold standard, and made all paper money redeemable in gold. Limiting the amount of money in circulation to what could be redeemed in available gold was deflationary, causing falling prices and increasing the value of the dollar.

89. **A** Jackson favored neither the North's nor the South's arguments over the protective tariff, but he enforced the Laws passed by Congress, including the protectionist Tariff of Abominations (1828) and the mildly different Tariff of 1832. As a southerner, he was expected to oppose protective tariffs; instead he strongly opposed nullification. Franklin D. Roosevelt believed in reducing tariffs in order to increase American foreign trade, international goodwill, and world prosperity. He had Congress pass the Reciprocal Trade Agreements Act of 1934, providing for the mutual lowering of duties on imports.

90. **E** A National Child Labor Committee was formed in 1904 to promote the abolition of child labor through legislation. A book by John Spargo, *The Bitter Cry of the Children*, revealed deplorable conditions, especially in the textile and coal industries. During the Progressive Era, many states passed laws to limit child labor, but the first federal law upheld as constitutional in this area was the Fair Labor Standards Act of 1938.

91. **D** For example, the Wisconsin (or direct) primary took the nomination of party candidates away from the party conventions and gave it to the voters. In education, Wisconsin was a leader in making

universities serve a wider public through extension courses and traveling lecturers.

92. **E** This 1913 act concentrated financial reserves, so that any single bank could be helped in time of temporary difficulty, such as a run on the bank. The twelve Federal Reserve Banks provided for local needs and made it easier to move money from one part of the country to another. The act provided for a new form of flexible currency known as Federal Reserve notes, and issued according to business needs. All U.S. currency now consists of Federal Reserve notes.

93. **B** Muckrakers of the early 20th century uncovered evidence that a very small group of individuals controlled American industry, transportation, and credit. The Pujo Committee, set up by Congress, investigated in 1912-1913, its report serving as an excellent background to Wilson's financial and antitrust legislation, including the Federal Reserve Act. The committee listed banks, which by their tremendous financial assets and interlocking directorates had control of huge banking resources, of sixteen major transportation companies, of nine industrial corporations, and of seven public utilities. This situation was called the "Money Trust."

94. **A** The Seneca Falls convention was the world's first women's rights convention. Organized by Elizabeth Cady Stanton and Lucretia Mott at Seneca Falls, New York, in 1848, it issued a ringing declaration of women's rights, which stated that all men *and women* are created equal.

95. **E** Presidents Theodore Roosevelt, William H. Taft, and their successors used the Marine intervention to enforce both the Roosevelt Corollary and "dollar diplomacy," making virtual protectorates of several Caribbean nations. Marines were stationed in the Dominican Republic from 1905 to 1907, and again from 1916 to 1924, to preserve order. Political disorder in Haiti brought about Marine occupation from 1915 to 1930. Nicaragua requested the Marines in 1912 to protect American lives and property.

96. **A** Followig the March 1916 U-boat sinking of the French passenger liner *Sussex*, Wilson demanded that the German government promise to give up its methods of U-boat warfare or risk war with the United States. Germany promised, with certain conditions, to sink no more merchant ships without warning. It offered to pay damages to Americans injured on the *Sussex*.

97. **E** Wilson won reelection in 1916 with the slogan, "He kept us out of war." He had earlier issued

a Neutrality Proclamation and urged Americans to be "impartial in thought as well as in action." After the May 1915 sinking of the British passenger liner *Lusitania*, Wilson insisted on our rights as a neutral.

Secretary of State William J. Bryan resigned because he thought such a course would lead to war. He favored proposed congressional laws forbidding American citizens to travel on ships of belligerents.

98. **D** The Germans had their own reasons for a lull in submarine activity from the spring of 1916 to February 1917, when a new submarine campaign began. On February 3, an American ship was torpedoed, and Wilson severed relations with Germany. On March 16, three more American vessels were sunk by U-boats, and Wilson prepared to ask Congress (on April 2) for a declaration of war.

ANSWER SHEET: TEST 2

1. Ⓐ Ⓑ Ⓒ Ⓓ Ⓔ	16. Ⓐ Ⓑ Ⓒ Ⓓ Ⓔ	31. Ⓐ Ⓑ Ⓒ Ⓓ Ⓔ
2. Ⓐ Ⓑ Ⓒ Ⓓ Ⓔ	17. Ⓐ Ⓑ Ⓒ Ⓓ Ⓔ	32. Ⓐ Ⓑ Ⓒ Ⓓ Ⓔ
3. Ⓐ Ⓑ Ⓒ Ⓓ Ⓔ	18. Ⓐ Ⓑ Ⓒ Ⓓ Ⓔ	33. Ⓐ Ⓑ Ⓒ Ⓓ Ⓔ
4. Ⓐ Ⓑ Ⓒ Ⓓ Ⓔ	19. Ⓐ Ⓑ Ⓒ Ⓓ Ⓔ	34. Ⓐ Ⓑ Ⓒ Ⓓ Ⓔ
5. Ⓐ Ⓑ Ⓒ Ⓓ Ⓔ	20. Ⓐ Ⓑ Ⓒ Ⓓ Ⓔ	35. Ⓐ Ⓑ Ⓒ Ⓓ Ⓔ
6. Ⓐ Ⓑ Ⓒ Ⓓ Ⓔ	21. Ⓐ Ⓑ Ⓒ Ⓓ Ⓔ	36. Ⓐ Ⓑ Ⓒ Ⓓ Ⓔ
7. Ⓐ Ⓑ Ⓒ Ⓓ Ⓔ	22. Ⓐ Ⓑ Ⓒ Ⓓ Ⓔ	37. Ⓐ Ⓑ Ⓒ Ⓓ Ⓔ
8. Ⓐ Ⓑ Ⓒ Ⓓ Ⓔ	23. Ⓐ Ⓑ Ⓒ Ⓓ Ⓔ	38. Ⓐ Ⓑ Ⓒ Ⓓ Ⓔ
9. Ⓐ Ⓑ Ⓒ Ⓓ Ⓔ	24. Ⓐ Ⓑ Ⓒ Ⓓ Ⓔ	39. Ⓐ Ⓑ Ⓒ Ⓓ Ⓔ
10. Ⓐ Ⓑ Ⓒ Ⓓ Ⓔ	25. Ⓐ Ⓑ Ⓒ Ⓓ Ⓔ	40. Ⓐ Ⓑ Ⓒ Ⓓ Ⓔ
11. Ⓐ Ⓑ Ⓒ Ⓓ Ⓔ	26. Ⓐ Ⓑ Ⓒ Ⓓ Ⓔ	41. Ⓐ Ⓑ Ⓒ Ⓓ Ⓔ
12. Ⓐ Ⓑ Ⓒ Ⓓ Ⓔ	27. Ⓐ Ⓑ Ⓒ Ⓓ Ⓔ	42. Ⓐ Ⓑ Ⓒ Ⓓ Ⓔ
13. Ⓐ Ⓑ Ⓒ Ⓓ Ⓔ	28. Ⓐ Ⓑ Ⓒ Ⓓ Ⓔ	43. Ⓐ Ⓑ Ⓒ Ⓓ Ⓔ
14. Ⓐ Ⓑ Ⓒ Ⓓ Ⓔ	29. Ⓐ Ⓑ Ⓒ Ⓓ Ⓔ	44. Ⓐ Ⓑ Ⓒ Ⓓ Ⓔ
15. Ⓐ Ⓑ Ⓒ Ⓓ Ⓔ	30. Ⓐ Ⓑ Ⓒ Ⓓ Ⓔ	45. Ⓐ Ⓑ Ⓒ Ⓓ Ⓔ

46. Ⓐ Ⓑ Ⓒ Ⓓ Ⓔ	61. Ⓐ Ⓑ Ⓒ Ⓓ Ⓔ	76. Ⓐ Ⓑ Ⓒ Ⓓ Ⓔ
47. Ⓐ Ⓑ Ⓒ Ⓓ Ⓔ	62. Ⓐ Ⓑ Ⓒ Ⓓ Ⓔ	77. Ⓐ Ⓑ Ⓒ Ⓓ Ⓔ
48. Ⓐ Ⓑ Ⓒ Ⓓ Ⓔ	63. Ⓐ Ⓑ Ⓒ Ⓓ Ⓔ	78. Ⓐ Ⓑ Ⓒ Ⓓ Ⓔ
49. Ⓐ Ⓑ Ⓒ Ⓓ Ⓔ	64. Ⓐ Ⓑ Ⓒ Ⓓ Ⓔ	79. Ⓐ Ⓑ Ⓒ Ⓓ Ⓔ
50. Ⓐ Ⓑ Ⓒ Ⓓ Ⓔ	65. Ⓐ Ⓑ Ⓒ Ⓓ Ⓔ	80. Ⓐ Ⓑ Ⓒ Ⓓ Ⓔ
51. Ⓐ Ⓑ Ⓒ Ⓓ Ⓔ	66. Ⓐ Ⓑ Ⓒ Ⓓ Ⓔ	81. Ⓐ Ⓑ Ⓒ Ⓓ Ⓔ
52. Ⓐ Ⓑ Ⓒ Ⓓ Ⓔ	67. Ⓐ Ⓑ Ⓒ Ⓓ Ⓔ	82. Ⓐ Ⓑ Ⓒ Ⓓ Ⓔ
53. Ⓐ Ⓑ Ⓒ Ⓓ Ⓔ	68. Ⓐ Ⓑ Ⓒ Ⓓ Ⓔ	83. Ⓐ Ⓑ Ⓒ Ⓓ Ⓔ
54. Ⓐ Ⓑ Ⓒ Ⓓ Ⓔ	69. Ⓐ Ⓑ Ⓒ Ⓓ Ⓔ	84. Ⓐ Ⓑ Ⓒ Ⓓ Ⓔ
55. Ⓐ Ⓑ Ⓒ Ⓓ Ⓔ	70. Ⓐ Ⓑ Ⓒ Ⓓ Ⓔ	85. Ⓐ Ⓑ Ⓒ Ⓓ Ⓔ
56. Ⓐ Ⓑ Ⓒ Ⓓ Ⓔ	71. Ⓐ Ⓑ Ⓒ Ⓓ Ⓔ	86. Ⓐ Ⓑ Ⓒ Ⓓ Ⓔ
57. Ⓐ Ⓑ Ⓒ Ⓓ Ⓔ	72. Ⓐ Ⓑ Ⓒ Ⓓ Ⓔ	87. Ⓐ Ⓑ Ⓒ Ⓓ Ⓔ
58. Ⓐ Ⓑ Ⓒ Ⓓ Ⓔ	73. Ⓐ Ⓑ Ⓒ Ⓓ Ⓔ	88. Ⓐ Ⓑ Ⓒ Ⓓ Ⓔ
59. Ⓐ Ⓑ Ⓒ Ⓓ Ⓔ	74. Ⓐ Ⓑ Ⓒ Ⓓ Ⓔ	89. Ⓐ Ⓑ Ⓒ Ⓓ Ⓔ
60. Ⓐ Ⓑ Ⓒ Ⓓ Ⓔ	75. Ⓐ Ⓑ Ⓒ Ⓓ Ⓔ	90. Ⓐ Ⓑ Ⓒ Ⓓ Ⓔ

91. Ⓐ Ⓑ Ⓒ Ⓓ Ⓔ
92. Ⓐ Ⓑ Ⓒ Ⓓ Ⓔ
93. Ⓐ Ⓑ Ⓒ Ⓓ Ⓔ
94. Ⓐ Ⓑ Ⓒ Ⓓ Ⓔ
95. Ⓐ Ⓑ Ⓒ Ⓓ Ⓔ

Test 2

Directions: Each of the questions or incomplete statements is followed by five suggested answers or completions. Select the one that is best in each case and then blacken the corresponding space on the answer sheet.

1. Where does the sole power lie to try a President against whom impeachment charges have already been brought?

   (A) House of Representatives
   (B) Senate
   (C) State legislatures
   (D) Supreme Court
   (E) The two houses of Congress

2. Which of the following statements is NOT true about the Demarcation Line of 1493?

   (A) The Pope had very limited knowledge of the geography of the New World.
   (B) The New World west of the Demarcation Line was given to Spain.
   (C) Portugal received only a portion of what is now Brazil.
   (D) Balboa, Cortez, and Sebastian Cabot explored for Spain.
   (E) Spain and Portugal were more vigorous and earlier in exploring the New World than were either England or France.

3. The act passed by Congress as a "frame-up" to lead to the impeachment of President Andrew Johnson was the

   (A) Civil Rights Act   (D) Pendleton Act
   (B) Civil Service Act   (E) Tenure of Office Act
   (C) Fugitive Slave Act

4. In order to become a law, a bill in Congress must

   (A) receive a two-thirds majority of the votes in Congress
   (B) receive a three-fourths majority of the votes in each house of Congress
   (C) receive a two-thirds majority of votes in each house of Congress
   (D) pass both houses of Congress in identical form

   (E) pass as amended in the last house of Congress to consider it

5. Which of the following statements does NOT represent a typical viewpoint of the Democratic Republicans in 1789-1800?

   (A) Sending thousands of troops into western Pennsylvania to collect small change from almost penniless corn farmers is ridiculous!
   (B) The treaty is an insult. Jay should be tarred and feathered.
   (C) It is too late to pay the domestic debt. The original bondholders have sold out to speculators. There's no sense in putting more money in the pockets of wealthy speculators.
   (D) The credit of the federal government and of the several states must be made secure by the payment in full of all public debts. How such a sound policy helps or hurts individuals is a matter of no lasting importance.
   (E) It is clear that government policies favor the interests of commerce, while the only attention paid to farmers is to make sure they pay taxes.

6. Which of the following statements is NOT true about the Fourteenth Amendment to the United States Constitution?

   (A) Its purpose was to force the ex-Confederate states to grant the ex-slaves equal treatment under the law with whites.
   (B) "...nor shall any State deprive any person of life, liberty, or property, without due process of law, nor deny to any person within its jurisdiction the equal protection of the laws" is a quotation from the Fourteenth Amendment.
   (C) "...nor shall any State deprive any citizen of the right to vote on account of race, color, or previous condition of servitude" is a quotation from the Fourteenth Amendment.
   (D) As long as the Reconstruction period lasted in each of the ex-Confederate states, the civil rights provisions of the Fourteenth Amendment were substantially enforced.

(E) After the Reconstruction period and until 1954, the "separate but equal" criterion prevailed.

7. Which of the following statements is NOT true about President Kennedy's administration?

(A) The Alliance for Progress was directed toward Latin America.
(B) Latin American governments were usually anxious to institute political and economic reforms in return for aid under the Alliance for Progress.
(C) Selling surplus food products to the Soviet Union and other communist nations gained considerable support from both major political parties.
(D) The Peace Corps program was a comparatively inexpensive foreign-aid program.
(E) President Kennedy backed the attempted Bay of Pigs invasion of Cuba.

Questions 8-11: Each of these slogans or quotations is associated with a specific individual. Select the name of the correct person.

8. "The only thing we have to fear is fear itself."

(A) Douglas MacArthur
(B) Franklin D. Roosevelt
(C) Theodore Roosevelt
(D) Harry S Truman
(E) Woodrow Wilson

9. "I regret that I was unable to shoot Henry Clay or to hang John Calhoun."

(A) William Garrison   (D) James Polk
(B) Andrew Jackson   (E) Daniel Webster
(C) Abraham Lincoln

10. "There is no right to strike against the public safety by anyone, anywhere, any time."

(A) Calvin Coolidge
(B) Warren Harding
(C) Cornelius Vanderbilt
(D) Charles Wilson
(E) Woodrow Wilson

11. "We should have open covenants openly arrived at."

(A) Douglas MacArthur
(B) Franklin D. Roosevelt

(C) Warren Harding
(D) Herbert Hoover
(E) Woodrow Wilson

12. All of these statements support the foreign policy of Jefferson and Madison EXCEPT

(A) The Embargo Act of 1807 kept American ships off the high seas and prevented impressment of our sailors by England.
(B) England and France needed our goods more than we needed their trade. They were at war and needed all the imports they could get.
(C) The Embargo Act and the Non-Intercourse Act were embarrassingly close to a peace-at-any price policy.
(D) Circumstances can make avoidance of war a wiser policy than insistence upon national rights.
(E) Had local officials aided the federal government in preventing smuggling, our rights as neutrals would soon have been observed by England and France.

13. Which of the following statements about the Hartford Convention is NOT true?'

(A) Only New England was represented at the convention.
(B) Every delegate there was a Federalist.
(C) Such a protest meeting held during the war was traitorous.
(D) The fact that the vote for the declaration of war in the Senate passed by only 19 to 13 strongly suggests that many Americans shared the views of the Hartford Convention.
(E) The convention killed the Federalist party as an influence on a national scale.

14. Which of the following statements about the Wagner-Connery Act is NOT true?

(A) The act encouraged the growth of unions so that, for the first time in our history, "big labor" came into being.
(B) The terms of the act were pro-labor and the law made no pretense of treating both labor and management equally.
(C) It was one of the major laws of the New Deal.
(D) Some labor leaders objected to certain provisions of the act and called it a "slave labor law."
(E) The law forbade employers to urge their workers not to join a union.

15. Which of the following statements is NOT true concerning the Marshall Plan?

(A) The plan was primarily a military alliance to assure peace in Europe.

(B) It was known as the European Recovery Plan (ERP).

(C) The fall of Czechoslovakia from an independent republic to a satellite of the USSR helped convince Congress to appropriate the billions of dollars the plan required.

(D) The Soviet Union's hostile reaction to the Marshall Plan made it very definite that the cold war was on in earnest.

(E) As it was first presented by the United States, the Communist bloc of nations in eastern Europe could have joined in the Marshall Plan.

Drawing by Dana Fradon;
©1972 The New Yorker Magazine, Inc.

"Founding Fathers! How come no Founding Mothers?"

16. Which is a valid generalization that can be drawn from the above cartoon?

(A) Women have not had a role in United States history.

(B) Women have become more appreciative of American art.

(C) Women have developed a consciousness with regard to their role in American society.

(D) Women artists are demanding greater respect for their contributions to the field.

(E) All of the above

17. In a United States presidential election, the electoral vote was distributed in this manner:

CANDIDATE	A	B	C	D
% OF ELECTORAL VOTE	38	38	16	8

Based on this information, which is a valid statement about the outcome of the election?

(A) Candidate A was declared the winner immediately after the election.
(B) Candidate A became President and Candidate B became Vice-President.
(C) Another presidential election was held after an additional month of campaigning.
(D) The President was chosen by the members of the House of Representatives.
(E) There was a runoff election between Candidates A and B.

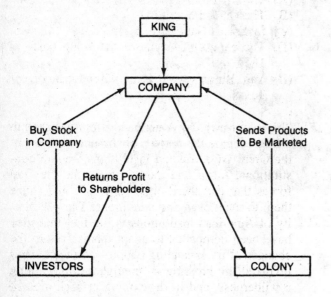

18. Which is a valid conclusion that can be drawn from the information in the above chart?

(A) The main purpose of the system was to benefit the colonies.
(B) Nationalism was the motivating factor in English colonization.
(C) The profit motive was a strong force in colonization.
(D) The opportunity to own land attracted many settlers to the colonies.
(E) The monarch was a major investor.

19. Which reason best explains the immigration policy adopted in 1921?

(A) Antipathy toward Europe had increased because of our losses in the war.
(B) There were already too many aliens in the United States.
(C) The United States was faced with large migrations from Europe.
(D) Cheap Asian laborers were replacing American laborers.
(E) Too many people of questionable health and moral standards were attempting to enter this country.

20. The chief aim of the sponsors of the literacy test for immigrants in 1917 was to bar immigrants who were

(A) born in southern and eastern Europe
(B) unable to speak English
(C) likely to work for low wages
(D) of low mental capacity
(E) of oriental background

21. Which immigrant group did NOT settle in large numbers in the area with which it is paired?

(A) Germans—Wisconsin
(B) Dutch—Indiana
(C) Scandinavians—Minnesota and the Dakotas
(D) Irish—New York
(E) Czechs—Iowa and Nebraska

22. Which common generalization about immigration to the United States is violated by the Irish immigration of the mid-19th century?

(A) Internal depression forces people to become emigrants.
(B) The country to which an immigrant comes is in need of a growing supply of labor.
(C) The basic motive of immigrants was the hope of raising themselves economically.
(D) Immigrants represent not the desperately poor and hopeless, but those who have some funds and wish to benefit themselves economically.
(E) The European immigration of the 19th century contributed to the population growth of urban areas.

23. Which person is paired with a plan he favored at the Constitutional Convention?

(A) John Dickinson of Delaware—establishment of a limited monarchy
(B) Elbridge Gerry of Massachusetts—a unicameral legislature

(C) Rufus King of Massachusetts—a parliamentary form of government

(D) Benjamin Franklin of Pennsylvania—the election of a President for life

(E) Alexander Hamilton of New York—popular control of the judiciary

24. Which factor was of greatest significance in bringing about the Albany Congress of 1754?

(A) The readiness of the colonies to unite for defense under the Crown

(B) The formal declaration of war with France by Britain

(C) A desire to adopt Benjamin Franklin's Plan of Union

(D) A desire for an alliance between the colonies and Native Americans

(E) The surrender of Washington to the French at Fort Duquesne

25. Which person would most likely have favored the right of preemption in 1800?

(A) A stockholder in a land company

(B) A frontier settler

(C) A plantation owner

(D) A New England merchant

(E) A land-bank operator

26. Whom did Lewis and Clark encounter as they traveled down the Missouri River on their return from the Pacific Coast?

(A) Small parties of trappers venturing far upriver in search of furs

(B) Squatters and their families clearing patches for their crude cabins

(C) Frontier people who with their laden pack-horses were driving livestock westward

(D) Missionaries en route to Oregon to convert the Native Americans

(E) Indians, who were surprised to encounter white people

27. A significant contribution to westward expansion made by the early trappers in the Rocky Mountain areas was their success in

(A) locating the best crossings of mountains and rivers, and blazing trails for later settlers

(B) Christianizing the Native Americans

(C) gaining the friendship of the Native American tribes by fair dealings for furs

(D) acting as scouts against the British in Oregon in the War of 1812

(E) eliminating many of the dangerous animals

that would otherwise have impeded settlement beyond the Rockies

28. "Manifest destiny" as a political idea found LEAST acceptance by

(A) the War Hawks at the time of the War of 1812

(B) New Englanders at the time of the Mexican War

(C) supporters of Andrew Jackson in his campaign in Florida

(D) campaign advisers for James Polk in 1844

(E) the backers of the Ostend Manifesto

29. "Manifest destiny" relates to James Polk as territorial expansion relates to

(A) William J. Bryan

(B) William H. Seward

(C) Cordell Hull

(D) James Monroe

(E) Charles E. Hughes

30. Which would NOT have the approval of an American expansionist during the period 1830-1860?

(A) The Slidell mission to Mexico

(B) The Ostend Manifest

(C) Jackson's Native American policy

(D) The campaign slogan of the Whig party in 1844

(E) Van Buren's policy on the annexation of Texas

31. "Up to our own day American history has been in a large degree the history of the colonization of the Great West...Behind institutions, behind constitutional forms and modifications, lie the vital forces that call these organs into life and shape them to meet changing conditions. The peculiarity of American institutions is the fact that they have been compelled to adapt themselves to the changes of an expanding people—to the changes involved in crossing a continent, in winning a wilderness, and in developing at each area of this progress out of the primitive economic and political conditions of the frontier into the complexity of city life."

The above quotation expresses an interpretation of American history first expounded in

(A) Walter P. Webb, *The Great Frontier*

(B) Frederic L. Paxson, *History of the American Frontier*

(C) Ray L. Billington, *Westward Expansion*

(D) Frederick Jackson Thrner, *The Significance of the Frontier in American History*

(E) Julius W. Pratt, *Expansionists of 1812*

32. Which presidential candidate was LEAST successful in obtaining the support of farm owners?

(A) Thomas Jefferson in 1800
(B) Andrew Jackson in 1832
(C) Abraham Lincoln in 1860
(D) Grover Cleveland in 1892
(E) Franklin D. Roosevelt in 1936

33. Throughout the 19th century, pressure for a loose interpretation of the Constitution and increased power for the federal government came most consistently from

(A) cotton farmers in the South
(B) shipping interests in New England
(C) railroad owners
(D) farmers on the western frontiers
(E) labor union leaders

34. It is often assumed that the North always championed a strong national government and opposed the doctrine of states rights. Northern support of the doctrine of states was manifested both in the adoption of resolutions at the Hartford Convention and in its

(A) support of personal liberty laws
(B) support of the Missouri Compromise
(C) opposition to the Compromise Tariff on 1833
(D) denouncement of the Supreme Court decision in *McCulloch* v. *Maryland*
(E) attacks on the court that sentenced John Brown to death

35. Which best accounts for the spirit of nationalism that was dominant in the United States between 1815 and 1824?

(A) Fear of European interference forced harmony.
(B) Economic rivalry was temporarily in abeyance.
(C) The Federalist party had replaced opposing factions.
(D) The people everywhere were elated by the great concessions that had been won by the Treaty of Ghent.
(E) The successful financing of the War of 1812 had developed cooperation among the states.

36. Which did NOT reflect the spirit of nationalism that characterized the United States during the period of 1816-1824?

(A) Decisions of the Supreme Court (1816-1824)
(B) The Monroe Doctrine
(C) The Tariff of 1816

(D) The Tallmadge Amendment (1819)
(E) The charter of the Second Bank of the United States

37. The constitutionality of federal regulation of "big business" and labor may be traced to the decision in

(A) *Marbury* v. *Madison*
(B) *Gibbons* v. *Ogden*
(C) *Martin* v. *Hunter's Lease*
(D) *Dartmouth* v. *Woodward*
(E) *Fletcher* v. *Peck*

38. On which point was Marshall's decision in *Gibbons* v. *Ogden* NOT clear-cut?

(A) Commerce should be defined as "traffic."
(B) Internal commerce was reserved to the state.
(C) Federal power and state power over interstate commerce were concurrent.
(D) Enumerated powers of Congress should not be construed narrowly.
(E) Congress's power to regulate interstate commerce may be limited by the Constitution.

39. Which was a factor considered by the Supreme Court in its decision in *United States* v. *Butler* (1936)?

(A) Proper exercise of the taxing power
(B) Violation of the Fourteenth Amendment
(C) Constitutionality of soil conservation practice
(D) Violation of Article IV, Section 2 of the Constitution
(E) Delegation of Legislative power by Congress to the Executive

40. Which pair contains two Supreme Court decisions that increased or upheld the power of the national government?

(A) *Gibbons* v. *Ogden—Lochner* v. *New York*
(B) *Fletcher* v. *Peck—Youngstown Sheet and Tube* v. *Sawyer*
(C) *United States* v. *Darby—National Labor Relations Board* v. *Jones and Laughlin Steel Corporation*
(D) *Dartmouth College* v. *Woodward—Pollock* v. *Farmers Loan and Trust Company*
(E) *Dred Scott* v. *Sandford—Plessy* v. *Ferguson*

41. The case of *Fletcher* v. *Peck* is to contracts as *Plessy* v. *Ferguson* is to

(A) religion   (D) taxation
(B) internal security   (E) segregation
(C) suffrage

42. Shays' Rebellion and the Whiskey Rebellion are similar in that each

    (A) was put down by federal troops
    (B) was a farmers' revolt
    (C) represented defiance of federal law
    (D) helped to lessen economic conflict
    (E) resulted in victory for the rebels

43. Sectionalism at the Constitutional Convention was most evident in the dispute over the

    (A) advisability of revising the Articles of Confederation
    (B) New Jersey and Virginia plans
    (C) regulation of foreign commerce
    (D) determination of office holding qualifications
    (E) right of states to issue paper currency

44. Which controversy is paired with the opposing side in that controversy?

    (A) The Paxton Boys' raid: shopkeepers v. tax collectors.
    (B) Dorr's Rebellion: slaves v. masters
    (C) Bacon's Rebellion: farmers v. merchants
    (D) The Regulator movement: tidewater v. frontier
    (E) The Flushing Remonstrance: Puritans v. Anglicans

45. Historians disagree on the major cause of the War of 1812. A state-by-state study of Congress's vote on the declaration of war would support as the chief cause

    (A) Britain's practice of impressment
    (B) Britain's failure to compensate slave owners for losses in the Revolution
    (C) Britain's refusal to repeal the Orders in Council
    (D) pro-French sentiment
    (E) expansionism

46. "Ordinarily, war seems to submerge sectional differences."

    The best example of a contradiction of this statement would be congressional criticism during

    (A) the Mexican War
    (B) the Spanish-American War
    (C) World War I
    (D) World War II
    (E) the Korean War

47. "By his act was revived a perilous dispute that was thought to have been settled."

    This statement best refers to

    (A) Daniel Webster's debate with Hayne
    (B) Andrew Jackson's veto of the Bank Charter
    (C) Stephen Douglas's championing of the Kansas-Nebraska Act
    (D) Abraham Lincoln's question for Douglas at Freeport
    (E) John Brown's raid

48. Who was the author of the phrases "a higher law" and "an irrepressible conflict," used by the anti-slavery forces?

    (A) John Brown
    (B) John Frémont
    (C) Abraham Lincoln
    (D) William H. Seward
    (E) William Lloyd Garrison

49. Which leader antagonized his own section by his stand on the issue with which he is paired?

    (A) James Polk—the Mexican War
    (B) Andrew Jackson—the rechartering of the Bank of the United States
    (C) John Quincy Adams—the Tariff of 1828
    (D) Daniel Webster—the Compromise of 1850
    (E) John C. Calhoun—*South Carolina Exposition and Protest*

50. Hinton Helper's *Impending Crisis* is primarily concerned with the

    (A) moral ambiguities of slavery in a democracy
    (B) economic effects of slavery on the South
    (C) inevitable clashes between the North and the South over slavery
    (D) threat of slave insurrections
    (E) criticism of the application of popular sovereignty to Kansas

Questions 51-58: Five persons were engaged in the following discussion of the American Civil War and its causes:

Speaker *A*:   The Civil War was the culmination of a conflict between agrarian and industrial interests.

Speaker *B*:   I don't believe so. The war was caused by people who wanted slavery completely eliminated.

Speaker *C*:   No so. The greatest instigators were the writers who played on the emotions of the people.

Speaker *D*:   Well, I feel that the differences between the North and the South could have been resolved by compromise.

Speaker *E*:   Possibly, but the South's recognition of the inevitability of Northern control of Congress made it almost impossible to prevent war.

51. The "people" referred to by Speaker *B* were in a majority in which section?

(A) New England
(B) California and Oregon
(C) Border states
(D) Kansas and Nebraska territories
(E) None of these

52. If Speaker *B* felt that war is caused by the urgings of leaders with uncompromising beliefs, whom would he most likely cite as an instigator of the American Revolution?

(A) Thomas Paine   (D) Samuel Adams
(B) Benjamin Franklin (E) Alexander Hamilton
(C) John Adams

53. Charles A. Beard was most in agreement with Speaker

(A) *A*   (B) *B*   (C) *C*   (D) *D*   (E) *E*

54. Which factor made almost impossible the compromise suggested by Speaker *D*?

(A) A judicial decision
(B) A presidential veto
(C) A state law
(D) An act of Congress
(E) A series of debates involving an election to the United States Senate

55. Who would probably have disagreed with Speaker *D*?

(A) Clay   (D) Seward
(B) Webster   (E) Crittenden
(C) Douglas

56. Speaker *C* was probably referring to the influence of

(A) Hinton R. Helper and Henry Thoreau
(B) James Lowell and Preston Brooks
(C) Robert Barnwell Rhett and Wendell Phillips
(D) Ralph Waldo Emerson and Alexander Stephens
(E) Harriet Beecher Stowe and Stephen Douglas

57. Which would NOT be cited by Speaker *A* to support his point of view?

(A) Force Acts
(B) *Exposition and Protest*
(C) Hartford Convention
(D) Chartering of the Second Bank of the United States
(E) Tariff of 1816

58. Which development can be cited in support of Speaker *E*?

(A) Supreme Court decisions
(B) Immigration
(C) The Mexican War
(D) Influence of the *Liberator*
(E) The senatorial election in Illinois in 1858

59. The original United States Constitution encouraged political democracy by

(A) providing for congressional immunity
(B) guaranteeing voting privileges to property owners
(C) insuring the use of the Electoral College
(D) providing for the formation of political parties
(E) providing for the direct election of United States Senators

60. In the Constitutional Convention, voting qualifications were made residual power because of the

(A) desire to follow the practice of English common law
(B) widespread variation of voting requirements in the states
(C) unwillingness of the federal government to bear the expense of the elections
(D) realization that more state and local officers than federal officers were to be elected
(E) conviction of the framers that the power to define citizenship should rest with the states

61. In respect to interstate agreements, the original Constitution of the United States states that

(A) such agreements are expressly forbidden
(B) a state may tax goods imported from another state if its goods are taxed by that state
(C) a state may extend to its native citizens greater privileges than those accorded to other residents

(D) a state may force the extradition of a criminal who has fled to another state
(E) a state is forbidden to enter into any compact with another state without the consent of Congress

62. What is the chronological order in which the following proposals became effective?

   I. Settlers in a territory should be allowed to decide whether they wanted slavery.
   II. Slavery should be barred north of a certain parallel.
   III. Importation of slaves into the United States should be forbidden.
   IV. Slaves should be freed throughout the United States.
   V. Slavery should be forbidden in the Northwest Territory.

   (A) I, II, III, V, IV   (D) III, V, I, II, IV
   (B) V, III, II, I, IV   (E) I, V, III, II, IV
   (C) V, II, III, I, IV

63. The Half-Breeds and Mugwumps were similar political groups in that both

   (A) worked to secure the removal of the Indians to reservations east of the Mississippi River
   (B) demanded the withdrawal of federal troops from the South
   (C) were made up of liberal groups in the Republican party
   (D) advocated direct election of United States Senators
   (E) denounced the "Crime of 1873"

64. Which person would most likely have been inclined to vote for William McKinley in 1896?

   (A) An owner of a silver mine
   (B) The president of a bank in Indiana
   (C) A member of the Knights of Labor
   (D) An Illinois farmer with a $5,000 mortgage on his farm
   (E) A person who favored vigorous enforcement of the Sherman Antitrust Act

65. An exponent of the "New Freedom" probably would have supported

   (A) a graduated income tax
   (B) an increase in tariff rates
   (C) government subsidies of railroads

(D) congressional review of Supreme Court decisions
(E) gradual elimination of governmental control over business

66. Franklin D. Roosevelt's first-term "New Deal" policies differed most markedly from Theodore Roosevelt's "Square Deal" and Wilson's "New Freedom" with respect to

   (A) tariff policy
   (B) enforcement of the antitrust laws
   (C) conservation of natural resources
   (D) protection of the consumer from harmful drugs
   (E) liberalization of credit to farmers

67. In *ex parte Milligan* the United States Supreme Court set an important precedent in the field of

   (A) civil rights
   (B) immigration
   (C) segregation
   (D) states' rights
   (E) government regulation of railroads

68. The percentage of the United States population living on farms in the 1980s was closest to

   (A) 10 percent
   (B) 25 percent
   (C) 45 percent
   (D) 65 percent
   (E) 80 percent

69. Between 1850 and 1950, in which direction did the center of population in the United States move?

   (A) East   (D) South
   (B) West   (E) Southeast
   (C) North

70. Between 1950 and 1990. in which direction did the center of population in the United States move?

   (A) East   (D) South
   (B) West   (E) Northwest
   (C) North

71. The state with the largest population in the 1980s was

   (A) California   (D) Massachusetts
   (B) Florida   (E) Texas
   (C) New York

Questions 72-76 are based on the map below.

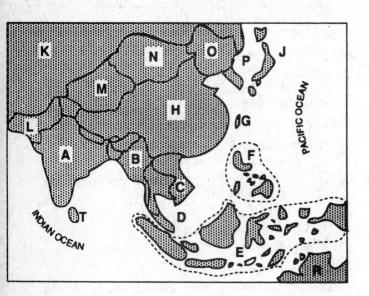

72. Once an enemy of the United States, now an ally, this nation is the industrial giant of Asia and a major trading partner of ours.

    (A) *O*   (D) *G*
    (B) *P*   (E) *F*
    (C) *J*

73 Formerly a Dutch colony, and independent since the end of World War II, this republic has the world's largest Muslim population.

    (A) *A*   (D) *K*
    (B) *E*   (E) *L*
    (C) *H*

74. This country, granted independence by the United States in 1946, saw its dictator toppled by the widow of its slain opposition leader.

    (A) *C*   (D) *F*
    (B) *D*   (E) *G*
    (C) *E*

75. Nationalists in this area, once a colony of France, defeated American troops and their domestic allies in the 1970s.

    (A) *A*   (D) *D*
    (B) *B*   (E) *F*
    (C) *C*

76. The Communist government of this country brutally suppressed a pro-democracy movement in its capital in June 1989.

    (A) *L*   (D) *O*
    (B) *M*   (E) *H*
    (C) *N*

77. While data are incomplete, it is fairly certain that the chief source of political party campaign funds is

    (A) the candidates themselves
    (B) small unsolicited contributions from people throughout the nation
    (C) trade unionists who contribute through their union locals
    (D) party dinners, such as the Lincoln Day or Jackson Day dinner
    (E) individuals who make contributions of $500 or more through political action committees

78. "The government ought to stop those aliens from coming in and taking jobs from Americans."

    This statement expresses an idea most closely related to

    (A) assimilation   (D) patriotism
    (B) environmentalism   (E) protectionism
    (C) nativism

79. The most distinctive function of a political party, as compared with other groups interested in government, is that it

    (A) helps to create public opinion
    (B) reflects public opinion
    (C) tries to persuade voters to support its candidates and policies
    (D) supplies personnel for nonelective public offices
    (E) selects candidates for public office

80. Professional politicians and political scientists would be most likely to agree that

    (A) the growth of third parties should be discouraged
    (B) presidential candidates should be chosen by national primaries rather than national conventions
    (C) a representative's first responsibility is to his constituents
    (D) policy-making positions in government should be excluded from civil service
    (E) free and equal radio and television time should be given to all candidates

81. Which territorial acquisition nearly doubled the size of the nation?

    (A) annexation of Texas

(B) Mexican Cession
(C) Louisiana Purchase
(D) Oregon Territory
(E) Results of treaties with Canada

82. A federal law insuring bank deposits was first passed during

(A) the Square Deal of Theodore Roosevelt
(B) the New Freedom of Woodrow Wilson
(C) the New Deal of Franklin D. Roosevelt
(D) the Fair Deal of Harry S Truman
(B) the Great Society of Lyndon B. Johnson

83. The conclusion of a peace treaty between Egypt and Israel was a foreign policy achievement of

(A) Dwight D. Eisenhower
(B) Richard Nixon
(C) Gerald Ford
(D) Jimmy Carter
(B) Ronald Reagan

84. The restoration of full diplomatic relations with China after 30 years of hostility was a foreign policy achievement of

(A) Richard Nixon   (D) Ronald Reagan
(B) Gerald Ford   (E) George Bush
(C) Jimmy Carter

85. Arab groups took American hostages during the presidencies of

(A) Carter and Reagan
(B) Ford and Carter
(C) Bush and Reagan
(D) Kennedy and Eisenhower
(E) Truman and Johnson

Questions 86-90 are based on the map below.

86. As a result of the compromise of 1850, this state entered the union prohibiting slavery.

(A) A   (D) F
(B) B   (E) E
(C) C

87. This state violated a treaty made between the United States and the Cherokee Indians.

(A) H   (D) D
(B) I   (E) E
(C) C

88. The Constitutional Convention of 1787 was held in this state.

(A) I   (D) L
(B) J   (E) M
(C) K

89. This is one of the states created out of the old Northwest Territory.

(A) B   (D) H
(B) D   (E) M
(C) G

90. The oldest settlement by people of European background in this area (state) was founded by John Jacob Astor.

(A) A   (D) I
(B) B   (E) L
(C) E

91. An investor in common stock who is interested primarily in capital appreciation would be most interested in a stock's

(A) par value   (D) dividends
(B) book value   (E) capital structure
(C) earnings

92. Which type of business combination involves an actual sale of stock?

(A) Pool   (D) Partnership
(B) Trust   (E) Holding company
(C) Interlocking
    directorate

93. Which policy would tend to encourage inflation?

(A) Balancing the national budget
(B) Raising the discount rate
(C) Increasing the margin rate
(D) Decreasing government spending
(E) Lowering the reserve ratio

94. Which tended to be the greatest stumbling block for the promotion of women's rights?

    (A) Lack of leadership
    (B) The Industrial Revolution
    (C) Frontier conditions
    (D) Common law
    (B) Influence of newspapers

95. In which respect was the administration of Woodrow Wilson similar to that of Franklin D. Roosevelt?

    (A) Legislation was enacted to deal with farm surpluses.
    (B) State claims to offshore oil were guaranteed.
    (C) Social Security legislation was extended.
    (D) Extensive changes were made in the currency system.
    (E) Few changes were made in the tariff laws.

ANSWER KEY: TEST 2

1. B	27. A	53. A	79. E
2. D	28. B	54. A	80. D
3. E	29. B	55. D	81. C
4. D	30. E	56. C	82. C
5. D	31. D	57. E	83. D
6. C	32. D	58. B	84. A
7. B	33. D	59. A	85. A
8. B	34. A	60. B	86. A
9. B	35. B	61. E	87. B
10. A	36. D	62. B	88. C
11. E	37. B	63. C	89. D
12. C	38. C	64. B	90. B
13. C	39. A	65. A	91. C
14. D	40. C	66. B	92. E
15. A	41. E	67. A	93. E
16. C	42. B	68. A	94. D
17. D	43. C	69. B	95. D
18. C	44. D	70. D	
19. C	45. E	71. A	
20. A	46. A	72. C	
21. B	47. C	73. B	
22. D	48. D	74. D	
23. A	49. D	75. C	
24. D	50. B	76. E	
25. B	51. E	77. E	
26. A	52. D	78. C	

ANALYSIS CHART: TEST 2

Era	Number of Questions	Number Right	Number Wrong	Number
Pre-Columbian to 1789: questions 2, 18, 23, 24, 42, 43, 44, 59, 60, 61	10			
1790 to 1898: questions 3, 5, 6, 9, 12, 13, 22, 25-31, 33-38, 41, 45, 47-58, 63, 64, 67, 74	38			
1899 to present: questions 7, 8, 10, 11, 14, 15, 19, 20, 39, 65, 66, 71, 79, 81-93, 95	27			

Era	Number of Questions	Number Right	Number Wrong	Number
Cross period: questions 32, 40, 46, 68-70, 72, 73, 75, 76, 94	11			
Nonchronological: questions 1, 4, 16, 17, 21, 62, 77, 78, 80	9			

FINDING THE REASONS FOR INCORRECT ANSWERS

Be sure to check the answer explanations before completing the following chart.

Era	Number Wrong	Lack of Knowledge	Misunderstand Problem	Careless Error	Not Answered
Pre-Columbian to 1789					
1790 to 1898					
1899 to present					
Cross period					
Nonchronological					

ANSWER EXPLANATIONS: TEST 2

1. **B** Article I, Section 3, Clause 6 of the Constitution states, "The Senate shall have the sole Power to try all impeachments...And no person shall be convicted without the concurrence of a two thirds of the Members present."

2. **D** Cabot was an Italian navigator who explored the coast of Newfoundland (Canada) in 1497 for England.

3. **E** Following the Civil War, the Radicals in Congress attempted to reduce the power of both the Judicial and Executive branches in order to push through their Reconstruction program. The Radicals also wanted to limit the President's power to fire Republican office-holders and replace them with his own supporters. To accomplish this, Congress passed the Tenure of Office Act in 1867, providing that the President could not remove important civil servants from office without the Senate's approval. President Andrew Johnson believed the Tenure of Office Act unconstitutional, and in August 1867 he removed Secretary of War Edwin Stanton (the only supporter of the Radicals in his Cabinet). The House voted eleven articles of impeachment against Johnson, but the Senate acquitted him.

4. **D** The committee system in Congress weeds out almost 95 percent of all bills introduced. The bicameral legislature provides a further check on legislation, as does the need for presidential approval.

5. **D** This point of view was that of Hamilton and other Federalist leaders, and was opposed by the Democratic Republicans.

6. **C** This is a paraphrase of the Fifteenth Amendment, which provides that race, color, or former status as a slave cannot be used by any state or the federal government as a reason to deny any person the right to vote.

7. **B** Such reforms would have had to be made at the expense of the political and economic supporters of the Latin American leadership. Otherwise, those reforms would have been made without prodding by the United States government.

8. **B** This sentence is from F.D.R.'s first inaugural address, in which he called for support of his proposed measures to deal with the Great Depression.

9. **B** Jackson believed that Clay had made a "corrupt bargain" that cost Jackson the Presidential election of 1824. He bitterly opposed the nullification ideas of Calhoun, who was Vice-President under Jackson until resigning in 1832 over opposition to the protective tariff act of that year.

10. **A** This terse telegraphic message was from Governor Calvin Coolidge of Massachusetts to Samuel Gompers regarding a strike by the Boston police force in 1920. Those words made Governor Coolidge a national figure overnight.

11. **E** This was the first of Woodrow Wilson's "Fourteen Points," opposing the secret treaties and alliances that he felt had led to World War I.

12. **C** Those two acts embodies the Jefferson and Madison policy of retreating from freedom of the seas rather than risk war with either of the belligerents, England or France.

13. **C** Although they were being hurt economically by the War of 1812, (the delegates of) the New England states were certainly not trying to help the enemy.

14. **D** The Wagner-Connery Act was hailed as the Magna Carta of labor; the Taft-Hartley Act of 1947 was denounced as a "slave labor law."

15. **A** The Marshall Plan, announced in 1947, was an economic one and was also known as the European Recovery Program. The North Atlantic Treaty Organization started in 1949 was a military alliance to oppose further Communist expansion in Europe.

16. **C** The women's rights movement began during the 1970s as a result of increased awareness of political and economic inequalities between American men and women, especially women working outside the home.

17. **D** The Constitution provides that if no Presidential candidate receives a majority of the Electoral College votes, the House of Representatives chooses the President from among the three candidates with the most electoral votes.

18. **C** The lower left side of the chart shows that investors expected to receive a share of the profits that the company made by selling products from the colony.

19. **C** The Immigration Act of 1921 reduced the number of persons who could be admitted from any country to 3 percent of the number of that nationality living in the United States in 1910. The effect was to severely restrict immigration from southern and eastern Europe, from which many were trying to escape the hardships of post-World War I Europe. When that war broke out in 1914, over two-thirds of all immigrants to the United States were coming from that part of the world.

20. **A** In those areas of Europe, living standards were low, and opportunities for education were limited there.

21. **B** The immigrant groups listed were all part of the "old immigration" that arrived before 1885. While New York was still a British colony, Dutch settlers continued to settle in the fertile Hudson Valley of New York State, as they had when it was part of New Netherlands.

22. **D** Between 1846 and 1860, a million and a half Irish braved the Atlantic to escape a potato famine in Ireland, which was destroying their staple food crop and creating nationwide poverty.

23. **A** This answer can be arrived at by a process of elimination. Dickinson is best known for his 1767 "letters from a Pennsylvania farmer," which attacked the Townshend duties.

24. **D** Brought about by French-sponsored Indian raids, the meeting considered Benjamin Franklin's "Albany Plan of Union" to centralize and unify the handling of defense problems and Indian affairs by the colonies.

25. **B** Preemption would give squatters on public lands the first right to buy the lands they had settled.

26. **A** This is the only logical answer, as it was too early for squatters, frontier settlers, or missionaries to

have arrived. The Louisiana Territory had been purchased from France in 1803, and Lewis and Clark explored it from 1804 to 1805. Sacajawea, a Shoshone Indian woman, helped them to establish peaceful contacts with Indian tribes along the route of their explorations.

27. **A**   Those accomplishments were necessary for the success of their endeavors.

28. **B**   New England was the seat of abolitionism, and the Mexican War was seen there as a means of extending the area open to slavery.

29. **B**   All of the choices were Secretaries of State. Seward fought for and achieved the purchase of Alaska from Russia in 1867.

30. **E**   Van Buren had served as President from 1836 to 1840 and was succeeded by William Henry Harrison, and upon Harrison's death by John Tyler. Both Van Buren and Henry Clay expected to be presidential candidates in 1844, and in letters to the newspapers made known their opposition to annexing Texas.

31. **D**   Turner and his students examined the effect on the American character of the availability of almost endless stretches of land. They concluded that the continuing opportunity to expand into the West had promoted democracy, nationalism, and individuality.

32. **D**   Cleveland was a "gold Democrat," while the farmers of the South and West were for the free and unlimited coinage of silver in order to produce inflation, which would make easier their burden of debt repayment.

33. **D**   Western farmers favored cheap land, rapid settlement, squatters' rights or preemption, and internal improvements, like roads and canals, built at federal expense. The Western farmers needed roads and canals to get their goods to market.

34. **A**   Personal liberty laws were passed in most of the free states in the early 1850's. These laws nullified the Fugitive Slave Law by forbidding state officials to assist in the capture of runaway slaves from the South.

35. **B**   This was the Era of Good Feelings, when James Monroe was President and the Federalist party was in decline. The nation as a whole supported a second Bank of the United States and a protective tariff. Every section hoped to become a manufacturing area, and state banks were in disrepute.

36. **D**   When Missouri in 1819 applied for admission to the Union as a slave state, Representative James Tallmadge of New York proposed an amendment to Missouri's bill for statehood that would gradually abolish slavery in Missouri. When the amendment passed in the House of Representatives, it brought forth a violent outcry from Southerners. The senate rejected the plan, and there were bitter debates in Congress.

37. **B**   In 1824, Chief Justice John Marshall ruled that Robert Fulton's monopoly of steamboat traffic on the Hudson River and other New York waterways was unconstitutional. Marshall wrote that whatever affects interstate commerce may come under federal control.

38. **C**   Marshall strengthened the power of the federal government at the expense of the states. His rulings established the idea that the Supreme Court could set aside the laws passed by state legislatures and the decisions of state courts.

39. **A**   In that decision, the Supreme Court declared unconstitutional the Agricultural Adjustment Act of 1933, a key New Deal measure, on the grounds that the taxes levied on processors of farm commodities were not levies to finance government, but were levies on one group to give benefits to another. In levying such a tax, the Court found that Congress had entered a field reserved for state action under the Tenth Amendment.

40. **C**   In *United States* v. *Darby* (1941), the Court upheld a 1938 law closing the channels of interstate commerce to goods produced by child labor. In *National Labor Relations Board* v. *Jones and Laughlin Steel Corporation* (1937), the Court upheld the constitutionality of the Wagner Act, which granted unions the right of collective bargaining, an permitted Congress to use the interstate commerce power to limit child labor.

41. **E**   The Supreme Court decision in *Fletcher* v. *Peck* (1810) declared that a land grant was a contract and that the state of Georgia could not invalidate one, even if it had been fraudulently secured. In *Plessy* v. *Ferguson* (1896), the Court upheld state laws establishing "separate but equal" schools for white and for black children. Each case involved fraudulent situations: the first, a bribed Georgia legislature; the second, unequal facilities called equal.

42. **B**   In 1786 Daniel Shays, an army captain in the Revolutionary War, led a group of angry fellow farmer debtors in forcing several Massachusetts courts to close, preventing judges from handing down judgments against other debtors. A few years later, in 1794, a group of frontier farmers in Pennsylvania refused to pay the whiskey tax, part of Hamilton's excise tax

program, and threatened the tax collectors. The Whiskey Rebellion was put down by a national militia, and the authority of the national government was established.

43. **C** The North wanted the new government to have full power to regulate all interstate and foreign commerce. The South feared being outvoted on matters of trade regulation by the more populous northern states and did not want interference with the slave trade.

44. **D** The grievances of the North Carolina Regulators of 1769 to 1771 related to bad government-unequal taxation, uncertainty of land titles, refusal of the assembly to allow taxes to be paid in produce, and the consequent action of having the government take over the farms of poor farmers. The tidewater legislators did not meet the needs of the frontier settlers. (These grievances are similar to those of Shays' Rebellion in Massachusetts.)

45. **E** Western and Southern leaders, especially from frontier areas, were anxious for United States' expansion into Canada and the Floridas. These "War Hawks" gained control of the House of Representatives in the election of 1810 and urged their program: to gain control of the Canadian fur trade and end the Native American menace there, and to end the Spanish influence in Florida.

46. **A** There was much opposition to the war in the North, especially among those who felt that acquiring Texas would lead to extending slavery. President Polk was criticized for sending troops into disputed territory.

47. **C** The Kansas-Nebraska Act of 1854 reopened the slavery controversy and aroused sectional hatreds by repealing the Missouri Compromise of 1820.

48. **D** In Seward's speech of October 1858, he echoed Lincoln's sentiment by saying, "It is an irrepressible conflict between opposing and enduring forces, and it means that the United States must and will, sooner or later, become entirely a slave-holding nation, or entirely a free-labor nation."

49. **D** In his Seventh of March (1850) speech to the United States Senate, Daniel Webster's eloquence convinced Northern Senators to vote for the compromise of 1850, despite its unpalatable provisions that permitted, the extension and protection of slavery. "The North could never have been induced to swallow a new fugitive slave law, had not Webster held the spoon." †

---

† Samuel E. Morison and Henry S. Commager, *Growth of the American Republic*, New York: Oxford University Press, 1962, vol. 1. p. 626.

50. **B** The thesis of his 1857 book was that while slavery enriched a few "slaveocrats," it doomed small Southern farmers to "galling poverty and ignorance."

51. **E** Only slave owners in the Deep South held that position.

52. **D** Samuel Adams was a radical leader who helped make Massachusetts a center of opposition to Great Britain from 1770 on. He helped form the "Committees of Correspondence."

53. **A** Beard wrote the influential Economic Origins of the Constitution in 1913 and believed generally in an economic interpretation of American history.

54. **A** The *Dred Scott* decision of 1857 brought the bitterness between North and South to a new high. It seemed to vindicate the Southern point of view and to open the way for the spread of slavery into the territories.

55. **D** See the explanation of question 48.

56. **C** Both were Northern abolitionists whose writings were bitterly antislavery.

57. **E** Passed during the Era of Good Feelings, the Tariff of 1816 had wide support throughout the nation. See also the explanation of question 35.

58. **B** Almost all the heavy immigration from northern and western Europe from 1815 to 1860 was destined for the cities of the Northeast and the farms of the West. Free labor was not about to compete with slave labor in the South. With ever-increasing population, the North and West gained more seats in the House of Representatives.

59. **A** Congressional immunity is considered necessary to insure that the members of Congress may act independently and speak freely. They are ordinarily free from arrest during sessions and are guaranteed freedom of speech within the halls of Congress—practices derived from those of the British Parliament.

60. **B** Residual powers are those reserved to the states and to the people, rather than delegated to the federal government.

61. **E** Until the twentieth century, interstate compacts were used only to settle boundary disputes between states. They have more recently been used to establish interstate agencies and to solve joint problems.

62. **B**   The Northwest Ordinance of 1787 forbade slavery in the Northwest Territory between the Ohio and Mississippi rivers. The United States Constitution, ratified in 1788, imposed a twenty-year ban on legislation prohibiting the importation of slaves. As soon as the ban could be lifted in 1808, importing slaves into the country was prohibited. The Missouri Compromise of 1820 banned slavery in states north of the southern boundary of Missouri, 36°30′ north latitude. The Kansas-Nebraska Act of 1854 permitted squatter sovereignty. All slaves in the United States were finally freed by the adoption of the Thirteenth Amendment in 1865.

63. **C**   The Half-Breeds were Republicans who parted company with President Grant and his cronies who hoped for a third term in 1876. In the election campaign of 1884, the pro-Blaine Republicans called the reform Republicans "Mugwumps" to ridicule them.

64. **B**   Since McKinley's program was opposed by those in each of the other four choices, the answer can be obtained by a process of elimination. McKinley's administration benefited from prosperity and supported big business. Placing the nation on a gold standard meant that bank loans would be repaid with money backed by gold, rather than with inflated paper currency.

65. **A**   The "New Freedom" was Woodrow Wilson's program of domestic reforms. During his administration, Congress passed and the states ratified the Sixteenth Amendment (1913), giving Congress the power to levy income taxes.

66. **B**   Roosevelt's approach from 1933 to 1936 was to try to establish a partnership between government and business through the establishment of NIRA (National Industrial Recovery Act) codes of fair competition.

67. **A**   Lambdin P. Milligan, a Copperhead suspected of being part of a plot to release Confederate prisoners in the North during the Civil War, was arrested and then tried by a military court, which sentenced him to be hanged. The Supreme Court overturned Milligan's conviction because he had been living in a peaceful area where regular courts were operating, and he had been denied a trial by jury. The Court denied that the war justified ignoring the individual's tights as guaranteed by the first ten amendments to the Constitution. The Court condemned Lincoln's use of military courts to try civilians.

68. **A**   Only about 7 percent of Americans lived on farms in the 1980s. In the first United States census in 1790, over 90 percent of Americans lived on farms.

69. **B**   The center of United States population moved steadily westward from Independence to the mid-twentieth century.

70. **D**   Since World War II, an aging population has sought the warm climate of the Sunbelt for retirement. They have been accompanied by the families of workers seeking jobs in the growing service industries.

71. **A**   California overtook New York as the state with most people, and with the largest state delegation in the United States House of Representatives.

72. **C**   Letter *J* on the map of East Asia is Japan, our World War II adversary and present partner in trade and in aid to underdeveloped nations.

73. **B**   Indonesia has ever 70 million followers of Islam. Before independence it was known as the Dutch East Indies, whose islands include Java, Sumatra, Borneo, and Celebes.

74. **D**   The people of the Republic of the Philippines overthrew Ferdinand Marcos in 1986, electing Corazon Aquino as President.

75. **C**   Vietnam, bordering on the South China Sea, saw the withdrawal of 500,000 United States troops from 1971 to 1973, and the victory of Communist forces from the Viet Cong and North Vietnam by 1975.

76. **E**   In Beijing, China, government troops and tanks brutally suppressed pro-democracy protesters in Tiananmen Square, and then continued their bloody crackdown nationwide.

77. **E**   Political action committees (PACs) have become the major conduit for large political corttributions, starting in the 1980s.

78. **C**   *Nativism* was a political program in the 19th century that favored the interests of the native-born over those of immigrants.

79. **E**   This has become the most important purpose of political parties, in contrast to other interest groups.

80. **D**   Policy is determined by the political leaders at the head of the administration of state and federal government, Policymakers should be held responsible for the consequences of their political and economic

decisions, whereas civil servants only carry out the policies and programs determined by elected or appointed political leaders.

81. **C** President Jefferson purchased the Louisiana Territory from France in 1803.

82. **C** The Federal Deposit Insurance Corporation (FDIC) was established in 1933 to prevent loss of deposits in case of bank failure.

83. **D** In 1978 President Carter hosted President Sadat of Egypt and Prime Minister Begin of Israel, helping to produce the Camp David (Maryland) Peace Accords, which led to the peace treaty of 1979.

84. **A** President Nixon flew to Beijing, China, in 1972 to restore more normal relations and to take advantage of the split between the Soviet Union and its former close Communist ally.

85. **A** In 1979, Iranian fundamentalist militants stormed the American embassy in Teheran and seized 52 Americans as hostages. A U.S. military mission to rescue them failed, and the hostages were not released until January 20, 1981, the day Ronald Reagan succeeded Jimmy Carter. During the Reagan years, eight or more Americans were kidnapped in Lebanon, their Arab captors demanding the release of jailed fellow Arab terrorists.

86. **A** California entered the Union free of slavery, while in the balance of the Mexican Cession, the Utah and New Mexico territories, the issue of slavery was to be decided by squatter sovereignty.

87. **B** Georgia was only one of the states that violated Indian land rights and treaty rights. When the Supreme Court ruled in favor of the Cherokees and against the state of Georgia, President Jackson refused to enforce the Court's decision, saying, "John Marshall has made his decision. Now let him enforce it."

88. **C** Philadelphia, Pennsylvania, hosted the Constitutional Convention, called to amend the Articles of Confederation, which had governed the states since their independence was effectively won in 1781.

89. **D** Indiana (letter *H*), Ohio, Michigan, Illinois, and Wisconsin were created out of the area of the original United States, which was northwest of the Ohio River and east of the Mississippi.

90. **B** The earliest settlers of the state of Oregon were merchants who could get furs. Beaver skins were in great demand in the East to make men's hats.

91. **C** This is determined by dividing the corporation's net earnings by the number of outstanding shares of common stock. Earnings will be greater than the amount of dividends distributed.

92. **E** A holding company is a corporation that holds a controlling interest (ownership of 51 percent or more of the voting stock). in other corporations.

93. **E** When the Federal Reserve lowers the percentage of deposits that a bank must keep in reserve, it increases the bank's ability to lend money. With more money in circulation, there is greater inflationary pressure on the prices of the same amount of goods and services.

94. **D** The common law, consisting largely of traditions that are very slow to change, needs specific legislation to move it along. The other choices, including positive leadership, can be shown to have promoted women's tights.

95. **D** During Wilson's first administration, Congress passed the Federal Reserve Act (1913), permitting the issue of Federal Reserve notes, which are usually backed by government securities or gold certificates. Under F.D.R., Congress passed the Banking Act of 1935, abandoning the gold standard and adopting a "managed" currency.

ANSWER SHEET: TEST 3

1. Ⓐ Ⓑ Ⓒ Ⓓ Ⓔ	16. Ⓐ Ⓑ Ⓒ Ⓓ Ⓔ	31. Ⓐ Ⓑ Ⓒ Ⓓ Ⓔ
2. Ⓐ Ⓑ Ⓒ Ⓓ Ⓔ	17. Ⓐ Ⓑ Ⓒ Ⓓ Ⓔ	32. Ⓐ Ⓑ Ⓒ Ⓓ Ⓔ
3. Ⓐ Ⓑ Ⓒ Ⓓ Ⓔ	18. Ⓐ Ⓑ Ⓒ Ⓓ Ⓔ	33. Ⓐ Ⓑ Ⓒ Ⓓ Ⓔ
4. Ⓐ Ⓑ Ⓒ Ⓓ Ⓔ	19. Ⓐ Ⓑ Ⓒ Ⓓ Ⓔ	34. Ⓐ Ⓑ Ⓒ Ⓓ Ⓔ
5. Ⓐ Ⓑ Ⓒ Ⓓ Ⓔ	20. Ⓐ Ⓑ Ⓒ Ⓓ Ⓔ	35. Ⓐ Ⓑ Ⓒ Ⓓ Ⓔ
6. Ⓐ Ⓑ Ⓒ Ⓓ Ⓔ	21. Ⓐ Ⓑ Ⓒ Ⓓ Ⓔ	36. Ⓐ Ⓑ Ⓒ Ⓓ Ⓔ
7. Ⓐ Ⓑ Ⓒ Ⓓ Ⓔ	22. Ⓐ Ⓑ Ⓒ Ⓓ Ⓔ	37. Ⓐ Ⓑ Ⓒ Ⓓ Ⓔ
8. Ⓐ Ⓑ Ⓒ Ⓓ Ⓔ	23. Ⓐ Ⓑ Ⓒ Ⓓ Ⓔ	38. Ⓐ Ⓑ Ⓒ Ⓓ Ⓔ
9. Ⓐ Ⓑ Ⓒ Ⓓ Ⓔ	24. Ⓐ Ⓑ Ⓒ Ⓓ Ⓔ	39. Ⓐ Ⓑ Ⓒ Ⓓ Ⓔ
10. Ⓐ Ⓑ Ⓒ Ⓓ Ⓔ	25. Ⓐ Ⓑ Ⓒ Ⓓ Ⓔ	40. Ⓐ Ⓑ Ⓒ Ⓓ Ⓔ
11. Ⓐ Ⓑ Ⓒ Ⓓ Ⓔ	26. Ⓐ Ⓑ Ⓒ Ⓓ Ⓔ	41. Ⓐ Ⓑ Ⓒ Ⓓ Ⓔ
12. Ⓐ Ⓑ Ⓒ Ⓓ Ⓔ	27. Ⓐ Ⓑ Ⓒ Ⓓ Ⓔ	42. Ⓐ Ⓑ Ⓒ Ⓓ Ⓔ
13. Ⓐ Ⓑ Ⓒ Ⓓ Ⓔ	28. Ⓐ Ⓑ Ⓒ Ⓓ Ⓔ	43. Ⓐ Ⓑ Ⓒ Ⓓ Ⓔ
14. Ⓐ Ⓑ Ⓒ Ⓓ Ⓔ	29. Ⓐ Ⓑ Ⓒ Ⓓ Ⓔ	44. Ⓐ Ⓑ Ⓒ Ⓓ Ⓔ
15. Ⓐ Ⓑ Ⓒ Ⓓ Ⓔ	30. Ⓐ Ⓑ Ⓒ Ⓓ Ⓔ	45. Ⓐ Ⓑ Ⓒ Ⓓ Ⓔ

46. Ⓐ Ⓑ Ⓒ Ⓓ Ⓔ	61. Ⓐ Ⓑ Ⓒ Ⓓ Ⓔ	76. Ⓐ Ⓑ Ⓒ Ⓓ Ⓔ
47. Ⓐ Ⓑ Ⓒ Ⓓ Ⓔ	62. Ⓐ Ⓑ Ⓒ Ⓓ Ⓔ	77. Ⓐ Ⓑ Ⓒ Ⓓ Ⓔ
48. Ⓐ Ⓑ Ⓒ Ⓓ Ⓔ	63. Ⓐ Ⓑ Ⓒ Ⓓ Ⓔ	78. Ⓐ Ⓑ Ⓒ Ⓓ Ⓔ
49. Ⓐ Ⓑ Ⓒ Ⓓ Ⓔ	64. Ⓐ Ⓑ Ⓒ Ⓓ Ⓔ	79. Ⓐ Ⓑ Ⓒ Ⓓ Ⓔ
50. Ⓐ Ⓑ Ⓒ Ⓓ Ⓔ	65. Ⓐ Ⓑ Ⓒ Ⓓ Ⓔ	80. Ⓐ Ⓑ Ⓒ Ⓓ Ⓔ
51. Ⓐ Ⓑ Ⓒ Ⓓ Ⓔ	66. Ⓐ Ⓑ Ⓒ Ⓓ Ⓔ	81. Ⓐ Ⓑ Ⓒ Ⓓ Ⓔ
52. Ⓐ Ⓑ Ⓒ Ⓓ Ⓔ	67. Ⓐ Ⓑ Ⓒ Ⓓ Ⓔ	82. Ⓐ Ⓑ Ⓒ Ⓓ Ⓔ
53. Ⓐ Ⓑ Ⓒ Ⓓ Ⓔ	68. Ⓐ Ⓑ Ⓒ Ⓓ Ⓔ	83. Ⓐ Ⓑ Ⓒ Ⓓ Ⓔ
54. Ⓐ Ⓑ Ⓒ Ⓓ Ⓔ	69. Ⓐ Ⓑ Ⓒ Ⓓ Ⓔ	84. Ⓐ Ⓑ Ⓒ Ⓓ Ⓔ
55. Ⓐ Ⓑ Ⓒ Ⓓ Ⓔ	70. Ⓐ Ⓑ Ⓒ Ⓓ Ⓔ	85. Ⓐ Ⓑ Ⓒ Ⓓ Ⓔ
56. Ⓐ Ⓑ Ⓒ Ⓓ Ⓔ	71. Ⓐ Ⓑ Ⓒ Ⓓ Ⓔ	86. Ⓐ Ⓑ Ⓒ Ⓓ Ⓔ
57. Ⓐ Ⓑ Ⓒ Ⓓ Ⓔ	72. Ⓐ Ⓑ Ⓒ Ⓓ Ⓔ	87. Ⓐ Ⓑ Ⓒ Ⓓ Ⓔ
58. Ⓐ Ⓑ Ⓒ Ⓓ Ⓔ	73. Ⓐ Ⓑ Ⓒ Ⓓ Ⓔ	88. Ⓐ Ⓑ Ⓒ Ⓓ Ⓔ
59. Ⓐ Ⓑ Ⓒ Ⓓ Ⓔ	74. Ⓐ Ⓑ Ⓒ Ⓓ Ⓔ	89. Ⓐ Ⓑ Ⓒ Ⓓ Ⓔ
60. Ⓐ Ⓑ Ⓒ Ⓓ Ⓔ	75. Ⓐ Ⓑ Ⓒ Ⓓ Ⓔ	90. Ⓐ Ⓑ Ⓒ Ⓓ Ⓔ

91. Ⓐ Ⓑ Ⓒ Ⓓ Ⓔ
92. Ⓐ Ⓑ Ⓒ Ⓓ Ⓔ
93. Ⓐ Ⓑ Ⓒ Ⓓ Ⓔ
94. Ⓐ Ⓑ Ⓒ Ⓓ Ⓔ
95. Ⓐ Ⓑ Ⓒ Ⓓ Ⓔ

Test 3

Directions: Each of the questions or incomplete statements is followed by five suggested answers or completions. Select the one that is best in each case and then blacken the corresponding space on the answer sheet.

Questions 1-4 refer to the following graph.

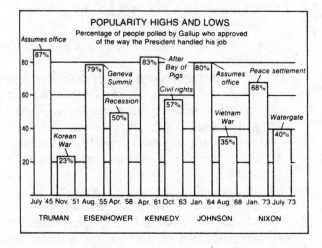

1. The President who reached the highest peak of popularity was

   (A) Truman   (D) Johnson
   (B) Eisenhower   (E) Nixon
   (C) Kennedy

2. Presidents who were considered most unpopular because of a foreign policy were

   (A) Johnson and Nixon
   (B) Truman and Johnson
   (C) Truman and Kennedy
   (D) Eisenhower and Kennedy
   (E) Eisenhower and Nixon

3. The President whose lowest popularity resulted from an economic problem was

   (A) Truman   (D) Johnson
   (B) Nixon   (E) Eisenhower
   (C) Kennedy

4. Which conclusion is most justified by the information in the chart?

   (A) The popularity of a President depends on how strong he is.
   (B) The popularity of most Presidents changes during their time in office.
   (C) A popular of President will usually be praised by future historians.
   (D) The popularity of Presidents really depends on what they accomplish before taking office.
   (E) The public does not appreciate the accomplishments of our Presidents.

5,6. In his Farewell Address, President Washington gave two bits of advice he thought the nation should follow. In substance, they are among the following statements. Identify them by letter.

   (A) Avoid making treaties with other nations.
   (B) Maintain at least two independent and strong political parties.
   (C) Avoid permanent entangling alliances.
   (D) It is better to err on the side of freedom for individuals than on the side of excessive power for the government.
   (E) Make sure that attachment to a political party does not become a stronger influence than attachment to the nation.

7. Which of these events occurred FIRST?

   (A) Final adjustment of the northeastern border of the United States between Maine and Canada
   (B) Establishment of the Mississippi River as the western border
   (C) Establishment of the present southwestern border between the Rio Grande River and the Pacific Ocean
   (D) Establishment of the northern border from the Lake of Woods to the Rocky Mountains
   (E) Establishment of the northern border from the Rockies to the West Coast

8. Which of the events in question 7 happened LAST?

Questions 9-10: In each of these questions, one item does not belong with the group because it lacks a factor common to the other four items. Identify the EXCEPTION in each group.

9. (A) Interstate Commerce Act
   (B) Esch-Cummins Act
   (C) *Wabash* v. *Illinois*
   (D) Hepburn Act
   (E) Pendleton Act

10. (A) Pullman strike
    (B) Molly Maguires
    (C) Force Bill
    (D) I.W.W. (Industrial Workers of the World)
    (E) Haymarket Square

11. Which of the following statements about the coal strike of 1902 is NOT true?

    (A) The strike was in the anthracite coal fields of eastern Pennsylvania.
    (B) J.P. Morgan played a part in bringing about a settlement.
    (C) President Theodore Roosevelt intervened on the part of the public.
    (D) Refusal of the mine operators to recognize the union as a bargaining agent was a major issue in the strike.
    (E) The intervention by the President in the strike was strongly resented by the union, but accepted willingly by the mine operators.

12. All of the following statements agree with the thinking of the New Deal liberal wing of the Democratic party EXCEPT

    (A) The key to economic health lies in the purchasing power of the lower-and middle-income groups.
    (B) Minimum-wage laws keep people from being employed and thus force them on the public relief rolls.
    (C) Cutting the gold content of the dollar by about 40 percent was a legitimate method of counteracting deflation in the 1930s.
    (D) A minimum wage set by law should be an hourly wage high enough to keep people off the public relief rolls.
    (E) High taxes in prosperous times tend to control inflation by leaving in the people's hands less money to spend.

13. All of the following statements agree with the thinking of the conservative wing of the Republican party EXCEPT

(A) The possibility of very high profits is a desirable factor to stimulate business enterprise into new ventures.
(B) Parity payments on agricultural products should be about 75 percent or less, and every effort should be made to get rid of parity payments altogether.
(C) Taxation results in the government spending the money it collects and has no influence in reducing or checking inflation.
(D) Parity payments on agricultural products should be in the range of about 80 percent to 100 percent.
(E) An ample supply of risk capital and political climate that encourages investment are the best stimulus for a healthy economy.

14. One of Wilson's "Fourteen Points" called for freedom of the seas in peace and war. Which of the following statements is FALSE?

(A) Freedom of the seas is rarely a problem in time of peace.
(B) The United States was not permitted freedom of the seas during the Napoleonic War, or from 1914 to its entrance into World War I.
(C) With freedom of the seas, in time of war all neutral nations would be allowed to trade with each other without molestation or hindrance.
(D) Under conditions expected to prevail if there is a World War III, the concept of freedom of the seas will have little, if any, meaning.
(E) With freedom of the seas, in wartime the operation of a blockade against neutral shipping would be prohibited.

15,16. When the Electoral College fails to elect the Vice-President, which two of the following statements are part of the constitutional provisions dealing with such a situation?

(A) The election goes to the House of Representatives
(B) The election goes to the Senate.
(C) Each state has one vote.
(D) Each state has two votes.
(E) Each state has as many votes as it has members in Congress.

Questions 17-18 refer to the following resolution.

"Resolved that the protective tariff policy which prevailed almost all the time from the Civil War to the depth of the Great Depression in 1933 was beneficial to our economy."

17. All of the following statements supports the *affirmative* of the resolution EXCEPT

   (A) Protected industries keep a full dinner pail for the workers.
   (B) Products of foreign pauper labor are kept out of the United States.
   (C) Protective tariffs tend to provoke international friction.
   (D) Without protection by tariffs for our manufacturers, England could have smothered our industries with its greater financial assets and its industrial "know-how" during the early and middle 1800s.
   (E) Promise of high profits, almost guaranteed by high tariffs, kept a flow of risk capital available for expansion and experimentation.

18. All of the following statements supports the negative of the resolution EXCEPT

   (A) Development of natural resources and growing population are the true explanation of our rising standard of living.
   (B) Protection encourages inefficiency in production and in marketing.
   (C) Our growth as an industrial and commercial nation was phenomenal during this period.
   (D) The tariff, as a single factor in the economy, had no more than a trifling effect on the ups and downs of our economy.
   (E) Protective rates levied by the United States invite corresponding rates against our products.

19. Which Supreme Court decision was soon followed by a President saying, "John Marshall has made his decision. Now let him enforce it"?

   (A) *Cherokee* v. *Georgia*
   (B) *Fletcher* v. *Peck*
   (C) *Marbury* v. *Madison*
   (D) *Schechter* v. *United States*
   (E) *United States* v. *E.C. Knight*

20. Which of the following groups of nations came into being before World War II as a result of World War I?

   (A) Estonia, Ethiopia, Poland
   (B) Hungary, Yugoslavia, Israel
   (C) Lithuania, Czechoslovakia, Finland
   (D) Congo, Egypt, Latvia
   (E) Botswana, Sri Lanka, Zaire

21. All of the following statements associated with the presidency of Herbert Hoover are true EXCEPT

   (A) The National Origins Immigration Formula went into effect.
   (B) As Hoover assumed the presidency, he felt that our American way of life was showing the way to banish poverty.
   (C) Hoover's 1928 opponent was John W. Davis.
   (D) Hoover did NOT close the banks after the 1929 crash.
   (E) As the depression deepened, Hoover claimed it was a postwar economic reaction made more severe by the widespread poverty in Europe.

22. Which of the following events occurred FIRST?

   (A) Hitler annexed Austria.
   (B) Italy attacked Ethiopia.
   (C) Japan attacked Manchuria and set up a puppet state.
   (D) Hitler violated the demilitarized Rhineland.
   (E) England and France deserted Czechoslovakia at Munich.

23. Which of the events in question 22 occurred LAST?

24. Which of the following was NOT associated with the Massachusetts Bay Colony?

   (A) Ann Hutchinson
   (B) Theocratic government
   (C) John Winthrop
   (D) Edmund Andros
   (E) James Oglethorpe

25. Which of the following quotations is NOT associated with the period of the American Revolution.

   (A) "I have not yet begun to fight."
   (B) "I know not what course others may take, but as for me, give me liberty or give me death."
   (C) "I only regret that I have but one life to lose for my country.
   (D) "I shall return."
   (E) "We must all hang together, or assuredly we shall all hang separately."

26. In the 18th century, a major objection of the American colonists to the Navigation and Trade Acts passed by the English Parliament was that the colonists were

   (A) required to maintain a favorable balance of trade between their exports and imports
   (B) required to export tobacco, indigo, and cotton only to England

(C) forbidden to engage in the fur trade west of the Appalachians

(D) forbidden to buy sugar and molasses from any source except the British West Indies

(E) forbidden to build oceangoing ships

27. England justified its refusal to evacuate the military posts according to the Treaty of 1783 on the grounds that

(A) the forts were needed to defend Canada

(B) Native American uprisings made the evacuation impossible

(C) the United States had not paid the debts owed to the Loyalists

(D) Napoleon threatened to develop an empire in North America

(E) Spain threatened to extend her claims along the Mississippi

28. Which of these actions taken in Washington most closely approached what is termed "appeasement"?

(A) Dismissal of Edmund Randolph

(B) Proclamation of neutrality

(C) Negotiation of the Pinckney Treaty

(D) Delivery of the Farewell Address

(E) Signing of the Jay Treaty

29. Which of these items departed most markedly from Washington's advice about our conduct in European affairs?

(A) The nonimportation and embargo legislation, 1807-1809

(B) The enunciation of the Monroe Doctrine, 1823

(C) The cash-and-carry legislation of the 1930s

(D) Wilson's European policy, 1914-1916

(E) Acheson's "containment" policy, 1947-1952

30. A feature of the American political system NOT adopted from practice in England is

(A) appeal of disputed court decisions to higher courts

(B) legislative control of government finances

(C) local government through town meetings

(D) the bicameral legislative system

(E) the office of sheriff for maintaining law and order

31. Farmers objected to the Land Ordinance of 1785 because

(A) the price per acre for land was too high

(B) the minimum amount of land that could be purchased cost $640 in cash.

(C) the purchaser could not subdivide his land for resale

(D) one-sixth of the land was reserved for soldiers who might cash in their warrants

(E) land could be sold only to companies, not to individuals

32. Which quotation would most likely be attributed to a frontier settler in the 1760s waging a losing fight against depression, unfair taxes, corrupt officials, and an Assembly controlled by eastern planters?

(A) "As a poor Piedmont farmer from South Carolina, I finally decided to join the Regulators, Association in their fight against these public grievances."

(B) "...and we Scotch-Irish of Southwest Pennsylvania cannot see why we should resist the excise tax on our liquor..."

(C) "...as a result, I joined up with Nathaniel Bacon and though the Governor hanged some twenty of our men, we finally got some relief from the Assembly."

(D) "In order to get the Quaker-controlled Assembly to do anything for us, we Paxton Boys had to take action into our own hands..."

(E) "Finally the Congress adopted the Continental Association, which, I think, will get us redress from the Crown..."

33. During both the Washington and the Jefferson administrations, the Western settlers' most urgent and consistent demand on the federal government was for the

(A) repeal of the whiskey tax

(B) guaranty of an outlet to the sea for their produce

(C) establishment of a national banking system

(D) reduction in the tariff

(E) removal of Native Americans to reservations

34. Which is more characteristic of the reforms of the Jacksonian period than of the period following the American Revolution?

(A) Abolition of quitrents

(B) Abolition of the law of primogeniture

(C) Decrease in the power of the state executives

(D) Elimination of property qualifications for officeholders

(E) Confiscation of Tory estates

35. Henry Clay was an ardent nationalist and expansionist in 1812, but in 1844 he was only luke-

warm, at best, on the annexation of Texas. What accounts for this change?

(A) He realized that his early nationalism had been too extreme.
(B) He had become a strong proponent of a liberal land policy.
(C) It was more popular to be anti-British than anti-Mexican.
(D) He had become concerned about alienating any one section of the nation.
(E) He was convinced that the annexation of Texas would provoke war.

36. Calhoun defended the doctrine of nullification because it

(A) was a principle stated in the Declaration of Independence
(B) was to him a constitutional means of redress for a state
(C) had been upheld by a Supreme Court decision
(D) was an extension of the doctrine of implied powers
(E) was basic to the philosophy of the land-owning class of the South

37. The decisions of the Supreme Court were most similar in significance in the cases of

(A) *Plessy* v. *Ferguson* and *Brown* v. *Board of Education*
(B) *Munn* v. *Illinois* and *Wabash* v. *Illinois*
(C) *United States* v. *E.C. Knight Co.* and *Northern Securities* v. *the United States*
(D) *Fletcher* v. *Peck* and *Dartmouth College* v. *Woodward*
(E) *Dennis et al.* v. *the United States* and *Muller* v. *Oregon*

38. The legal basis for Congress's power to enact immigration legislation is the power to

(A) regulate commerce
(B) define citizenship
(C) insure internal security
(D) promote the general welfare
(E) establish rules of naturalization

39. Which policy of the United States government is paired with the constitutional interpretation by which it may be justified?

(A) Purchase of new territory—a strict interpretation
(B) Creation of federal district courts—a loose interpretation

(C) Control of hydroelectric projects—a strict interpretation
(D) Minimum wage legislation—a loose interpretation
(E) Levying of the present federal income tax—a loose interpretation

40. The original purpose of the Fourteenth Amendment differed from the purpose of the Bill of Rights in that this amendment

(A) restricted the powers of the states
(B) restricted the powers of the federal government
(C) restricted the rights of an individual accused of a federal crime
(D) protected the rights of corporations
(E) protected states' rights in regulating business

41. Congressional opinion was most divided in respect to the War Resolution for

(A) the War of 1812
(B) the Mexican War
(C) the Spanish-American War
(D) World War I
(E) World War II

42. The political purpose for proposing the Tariff of 1828 was to

(A) "get even" with the New Englanders for the Hartford Convention
(B) secure the support of the shipping interests of New England by depriving manufacturers of the protection they desired
(C) assure the Jacksonians of Southern support in the election of 1828
(D) gain the favor of producers of such raw materials as wool, hemp, and flax
(E) discredit the administration of President John Quincy Adams

43. Henry Clay played a prominent role in arranging a compromise settlement for the

(A) Maine boundary dispute
(B) tariff problem in Jackson's administration
(C) admission of Texas
(D) bank problem in 1832-1836
(E) Oregon settlement with England in 1846

44. The interests of the creditor class were best served by

(A) Jackson's transfer of funds to state banks
(B) Franklin D. Roosevelt's devaluation program
(C) Cleveland's request for repeal of the Sherman Silver Purchase Act

(D) Lincoln's signing of the Legal Tender Bills
(E) Madison's failure to support Henry Clay's "American system"

45. Which statement is LEAST accurate in its description of slavery in the 1850s?

(A) Slavery on a Georgia rice plantation was generally much more rigorous than on a Virginia tobacco plantation.
(B) Slavery under the personal supervision of a benevolent master was likely to be different from slavery on property managed by a hard-handed overseer.
(C) Household slaves usually enjoyed much better treatment than did field slaves.
(D) Under the patriarchal system of Virginia and South Carolina, the slaves on the plantations led an easygoing life.
(E) Slaves were generally provided with clothes, shelter, and enough corn meal and salt pork to keep them in good health.

46. Which group of men represented Southern interests in the United States Congress before the Civil War?

(A) Henry Clay, Robert Hayne, Daniel Webster
(B) Henry Clay, Thomas H. Benton, William Crawford
(C) Preston Brooks, Thomas H. Benton, John C. Calhoun
(D) Jefferson Davis, Stephen A. Douglas, Charles Sumner
(E) Alexander Stephens, William Crawford, John C. Calhoun

47. In 1860 the slavery plank of the Republican platform corresponded most closely with the principles of the

(A) Liberty party
(B) Whig party
(C) Free Soil party
(D) Kansas-Nebraska Act
(E) Freeport Doctrine

Questions 48-52: Each of these questions contains a statement. For each, indicate which of the following persons was most closely associated with that statement in the years between 1820 and 1861.

(A) William Lloyd Garrison
(B) Abraham Lincoln
(C) John C. Calhoun
(D) Henry Clay
(E) Stephen Douglas

48. "No matter what the decision of the Supreme Court may be...the right of the people to make a slave Territory or a free Territory is perfect...under the Nebraska Bill."

49. "We consider the slaveholder to be a greedy, relentless tyrant."

50. "The infant industries of this country must be protected from foreign competition by a protective tariff."

51. "Slavery is an evil but we have allowed it. In good conscience all that we can do is to stop it from spreading."

52. "All great civilizations of the past have been based upon the theory that a leisure class developed the arts and sciences to a high point."

Questions 53-59 are based on the map below.

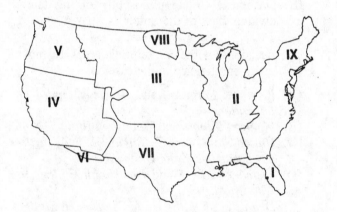

53. This territory was purchased by President Jefferson from France in 1803.

(A) I   (D) IV
(B) II   (E) V
(C) III

54. This territory was ceded by Mexico in 1848.

(A) III   (D) IV
(B) VI   (E) VII
(C) V

55. The western border of this territory was the Mississippi River.

(A) I   (D) VII
(B) II   (E) VIII
(C) III

56. This territory was purchased from Mexico for the right-of-way of a proposed railroad.

   (A) III   (D) VI
   (B) IV   (E) VII
   (C) V

57. In this territory Andrew Jackson pursued raiding Native Americans

   (A) I   (D) IV
   (B) II   (E) VII
   (C) III

58. The Webster-Ashburton Treaty of 1842 settled the northern border of this territory.

   (A) II   (D) V
   (B) III   (E) IX
   (C) IV

59. Here was an independent republic that applied for admission into the Union in 1845.

   (A) III   (D) VI
   (B) IV   (E) VII
   (C) V

60. Edward Bellamy and Henry George shared the belief that

   (A) the disadvantages of the competitive system outweighed its advantages
   (B) the clue to real reform lay in the tax structure
   (C) progress accompanied the poverty engendered by private land ownership
   (D) the nation's material progress had not been accompanied by social justice
   (E) the evils of their day were essentially incurable

61. Which of these was a general characteristic of the period 1920-1930 in the United States?

   (A) Strong executive leadership
   (B) A retreat from a policy of laissez-faire
   (C) Apathy toward reform
   (D) Increase in federal tax rates
   (E) Increase in the number of antitrust suits

62. Although the New Freedom and the New Deal were similar in many ways, they were dissimilar in respect to advocating

   (A) improved relations with Latin America
   (B) increased controls over the banking system of the nation
   (C) legislation to aid the farmer
   (D) contributions to the cause of conservation
   (E) extension of government control over business

63. Which was NOT included in the legislative program of both the New Freedom and the New Deal?

   (A) Tariff reduction
   (B) Banking reform
   (C) Labor reform
   (D) Regulation of big business
   (E) Public relief measures

64. During which period did the power of the legislative branch most increase at the expense of the executive branch?

   (A) 1801-1809   (D) 1921-1933
   (B) 1829-1837   (E) 1934-1941
   (C) 1901-1909

65. On the basis of a study of the Anti-Mason, Liberty, Free Soil, and Populist parties, one could conclude that

   (A) founders of third parties should anticipate no greater success than drawing the attention of major parties to needed reforms
   (B) sticking to principles rather than resorting to expediency is one way to win elections
   (C) only third parties organized west of the Mississippi have had any permanent influence on the nation's legislative program
   (D) third parties provide leadership training for presidential candidates
   (E) third parties included liberal and conservative wings

66. John C. Calhoun, William H. Seward, and Robert A. Taft were unable to win a presidential nomination although each had a long, successful political career. The best explanation probably is that each

   (A) was too conservative and unwilling to take sides on controversial issues
   (B) was too heavily indebted to "big money" interests
   (C) had little support outside his own small state
   (D) took a strong stand on controversial issues and antagonized large groups
   (E) failed to build a national political machine

67. Adoption of the presidential primary was most actively promoted during the

   (A) Jacksonian Era
   (B) Reconstruction Era
   (C) Progressive Era
   (D) New Deal period
   (E) post-World War II period

68. Which is an example of a President's maintaining a consistent position before and after election to office?

    (A) Jefferson's defense of the constitutionality of the Louisiana Purchase
    (B) Cleveland's attempt to reduce the tariff
    (C) Polk's settlement of the Oregon question
    (D) Arthur's support of the Pendleton Act
    (E) Franklin D. Roosevelt's defense of an unbalanced budget

69. Which aspect of the Federal Reserve system caused some Democrats to criticize President Wilson's establishment of the Federal Reserve System as a betrayal of the traditional monetary and banking principles of the Democratic party?

    (A) Creation of short-term credit facilities
    (B) Provisions for an elastic currency
    (C) Creation of a centralized bank owned by member backing
    (D) Issuance of Federal Reserve notes without specie backing
    (E) Provision for allowing state banks to join the Federal Reserve System

70. Over which segment of the American economy did the federal government take control during World War I?

    (A) Banking   (D) Steel manufacturing
    (B) Transportation   (E) Agriculture
    (C) Mining

71. Which was NOT a characteristic of the economic life of the 1920s?

    (A) New methods of production
    (B) Swift maturity of new industries
    (C) Installment buying and borrowing to finance consumer growth
    (D) Investment by banks in real estate, mortgages, bonds, and stocks
    (E) A government tax policy that retards accumulation of large personal fortunes

72. An important result of the Hawley-Smoot Tariff Act was

    (A) an increase in farm income
    (B) a great increase in the development of foreign trade
    (C) a general improvement in business conditions
    (D) tariff reprisals from a number of foreign countries

    (E) new prosperity for factory workers in the United States

73. Which was LEAST stimulating to the development of manufacturing in the United States immediately following the War of 1812?

    (A) Capital investment by New England shipping interests
    (B) Expansion of cotton culture in the South
    (C) Development of the corporate form of business
    (D) The federal government's trade policy
    (E) Opening of the West

74. Which came closest to being a victory for workers?

    (A) Anthracite Coal Strike (1902)
    (B) Haymarket Riot (1886)
    (C) Danbury Hatters' Strike (1902)
    (D) Pullman Strike (1894)
    (E) Homestead Strike (1892)

75. Which type of governmental assistance was most helpful to labor during the period 1876-1914?

    (A) Presidential support in nationwide strikes
    (B) Amendments to the federal Constitution
    (C) Supreme Court decisions
    (D) Federal legislation
    (E) State legislation

76. Which statement about the Industrial Workers of the World (IWW) is FALSE?

    (A) In the beginning the union was essentially one of unskilled migratory laborers in the western mines, lumber camps, and harvest fields.
    (B) The union was distrustful of political activity and for many years advocated direct action as exemplified by the general strike and sabotage.
    (C) Legislative action by sixteen states outlawing its activities weakened this union tremendously.
    (D) The federal government tried over one hundred of its leaders for conspiracies and secured convictions in a great many of the cases.
    (E) This union agitated for early entrance of the United States into World War I and advocated strenuous war measures.

77. Which provision favorable to labor was included in the Clayton Antitrust Act (1914)?

(A) Outlawing the closed shop
(B) Outlawing blanket injunctions in labor disputes
(C) Guaranteeing the right of collective bargaining
(D) Recognizing the right of peaceful picketing, boycotts, and strikes
(E) Abolishing labor by children under fourteen in interstate industries

78. The tendency of American farmers to be individualistic and to identify themselves as a business people explains their

(A) support of cheap money
(B) agitation for the protective tariff
(C) resistance to compulsory restriction of production
(D) opposition to nationalization of railroads
(E) unwillingness to join a farm organization

79. Which problem that confronted the farmer from 1870-1890 was practically nonexistent by 1935?

(A) Low real income
(B) Discriminatory practices of railroads
(C) Existence of large farm surpluses
(D) Inadequate farm credit facilities
(E) Supreme Court opposition to legislation that favored agriculture

80. Which feature of the New Deal, designed to restore agricultural prosperity, was most similar in approach to a proposal sponsored by William Jennings Bryan?

(A) The first AAA
(B) Civilian Conservation Corps
(C) NIRA
(D) Gold Reserve Act of 1934
(E) Commodity Credit Corporation

81. Which attempt by the federal government to aid farmers was declared unconstitutional by the Supreme Court?

(A) Encouraging farmers to cut down production of staples such as corn, wheat, rice, and tobacco
(B) Establishment of acreage quotas by the Secretary of Agriculture
(C) Purchase of surplus commodities
(D) Raising money for farmers by taxing the first processor of basic farm products
(E) Granting farmers a moratorium to pay their debts when threatened with foreclosure

82. Which period of time is paired with the chief source of federal revenue during that period?

(A) 1789-1800—excise taxes
(B) 1840-1850—sale of public land
(C) 1860-1865—tariff
(D) 1910-1914—corporation taxes
(E) 1945-1962—personal income taxes

Questions 83-89 refer to the following passage.

It required no very profound economic insight to grasp the import of the Hamiltonian program: holders of the old debt—continental and state—were simply to exchange their depreciated paper at face value for new bonds bearing interest and guaranteed by a government that possesses ample taxing power. Prime public securities, such as were now to be issued, would readily pass as money from hand to hand, augmenting the fluid capital of the country and stimulating commerce, manufacturing, and agriculture. If the government bonds failed to realize all expectations in the line of capital expansion, notes issued by the United States Bank were to supply the deficiency. At last, American business enterprise, which had suffered from the want of currency and credit, was to be abundantly furnished with both and at the same time protected against foreign competition by favorable commercial legislation. Naturally, those who expected to reap the benefits from Hamilton's system were delighted with the prospects. On the other hand, since the whole financial structure rested on taxation, mere owners of land and consumers of goods, on whom most of the burden was to fall, got into their heads that they were to pay the bills of the new adventure.

83. The words "commercial legislation," as used by the author, have specific reference to

(A) a tariff
(B) a national bank
(C) assumption of state debts
(D) an increase in credit and currency
(E) subsidies to American agriculture

84. The economic device employed by Alexander Hamilton to refinance government indebtedness is called

(A) amortization
(B) funding the debt
(C) deficit financing
(D) progressive taxation
(E) issuance of fiat money

85. The Hamilton program most likely had the greatest appeal for

(A) a debtor in Massachusetts
(B) a bank clerk in New York

(C) a land owner in Virginia

(D) an apprentice in Boston

(E) a mortgageholder in Philadelphia

86. According to the author, the Hamilton program was designed to

(A) increase consumer purchasing power

(B) encourage business by lowering taxes

(C) provide for a greater expansion of money and credit

(D) provide relief for those having difficulty making mortgage payments

(E) maintain a high price level by increasing the amount of money in circulation

87. In general, one can say that the author considers Hamilton's program to be

(A) desirable, because it provided for the purchase of state bonds at the market price

(B) undesirable, because it did not follow the benefit theory of taxation

(C) undesirable, because it was not understood by the average American

(D) both desirable and undesirable, because it did not benefit all economic groups equally

(E) both desirable and undesirable, because although some parts of the program were constitutional, other parts were not

88. The term *Hamiltonian program* refers to

(A) refinancing of the debt during the Critical period

(B) a set of proposals submitted to Congress by the Secretary of the Treasury

(C) reorganization of the finances at the Constitutional Convention

(D) the exchange of Continental dollars for new currency at face value

(E) the assumption by the states of all state and national debts

89. Alexander Hamilton's financial program was most vulnerable to criticism in respect to

(A) use of import duties to raise money

(B) establishment of a sinking fund to repay the debt

(C) sales of government bonds above par in Europe

(D) creation of fortunes by speculators in government bonds

(E) rapid subscription of the stock in the National Bank

90. South Carolina's stand on the tariff controversy in 1828 reflected the fact that

(A) South Carolina had always voted against tariffs

(B) South Carolina's economy was declining because of its planting system

(C) South Carolina's political leaders were rivals of Andrew Jackson

(D) cotton sales were declining

(E) there was no precedent for a protective tariff before 1828

91. Which best represents the objectives that Henry Clay expressed in his "American system"?

(A) The Republican platform of 1860

(B) The Populist platform of 1892

(C) Woodrow Wilson's New Freedom

(D) Franklin D. Roosevelt's New Deal

(E) The policies of Dwight D. Eisenhower

92. Which reform was achieved in many states during the Jacksonian era?

(A) Granting of equal property rights for women

(B) Enactment of compulsory school-attendance laws

(C) Disestablishment of state-supported churches

(D) Legislation providing for factory inspection

(E) Abolition of imprisonment for debt

93. In the history of American education, the first half of the 19th century was marked by the

(A) introduction of church-supported elementary schools

(B) widespread establishment of public high schools

(C) struggle for the establishment of tax-supported public schools

(D) struggle over the compulsory-education issue

(E) controversy over coeducation in public schools

94. Changes in the high school curriculum for large numbers of students who were not going to college began about the same time that

(A) limitations were placed on the working hours of children

(B) the federal Department of Health, Education, and Welfare was established

(C) federal aid was first given to colleges of agriculture and mechanics

(D) compulsory education laws were passed

(E) coeducational colleges for women were opened

95. The Bush administration succeeded in easing tensions in all the following areas EXCEPT

    (A) Kuwait
    (B) Bosnia
    (C) Panama
    (D) Somalia
    (E) Middle East

ANSWER KEY: TEST 3

1.	A	27.	C	53.	C	79.	B
2.	B	28.	E	54.	D	80.	D
3.	E	29.	E	55.	B	81.	D
4.	B	30.	C	56.	D	82.	E
5.	C or E	31.	B	57.	A	83.	A
6.	E or C	32.	A	58.	E	84.	B
7.	B	33.	B	59.	E	85.	E
8.	C	34.	D	60.	D	86.	C
9.	E	35.	D	61.	C	87.	D
10.	C	36.	B	62.	A	88.	B
11.	E	37.	D	63.	E	89.	D
12.	B	38.	A	64.	D	90.	B
13.	D	39.	D	65.	A	91.	A
14.	E	40.	A	66.	D	92.	E
15.	B or D	41.	A	67.	C	93.	C
16.	D or B	42.	E	68.	B	94.	A
17.	C	43.	B	69.	C	95.	B
18.	D	44.	C	70.	B		
19.	A	45.	D	71.	E		
20.	C	46.	E	72.	D		
21.	C	47.	C	73.	C		
22.	C	48.	E	74.	A		
23.	E	49.	A	75.	E		
24.	E	50.	D	76.	E		
25.	D	51.	B	77.	D		
26.	B	52.	C	78.	C		

ANALYSIS CHART: TEST 3

Era	Number of Questions	Number Right	Number Wrong	Number Unanswered
Pre-Columbian to 1789: questions 24-27, 31, 32	6			
1790 to 1898: questions 5-10, 19, 28, 33-36, 40, 42-60, 65, 73, 79, 83-93,95	47			
1899 to present: questions 1-4, 11-14, 17, 18, 20-23, 61-63, 67, 69-72, 74-77, 80, 81, 94	29			
Cross period: questions 29, 37, 41, 64, 66, 68 82	17			
Nonchronological: questions 15, 16, 30, 38, 39, 78	6			

FINDING THE REASONS FOR INCORRECT ANSWERS

Be sure to check the answer explanations before completing the following chart.

Era	Number Wrong	Lack of Knowledge	Micunderstand Problem	Careless Error	Not Answered
Pre-Columbian to 1789					
1790 to 1898					
1899 to present					
Cross period					
Nonchronological					

ANSWER EXPLANATIONS: TEST 3

1. **A** Harry S Truman had 87 percent of the people approving his handling of the presidency in July 1945, after he assumed office.

2. **B** Truman hit bottom, with only 23 percent of those polled approving his Korean War Policies, in November 1951. Lyndon Johnson's low point came in August 1968, when continued United States involvement in the Vietnam War influenced him not to run for reelection that year.

3. **E** Dwight Eisenhower's popularity suffered during the economic recession of 1957-1958. There had been a tremendous growth in the use of consumer credit, and Eisenhower, concerned about inflation, worked to hold down government spending for domestic and military projects. His attempts to balance the federal budget in those years set off a recession, or slowdown in the economy.

4. **B** There was a large change between the percentage of those polled who approved of presidential policies at the popularity high and those who did so at the popularity low of each President charted.

5,6. **C** and **E** Washington wrote that the United States should "steer clear of permanent alliances with any portion of the foreign world." At that time, in 1796, the disputes between Britain and France were a threat to the very existence of our new nation. Washington also warned against the formation of permanent political parties, having in mind the bitter struggle that had developed between the followers of Hamilton and Jefferson.

7. **B** The American Revolution was ended by the Treaty of Paris in 1783, which made the western boundary of the United States the Mississippi River.

8. **C** The Treaty of Guadalupe Hidalgo ended the Mexican War in 1848 and accepted the United States claim of the Rio Grande as the border between Texas and Mexico. It also gave the territories of California and New Mexico to the United States.

9. **E** The common factor is government control over the practices and prices of the railroads. The Pendleton Act of 1883 established the Civil Service System for government jobs.

10. **C** The common factor is American labor history. The Force Bill of 1832 was requested by President Andrew Jackson to give him the power to enforce the tariff in South Carolina. Fortunately, a compromise was worked out by Henry Clay.

11. **E** The United Mine Workers, led by John Mitchell, welcomed President Theodore Roosevelt's

offer to meet with the coal company representatives at the White House. Anthracite coal workers had walked out of eastern Pennsylvania mines because of low wages and frequent layoffs.

12. B   A New Deal accomplishment was the 1938 passage of the Fair Labor Standards Act, including a minimum wage (then 40 cents an hour) and a maximum work week of 40 hours for all workers involved in interstate commerce.

13. D   Payment of a *parity price* would give the farmer the same purchasing power from the sale of his products that he had during a selected base period. This formula is used in calculating the size of crop loads and the level of support prices. Conservative Republicans want to end such government assistance to farmers, as part of a program to reduce the role of the federal government in the economy.

14. E   It is virtually impossible to effectively prohibit a belligerent with the power to do so from blockading its enemies against *all* shipping.

15,16. B and D   When no candidate receives a majority of the votes of the Electoral College, the Senate chooses the next Vice-President from the two candidates with the largest number of electoral votes. Each Senator may vote and an absolute majority (51 votes) is needed to elect the new Vice-President. This procedure is provided for by the Twelfth Amendment (1804).

17. C   A nation that considers itself harmed by the protectionist measures of another will retaliate. For example, were the United States to place a high protective tariff on Italian cloth, Italy might well place a high tariff, or import quotas, on United States computers.

18. D   This statement supports the affirmative, indicating that the protective tariff historically has not harmed our economy.

19. A   Despite a United States treaty of 1791 guaranteeing the independence of the Cherokee nation, the state of Georgia kept chopping away at the Cherokee lands. The discovery of gold in Cherokee country in 1828 brought the controversy to a head. When Chief Justice John Marshall decided in a test case that the laws of Georgia had no force within Cherokee territory, President Jackson decided to let Georgia have its own way, and made the quoted comment.

20. C   The Treaty of Versailles (1919) liberated various peoples from alien rule. Lithuania and Finland had been ruled by Russia; Czechoslovakia was created out of the old Austro-Hungarian empire.

21. C   Davis ran against Calvin Coolidge in 1924. Hoover's 1928 opponent was Al Smith, a four-time Governor of New York.

22. C   This was the first of a series of acts of aggression by totalitarian nations during the 1930s that led to World War II.

23. E   In 1938 the governments of England and France practiced a policy of appeasement of Hitler, hoping that allowing him to annex the area of Czechoslovakia where Sudeten Germans lived would satisfy his expansionist desires.

24. E   General James Oglethorpe was the first Governor of the Georgia colony, bringing over the first group of settlers and founding the city of Savannah.

25. D   These were the words of General Douglas MacArthur, when forced to abandon the Philippines to the Japanese invaders early in 1942 during World War II.

26. B   Applying the theory of mercantilism to its colonies, England passed a series of Navigation Acts in the late 17th and early 18th centuries. One required that certain specific or "enumerated commodities," such as cotton, indigo, sugar, and tobacco, had to be sent only to England or to English colonies.

27. C   It became the firm belief of American frontiersmen that British garrisons incited the Native Americans to harass the American frontier. In any event, the British did supply the Indians with arms and ammunition for hunting "game," which was sometimes human.

28. E   Washington sent John Jay to England in 1795 to settle the disputes with Britain and to secure commercial privileges. While Britain did agree to surrender the Northwest posts and to submit some thornier problems to arbitration, the treaty did nothing about the impressment of American sailors and little to promote United States trade with the British West Indies.

29. E   Dean Acheson was President Truman's Secretary of State when the Truman Doctrine was adopted in 1947. The aim of the doctrine was to halt further Communist expansion. This marked a decisive break with the policy of isolation and noninterference in European affairs by the United States, which became the acknowledged leader of the anti-Communist world in the Cold War.

30. **C** Although elected by a local constituency, members of Parliament represented the entire nation. The New England town meeting was an American contribution, based on both the size of the community and the democratic spirit of its leaders.

31. **B** The Land Ordinance of 1785 provided that buyers had to take at least a whole section, one square mile or 640 acres, at a dollar an acre. The price per acre was attractive, but the size of lots was intended to make the land inviting to speculators and to increase the amount of revenue to the central government.

32. **A** Back-country discontent in the 1760s was most pronounced in the Carolinas, where there were neither courts, schools, nor police west of the pine barrens. The people wanted government services and formed associations known as "Regulators" to refuse payment of taxes until they got the services.

33. **B** The Westerners could not profitably carry their bulky goods—lumber, grain, deer hides—over the mountains to the Atlantic Coast. They had to ship them down the Ohio and Mississippi rivers on rafts and flatboats. They needed permission from Spain to put their goods ashore at New Orleans or elsewhere, and to load them on oceangoing ships without payment of duty. The Westerners demanded that Congress make a treaty with Spain to grant them the "right of deposit."

34. **D** Following the Revolution, most states kept high property qualifications, about $4,000 in New Jersey and Maryland, for membership in the upper house of the legislature. During the 1830s and 1840s—a period of democratic changes called Jacksonian Democracy—property qualifications for voting and officeholding were greatly reduced or eliminated in many states.

35. **D** Annexing Texas meant spreading slavery, therefore alienating New England and Western states opposed to any such expansion.

36. **B** The Virginia and Kentucky Resolutions framed by Madison and Jefferson in 1798-1799 contained the arguments later used by Calhoun to oppose the Tariff of 1828: The Constitution is a compact among sovereign states, which are as a body superior to the federal government. Each state, then, has the right to decide when a federal law is unconstitutional. This is the doctrine of states' rights. If a state claims that Congress has exceeded its power, it has the right to declare a federal law null and void within its borders. The Union victory in the Civil War ended the South's use of states' rights arguments.

37. **D** In 1810, in the decision in *Fletcher* v. *Peck*, the Supreme Court said that no state has the right to invalidate a contract. In the *Dartmouth College* case in 1819, the Court ruled that a college charter was also a contract and therefore could not legally be impaired.

38. **A** The interstate commerce clause has proved the most elastic of the powers of Congress, having been stretched to cover many areas of legislation.

39. **D** The Fair Labor Standards Act of 1938 legislates minimum wages for those involved in interstate commerce, clearly a loose interpretation of the right of Congress to regulate commerce among the states.

40. **A** The purpose of the Bill of Rights was to protect persons from abuses by the central government. The Fourteenth Amendment was to protect the freed slaves from abuses by the governments of the former slave states.

41. **A** While Western and Southern "War Hawks" favored war, New England was bitterly opposed, calling it "Mr. Madison's War," refusing to buy war bonds, and refusing to allow their state militias to be used outside their own borders. The high point of New England opposition came at the Hartford Convention, which condemned the war, supported states' rights, and favored the doctrine of nullification.

42. **E** The Tariff bill of 1828 contained rates so high that they were designed to disgust several members of Congress from the Northeast, who would then join Southerners in voting its defeat. The trick misfired, and the Tariff of Abominations was passed.

43. **B** After passage of the Tariff of 1832, South Carolina nullified the tariff, threatening to prevent the collection of import duties within its borders. Jackson had Congress pass a Force Bill, and Henry Clay pushed through the Compromise Tariff of 1833. The latter provided for annual reductions of tariff rates for ten years, down to the moderate protective level of 1816.

44. **C** The purpose of the Sherman Silver Purchase Act of 1890 was to have the government buy up the total output of United States silver mines, paying for it in Treasury notes which would be legal tender. Farmers expected that the increased amount of money in circulation would result in higher prices for farm products and an easier way to pay off mortgages by using inflated money. The silver-mining industry wanted a guaranteed market for silver. The Treasury notes were redeemable in gold or silver, and during the Panic of 1893, holders of the silver certificates

demanded gold, cutting into government gold reserves. Cleveland induced Congress to repeal the Sherman Silver Purchase Act and had the Treasury borrow a large sum of gold from an Eastern banking syndicate. The bankers made a large profit, and Cleveland was denounced as a "tool of Wall Street."

45. **D** Owning nothing of their own, prohibited from learning to read and write, subject to separation from immediate family members, and constantly suspected of trying to run away, slaves in the Old South led lives of increasing tension in the 1850s.

46. **E** Alexander Stephens of Georgia was elected Vice-President of the Southern Confederacy in 1861. Also from Georgia, William Crawford was an unsuccessful presidential candidate in 1824, in competition with John Quincy Adams, Henry Clay, and Andrew Jackson. Calhoun of South Carolina led the movement for Southern secession in 1860-1861.

47. **C** The plank was opposed to the spread of slavery, rather than to the institution of slavery.

48. **E** Douglas was the Senate sponsor of the Kansas-Nebraska Act, which applied squatter sovereignty to those territories.

49. **A** Garrison, the Boston editor of the abolitionist *Liberator*, demanded immediate freedom for slaves, without compensation for the owners.

50. **D** The protective tariff of 1816 was part of Henry Clay's program for economic development, known as the "American system." It was supported by the West and the South, as well as the expected Northeast, in order to make the nation economically and politically independent of Europe.

51. **B** This was Lincoln's and the Republican party's position. See also the explanation of question 47.

52. **C** This would be the position of a defender of slavery as an institution. Calhoun is the only candidate on the list.

53. **C** The immediate need of the Americans was to reopen the port of New Orleans. There the goods floated down the Mississippi by Western farmers were transhipped to the port cities of the Atlantic seaboard. Envoys Monroe and Livingston closed the deal for $15 million in gold—a bargain!

54. **D** Under the terms of the Treaty of Guadalupe Hidalgo, which ended the Mexican War, this Mexican Cession included the present states of California,

Nevada, Utah, Arizona, and parts of Colorado and New Mexico.

55. **B** This was the Native American Reserve, the land west of the original thirteen states. The Treaty of Paris (1783) ceded to the United States all British land between the Atlantic Coast and the Mississippi River, as far north as the Great Lakes and as far south as Florida.

56. **D** In 1853 the United States paid Mexico $10 million for a strip of land south of the Gila River in Arizona and New Mexico. It provided a favorable route for a planned southern transcontinental railroad.

57. **A** Florida then belonged to Spain, which was outraged at Jackson's violation of the Florida border.

58. **E** That treaty settled the conflicting claim to 12,000 square miles of land lying between the state of Maine and the province of New Brunswick, Canada. Secretary of State Daniel Webster helped to negotiate a compromise boundary that gave the United States the fertile Aroostook Valley, where excellent potatoes are still grown.

59. **E** This was Texas, the Lone Star Republic. During the 1844 presidential campaign, James Polk demanded the "reannexation of Texas," arguing that Texas had been part of the original Louisiana Purchase. Polk was elected, and Congress admitted Texas to the Union. Mexican resentment contributed to the causes of the Mexican War in 1846.

60. **D** Bellamy wrote the Utopian romance *Looking Backward*, late in the 19th century. Henry George wrote *Progress and Poverty*, advocating a single tax on the increased value of land. Each in his way tried to improve social justice.

61. **C** The election of Warren Harding in 1920 signaled a "return to normalcy" and a turning away from the idealism and problems of World War I. Americans cast a protest vote against demands for reform, government regulation, high taxes, the high cost of living, and the League of Nations.

62. **A** Wilson's domestic reform program, the New Freedom, did not include improving our relations with Latin America, then characterized by military intervention and dollar diplomacy. Franklin D. Roosevelt's New Deal Policies included our becoming a good neighbor toward Latin America. That meant ending United States Marine occupation in Haiti and agreeing to a multilateral approach to interpreting the Monroe Doctrine.

63. **E** These were part only of the New Deal of Franklin Roosevelt, and included the Civilian Conservation Corps to provide jobs for needy youth, the Works Progress Administration to provide jobs for unemployed adults, grants to the states to provide direct relief to destitute families, and credit extended to farmers and homeowners to prevent mortgage foreclosure.

64. **D** This was the period of Republican Presidents Harding, Coolidge, and Hoover, during the "return to normalcy." Each of the other periods saw strong Presidents—Jefferson, Jackson, and the two Roosevelts—increase Executive power at the expense of Congress.

65. **A** In 1844, votes for the Liberty party, which favored the abolition of slavery, cost Henry Clay the presidency. Ex-Liberty party members joined the Free Soil party for the 1848 election, and opposed to the expansion of slavery, they helped elect Zachary Taylor. The Populist party platform of 1892 included such reforms as direct election of United States Senators, a graduated income tax, and an eight-hour day for labor.

66. **D** From 1828 on, Calhoun was a minority spokesman for nullification. He resigned as Vice-President in 1832 over the protective tariff. On the issue of slavery, Seward appealed to a "higher law" than that of Congress or the Constitution, making him an unsatisfactory Republican party candidate in 1860. Taft, "Mr. Republican," was too conservative for the 1952 Republican nomination, having introduced the anti-union Taft-Hartley Act and having led to the opposition to the Marshall Plan.

67. **C** The Progressives of the early 20th century brought many political reforms, including the presidential primary, to their states. Other reforms were women's suffrage, initiative and referendum, and factory and minimum-wage legislation.

68. **B** Tariff reform was a constant with Cleveland. At the time, there was a budget surplus for each of seven years and more taxes than required to meet government expenses; and the largest single source of revenue was the tariff. Cleveland maintained that excessive government income is overtaxation.

69. **C** The Democrats were traditionally opposed to the concentration of power in big banking business, as represented by J.P. Morgan and Company.

70. **B** In order to mobilize its industrial resources efficiently, the government placed both railroads and telephone and telegraph lines under its control during the war.

71. **E** High personal income taxes and inheritance taxes did not become common until World War II and afterwards, when the need for state and federal income rose dramatically.

72. **D** The Hawley-Smoot Tariff Act of 1930 pushed protection to a new high and brought about prompt foreign retaliation. Twenty-five nations put up tariff barriers against American goods, and our foreign trade fell 50 percent within 18 months.

73. **C** Development of corporations was most important during the period from 1860 to 1900.

74. **A** The others were all disasters for workers and their labor unions. In 1902, President Theodore Roosevelt got J.P. Morgan, the financial power behind the coal mines, to press the mine owners to arbitrate the issues between miners and management in the Anthracite Coal Strike. The miners received a 10 percent raise and some other improvements.

75. **E** Most states by 1914 had compulsory school attendance laws and a minimum age (twelve to fourteen years) for lawful employment. Women and children were prohibited from mining and other dangerous occupations.

76. **E** The I.W.W. leaders opposed America's entry into World War I.

77. **D** The Clayton Act helped labor unions by barring federal court injunctions previously used to halt peaceful strikes, picketing, boycotts, or union meetings.

78. **C** When farm prices are high, farmers want to maximize their production and thereby increase their profits. When prices are low, they want to grow more in order to be able to pay back the debts incurred in purchasing seed, machinery, and land.

79. **B** Railroads needed government regulation to protect the consumer and farmer when railroads had monopoly of the carrying trade. By the early 1930s, the railroads had lost much of their revenue to the competition of trucks, buses, airplanes, internal waterways, and pipelines.

80. **D** The act fixed the value of the dollar in 1934 at 59 percent of its former (1900) value in terms of gold. The purpose of the law was to raise prices, which some economists held was closely influenced by the gold content of the monetary medium. The government policy failed to raise prices to the extent expected, partly because 90 percent of the nation's

business was already being conducted on bank credit rather than with currency. Bryan urged the free and unlimited coinage of silver (in 1896) in order also to inflate the price of commodities and help the impoverished farmer.

81. **D**   That means was tried in the Agricultural Adjustment Act of 1933, which was struck down by the Supreme Court in January 1936.

82. **E**   Beginning in 1943, the federal government deducted taxes from workers' checks before they received their pay. By increasing the number of taxpayers and making the means of collection less painful for them, the government gained a large new source of revenue for its wartime and postwar programs.

83. **A**   The protective tariff favored by Hamilton was to help defend American infant industries against foreign competition.

84. **B**   Provision was made for paying the debt in full by issuing new bonds.

85. **E**   Creditors stood to benefit from the improved business conditions promised by Hamilton's financial program.

86. **C**   Government securities "would readily pass as money from hand to hand, augmenting the fluid capital of the country and stimulating commerce."

87. **D**   Opponents argued that some states had already paid their debts or had only small ones, that payment of the debt would result in increased taxes, and that redeeming bonds at face value would benefit the speculators who had bought them up at a fraction of their stated value, rather than benefit the original owners.

88. **B**   His program included proposals to pay the national debt, to assume the state debts, to establish sources of income (including import duties, the sale of western lands, and excise taxes), and to organize a sound banking and currency system.

89. **D**   See the answer to question 87.

90. **B**   Most of the Old South's economic difficulties resulted from its being unable to compete in cotton production with the better lands of the Southwest. However, it blamed its ills largely on the protective tariff on the ground that the agricultural South had imported its manufactured goods and would have to pay higher prices with a tariff in place.

91. **A**   The Republican party platform of 1860 revived Henry Clay's American system of internal improvements and protective tariff, and promised settlers a free quarter-section of public land.

92. **E**   This was in keeping with the other social reform movements of the Jacksonian era, from 1828 to 1840. State support of churches was ended at the time of the adoption of the Bill of Rights in 1791, and the other reforms came about later.

93. **C**   By 1850, the public elementary schools were generally superior to the private schools thirty years earlier; and public high schools gave good training in mathematics, the classics, modern languages, and history.

94. **A**   See the answer to question 75.

95. **B**   Neither the Bush administration nor the governments of Western Europe intervened to protect the Moslem Bosnian population from military attacks and "ethnic cleansing" carried out by Serbian and Croatian militias in parts of what had been Yugoslavia.

ANSWER SHEET: TEST 4

1. (A) (B) (C) (D) (E)   16. (A) (B) (C) (D) (E)   31. (A) (B) (C) (D) (E)
2. (A) (B) (C) (D) (E)   17. (A) (B) (C) (D) (E)   32. (A) (B) (C) (D) (E)
3. (A) (B) (C) (D) (E)   18. (A) (B) (C) (D) (E)   33. (A) (B) (C) (D) (E)
4. (A) (B) (C) (D) (E)   19. (A) (B) (C) (D) (E)   34. (A) (B) (C) (D) (E)
5. (A) (B) (C) (D) (E)   20. (A) (B) (C) (D) (E)   35. (A) (B) (C) (D) (E)
6. (A) (B) (C) (D) (E)   21. (A) (B) (C) (D) (E)   36. (A) (B) (C) (D) (E)
7. (A) (B) (C) (D) (E)   22. (A) (B) (C) (D) (E)   37. (A) (B) (C) (D) (E)
8. (A) (B) (C) (D) (E)   23. (A) (B) (C) (D) (E)   38. (A) (B) (C) (D) (E)
9. (A) (B) (C) (D) (E)   24. (A) (B) (C) (D) (E)   39. (A) (B) (C) (D) (E)
10. (A) (B) (C) (D) (E)   25. (A) (B) (C) (D) (E)   40. (A) (B) (C) (D) (E)
11. (A) (B) (C) (D) (E)   26. (A) (B) (C) (D) (E)   41. (A) (B) (C) (D) (E)
12. (A) (B) (C) (D) (E)   27. (A) (B) (C) (D) (E)   42. (A) (B) (C) (D) (E)
13. (A) (B) (C) (D) (E)   28. (A) (B) (C) (D) (E)   43. (A) (B) (C) (D) (E)
14. (A) (B) (C) (D) (E)   29. (A) (B) (C) (D) (E)   44. (A) (B) (C) (D) (E)
15. (A) (B) (C) (D) (E)   30. (A) (B) (C) (D) (E)   45. (A) (B) (C) (D) (E)

46. (A) (B) (C) (D) (E)   61. (A) (B) (C) (D) (E)   76. (A) (B) (C) (D) (E)
47. (A) (B) (C) (D) (E)   62. (A) (B) (C) (D) (E)   77. (A) (B) (C) (D) (E)
48. (A) (B) (C) (D) (E)   63. (A) (B) (C) (D) (E)   78. (A) (B) (C) (D) (E)
49. (A) (B) (C) (D) (E)   64. (A) (B) (C) (D) (E)   79. (A) (B) (C) (D) (E)
50. (A) (B) (C) (D) (E)   65. (A) (B) (C) (D) (E)   80. (A) (B) (C) (D) (E)
51. (A) (B) (C) (D) (E)   66. (A) (B) (C) (D) (E)   81. (A) (B) (C) (D) (E)
52. (A) (B) (C) (D) (E)   67. (A) (B) (C) (D) (E)   82. (A) (B) (C) (D) (E)
53. (A) (B) (C) (D) (E)   68. (A) (B) (C) (D) (E)   83. (A) (B) (C) (D) (E)
54. (A) (B) (C) (D) (E)   69. (A) (B) (C) (D) (E)   84. (A) (B) (C) (D) (E)
55. (A) (B) (C) (D) (E)   70. (A) (B) (C) (D) (E)   85. (A) (B) (C) (D) (E)
56. (A) (B) (C) (D) (E)   71. (A) (B) (C) (D) (E)   86. (A) (B) (C) (D) (E)
57. (A) (B) (C) (D) (E)   72. (A) (B) (C) (D) (E)   87. (A) (B) (C) (D) (E)
58. (A) (B) (C) (D) (E)   73. (A) (B) (C) (D) (E)   88. (A) (B) (C) (D) (E)
59. (A) (B) (C) (D) (E)   74. (A) (B) (C) (D) (E)   89. (A) (B) (C) (D) (E)
60. (A) (B) (C) (D) (E)   75. (A) (B) (C) (D) (E)   90. (A) (B) (C) (D) (E)

91. (A) (B) (C) (D) (E)
92. (A) (B) (C) (D) (E)
93. (A) (B) (C) (D) (E)
94. (A) (B) (C) (D) (E)
95. (A) (B) (C) (D) (E)

Test 4

Directions: Each of the questions or incomplete statements is followed by five suggested answers or completions. Select the one that is best in each case and then blacken the corresponding space on the answer sheet.

Questions 3-4 refer to the following cartoon.

from HERBLOCK'S SPECIAL FOR TODAY (Simon & Schuster, 1958)

1. All of the following are special privileges or restrictions of members of Congress contained in the Constitution EXCEPT

   (A) In some instances they are not subject to arrest when other citizens would be.
   (B) Attendance at half the meetings of Congress each session is compulsory unless due to physical disability.
   (C) While a member of Congress, they can't hold another federal office.
   (D) Any pay raise Congress passes for its members does not apply to any member until his or her election after the new salary became law.
   (E) Members of Congress are not subject to the same restraints or penalties for the abuse of freedom of speech as are other citizens.

2. All of the following statements about the *Marbury v. Madison* case (1803) are true EXCEPT

   (A) The case was the first to involve the principle of judicial review by the Supreme Court.
   (B) The case involved the Judiciary Act of 1789.
   (C) The Court upheld a law of Congress that was challenged by Jefferson.
   (D) The Court declared an act of Congress unconstitutional.
   (E) Chief Justice Marshall and President Jefferson held opposing political views.

3. The cartoonist most likely believes that proposals to increase public contributions would

   (A) prove to be too expensive for taxpayers
   (B) increase the influence of lobbies and pressure groups
   (C) lighten the financial burden of big campaign contributors
   (D) increase the independence of political candidates
   (E) increase the use of cars in campaigning

347

4. The interest in the financing of political campaigns exists because there is concern about the

   (A) influence campaign contributors have on elected officials
   (B) influence campaign spending has on the impartiality of the media
   (C) burden placed on small campaign contributors
   (D) effect campaign expenditures have on the economy
   (E) costs of television campaigning

5. All of the following items are associated with the early days of the colony of Virginia EXCEPT

   (A) A terrible starving time
   (B) John Rolfe
   (C) Governor Berkeley
   (D) Religious Toleration Act of 1649
   (E) Pocahontas

6. In all of the pairs below, the words or phrase in parentheses helps to bring into effect, to support, or to make more effective the item with which it is paired EXCEPT

   (A) Proclamation Line of 1763 (Chief Pontiac's War)
   (B) Mercantilism (laws forbidding trades and crafts in the colonies)
   (C) Favorable balance of trade for England (Trade and Navigation Acts)
   (D) Dependence of the American colonies on England (expulsion of the French from America)
   (E) American colonial boycott against England (Sons of Liberty)

7,8. A writ of habeas corpus will, under most conditions, protect the individual in which two of the following ways?

   (A) Assure him of the services of a competent lawyer
   (B) Afford the opportunity to get out on bail within a brief period after arrest
   (C) Guarantee a prisoner the right to have his or her accusers cross-examined
   (D) Make it very unlikely that a person will be deliberately arrested on false charges
   (E) Make it illegal to try persons a second time for acts for which they have been tried and found innocent

9. All of the following are freedoms contained in the First Amendment to the Constitution EXCEPT

   (A) Freedom of assembly
   (B) Freedom of enterprise
   (C) Freedom to petition
   (D) Freedom of the press
   (E) Freedom of speech

10. In all of the following pairs, the words or phrase in parentheses helps to bring to an end, to oppose, or to make less effective the item with which it is paired EXCEPT

   (A) The *compact theory* of the Union (Daniel Webster)
   (B) The likelihood of Douglas being elected President (Lincoln-Douglas debates)
   (C) Pendleton Act (C. Julius Guiteau)
   (D) Pacification of the Philippines (Aguinaldo)
   (E) The philosophy of caveat emptor (United States Department of Agriculture and the American Medical Association)

11. "Resolved that the Civil War was an irrepressible conflict."

   All of the following statements support the *negative* of this resolution EXCEPT

   (A) Northern defiance of the federal Fugitive Slave Law of 1850 by operating the Underground Railway and passing personal liberty laws created an intolerable situation.
   (B) Because of the conditions of weather and soil prevailing in the Mexican Cession and in the Kansas-Nebraska Territory, the furor over slavery made no sense.
   (C) Many Southerners were finding out that slave labor was more expensive and more trouble than hired labor. Helper's *Impending Crisis* pictured slavery as a weakness, not a strength, of the Southern economy.
   (D) Comparatively few Southerners owned slaves. Confederate soldiers would have stayed home gladly if only the federal laws were obeyed and the Northerners minded their own business. "Let us alone," not "Slavery forever," was their cry.
   (E) There was no need to stir up the Kansas-Nebraska struggle in the middle 1850s. Calm and prosperity marked the early years of the 1850s. The unnecessary Kansas-Nebraska Act of 1854 then set off a chain of violent actions and reactions that led to secession.

12,13. Which two of the following statements about the Bland-Allison Act are true?

   (A) It was generally favored by farmers of the West.

(B) The Greenback party opposed it.
(C) Some termed its passage the "Crime of '73."
(D) The bill was vetoed by the President.
(E) The bill provided for unlimited (or free) coinage of silver at 16 to 1.

14. In all of the following pairs, the words or phrase in parentheses helps to bring into effect, to support, or to make more effective the items with which it is paired EXCEPT

(A) Abolitionist, sentiment (Seward's "higher law")
(B) G.O.P. control in the South 1867-1875 (waving the bloody shirt)
(C) Dewey's occupation of the city of Manila (Admiral Cervera)
(D) The split between Taft and Theodore Roosevelt (Pinchot-Ballinger)
(E) Blame's leadership in the Republican party ("Stalwarts")

15. All of the following statements are true about the Kentucky Resolutions written by Jefferson EXCEPT

(A) They declared the Sedition Act unconstitutional.
(B) While an important political pronouncement, these resolutions were not the formal act of any government.
(C) The immediate purpose of the resolutions, and probably their only purpose, was to win the election of 1800 for the Republicans.
(D) James Madison wrote the Virginia Resolutions, which pointed in the same direction as the Kentucky Resolutions but were more moderate in tone.
(E) Jefferson's reasoning in these resolutions would apply to secession as logically as to nullification, but Jefferson did not claim the right of a state to secede.

16. In all of the following pairs, the words or phrase in parentheses helps to bring to an end, to oppose, or to make *less effective* the item with which it is paired EXCEPT

(A) Napoleon's plans for an empire in the Western Hemisphere (Toussaint L'Ouverture)
(B) The action of the New Hampshire legislature that changed Dartmouth College, a private institution, into Dartmouth University, a state institution (*Dartmouth College* case)
(C) Abolitionist' sentiment (Seward's "higher law")

(D) The strength of organized labor (Haymarket Riot)
(E) Prosperity in Hawaii (2¢ bounty for American sugar passed with the McKinley Tariff)

17. All of the following statements are true about the Homestead Act of 1862 EXCEPT

(A) The purpose of the act was to encourage more rapid settlement of the West.
(B) An adult could acquire 160 acres by living on it and working it for five years with no money payment required other than a modest registration fee.
(C) Land could be purchased at $1.25 per acre with a six months' residence provision.
(D) The residence provisions of the law were carefully administered to assure that only true homesteaders acquired land under this act.
(E) Homesteading was one way to avoid the Civil War draft back home and also to escape the embarrassment of not enlisting.

18. This presidential candidate had the greatest electoral and popular vote, but an opponent won.

(A) John Quincy Adams
(B) Andrew Jackson
(C) Martin Van Buren
(D) James Polk
(E) Benjamin Harrison

19. His Vice-President belonged to the opposing political party.

(A) John Adams
(B) James Buchanan
(C) Grover Cleveland
(D) Thomas Jefferson
(E) Franklin D. Roosevelt

20. This President served two nonconsecutive terms.

(A) John Quincy Adams
(B) Grover Cleveland
(C) William H. Harrison
(D) Andrew Jackson
(E) Franklin D. Roosevelt

21. Which of the statements below associated with the Lincoln-Douglas debates is NOT true?

(A) Lincoln pointed out the incompatibility of the *Dred Scott* decision and the Kansas-Nebraska bill.
(B) Douglas had to win reelection to the United States Senate in 1858 in order to be in line for the Democratic presidential nomination.

(C) Douglas went against the Supreme Court and stuck to the "popular sovereignty" principle of his Kansas-Nebraska bill.
(D) Douglas defeated Lincoln for the senatorship.
(E) The Freeport Doctrine was heartily disliked by Southern Democrats.

22. This President broke the two-term tradition.

(A) Thomas Jefferson
(B) Andrew Jackson
(C) Lyndon Johnson
(D) Franklin D. Roosevelt
(E) Theodore Roosevelt

23. Which of these items promoted vigorous nationalism and at the same time provoked the LEAST sectional dispute and disunity?

(A) Alexander Hamilton's financial program
(B) The Battle of the Alamo
(C) Henry Clay's "American system"
(D) James K. Polk's "manifest destiny"
(E) Washington's demand for Genêt's recall

24. Which was a deterrent to the growth of nationalism in the United States?

(A) The mobility of the population
(B) The influx of immigrants in the 19th century
(C) The Nineteenth Amendment
(D) The compact theory of government
(E) American literature

25. Basing your choice on your knowledge of the *McCulloch* v. *Maryland* case, select the quotation that is most likely to be a part of that decision.

(A) "Let the end be legitimate...within the scope of the Constitution, and all means which are appropriate...which are not prohibited...are constitutional."
(B) "My construction of the Constitution is...that each department is truly independent of the others and has equal rights to decide for itself what is the meaning of the Constitution."
(C) "The authority, therefore, given to the Supreme Court...to issue writs of mandamus to public officers, appears not to be warranted by the Constitution..."
(D) "...the right of property in a slave is distinctly and expressly affirmed in the Constitution."
(E) "The claim of the police power would be a mere pretext—become another and delusive name for the supreme sovereignty of the state to be exercised free from constitutional restraint."

26. Which decision of the Supreme Court expanded the contract clause of the federal Constitution?

(A) *Marbury* v. *Madison*
(B) *McCulloch* v. *Maryland*
(C) *Gibbons* v. *Ogden*
(D) *Dartmouth* v. *Woodward*
(E) *Wabash* v. *Illinois*

27. Which section of the United States Constitution was cited by the South in its challenge to the power of the United States Supreme Court to order desegregation in the public schools?

(A) The Tenth Amendment which deals with state and federal powers.
(B) Section 5 of the Fourteenth Amendment, which deals with exercise of congressional powers.
(C) The sections of Article I that deal with the powers of Congress.
(D) The sections of Article III that deal with the powers of the Judiciary.
(E) The sections of Article IV that deal with the relations of the states to the federal government.

28. When it was drawn up, the Constitution differed most from existing state constitutions in its provision for

(A) a bicameral legislature
(B) an appointive judiciary, with tenure for good behavior
(C) a separation of powers
(D) the origin of revenue bills in the lower House
(E) an Executive with strong powers

29. The title "Our Intellectual Declaration of Independence" was applied to

(A) Thoreau's "Civil Disobedience"
(B) Cooper's *Leatherstocking Tales*
(C) Emerson's "The American Scholar"
(D) Melville's *Moby Dick*
(E) Hawthorne's *The House of the Seven Gables*

30. The Embargo Act of 1807 and the neutrality legislation of the 1930s were alike in that both

(A) prevented American ships from sailing for foreign ports
(B) prevented American citizens from lending money to belligerent countries
(C) relieved the federal government of the necessity of enforcing the right of freedom of the seas
(D) were intended to coerce America's traditional enemy, Great Britain

(E) prohibited Americans from traveling on ships of belligerent nations

31. Members of Congress who wanted to punish the former leaders of the Confederacy approved of

(A) Lincoln's "Ten percent plan"
(B) President Johnson's policy toward the South
(C) the Fourteenth Amendment
(D) the "grandfather clauses"
(E) the Amnesty Act of 1872

32. A major purpose of the Reconstruction Act (1867) in the United States was to

(A) hasten the industrialization of the South
(B) break down the one-crop economy of the South
(C) "bind up the nation's wounds"
(D) prevent the readmission of the Southern states to the Union
(E) enable the Republican party to retain control of Congress

33. The "grandfather clause" is most similar in purpose and principle to the

(A) "Jim Crow" laws   (D) poll tax
(B) liberty laws   (E) gag rule
(C) Fourteenth Amendment

34. The quotation "...the best test of truth is the power of the thought to get itself accepted in the competition of the market..." expresses the views found in the

(A) Alien and Sedition Acts
(B) Espionage Act of 1918
(C) platform of the Know-Nothing party
(D) Opinions of Justice Oliver Wendell Holmes
(E) prosecutor's speech at the Haymarket Riot trial

35. Which issue did NOT involve sectional differences?

(A) Admission of Hawaii
(B) Passage of the Embargo Act
(C) Declaration of war against Spain
(D) Annexation of Texas
(E) Election of McKinley in 1896

Questions 36-46: Five persons were engaged in a discussion prior to the ratification of the Constitution. The following statements were made:

Speaker A: I favor adoption of the new Constitution. It provides for the dualism in government which we have long needed. True, the document is full of compromises; but these are necessary if there is to be an effective government at all. We must recognize that compromise is the essence of the democratic process.

Speaker B: In spite of the fact that George Mason from this state refused to sign it, I hope that the new Constitution will be adopted. The recent outbreak in one of the states was a terrifying experience. A vigorous government can prevent such occurrences in the future.

Speaker C: The proposed government, in my opinion, will assure more adequate protection for the rights of private property. Its monetary provisions should result in the revival of trade and commerce. I do have some qualms, however. I feel strongly that the legislature should be further removed from control by the people. The upper house should be appointed by the governors of the states for a longer term, possibly for life. This would create a stability in the Legislative branch which could affect the whims and caprices of the popularity elected lower house. The President, too, should have a much longer term in office.

Speaker D: It is my feeling that the proposed new government is not democratic enough. It will assume too many powers for the central government which rightfully belong to the states. It is too aristocratic and does not give sufficient guarantees to the rights of the people. The whole thing is arranged to give advantage to the wealthy owners of property whose interests were so well-represented at the convention.

Speaker E: To me the proposed constitution poses a dilemma. I go along with our Minister to France, however, and favor its adoption in hopes that the amending process will take care of discrepancies which appear in it.

36. Speaker B was apparently a resident of the state of

(A) New York   (D) Virginia
(B) Massachusetts   (E) Rhode Island
(C) New Jersey

37. The outbreak referred to by Speaker B was

(A) Bacon's Rebellion
(B) Leisler's Rebellion
(C) Dorr's Rebellion
(D) Shays' Rebellion
(E) the Whiskey Insurrection

38. The people who instigated the outbreak mentioned by Speaker *B* probably would NOT have favored

    (A) the appointment of state judges for life or good behavior
    (B) the issuance of cheap money
    (C) the cessation of court foreclosures on mortgages
    (D) lower property qualifications for office-holding
    (E) increased representation of the frontier in the state legislature

39. Which speaker expressed ideas similar to those of Alexander Hamilton?

    (A) *A* (B) *B* (C) *C* (D) *D* (E) *E*

40. Which speaker apparently most admired the British form of government?

    (A) *A* (B) *B* (C) *C* (D) *D* (E) *E*

41. Which speaker agreed most completely with the view of the Constitution held by Thomas Jefferson at the time?

    (A) *A* (B) *B* (C) *C* (D) *D* (E) *E*

42. The dualism mentioned by Speaker *A* refers to

    (A) the system of checks and balances
    (B) the principle of division of powers
    (C) the principle of separation of powers
    (D) acceptance of both states and implied powers
    (E) two methods of amending the federal Constitution

43. Which speaker expressed an opinion similar to the feelings of Patrick Henry about the Constitution?

    (A) *A* (B) *B* (C) *C* (D) *D* (E) *E*

44. Which speaker expressed an opinion about the Constitution most similar to one held by Benjamin Franklin?

    (A) *A* (B) *B* (C) *C* (D) *D* (E) *E*

45. Which speaker made a statement similar to the thesis advanced by Charles A. Beard in his book *An Economic Interpretation of the Constitution*?

    (A) *A* (B) *B* (C) *C* (D) *D* (E) *E*

46. Which speaker pointed up the conflict of interests most similar to that presented by Vernon L. Parrington in his comments on the Constitutional Convention in *Main Currents in American Thought*?

    (A) *A* (B) *B* (C) *C* (D) *D* (E) *E*

47. A significant achievement of the Congress under the Articles of Confederation was its

    (A) requirement that individual states relinquish their claims to western lands
    (B) decision to declare independence from Britain
    (C) encouragement of domestic industry by its protective policies
    (D) negotiation of a commercial treaty with Great Britain for reopening tie West Indian trade
    (E) creation of a postal system

48. Jacksonian democracy represented a trend away from the Jeffersonian ideal in its

    (A) attitude toward the National Bank
    (B) feeling about the common people
    (C) tendency toward centralization of government
    (D) sympathy for agrarian problems
    (E) dislike of aristocratic customs

49. During the Jacksonian era, the foremost demand of workers' parties was for

    (A) secret balloting
    (B) minimum-wage laws
    (C) the abolition of slavery
    (B) a tax-supported public school system
    (E) outlawing the use of the injunction in industrial disputes

50. Which is NOT an illustration of the influence of conservative political thought in the United States?

    (A) Alexander Hamilton's defense of the federal Constitution
    (B) The writings of the Connecticut (Hartford) wits
    (C) John Marshall's decision in *Fletcher* v. *Peck*
    (D) The Sedition Act of 1798
    (E) The publication of Edward Bellamy's *Looking Backward*

51. In the 1850s, the platform of the Know-Nothing party advocated

    (A) enforcement of the principle that only citizens should be allowed to vote and hold office in each state or territory
    (B) abandonment of the principle of dual citizenship
    (C) supervision of the naturalization process by state judges
    (D) administration of the Burlingame Treaty by the Attorney General
    (E) an end to the admission of additional states into the Union

52. An important result of the Populist movement was that it

    (A) split the Republican party
    (B) helped to discredit the muckrakers
    (C) helped to liberalize the Democratic party platform of 1896
    (D) promoted the acceptance of industrial unionism
    (E) succeeded in gaining enough votes in agricultural states to form the "farm bloc"

53. Which presidential election disproves the statement that a defeated presidential candidate of a major political party is a poor risk to entrust with a second nomination?

    (A) 1844   (D) 1908
    (B) 1892   (E) 1948
    (C) 1900

54. Two results of the presidential election of 1896 were

    (A) the repudiation of imperialism and the end of military reconstruction in the South
    (B) the triumph of the gold standard and the continuance of the high-protective-tariff policy
    (C) extensive land grants to railroads and the development of a large navy
    (D) an administration favorable to the business interests and national legislation restricting the activities of organized labor
    (E) grants-in-aid for promoting agricultural education and vocational training

Questions 55-59 are based on the map below.

55. This state was the scene of a massacre at the hands of Mexican forces led by Santa Anna.

    (A) A   (D) F
    (B) C   (E) I
    (C) E

56. As a result of the Missouri Compromise of 1820, this state entered the Union as a free state.

    (A) A   (D) H
    (B) B   (E) M
    (C) E

57. Before its admission to the Union, this state was the scene of a bloody civil war between proslavery and antislavery forces.

    (A) C   (C) F
    (B) D   (E) H
    (C) E

58. The meeting place of the Union Pacific and Central Pacific railroads, where Leland Stanford drove a golden spike in May 1869 is located in this state.

    (A) C   (D) F
    (B) D   (E) G
    (C) E

59. The Declaration of Independence was signed in this state.

    (A) G   (D) K
    (B) H   (E) L
    (C) J

60. At the outbreak of the Civil War, which statement below was true?

    (A) All eleven Confederate states seceded at the same time.
    (B) Slavery had been abolished in all Union states.
    (C) Slavery had not yet become an issue in the territories.
    (D) The issue of expanding slavery into the territories was more political than economic.
    (E) The Fugitive Slave Law did not apply to the territories.

61. The federal government encouraged late 19th-century railroad construction in which two main ways?

    (A) Cash subsidies and land grants
    (B) High wages and land grants
    (C) High minimum wages and subsidies
    (D) Monopolies and subsidies
    (E) Monopolies and land grants

Questions 62-66 refer to the following graph.

Knocking on America's Doors.

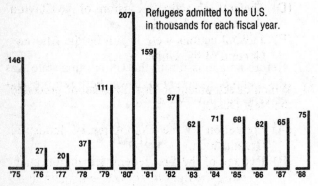

*Surge due in part to boatlift from Mariel, Cuba.

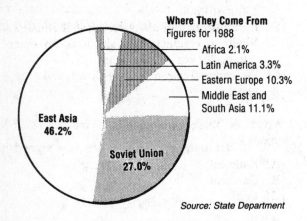

Where They Come From
Figures for 1988

— Africa 2.1%
— Latin America 3.3%
— Eastern Europe 10.3%
— Middle East and South Asia 11.1%

East Asia 46.2%

Soviet Union 27.0%

Source: State Department

62. In which two years did an equal number of refugees enter the United States?

(A) 1976 and 1977   (D) 1983 and 1986
(B) 1975 and 1981   (E) 1985 and 1987
(C) 1984 and 1986

63. Many of the 1980 refugees were fleeing the regime of

(A) Fidel Castro   (D) Manuel Noriega
(B) Pol Pot   (E) Daniel Ortega
(C) Deng Xiao-ping

64. In which year was the total number of refugees admitted to the U.S. equal to those who entered in 1982 and 1983 combined?

(A) 1975   (D) 1981
(B) 1979   (E) 1988
(C) 1980

65. The *second* largest number of refugees in 1988 came from

(A) East Asia   (D) Middle East
(B) Latin America   and South Asia
(C) Eastern Europe   (E) Soviet Union

66. Approximately ten percent of all 1988 refugees to the United States came from

(A) Africa   (D) Latin America
(B) Eastern Europe   (E) Soviet Union
(C) Middle East

Questions 67-68 refer to the following chart.

TRENDS IN POLITICAL AFFILIATION IN THE UNITED STATES

Year	Republican	Democratic	Independent
1979	22%	45%	33%
1978	23	49	28
1975	22	45	33
1972	28	43	29
1968	27	46	27
1964	25	53	22
1960	30	47	23
1952	34	41	25
1949	32	48	20
1944	39	41	20
1940	38	42	20
1937	34	50	16

67. Which statement is best supported by the information in the chart?

(A) Since 1937, Americans have been moving away from traditional political party affiliations.
(B) During the 1940s a greater percentage of Americans were Independent than were members of either major party.
(C) Membership in the Democratic party was at its lowest point during the 1960s.
(D) The Republican party made great gains in membership during the 1970s.
(E) The Republican party made great gains in the early 1980s.

68. Which development will most likely occur as a result of the trend shown in the chart?

(A) The United States will have only one political party.
(B) More Democrats will be voting in their party's primary elections.
(C) Interest in politics and voting will increase.
(D) Established political party organizations will have less control over election results.
(E) Young voters will register in larger numbers.

69. In the United States today, establishing priorities for federal government spending has been made more difficult by the fact that

    (A) the public strongly supports government regulation of business
    (B) the major labor unions favor socialism over capitalism
    (C) antitrust acts prevent the federal government from engaging in business activities
    (D) the need to support a strong military conflicts with the need to provide social services
    (E) neither political party wants to reduce the deficit in the federal budget

70. Which represents Samuel Gompers' strongest conviction for improving labor conditions?

    (A) National laws establishing minimum wages and maximum hours.
    (B) An alliance of workers and farmers into a strong political-action group.
    (C) Establishment of federal court of arbitration for labor disputes.
    (D) Government guarantees of the right of labor unions to use economic pressure against management.
    (E) Uniting skilled and unskilled workers into a single organization.

71. Which principle of American government might have been used as the basis for declaring unconstitutional a New York State law fixing the hours of work in bakeries?

    (A) Division of powers between the state and federal governments.
    (B) Police powers reserved to the states.
    (C) Promotion of the general welfare.
    (D) Powers implied by the elastic clause.
    (E) Protection of the inviolability of a contract.

72. What reason was given by President Cleveland for intervening with federal troops in the Pullman Strike of 1894?

    (A) The Governor of Illinois requested the troops.
    (B) The strike endangered the national health and safety.
    (C) The strike interfered with the United States' mails and interstate commerce.
    (D) The strike endangered the national defense.
    (E) Federal property was being destroyed.

73. Which was common to both the *Pullman* case and the *Danbury Hatters'* case?

    (A) The Sherman Anti-Trust Act was used against a labor union.

(B) The federal court issued an injunction to restrict the activities of a labor union.
(C) The federal courts upheld the use of United States troops to intervene in the dispute.
(D) The anti-injunction provisions of the Clayton Act were weakened.
(E) Judicial actions were begun by the Attorney General of the United States.

74. Which development in organized labor preceded the New Deal?

    (A) Formation of the Committee of Industrial Organization.
    (B) Passage of the first federal legislation guaranteeing the right of collective bargaining.
    (C) Passage of the first federal legislation exempting labor organizations from the antitrust laws.
    (D) Establishment of a National Labor Relations Board to conduct shop elections for determining the bargaining agent.
    (E) Widespread use of the sit-down strike as a weapon.

75. Which of these industries was the last to be unionized?

    (A) Railroad   (D) Textile
    (B) Garment   (E) Steel
    (C) Coal

76. Which item pairs two persons holding dissimilar views on labor unions?

    (A) John L. Lewis—Eugene Debs
    (B) Samuel Gompers—William Green
    (C) George Norris—Calvin Coolidge
    (D) Theodore Roosevelt—Franklin D. Roosevelt
    (E) Robert Wagner, Sr.—John Altgeld

77. Which group gives the names of presidents of the CIO in correct chronological order?

    (A) John L. Lewis, Philip Murray, George Meany
    (B) John L. Lewis, Philip Murray, Walter Reuther
    (C) John L. Lewis, William Green, Walter Reuther
    (D) William Green, Walter Reuther, John L. Lewis
    (E) Samuel Gompers, John L. Lewis, Walter Reuther

78. In which pair did the second item nullify or reverse the effect of the first item?

    (A) Use of injunction by management—Supreme Court decision in *Lochner* v. *New York*

(B) Decision in the *Danbury Hatters'* case—Clayton Antitrust Act
(C) Adamson Act—Norris-LaGuardia Act
(D) Section 7A of NIRA—National Labor Relations Act
(E) Fair Labor Standards Act—Taft-Hartley Act

79. Judged solely on the basis of legislation enacted during his administration, which President did the LEAST for the farmer?

(A) Abraham Lincoln
(B) Woodrow Wilson
(C) Warren Harding
(D) Calvin Coolidge
(E) Herbert Hoover

80. Since 1865 the American farmer has consistently favored

(A) inflation
(B) a soil-bank program
(C) parity price supports
(D) an export subsidy program
(E) government ownership of national transportation systems

81. The basic case of the "agrarian crusade" in the United States during the 19th century was most similar to that of

(A) Shays' Rebellion
(B) the Whiskey Rebellion
(C) the Hartford Convention
(D) Nat Turner's Insurrection
(E) South Carolina's Ordinance of Secession

82. An advocate of "hard money" would be most likely to approve the

(A) Bland-Allison Act
(B) First Agricultural Adjustment Act
(C) redemption of greenbacks
(D) Legal Tender Acts
(E) policy of deficit financing by the federal government

83. Which is an example of agrarian protest?

(A) Leisler's Revolt
(B) Coxey's Army
(C) The Haymarket Riot
(D) Dorr's Rebellion
(E) Bacon's Rebellion

84. Makers of the farm policies of the New Deal, in their efforts to "restore" agriculture, gave LEAST attention to

(A) regaining foreign markets
(B) reducing crop acreage
(C) resettling marginal farmers
(D) extending farm mortgage relief
(E) devaluating the currency

85. The basic weakness of the agrarian crusades of the 19th century was their failure to appreciate the

(A) significance of the agricultural revolution
(B) value of political action
(C) need for conservation measures
(D) extent of the movement of labor from the farm to the city
(E) need to enlist the support of the tenant farmers

86. Which trend did NOT characterize both agriculture and business after the Civil War?

(A) Formation of organizations to control prices
(B) Introduction of labor-saving devices
(C) Increase in importance of world markets
(D) Increase in capital investments
(E) Attempts to have their interests protected by the federal government

87. During the 20th century, which contributed LEAST to the shift in agriculture from diversified to specialized farming?

(A) Chemical fertilizers
(B) High cost of machinery
(C) Increase in land value
(D) Shortage of labor
(E) Increase in farm tenancy

88. The political and economic philosophy of which President would probably be LEAST attractive to the Utopian planners?

(A) Theodore Roosevelt
(B) Woodrow Wilson
(C) William McKinley
(D) Franklin D. Roosevelt
(E) Thomas Jefferson

89. Theodore Roosevelt's chief criticism of the muckrakers was that they

(A) influenced only a limited number of voters
(B) supplied the Democrats with good political issues
(C) undermined reforms already in progress
(D) lacked sufficient documentation for many of their writings
(E) were more adept at exposing abuses than at constructive effort

90. During his administration he brought forty-five indictments against the trusts, added over a

million acres to the National Forest Reserves, and personally sponsored an amendment for an income tax law. He alienated the Progressive reformers, however, by his action on the tariff. This statement refers to

(A) William Jennings Bryan
(B) William McKinley
(C) Theodore Roosevelt
(D) William H. Taft
(E) Woodrow Wilson

91. Franklin D. Roosevelt's disagreement with the Supreme Court differed from those of the other Presidents because he alone

(A) feared the growing power of the federal Judiciary
(B) was angered by the Court's invalidation of major parts of his legislative program
(C) was confronted by a Court with judges appointed by a President of the opposition party
(D) was censured by the Court for his illegal exercise of Executive power
(E) proposed to limit the doctrine of judicial review

92. The correct order, from most to fewest popular votes in the 1992 Presidental election, was

(A) Clinton, Bush, Buchanan
(B) Clinton, Buchanan, Bush
(C) Clinton, Perot, Bush
(D) Clinton, Bush, Perot
(E) Bush, Perot, Clinton

93. Which statement applies to Abraham Lincoln, Andrew Jackson, and Franklin D. Roosevelt?

(A) Basic policy-making decisions were carefully worked out with their cabinets.
(B) Each held a rank in the Army.
(C) Their actions were often criticized as exceeding their constitutional powers.

(D) Their administrations were characterized by a minimum of friction with the other branches of government.
(E) They were successful in business ventures prior to becoming President.

94. During President Eisenhower's administration, a most significant gain was made in the status of the office of

(A) President
(B) Vice-President
(C) Speaker of the House of Representatives
(D) Chief Justice
(E) Secretary of State

95. Which of the following statements is supported by the information provided on the graph?

(A) China's carbon emissions were three-fourths those of the United States in 1993.
(B) Germany was a greater polluter than Japan.
(C) India opposed adoption of a 1997 treaty on global warming.
(D) In 1993, the United States produced more carbon gas emissions than any other nation shown.
(E) In 1993, the United States was the world's biggest user of energy.

Emissions of Carbon Gases from Energy Production, 1993
In millions of metric tons

United States	1,328
Former Soviet Union	998
China	647
Japan	291
Germany	269
India	164
Britain	159

Source: Center for Clean Air Policy

ANSWER KEY: TEST 4

1.	B	25.	A	49.	D	73.	A
2.	C	26.	D	50.	E	74.	C
3.	D	27.	A	51.	A	75.	E
4.	A	28.	E	52.	C	76.	C
5.	D	29.	C	53.	B	77.	B
6.	D	30.	C	54.	B	78.	B
7.	B or D	31.	C	55.	C	79.	D
8.	D or B	32.	E	56.	E	80.	A
9.	B	33.	D	57.	D	81.	A
10.	C	34.	D	58.	A	82.	C
11.	A	35.	C	59.	E	83.	E
12.	A or D	36.	D	60.	D	84.	A
13.	D or A	37.	D	61.	D	85.	A
14.	C	38.	A	62.	D	86.	A
15.	B	39.	C	63.	A	87.	D
16.	C	40.	C	64.	D	88.	C
17.	D	41.	E	65.	E	89.	E
18.	B	42.	B	66.	B	90.	D
19.	A	43.	D	67.	A	91.	B
20.	B	44.	A	68.	D	92.	D
21.	C	45.	D	69.	D	93.	C
22.	D	46.	D	70.	D	94.	B
23.	E	47.	E	71.	E	95.	D
24.	D	48.	C	72.	C		

ANALYSIS CHART: TEST 4

Era	Number of Questions	Number Right	Number Wrong	Number Unanswered
Pre-Columbian to 1789: questions 5, 6, 28, 36-47	16			
1790 to 1898: questions 2, 10-21, 23-26, 29, 31-33, 35, 48-52, 54-66, 70, 72, 73, 81, 82, 85, 86	47			
1899 to present: questions 3, 4, 22, 27, 67-69, 74-80, 83, 84, 87, 89-93, 94, 95	22			
Cross period: questions 30, 34, 53	3			
Nonchronological: questions 1, 7-9, 71, 88, 93	7			

FINDING THE REASONS FOR INCORRECT ANSWERS

Be sure to check the answer explanations before completing the following chart.

Era	Number Wrong	Lack of Knowledge	Misunderstand Problem	Careless Error	Not Answered
Pre-Columbian to 1789					
1790 to 1898					
1899 to present					
Cross period					
Nonchronological					

ANSWER EXPLANATIONS: TEST 4

1. **B** The only penalty for such poor attendance will be having to explain to one's constituents absence from key votes, especially when running for reelection.

2. **C** Chief Justice Marshall wrote in his famous decision that a key clause of the Judiciary Act of 1789 was unconstitutional because it violated the separation of powers.

3. **D** The cartoon shows political candidates tied to big campaign contributors. Proposals to increase public contributions are offered to free the candidates from the consequences of accepting large contributions from special interests.

4. **A** Politicians who accept large contributions find themselves indebted to those contributors.

5. **D** In *Maryland*, the Toleration Act of 1649 legally recognized the right of all Christians to practice their religion in that colony.

6. **D** Since the Americans no longer needed Great Britain's protection against the French, there was a more independent attitude by the colonists toward England after the French and Indian War.

7, 8. **B and D** A writ of habeas corpus is a court order compelling the authorities to bring a prisoner into open court without delay and to prove that there are legal reasons for holding him or her in custody. Release on bail until trial is a typical remedy.

9. **B** The First Amendment freedoms are guarantees of specific political rights. Freedom of enterprise, a key element of the market system of economic organization, is a more generalized idea, not a specific right.

10. **C** Guiteau was the assassin of President James Garfield in 1881. Since Guiteau was a disappointed office seeker in a corrupt system of appointments, Congress was finally pushed to pass the Pendleton Act of 1883, creating the basis for a federal Civil Service System.

11. **A** The North was becoming progressively more antislavery, and the South was embittered by the North's failure to adhere to the spirit of the Compromise of 1850.

12, 13. **A and D** From the mid-1870s to the late 1890s, the American farmer supported a movement to have as much silver as was brought to the mint coined into silver dollars. The farmer hoped that would swell the amount of currency in circulation, thereby lowering its value and raising the prices of farm products. President Hayes vetoed the Bland-Allison Act of 1878, providing for government purchase and coinage of $2 million to $4 million worth of silver a month, but Congress passed it over his veto.

14. **C**   Admiral Cervera was in charge of the Spanish fleet in the Caribbean at the time of the Spanish American War. United States Commodore George Dewey's fleet occupied Manila Bay in the Philippines during that war, almost half a world away from the Caribbean.

15. **B**   The Kentucky and Virginia Resolutions were passed as official pronouncements of the legislatures of those state governments.

16. **C**   In seeking to abolish slavery in the 1850s, William Seward claimed that there was a *higher law* than the [fugitive slave] law of Congress and the Constitution of the United States, which tolerated slave owning.

17. **D**   The purpose of the act was frustrated to a large degree by land companies and other speculators buying the better lands for $1.25 an acre for resale. The provisions of residence and of being the head of a family were often fraudulently administered.

18. **B**   In the election of 1824, Jackson had 99 electoral votes to John Quincy Adams' 84, and 154,000 popular votes to Adams' 109,000. Since none of the four candidates received a majority of the 261 electoral votes cast, the choice went to the House of Representatives.

19. **A**   In the election of 1796, John Adams, a Federalist, received 71 electoral votes. Thomas Jefferson, leader of the Republican party, received 68 votes. The election of the two rival candidates as President and Vice-President resulted from the original provisions of the Constitution, later changed by the Twelfth Amendment.

20. **B**   Cleveland, a Democrat, served from 1885 to 1889, and from 1893 to 1897. Benjamin Harrison, a Republican, defeated Cleveland in 1888 without winning the popular vote.

21. **C**   In the Freeport Doctrine, Douglas admitted that a territorial legislature could practically nullify the *Dred Scott* decision, and discourage slavery by failing to pass regulations to keep slaves under control.

22. **D**   Franklin D. Roosevelt was elected four times to the presidency: in 1932, 1936, 1940, and 1944. No other President was elected more than twice.

23. **E**   Citizen Edmond Genêt was the new French minister who put President Washington's Proclamation of Neutrality between France and England to a test. He tried to hire American crews for the French privateers he was outfitting. Hamilton, the Federalist, and Jefferson, the Republican, warned him to no avail, until he lost his post.

24. **D**   This was the theoretical underpinning of nullification, based on states' rights, the opposite of national feeling.

25. **A**   In his 1819 Supreme Court decision, Marshall held that Congress could establish a bank under its implied powers and that a state could not tax a federal agency since "the power to tax involves the power to destroy." He upheld the constitutionality of the Bank of the United States and struck down a Maryland law intended to destroy a branch bank by taxing its bank-notes.

26. **D**   In the *Dartmouth College* case of 1819, Marshall ruled that a college charter was a contract that could not legally be impaired or unilaterally changed by the legislature of New Hampshire.

27. **A**   The Tenth Amendment states that "the powers not delegated to the United States by the Constitution nor prohibited by it to the States, are reserved to the States respectively, or to the people."

28. **E**   Despite tremendous powers, no American President has sought to become a dictator. This a tribute to the American way of life as well as to the principles of separation of powers and of checks and balances.

29. **C**   In his Phi Beta Kappa address at Harvard in 1837, Emerson urged American scholars to write about American themes rather than copy European models, to find inspiration in nature, and to have confidence in themselves.

30. **C**   In 1807, Jefferson reasoned that England and France needed American food and raw materials so badly that they would agree to respect our rights if faced with an economic boycott. He had Congress pass the Embargo Act, which forbade the departure of all American merchant ships for foreign ports. Under the Neutrality Acts of 1935 and 1937, American citizens were forbidden to travel on ships of belligerents.

Nations at war that bought goods other than munitions here had to pay cash and transport the merchandise in their own vessels—the principle of "cash and carry."

31. **C** The Fourteenth Amendment was adopted in 1868. It says that any state denying the right to vote to any adult male shall have its representation in the House of Representatives reduced. This was an unsuccessful attempt to coerce the ex-Confederate states into allowing black Americans to vote. Also, any person who held a public office requiring an oath of allegiance to the Constitution and who later joined the armed forces of the Confederacy is prevented from holding any such office again.

32. **E** The act required each of the ten ex-Confederate states to replace its government with another to be established through a state constitutional convention chosen by universal manhood suffrage. The Republican Congress would then decide whether those elected to the federal legislature according to the new state constitutions would be allowed to take their seats in Congress.

33. **D** A poll tax requires a monetary payment as a condition of voting. The Twenty-fourth Amendment, ratified in 1964, forbids a poll tax in federal elections. It had been used until then in four Southern states to deprive blacks of their right to vote. "Grandfather clauses" in Southern state constitutions were designed to protect poor whites from discrimination aimed at blacks. These clauses gave the right to vote to all persons whose fathers and grandfathers could vote in 1867, even if the person could not meet other voting requirements, such as paying the poll tax. This practice was declared unconstitutional in 1915.

34. **D** This is the only democratic expression among the choices.

35. **C** Public opinion throughout the nation was whipped into a fury by the exaggerations and distortions of the American press, particularly by the yellow journalism of Hearst's *New York Journal* and Pulitzer's *New York World*.

36. **D** George Mason was delegate from Virginia and the author of that state's earlier Bill of Rights. The "outbreak" referred to is Shays' Rebellion of 1786 in Massachusetts.

37. **D** In trying to pay off the state's debt, the Massachusetts legislature levied heavy taxes, which burdened farmers could not pay. The farmers protested loudly when people went to jail or lost their land for inability to pay private or public debts. A farmers' rebellion against the Massachusetts government resulted.

38. **A** Those judges tended to represent the propertied class of the cities whom the farmers in debt saw as their persecutors.

39. **C** Hamilton wanted to protect property rights, and mistrusted the populace.

40. **C** The upper house of the British Parliament, the House of Lords, was then also "removed from control by the people" and possessed greater powers than now.

41. **E** Jefferson and Franklin had faith in the amending process and the promised Bill of Rights to point the nation in the direction in which it should go.

42. **B** This is the division of powers between those exercised by a central government and those exercised by the states. The separation of powers refers to the allocation of both the state and federal levels of various powers among the Executive, Legislative, and Judicial branches.

43. **D** Patrick Henry and Samuel Adams were satisfied with the government under the Articles of Confederation and did not want the central government strengthened.

44. **A** Franklin was the convention's leader in seeking compromise between opposing positions. He proposed that each session of the Constitutional Convention be opened with a prayer for divine aid in compromise.

45. **D** The speaker echoes the conclusions of Professor Beard in his famous book—that the Constitution favored wealthy property owners.

46. **D** He speaks of the conflict of interest between the rights of the people and the powers of the central government.

47. **E** Under the Articles of Confederation, Congress was given the power to establish post offices and to charge postage—the only taxing power it had.

48. **C** Jefferson believed that a weak central government would protect the country from the evil effects of minority rule. He said, "That government is best which governs least."

49. **D** This was substantially achieved by 1850.

50. **E** This was a 19th-century socialist novel, telling the story of an American who awoke in the year 2000 in a socialist paradise, with work and leisure for all and with no poverty and no crime.

51. **A** Members of this secret political society tried to keep recent immigrants from serving in political office. They demanded restrictions on immigration and the extension of the naturalization period to 21 years.

52. **C** The Democrats took both the candidate, William J. Bryan, and various platform planks of the Populist party.

53. **B** It was then that Grover Cleveland, who had served from 1885 to 1889 before losing to Benjamin Harrison, regained the presidency.

54. **B** McKinley, the Republican candidate, ran on a platform of a protective tariff and the gold standard. He defeated both Bryan and the idea of free silver.

55. **C** In 1836, Americans who had been invited to settle in Mexico's northern province of Texas rebelled for independence. At the Alamo, a fortified church mission at San Antonio, a small Texan force was overwhelmed by a Mexican army under General Santa Anna.

56. **E** Maine's entry as a state free of slavery was balanced by the acceptance of Missouri as a slave state. The number of proslavery and antislavery votes in the Senate thus remained equal.

57. **D** "Bleeding Kansas" was the result of the Kansas-Nebraska Act of 1854, whose provision for popular sovereignty in that territory produced two governments—a proslavery one based on fraud and an antislavery one without any legal basis.

58. **A** Promontory Point, Utah, was the meeting place of the two work crews that helped unite a continent with steel rails.

59. **E** The Declaration was adopted by the Second Continental Congress in Philadelphia and first read to a crowd outside the red brick Pennsylvania State House, now Independence Hall.

60. **D** In attempting to mandate slavery in areas where it was too cold to grow plantation crops, the South showed it really wanted control over the Senate. (See also the explanation of question 56, above.)

61. **A** The federal government provided subsidies of from $16,000 to $48,000 per mile of track laid, in addition to grants of land on either side of the right-of-way.

62. **D** The bar graph shows that in 1983 and again in 1986, 62,000 refugees were admitted into the United States.

63. **A** The notation under the bar graph refers to President Castro's allowing (and forcing) Cubans he didn't want in Cuba to leave from the port of Mariel that year.

64. **D** The bar graph shows that the total number of refugees for 1981 is equal to the sum for 1982 and 1983 (159 = 97 + 62).

65. **E** The circle graph shows that 27 percent of refugees admitted in 1988 came from the Soviet Union. The largest percentage, 46.2 percent, came from East Asia.

66. **B** The pie graph shows that 10.3 percent of 1988 refugees came from eastern Europe.

67. **A** Reading the last column from the bottom to the top, we see that the percentage of Independent voters has more than doubled (from 16 percent to 33 percent) from 1937 to 1979.

68. **D** Election results are likely to depend more on the appeal of the candidates and their stand than on the political party that sponsors them.

69. **D** This conflict between "guns and butter" reflects American government commitments abroad as a world leader opposed to the spread of communism, and commitments to support the general welfare of the American people.

70. **D** More specifically, Gompers worked to end "government by injunction," and labor succeeded in writing into the Clayton Act of 1914 a clause prohibiting the use of unrestrained injunctions in cases between employers and employees.

71. **E** Before the 1938 Fair Labor Standards Act, which established minimum wages and maximum hours (in interstate commerce) nationally, a worker's "right" to enter into a contract to work very long hours at low wages would be upheld by the courts, because that position was favored by the social class from which came the judges, not the laborers.

72. **C** That intervention by federal troops led to rioting, and was an action opposed by both the mayor of Chicago and the governor of Illinois, who claimed they had matters in hand.

73. **A** Each of those strikes was labeled a conspiracy in restraint of trade and in violation of the Sherman Antitrust Act. In the first, Eugene Debs was sent to jail, and the American Railway Union collapsed. In the second, the union was assessed treble damages, authorized by the Sherman Act, and it went bankrupt.

74. **C** The Clayton Antitrust Act of 1914 specifically exempted labor unions from being considered conspiracies in restraint of trade, a situation punishable under the Sherman Act. The Clayton Act forbade federal courts from halting peaceful strikes, picketing, boycotts, or union meetings. The New Deal program started in 1933.

75. **E** The first four choices involve skilled trades that were organized earlier. The steel industry contained both skilled and unskilled workers, and its unions, crushed in the steel strike of 1919, were not effectively reorganized until the 1930s by the new Congress of Industrial Organizations (CIO).

76. **C** Senator George Norris was co-author of the Norris-LaGuardia anti-injunction act of 1932, to protect labor unions in an area where the Clayton Act had been unsuccessful. As governor of Massachusetts in 1919, Coolidge had vigorously opposed the Boston police strike.

77. **B** John L. Lewis of the United Mine Workers helped organize the CIO in 1935. The next CIO president, Philip Murray, held the office for sixteen years until his death in 1952. His successor, Walter Reuther, had headed the United Auto Workers.

78. **B** See the explanations of questions 73 and 74.

79. **D** During the Coolidge years, the farm block supported the McNary-Haugen bills, twice passed by Congress and twice vetoed by Coolidge. Those bills would have had the federal government buy up crop surpluses and sell them abroad. That would have raised farm prices helping farmers just as the tariff helped manufacturers. Farmers continued to be squeezed between rising costs and falling prices.

80. **A** Inflation would help the farmer repay his annual bank loans for machinery, seed, fertilizer, etc., with cheaper money. To repay a $1,000 loan when wheat sells at $1 a bushel requires 1,000 bushels, whereas if wheat sells at $2 a bushel, the same loan can be repaid with the proceeds from the sale of only 500 bushels of wheat.

81. **A** Shays' Rebellion in Massachusetts in 1786 was carried out by angry debtor farmers who wanted the state legislature to have cheap money issued so that they could more easily pay their debts. They stormed courthouses and prevented judges from handing down judgments against persons who could not meet their debt payments.

82. **C** In 1866, the federal government began to withdraw from circulation the unbacked paper currency, or "greenbacks," that it had issued during the Civil War. In 1875, Congress made the greenbacks redeemable in gold, ending their status as a form of "cheap money."

83. **E** In 1676 a Virginia frontier planter, Nathaniel Bacon, led a rebellion against the colonial government for its failure to provide frontier settlers with protection against Native Americans.

84. **A** New Deal programs of the 1930s concentrated on reducing farm acreage and encouraging soil conservation.

85. **A** The introduction of labor-saving farm equipment and of scientific agriculture after the Civil War led to a tremendous expansion of production. Since the 1920s there has been over production of staple crops—surpluses that cannot be sold in the regular markets.

86. **A** Trusts, pools, and monopolies were methods available to railroads and manufacturers to control prices. The individual wheat or tobacco farmer contributed too small a portion of the total supply of a product to influence prices.

87. **D** Year-round farm labor has not been in short supply. The agricultural revolution has continued to cut into the amount of farm labor needed to produce food and fiber in the United States and in other industrialized countries.

86. **C** President McKinley was a laissez-faire Republican, opposed to government economic planning.

89. **E** The muckrakers were writers who exposed evils in the economy and in government, leaving it to others to propose and pass corrective legislation.

90. **D** Taft continued and extended the antitrust actions of Theodore Roosevelt. The passage of the

Payne-Aldrich Tariff of 1908, which Taft failed to veto, angered the Progressives in the Republican party because rates were not much reduced.

91. **B** The Court had struck down two key laws, among others, including the National Industrial Recovery Act and the Agricultural Adjustment Act, seeming to invalidate F.D.R.'s programs to help industry and agriculture out of the depression.

92. **D** Of more than 100 million votes cast, Clinton received 43 percent, Bush took 38 percent, and Perot garnered 19 percent.

93. **C** Each was a very strong President, whose exercise of power was resented by Conservatives.

There were conflicts between each of these Presidents and the Supreme Court.

94. **B** Elected in 1952, Eisenhower tried to spread decision-making responsibilities. While in office, he suffered a heart attack, had abdominal surgery, and later bad a slight stroke. Vice-President Richard Nixon incurred greater responsibilities, including those for foreign travel.

95. **D** Total U.S. carbon gas emissions from energy production was 1,328 million metric tons, the largest amount shown on the graph. Choices C and E are not referred to in the graph.

ANSWER SHEET: TEST 5

1. Ⓐ Ⓑ Ⓒ Ⓓ Ⓔ	16. Ⓐ Ⓑ Ⓒ Ⓓ Ⓔ	31. Ⓐ Ⓑ Ⓒ Ⓓ Ⓔ
2. Ⓐ Ⓑ Ⓒ Ⓓ Ⓔ	17. Ⓐ Ⓑ Ⓒ Ⓓ Ⓔ	32. Ⓐ Ⓑ Ⓒ Ⓓ Ⓔ
3. Ⓐ Ⓑ Ⓒ Ⓓ Ⓔ	18. Ⓐ Ⓑ Ⓒ Ⓓ Ⓔ	33. Ⓐ Ⓑ Ⓒ Ⓓ Ⓔ
4. Ⓐ Ⓑ Ⓒ Ⓓ Ⓔ	19. Ⓐ Ⓑ Ⓒ Ⓓ Ⓔ	34. Ⓐ Ⓑ Ⓒ Ⓓ Ⓔ
5. Ⓐ Ⓑ Ⓒ Ⓓ Ⓔ	20. Ⓐ Ⓑ Ⓒ Ⓓ Ⓔ	35. Ⓐ Ⓑ Ⓒ Ⓓ Ⓔ
6. Ⓐ Ⓑ Ⓒ Ⓓ Ⓔ	21. Ⓐ Ⓑ Ⓒ Ⓓ Ⓔ	36. Ⓐ Ⓑ Ⓒ Ⓓ Ⓔ
7. Ⓐ Ⓑ Ⓒ Ⓓ Ⓔ	22. Ⓐ Ⓑ Ⓒ Ⓓ Ⓔ	37. Ⓐ Ⓑ Ⓒ Ⓓ Ⓔ
8. Ⓐ Ⓑ Ⓒ Ⓓ Ⓔ	23. Ⓐ Ⓑ Ⓒ Ⓓ Ⓔ	38. Ⓐ Ⓑ Ⓒ Ⓓ Ⓔ
9. Ⓐ Ⓑ Ⓒ Ⓓ Ⓔ	24. Ⓐ Ⓑ Ⓒ Ⓓ Ⓔ	39. Ⓐ Ⓑ Ⓒ Ⓓ Ⓔ
10. Ⓐ Ⓑ Ⓒ Ⓓ Ⓔ	25. Ⓐ Ⓑ Ⓒ Ⓓ Ⓔ	40. Ⓐ Ⓑ Ⓒ Ⓓ Ⓔ
11. Ⓐ Ⓑ Ⓒ Ⓓ Ⓔ	26. Ⓐ Ⓑ Ⓒ Ⓓ Ⓔ	41. Ⓐ Ⓑ Ⓒ Ⓓ Ⓔ
12. Ⓐ Ⓑ Ⓒ Ⓓ Ⓔ	27. Ⓐ Ⓑ Ⓒ Ⓓ Ⓔ	42. Ⓐ Ⓑ Ⓒ Ⓓ Ⓔ
13. Ⓐ Ⓑ Ⓒ Ⓓ Ⓔ	28. Ⓐ Ⓑ Ⓒ Ⓓ Ⓔ	43. Ⓐ Ⓑ Ⓒ Ⓓ Ⓔ
14. Ⓐ Ⓑ Ⓒ Ⓓ Ⓔ	29. Ⓐ Ⓑ Ⓒ Ⓓ Ⓔ	44. Ⓐ Ⓑ Ⓒ Ⓓ Ⓔ
15. Ⓐ Ⓑ Ⓒ Ⓓ Ⓔ	30. Ⓐ Ⓑ Ⓒ Ⓓ Ⓔ	45. Ⓐ Ⓑ Ⓒ Ⓓ Ⓔ

46. Ⓐ Ⓑ Ⓒ Ⓓ Ⓔ	61. Ⓐ Ⓑ Ⓒ Ⓓ Ⓔ	76. Ⓐ Ⓑ Ⓒ Ⓓ Ⓔ
47. Ⓐ Ⓑ Ⓒ Ⓓ Ⓔ	62. Ⓐ Ⓑ Ⓒ Ⓓ Ⓔ	77. Ⓐ Ⓑ Ⓒ Ⓓ Ⓔ
48. Ⓐ Ⓑ Ⓒ Ⓓ Ⓔ	63. Ⓐ Ⓑ Ⓒ Ⓓ Ⓔ	78. Ⓐ Ⓑ Ⓒ Ⓓ Ⓔ
49. Ⓐ Ⓑ Ⓒ Ⓓ Ⓔ	64. Ⓐ Ⓑ Ⓒ Ⓓ Ⓔ	79. Ⓐ Ⓑ Ⓒ Ⓓ Ⓔ
50. Ⓐ Ⓑ Ⓒ Ⓓ Ⓔ	65. Ⓐ Ⓑ Ⓒ Ⓓ Ⓔ	80. Ⓐ Ⓑ Ⓒ Ⓓ Ⓔ
51. Ⓐ Ⓑ Ⓒ Ⓓ Ⓔ	66. Ⓐ Ⓑ Ⓒ Ⓓ Ⓔ	81. Ⓐ Ⓑ Ⓒ Ⓓ Ⓔ
52. Ⓐ Ⓑ Ⓒ Ⓓ Ⓔ	67. Ⓐ Ⓑ Ⓒ Ⓓ Ⓔ	82. Ⓐ Ⓑ Ⓒ Ⓓ Ⓔ
53. Ⓐ Ⓑ Ⓒ Ⓓ Ⓔ	68. Ⓐ Ⓑ Ⓒ Ⓓ Ⓔ	83. Ⓐ Ⓑ Ⓒ Ⓓ Ⓔ
54. Ⓐ Ⓑ Ⓒ Ⓓ Ⓔ	69. Ⓐ Ⓑ Ⓒ Ⓓ Ⓔ	84. Ⓐ Ⓑ Ⓒ Ⓓ Ⓔ
55. Ⓐ Ⓑ Ⓒ Ⓓ Ⓔ	70. Ⓐ Ⓑ Ⓒ Ⓓ Ⓔ	85. Ⓐ Ⓑ Ⓒ Ⓓ Ⓔ
56. Ⓐ Ⓑ Ⓒ Ⓓ Ⓔ	71. Ⓐ Ⓑ Ⓒ Ⓓ Ⓔ	86. Ⓐ Ⓑ Ⓒ Ⓓ Ⓔ
57. Ⓐ Ⓑ Ⓒ Ⓓ Ⓔ	72. Ⓐ Ⓑ Ⓒ Ⓓ Ⓔ	87. Ⓐ Ⓑ Ⓒ Ⓓ Ⓔ
58. Ⓐ Ⓑ Ⓒ Ⓓ Ⓔ	73. Ⓐ Ⓑ Ⓒ Ⓓ Ⓔ	88. Ⓐ Ⓑ Ⓒ Ⓓ Ⓔ
59. Ⓐ Ⓑ Ⓒ Ⓓ Ⓔ	74. Ⓐ Ⓑ Ⓒ Ⓓ Ⓔ	89. Ⓐ Ⓑ Ⓒ Ⓓ Ⓔ
60. Ⓐ Ⓑ Ⓒ Ⓓ Ⓔ	75. Ⓐ Ⓑ Ⓒ Ⓓ Ⓔ	90. Ⓐ Ⓑ Ⓒ Ⓓ Ⓔ

91. Ⓐ Ⓑ Ⓒ Ⓓ Ⓔ
92. Ⓐ Ⓑ Ⓒ Ⓓ Ⓔ
93. Ⓐ Ⓑ Ⓒ Ⓓ Ⓔ
94. Ⓐ Ⓑ Ⓒ Ⓓ Ⓔ
95. Ⓐ Ⓑ Ⓒ Ⓓ Ⓔ

Test 5

Directions: Each of the questions or incomplete statements is followed by five suggested answers or completions. Select the one that is best in each case and then blacken the corresponding space on the answer sheet.

Questions 1-2 refer to the following cartoon.

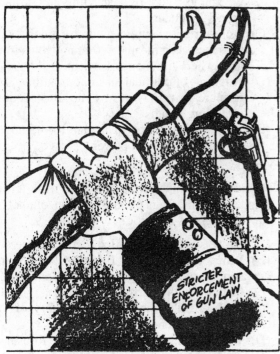

Liederman in The Long Island Press

1. The arm dropping the gun represents a

   (A) hunter
   (B) criminal
   (C) police officer
   (D) soldier
   (E) teacher

2. The cartoon is in favor of

   (A) prison reform
   (B) legalization of heroin
   (C) control of firearms
   (D) death penalty
   (E) export controls

Questions 3-4 refer to the following illustration.

THE VERRAZANO - NARROWS BRIDGE
from New York Convention and Visitors Bureau

3. In the American tradition, the name of this bridge is derived from the

   (A) architect's and/or engineer's name
   (B) history and/or geography of the surrounding area
   (C) direction and/or name of the connecting highway
   (D) private and/or public owners of the land upon which it is built
   (E) prominent generous donors

4. This architectural achievement is a good example of the growing interrelationship between the artist and the

   (A) consuming public
   (B) federal government
   (C) world of science and technology
   (D) traditions of the classic art world
   (E) local communities

5. Some Presidents have had programs that they drove, or tried to drive, through Congress. They looked upon themselves as representing the people. They interpreted their election to be an order by the people to carry out the program they had favored in their campaign for office. They expected to rule as well as reign.

   All of the following Presidents were of that type EXCEPT

   (A) Andrew Jackson
   (B) William McKinley
   (C) Theodore Roosevelt
   (D) Franklin D. Roosevelt
   (E) Harry S Truman

6. Other Presidents saw themselves as the leader of their party. They saw their job to be that of a chief executive to carry out the laws of the land. It was Congress who made policy by passing laws. They willingly kept in the background.

   All of the following were examples of this second type EXCEPT

   (A) Grover Cleveland   (D) Herbert Hoover
   (B) Calvin Coolidge   (E) Martin Van Buren
   (C) Ulysses S. Grant

Questions 7-8: One item in each group of answer choices is out of place. It lacks a factor common to all the other items in its group. Select the ODD item.

7. (A) A.A.A.   (D) Okies
   (B) Free Soilers   (E) Soil Bank
   (C) Parity

8. (A) Nineteenth Amendment
   (B) W.C.T.U.
   (C) Referendum
   (D) Seventeenth Amendment
   (E) Australian ballot

9. "Waving the bloody shirt" means which of the following?

   (A) Yellow journalism tending to provoke war
   (B) Activities of members of Congress known as "War Hawks" in 1811-1812
   (C) Campaign oratory of Radical Republicans in the 1860s and 1870s
   (D) Upton Sinclair's lurid, and largely accurate, account of the slaughterhouses of the Chicago stockyards
   (E) Opposing war on the moral basis that all intentional killing of people by people is murder

10. "Gerrymandering" means which of the following?

    (A) Straightening the useless and dangerous curves in major highways
    (B) Avoiding some of the meanderings of navigable rivers by deepening and straightening the channels
    (C) Appropriating public funds for unnecessary prospects as a means of winning votes in the area where the money is spent
    (D) Attempts of political machines in urban areas to increase their votes by illegal procedures at polling booths
    (E) Unfair redistricting of a state to the advantage of the party in power

11. President Taft had been referred to as a "crown prince" in American politics. Which of the following explains this title?

    (A) He was a quiet, dignified, deliberate person.
    (B) When nominated in 1908, he had the full support of both Progressive and Conservative factions in the party.
    (C) He had filled the post of Secretary of War with competence.
    (D) The outgoing President, Theodore Roosevelt, had recommended Taft as his successor.
    (E) Taft displayed a forcefulness in leadership that was somewhat of a surprise in a man of quiet manner and judicial mind.

12. "Corruption dominates the ballot box, the Legislatures, the Congress, and touches even the ermine of the bench...Newspapers are largely subsidized or muzzled, public opinion silenced, business prostrated, homes covered with mortgages, labor impoverished, and the land concentrating in the hands of capitalists...We have witnessed for more than a quarter century the struggles of the two great political parties for power and plunder, which grievous wrongs have been inflicted upon the suffering people."

Which is the source of the above quotation?

(A) Communist party platform (Earl Browder, 1936)
(B) Progressive party platform (Henry Wallace, 1948)
(C) Progressive party platform (Theodore Roosevelt, 1912)
(D) Socialist party platform (Eugene Debs, 1920)
(E) Populist party platform (James Weaver, 1892)

13. "Manifest destiny" would apply to which of the following?

(A) Joining in World War I against Germany
(B) Entering upon a program to beat the USSR in the race to the moon
(C) Becoming the leading republic of modern times
(D) Expanding westward from the Mississippi River to the Pacific Ocean
(E) Assuming the burden of aiding backward nations

14. The Open Door policy refers to which of the following?

(A) A very liberal immigration policy
(B) Reciprocal trade agreements with the European Common Market
(C) Admission of political refugees from any other nation
(D) Equal trade opportunities with other nations in China
(E) Prison reform, advocating an expanded parole system

15. "Logrolling" means which of the following?

(A) An agreement by one group of legislators to support or oppose a particular bill in return for support or opposition for another bill
(B) Arranging to break up a jam of legislation and get action on the more important bills
(C) Members of Congress voting themselves a pay raise
(D) A President bringing strong political pressure on congressional leaders in his party to press for the laws he wants
(E) Giving "spoils" jobs to persons unfit for their duties

16. By which of these treaties did France give up all the lands it possessed on the continent of North America?

(A) Treaty of Utrecht
(B) Treaty of San Ildefonso
(C) Treaty of Ghent
(D) Treaty of Paris
(E) Treaty of Versailles

17. A fort built by George Washington was

(A) Fort Apache   (D) Fort Pitt
(B) Fort Duquesne   (E) Fort William Henry
(C) Fort Necessity

18. In which of the following pairs, the words or phrase in parentheses helps to bring into effect, to support, or to make more effective the item with which it is paired.

(A) Orderly control of the freed slaves (Underground Railway)
(B) Interstate Commerce Act (*Wabash* v. *Illinois*)
(C) The rise of McKinley to the presidency (Marcus Hanna)
(D) Pure Food & Drug Act and Meat Inspection Act (muckrakers)
(E) Sherman Antitrust Act (Clayton Antitrust Act)

19. All of the following statements about the Hawaiian Islands in the 1890s are true EXCEPT

(A) The two cents per-pound bounty of American sugar had a severely adverse effect on the Hawaiian economy.
(B) The American minister at Honolulu favored, and United States Marines aided, the rebellious Hawaiians to overthrow Queen Liliuokalini.
(C) After investigation, President Cleveland approved the annexation of the Hawaiian Islands.
(D) The Hawaiian Islands were annexed by the United States, not by treaty but by a joint resolution of Congress.
(E) In 1900, all inhabitants of the Hawaiian Islands became United States citizens.

20. The treaty banning nuclear test explosions anywhere other than underground went into effect on October 10, 1963. Which statement supports the treaty?

(A) The United States proposed the same idea to the Soviet Union many months before, and no action was taken.
(B) Both the United States and the Soviet Union were concerned over the tremendous cost of the race to the moon.
(C) The United States was able to detect any violation of this treaty and thus did not have to rely on the integrity of the Soviet Union.

(D) Such a treaty required the approval of the Senate.

(E) There can be no victor in a nuclear war.

21. In all of the following pairs, the words or phrase in parentheses helps to bring to an end, to oppose, or to make less effective the item with which it is paired EXCEPT

(A) Gag Resolution (John Quincy Adams)
(B) Monroe Doctrine (England's preference for developing trade rather than enlarging its empire in Latin America)
(C) Friendly relations between the United States and the Latin American republics (Roosevelt Corollary to the Monroe Doctrine)
(D) Huerta's efforts to maintain his position as president of Mexico (President Wilson)
(E) Federal income tax law of 1894 (Supreme Court five-to-four decision)

Questions 22-23: Which of the following Americans is responsible for each of these quotations?

(A) Henry Clay   (D) Thomas Jefferson
(B) Stephen Decatur   (E) David Farragut
(C) Alexander Hamilton

22. "Our country! In her intercourse with foreign nations may she always be right; but our country, right or wrong."

23. "Damn the torpedoes."

24. Which of the following states did NOT secede from the Union before Lincoln's inauguration?

(A) Alabama   (D) Texas
(B) Florida   (E) Virginia
(C) Georgia

25. Which of the following items occurred FIRST?

(A) Burning of the *Gaspée* on the Rhode Island coast
(B) Stamp Act Congress
(C) Declaratory Act
(D) Boston Tea Party
(E) Boston Massacre

26. Which of the items in question 25 occurred LAST?

27. The President of the United States, according to the Constitution, is inaugurated on

(A) January 3   (D) February 22
(B) January 20   (E) March 4
(C) February 12

28. In all of the following pairs, the words or phrase in parentheses helps to bring into effect, to support, or to make more effective the item with which it is paired EXCEPT

(A) Repeal of the Volstead Act (ineffective enforcement)
(B) The strength of the Republican party (admission of six northwestern states to the Union in 1889 and 1890)
(C) Spheres of influence in China (clipper ships)
(D) Repeal of the Berlin and Milan Decrees (Macon Act)
(E) Monroe Doctrine (England's preference for developing trade rather than enlarging her empire in Latin America)

29. Which one of the following men favored tariffs primarily for protection, rather than for revenue?

(A) Cleveland   (D) Payne
(B) Morrill   (E) Underwood
(C) McKinley

30. All of the following statements are true about the American Federation of Labor EXCEPT

(A) Samuel Gompers was its first president.
(B) John Mitchell and Eugene Debs were prominent leaders in the AFL.
(C) It followed a policy for many decades of non alliance with any political party.
(D) It has been a craft, rather than an industrial, union.
(E) From the 1880s to World War I, it was the largest labor union in the United States.

31. Which of the following occurred LAST?

(A) Adjustment of the Maine-New Brunswick border
(B) Acquisition of Texas by the United States
(C) Gadsden Purchase
(D) California gold rush
(E) Settlement of the Oregon boundary

32. This Supreme Court case gave some vitality to the Sherman Antitrust Act

(A) *McCullough* v. *Maryland*
(B) *Munn* v. *Illinois*
(C) *Northern Securities* case
(D) *Brown* v. *Board of Education of Topeka, Kansas*
(E) *Schechter* v. *United States*

33. Which of the following statements about the Roosevelt Corollary to the Monroe Doctrine is true?

   (A) It was first applied to Mexico
   (B) It served as a foundation for better trade relations with Latin America.
   (C) It is a policy that, under another name, is still in effect today.
   (D) It was intended to assure fair treatment for European nations in their dealings with Latin American republics.
   (E) It could apply to the South American colonies of British and French Guiana.

34. Which of the following statements is correct?

   (A) The President may do whatever he thinks is right and for the national welfare so long as there is no prohibition in the Constitution or law as to prevent such action.
   (B) The President must restrict his official actions to carrying out powers specifically granted the President in the Constitution.
   (C) The President may do whatever the Constitution specifically provides and anything reasonably implied by Constitutional provisions. Any dispute about the implication may be settled in the courts.
   (D) In time of war or other major emergencies, the President may do as he thinks best, without regard to the Constitution.
   (E) Whenever a President is in doubt about the extent of his legal powers, he may confer with the Supreme Court for authoritative advice.

35. In the judgment of history, which of the following is considered the greatest and most lasting achievement of Theodore Roosevelt?

   (A) Conservation and reclamation
   (B) Panama Canal
   (C) Contributions to world peace (Nobel Peace Prize)
   (D) His part in the Spanish-American War
   (E) His vigorous championship of the people

36. Which President's domestic program was known as the Square Deal?

   (A) Franklin D. Roosevelt
   (B) Theodore Roosevelt
   (C) Woodrow Wilson
   (D) Lyndon Johnson
   (E) John F. Kennedy

37. The domestic program of Ronald Reagan can be called

   (A) the New Deal   (D) the New Freedom
   (B) the Fair Deal   (E) the War on Poverty
   (C) the New Populism

38. With whom is the following quotation associated?

   "Let error be free so long as reason is free to combat it."

   (A) Andrew Jackson   (D) Harry S. Truman
   (B) Thomas Jefferson   (E) George Washington
   (C) Abraham Lincoln

39. "The press was to serve the governed, not the government." This statement was made by

   (A) Neil Armstrong   (D) Ralph Nader
   (B) Hugo Black   (E) Simon Wiesenthal
   (C) Rachel Carson

40. With which of the following is the expression "one man, one vote"' most closely associated?

   (A) Amtrak
   (B) Immigration Act (1965)
   (C) *Wade* v. *Roe*
   (D) Watergate
   (E) *Wesberry* v. *Sanders*

41. The Supreme Court ruling that congressional election districts within each state must be of approximately equal population is most closely associated with

   (A) Alaska statehood (1959)
   (B) the Alliance for Progress (1961)
   (C) *Baker* v. *Carr* (1962)
   (D) the Civil Rights Act (1964)
   (E) the election of 1968

42. Which one of the following statements about the 1960s is FALSE?

   (A) Shortly before the Bay of Pigs fiasco, President Kennedy's statement about United States' intentions and plans toward Cuba was considerably less than frank and straightforward.
   (B) The *New York Times* and the *Washington Post* were the first newspapers to publish excerpts from the *Pentagon Papers*.
   (C) By 1970 the majority of persons on payrolls were members of labor unions
   (D) President Kennedy listed the four rights of consumers as the right to safety, to be informed, to choose, and to be heard.
   (E) Caveat venditor and caveat emptor refer to opposite members of a business transaction.

43. Which of the following statements is TRUE about the 1960s?

   (A) Inadequate technology was the major factor in preventing faster improvement in pollution problems.
   (B) Some communities had a strong preference for pollution with employment over no pollution with unemployment.
   (C) Religious bigotry fortunately was not a major factor in the election of 1960.
   (D) The decade of the 1960s marked the growth of a substantial middle class in several Latin American countries.
   (E) Peace Corps volunteers were guaranteed at least a comfortable standard of living wherever they worked.

44. Which one of the following statements about the 1960s is FALSE?

   (A) After the missile crisis in Cuba, the United States had the right of on-site inspection to prevent another similar crisis.
   (B) Early in the 1968 campaign, Senators Robert F. Kennedy of New York and Eugene McCarthy of Minnesota urged a rapid withdrawal from Vietnam so long as the military maneuver could be accomplished in an orderly manner.
   (C) Edmund Muskie of Maine was on the Democratic ticket with Hubert Humphrey in the campaign of 1968.
   (D) In 1968 Richard Nixon and Spiro Agnew, the Republican ticket, advocated a negotiated peace with North Vietnam.
   (E) In 1968 George Wallace led the American Independent party and advocated pressing for a military victory in Vietnam.

45. All of the following statements are true about President Nixon's visit in 1972 to China and the Soviet Union EXCEPT

   (A) Television coverage showed pockets of poverty in China markedly worse than in our urban ghettos and Appalachia.
   (B) The streets and great squares of China were very clean, and the people seemed mildly curious and quietly friendly toward the American visitors.
   (C) President Nixon was granted an interview by Chairman Mao Tse-tung.
   (D) Most of the agreements signed at Moscow had already been worked out over the previous two to three years.
   (E) It was not clear which of the "troika" of

Brezhnev, Kosygin, and Podgorney was actually the number-one man.

46. A business conglomerate is an example of

   (A) a combination of two or more firms producing unrelated goods or services
   (B) a horizontal combination
   (C) a monopoly
   (D) an oligopoly
   (E) a vertical combination

47. All of the following treaties are associated with the story of the Panama Canal EXCEPT

   (A) Clayton-Bulwer Treaty
   (B) Hay-Pauncefote Treaty
   (C) Proposed Hay-Herran Treaty
   (D) Hay-Bunau-Varilla Treaty
   (E) Treaty of Paris (1898)

48. The head of state who announced to his parliament, "I am ready to go to the Israeli parliament itself to discuss peace," was

   (A) King Hussein
   (B) King Saud
   (C) Colonel Nasser
   (D) Colonel Qaddafi
   (E) President Sadat

49. The name of the legislative body in Israel is the

   (A) Congress
   (B) Duma
   (C) Knesset
   (D) Reichstag
   (E) Parliament

Questions 50-51 refer to the following illustration.

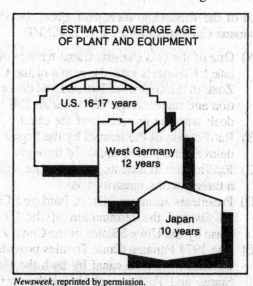

ESTIMATED AVERAGE AGE OF PLANT AND EQUIPMENT

U.S. 16-17 years

West Germany 12 years

Japan 10 years

Newsweek, reprinted by permission.

50. Which statement most accurately summarizes the information in the illustration?

(A) Modernization policies adopted by the Japanese and West German governments reflect strong religious beliefs of workers.
(B) United States' plants and equipment are more productive than those of Japan and West Germany.
(C) Most plants and equipment in the United States, Japan, and West Germany have become obsolete.
(D) Modernization of United States' industry has not kept pace with that of Japanese and West German industry.
(E) All of the above

51. Which would be the most effective remedy for the situation referred to in the illustration?

(A) Increased productivity of the United States labor force
(B) Congressional legislation to increase corporate taxes
(C) Increased capital investment by United States industry
(D) Congressional legislation to eliminate all imports to the United States
(E) A nationwide "Buy American" campaign

52. Which of the following was the most effective spokesman opposing ratification of the two Panama Canal treaties of the late 1970s?

(A) Jimmy Carter
(B) Barry Goldwater
(C) Henry Kissinger
(D) Richard Nixon
(E) Ronald Reagan

53. All of the following statements about the 1970s Panama Canal treaties are true EXCEPT

(A) One of the two Panama Canal treaties of the late 1970s dealt with the return of the Canal Zone to the control of Panama and the operation and maintenance of the canal. The other dealt with the protection of the canal.
(B) Ratification of the treaties by the Senate was delayed and barely squeaked through.
(C) Ratification of a treaty in the Senate requires a three-fourths majority vote.
(D) Presidents Johnson, Nixon, Ford and Carter all favored the termination of the 99-year lease by the United States of the Canal Zone.
(E) The 1977 Panama Canal Treaties provide for the defense of the canal by both the United States and Panama acting jointly or inde-

pendently as each deems necessary, even including military force in the Republic of Panama.

54. Which of the following was NOT a member of OPEC in the 1960s and 1970s?

(A) Algeria
(B) Ecuador
(C) England
(D) Indonesia
(E) Iran

55. All of the following are true about the Camp David Accord that President Carter helped Egypt and Israel to achieve EXCEPT

(A) These conclusions became the framework on which the treaty signed by Egypt and Israel was based.
(B) Egypt's ambassador to the United States resigned in protest against the Camp David agreements.
(C) Mass demonstrations in Cairo protested against the Camp David conference.
(D) Egypt was the only Arab state to officially approve the work of the Camp David conference.
(E) Four wars within twenty-five years was a major factor pressuring both Egypt and Israel to persist with negotiating, difficult and slow as it was.

56. Which of the following was NOT a member of OPEC from the 1960s to the 1980s?

(A) Argentina
(B) Brazil
(C) Cuba
(D) Mexico
(E) Venezuela

57. All but one of the following statements about the malfunctioning of the Three Mile Island nuclear plant are "true, but nothing effective can be done" about them. Find the EXCEPTION, the ease in which something can and should be done.

(A) Workers exposed to "tolerable" amounts of radioactive radiation during the 1950s now have a higher-than-usual incidence of cancer.
(B) Nuclear wastes remain active for thousands of years.
(C) Nuclear power plants have a life of about 35 years. If torn down, nuclear wastes have to be disposed of. If the plants are not dismantled, they must be sealed. In either case the problem of the thousand years or more of radioactive radiation remains.
(D) Regulation of the operation of nuclear power plants is inadequate.
(E) Nuclear power plants drastically depress property values over a very considerable area.

Immigrants to the United States by Area of Origin

Area of Origin	Year 1959	1979
Europe	60.9%	13.4%
Asia	8.8	41.4
Africa	1.1	2.6
Oceania	0.5	1.0
Latin America	19.8	38.6
Canada	8.9	3.0

U.S. News & World Report (adapted)

58. Which is a valid conclusion based on the above chart?

(A) Total immigration to the United States doubled between 1959 and 1979.
(B) The sources of immigration to the United States have changed greatly.
(C) Illegal immigration to the United States has decreased significantly.
(D) The United States was less ethnically diverse in 1979 than in 1959.
(E) None of the above

Questions 59-60: All of the events in each group occurred during the Jacksonian era EXCEPT

59. (A) Oberlin was founded as the first coeducational college.
(B) Eugene V. Debs founded the American Railway Union.
(C) Mary Lyon founded the college now known as Mount Holyoke.
(D) the Grimke sisters preached abolition.
(E) Frances Write lectured on women's rights.

60. (A) Clara Barton founded the American Red Cross.
(B) Lucretia Mott worked for women's rights.
(C) Garrison founded the *Liberator*.
(D) Horace Mann organized a school system for Massachusetts.
(E) Property qualifications for voting decreased.

61. Which of these items is associated with government land policy?

(A) Granger Laws
(B) Esch-Cummins Act
(C) Controversy between Gifford Pinchot and Richard Ballinger
(D) Wagner-Connery Act
(E) Controversy between President Cleveland and Governor Altgeld

62. Which of these items is NOT associated with government land policy?

(A) Theodore, Roosevelt's conference with several Governors
(B) Compromise of 1850
(C) Northwest Ordinance of 1787
(D) Interstate Commerce Act
(E) Building of Central Pacific and Union Pacific railroads

63. Which of the following statements about the Kansas-Nebraska Bill is not true?

(A) It realigned political parties, with the result that the two major partie were almost completely sectional (North and South), and their geographical division was based on differences over slavery.
(B) It stimulated a rapid settlement of Kansas.
(C) The terms of the Kansas-Nebraska Bill were incompatible with those of the Missouri Compromise.
(D) The bill was primarily the work of the "Little Giant," Daniel Webster.
(E) The 40th parallel separated Kansas from Nebraska.

64. Which of the following best describes the Crédit Mobilier?

(A) Home loan association to stimulate settlement under the Homestead Act of 1862
(B) The first widespread plan of installment buying
(C) A corporation to finance railroad building
(D) A credit union organized by workers
(E) The mobilizing of credit in order to alleviate the effects of the panic and depression of 1873

65. If two or more railroads agreed to charge the same rates for their services and to divide among them their income according to a prearranged formula, they were engaging in what practice made illegal by the Interstate Commerce Act of 1887?

(A) Cartelizing   (D) Pooling
(B) Logrolling   (E) Rebating
(E) Merging

Questions 66-67: All of the Presidents in each group were victims of attempted or actual assassination EXCEPT

66. (A) Franklin D. Roosevelt
    (B) Harry S Truman
    (C) Dwight Eisenhower
    (D) John F. Kennedy
    (E) Ronald Reagan

67. (A) Abraham Lincoln
    (B) James Garfield
    (C) William McKinley
    (D) Theodore Roosevelt
    (E) Warren Harding

68. In which of the following periods were the black codes effective?

    (A) From the *Dred Scott* case to the firing on Fort Sumter
    (B) From the Reconstruction Acts of 1867-1868 to the Hayes-Tilden election
    (C) From the Kansas-Nebraska Bill to the *Dred Scott* case
    (D) From Appomattox to the Reconstruction Acts of 1867-1868
    (E) From the first issue of Garrison's *Liberator* to John Brown at Harper's Ferry

Questions 69-71: One name in each group is out of place. It lacks a factor common to all the other names in its group. Select the ODD name.

69. (A) Charles Guiteau   (D) Leon Czolgosz
    (B) John Booth   (E) Lee Oswald
    (C) Carl Schurz

70. (A) Frances Wright   (D) Henry George
    (B) William Ladd   (E) Jane Addams
    (C) Samuel Morse

71. (A) William L. Garrison
    (B) Harriet Beecher Stowe
    (C) James G. Blaine
    (D) John Brown
    (E) Henry Clay

72,73. Which *two* of the following statements about the Knights of Labor are true?

    (A) The membership of the Knights of Labor was an exceedingly heterogeneous group.'
    (B) It grew very rapidly and faded out of the labor picture almost as quickly as it had developed.
    (C) Its program was limited to very practical economic ends, such as more pay, shorter hours, and better working conditions
    (D) Samuel Gompers was one of its early leaders.

    (E) While its membership included people of many occupations, it was largely restricted to those with highly developed skills and much better pay than the general run of workers.

74. Which of the following statements is the most substantial explanation of the ineffectiveness of the Interstate Commerce Commission during its first two decades?

    (A) The commissioners' salaries were too low to attract really competent people.
    (B) The provisions of the Interstate Commerce Act were too vaguely worded to permit effective enforcement.
    (C) The railroads could challenge in the courts the orders for the commission before obeying them.
    (D) Public opinion did not support the Interstate Commerce Commission.
    (E) The Congress refused to appropriate sufficient funds for the Interstate Commerce Commission.

75. All of the following statements associated with the early part of World War II are true EXCEPT

    (A) "Peace in our time" is associated with the Munich Conference.
    (B) Warsaw was the first city to be the victim of the "blitzkrieg."
    (C) Germany, Italy, and France formed the Axis powers of World War II.
    (D) The United States transferred 50 "over-age" destroyers to the British Navy months before Congress declared war.
    (E) Even though the U.S.S.R. had taken part of Finland and all of Estonia, Latvia, and Lithuania, the United States extended the Lend Lease program to include the Soviet Union.

76. All of these statements about the presidential campaign of 1948 are true EXCEPT

    (A) The Dixiecrats were a special group of Southern Democrats who would not support Truman.
    (B) Truman was a heavy favorite to defeat his Republican rival, Governor Thomas Dewey of New York.
    (C) Henry Wallace broke from the Democratic party and became a candidate on the Progressive party ticket.
    (D) Not only did Truman win the election, but his party made gains in both houses of Congress and picked up most of the governorships.

(E) The Democrats lost electoral votes from the states once known as the "solid South."

77. The name "Gresham" should be associated with which one of the following?

(A) Naval power   (D) Monetary problems
(B) Air power   (E) International peace
(C) Atomic power

78. One of the ways by which the Federal Reserve System directly exercises control over the monetary system of the United States is

(A) adjustment of the gold content of the dollar
(B) regulation of the interest rates for loans by Federal Reserve banks to member banks
(C) specification of the interest rates banks may charge high-risk borrowers
(D) management of government spending and the size of the national debt
(E) limitation of the amount of money that depositors can keep in banks

79. When President Harry S Truman announced on August 6, 1945, "We have spent two billion dollars on the greatest scientific gamble in history—and won," he was referring to the

(A) building of the first jet airplane
(B) successful firing of the first military rocket
(C) construction of an atomic bomb and its explosion on Hiroshima
(D) first successful operation of a military radar system
(E) success of the Allied war effort in the European theater

80. In the post-World War II period, all of the following policies were used by the federal government to combat inflation EXCEPT

(A) government pressure on certain industries to rescind price increases
(B) an increase in interest rates
(C) the urging of manufacturers and unions to act with restraint
(D) a tax increase
(E) government seizure of industries that exceeded price guidelines

81. The removal of General Douglas MacArthur from command of the United States-United Nations forces during the Korean War exemplifies the constitutional principle of

(A) separation of powers
(B) federal supremacy
(C) freedom of speech

(D) impeachment for high crimes and misdemeanors
(E) civilian control of the military

82. "Let the Negro have a country of his own. Help him to return to his original home, Africa, and there give him the opportunity to climb from the lowest to the highest positions in a state of his own."

Which of the following espoused this position?

(A) David Walker
(B) Booker T. Washington
(C) W. Monroe Trotter
(D) Marcus Garvey
(E) Father Divine

83. "The Model A Ford is a favorite American car; farmers in the Midwest have organized a Farm Holiday Association to hold goods off the market; Samuel Insull and other business tycoons have suddenly been discredited; governors of several states have declared a bank holiday, and the President has declared a war debt moratorium."

Who is the President of the United States referred to?

(A) Theodore Roosevelt
(B) William H. Taft
(C) Herbert Hoover
(D) Franklin D. Roosevelt
(E) Harry S Truman

84. Alexander Hamilton approved of Jay's Treaty because it

(A) admitted United States' goods freely to British ports without restrictions
(B) incorporated United States ideas about the rights of neutrals
(C) reflected the ideas of Madison and Jefferson as well as his own
(D) united public opinion in support of the President's treaty-making power
(E) provided a framework for peaceful United States' relations with Great Britain

85. President Wilson's primary objective at the Versailles Peace Conference was to

(A) secure recognition of the Monroe Doctrine
(B) insure that the Allied powers paid their war debts
(C) establish an international organization to prevent future wars
(D) make Germany pay for the war
(E) organize a relief program for war-torn Europe

86. National legislation was passed during the New Deal era to provide for all of the following EXCEPT

(A) aid to dependent children
(B) conservation
(C) medical insurance
(D) bank deposit insurance
(E) unemployment compensation

87. Which of the following Presidents encountered the LEAST opposition to his foreign policies?

(A) George Washington
(B) James Madison
(C) Andrew Jackson
(D) James K. Polk
(E) Woodrow Wilson

88. An important factor in the continuing expansion of American industry between the Civil War and World War I was

(A) the demand from Asia for American manufactured goods
(B) the rivalry with Canada for the wheat markets of the world
(C) the returns from American investments in Europe
(D) the growing size of the American market
(E) a boom in canal building

89. The idea that form follows function in architecture is associated with

(A) Thomas Jefferson's plan of Monticello
(B) the Greek revival of the early nineteenth century
(C) the Victorian gothic of the post-Civil War period
(D) the Chicago School of the late nineteenth century
(E) the builders of post-World War II suburban developments

90. Summer 1993 flooding in the upper Mississippi Valley took a heavy toll in each of the following states EXCEPT

(A) Iowa
(B) Illinois
(C) Missouri
(D) Nebraska
(E) Oklahoma

91. It was the position of the Virginia and Kentucky Resolutions that the

(A) Supreme Court should judge the constitutionality of congressional measures

(B) states should secede from the Union when they believed congressional measures to be unconstitutional
(C) states should judge the constitutionality of congressional measures
(D) Tariff of Abominations was null and void
(E) appointment of "midnight judges" was unconstitutional

92. The peace treaty with Japan following World War II provided for which of the following?

(A) Reparations payment of $10 billion
(B) Japanese renunciation of all claims to Korea and Formosa
(C) Russian participation in the occupation of Japan
(D) Japanese membership in SEATO
(E) Renunciation of the throne by the emperor

Questions 93-95 refer to the following map.

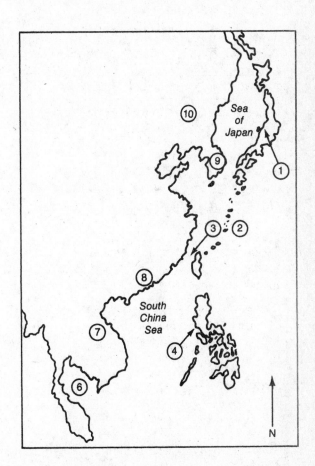

93. During the late 1960s and early 1970s, thousands of United States troops were fighting Communist forces in area

(A) 1   (B) 4   (C) 7   (D) 8   (E) 10

94. American commercial interest in the Far East was first focused on area

   (A) 6   (B) 7   (C) 8   (D) 9   (E) 10

95. The Stimson Doctrine of 1932 was concerned with area

   (A) 1   (B) 6   (C) 7   (D) 9   (E) 10

ANSWER KEY: TEST 5

1.	B	25.	B	49.	C	73.	B or A
2.	C	26.	D	50.	D	74.	C
3.	B	27.	B	51.	C	75.	C
4.	C	28.	C	52.	E	76.	B
5.	B	29.	B	53.	C	77.	D
6.	A	30.	B	54.	C	78.	B
7.	D	31.	C	55.	C	79.	C
8.	B	32.	C	56.	A	80.	E
9.	C	33.	D	57.	D	81.	E
10.	E	34.	C	58.	B	82.	D
11.	D	35.	A	59.	B	83.	C
12.	E	36.	B	60.	A	84.	E
13.	D	37.	C	61.	C	85.	C
14.	D	38.	B	62.	D	86.	C
15.	A	39.	B	63.	D	87.	D
16.	D	40.	E	64.	C	88.	D
17.	C	41.	C	65.	D	89.	D
18.	A	42.	C	66.	C	90.	E
19.	C	43.	B	67.	E	91.	C
20.	C	44.	A	68.	B	92.	B
21.	B	45.	A	69.	C	93.	C
22.	B	46.	A	70.	C	94.	C
23.	E	47.	E	71.	C	95.	E
24.	E	48.	E	72.	A or B		

ANALYSIS CHART: TEST 5

Era	Number of Questions	Number Right	Number Wrong	Number Unanswered
Pre-Columbian to 1789: questions 3, 16, 17, 25, 26	5			

1790 to 1898:
    questions 9, 12, 13, 18, 19, 22-24,
    28, 29, 31, 38, 59, 60, 63-65
    68-74, 84, 88, 89, 91, 92, 95
	30			

1899 to present:
    questions 1, 2, 4, 7, 8, 11, 14, 32,
    33, 35-37, 39-46, 48-58, 66, 75,
    76, 78-83, 85, 86, 90, 93, 94
	45			

Cross period:
    questions 5, 6, 21, 30, 47, 61, 62,
    67, 87
	9			

Nonchronological: questions 10, 15, 20, 27, 34, 77	6			

FINDING THE REASONS FOR INCORRECT ANSWERS

Be sure to check the answer explanations before completing the following chart.

Era	Number Wrong	Lack of Knowledge	Misunderstand Problem	Careless Error	Not Answered
Pre-Columbian to 1789					
1790 to 1898					
1899 to present					
Cross period					
Nonchronological					

ANSWER EXPLANATIONS: TEST 5

1. B The dark sleeve and brass buttons on the cuff suggest a police officer, the long arm of the law.

2. C The graph, which is part of the cartoon, shows a rising number of crimes committed with hand guns. The arm of the police officer is shown stopping the commission of another crime in which a gun is used. This strong arm represents stricter enforcement of gun laws.

3. B Giovanni da Verrazano was an Italian navigator who reached New York harbor in 1524 on a voyage financed by France. He was one of many explorers searching for a water passage through America to the Pacific. The Narrows refers to the part of New York harbor that lies between Brooklyn and Staten Island, and is connected by the Verrazano-Narrows Bridge.

4. C This longest suspension bridge is classically simple in appearance. The problems of design and construction and the technological advances needed to complete the span are not evident to the viewer.

5. B William McKinley of Ohio gave the Republicans of 1897-1901 the kind of government they wanted: one with a high protective tariff and maintenance of the gold standard. He was too weak to prevent the Spanish-American War. He followed his party leaders, rather than leading the American people.

6. A Grover Cleveland had won a reputation for honesty and stubborn integrity as mayor of Buffalo and as governor of New York. As President, he compelled cattle ranchers and lumber companies to return land they had illegally taken. He forced railroads that had received land grants from the government to open millions of acres to settlement to return the land to the federal government. He vetoed over 200 private pension bills passed by Congress for Civil War veterans because he found the claims to be fraudulent.

7. D The common factor is government farm policy. The Okies were impoverished migrant farm workers, especially from Oklahoma, who were forced to leave their farms during the depression of the 1930s. Their plight was depicted in John Steinbeck's novel *The Grapes of Wrath*.

8. B The common factor is increasing participation in government. The Women's Christian Temperance Union is associated with the movement to restrict the sale and consumption of alcoholic beverages.

9. C From 1865 to 1877 the Radical Republicans in Congress used the memory of the Civil War to regain power after four years of subjugation to a wartime President. This oratory also included depicting the Democrats as too closely associated with the late rebellion.

10. **E**   This practice was declared unconstitutional in the United States Supreme Court decisions in *Baker* v. *Carr* (1962, with reference to districts for state legislatures), and in *Wesberry* v. *Saunders* (1964, including congressional districts). From these decisions came the expression, "one man, one vote."

11. **D**   A crown prince is next in line for a monarchy, as is Prince Charles of England. Taft was Theodore Roosevelt's Secretary of War, and T.R.'s choice of successor. The 1908 Republican Convention was happy to nominate the choice of a popular outgoing President, and T.R. campaigned successfully for Taft.

12. **E**   The Populist party was formed to represent the Western farmers, who were suffering from ruinously low prices caused by overproduction, and the people in silver-mining towns, who had the same complaint. In 1892 at Omaha, Nebraska, the Populists nominated James Weaver for President and wrote a famous platform. It was scorching blast at the status quo, but more famous as a prophecy of things to come: a graduated income tax, the direct election of United States Senators, a secret ballot, an eight-hour day for labor, etc.

13. **D**   From 1820 to the 1850s, westward expansion was linked to patriotism and to the belief that Americans had a duty to settle the entire continent.

14. **D**   At the turn of the century, the United States wanted a larger share of the rich China market and was concerned that European nations and Japan had special trading privileges in their "spheres of influence" to permit other nations to do business there, and not to charge higher rail, harbor, and tariff rates to other nationals than to their own merchants. Although the nations involved more or less refused, Hay in 1900 announced an Open Door policy in China.

15. **A**   Logrolling is the exchange of political favors, especially the trading of influence or votes among legislators to achieve passage of projects of interest to one another.

16. **D**   The Treaty of Paris, 1763, ended the French and Indian War. In it, France gave up all of Canada to England.

17. **C**   In 1754, Major George Washington, sent by the Governor of Virginia to counter the French in the Allegaheny-Monongahela rivers area, built Fort Necessity near the French Fort Duquesne. In the ensuing battle at Great Meadows, Fort Necessity was surrendered. (This was near the present city of Pittsburgh, Pennsylvania.)

18. **A**   The Underground Railway was a system of safe houses and barns (or stations) in which fugitive slaves were hidden as they fled through the Northern states to Canada. In the 1850s, with the publication of *Uncle Tom's Cabin* and the passage of the Kansas-Nebraska Act, an enlarged group of abolitionists operated this escape route. Helping to free escaped slaves was not on the same wavelength with the orderly control of freed slaves.

19. **C**   Grover Cleveland *disapproved* annexation of the Hawaiian Islands. He found that the revolution had been engineered largely by Americans who had invested heavily in the island sugar plantations.

20. **C**   The United States has relied on aerial surveillance to detect air, sea or surface violations of the treaty.

21. **B**   England supported the idea of the Monroe Doctrine, helping to bring it about. Like the United States, England wanted more trade with the newly independent nations of Latin America.

22. **B**   Captain Stephen Decatur of the United States Navy was a hero of the War of 1812. Later, the British allowed him to use their Mediterranean stronghold at Gibraltar as a naval base for American ships operating against the Barbary pirates.

23. **E**   During the Civil War, Admiral David Farragut commanded a Union naval force that forced its way forty miles up the Mississippi from the Gulf of Mexico to capture New Orleans in the spring of 1862, and Baton Rouge soon after. That control enabled the Union in 1863 to split Texas, Louisiana, and Arkansas from the rest of the Confederacy.

24. **E**   The Confederate bombardment of Fort Sumter, in the harbor of Charleston, South Carolina, on April 12, 1861, resulted in a wave of patriotic feeling in both the North and South. Lincoln called for 75,000 volunteers to suppress the rebellion. On April 4, a Virginia convention had voted strongly against secession, but faced with the prospect of fighting their Southern neighbors, Virginia left the Union, along with North Carolina, Tennessee, and Arkansas.

25. **B**   The Stamp Act Congress took place in October 1765, with nine American colonies protesting to the king and British Parliament both taxation without representation and their conviction that only their own assemblies could levy taxes for revenue purposes. The May 1766 repeal of the Stamp Act was accompanied by passage of the Declaratory Act, which affirmed Parliament's right to make such laws and rejected the

colonists' arguments. The Boston Massacre of March 1770 resulted from the inflamed tempers of both citizens and British soldiers. The *Gaspée* was a British revenue ship that ran aground in Narragansett Bay, Rhode Island, while pursuing a suspected smuggler. The stranded ship was burned in June 1772. The Boston Tea Party of December 1773 was a commando raid in native costume to protest the tea trade monopoly granted to the British East India Tea Company that took profits away from colonial merchants.

26. **D** See the answer to question 25.

27. **B** The Twentieth Amendment to the United States Constitution changed the date of the inauguration of the President and Vice-President from March 4 to January 20, thus shortening the time between election and inauguration. (It also moved up the date when the new Congress meets, now January 3.)

28. **C** The heyday of the fast clipper ships was between 1845 and 1860, after which sailing ships were replaced by steam. Colonial powers established spheres of influence in China in the 1890s.

29. **B** The Morrill Tariff of 1891 had high rates intended to encourage American manufacturing.

30. **B** John Mitchell was president of the United Mine Workers during the 1902 Pennsylvania anthracite coal strike, Eugene Debs was president of the American Railway Union during the 1894 Pullman strike, and the Socialist party candidate for President five times.

31. **C** The Gadsden area was purchased in 1853 from Mexico because it contained a pass through the mountains suitable for a railroad. The generous price was $10 million. All the other events occurred during the 1840s.

32. **C** Theodore Roosevelt, the trustbuster, had his attorney general bring suit against the Northern Securities Company formed by J. P. Morgan, Hill, and Harriman. That company combined under one management the railroads of the Northwest, an area roughly one-fourth of the entire United States. The Supreme Court in a 1904 decision ordered the merger dissolved and gave the government its first major victory over a business combination.

33. **D** This policy, stated in 1904 by the President, declared that, in cases of chronic wrongdoing by Latin American nations, or their inability to maintain order or to fulfill their obligations to other nations, the United States had the right to exercise "international

police power." Thus the United States became the debt collector in Latin America for its European creditors. The policy was to severely harm our relations with our southern neighbors.

34. **C** Only this choice indicates the legitimate degree of constitutional restraint upon the actions of the President.

35. **A** Theodore Roosevelt was the first to get the entire nation interested in conservation. At his urging, Congress passed the Newlands Act (1902) to fund irrigation and reclamation projects. His 1908 Governors' conference called for active efforts to fight forest fires, improve inland waterways, eliminate waste in mining, and conserve water-power facilities. In 1909 he set aside in national reserves and parks some 234 million acres of federal lands rich in timber, minerals, and scenic beauty.

36. **B** T.R.'s program of domestic reform is called the "Square Deal" from his promise to bring a square deal and equal opportunity to every American.

37. **C** The original Populist party of 1892 was formed to protest agrarian suffering amidst plenty and to offer a corrective program. The early 1980s was also a period favorable to the growth of widespread and outspoken discontent. There was distrust of those in positions of political and economic power; there, was discontent with inflation, with rising taxes, with increasing crime, with unemployment, with abortion on demand, and with the flight from the public schools. President Reagan offered a program centered on getting the government out of regulation, cutting taxes, and maintaining a strong military posture toward the Soviet Union.

38. **B** This is typical of Jefferson's belief in the power of reason and in the need to educate the common people to use that reason.

39. **B** Hugo Black was a distinguished 20th-century Supreme Court Justice, who with Justice William O. Douglas wrote many important dissenting (minority) opinions. None of the other choices is a likely alternative.

40. **E** You should know this one from the explanation of question 10.

41. **C** If in doubt, reread the explanation of question 10.

42. **C** The 1960s saw a decline in the percentage of American workers who were union members, from about 25 percent to about 22 percent.

43. **B** This is especially true when the degree of pollution can be pictured as not immediately threatening to life or health. For example, not many asbestos workers wanted to see their factories close when they had no alternative local source of a job.

44. **A** Aerial, not on-site, inspection was relied on.

45. **A** The American President and television crews were shown only those aspects of Chinese life that revealed Chinese leaders and policies in a favorable light.

46. **A** Such diversification permits the company to overcome market and profit weaknesses in any one area.

47. **E** The treaty of Paris ended the Spanish-American War. Under the treaty, Puerto Rico was ceded to the United States, but Panama was not mentioned.

48. **E** President Anwar Sadat of Egypt became the first Arab leader ever to visit Israel, where he addressed the Knesset early in 1978, saying that we Arabs "welcome you to live among us in peace and security."

49. **C** The Knesset, or Israeli parliament, meets in a modern capitol building (also called the Knesset) in Jerusalem.

50. **D** Japanese and German manufacturers have invested a larger percentage of their earnings than have Americans into capital improvements, including modernization. They have been effective in trying to catch up with and surpass their United States competition. The result is that they now have newer factories with more advanced technology.

51. **C** President Reagan cited as a major reason for lowering corporate income-tax rates that such a tax policy would enable United States' industries to increase capital investment to improve plant and equipment.

52. **E** After thirteen years of talks spanning four United States presidential administrations, the United States and Panama agreed to replace the 1903 Hay-Bunau-Varilla pact with new treaties that will transfer ownership and control of the canal to Panama by the year 2000. President Carter used much political pressure to get the Senate to ratify the treaties in 1977. Ronald Reagan, then emerging as a likely challenger to Carter in the 1980 election, opposed United States surrender of the canal and the extension of large-scale economic aid to Panama from the canal tolls.

53. **C** A treaty must be ratified by two-thirds of the Senators present and voting. The Senate ratified the two 1977 Panama Canal treaties by identical votes of 68 to 32, one vote more than required by the Constitution.

54. **C** England was never an OPEC member. Neither is the United Kingdom a producer or exporter of oil.

55. **C** The Egyptian people hailed President Anwar Sadat's initiative and courage in seeking a peace settlement with Israel that would relieve Egypt of a crushing military burden.

56. **A** Argentina was never an OPEC member. Venezuela is the South American nation that helped to organize OPEC.

57. **D** Much more attention has since been paid to (and is being concentrated on) matters of safety in the building and operation of nuclear energy facilities. One such plant was the Shoreham nuclear energy plant of the Long Island Lighting Company, where failure to gain approval of a disputed emergency evacuation plan never allowed the plant to open.

58. **B** The European portion, traditionally the greatest source of United States immigration, dropped from 16 percent to less than one-quarter of that over twenty years. Asian immigration, aided by changes in the 1952 and 1965 immigration laws, increased four and a half times. Latin American immigration, largely from Mexico, Cuba, and Central America, almost doubled.

59. **B** Eugene V. Debs founded the American Railway Union in 1893. Both skilled and unskilled workers could join, and union membership soon rose to 150,000. Jailed for violating an injunction during the 1894 Pullman strike, Debs was later to run for President five times on the Socialist ticket.

60. **A** The Jacksonian era was a period of broad reform movements and democratic changes during the 1830s and 1840s, including improvements in public education, the rights of women, treatment of the poor and insane, and the antislavery movements. Clara Barton served as a nurse and medical aide during the Civil War (1861-1865). In 1881 she founded the American Red Cross.

61. **C** Starting during the administration of Theodore Roosevelt, his friend Gifford Pinchot built the United States Forest Service into a major force for conservation. Pinchot thought that President Taft, Roosevelt's successor, and Taft's Secretary of the Inte-

rior, Richard Ballinger, were reversing Roosevelt's conservation effort. Pinchot accused Ballinger of permitting valuable coal lands and water-power land to fall into private hands. After investigation, Taft fired Pinchot and thus widened the split between Progressive and Old Guard Republicans.

62. **D**   The Interstate Commerce Act of 1887 created the Interstate Commerce Commission to regulate rail (and then motor) transportation as well as inland and coastal shipping.

63. **D**   Stephen Douglas, the Senator from Illinois, introduced the bill, which increased sectional bitterness, led to a bloody struggle between proslavery and antislavery forces in Kansas, and caused Douglas to be denounced as a traitor by Northern antislavery interests.

64. **C**   The Crédit Mobilier was the company that built the Union Pacific Railroad (completed in 1869), enjoyed extremely favorable treatment from Congress, and earned huge profits. When it was revealed that several members of Congress had received company stock as a gift, an attempt was made in Congress to block investigation of these suspicious dealings. It was then found that high public officials, including the Vice President of the United States, were involved in the ugly scandal.

65. **D**   Pools were a method of business combination popular in the 1870s, especially among railroads. A pool was a gentlemen's agreement among business rivals to fix prices or divide profits or markets.

66. **C**   Eisenhower was the popular World War II general who served as a fatherly and popular President from 1953 to 1961.

67. **E**   Elected in 1921 as part of a national desire to "return to normalcy" after World War I, Warren Harding died in office of natural causes in 1923.

68. **B**   The black codes were restrictive state laws passed by the Southern legislatures during Reconstruction (1866-1876) to control and regulate the freed black people. While allowed to own property and marry among themselves, Southern blacks were not permitted to serve as jurors or to vote. They were required to make long-term work contracts with employers. Those without steady jobs could be arrested as vagrants and forced to work for the highest bidder.

69. **C**   Carl Schurz is the only one in this group who did not assassinate a United States President. Schurz was a German-born political reformer who served as

an ambassador under President Lincoln and who headed the Department of the Interior under President Hayes.

70. **C**   The only one who was not a 19th-century social reformer was Samuel Morse. A painter and inventor, he perfected the electric telegraph in 1844, established the Morse Code as the language of telegraphic communication, and built a line from Baltimore to Washington. By 1861, thousands of miles of telegraph lines had been laid, and an Atlantic cable connected the United States with Great Britain.

71. **C**   The common thread was opposition to slavery in the era before the Civil War. Blaine was a Republican party leader, Secretary of State, and unsuccessful presidential aspirant in the 1880s. He opposed Cleveland in the campaign of 1884.

72, 73. **A** and **B**   In an era of individual craft unions of skilled workers, the aim of the Knights of Labor was to organize all workers into one big union, including both the skilled and unskilled. Starting in 1869, the Knights quickly developed into the first important national labor organization.

In 1881 the Knights dropped its policy of secret membership and won a number of big strikes. This helped it grow rapidly to a peak membership of 700,000 by 1886. Its decline in numbers and influence was also rapid, partly because the Knights were unjustly associated by some with the violence of the Haymarket Affair.

74. **C**   The ICC had to rely upon the courts to enforce its decisions, and in most cases the courts ruled in favor of the railroads. In addition, evasion of the law was widespread.

75. **C**   Japan, Germany, and Italy were the Axis powers, France was allied to Great Britain and later also to the United States.

76. **B**   Most of the polls indicated that Dewey would easily defeat Truman in 1948. *The Chicago Daily Tribune* was so sure that Dewey would win that it ran the bold headline "Dewey Defeats Truman" before the final results were in.

77. **D**   Gresham's Law, familiar to students of economics, says that bad money tends to drive out good money. For instance, given a choice between using paper money or gold, people will use the paper and save the gold.

78. **B**   The Fed's rate of interest for member-bank borrowing is called the discount rate. As the Fed raises

or lowers its discount rate, banks tend to do the same. The amount of money that consumers and businesses borrow is influenced by the bank rate of interest. As loans become more costly, the public is likely to borrow less. Thus, the discount rate is used by the Fed to attempt to influence the volume of credit in our economy.

79. **C**   The gamble was to develop a successful "ultimate" weapon before the Germans did. During World War II, Nazi German research was far ahead in the use of rocketry.

80. **E**   Fines, adverse publicity, and the pressure of public opinion during a war in which 18 million Americans were in uniform were sufficient deterrents against excessive greed in pricing.

81. **E**   The Constitution makes the President the Commander-in-Chief of the armed forces.

82. **D**   Garvey called for a new African empire, free of European colonialism. His "back to Africa" movement stressed racial pride and self-esteem. He told his audiences, "You were once great; you shall be great again!" Immediately after World War I, he attracted millions to his cause, using uniforms, pageantry, and parades.

83. **C**   Caught between plummeting farm prices and high debts, the farmers' income was cut by more than half between 1929 and 1932. In several parts of the country, a Farm Holiday Association proposed a national farm strike unless the debt burden was eased and agricultural prices rose. Samuel Insull headed a public utilities holding company empire that collapsed in 1929, wiping out the investments of some 175,000 stockholders and exposing the evils of such companies. In 1931 Hoover arranged an international moratorium by which all payments of German war debts and reparations resulting from World War I was suspended for a year. It came too late to accomplish its objectives: to save the German Republic from collapse, to protect American investments in Germany, and to stimulate international trade.

84. **E**   President Washington sent John Jay to England in 1795 to settle post-Revolutionary War disputes with Britain and secure commercial privileges. The treaty provisions accomplished much of this and won the approval of Hamilton, Washington's Secretary of the Treasury and a supporter of Britain against France. However, the Jay Treaty was unpopular at home because it did nothing about the impressment of American sailors into the British Navy and did little to promote United States trade with the British West Indies.

85. **C**   It has been said that Wilson gave up thirteen of his Fourteen Points (of United States' World War I aims) in order to obtain the fourteenth, the creation of the League of Nations, which he felt could assure future world peace.

86. **C**   The United States still has no national system of medical insurance for all. In 1965, President Lyndon Johnson had Congress pass a Medicare plan to provide hospital and medical care for the elderly under Social Security. This was later supplemented by Medicaid, a joint federal-state program to pay medical bills for low-income persons and families.

87. **D**   The westward movement and settlement of the Louisiana Territory overshadowed foreign policy concerns during Jackson's administration. The other Presidents all encountered serious controversies over foreign affairs: Washington over his policy of neutrality between Britain and France; Madison over the War of 1812; Polk over annexation of Texas and the Mexican War; Wilson over United States membership in the League of Nations and signing the Treaty of Versailles.

88. **D**   This was a period of large families, large-scale European immigration, continued westward migration, and the growth of large cities.

89. **D**   This concept, stated by Louis Sullivan, means that architects should not follow tradition but should create buildings whose designs reveal the buildings' purpose and method of construction.

90. **E**   The Mississippi River system does not flow through or near the state of Oklahoma, which does share a border with Kansas to the north and Missouri to the northeast. Those states suffered flood damage.

91. **C**   To protest the unpopular Alien and Sedition Acts of 1798, Jefferson and Madison drew up the Virginia and Kentucky Resolutions, which were adopted by the legislatures of those states. The resolutions declared that the Alien and Sedition Acts were unconstitutional, and therefore null and void: that the Constitution was a compact drawn up among the states, granting the federal government only specific powers; that each state had the right to judge whether an act of Congress was unconstitutional. If a state judged an act unconstitutional, it did not have to obey it. This theory of states' rights or nullification underlay the secession of Southern slave states in 1861.

92. **B**   Japan had obtained Formosa and special rights in Korea as a result of defeating China in the Sino-Japanese War (1894-1895). Japan annexed Korea in 1910.

93. **C** Up to 500,000 American troops were trying to prevent a communist takeover of South Vietnam. Because of growing opposition at home, most of those were withdrawn by late 1972. The remaining South Vietnamese forces were unable to prevent the North Vietnamese and Viet Cong from gaining full control of the South by 1975.

94. **C** American trade with China dates from 1844 and the visit there of American diplomat Caleb Cushing with a group of warships.

95. **E** United States Secretary of State Henry Stimson authored the document about Manchuria, which had been seized in 1931 by the Japanese. The United States condemned the act of aggression and stated that our government would not recognize the new government of Manchukuo, seized in violation of existing treaties.

1. Ⓐ Ⓑ Ⓒ Ⓓ Ⓔ   16. Ⓐ Ⓑ Ⓒ Ⓓ Ⓔ   31. Ⓐ Ⓑ Ⓒ Ⓓ Ⓔ
2. Ⓐ Ⓑ Ⓒ Ⓓ Ⓔ   17. Ⓐ Ⓑ Ⓒ Ⓓ Ⓔ   32. Ⓐ Ⓑ Ⓒ Ⓓ Ⓔ
3. Ⓐ Ⓑ Ⓒ Ⓓ Ⓔ   18. Ⓐ Ⓑ Ⓒ Ⓓ Ⓔ   33. Ⓐ Ⓑ Ⓒ Ⓓ Ⓔ
4. Ⓐ Ⓑ Ⓒ Ⓓ Ⓔ   19. Ⓐ Ⓑ Ⓒ Ⓓ Ⓔ   34. Ⓐ Ⓑ Ⓒ Ⓓ Ⓔ
5. Ⓐ Ⓑ Ⓒ Ⓓ Ⓔ   20. Ⓐ Ⓑ Ⓒ Ⓓ Ⓔ   35. Ⓐ Ⓑ Ⓒ Ⓓ Ⓔ
6. Ⓐ Ⓑ Ⓒ Ⓓ Ⓔ   21. Ⓐ Ⓑ Ⓒ Ⓓ Ⓔ   36. Ⓐ Ⓑ Ⓒ Ⓓ Ⓔ
7. Ⓐ Ⓑ Ⓒ Ⓓ Ⓔ   22. Ⓐ Ⓑ Ⓒ Ⓓ Ⓔ   37. Ⓐ Ⓑ Ⓒ Ⓓ Ⓔ
8. Ⓐ Ⓑ Ⓒ Ⓓ Ⓔ   23. Ⓐ Ⓑ Ⓒ Ⓓ Ⓔ   38. Ⓐ Ⓑ Ⓒ Ⓓ Ⓔ
9. Ⓐ Ⓑ Ⓒ Ⓓ Ⓔ   24. Ⓐ Ⓑ Ⓒ Ⓓ Ⓔ   39. Ⓐ Ⓑ Ⓒ Ⓓ Ⓔ
10. Ⓐ Ⓑ Ⓒ Ⓓ Ⓔ   25. Ⓐ Ⓑ Ⓒ Ⓓ Ⓔ   40. Ⓐ Ⓑ Ⓒ Ⓓ Ⓔ
11. Ⓐ Ⓑ Ⓒ Ⓓ Ⓔ   26. Ⓐ Ⓑ Ⓒ Ⓓ Ⓔ   41. Ⓐ Ⓑ Ⓒ Ⓓ Ⓔ
12. Ⓐ Ⓑ Ⓒ Ⓓ Ⓔ   27. Ⓐ Ⓑ Ⓒ Ⓓ Ⓔ   42. Ⓐ Ⓑ Ⓒ Ⓓ Ⓔ
13. Ⓐ Ⓑ Ⓒ Ⓓ Ⓔ   28. Ⓐ Ⓑ Ⓒ Ⓓ Ⓔ   43. Ⓐ Ⓑ Ⓒ Ⓓ Ⓔ
14. Ⓐ Ⓑ Ⓒ Ⓓ Ⓔ   29. Ⓐ Ⓑ Ⓒ Ⓓ Ⓔ   44. Ⓐ Ⓑ Ⓒ Ⓓ Ⓔ
15. Ⓐ Ⓑ Ⓒ Ⓓ Ⓔ   30. Ⓐ Ⓑ Ⓒ Ⓓ Ⓔ   45. Ⓐ Ⓑ Ⓒ Ⓓ Ⓔ

46. Ⓐ Ⓑ Ⓒ Ⓓ Ⓔ   61. Ⓐ Ⓑ Ⓒ Ⓓ Ⓔ   76. Ⓐ Ⓑ Ⓒ Ⓓ Ⓔ
47. Ⓐ Ⓑ Ⓒ Ⓓ Ⓔ   62. Ⓐ Ⓑ Ⓒ Ⓓ Ⓔ   77. Ⓐ Ⓑ Ⓒ Ⓓ Ⓔ
48. Ⓐ Ⓑ Ⓒ Ⓓ Ⓔ   63. Ⓐ Ⓑ Ⓒ Ⓓ Ⓔ   78. Ⓐ Ⓑ Ⓒ Ⓓ Ⓔ
49. Ⓐ Ⓑ Ⓒ Ⓓ Ⓔ   64. Ⓐ Ⓑ Ⓒ Ⓓ Ⓔ   79. Ⓐ Ⓑ Ⓒ Ⓓ Ⓔ
50. Ⓐ Ⓑ Ⓒ Ⓓ Ⓔ   65. Ⓐ Ⓑ Ⓒ Ⓓ Ⓔ   80. Ⓐ Ⓑ Ⓒ Ⓓ Ⓔ
51. Ⓐ Ⓑ Ⓒ Ⓓ Ⓔ   66. Ⓐ Ⓑ Ⓒ Ⓓ Ⓔ   81. Ⓐ Ⓑ Ⓒ Ⓓ Ⓔ
52. Ⓐ Ⓑ Ⓒ Ⓓ Ⓔ   67. Ⓐ Ⓑ Ⓒ Ⓓ Ⓔ   82. Ⓐ Ⓑ Ⓒ Ⓓ Ⓔ
53. Ⓐ Ⓑ Ⓒ Ⓓ Ⓔ   68. Ⓐ Ⓑ Ⓒ Ⓓ Ⓔ   83. Ⓐ Ⓑ Ⓒ Ⓓ Ⓔ
54. Ⓐ Ⓑ Ⓒ Ⓓ Ⓔ   69. Ⓐ Ⓑ Ⓒ Ⓓ Ⓔ   84. Ⓐ Ⓑ Ⓒ Ⓓ Ⓔ
55. Ⓐ Ⓑ Ⓒ Ⓓ Ⓔ   70. Ⓐ Ⓑ Ⓒ Ⓓ Ⓔ   85. Ⓐ Ⓑ Ⓒ Ⓓ Ⓔ
56. Ⓐ Ⓑ Ⓒ Ⓓ Ⓔ   71. Ⓐ Ⓑ Ⓒ Ⓓ Ⓔ   86. Ⓐ Ⓑ Ⓒ Ⓓ Ⓔ
57. Ⓐ Ⓑ Ⓒ Ⓓ Ⓔ   72. Ⓐ Ⓑ Ⓒ Ⓓ Ⓔ   87. Ⓐ Ⓑ Ⓒ Ⓓ Ⓔ
58. Ⓐ Ⓑ Ⓒ Ⓓ Ⓔ   73. Ⓐ Ⓑ Ⓒ Ⓓ Ⓔ   88. Ⓐ Ⓑ Ⓒ Ⓓ Ⓔ
59. Ⓐ Ⓑ Ⓒ Ⓓ Ⓔ   74. Ⓐ Ⓑ Ⓒ Ⓓ Ⓔ   89. Ⓐ Ⓑ Ⓒ Ⓓ Ⓔ
60. Ⓐ Ⓑ Ⓒ Ⓓ Ⓔ   75. Ⓐ Ⓑ Ⓒ Ⓓ Ⓔ   90. Ⓐ Ⓑ Ⓒ Ⓓ Ⓔ

91. Ⓐ Ⓑ Ⓒ Ⓓ Ⓔ
92. Ⓐ Ⓑ Ⓒ Ⓓ Ⓔ
93. Ⓐ Ⓑ Ⓒ Ⓓ Ⓔ
94. Ⓐ Ⓑ Ⓒ Ⓓ Ⓔ
95. Ⓐ Ⓑ Ⓒ Ⓓ Ⓔ

Test 6

---

1. All of the following statements about mercantilism are true EXCEPT

   (A) Lord Grenville in England advocated mercantilism.
   (B) Colonial trade was to be regulated in a manner that would create a favorable balance of trade for the mother country.
   (C) While England was following the mercantile theory of trade, it was also treating the American colonies with "salutary neglect" in regard to the trade and navigation acts.
   (D) Laissez-faire was a basic concept of mercantilism.
   (E) An assumption inherent in mercantilism was that in business deals, one party got the better of the other.

2. "Resolved that the fixing of the Proclamation Line of 1763 was justified."

   All of the statements below supports this resolution EXCEPT

   (A) British troops could not provide effective protection west of the Alleghenies.
   (B) The destruction of several English forts in the Ohio region by Native Americans under Chief Pontiac could have been only the beginning of a serious military problem.
   (C) The area east of the Alleghenies to the Atlantic Coast left plenty of land for the settlers of the 1700s.
   (D) Settlers who had already gone west of the mountains could not be expected to give up their land claims and their livelihood.
   (E) Keeping Native Americans in a designated area by military force was impractical and necessitated an agreement they would willingly accept.

3. What is the minimum number of years of citizenship required of a United States Senator?

   (A) 6 (B) 7 (C) 9 (D) 14 (E) 15

4. For how many years must one have been a United States resident in order to be eligible for the presidency?

   (A) 6   (D) 14
   (B) 7   (E) Lifelong resident
   (C) 9

5. Which of the following is NOT in the Preamble of the Constitution?

   (A) To form a more perfect union
   (B) To protect life, liberty, and property
   (C) To promote the general welfare
   (D) To secure the blessings of liberty
   (E) To provide for the common defense

6. Which of the following is a correct paraphrase of the implied-powers (or elastic) clause of the Constitution?

   Congress shall have power to make all laws necessary and proper

   (A) to promote the general welfare of the United States
   (B) to provide for the common defense, pay the public debt, and promote the general welfare
   (C) to carry out the provisions of this Constitution
   (D) to carry out the list of powers of which the implied-powers clause is the last
   (E) to maintain the Union

7. Which of the following statements about the Alien, Sedition, and Naturalization Acts of John Adams' administration expresses a Federalist point of view?

   (A) "The XYZ affair and malicious statements about our government or its officials present no threat to the national safety."
   (B) "There is a real danger that the revolutionary spirit of the French Reign of Terror may spread to America."
   (C) "Newspaper editors, not Jacobins or aliens, were the intended victims of the Sedition Act."
   (D) "The political strife over these acts illustrates the excesses in party factionalism so strongly deplored by President Washington."
   (E) "The Sedition Act brought forth the Kentucky and Virginia Resolutions."

8. In all of the following pairs, the words or phrase in parentheses helps to bring into effect, to support, or to make more effective the item with which it is paired EXCEPT

    (A) The Embargo Act (The *Chesapeake* incident)
    (B) The Spanish Step Line (Treaty of 1819)
    (C) Organized Labor (Panic of 1837)
    (D) Westward movement of settlers (Kansas-Nebraska Bill)
    (E) The Eighteenth Amendment (Volstead Act)

9. In all of the following pairs, the words or phrase in parentheses helps to bring into effect, to support, or to make more effective the item with which it is paired EXCEPT

    (A) The strength of Jefferson's Republican party (the Alien, Naturalization, and Sedition Acts; the "midnight judges," and the Kentucky and Virginia Resolutions)
    (B) The doctrine of states' rights (strict construction of the Constitution)
    (C) Pendleton Act (C. Julius Guiteau)
    (D) The philosophy of caveat emptor (United States Department of Agriculture)
    (E) The right of a state to fix maximum rates for the use of grain storage elevators (*Munn* v. *Illinois*)

10. All of the following statements are true about United States difficulties with Mexico over oil in the period of 1920-1945 EXCEPT

    (A) The United States did not follow a policy of dollar diplomacy.
    (B) As President Wilson had done in opposing Huerta, we continued to exert influence in Mexican politics to assure the election of friendly Mexican presidents.
    (C) Ambassador Dwight Morrow established workable relations with Mexico by convincing them that our government would insist on a fair payment for all American oil properties, but would not hinder the transfer of such properties to the Mexican government.
    (D) Mexican moves toward confiscation were met through decreasing our purchases of Mexican silver.
    (E) After many years and several incidents, foreign oil companies were squeezed out of Mexico but were paid for their properties.

11, 12. Pick out the *two* statements that make the most sense.

    (A) The Specie Circular caused the Panic of 1837.

    (B) The Specie Circular precipitated the Panic of 1837.
    (C) The Panic of 1837 was merely the low spot of an economic cycle that regularly recurs according to natural economic law.
    (D) Overspeculation in land, unsound financial policies of many wildcat banks, irresponsible financing of state governments, and other discernible factors combined to cause the Panic in 1837.
    (E) Jackson's defiance of the federal courts, his illegal refusal to deposit government funds in the Second Bank of the United States, his open dislike of the wealthy and aristocratic class frightened the business community into activity and hence depression.

13. Two slave states that did NOT join the Confederate States of America were

    (A) Alabama and Mississippi
    (B) Georgia and Kentucky
    (C) Missouri and Delaware
    (D) North Carolina and West Virginia
    (E) Virginia and Florida

14. The President whose election depended upon the decision of an Electoral Commission was

    (A) Grover Cleveland
    (B) Benjamin Harrison
    (C) Rutherford B. Hayes
    (D) Andrew Jackson
    (E) Richard Nixon

15. The World War II American cartoonist who created the characters of G.I. Joe and Willy was

    (A) Charles Addams   (D) Herbert Low
    (B) Whitney Darrow   (E) Bill Mauldin
    (C) Chester Gould

16. The 19th-century American cartoonist who created the Tammany tiger, the G.O.P. elephant, and the Democratic donkey was

    (A) Rollin Kirby   (D) Thomas Nast
    (B) Herbert Low   (E) Charles Schultz
    (C) Bill Mauldin

17. Which of the following treaties was signed FIRST?

    (A) Hay-Bunau-Varilla Treaty
    (B) Kellogg-Briand Treaty
    (C) Treaty of Ghent
    (D) Pinckney Treaty
    (E) Webster-Ashburton Treaty

18. Which of the treaties in question 17 was signed LAST?

19. All of the following statements are true EXCEPT

    (A) the day after his inauguration, President Franklin D. Roosevelt declared a bank holiday. Many banks and loan associations had already been closed by order of Governors in some 21 states.
    (B) the Federal Securities Act of 1933 and the Securities and Exchange Commission were reforms in the marketing of stocks and bonds to eliminate fraudulent practices.
    (C) in the early 1930s, all gold coin and gold certificates were called in and all debts were made payable in legal tender.
    (D) as a result of the financial measures of the New Deal, gold ceased to be an important factor in our currency system.
    (E) the New Deal financial legislation separated investment banking from commercial banking.

Questions 20-21 refer to the following graph.

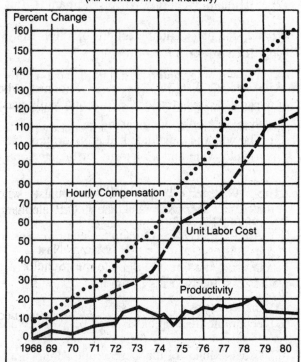

PRODUCTIVITY vs. LABOR COSTS
(All workers in U.S. Industry)

20. According to the graph, which occurred from 1968 to 1980?

    (A) Wage increases have not been accompanied proportionally by productivity increases.
    (B) Unit labor costs have tripled.
    (C) Productivity has kept pace with labor costs.
    (D) Workers' per capita income has decreased proportionally because of inflation.
    (E) Total labor costs have hurt the profits of United States industry.

21. Based on the graph, which is the most valid conclusion about the period 1968-1980?

    (A) The gross national product increased significantly.
    (B) The rate of inflation was low.
    (C) In order to maintain profit margins, businesses had to raise prices.
    (D) Increases in hourly wages did not significantly affect unit labor costs.
    (E) A rise in the value of the dollar can be predicted.

22. In all of the following pairs, the words or phrase in parentheses helps to bring to an end, to oppose, or to make less effective the item with which it is paired EXCEPT

    (A) American shipping companies (Embargo and Non-Intercourse Act)
    (B) Mutual suspicions and hostility of the United States and Great Britain toward each other over Central America (Clayton-Bulwer Treaty)
    (C) The continuance of slavery (Emancipation Proclamation)
    (D) The right of Cuba to govern itself (Platt Amendment)
    (E) Segregation in public schools (*Plessy* v. *Ferguson*)

23. All of these Presidents served only one term EXCEPT

    (A) John Adams   (D) James Polk
    (B) James Madison   (E) Herbert Hoover
    (C) John Quincy Adams

24. Which statement in the United States Constitution is NOT consistent with British governmental practices?

    (A) All legislative powers herein granted shall be vested in a Congress of the United States, which shall consist of a Senate and a House of Representatives.

(B) The privilege of the writ of habeas corpus shall not be suspended, unless...the public safety may require it.

(C) The Congress, whenever two-thirds of both houses shall deem it necessary, shall propose amendments to this Constitution....

(D) All bills for raising revenue shall originate in the House of Representatives; but the Senate may propose or concur with other amendments as on other bills.

(E) The Congress shall have power to lay and collect taxes, duties, imposts, and excises....

25. The government provided by the United States Constitution differs basically from the British parliamentary system in its

(A) direct election of members of the legislature
(B) failure to provide explicitly for political parties
(C) division of responsibility for lawmaking between the Executive and Legislative branches
(D) guarantees of civil liberties
(E) establishment of freedom of speech and debate for members of the legislature

26. Which quotation expresses the political ideas of Thomas Jefferson?

(A) "You cannot extend the mastery of the federal government over the daily life of a people without somewhere making it the master of peoples' souls and thoughts."

(B) "Our Constitution is so simple and practical that it is possible always to meet extraordinary needs by changes in emphasis and arrangement...."

(C) "The 'New Nationalism' calls for an extension of the power of the federal government...the steward of human welfare."

(D) "Sound policy requires such an adjustment of imposts (tariffs) as to encourage the development of the industrial interests...."

(E) "I consider...the power to annul a law of the United States, assumed by one State, incompatible with the existence of the Union...."

27. Historically, which would be sound political advice to a successful mayor of a city in a Northern state who wants to be elected to the presidency?

(A) Accept the offer of a federal Cabinet post
(B) Accept an appointment to a federal judge-ship
(C) Run for the United States Senate

(D) Run for Governor
(B) Run for Vice-President

28. In holding President Hoover responsible for the depression during his administration, the American people were repeating the criticism leveled earlier in our history at President

(A) Martin Van Buren
(B) Franklin Pierce
(C) Andrew Jackson
(D) Warren Harding
(E) Rutherford B. Hayes

29. Which group contains the names of Presidents, all of whom had been Governors?

(A) Woodrow Wilson, Franklin D. Roosevelt, Herbert Hoover, Ulysses Grant, Harry S Truman
(B) Calvin Coolidge, William McKinley, Franklin D. Roosevelt, Warren G. Harding, William H. Taft
(C) Benjamin Harrison, Grover Cleveland, Franklin D. Roosevelt, Herbert Hoover, Rutherford B. Hayes
(D) Franklin D. Roosevelt, Grover Cleveland, Rutherford B. Hayes, Calvin Coolidge, Woodrow Wilson
(E) Benjamin Harrison, Grover Cleveland, Harry S Truman, Woodrow Wilson, William H. Taft

30. What do the presidential elections of 1860, 1888, and 1912 have in common?

(A) The winning candidate did not have a majority of the electoral vote.
(B) The losing candidate had fewer popular votes than did the winning candidate.
(C) The winning candidate had a majority of the popular vote and a majority of the electoral vote.
(D) The winning candidate had a majority of the electoral vote but did not have a majority of the popular vote.
(E) A third party received some electoral votes.

31. In analyzing the Great Depression, a Republican would most likely stress as the basic cause the

(A) inadequacies of laissez-faire policy
(B) economic dislocations caused by World War I
(C) fiscal policies of the Democratic administrations preceding the depression
(D) careless exploitation of the nation's natural resources during the 1920s
(E) stock market crash of 1929

Questions 32-40 consist of phrases pertaining to the following list of banks and banking acts. Answer each item by indicating which bank on banking act is most closely related to that phrase.

(A) Independent Treasury Act
(B) Second Bank of the United States
(C) National Bank Act
(D) Federal Reserve Act
(E) Glass-Steagall Act

32. Earned a profit for the federal government as a result of its operations

33. Resulted from the banking reforms indicated by the Great Depression

34. Was intended to provide a more elastic currency

35. Was an integral part of Henry Clay's "American system"

36. Was established primarily to facilitate the sale of United States bonds to finance a war

37. Was intended to facilitate the movement of credit from one part of the country to another

38. Was an essential reform of the New Freedom program

39. Was the predominant issue in a presidential election

40. Was opposed by the Populist party

41. The Taft-Hartley Act of 1947 is an important milestone in the history of labor-management relations because it marked the

(A) reversal of the basic labor policies of the New Deal
(B) achievement of labor's demand for union security
(C) further assumption by the federal government of the responsibility for balancing the power of labor and management
(D) acceptance by management and labor of the need to keep essential industries operating during periods of industrial strife
(E) beginning of government arbitration as a means of preventing strikes in essential industries

42. The Taft-Hartley Act substituted the union shop for the closed shop. This change makes it more difficult to insure employment of members of which union?

(A) Building trades
(B) Barbers
(C) Auto workers
(D) Clothing workers
(E) Government employees

43. The following are some of the important gains made by labor in the period since the Civil War:

I. An act of Congress recognizing the right to bargain collectively
II. Legislation limiting the use of injunctions in labor disputes
III. The passing of the first Workers' Compensation Act
IV. An act of Congress prohibiting the use of child labor in interstate commerce, upheld by the Supreme Court
V. The first law to restrict immigration that was competing with American labor

Which represents the correct chronological order in which these gains were made?

(A) V, III, II, I, IV   (D) V, III, II, IV, I
(B) I, III, II, V, IV   (E) V, III, I, II, IV
(C) III, V, I, II, IV

44. Which of these has been a major concern of organized labor in both the 19th and the 20th centuries?

(A) Industrial v. a craft organization
(B) Political action committees
(C) Labor cooperatives
(D) The closed shop as the best guarantee of job security
(E) Serious corruption among union leaders

45. In what special respect did the New Deal program to promote prosperity for agriculture depart from traditional plans proposed by farm groups from 1865 to 1914?

(A) Abandonment of the protective tariff
(B) Reliance on monetary measures to raise prices for farm products
(C) Promotion of artificial scarcity of crops
(D) Sales of surpluses abroad
(E) Provision for relief from mortgage foreclosure

46. One reason the federal government adopted a policy of parity-price supports for agriculture was to

(A) encourage production of surplus commodities
(B) increase the sale of United States farm products in foreign countries
(C) increase federal expenditures in areas of low employment
(D) increase government control over agriculture
(E) increase the real income of farmers

47. During the 1880s and 1890s, farmers were more successful than industrial workers in achieving

(A) restriction of output
(B) increased tariff protection
(C) restriction of immigration
(D) formation of a national organization
(E) effectively controlled blocs in the state legislatures

48. The National Origins Act passed in 1924 was designed to

(A) restrict immigration
(B) increase immigration
(C) establish a lower tariff
(D) deport Communists
(E) provide citizenship to Native Americans

49. Under flexible price supports, the percentage of parity is determined by the

(A) Bureau of Statistics' cost of living index
(B) Dow-Jones averages of leading stocks
(C) Commodity Credit Corporation
(D) supply of crops on hand
(E) amount of money appropriated by Congress

50. Which type of New Deal legislation found LEAST favor with the New Republicanism of the Eisenhower administration?

(A) Conservation
(B) Social Security
(C) Federal support of farm prices
(D) Reciprocal trade agreements
(E) Promotion of public power facilities

51. Which of these New Deal measures would have been opposed by those who supported the Progressive movement?

(A) Attempts to solve the farmers' problem of low prices

(B) Guarantees of the right of collective bargaining
(C) Suspension of the monopoly laws under the NRA
(D) Increased regulation of banking
(E) Minimum wage and hour laws

52. Before 1940 some conservative Democrats accused President Franklin D. Roosevelt of violating the traditional principles of Jefferson and the Democratic party by

(A) lowering the tariff through reciprocal agreements
(B) excessive involvement in foreign affairs
(C) failing to strive for economy in government
(D) failing to promote the interest of farmers
(E) attacking the Supreme Court

53. In 1937, the attempt of the President to increase the number of members of the Supreme Court resulted in

(A) a bitter split in Congress along party lines
(B) a loss of public support for the Court
(C) a controversy over the constitutionality of the proposal
(D) the Court's refusal to reverse previous decisions on New Deal legislation
(E) the resignation of several Supreme Court Justices

54. Which did Midwestern farmers of the 1870s favor?

(A) Tariff policy followed in the McKinley administration
(B) Reconstruction Finance Corporation
(C) The Court decision in *Munn* v. *Illinois*
(D) Parity-price supports
(E) The denial of the Fourteenth Amendment to corporations

55. Which contributed most to federal regulation of railroads?

(A) Demands from manufacturers for the elimination of certain railroad abuses
(B) Demands from people who had purchased railroad securities
(C) Issuance of watered stock by the railroad corporations
(D) Political pressure from labor unions
(E) Breakdown of state control and regulation

Questions 56-60 are based on the map below.

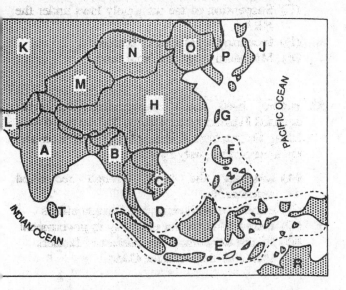

56. This island, the last stronghold of the Chinese Nationalists, sends many of its manufactured exports to the United States.

    (A) *E* (B) *F* (C) *G* (D) *J* (E) *T*

57. This nation, a former colony of Great Britain, became independent at the end of World War II. Considered neutralist in its foreign policies, it has the largest population governed by a democratic constitution.

    (A) *A* (B) *B* (C) *E* (D) *H* (E) *K*

58. This nation, formed at the time that India became independent in 1947, was divided from it along religious lines.

    (A) *B* (B) *C* (C) *L* (D) *K* (E) *T*

59. This country, a former protectorate of Japan, was granted independence after World War II, but became divided and experienced a bloody war in the early 1950s

    (A) *C* (B) *D* (C) *G* (D) *O* (E) *P*

60. This is the location of Sri Lanka, whose Tamil rebels disrupt the national peace and economic development.

    (A) *A* (B) *B* (C) *L* (D) *K* (E) *T*

61. The prohibition of child labor in the United States was the result of

    (A) an act of Congress
    (B) a Supreme Court decision
    (C) an action by a federal agency
    (D) an amendment to the United States Constitution
    (E) presidential action

62. An order raising the rediscount rate would require

    (A) an act of Congress
    (B) a Supreme Court decision
    (C) an action by a federal agency
    (D) an amendment to the United States Constitution
    (E) presidential action

63. Raising the amount of federal insurance of bank deposits from $10,000 to $100,000 required

    (A) an act of Congress
    (B) a Supreme Court decision
    (C) an action by a federal agency
    (D) an amendment to the United States Constitution
    (E) presidential action

64. Denial of the right of the states to levy poll taxes was a result of

    (A) an act of Congress
    (B) a Supreme Court decision
    (C) an action by a federal agency
    (D) an amendment to the United States Constitution
    (E) presidential action

Questions 65-74: Five people were evaluating the New Deal and its importance in American history. The following statements were made:

Speaker *A*: The attempt to promote economic recovery by "pump priming" and deficit financing was economically wasteful and was eventually abandoned.

Speaker *B*: Most New Deal legislation was clearly socialistic, doctrinaire, and unconstitutional.

Speaker *C*: The domestic program of the New Deal was, in many respects, an old attack on an old problem.

Speaker *D*: The New Deal was experimental during the early years, but by 1936, experimentalism had run its course and traditional methods were again in favor.

Speaker *E*: It is difficult to evaluate the New Deal without deciding on the relative importance of temporary, as compared with permanent, legislation that was passed.

65. Which speaker could cite the New Freedom as a historical example to support his statement?

(A) *A* (B) *B* (C) *C* (D) *D* (E) *E*

66. Which speaker is attacking a theory advanced by John Maynard Keynes?

(A) *A* (B) *B* (C) *C* (D) *D* (E) *E*

67. An example of the problem cited by Speaker E would involve a discussion of

(A) the Reconstruction Finance Corporation and the Tennessee Valley Authority
(B) the National Industrial Recovery Act and the National Labor Relations Act
(C) the bank holiday and the Resettlement Administration
(D) Social Security and unemployment insurance
(E) the Works Progress Administration (WPA) and the Public Works Administration (PWA)

68. Which speaker's arguments are primarily appeals to emotions?

(A) *A* (B) *B* (C) *C* (D) *D* (E) *E*

69. The WPA is an example of legislation that could best be cited by Speaker

(A) *A* (B) *B* (C) *C* (D) *D* (E) *E*

70. Franklin D. Roosevelt's Supreme Court plan can be cited in opposition to Speaker

(A) *A* (B) *B* (C) *C* (D) *D* (E) *E*

71. Which pair of speakers seem to be most nearly in agreement?

(A) *A* and *E*   (D) *D* and *E*
(B) *C* and *B*   (E) *A* and *C*
(C) *B* and *D*

72. A defender of the New Deal would be most likely to label as "reactionary" Speaker

(A) *A* (B) *B* (C) *C* (D) *D* (E) *E*

73. Which speaker's remarks would be most acceptable to both a supporter and a critic of the New Deal?

(A) *A* (B) *B* (C) *C* (D) *D* (E) *E*

74. None of the speakers mentioned the

(A) New Deal's dependence on trial and error
(B) vast increase in government spending
(C) growth of economic democracy

(D) international phases of the New Deal
(E) conflict between the Executive and the Judicial branches

Questions 75-80 refer to the following three paragraphs.

I. It is a false liberalism that interprets itself into the government operation of commercial business. Every step of bureaucratizing of the business of our country poisons the very roots of liberalism—that is, political equality, free speech, free assembly, free press, and equality of opportunity. It is the road not to more liberty but to less liberty. Liberalism should be found not striving to spread bureaucracy but striving to set bounds to it. True liberalism seeks all legitimate freedom, first in the confident belief that without such freedom, the pursuit of all other blessings and benefits is vain. That belief is the foundation of all American progress, political as well as economic.

II. American industry is not free, as once it was free; American enterprise is not free; the man with only a little capital is finding it harder to get into the field, more and more impossible to compete with the big fellow. Why? Because the laws of this country do not prevent the strong from crushing the weak. That is the reason, and because the strong have crushed the weak, the strong dominate the industry and the economic life of this country....What this country needs above everything else is a body of laws which will look after the men who are on the make rather than the men who are already made.

III. Every man has a right to his own property, which means a right to be assured to the fullest extent attainable, of the safety of his savings. By no other means can men carry the burdens of those parts of life which in the nature of things afford no chance of labor—childhood, sickness, old age. In all thought of property, this right is paramount; all other property rights must yield to it. If, in accord with this principle, we must restrict the operation of the speculator, the manipulator, even the financier, I believe we must accept the restriction as needful not to hamper individualism but to protect it.

75. All three paragraphs are concerned chiefly with

(A) liberalism v. property rights
(B) liberalism v. conservatism
(C) freedom v. property rights
(D) individualism v. liberalism
(E) individualism v. social control

76. Liberalism as defined in paragraph I is most akin to the ideas advocated or expressed by people associated with the

(A) New Deal philosophy
(B) Progressive movement of the 20th century
(C) laissez-faire school of political thought
(D) New Freedom of the common people
(E) American labor movement

77. Which group lists three men who would have been in close agreement with the thoughts expressed in paragraph I?

(A) Carnegie, Lincoln, Wilson
(B) Jackson, Theodore Roosevelt, Truman
(C) Rockefeller, Gompers, Henry George
(D) LaFollette, George Norris, William H. Taft
(E) Jefferson, McKinley, Hoover

78. The thoughts expressed in paragraph II indicate that the statement was probably made in the year

(A) 1836   (D) 1912
(B) 1864   (E) 1952
(C) 1876

79. The author of paragraph II would have favored most the legislation exemplified by the

(A) Federal Trade Commission Act
(B) National Labor Relations Act
(C) Social Security Act
(D) Food, Drugs, and Cosmetics Act
(E) Smoot-Hawley Tariff Act

80. Which is an implication of the thoughts expressed in paragraph III?

(A) Property rights must be protected at all costs.
(B) Regulation of securities and banking may be needed.
(C) Social Security legislation is needed to protect property rights.
(D) Property rights must be abolished if they hamper individual rights.
(E) We can protect individualism by defending property rights.

81. The agreement to exchange fifty American destroyers for British bases in 1940 was criticized in the United States mainly because

(A) it would anger Germany and Italy
(B) it was a violation of international law
(C) the bases were really of little actual value
(D) it was negotiated without the advice and consent of the Senate

(E) our fleet strength was weakened at a key point in our history

82. Which action by the United States showed most clearly its resolution to preserve the political independence and territorial integrity of China?

(A) Intervening in the Korean War (1950)
(B) Issuing the Stimson Doctrine
(C) Protesting against the attack on the *Panay*
(D) Concluding the Gentlemen's Agreement with Japan
(E) Sending the American fleet to the Orient (1907)

83. Under the Puerto Rican Constitution of 1952, it was agreed that the United States would

(A) grant citizenship to Puerto Ricans
(B) retain control over Puerto Rican foreign affairs
(C) retain control over taxation in Puerto Rico
(D) grant independence to Puerto Rico at an unspecified date
(E) give Puerto Rico tariff concessions for a period of ten years

84. During the period since the end of World War II, the United States has departed most sharply from its traditional attitude toward Europe by

(A) initiating disarmament negotiations
(B) supporting foreign independence movements
(C) lowering its tariff barriers
(D) employing nonrecognition to show disapproval of aggressor
(E) forming a system of defensive alliances

85. In its relations with the Arab world since 1945, the United States' most fateful decision was that resulting in the

(A) creation of Central Treaty Organization
(B) support of the United Nations resolution partitioning Palestine
(C) dispatch of troops to Lebanon at the time of the Iraqi Revolution
(D) building of air bases in Morocco and Iran
(E) sending of technical-assistance missions to the United Arab Republic

86. The Korean War (1950-1953) and the Boxer Rebellion were alike in that both

(A) were provoked by a nation that did not become a belligerent
(B) ended in a stalemate

(C) aided directly in the advance of communism in East Asia

(D) involved the joint participation of forces of the United States and other nations

(E) resulted in loss of territory for China

87. The legal basis for President Truman's order for American air and naval forces to support South Korea was

(A) an inherent power of the presidency
(B) a joint resolution of Congress
(C) the federal Constitution
(D) the United Nations Charter
(E) the United States treaty with the Republic of Korea

88. Which of these immediately preceded the signing of the North Atlantic Treaty?

(A) Outbreak of war in Korea
(B) Failure of the United Nations to settle the Berlin blockade
(C) Communist coup d'état in Czechoslovakia
(D) Failure to renew the Marshall Plan
(E) Suppression of the Hungarian Revolution

89. The Nuremberg Trials at the end of World War II were important because they

(A) demonstrated that the Soviet Union lacked good faith in carrying out its agreements
(B) set the precedent that leaders were responsible for the deeds of their nations
(C) established Hitler's responsibility for World War II
(D) revealed that most accounts of Nazi atrocities could not be documented
(E) extended the American legal concept of *ex post facto* to international law

90. The Act of Chapultepec marked a turning point in our Latin American relations because it

(A) made the Monroe Doctrine a responsibility of all the Pan-American republics
(B) reaffirmed the Roosevelt Corollary to the Monroe Doctrine
(C) initiated the first program of technical aid to underdeveloped areas
(D) extended the principle of reciprocal trade to Latin American nations
(E) provided for the eventual withdrawal of United States military forces from the Caribbean area

91. Which event occurred AFTER the United States declaration of war for the war with which the event is paired?

(A) Battle of the Alamo—Mexican War
(B) *Chesapeake-Leopard* affair—War of 1812
(C) Occupation of Puerto Rico—Spanish-American War
(D) Sinking of the *Lusitania*—World War I
(E) Sinking of the *Panay*—World War II

Questions 92-94 refer to the following cartoon.

— Art Bimrose, *The Oregonian*

92. Which would be the best title for this cartoon?

(A) "The End of Intervention"
(B) "Farewell to Isolation"
(C) "The Birth of Neutrality"
(D) "The Start of Coexistence"
(E) "Ready and Willing"

93. This cartoon probably describes events that took place during the years

(A) 1790-1820   (D) 1940-1965
(B) 1820-1850   (E) 1965-1985
(C) 1870-1890

94. The conclusions that may best be drawn from this cartoon is that the United States

(A) willingly assumed a major role in world affairs
(B) refused to play a major role in world affairs
(C) reluctantly assumed a leading role in world affairs
(D) forced the world to accept United States leadership
(E) at first was hesitant, then was comfortable in its new role

95. At which three wartime conferences did the heads of government of the United States, the United Kingdom, and the Soviet Union meet together?

(A) Atlantic Conference, Teheran Conference, Yalta Conference
(B) Quebec Conference, Potsdam Conference, Yalta Conference
(C) Quebec Conference, Potsdam Conference, Casablanca Conference
(D) Teheran Conference, Yalta Conference, Potsdam Conference
(E) Atlantic Conference, Casablanca Conference, Quebec Conference

ANSWER KEY: TEST 6

1. D	25. C	49. D	73. E
2. D	26. A	50. E	74. D
3. C	27. D	51. C	75. E
4. D	28. A	52. C	76. C
5. B	29. D	53. C	77. E
6. D	30. D	54. C	78. D
7. B	31. B	55. E	79. A
8. C	32. B	56. C	80. B
9. D	33. E	57. A	81. D
10. B	34. D	58. C	82. B
11. D or B	35. B	59. E	83. B
12. B or D	36. C	60. E	84. E
13. C	37. D	61. A	85. B
14. C	38. D	62. C	86. D
15. E	39. B	63. A	87. C
16. D	40. C	64. D	88. C
17. D	41. C	65. C	89. B
18. B	42. A	66. A	90. A
19. D	43. A	67. B	91. C
20. A	44. D	68. B	92. B
21. C	45. C	69. A	93. D
22. E	46. E	70. D	94. C
23. B	47. E	71. D	95. D
24. C	48. A	72. B	

ANALYSIS CHART: TEST 6

Era	Number of Questions	Number Right	Number Wrong	Number Unanswered
Pre-Columbian to 1789: questions 1, 2, 5, 6	4			
1790 to 1898: questions 7-9, 11-14, 16, 22, 23, 26, 32, 35, 36, 39, 40, 43, 47, 54, 56, 91	21			
1899 to present: questions 10, 15, 18-21, 28, 31, 33, 34, 37, 38, 41, 42, 45, 46, 48-53, 55, 57-76, 78-90, 92-95	60			
Cross period: questions 17, 27, 29, 30, 44, 77	6			
Nonchronological: questions 3, 4, 24, 25	4			

FINDING THE REASONS FOR INCORRECT ANSWERS

Be sure to check the answer explanations before completing the follwing chart.

Era	Number Wrong	Lack of Knowledge	Misunderstand Problem	Careless Error	Not Answered
Pre-Columbian to 1789					
1790 to 1898					
1899 to present					
Cross period					
Nonchronological					

ANSWER EXPLANATIONS: TEST 6

1. **D** Laissez-faire is a government policy of hands-off business. Under mercantilism, governments regulated trade so as to amass gold and silver.

2. **D** By the Royal Proclamation of 1763, colonists were ordered to remain east of the Allegheny Mountains, and those settlers already west of the Alleghenies were ordered to leave.

3. **C** Article I, Section 3, Clause 3 of the Constitution fixes the qualifications for Senators, including nine years as a citizen and an inhabitant of the state for which he or she shall be chosen.

4. **D** Article II, Section 1, Clause 5 fixes the qualifications for President and Vice-President, including natural-born citizenship and fourteen years of residency.

5. **B** The Declaration of Independence lists as among human rights those of life, liberty, and the pursuit of happiness. Of these, the Preamble to the Constitution mentions only "the blessings of liberty."

6. **D** Article I, Section 8 of the Constitution lists in eighteen clauses the powers granted to Congress. The last, or elastic clause, gives Congress the power to "make all Laws which shall be necessary and proper for carrying into Execution the foregoing Powers."

7. **B** The Federalists tried to use the ill-feeling toward France that resulted from the XYZ affair to weaken the Republican party and to silence opposition.

8. **C** The Panic of 1837 was one of the most severe business depressions in American history. Banks and businesses closed. Farmers lost their farms through mortgage foreclosures. Eastern factory workers lost their jobs, and fledgling unions were weakened or destroyed.

9. **D** *Caveat emptor* is Latin for "Let the buyer beware," meaning that it is the consumer's own fault for getting stuck with a bad product. In 1862, a commissioner of agriculture was created to collect and diffuse useful information on agriculture. Ever since, that department has provided farmers and consumers with useful information to make the growing, buying, storage, and cooking of food economical and to maximize nutritional value.

10. **B** Despite problems, cordial relations were restored between the two nations, thanks to the efforts of United States Ambassador Dwight Morrow in the 1920s and Secretary of State Cordell Hull in the 1930s.

11, 12. **B** and **D** The causes of the Panic of 1837 are described in choice **D**. To break the speculative boom, President Jackson issued the Specie Circular of 1836, directing all purchasers of public lands, except actual settlers living there, to pay in gold or silver coin rather than in state bank notes. This action created a demand for specie, which put a strain on those banks that had lent money too freely. Stronger banks began to call in loans; weaker banks failed.

13. **C** Called border states, these two lay between the Deep South, where cotton was "king," and the antislavery North.

14. **C** In the presidential election of 1876, the electoral votes of four states were in dispute. Excluding them, Samuel J. Tilden lacked one electoral vote for victory. The House of Representatives created an electoral commission of eight Republicans and seven Democrats to decide the issue, and they all voted for their own party. Hayes won the election.

15. **E** Many of Mauldin's most famous wartime cartoons were collected in his popular book *Up Front*. He continued to be an incisive political cartoonist into the 1980s.

16. **D** Thomas Nast was famous for his cartoons attacking the New York City Tweed Ring, the object of reforms of Governor Samuel J. Tilden.

17. **D** In 1795 the Pinckney Treaty with Spain gave the new American nation the right of free navigation on the Mississippi and the right of deposit at the port of New Orleans.

18. **B** The Kellogg-Briand Treaty of 1928 was an agreement among fifteen nations renouncing war as a "means of settling international disputes" and calling for their peaceful solution.

19. **D** From 1933 on, the United States was on a modified gold standard. People holding gold had to exchange it for paper money. Foreign governments could buy or sell dollars at the price of $35 for an ounce of gold, and the Federal Reserve System was required to hold some gold as a reserve for the dollars it circulated.

20. **A** While wages rose more than 160 percent from 1968 to 1981, productivity, or the output per worker per hour, rose only about 20 percent and then dropped off after 1978.

21. **C** Profits are determined by subtracting costs from receipts. As the labor costs per item produced (unit labor costs) rose about 115 percent, a substantial rise in prices was necessary to keep making a profit.

22. **E** The Supreme Court decision in *Plessy* v. *Ferguson* in 1896 permitted the continuation of racial segregation in public schools under the "separate but equal" doctrine that was reversed in *Brown* v. *Topeka*, 1954.

23. **B** Madison, a Democratic-Republican, served from 1809 to 1817. He was supported by the South and the West, and opposed by New England because of the War of 1812.

24. **C** Unlike the single document called the United States Constitution, the basis for British law lies in various documents as well as in the common law.

25. **C** In a parliamentary system of government, such as Britain's, the head of the executive branch is usually the leader of the political party that controls a majority in the legislative branch. Thus, there is no separation of powers between the two branches.

26. **A** Jefferson said, "That government is best which governs least."

27. **D** The governorship of such states as New York, New Jersey, and Massachusetts was a stepping-stone to the presidency for both Roosevelts, Woodrow Wilson, and Calvin Coolidge, and more recently, Carter, Reagan, and Clinton headed the state governments of Georgia, California, and Arkansas.

28. **A** Van Buren was President during the Panic of 1837. See also the explanations of questions 8, 11, and 12.

29. **D** Hayes had been governor of Ohio for three terms. Cleveland served as governor of New York. See also the explanation of question 27.

30. **D** In 1860 Lincoln defeated three opponents: Douglas, Bell, and Breckinridge. In 1888, running for a second term, Cleveland won the popular vote but lost to Benjamin Harrison (who had the most electoral votes). In 1912, Woodrow Wilson divided votes with Theodore Roosevelt, William H. Taft, and Eugene Debs. None of the winning candidates received a majority of the popular votes.

31. **B** By a process of elimination, this is the only choice that could be used by a Republican, whose party dominated American politics from 1920 to 1933.

32. **B** Since 1819 the Second Bank of the United States had been well-managed by Nicholas Biddle. In the Eastern states it had become a necessary part of business mechanism.

33. **E** The Glass-Steagall Act of 1933 provided for several reforms in the banking system. It provided for a Federal Deposit Insurance Corporation (FDIC) to insure bank savings deposits. The FDIC protected the savings of small depositors and promoted stability in the banking system by increasing public confidence.

34. **D** The Federal Reserve Act of 1913 set up twelve federal reserve banks to provide for local needs and make it easier to move money from one part of the country to another. Federal Reserve notes were a new form of flexible currency, to be issued according to business needs by these twelve "banks for bankers."

35. **B** Part of Henry Clay's "American system" included a national bank that would supply a national currency. In 1832 Clay campaigned for the recharter of the Second B.U.S., but lost to Jackson.

36. **C** Congress set up the National Banking System in 1863 to hasten sales of government bonds during the Civil War. Under this system, a state bank or group of five persons with adequate capital could organize a national bank, provided they invested one-third of the minimum capital in government bonds, to be deposited in the United States Treasury. They could then issue national bank notes against this reserve. The system raised much money.

37. **D** See the answer to question 34.

38. **D** The Federal Reserve Act of 1913 was a major reform measure in providing greater banking stability in time of crisis, greater flexibility of currency with Federal Reserve notes, central control of banking practices, and an end to overconcentration of bank capital in New York City.

39. **B** Although the B.U.S. was not due for recharter until 1836, Andrew Jackson made it a key issue in the 1832 campaign against Henry Clay. See also the answer to question 35.

40. **C** One plank in the Populist party's 1892 platform was the establishment of a subtreasury system to make credit easier to obtain. This item had great appeal to the farmers, who were debtors.

41. **C** Some people felt that the liberal Wagner Act, or National Labor Relations Act, of 1935 had put restraints on employers but did not put checks on labor unions. Taft-Hartley was supposed to correct that imbalance.

42. **A** In a closed shop, workers had to join the union before they could secure a job. In the construc-

tion trades, such as in the carpenters', plumbers', and electricians' unions, the closed shop meant that the carrier of a union card already had the union's guarantee of a high level of skill in the trade. These highly skilled workers, after passage of Taft-Hartley, were in competition with workers of questionable skill willing to accept a lower wage.

43. **A** To satisfy the complaint of American workers about the unwelcome competition of Chinese workers, Congress passed an 1882 bill cutting off all immigration from China for ten years. In 1916 Congress passed a Workers' Compensation Act. In 1932 it passed the Norris-LaGuardia (anti-injunction) Act. The right to collective bargaining was recognized in the 1935 Wagner Act, for which see the answer to question 41. The Fair Labor Standards Act of 1938 prohibited the employment of children under age sixteen in interstate commerce and was upheld by the Supreme Court.

44. **D** The closed shop, described in the answer to question 42, provides the greatest degree of union worker security.

45. **C** The Agricultural Adjustment Act of 1933 paid farmers to remove arable land from cultivation, rather than starting with the purchase of their surplus.

46. **E** Parity is that price that will give farmers the same purchasing power from the sale of their goods that they had over a selected base period.

47. **E** During this period, the Grangers, or Patrons of Husbandry, helped elect many officials in Western states and influenced state legislatures, especially in the Middle West, to pass laws prohibiting abuses by railroads and grain-elevator operators.

48. **A** The National Origins Act of 1924 was designed to limit immigration to the United States and to reduce the number of immigrants from southern and eastern Europe.

49. **D** Since the supply of crops, given a constant demand, determines their price, that supply will determine the percentage of parity needed to give the farmer a decent income.

50. **E** Eisenhower's administration supported private rather than public development of hydroelectric power and atomic energy. The Atomic Energy Act of 1954 permitted private industry to develop atomic power. Private power companies were encouraged to build their own dams.

51. **C** Progressives argued that effective enforcement of the Sherman Antitrust Act of 1890 would break up undesirable monopolies and create new economic opportunities. They realized that the formation of trusts ruined many small businesses, reduced competition, and often led to higher prices.

52. **C** In dealing with a sick economy, F.D.R.'s New Deal greatly expanded the federal government's regulatory powers beyond anything previously undertaken. It also raised government spending to an unprecedented level in its efforts to lift the country out of the depression.

53. **C** Congress has the constitutional authority to determine the number of Justices on the Supreme Court. In 1937, F.D.R. wanted the power to appoint (up to a total of fifteen) a new Supreme Court Justice for each one who did not retire upon reaching the age of seventy. This would have counterbalanced those Justices who were anti-New Deal.

54. **C** That Supreme Court decision in 1876 upheld the right of states to regulate private property, like railroads and grain elevators, for the public good. The other choices all involve issues that arose later on.

55. **E** In 1886 the Supreme Court reversed itself on *Munn* v. *Illinois*, by declaring in *Wabash* v. *Illinois* that where railroads and other forms of commerce crossed state lines, the states could not restrict them. Only Congress has the power to regulate interstate commerce. The next year Congress passed the Interstate Commerce Act.

56. **C** Taiwan, also called the Republic of China (R.O.C.), has become industrialized since World War II with American assistance.

57. **A** India, with a population three times that of the United States, now sees other political parties challenging the long supremacy of the Congress party at the polls.

58. **C** Pakistan is an Islamic republic that has fought three wars with its neighbor, India, during their brief existence. Mutual suspicions and distrust continue to mar their relations.

59. **E** Korea remains a nation divided between North and South Korean governments. The United States keeps 39,000 American troops in South Korea to help provide military security against Communist North Korea.

60. **E** Sri Lanka, formerly Ceylon, exports tea to the rest of the world. Since 1975 many Tamil people, whose traditional home is South India, have been fighting for an autonomous state in northern and eastern Sri Lanka.

61. **A** Some child labor, especially agricultural and part time employment, exists in many states. The Fair Labor Standards Act of 1839 restricts but does not eliminate child labor. That is also true of compulsory education laws.

62. **C** Each of the twelve federal reserve banks has the power to raise the rediscount rate for its member banks, thereby making credit expensive and tending to discourage the extension of loans.

63. **A** Congress determines the maximum amount of insurance on savings accounts in member banks of the Federal Deposit Insurance Corporation.

64. **D** In 1964, the Twenty-fourth Amendment to the Constitution abolished the poll tax, a fee that persons were required to pay in order to vote in a number of Southern states.

65. **C** The "Roosevelt revolution" was the culmination of half a century of historical development. To aid banks, Franklin D. Roosevelt used the Federal Reserve System begun under Wilson. The farm relief program of Wilson's New Freedom anticipated much that the Roosevelt administration enacted. The fight that Wilson waged against the "money power" and Wall Street was more bitter than anything that came during the New Deal.

66. **A** John Maynard Keynes was an English economist whose ideas were widely known and discussed during the 1930s. To start the business cycle upward during the depression, he insisted that government must "prime the pump" by providing employment that would sustain buying power. This would mean *deficit spending*, but it would also restore the economic balance.

67. **B** The National Industrial Recovery Act was temporary, aimed at promoting recovery by introducing self-regulations of business, curtailing overproduction, increasing wages, shortening hours of labor, and raising prices. The keys were codes of fair competition, which industry was to accept voluntarily. The National Labor Relations Act was to recognize permanently the right of labor unions to engage in collective bargaining with employers.

68. **B** The terms *socialistic, doctrinaire*, and *unconstitutional* are all emotionally loaded, casting more heat than light.

69. **A**   The Works Progress Administration was established in 1935 as the government agency to coordinate all federal public-works construction projects. It provided jobs for almost four million of the unemployed, building new roads, bridges, airports, parks, and public buildings, as well as repairing others.

70. **D**   F.D.R.'s 1937 Court-packing plan was novel. It is discussed in the answer to question 53.

71. **D**   The first three speakers are all negative about the New Deal, but for very different reasons. The last two speakers take a balanced view of the New Deal.

72. **B**   A reactionary is one who wants to return to the "good old ways" of doing things.

73. **E**   The supporter would cite the permanent reforms, and the critic would cite much temporary "wasteful meddling" by government with the nation's business.

74. **D**   These included attempts to improve international trade by lowering tariffs, a "good neighbor policy" toward Latin America, and the recognition of the Communist government of the Soviet Union.

75. **E**   Social control refers to the various ways by which a society exerts pressure on an individual to conform to the norms of that society. Actions taken and laws passed by government are examples of strong social control. (This choice would fit as a title for each of the three paragraphs.)

76. **C**   Laissez-faire is the doctrine that an economic system functions best without governmental interference.

77. **E**   Jefferson, as a strict constructionist of the Constitution, and the two more recent Presidents, as economic conservatives, believed in a minimum of government intervention in the lives of the people.

78. **D**   In the presidential campaign of 1912, both Wilson and Theodore Roosevelt called for government to deal with the problem of trusts. Wilson emphasized trustbusting, while Roosevelt urged instead stricter regulation of those business organizations that had "not offended otherwise than by...size."

79. **A**   This 1914 law, part of Wilson's New Freedom, created a federal trade commission that could order a corporation to stop unfair methods of competition.

80. **B**   The speaker is concerned primarily with the safety of one's savings. Laws regulating the conduct of the nation's securities business and protecting the bank savings deposits, of individuals were passed in the 1930s, and amended since.

81. **D**   This was an *executive agreement* concluded by the President; it did not require participation by the Senate or the House. Had it been in the form of a treaty, ratification by a two-thirds vote of the Senate would be necessary.

82. **B**   In 1932 the Stimson Doctrine, named after United States Secretary of State Henry Stimson, said that the United States would refuse to recognize any territorial changes that violated existing treaties. This political objection to Japan's 1931 seizure of the rich Chinese province of Manchuria was in lieu of any military or economic sanction.

83. **B**   Puerto Ricans are U.S. citizens. Puerto Rico is a commonwealth, which in this case means it has self-government in domestic affairs, while control of military protection and foreign affairs remain with the United States.

84. **E**   The North Atlantic Treaty Organization of 1949 has been very successful in preventing further Soviet expansion westward in Europe. NATO also protects Greece and Turkey, which are member states.

85. **B**   This led to the 1948 creation of the State of Israel, which no Arab state but Egypt has recognized, and with which the other Arab states have been at war ever since.

86. **D**   The Korean War (1950-1953) was unique in that it was a police action called for by the Security Council of the United Nations and directed against aggression by North Korea against South Korea. The Boxer Rebellion of 1900 was a bloody Chinese uprising against foreigners that was put down by an international army of European, Japanese, and American soldiers.

87. **C**   The President is not bound by the United Nations Charter. He is Commander-in-Chief of the United States armed forces under the Constitution and in that legal capacity responded to the call for aid to South Korea.

88. **C**   The 1948 Communist seizure of the democratic government of Czechoslovakia made Western nations realize the need for a policy of strict containment of Communist expansion.

89. **B**   During 1945 and 1946 an international military court at Nuremberg, Germany, tried top Nazi

officials for war crimes. Ten were hanged, eight were sentenced to prison, and one committed suicide.

90. **A**   This pact was signed at a Pan-American Conference in Mexico City in 1945.

91. **C**   The Treaty of Paris, signed in 1898, ended the Spanish-American War and provided that Spain cede Puerto Rico to the United States.

92. **B**   Uncle Sam is pictured as being pushed unwillingly on stage by the world into a role of world leadership.

93. **D**   This period covers the United States' role in World War II and the Cold War.

94. **C**   The cartoon shows Uncle Sam dragging his heels and looking unhappy. He is being pushed and is frowning.

95. **D**   Franklin D. Roosevelt, Winston Churchill, and Joseph Stalin attended the conferences at Teheran, Iran, in 1943 and at Yalta in the Soviet Union in February 1945. Harry S. Truman, Clement Atlee, and Stalin were at the Potsdam, Germany, Conference in July 1945.

ANSWER SHEET: TEST 7

1. Ⓐ Ⓑ Ⓒ Ⓓ Ⓔ   16. Ⓐ Ⓑ Ⓒ Ⓓ Ⓔ   31. Ⓐ Ⓑ Ⓒ Ⓓ Ⓔ
2. Ⓐ Ⓑ Ⓒ Ⓓ Ⓔ   17. Ⓐ Ⓑ Ⓒ Ⓓ Ⓔ   32. Ⓐ Ⓑ Ⓒ Ⓓ Ⓔ
3. Ⓐ Ⓑ Ⓒ Ⓓ Ⓔ   18. Ⓐ Ⓑ Ⓒ Ⓓ Ⓔ   33. Ⓐ Ⓑ Ⓒ Ⓓ Ⓔ
4. Ⓐ Ⓑ Ⓒ Ⓓ Ⓔ   19. Ⓐ Ⓑ Ⓒ Ⓓ Ⓔ   34. Ⓐ Ⓑ Ⓒ Ⓓ Ⓔ
5. Ⓐ Ⓑ Ⓒ Ⓓ Ⓔ   20. Ⓐ Ⓑ Ⓒ Ⓓ Ⓔ   35. Ⓐ Ⓑ Ⓒ Ⓓ Ⓔ
6. Ⓐ Ⓑ Ⓒ Ⓓ Ⓔ   21. Ⓐ Ⓑ Ⓒ Ⓓ Ⓔ   36. Ⓐ Ⓑ Ⓒ Ⓓ Ⓔ
7. Ⓐ Ⓑ Ⓒ Ⓓ Ⓔ   22. Ⓐ Ⓑ Ⓒ Ⓓ Ⓔ   37. Ⓐ Ⓑ Ⓒ Ⓓ Ⓔ
8. Ⓐ Ⓑ Ⓒ Ⓓ Ⓔ   23. Ⓐ Ⓑ Ⓒ Ⓓ Ⓔ   38. Ⓐ Ⓑ Ⓒ Ⓓ Ⓔ
9. Ⓐ Ⓑ Ⓒ Ⓓ Ⓔ   24. Ⓐ Ⓑ Ⓒ Ⓓ Ⓔ   39. Ⓐ Ⓑ Ⓒ Ⓓ Ⓔ
10. Ⓐ Ⓑ Ⓒ Ⓓ Ⓔ   25. Ⓐ Ⓑ Ⓒ Ⓓ Ⓔ   40. Ⓐ Ⓑ Ⓒ Ⓓ Ⓔ
11. Ⓐ Ⓑ Ⓒ Ⓓ Ⓔ   26. Ⓐ Ⓑ Ⓒ Ⓓ Ⓔ   41. Ⓐ Ⓑ Ⓒ Ⓓ Ⓔ
12. Ⓐ Ⓑ Ⓒ Ⓓ Ⓔ   27. Ⓐ Ⓑ Ⓒ Ⓓ Ⓔ   42. Ⓐ Ⓑ Ⓒ Ⓓ Ⓔ
13. Ⓐ Ⓑ Ⓒ Ⓓ Ⓔ   28. Ⓐ Ⓑ Ⓒ Ⓓ Ⓔ   43. Ⓐ Ⓑ Ⓒ Ⓓ Ⓔ
14. Ⓐ Ⓑ Ⓒ Ⓓ Ⓔ   29. Ⓐ Ⓑ Ⓒ Ⓓ Ⓔ   44. Ⓐ Ⓑ Ⓒ Ⓓ Ⓔ
15. Ⓐ Ⓑ Ⓒ Ⓓ Ⓔ   30. Ⓐ Ⓑ Ⓒ Ⓓ Ⓔ   45. Ⓐ Ⓑ Ⓒ Ⓓ Ⓔ

46. Ⓐ Ⓑ Ⓒ Ⓓ Ⓔ   61. Ⓐ Ⓑ Ⓒ Ⓓ Ⓔ   76. Ⓐ Ⓑ Ⓒ Ⓓ Ⓔ
47. Ⓐ Ⓑ Ⓒ Ⓓ Ⓔ   62. Ⓐ Ⓑ Ⓒ Ⓓ Ⓔ   77. Ⓐ Ⓑ Ⓒ Ⓓ Ⓔ
48. Ⓐ Ⓑ Ⓒ Ⓓ Ⓔ   63. Ⓐ Ⓑ Ⓒ Ⓓ Ⓔ   78. Ⓐ Ⓑ Ⓒ Ⓓ Ⓔ
49. Ⓐ Ⓑ Ⓒ Ⓓ Ⓔ   64. Ⓐ Ⓑ Ⓒ Ⓓ Ⓔ   79. Ⓐ Ⓑ Ⓒ Ⓓ Ⓔ
50. Ⓐ Ⓑ Ⓒ Ⓓ Ⓔ   65. Ⓐ Ⓑ Ⓒ Ⓓ Ⓔ   80. Ⓐ Ⓑ Ⓒ Ⓓ Ⓔ
51. Ⓐ Ⓑ Ⓒ Ⓓ Ⓔ   66. Ⓐ Ⓑ Ⓒ Ⓓ Ⓔ   81. Ⓐ Ⓑ Ⓒ Ⓓ Ⓔ
52. Ⓐ Ⓑ Ⓒ Ⓓ Ⓔ   67. Ⓐ Ⓑ Ⓒ Ⓓ Ⓔ   82. Ⓐ Ⓑ Ⓒ Ⓓ Ⓔ
53. Ⓐ Ⓑ Ⓒ Ⓓ Ⓔ   68. Ⓐ Ⓑ Ⓒ Ⓓ Ⓔ   83. Ⓐ Ⓑ Ⓒ Ⓓ Ⓔ
54. Ⓐ Ⓑ Ⓒ Ⓓ Ⓔ   69. Ⓐ Ⓑ Ⓒ Ⓓ Ⓔ   84. Ⓐ Ⓑ Ⓒ Ⓓ Ⓔ
55. Ⓐ Ⓑ Ⓒ Ⓓ Ⓔ   70. Ⓐ Ⓑ Ⓒ Ⓓ Ⓔ   85. Ⓐ Ⓑ Ⓒ Ⓓ Ⓔ
56. Ⓐ Ⓑ Ⓒ Ⓓ Ⓔ   71. Ⓐ Ⓑ Ⓒ Ⓓ Ⓔ   86. Ⓐ Ⓑ Ⓒ Ⓓ Ⓔ
57. Ⓐ Ⓑ Ⓒ Ⓓ Ⓔ   72. Ⓐ Ⓑ Ⓒ Ⓓ Ⓔ   87. Ⓐ Ⓑ Ⓒ Ⓓ Ⓔ
58. Ⓐ Ⓑ Ⓒ Ⓓ Ⓔ   73. Ⓐ Ⓑ Ⓒ Ⓓ Ⓔ   88. Ⓐ Ⓑ Ⓒ Ⓓ Ⓔ
59. Ⓐ Ⓑ Ⓒ Ⓓ Ⓔ   74. Ⓐ Ⓑ Ⓒ Ⓓ Ⓔ   89. Ⓐ Ⓑ Ⓒ Ⓓ Ⓔ
60. Ⓐ Ⓑ Ⓒ Ⓓ Ⓔ   75. Ⓐ Ⓑ Ⓒ Ⓓ Ⓔ   90. Ⓐ Ⓑ Ⓒ Ⓓ Ⓔ

91. Ⓐ Ⓑ Ⓒ Ⓓ Ⓔ
92. Ⓐ Ⓑ Ⓒ Ⓓ Ⓔ
93. Ⓐ Ⓑ Ⓒ Ⓓ Ⓔ
94. Ⓐ Ⓑ Ⓒ Ⓓ Ⓔ
95. Ⓐ Ⓑ Ⓒ Ⓓ Ⓔ

Test 7

Questions 1-4 refer to the following chart.

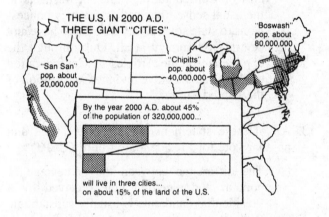

1. Which best explains why many people settled in the areas known as "Boswash," "Chipitts," and "San San"?

   (A) The climate of these areas has tended to attract settlers.
   (B) Expanding industries in these areas created job opportunities.
   (C) An abundant supply of energy in these areas attracted industry.
   (D) Low property taxes in these areas attracted people from rural areas.
   (E) All of the above

2. The information given in the chart could best be used to support the

   (A) cancellation of federal urban programs
   (B) reduction of federal personal income taxes
   (C) establishment of a two-story political system
   (D) need for planning for urban-suburban growth
   (E) need to rebuild a national railroad system

3. What change is most likely to occur in public schools in the three giant "cities"?

   (A) Development of wider choices in education
   (B) Increased emphasis upon memorization of facts
   (C) Separate schools for boys and girls
   (D) Legalized racial segregation
   (E) Under utilization of buildings

4. Solutions to problems arising in the three giant "cities" will probably depend on

   (A) unionization of white-collar workers
   (B) decreased federal government involvement in planning
   (C) getting more people to live on farms
   (D) increased cooperation between governments
   (E) growth of voluntarism

5. All of the following statements about the Trade and Navigation acts of the colonial period are true EXCEPT

   (A) The regulations concerning the tobacco trade practically assured the British Isles as a market for Virginia and Maryland tobacco.
   (B) The beaver trade centered in the Hudson Valley resulted in scores of small establishments in Connecticut and New York coastal towns that were well-known for the manufacture of fine beaver hats and cloaks.
   (C) No real trouble between England and the American colonies developed over Trade and Navigation acts until after the French and Indian War.
   (D) The rival colonial powers had similar Trade and Navigation laws to control the trade of their respective colonies.
   (E) Had the Sugar and Molasses acts passed by the British Parliament been enforced, they would have had a substantial adverse effect on the New England rum trade.

6. How are the *number* of judges on the Supreme Court determined?

   (A) By Congress
   (B) By the Senate
   (C) By the Constitution
   (D) By a convention that at least three-fourths of the states must attend

(E) By a convention that at least two-thirds of the states must attend

7. How is a new state admitted into the Union?

   (A) By Congress
   (B) By the President
   (C) By the Senate
   (D) By the Supreme Court if it approves of its constitution
   (E) By Congress with the approval of the Supreme Court

8. Which of the following statements about the French and Indian War contains the most significance for a history student?

   (A) The British Navy proved that England was mistress of the seas.
   (B) Pitt was one of England's war ministers.
   (C) The expulsion of the French from America set the stage for the American Revolution.
   (D) Tactics suitable for the wars in Europe were often unsuitable for battles in the American colonies.
   (E) As the British demonstrated at Quebec, trying the impossible is sometimes the road to fame.

9, 10. Which two of the following statements best explain the reaction of the American colonies to the tax on tea that led to the Boston Tea Party?

   (A) Basically the colonials objected to paying taxes levied by Parliament.
   (B) Selling British tea only through agents of the East India Tea Company deprived local colonial merchants of business and led them to join the Sons of Liberty in angry protest against the tax.
   (C) Since the Boston Massacre, a continuous chain of violent outbreaks made the Tea Party an almost predictable occurrence.
   (D) England prevented foreign tea from getting into the colonies, and the tax made the British tea very costly.
   (E) Parliament was trying to rescue the British East India Company from bankruptcy at the expense of the colonists.

11. Which of the following battles is considered the turning point of the Revolutionary War?

   (A) Bennington
   (B) Germantown
   (C) Princeton
   (D) Saratoga
   (E) Trenton

12. Which of the following statements about the Articles of Confederation is the most significant?

   (A) There was neither an effective Executive department nor a satisfactory Judicial department.
   (B) The government told each state how much it should contribute in support of the central government, but had no power to actually collect the amount due.
   (C) The Congress had so little power that members of state legislatures enjoyed greater prestige than did members of Congress.
   (D) Conditions of interstate and foreign commerce were chaotic because the central government had no power to enforce uniformity.
   (E) The many weaknesses written into the Articles of Confederation were not mistakes in the usual sense; they were necessary concessions to state sovereignty in order to have any central government at all. Only through the experience of the Articles of Confederation could the states move into the Constitution of the United States.

13. All of these statements about the electoral and popular vote for President are true EXCEPT

   (A) The difference between the percentage of popular and electoral vote received by a Presidential candidate is usually substantial.
   (B) With the possible exception of President Washington's elections, the Electoral College has never functioned as intended by those who wrote the Constitution.
   (C) The Constitution does *not* require the "unit rule," which gives all of the electoral votes of any state to whichever candidate gets the most popular votes in that state.
   (D) While it is theoretically possible for a presidential candidate to get a larger popular vote than his victorious opponent, it has never happened.
   (E) The Electoral College system of electing a President gives an advantage to the least populous states.

14. In all of the following pairs, the words or phrase in parentheses helps to bring into effect, to support, or to make more effective the item with which it is paired EXCEPT

   (A) an unwritten law founded in tradition (Washington and Jefferson refused to run for a third term)
   (B) the new republics in Latin American (Monroe Doctrine)

(C) the *McCulloch* v. *Maryland* decision (Civil War in Kansas)

(D) investment by American corporations in Latin America (dollar diplomacy)

(E) election of President Hayes (Electoral commission)

15. Which of the following events occurred FIRST?

(A) Hawaiian Islands annexed
(B) Texas became a state
(C) Mexican Cession
(D) Virgin Islands purchased
(E) Florida purchased

16. Which of the events in question 15 occurred LAST?

17. Which of the following events occurred FIRST?

(A) Louisiana Purchase
(B) Gadsden Purchase
(C) Webster-Ashburton Treaty
(D) Oregon boundary dispute settled
(E) Purchase of Alaska

18. Which of the events in question 17 occurred LAST?

19. All of the following statements about the Monroe Doctrine are true EXCEPT

(A) The idea of the doctrine was suggested by George Canning, British foreign secretary.
(B) It was an early indication that the United States was abandoning its traditional policy of isolation.
(C) Monroe approved of Canning's suggestion, and he also received approval of the idea from ex-Presidents John Adams and Thomas Jefferson.
(D) If the Holy Alliance attempted to violate the doctrine, Monroe was sure that the British fleet would oppose such an act.
(E) England was not interested at the time in extending its colonial empire in Latin America.

20. In all of the pairs below, the words or phrase in parentheses helps to bring to an end, to oppose, or to make less effective the item with which it is paired EXCEPT

(A) Missouri Compromise (*Dred Scott* decision)
(B) The "Crime of Reconstruction" (Tweed Ring)
(C) Cutthroat rate wars (Pooling)

(D) Cleveland's support of this party in 1896 (Free Silver at sixteen to one)
(E) Clayton-Bulwer Treaty (Hay-Pauncefote Treaty)

21. Which of the following occurred during the Jacksonian Era?

(A) Samuel Gompers organized the AFL.
(B) Emma Willard founded the first women's college.
(C) Eugene V. Debs founded the American Railway Union.
(D) Clara Barton founded the American Red Cross.
(E) Walter Reed controlled yellow fever.

22. Of the following items associated with World War I, which occurred FIRST?

(A) Wilson's reelection
(B) Bolshevik Revolution
(C) England's declaration of war on Germany
(D) Germany's declaration of war on France
(E) Entrance of the United States into the war

23. Of the items in question 22, which occurred LAST?

24. Of the following famous writings that have influenced American history, which was written FIRST?

(A) *Uncle Tom's Cabin*
(B) *Common Sense*
(C) *Progress and Poverty*
(D) *The Grapes of Wrath*
(E) *The Liberator*

25. Of the items in question 24, which was written LAST?

Questions 26-27: One item in each group is out of place. It lacks a factor common to all of the other items in its group. Select the ODD items.

26. (A) Zachary Taylor   (D) Millard Fillmore
    (B) John Tyler   (E) Franklin Pierce
    (C) John C. Calhoun

27. (A) Teapot Dome   (D) Crédit Mobilier
    (B) Tweed Ring   (E) Mugwumps
    (C) Whiskey Ring

28. The wording of the Agricultural Adjustment Act (AAA) made it clear that Congress depended upon which of the following constitutional

powers as a support of its right to pass such a law.

(A) The "general welfare" clause in the preamble
(B) The "general welfare" clause in the taxing power
(C) The elastic clause (implied powers clause)
(D) The "supreme law of the land" clause
(E) The interstate commerce clause

29. Which of the following statements best expresses Theodore Roosevelt's views on presidential powers?

(A) The President may do whatever he thinks is right and for the national welfare so long as there is no prohibition in the Constitution or laws to prevent such action.
(B) The President must restrict his official actions to carrying out powers specifically granted to him in the Constitution.
(C) The President may do anything the Constitution specifically permits or anything else reasonably implied by Constitutional provisions.
(D) In time of war or other national emergency, the President may do as he thinks best, without regard to the Constitution.
(E) Whenever a President is in doubt about the extent of his legal powers, he may confer with the Supreme Court for authoritative advice.

30. Which Supreme Court case resulted in a setback for the Grangers?

(A) *Chisholm* v. *Georgia*
(B) *Wabash* v. *Illinois*
(C) *Insular* cases
(D) *Munn* v. *Illinois*
(E) *McCulloch* v. *Maryland*

31. Which of the Supreme Court decisions in question 30 resulted in the Eleventh Amendment to the United States Constitution?

32. "I preach to you, my countrymen, that our country calls not for a life of ease but for the life of strenuous endeavor. Nothing in this world is worth doing unless it means effort, pain, difficulty....Let us therefore boldly face the life of strife."

Which of the following Presidents is quoted here?

(A) Jefferson   (D) Theodore Roosevelt
(B) Grant   (E) Kennedy
(C) McKinley

33. All of the following statements are true about the Prohibition Amendment EXCEPT

(A) It was proposed and ratified while Wilson was President.
(B) A national plebiscite, while many men were in the armed forces overseas, was a factor in the adoption of this amendment.
(C) The Anti-Saloon League had worked for years to achieve Prohibition
(D) Intoxicating liquor was defined by the Volstead Act.
(E) President Wilson vetoed the Volstead Act.

34. This Supreme Court case reversed a previous decision on "separate but equal" segregated facilities.

(A) *Brown* v. *Board of Education of Topeka, Kansas*
(B) *Roe* v. *Wade*
(C) *Miranda* v. *Arizona*
(D) *Plessy* v. *Ferguson*
(E) *Ex parte Milligan*

35. This Supreme Court case upheld segregation in public transportation.

(A) *Dred Scott* case
(B) *Gideon* v. *Wainwright*
(C) *Plessy* v. *Ferguson*
(D) *Brown* v. *Board of Education of Topeka, Kansas*
(E) *Roe* v. *Wade*

36. All of the following statements about automation contains a sound opinion, upon which most well-informed people would agree EXCEPT

(A) It is difficult to determine just how much unemployment is due to automation, particularly when considering those entering the labor market for the first time.
(B) Whatever problems automation presents, the answers lie in going ahead with automation while doing our best to handle the problems it creates.
(C) An employer who cuts his labor force by automation should be required to retrain the displaced workers and pay them their accustomed wages.
(D) Automation creates highly skilled jobs, for which there are too few capable workers.
(E) Retraining programs, both by industry and government, constitute one constructive measure dealing with unemployment caused by automation.

37. The following statements refer to the Truman-MacArthur controversy between the President and the general he appointed as Chief United Nations Commander in Korea in 1952. All of the following support Truman EXCEPT

    (A) General MacArthur, in writing a letter to Republican minority leader Congressman Joseph Martin, urging his campaign policies, opposing the President's policies, and containing the phrase, "There is no substitute for victory," was guilty of gross indiscretion and probably insubordination.
    (B) General Bradley, Chief of Staff, said of the MacArthur policies that they would lead the United States into the "wrong war, at the wrong time, in the wrong place, with the wrong enemy."
    (C) When it became clear that MacArthur, who had been appointed Commander of the UN forces by Truman, was unwilling to carry out Truman's objectives and policies, there was little the President could do other than dismiss MacArthur from his command.
    (D) The decision to limit the fighting to Korea when the United States had atomic bombs and great superiority on the sea and in the air made acceptance of a stalemate without victory a needless humiliation.
    (E) Driving the combined Chinese and North Korean forces back to the 38th parallel, as was finally done, and making them stay there was not a stalemate; it was a complete victory carrying out precisely the stated objectives of the United Nations.

38. Dollars that ranged in value from a few cents to 100 cents were simultaneously circulating, in the United States until

    (A) the Constitution of 1787, prohibiting the states from issuing bills of credit, was ratified
    (B) the First United States Bank was established
    (C) the Independent Treasury System was established
    (D) Jackson issued the Specie Circular
    (E) Congress taxed state bank notes out of existence in 1865

39. Which pair of laws best represents an attempt to conciliate conflicting economic interests?

    (A) Tariff Act of 1789 and United States Banking Act of 1791
    (B) Morrill Tariff of 1861 and Homestead Act of 1862

    (C) Resumption Act of 1875 and Gold Standard Act of 1900
    (D) Underwood Tariff of 1913 and Federal Reserve Act of 1913
    (E) Agricultural Adjustment Act of 1933 and Gold Reserve Act of 1934

40. If the Greenback party had been able to carry out its monetary plank, the effect on the money supply would have been much the same as when the Federal Reserve System

    (A) raises the rediscount rate
    (B) lowers the rediscount rate
    (C) raises the reserve ratio of member banks
    (D) raises the margin requirements for stock purchases
    (E) sells securities through the Open Market Committee

41. Which choice pairs two persons who would be in closest agreement as to the role the government should play in the economy?

    (A) William G. Sumner—Lester Ward
    (B) Frank Norris—Stephen J. Field
    (C) Edward Bellamy—Marcus A. Hanna
    (D) Henry George—Andrew Carnegie
    (E) Eugene V. Debs—Upton Sinclair

42. Which writer was LEAST critical of American society and culture in the 1920s?

    (A) Booth Tarkington
    (B) John Dos Passos
    (C) Sinclair Lewis
    (D) Theodore Dreiser
    (E) Henry L. Mencken

43. An important economic development of the 1950s was the

    (A) merger of the AFL with the CIO
    (B) rapid growth of federal power projects
    (C) steady decrease in United States imports
    (D) sale of federal atomic plants to private industry
    (E) trend away from consolidation in American industry

44. Who helped to suppress malaria and yellow fever in the Panama Canal Zone?

    (A) Gorgas
    (B) Bunau-Varilla
    (C) Goethals
    (D) de Lesseps
    (E) Bulwer

Questions 45-53: Five persons were engaged in the following discussion prior to a presidential election:

Speaker 1: I'll vote for the candidate who has made a professional study of the science of government and has already demonstrated his executive ability as a "reform" Governor.

Speaker 2: I'll vote to return to office the person who encouraged the passage of legislation that would punish the "malefactors of great wealth."

Speaker 3: I'll vote for the incumbent, because his administration has successfully prosecuted more antitrust cases than has any other.

Speaker 4: I'll vote for the person who sided with the workers during the Pullman strike.

Speaker 5: I haven't decided how I'll vote because it is difficult to choose between two individuals who were once members of the same party.

45. Which term best identifies the political movement associated with this election?

(A) Progressivism　　(D) Unionism
(B) Federalism　　　(E) Socialism
(C) Utopianism

46. Speaker 1 is going to vote for

(A) William J. Bryan
(B) Theodore Roosevelt
(C) William McKinley
(D) William H. Taft
(E) Woodrow Wilson

47. Speaker 2 is going to vote for

(A) William J. Bryan
(B) Theodore Roosevelt
(C) Grover Cleveland
(D) Charles E. Hughes
(E) Woodrow Wilson

48. Speaker 3 is going to vote for

(A) Charles E. Hughes
(B) Theodore Roosevelt
(C) Grover Cleveland
(D) William H. Taft
(E) Woodrow Wilson

49. Speaker 4 is going to vote for

(A) William J. Bryan
(B) Norman Thomas

(C) Terence V. Powderly
(D) John Mitchell
(E) Eugene V. Debs

50. Speaker 5 is going to vote for either

(A) William J. Bryan or Woodrow Wilson
(B) William H. Taft or William McKinley
(C) William H. Taft or Theodore Roosevelt
(D) Robert La Follette or Theodore Roosevelt
(E) Eugene V. Debs or Terence V. Powderly

51. Who won this election?

(A) William J. Bryan
(B) William McKinley
(C) Theodore Roosevelt
(D) William H. Taft
(E) Woodrow Wilson

52. An important issue in this election was

(A) banking reform
(B) free silver
(C) neutrality
(D) imperialism
(E) restrictive immigration

53. Which is *not* considered one of foundations of the free enterprise system?

(A) Free markets　　(D) Trade associations
(B) Profit motivation　(E) Private property
(C) Competition

54. Which New Deal measure illustrates acceptance of the Keynesian theory?

(A) Securities and Exchange Commission
(B) Social Security Act
(C) Works Progress Administration
(D) Federal Deposit Insurance Corporation
(E) Home Owners Loan Corporation

55. Which statement best expresses Theodore Roosevelt's attitude toward trusts at the time he became President?

(A) All corporations, trusts, and combinations are bad.
(B) Legislation must be enacted immediately to prohibit the growth of large corporations.
(C) Those who want to impose controls on corporations seek to destroy the very lifeblood of our industry.
(D) We do not wish to destroy corporations, but we do wish to make them subserve the public good.

(E) Only through the growth of large corporations and combines can America compete....We must have complete faith in management....

56. The significance of the Supreme Court decision in the *Northern Securities* case was that it

(A) guaranteed the end of business combinations
(B) had great influence on the economic development of business
(C) proved that new laws were needed before the Department of Justice could act against other combinations
(D) immediately raised serious questions concerning Theodore Roosevelt's antitrust pronouncements
(E) boosted the morale of the antitrust forces

Questions 57-61 are based on the following map.

57. There is worldwide environmental concern over the burning of large tracts of tropical forest in this nation.

(A) A   (B) D   (C) E   (D) F   (E) K

58. This birthplace of Simón Bolívar is a major producer of oil and a member of OPEC.

(A) A   (B) B   (C) C   (D) D   (E) E

59. The crest of the Andes Mountains is the border between these nations, where South American summer occurs during the North American winter.

(A) A and C   (D) G and K
(B) C and D   (E) J and K
(C) D and F

60. This nation held the capital of the Inca civilization destroyed by Pizzaro.

(A) A   (D) D
(B) B   (E) E
(C) C

61. This landlocked nation, named after a great liberator, is among the highest inhabited areas on earth.

(A) F   (D) K
(B) G   (E) L
(C) H

62. The first federal law regulating the manufacture and sale of food and drugs was passed during

(A) the Square Deal of Theodore Roosevelt
(B) the New Freedom of Woodrow Wilson
(C) the New Deal of Franklin D. Roosevelt
(D) the Fair Deal of Harry S Truman
(E) the Great Society of Lyndon B. Johnson

63. A federal law guaranteeing to labor the right of collective bargaining was part of

(A) the Square Deal of Theodore Roosevelt
(B) the New Freedom of Woodrow Wilson
(C) the New Deal of Franklin D. Roosevelt
(D) the Fair Deal of Harry S Truman
(E) the Great Society of Lyndon B. Johnson

64. A policy for the containment of communism originated during the presidency of

(A) Franklin D. Roosevelt
(B) Harry S Truman
(C) Dwight D. Eisenhower
(D) John F. Kennedy
(E) Richard Nixon

65. An act exempting labor organizations from prosecution under the Sherman Antitrust Law was part of

(A) the Square Deal of Theodore Roosevelt
(B) the New Freedom of Woodrow Wilson
(C) the New Deal of Franklin D. Roosevelt
(D) the Fair Deal of Harry S Truman
(E) the Alliance for Progress of John F. Kennedy

66. A federal law providing for old-age and survivors insurance was an important part of

   (A) the Square Deal of Theodore Roosevelt
   (B) the New Freedom of Woodrow Wilson
   (C) the New Deal of Franklin D. Roosevelt
   (D) the Fair Deal of Harry S Truman
   (E) the Alliance for Progress of John F. Kennedy

67. English neutrality during the American Civil War was greatly influenced by

   (A) large war profits gained by English manufacturers
   (B) steady Southern military successes in the first three years of the war
   (C) increased importance of the American merchant marine
   (D) self-sufficiency of crop harvests in England
   (E) indifference of the English people to a foreign civil war

68. Why did the United States find it necessary to implement the Monroe Doctrine in the two decades following its pronouncement?

   (A) France mediated several disputes between England and Brazil.
   (B) None of the intrusions by European powers seemed seriously to endanger the security of the United States.
   (C) Both houses of Congress were opposed to any overt action by the United States.
   (D) No European power attempted to colonize in the Western Hemisphere.
   (E) The revolutions in Europe during this period caused the dissolution of the Holy Alliance.

69. During the Civil War the United States seized goods consigned to British colonial ports but destined for ports in the South. What justification was given for this seizure?

   (A) Ostend Manifesto
   (B) Doctrine of continuous voyage
   (C) Rights under a "paper" blockade
   (D) Rights established by the Jay Treaty
   (E) Privilege under letters of marque and reprisal

70. The Platt Amendment, the Ostend Manifesto, and the Roosevelt Corollary had an underlying similarity in that all three

   (A) expressed the expanding interests of the United States
   (B) carried out the ideas expressed in the original Monroe Doctrine
   (C) represented a radical departure from the previous attitude toward Latin America

   (D) were concerned chiefly with South America
   (E) established governing procedures for colonial dependencies

71. According to historian Thomas Bailey, which statement most nearly describes how Americans supported the Revolutionary War?

   (A) Most city dwellers supported the Revolution, and most rural dwellers were indifferent.
   (B) Most rural dwellers supported the Revolution, and most city dwellers were indifferent.
   (C) A vast majority of Americans supported the Revolution.
   (D) Somewhat more than one-third supported the Revolution; somewhat less than one-third were loyal to England; the remainder were indifferent.
   (E) About 80 percent supported the Revolution; the others were either indifferent or loyal to England.

72. Which of these "residues" of the Revolutionary War was *not* repudiated later?

   (A) Treaty of Alliance with France
   (B) Continental currency
   (C) Foreign debt
   (D) Promises of compensation to Loyalists
   (E) Privilege of individual British subjects to recover prewar debts owed by American colonists

73. Evidence of division of interests in the United States during the War of 1812 was shown by the

   (A) objections of the agrarian faction to a war they claimed would benefit only the mercantile faction
   (B) efforts of a Southern-Western coalition to stem Eastern belligerence at the last minute
   (C) charges that the war declaration was promoted by owners of infant industries
   (D) unenthusiastic support for the war effort by shipping states
   (E) unsuccessful bid of the Federalist party to return to power by supporting war measures

74. Following the sinking of the Maine, the only significant check upon the popular demand for war came from

   (A) the clergy
   (B) business groups
   (C) farm organizations
   (D) Congress
   (E) President Cleveland

PRACTICE TEST 7   417

75. The "yellow journalism" of the period before the outbreak of the Spanish-American War had much the same effect on opinion in the United States as

(A) calling the Hartford Convention (1814)
(B) Emancipation Proclamation (1863)
(C) reports of German atrocities in Belgium (1914-1917)
(D) Fourteen Points (1918)
(E) drafting of the Atlantic Charter (1941)

76. Which person would have been most likely to oppose the United States' entrance into World War I (1917)?

(A) A member of Congress from New York
(B) An admirer of Theodore Roosevelt
(C) An owner of British bonds
(D) An editor of a Midwestern newspaper
(E) An American manufacturer who had sold goods to a French merchant on credit

77. The War of 1812 and World War I are similar in that in both wars, the United States

(A) adopted national conscription
(B) won a decisive victory after the treaty was arranged
(C) proposed a world organization to promote peace at the end of the war
(D) vigorously upheld a traditional interpretation of the rights of neutrals
(E) signed a treaty of alliance with France after an initial period of neutrality

78. Which man was an ardent sectionalist at the time Henry Clay was promoting his "American system"?

(A) James Monroe
(B) James Madison
(C) John C. Calhoun
(D) John Quincy Adams
(E) Daniel Webster

79. On the basis of significant legislation passed during his administration, President Lincoln seemed most influenced by the principles of

(A) Alexander Hamilton
(B) Thomas Jefferson
(C) William Lloyd Garrison
(D) Andrew Jackson
(E) Daniel Webster

80. In foreign affairs, President Lincoln's most significant achievement was his success in

(A) gaining the support of the czar of Russia for the Union cause
(B) negotiating the demilitarization of the Canadian-American boundary
(C) meeting the challenge to the Monroe Doctrine in Mexico
(D) establishing claims to islands in the Pacific
(E) restraining foreign powers from recognizing the Confederacy

81. Between what two men was there the most serious controversy over the conduct of a war?

(A) Woodrow Wilson and General Pershing
(B) Abraham Lincoln and General McClellan
(C) Franklin D. Roosevelt and General Eisenhower
(D) Theodore Roosevelt and General Wood
(E) William McKinley and Admiral Dewey

82. Which war did not supply a military hero later nominated for the presidency by one of the major parties?

(A) War of 1812   (D) World War I
(B) Mexican War   (E) World War II
(C) Spanish-American War

83. "Conspicuous consumption of valuable goods is a means of reputability to the gentleman of leisure."

This statement reflects the thinking of

(A) Thorstein Veblen
(B) John D. Rockefeller
(C) J. P. Morgan
(D) Ward McAllister
(E) Cornelius Vanderbilt

84. The social-gospel idea in American Protestantism was fostered most strongly by

(A) Brigham Young
(B) William Miller
(C) Henry Ward Beecher
(D) Mary Baker Eddy
(E) Walter Rauschenbusch

85. Which author's work is better known for romance than for literary realism?

(A) William Dean Howells
(B) Nathaniel Hawthorne
(C) Stephen Crane
(D) Theodore Dreiser
(E) Frank Norris

86. The expansionist policy of the 1890s was especially criticized by

(A) Joseph Pulitzer
(B) Thomas Hart Benton
(C) William Randolph Hearst
(D) Henry Cabot Lodge
(E) Finley Peter Dunne

87. Which statement concerning the political careers of Theodore Roosevelt and Franklin D. Roosevelt is FALSE?

(A) Both served as Governor of New York.
(B) Both served in the Navy Department.
(C) Both served as Vice-President of the United States.
(D) Both were proponents of the conservation movement.
(E) Both were advocates of a strong Executive department.

88. "The country needs and, unless I mistake its temper, the country demands bold, persistent experimentation. It is common sense to take a method and try it. If it fails, admit it frankly and try another. But above all, try something."

This statement best represents the philosophy of

(A) Thomas Jefferson
(B) Franklin D. Roosevelt
(C) Benjamin Franklin
(D) Theodore Roosevelt
(E) Abraham Lincoln

89. Who exerted conservative leadership of the Republican party in the 20th century?

(A) Theodore Roosevelt
(B) Wendell Wilkie
(C) Robert Taft
(D) Robert La Follette
(E) Earl Warren

90. Which group contains three persons who achieved success in the same field?

(A) Frederick Turner, William Prescott, James F. Rhodes
(B) James Birney, Joseph Pulitzer, William L. Garrison
(C) Susan B. Anthony, Carrie C. Catt, Emily Dickinson
(D) Louis Agassiz, Carl Schurz, Luther Burbank
(E) Mark Sullivan, Frank Lloyd Wright, Charles W. Peale

91. Which United States Senator gradually reversed his stand on the issue with which he is paired?

(A) George Norris—government ownership of public power
(B) Robert La Follette—government regulation of trusts
(C) Robert Wagner, Sr.—protection of the rights of labor
(D) Arthur Vandenberg—isolation in foreign affairs
(E) Robert Taft—federal aid for public housing

92. Which group contains a man who is incorrectly included in the group?

(A) Third party leaders: John Bell, James B. Weaver, Norman Thomas
(B) Leaders of the Republican party: James Garfield, Theodore Roosevelt, Benjamin Harrison
(C) Leaders of the Democratic party: Woodrow Wilson, Grover Cleveland, Andrew Jackson
(D) Governors of the state of New York: Charles E. Hughes, Alfred E. Smith, William McKinley
(E) Unsuccessful presidential candidates: Henry Clay, William J. Bryan, James G. Blaine

Questions 93-94 are based on the following graph.

Carbon Emissions Relative to Economic Activity, 1993
Metric tons of carbon emitted for each million dollars of gross domestic product

Former Soviet Union	502
Germany	281
China	273
Britain	242
United States	238
India	183
Japan	144

Source: Center for Clean Air Policy

93. According to the graph above, which two nations had the most similar degree of efficiency in controlling pollution in 1993?

(A) India and Japan
(B) Britain and the United States
(C) China and Germany
(D) United States and Japan
(E) Britain and the former Soviet Union

94. According to the graph, which one of the following statements is NOT true?

 (A) The former Soviet Union was the "dirtiest" country, as measured by carbon emissions per dollar of goods produced.
 (B) India was less of a polluter than Japan.
 (C) Germany was a "dirtier" producer than either Britain or China.
 (D) Compared with other nations shown, Japan had a relatively good pollution record in 1993.
 (E) The combined total carbon emissions of Britain and the U.S. were less than that of the former Soviet Union.

Pletcher, Times - Picayune, La

"Either one's poison to me!"

95. The main idea of the above cartoon is that the problems of the United States Social Security System

 (A) are being ignored by Congress
 (B) are caused primarily by rising medical costs
 (C) have led to economic recession
 (D) involve choices between unpopular alternatives
 (E) involve having too many people in hospitals

ANSWER KEY: TEST 7

1.	B	25.	D	49.	E	73.	D
2.	D	26.	C	50.	C	74.	B
3.	A	27.	B	51.	E	75.	C
4.	D	28.	E	52.	A	76.	D
5.	B	29.	A	53.	D	77.	D
6.	A	30.	B	54.	C	78.	E
7.	A	31.	A	55.	D	79.	A
8.	C	32.	D	56.	E	80.	E
9.	A or B	33.	B	57.	C	81.	B
10.	B or A	34.	A	58.	B	82.	D
11.	D	35.	C	59.	E	83.	A
12.	E	36.	C	60.	D	84.	E
13.	D	37.	D	61.	A	85.	B
14.	C	38.	B	62.	A	86.	E
15.	E	39.	B	63.	C	87.	C
16.	D	40.	B	64.	B	88.	B
17.	A	41.	B	65.	B	89.	C
18.	E	42.	A	66.	C	90.	A
19.	B	43.	A	67.	A	91.	D
20.	B	44.	A	68.	B	92.	D
21.	B	45.	A	69.	B	93.	B
22.	D	46.	E	70.	A	94.	B
23.	B	47.	B	71.	D	95.	D
24.	B	48.	D	72.	C		

ANALYSIS CHART: TEST 7

Era	Number of Questions	Number Right	Number Wrong	Number Unanswered
Pre-Columbian to 1789: questions 5, 8-12, 24, 71, 72	9			
1790 to 1898: questions 14, 15, 17-21, 26, 27, 30, 31, 35, 38,41, 67-69, 73, 74, 78-81, 84-86 ,90	27			
1899 to present: questions 1-4, 16, 22, 23, 25, 28, 29, 32-34, 36, 37, 42-52, 54-61, 65, 66, 76, 83, 87-89, 91, 93-95	45			
Cross period: questions 39, 40, 70, 75, 77, 82, 92	7			
Nonchronological: questions 6, 7, 13, 53, 62-64	7			

FINDING THE REASONS FOR INCORRECT ANSWERS

Be sure to check the answer explanations before completing the following chart.

Era	Number Wrong	Lack of Knowledge	Micunderstand Problem	Careless Error	Not Answered
Pre-Columbian to 1789					
1790 to 1898					
1899 to present					
Cross period					
Nonchronological					

ANSWER EXPLANATIONS: TEST 7

1. **B** The East Coast megalopolis stretches from southern New Hampshire west to Lake Erie, and from Boston through New York past Washington, D.C. The California megalopolis includes San Francisco, Los Angeles, and San Diego.

2. **D** Regional planning needs include various communities and even several states at a time.

3. **A** The larger the available student body, the greater the likelihood of educational alternatives: magnet public schools, private and parochial schools, technical schools, etc.

4. **D** Regional planning requires cooperation among various communities, counties, states, and even the federal government.

5. **B** Mercantilism dictated that any goods commonly produced in England must not be produced in the colonies. The colonists were encouraged to skin the beavers in Albany, New York, sell the skins to a London furrier, and let the furrier sell the hats and capes wherever there was a market for them. Parliament attempted to limit colonial industry. The Hat Act of 1732 prohibited the sale of hats and felts outside of the colony where they were made.

6. **A** Congress has used this power to increase the number of Supreme Court Justices to the present nine.

7. **A** Article IV. Section 3, of the Constitution says that new states may be admitted by Congress into the Union.

8. **C** With the elimination of the French, the Americans no longer needed British protection.

9,10. **A** and **B** Since Americans did not elect members of the British Parliament, they said that Britain had no right to tax the colonies: No taxation without representation. The colonists believed they could be rightfully taxed only by their own colonial legislatures. In 1770, the new prime minister repealed all but the tax on tea to emphasize Parliament's right to levy such taxes. When England gave a monopoly on all tea sold in America to the British East India Company, the colonial merchants saw the profits from an extensive tea trade set beyond their reach. If this could be done with tea, why not with other items? The Sons of Liberty denounced everyone who handled tea.

11. **D** General Burgoyne and his overburdened troops were trapped at Saratoga, New York, and surrendered in October 1777. This led to an alliance with France and proved to be the turning point of the Revolutionary War.

12. **E** Each protection of the sovereign power of the states and each limitation of the power of the United States was carefully calculated. Had the power of the

central government been made greater, the states would have refused to form the Union.

13. **D**   In 1824 Jackson had a plurality of popular votes, but John Quincy Adams became President; in 1888 Cleveland had more popular votes than Benjamin Harrison, but Harrison carried the electoral vote and the presidency.

14. **C**   The chronology and the logic are both wrong. "Bleeding Kansas" was an event of the 1850s as a result of the Kansas-Nebraska Act permitting squatter sovereignty on the issue of slavery. The Supreme Court case of *McCulloch* v. *Maryland* was decided in 1819, prohibiting a state from taxing a federal agency.

15. **E**   The United States purchased Florida from Spain in 1819. Texas became a state in 1846, and the dispute over its southern boundary led to the Mexican War are the loss by Mexico of the Mexican Cession in 1848. The Hwaiian Islánds were annexed in 1898. The Virgin Islands were purchased from Denmark in 1917 to prevent their falling into the hands of Germany.

16. **D**   See the answer to question 15.

17. **A**   The Louisiana Purchase was made in 1803, doubling the size of the young republic. The boundaries of Maine and Oregon were settled in the 1840s, and the Gadsden Purchase from Mexico was made in 1853. Alaska was bought from Russia in 1867 and was called "Seward's Icebox."

18. **E**   See the answer to question 17.

19. **B**   The Monroe Doctrine was a logical extension of the policy of isolation set forth in Washington's Proclamation of Neutrality and Farewell Address. It stated that any attempt by a European power to intervene in the Western hemisphere would be considered dangerous to the peace and safety of the United States.

20. **B**   The two items are unrelated. The "Crime of Reconstruction" refers to the military occupation of the former Confederate states from 1866 to 1877. The Tweed Ring refers to the corrupt political machine that controlled the government of New York City during the 1860s and 1870s.

21. **B**   The Jacksonian Era occurred from the 1820s to the 1840s. It was one of political and social reform movements, including education for women. Emma Willard founded an academy for girls in Troy, New York, in 1821. It was called the Troy Female Seminary.

22. **D**   World War I broke out when Austria-Hungary declared war on Serbia on July 28, 1914, for harbor-ing the terrorist group that assassinated the Archduke Francis Ferdinand. When Russia mobilized in the hope of protecting Serbia, Germany, backing its ally Austria, declared war on Russia and on France, Russia's ally (August 1-3, 1914). When German armies crashed through neutral Belgium to crush France, England honored its pledge to defend neutral Belgium by declaring war on Germany. The United States entered the war in April 1917, and the Bolshevik Revolution took place in November 1917.

23. **B**   See the answer to question 22.

24. **B**   In 1775, Thomas Paine, a middle-class English Quaker, published the pamphlet entitled *Common Sense*, urging independence from England.

25. **D**   The only 20th-century writing in the group is John Steinbeck's novel *The Grapes of Wrath*, the story of an impoverished farm family's flight from the Dust Bowl in the 1930s.

26. **C**   All the others were pre-Civil War 19th-century Presidents. Calhoun, whose importance was greater than any of these others, resigned as Andrew Jackson's Vice-President to fight the cause of the South.

27. **E**   All the others were examples of corruption and scandal. The Mugwumps were Republicans who would not support James G. Blaine for President in 1884 because of his prior involvement with scandal as Speaker of the House.

28. **E**   The Act created the Agricultural Adjustment Administration, which would secure promises from farmers to reduce the production of such staple crops as wheat, corn, rice, and pork. In return, the farmers would receive cash payments from the government, financed by a tax on such processors of farm products as meat packers, millers, and cotton ginners—all of whom were engaged in interstate commerce.

29. **A**   Theodore Roosevelt was an energetic Chief Executive, who used his tremendous personal popularity to arouse the interest of the American people in reform.

30. **B**   The Supreme Court decision in *Wabash* v. *Illinois* in 1886 declared that where railroads and other businesses crossed state lines, Congress, not the states, had the power to regulate them. The ruling invalidated state laws prohibiting abuses by railroads and grain elevator operators.

31. **A**   The Eleventh Amendment provides that a lawsuit brought by a United States citizen or citizen

of a foreign nation against a state must be tried in a state court, not in a federal court. In *Chisholm v. Georgia*, decided in 1793, the Supreme Court had allowed a lawsuit brought by citizens of South Carolina against a citizen of Georgia to be tried in a federal court,

32. **D** "The strenuous life" is a phrase long associated with the ideas of Theodore Roosevelt.

33. **B** Not so. The amendment was proposed by a two-thirds vote of each house of Congress and ratified by the legislature of three-fourths of the states.

34. **A** In 1954 the Supreme Court decided that in the field of public education, the doctrine of "separate but equal" has no place. This reversed the 1896 decision in *Plessy* v. *Ferguson*.

35. **C** The *Plessy* decision was used to justify racial segregation in Southern school systems until 1954.

36. **C** This opinion is not one upon which ready agreement of most of the people is likely to be obtained. It is quite controversial.

37. **D** This says that the decision of President Truman, with which General MacArthur disagreed, caused the United States humiliation.

38. **E** In 1862 there were about 1,600 banks established under the laws of the various states, whose notes circulated at a discount varying with the confidence in the bank and the distance from bank of issue. Partly to eliminate this chaotic paper currency, the National Banking System was established in 1863.

39. **B** The North helped to finance the Civil War by raising the protective tariff rates in the Morrill Act of 1861. To help Westerners acquire a home and farm, the Homestead Act of 1862 provided 160 acres free to citizens who would occupy and cultivate that parcel for five years.

40. **B** Both actions would be inflationary. The Greenback party of the 1870s called for the issuance of more unbacked paper money. By lowering the rate it charges member banks for loans, the Federal Reserve encourages more borrowing. With more money and credit in circulation, the value of each dollar drops.

41. **E** Both were Socialists, who believed the government should play a larger role in protecting Americans from the evils of big business and in regulating the economy.

42. **A** While each of the others was a critic of American society, Booth Tarkington was a popular regional novelist and author of stories of boyhood, like *Penrod* and *Seventeen*.

43. **A** In 1955, after 20 years of rivalry, the two labor federations agreed to unite. The AFL-CIO consists of some 140 national and international unions with some 12 million members.

44. **A** The medical work and splendid organization accomplished under Colonel William Gorgas changed a tropical jungle area into a livable zone in which the building of the Panama Canal could proceed.

45. **A** Roosevelt's new party was even named the Progressive party.

46. **E** Wilson had been professor of political economy at Princeton, where he became president. His area of specialization was congressional government. As a reform Governor of New Jersey, Wilson achieved many reforms, including a workers' compensation law, a direct primary, a utility control act, and election reforms.

47. **B** Disturbed by the power position of the trusts and the plight of many workers and their families, Roosevelt called for a "square-deal" for ordinary citizens and promised to take action against the "malefactors of great wealth."

48. **D** Taft, President from 1909 to 1931, initiated 90 antitrust suits, 36 more than the record set by Roosevelt.

49. **E** Eugene V. Debs led the American Railway Union during their 1894 Pullman strike. He was five times a presidential candidate on the Socialist ticket.

50. **C** Roosevelt broke with Taft and the Republican party over issues of reform and business regulation.

51. **E** Wilson, the Democrat, took advantage of the split among Republicans supporting Taft or Roosevelt.

52. **A** The financial panic of 1907 revealed two weaknesses of the National Banking Systems: inelastic currency and lack of provision for pooling funds. A national monetary commission recommended reform.

53. **D** A trade association is an organization of firms engaged in a similar business enterprise and formed to exchange ideas and modify unbridled competition.

54. **C** The WPA provides public-works jobs for the unemployed, providing them with wages to spend to help the economy recover. Keynes believed in deficit

spending by government to "prime the pump" of business activity.

55. **D**   He wished to control the trusts rather than to destroy them.

56. **E**   In this 1904 decision, the Supreme Court ordered dissolved a merger of the railroads of the Northwest, giving the government its first substantial victory over a business combination and breathing life into the Sherman Act, which had been considered dead for fourteen years.

57. **C**   The government of Brazil has built roads into the previously inaccessible Amazon jungle, enabling land-hungry farmers and developers to burn large areas to clear the forest. Their actions endanger many species of plants and animals. By adding much carbon dioxide to the atmosphere, they contribute to the dangerous "greenhouse effect."

58. **B**   Lake Maracaibo, in northern Venezuela, is a "lake of oil," whose earnings are vital to the nation's economic development.

59. **E**   Chile is on the Pacific Ocean side, and Argentina borders the Atlantic Ocean.

60. **D**   In Peru, the Inca capital of Cuzco is the oldest continually lived-in city on the American continent.

61. **A**   Bolivia, named after Simón Bolívar, contains a wide plateau, the *Altiplano*, which is from 10,000 to 13,000 feet high. Here live 80 percent of the people of Bolivia.

62. **A**   Congress passed the Pure Food and Drug Act and the Meat Inspection Act in 1906.

63. **C**   The National Labor Relations Act, or Wagner-Connery Act, made this provision in 1935, as part of the New Deal.

64. **B**   The North Atlantic Treaty Organization, NATO, was created in 1949 to prevent further Communist expansion in Europe. The Truman Doctrine of 1947 was more modest, providing economic and military aid to the Greece and Turkey to prevent Communist subversion there.

65. **B**   The Clayton Antitrust Act of 1914 exempted labor unions from prosecution as conspiracies in restraint of trade.

66. **C**   The Social Security Act of 1935 provided for the payment of benefits in January 1937.

67. **A**   British manufacturers and shippers made money by selling war materiel to the North. After several bad harvests at home, the British also became dependent on American wheat.

68. **B**   One factor was that the British Navy backed the American statements in the Monroe Doctrine in support of Latin American independence.

69. **B**   Under this doctrine, goods ultimately destined for the South were seized as contraband of war.

70. **A**   The Ostend Manifesto was a Southern attempt in 1854 to annex Cuba because it offered possibilities for the expansion of slavery. The Platt Amendment to the Cuban Constitution of 1903 gave the United States the right to intervene there to preserve order and independence. The next year, Theodore Roosevelt's Corollary to the Monroe Doctrine proclaimed the right of the United States to exercise "international police power" whenever Latin American republics were unable to maintain order or repay their debts to other nations.

71. **D**   This shows the importance of the leadership of the Patriots, an educated and idealistic group.

72. **C**   Payment of the foreign debt was important to establish the credit of the new nation. Also, it was owed primarily to friends: Holland and France.

73. **D**   The New England states, whose trade was disrupted by the war, were even hostile, as evidenced by the Hartford Convention.

74. **B**   As shown in the answer to question 73, business interests lose when war conditions disrupt or destroy their commerce.

75. **C**   Both helped to convince a reluctant American people that alleged barbarous actions of others justified our going to war.

76. **D**   Isolationist and pro-German sentiment were strongest in the Midwest, where many immigrants of German descent had settled.

77. **D**   In both cases, the United States claimed violation of its rights to freedom of the seas. The impressment of American sailors into the British Navy helped bring on the War of 1812. The German U-boat sinking of passenger and merchant vessels from 1915 to 1917, with loss of American lives, helped bring the United States into World War I.

78. **E** Webster interested himself as a young lawyer particularly in matters affecting New England. When the state of New Hampshire tried to make Dartmouth College a state institution, Webster's oratory before the Supreme Court helped nullify the state's action.

79. **A** The legislation referred to is the creation of the National Banking System, under which national banks had to invest one-third of the minimum capital required for their organization in government bonds, deposited in the United States Treasury. Both Hamilton, as the first Secretary of the Treasury, and Lincoln, as a wartime President, had great need to raise money for the government.

80. **E** When the Confederacy went to war, it hoped to receive strong British support because Britain was supposedly dependent on Southern cotton, Lincoln succeeded in keeping Britain officially neutral.

81. **B** Lincoln twice removed General George McClellan from command of the Army of the Potomac. McClellan was chosen by the Democrats to run against Lincoln in the presidential election of 1864.

82. **D** Subsequent nominees were political and business leaders.

83. **A** This idea of Veblen's was presented in his 1899 book *The Theory of the Leisure Class.* An American social scientist, Veblen analyzed the psychological bases of social institutions and helped found the field of institutional economics.

84. **E** A professor at the Rochester Theological Seminary early in this century, Rauschenbusch wrote influential books on the social interpretation of Christianity. The "social gospel" ministers urged their parishioners to practice their faith by helping underprivileged people.

85. **B** Hawthorne's most famous works include *The Scarlet Letter* and *The House of the Seven Gables.* He blended realistic detail with romantic theme, darkhued atmosphere, and rich symbolism.

86. **E** An American humorist and journalist, Dunne used his Irish-American character, *Mr. Dooley*, to deflate politician's pretensions. He opposed the Spanish-American War with his humor.

87. **C** Theodore Roosevelt served as Vice-President until McKinley's assassination in 1901. Franklin Roosevelt ran for the office in 1920 but was defeated.

88. **B** Bold experimentation was a hallmark of the New Deal in its attempts to end the Great Depression of the 1930s.

89. **C** Known as "Mr. Republican," Taft was bypassed in 1952 for the Republican presidential nomination, and General Dwight Eisenhower was their victorious candidate.

90. **A** All three were, famous American historians. Turner wrote about the influence of the frontier in American history. Prescott wrote in a vivid style the histories of the conquests of Mexico and Peru. Rhode's major work was a multi-volume history of the United States from the Compromise of 1850.

91. **D** An influential Republican leader, Senator Vandenberg supported Truman's Containment policies against Soviet expansion and obtained the support of other Republican legislators for a bipartisan foreign policy.

92. **D** McKinley had been Governor of Ohio, and before that he served as a member of Congress from Ohio.

93. **B** The relative carbon emissions of Britain and the United States were only four metric tons apart, closer than any other pair among the choices.

94. **B** India's relative pollution was greater than that of Japan, 183 to 144 metric tons of carbon emissions.

95. **D** Having to choose between increasing taxes and reducing benefits, "Dr. Congress" complains that "either one's poison to me!"

Appendix

The Declaration of Independence[†]

In Congress, July 4, 1776

THE UNANIMOUS DECLARATION OF THE THIRTEEN UNITED STATES OF AMERICA

When, in the Course of human events, it becomes necessary for one people to dissolve the political bands which have connected them with another, and to assume among the powers of the earth, the separate and equal station to which the Laws of Nature and of Nature's God entitle them, a decent respect to the opinions of mankind requires that they should declare the causes which impel them to the separation.

We hold these truths to be self-evident, that all men are created equal, that they are endowed by their Creator with certain unalienable Rights, that among these, are Life, Liberty, and the pursuit of Happiness. That, to secure these rights, Governments are instituted among Men, deriving their just powers from the consent of the governed, that, whenever any Form of Government becomes destructive of these ends, it is the Right of the People to alter or to abolish it, and to institute new Government, laying its foundation on such principles, and organizing its powers in such form, as to them shall seem likely to effect their Safety and Happiness. Prudence, indeed, will dictate that Governments long established, should not be changed for light and transient causes; and, accordingly, all experience hath shewn, that mankind are more disposed to suffer, while evils are sufferable, than to right themselves by abolishing the forms to which they are accustomed. But, when a long train of abuses and usurpations, pursuing invariably the same Object, evinces a design to reduce them under absolute Despotism, it is their right, it is their duty, to throw off such Government and to provide new Guards for their future security.—Such has been the patient sufferance of these Colonies; and such is now the necessity which constrains them to alter their former Systems of Government. The history of the present King of Great Britain is a history of repeated injuries and usurpations, all having in direct object the establishment of an absolute Tyranny over these States. To prove this, let Facts be submitted to a candid world.—

[†] *Spelling and capitalization follow the parchment copy.*

He has refused his Assent to Laws the most wholesome and necessary for the public good.

He has forbidden his Governors to pass Laws of immediate and pressing importance, unless suspended in their operation till his Assent should be obtained; and when so suspended, he has utterly neglected to attend to them.

He has refused to pass other laws for the accommodation of large districts of people, unless those people would relinquish the right of Representation in the Legislature; a right inestimable to them and formidable to tyrants only.

He has called together legislative bodies at places unusual, uncomfortable, and distant from the depository of their public Records, for the sole purpose of fatiguing them into compliance with his measures.

He has dissolved Representative Houses repeatedly, for opposing with manly firmness his invasions on the rights of the people.

He has refused for a long time, after such dissolutions, to cause others to be elected; whereby the Legislative powers, incapable of Annihilation, have returned to the People at large for their exercise; the State remaining, in the meantime, exposed to all the dangers of invasion from without, and convulsions within.

He has endeavored to prevent the population of these States; for that purpose, obstructing the Laws for Naturalization of Foreigners; refusing to pass others to encourage their migrations hither, and raising the conditions of new Appropriations of Lands.

He has obstructed the Administration of Justice, by refusing his Assent to Laws for establishing Judiciary powers.

He has made Judges dependent on his Will alone, for the tenure of their offices, and the amount and payment of their salaries.

He has erected a multitude of New Offices, and sent hither swarms of Officers to harass our people, and eat out their substance.

He has kept among us, in times of peace, Standing Armies, without the Consent of our legislatures.

He has affected to render the Military independent of, and superior to, the Civil power.

He has combined, with others, to subject us to a jurisdiction foreign to our constitution, and unacknowledged by our laws; giving his Assent to their Acts of pretended Legislation:

For quartering large bodies of armed troops among us:

For protecting them by a mock Trial, from punishment, for any Murders which they should commit on the Inhabitants of these States:

For cutting off our Trade with all parts of the world:

For imposing Taxes on us without our Consent:

For depriving us, in many cases, of the benefits of Trial by Jury:

For transporting us beyond Seas to be tried for pretended offenses:

For abolishing the free System of English Laws in a neighboring Province, establishing therein an Arbitrary government, and enlarging its Boundaries, so as to render it at once an example and fit instrument for introducing the same absolute rule into these Colonies:

For taking away our Charters, abolishing our most valuable Laws, and altering, fundamentally, the Forms of our Governments:

For suspending our own Legislatures, and declaring themselves invested with power to legislate for us in all cases whatsoever.

He has abdicated Government here, by declaring us out of his Protection, and waging War against us.

He has plundered our seas, ravaged our Coasts, burnt our towns, and destroyed the lives our our people.

He is, at this time, transporting large Armies of foreign Mercenaries to compleat the works of death, desolation, and tyranny, already begun with circumstances of Cruelty & perfidy scarcely paralleled in the most barbarous ages, and totally unworthy the Head of a civilized nation.

He has constrained our fellow Citizens, taken Captive on the high Seas, to bear Arms against their Country, to become the executioners of their friends and Brethren, or to fall themselves by their Hands.

He has excited domestic insurrections amongst us, and has endeavored to bring on the inhabitants of our frontiers, the merciless Indian Savages, whose known rule of warfare, is, an undistinguished destruction of all ages, sexes and conditions.

In every stage of these Oppressions, We have Petitioned for Redress, in the most humble terms; our repeated Petitions have been answered only by repeated injury. A Prince, whose character is thus marked by every act which may define a Tyrant, is unfit to be the ruler of a free people.

Nor have we been wanting in attentions to our British brethren. We have warned them, from time to time, of attempts made by their legislature to extend an unwarrantable jurisdiction over us. We have reminded them of the circumstances of our emigration and settlement here. We have appealed to their native justice and magnanimity, and we have conjured them by the ties of our common kindred to disavow these usurpations, which would inevitably interrupt our connections and correspondence. They too have been deaf to the voice of justice and of consanguinity. We must, therefore, acquiesce in the necessity, which denounces our Separation, and hold them, as we hold the rest of mankind, Enemies in War, in Peace Friends.

We, therefore, the Representatives of the united States of America, in General Congress, Assembled, appealing to the Supreme Judge of the world for the rectitude of our intentions, do, in the Name, and by Authority of the good People of these Colonies, solemnly publish and declare, That these United Colonies are, and of Right ought to be, Free and Independent States; that they are Absolved from all Allegiance to the British Crown, and that all political connection between them and the State of Great Britain is, and ought to be, totally dissolved: and that, as Free and Independent States, they have full Power to levy War, conclude Peace, contract Alliances, establish Commerce, and to do all other Acts and Things which Independent States may of right do. And, for the support of this Declaration, with a firm reliance on the protection of divine Providence, we mutually pledge to each other our Lives, our Fortunes, and our sacred Honor.

The foregoing Declaration was, by order of Congress, engrossed, and signed by the following members:

John Hancock

NEW HAMPSHIRE
Josiah Bartlett
William Whipple
Matthew Thornton

MASSACHUSETTS BAY
Samuel Adams
John Adams
Robert Treat Paine
Elbridge Gerry

RHODE ISLAND
Stephen Hopkins
William Ellery

CONNECTICUT
Roger Sherman
Samuel Huntington
William Williams
Oliver Wolcott

NEW YORK
William Floyd
Philip Livingston
Francis Lewis
Lewis Morris

NEW JERSEY
Richard Stockton
John Witherspoon
Francis Hopkinson
John Hart
Abraham Clark

PENNSYLVANIA
Robert Morris
Benjamin Rush
Benjamin Franklin
John Morton
George Clymer
James Smith
George Taylor
James Wilson
George Ross

DELAWARE
Caesar Rodney
George Read
Thomas M'Kean

MARYLAND
Samuel Chase
William Paca
Thomas Stone
Charles Carroll, of Carrollton

VIRGINIA
George Wythe
Richard Henry Lee
Thomas Jefferson
Benjamin Harrison
Thomas Nelson, Jr.
Francis Lightfoot Lee
Carter Braxton

NORTH CAROLINA
William Hooper
Joseph Hewes
John Penn.

SOUTH CAROLINA
Edward Rutledge
Thomas Heyward, Jr.
Thomas Lynch, Jr.
Arthur Middleton

GEORGIA
Button Gwinnett
Lyman Hall
George Walton

RESOLVED, That copies of the Declaration be sent to the several assemblies, conventions, and committees, or councils of safety, and to the several commanding officers of the continental troops; that it be proclaimed in each of the united States, at the head of the army.

The Constitution of the United States

General objectives of the Constitution

WE THE PEOPLE of the United States, in Order to form a more perfect Union, establish Justice, insure domestic Tranquility, provide for the common defence, promote the general Welfare, and secure the Blessings of Liberty to ourselves and our Posterity, do ordain and establish this CONSTITUTION for the United States of America.

ARTICLE I • LEGISLATIVE DEPARTMENT

A bicameral Congress

SECTION 1. All legislative Powers herein granted shall be vested in a Congress of the United States, which shall consist of a Senate and House of Representatives.

Selection and term of Representatives

SECTION 2. [1]The House of Representatives shall be composed of Members chosen every second Year by the People of the several States, and the Electors in each State shall have the Qualifications requisite for Electors of the most numerous Branch of the State Legislature.

Qualifications of Representatives

[2]No person shall be a representative who shall not have attained to the Age of twenty five Years, and been seven Years a Citizen of the United States, and who shall not, when elected, be an Inhabitant of that State in which he shall be chosen.

Apportionment of Representatives among states—see Section 2 of Fourteenth Amendment: a decennial census; maximum and minimum size of House

[3][Representatives and direct Taxes shall be apportioned among the several States which may be included within this Union, according to their respective Numbers, which shall be determined by adding to the whole Number of free Persons, including those bound to Service for a Term of Years, and excluding Indians not taxed, three fifths of all other Persons.].* The actual Enumeration shall be made within three Years after the first Meeting of the Congress of the United States, and within every subsequent Term of ten Years, in such Manner as they shall by Law direct. The Number of Representatives shall not exceed one for every thirty Thousand, but each State shall have a Least one Representative; and until such enumeration shall be made, the State of New Hampshire shall be entitled to chuse three, Massachusetts eight, Rhode-Island and Providence Plantations one, Connecticut five, New York six, New Jersey four, Pennsylvania eight, Delaware one, Maryland six, Virginia ten, North Carolina five, South Carolina five, and Georgia three.

Filling of vacancies

[4]When vacancies happen in the Representation from any State, the Executive Authority thereof shall issue Writs of Election to fill such Vacancies.

Choice of Speaker and other officers; sole power of impeachment

[5]The House of Representatives shall chuse their Speaker and other Officers; and shall have the sole Power of Impeachment.

Composition of Senate; see Seventeenth Amendment for selection of Senators.

SECTION 3. The Senate of the United States shall be composed of two Senators from each State, [chosen by the Legislature thereof,]** for six Years; and each senator shall have one Vote.

NOTE:—This text of the Constitution follows the engrossed copy signed by Gen. Washington and the deputies from 12 States. The superior number preceding the paragraphs designates the number of the clause; it was not in the original.
* The part included in heavy brackets was changed by section 2 of the fourteenth amendment.
**The part included in heavy brackets was changed by section 1 of the seventeenth amendment.

Terms of Senators—overlapping

[2]Immediately after they shall be assembled in Consequence of the first Election, they shall be divided as equally as may be into three Classes. The Seats of the Senators of the first Class shall be vacated at the Expiration of the second Year, of the second Class at the Expiration of the fourth Year, and of the third Class at the Expiration of the sixth Year, so that one third may be chosen every second Year;

Vacancies—see Seventeenth Amendment

[and if Vacancies happen by Resignation, or otherwise, during the Recess of the Legislature of any State, the Executive thereof may make temporary Appointments until the next Meeting of the Legislature, which shall then fill such Vacancies].*

Qualifications

[3]No Person shall be a Senator who shall not have attained to the Age of thirty Years, and been nine Years a Citizen of the United States, and who shall not, when elected, be an Inhabitant of that State for which he shall be chosen.

Vice President to preside; choice of other officers

[4]The Vice President of the United States shall be President of the Senate, but shall have no Vote, unless they be equally divided.

[5]The Senate shall chuse their other Officers, and also a President pro tempore, in the Absence of the Vice President, or when he shall exercise the Office of President of the United States.

Trial of impeachments by Senate; penalties if impeached and convicted.

[6]The Senate shall have the sole Power to try all Impeachments. When sitting for that Purpose, they shall be on Oath or Affirmation. When the President of the United States is tried, the Chief Justice shall preside: And no Person shall be convicted without the Concurrence of two thirds of the Members present.

[7]Judgment in Cases of Impeachment shall not extend further than to removal from Office, and disqualification to hold and enjoy any Office of honor, Trust or Profit under the United States: but the Party convicted shall nevertheless be liable and subject to Indictment, Trial, Judgment and Punishment, according to Law.

Times, places and manner of holding Congressional elections.

SECTION 4.   [1]The Times, Places and Manner of holding Elections for Senators and Representatives, shall be prescribed in each State by the Legislature thereof; but the Congress may at any time by Law make or alter such Regulations, except as to the Places of chusing Senators.

Congressional sessions—see Twentieth Amendment

[2]The Congress shall assemble at Least once in every Year, and such Meeting shall [be on the first Monday in December,]** unless they shall by Law appoint a different Day.

Judging elections and qualifications; size of a quorum; expulsion of members of Congress

SECTION 5.   [1]Each House shall be the Judge of the Elections, Returns and Qualifications of its own Members, and a Majority of each shall constitute a Quorum to do Business; but a smaller Number may adjourn from day to day, and may be authorized to compel the Attendance of absent Members, in such Manner, and under such Penalties as each House may provide.

Rules of proceeding and keeping of journal.

[2]Each House may determine the Rules of its Proceedings, punish its Members for disorderly Behavior, and, with the Concurrence of two thirds, expel a Member.

[3]Each House shall keep a Journal of its Proceedings, and from time to time publish the same, excepting such Parts as may in their Judgment require Secrecy; and the Yeas and Nays of the Members of either House on any question shall, at the Desire of one fifth of those Present, be entered on the Journal.

Adjournment

[4]Neither House, during the Session of Congress, shall, without the Consent of the other, adjourn for more than three days, nor to any other Place than that in which the two Houses shall be sitting.

---

* The part included in heavy brackets was changed by clause 2 of the seventeenth amendment.

**The part included in heavy brackets was changed by section 2 of the twentieth amendment.

Compensation and immunities of members of Congress

SECTION 6.   [1]The Senators and Representatives shall receive a Compensation for their Services, to be ascertained by Law, and paid out of the Treasury of the United States. They shall in all Cases, except Treason, Felony and Breach of the Peace, be privileged from Arrest during their Attendance at the Session of their respective Houses, and in going to and returning from the same; and for any Speech or Debate in either House, they shall not be questioned in any other Place.

Limitations on appointment of members of Congress to civil offices; no national office-holder to be a member of Congress

[2]No Senator or Representative shall, during the Time for which he was elected, be appointed to any civil Office under the Authority of the United States, which shall have been created, or the Emoluments whereof shall have been encreased during such time; and no Person holding any Office under the United States, shall be a Member of either House during his Continuance in Office.

Origin of revenue bills

SECTION 7.   [1]All Bills for raising Revenue shall originate in the House of Representatives; but the Senate may propose or concur with Amendments as on other Bills.

Veto power of President: overriding of veto

[2]Every Bill which shall have passed the House of Representatives and the Senate, shall, before it becomes a Law, be presented to the President of the United States; If he approve he shall sign it, but if not he shall return it, with his Objections to that House in which it shall have originated, who shall enter the Objections at large on their Journal, and proceed to reconsider it. If after such Reconsideration two thirds of that House shall agree to pass the Bill, it shall be sent, together with the Objections, to the other House, by which it shall likewise be reconsidered, and if approved by two thirds of that House, it shall become a Law. But in all such Cases the Votes of both Houses shall be determined by Yeas and Nays, and the Names of the Persons voting for and against the Bill shall be entered on the Journal of each House respectively. If any Bill shall not be returned by the President within ten days (Sundays excepted) after it shall have been presented to him, the Same shall be a Law, in like Manner as if he had signed it, unless the Congress by their Adjournment prevent its Return, in which Case it shall not be a Law.

[3]Every Order, Resolution, or Vote to which the Concurrence of the Senate and House of Representatives may be necessary (except on a question of Adjournment) shall be presented to the President of the United States; and before the Same shall take Effect, shall be approved by him, or being disapproved by him, shall be repassed by two thirds of the Senate and House of Representatives, according to the Rules and Limitations prescribed in the Case of a Bill.

Enumerated powers of Congress:

Taxation

SECTION 8.   [1]The Congress shall have Power To lay and collect Taxes, Duties, Imposts and Excises, to pay the Debts and provide for the common Defence and general Welfare of the United States; but all Duties, Imposts and Excises shall be uniform throughout the United States;

Borrowing of money
Regulation of commerce

[2]To borrow Money on the credit of the United States;

[3]To regulate Commerce with foreign Nations, and among the several States, and with the Indian Tribes;

Naturalization and bankruptcy

[4]To establish an uniform Rule of Naturalization, and uniform Laws on the subject of Bankruptcies throughout the United States;

Coining of money; weights and measures

[5]To coin Money, regulate the Value thereof, and of foreign Coin, and fix the Standard of Weights and Measures;

Punishment of counterfeiting

[6]To provide for the Punishment of counterfeiting the Securities and current Coin of the United States;

Postal service

[7]To establish Post Offices and post Roads;

Patents and copyrights

[8]To promote the Progress of Science and useful Arts, by securing for limited Times to Authors and Inventors the exclusive Right to their respective Writings and Discoveries;

Creation of courts
Piracies and high seas felonies

[9]To constitute Tribunals inferior to the supreme Court;

[10]To define and punish Piracies and Felonies committed on the high Seas, and Offences against the Law of Nations;

Declaration of War

[11]To declare War, grant Letters of Marque and Reprisal, and make Rules concerning Captures on Land and Water;

Provide armed forces and for calling forth and organizing the militia

[12]To raise and support Armies, but no Appropriation of Money to that Use shall be for a longer Term than two Years;

[13]To provide and maintain a Navy;

[14]To make Rules for the Government and Regulation of the land and naval Forces;

[15]To provide for calling forth the Militia to execute the Laws of the Union, suppress Insurrections and repel Invasions;

[16]To provide for organizing, arming, and disciplining the Militia and for governing such Part of them as may be employed in the Service of the United States, reserving to the States respectively, the Appointment of the Officers, and the Authority of training the Militia according to the discipline prescribed by Congress;

Congress to govern the District of Columbia and other places owned by national government

[17]To exercise exclusive Legislation in all Cases whatsoever, over such District (not exceeding ten Miles square) as may, by Cession of particular States, and the Acceptance of Congress, become the Seat of the Government of the United States, and to exercise like Authority over all Places purchased by the Consent of the Legislature of the State in which the Same shall be, for the Erection of Forts, Magazines, Arsenals, dock-Yards, and other needful Buildings;—And

Necessary and proper (elastic) clause

[18]To make all Laws which shall be necessary and proper for carrying into Execution the foregoing Powers, and all other Powers vested by this Constitution in the Government of the United States, or in any Department or Officer thereof.

Express limitations on national government— Congress in particular

SECTION 9.   [1]The Migration or Importation of such Persons as any of the States now existing shall think proper to admit, shall not be prohibited by the Congress prior to the Year one thousand eight hundred and eight, but a Tax or duty may be imposed on such Importation, not exceeding ten dollars for each Person.

[2]The Privilege of the Writ of Habeas Corpus shall not be suspended, unless when in Cases of Rebellion or Invasion the public Safety may require it.

[3]No Bill of Attainder or ex post facto Law shall be passed.

*[4]No Capitation, or other direct, Tax shall be laid, unless in Proportion to the Census or Enumeration herein before directed to be taken.

[5]No Tax or Duty shall be laid on Articles exported from any State.

[6]No Preference shall be given by any Regulation of Commerce or Revenue to the Ports of one State over those of another: nor shall Vessels bound to, or from, one State be obliged to enter, clear, or pay Duties in another.

[7]No Money shall be drawn from the Treasury, but in Consequence of Appropriations made by Law; and a regular Statement and Account of the Receipts and Expenditures of all public Money shall be published from time to time.

[8]No Title of Nobility shall be granted by the United States: And no Person holding any Office of Profit or Trust under them, shall, without the Consent of the Congress, accept of any present, Emolument, Office, or Title, of any kind of whatever, from any King, Prince, or foreign State.

Express limitations on states

SECTION 10.   [1]No State shall enter into any Treaty, Alliance, or Confederation; grant Letters of Marque and Reprisal, coin Money, emit Bills of Credit; make any Thing but gold and silver Coin a Tender in Payment of Debts; pass any Bill of Attainder, ex post facto Law, or Law impairing the Obligation of Contracts, or grant any Title of Nobility.

[2]No State shall, without the Consent of the Congress, lay any Imposts or Duties on Imports or Exports, except what may be absolutely necessary for executing it's inspection Laws: and the net Produce of all Duties and Imposts, laid by any State on Imports or Exports, shall be for the Use of the Treasury of the United States; and all such Laws shall be subject to the Revision and Controul of the Congress.

---

*See also the sixteenth amendment.

[3]No State shall, without the Consent of Congress, lay any Duty of Tonnage, keep Troops, or Ships of War in time of Peace, enter into any Agreement or Compact with another State, or with a foreign Power, or engage in War, unless actually invaded, or in such imminent Danger as will not admit of delay.

ARTICLE II • EXECUTIVE DEPARTMENT

Executive power vested in President; term of office— see Twenty-second Amendment
Selection of Presidential electors and number Per state

SECTION 1.   [1]The executive Power shall be vested in a President of the United States of America. He shall hold his Office during the Term of four Years, and, together with the Vice President, chosen for the same Term, be elected as follows:

[2]Each State shall appoint, in such Manner as the Legislature thereof may direct, a Number of Electors, equal to the whole Number of Senators and Representatives to which the State may be entitled in the Congress: but no Senator or Representative, or Person holding an Office of Trust or Profit under the United States, shall be appointed an Elector.

Replaced by Twelfth Amendment

[The Electors shall meet in their respective States, and vote by Ballot for two Persons, of whom one at least shall not be an Inhabitant of the same State with themselves. And they shall make a List of all the Persons voted for, and of the Number of Votes for each; which List they shall sign and certify, and transmit sealed to the Seat of the Government of the United States, directed to the President of the Senate. The President of the Senate shall, in the Presence of the Senate and House of Representatives, open all the Certificates, and the Votes shall then be counted. The Person having the greatest Number of Votes shall be the President, if such Number be a Majority of the whole Number of Electors appointed; and if there be more than one who have such Majority, and have an equal Number of Votes, then the House of Representatives shall immediately chuse by Ballot one of them for President; and if no Person have a Majority, then from the five highest on the List the said House shall in like Manner chuse the President. But in chusing the President, the Votes shall be taken by States, the Representation from each State having one Vote; A quorum for this Purpose shall consist of a Member or Members from two thirds of the States, and a Majority of all the States shall be necessary to a Choice. In every Case, after the Choice of the President, the Person having the greatest Number of Votes of the Electors shall be the Vice President. But if there should remain two or more who have equal Votes, the Senate shall chuse from them by Ballot the Vice President.]*

Congress to determine the time of choosing electors and the casting of electoral votes
Required qualifications of President

[3]The Congress may determine the Time of chusing the Electors, and the Day on which they shall give their Votes; which Day shall be the same throughout the United States.

[4]No Person except a natural born Citizen, or a Citizen of the United States, at the time of the Adoption of this Constitution, shall be eligible to the Office of President; neither shall any Person be eligible to that Office who shall not have attained to the Age of thirty five Years, and been fourteen Years a Resident within the United States.

Succession to the Presidency; also see the Twenty-fifth Amendment

[5]In Case of the Removal of the President from Office, or of his Death, Resignation, or Inability to discharge the Powers and Duties of the said Office, the Same shall devolve on the Vice President, and the Congress may by law provide for the Case of Removal, Death, Resignation or Inability, both of the President and Vice President declaring what Officer shall then act as President, and such Officer shall act accordingly, until the Disability be removed, or a President shall be elected.

Compensation of the President

[6]The President shall, at stated Times, receive for his Services, a Compensation, which shall neither be encreased nor diminished during the Period for which he shall have been elected, and he shall not receive within that Period any other Emolument from the United States, or any of them.

---

*This paragraph has been superseded by the twelfth amendment.

Presidential oath of office

[7]Before he enter on the Execution of his Office, he shall take the following Oath or Affirmation: "I do solemnly swear (or affirm) that I will faithfully execute the Office of President of the United States, and will to the best of my Ability, preserve, protect and defend the Constitution of the United States."

Powers of the President: Commander in Chief

SECTION 2.   [1]The President shall be Commander in Chief of the Army and Navy of the United States, and of the Militia of the several States, when called into the actual Service of the United States; he may require the Opinion, in writing, of the principal Officer in each of the executive Departments, upon any Subject relat-

Granting of pardons and reprieves

ing to the Duties of their respective Offices, and he shall have Power to grant Reprieves and Pardons for Offences against the United States, except in Cases of Impeachment.

Treaty-making with advice and consent of Senate

[2]He shall have Power, by and with the Advice and Consent of the Senate, to make Treaties, provided two thirds of the Senators present concur; and he shall nominate, and by and with the Advice and Consent of the Senate, shall appoint

Appointment of officials with advice and consent of Senate; appointment of inferior officers by President alone if Congress so provides

Ambassadors, other public Ministers and Consuls, Judges of the supreme Court, and all other Officers of the United States, whose Appointments are not herein otherwise provided for, and which shall be established by Law: but the Congress may by Law vest the Appointment of such inferior Officers, as they think proper, in the President alone, in the Courts of Law, or in the Heads of Departments.

Temporary filling of vacancies

[3]The President shall have Power to fill up all Vacancies that may happen during the Recess of the Senate, by granting Commissions which shall expire at the End of their next Session.

Make recommendations to Congress and provide information

SECTION 3.   He shall from time to time give to the Congress Information of the State of the Union, and recommend to their Consideration such Measures as he shall judge necessary and expedient; he may, on extraordinary Occasions, convene

Call special sessions of Congress

both Houses, or either of them, and in Case of Disagreement between them, with Respect to the Time of Adjournment, he may adjourn them to such Time as he

Receive ambassadors and other public ministers

shall think proper; he shall receive Ambassadors and other public Ministers; he shall take Care that the Laws be faithfully executed, and shall Commission all the

Enforce the laws

Officers of the United States.

Civil officers, including President and Vice President, to be removed from office if impeached and convicted

SECTION 4.   The President, Vice President and all civil Officers of the United States, shall be removed from Office on Impeachment for, and Conviction of, Treason, Bribery, or other high Crimes and Misdemeanors.

ARTICLE III • JUDICIAL DEPARTMENT

Structure of national judiciary

SECTION 1.   The judicial Power of the United States, shall be vested in one supreme Court, and in such inferior Courts as the Congress may from time to time ordain and establish. The Judges, both of the supreme and inferior Courts, shall

Tenure and compensation of judges

hold their Offices during good Behaviour, and shall, at stated Times, receive for their Services, a Compensation, which shall not be diminished during their Continuance in Office.

Jurisdiction of the national judiciary

SECTION 2.   [1]The judicial Power shall extend to all Cases, in Law and Equity, arising under this Constitution, the Laws of the United States; and Treaties made, or which shall be made, under their Authority;—to all Cases affecting Ambassadors, other public Ministers and Consuls;—to all Cases of admiralty and maritime Jurisdiction;—to Controversies to which the United States shall be a Party;—to Controversies between two or more States;—between a State and Citizens of another State;*—between Citizens of different States—between Citizens of the same State claiming Lands under Grants of different States, and between a State, or the Citizens thereof, and foreign States, Citizens or Subjects.

---

*This clause has been affected by the eleventh amendment.

Original and appellate jurisdiction of the Supreme Court

²In all Cases affecting Ambassadors, other public Ministers and Consuls, and those in which a State shall be Party, the supreme Court shall have original Jurisdiction. In all the other Cases before mentioned, the supreme Court shall have appellate Jurisdiction, both as to Law and Fact, with such Exceptions, and under such Regulations as the Congress shall make.

Jury trial in criminal cases other than impeachment

³The Trial of all Crimes, except in Cases of Impeachment, shall be by Jury; and such Trial shall be held in the State where the said Crimes shall have been committed; but when not committed within any State, the Trial shall be at such Place or Places as the Congress may by Law have directed.

Definition of treason and requisites for conviction

SECTION 3.   ¹Treason against the United States, shall consist only in levying War against them, or in adhering to their Enemies, giving them Aid and Comfort. No Person shall be convicted of Treason unless on the Testimony of two Witnesses to the same overt Act, or on Confession in open Court.

Punishment for treason

²The Congress shall have Power to declare the Punishment of Treason, but no Attainder of Treason shall work Corruption of Blood, or Forfeiture except during the Life of the Person attainted.

ARTICLE IV • RELATION OF THE STATES TO EACH OTHER

Interstate obligations: full faith and credit, privileges and immunities of citizens, rendition of fugitives from justice

SECTION 1.   Full Faith and Credit shall be given in each State to the public Acts, Records, and judicial Proceedings of every other State. And the Congress may by general Laws prescribe the Manner in which such Acts, Records and Proceedings shall be proved, and the Effect thereof.

SECTION 2.   ¹The Citizens of each State shall be entitled to all Privileges and Immunities of Citizens in the several States.

²A Person charged in any State with Treason, Felony, or other Crime, who shall flee from Justice, and be found in another State, shall on Demand of the executive Authority of the State from which he fled, be delivered up, to be removed to the State having Jurisdiction of the Crime.

Obsolete

³[No Person held to Service or Labour in one State, under the Laws thereof, escaping into another, shall, in Consequence of any Law or Regulation therein, be discharged from such Service or Labour but shall be delivered up on Claim of the Party to whom such Service or Labour may be due.]*

Admission of new states

SECTION 3.   ¹New States may be admitted by Congress into this Union; but no new State shall be formed or erected within the Jurisdiction of any other State; nor any State be formed by the Junction of two or more States, or Parts of States, without the Consent of the Legislature of the States concerned as well as the Congress.

Government of territories

²The Congress shall have Power to dispose of and make all needful Rules and Regulations respecting the Territory or other Property belonging to the United States; and nothing in this Constitution shall be so construed as to Prejudice any Claims of the United States, or of any particular State.

Guarantee of republican form of government and protection against invasion and domestic violence

SECTION 4.   The United States shall guarantee to every State in this Union a Republican Form of Government, and shall protect each of them against Invasion; and on Application of the Legislature, or of the Executive (when the Legislature cannot be convened) against domestic Violence.

ARTICLE V • AMENDMENTS

Proposal and ratification of amendments

The Congress, whenever two thirds of both Houses shall deem it necessary, shall propose Amendments to this Constitution, or, on the Application of the

---

*This paragraph has been superseded by the thirteenth amendment.

Legislatures of two thirds of the several States, shall call a Convention for proposing Amendments, which, in either Case, shall be valid to all Intents and Purposes, as Part of this Constitution, when ratified by the Legislatures of three fourths of the several States, or by Conventions in three fourths thereof, as the one or the other Mode of Ratification may be proposed by the Congress; Provided, [that no Amendment which may be made prior to the Year One thousand eight hundred and eight shall in any Manner affect the first and fourth Clauses in the Ninth Section of the first Article; and]** that no State, without its Consent, shall be deprived of its equal Suffrage in the Senate.

ARTICLE VI • GENERAL PROVISIONS

Validity of debts contracted prior to adoption of the Constitution

[1]All Debts contracted and Engagements entered into, before the Adoption of this Constitution, shall be as valid against the United States under this Constitution, as under the Confederation.

Supremacy of the national constitution, laws, and treaties

[2]This Constitution, and the Laws of the United States which shall be made in Pursuance thereof; and all Treaties made, or which shall be made, under the Authority of the United States, shall be the supreme Law of the Land; and the Judges in every State shall be bound thereby, any Thing in the Constitution or Laws of any State to the Contrary notwithstanding.

Oath of office to support Constitution: required of all officials, national and state; no religious qualification

[3]The Senators and Representatives before mentioned, and the Members of the several State Legislatures, and all executive and judicial Officers, both of the United States and of the several States, shall be bound by Oath or Affirmation, to support this Constitution; but no religious Test shall ever be required as a Qualification to any Office or public Trust under the United States.

ARTICLE VII • RATIFICATION OF THE CONSTITUTION

Schedule

The Ratification of the Conventions of nine States, shall be sufficient for the Establishment of this Constitution between the States so ratifying the Same.

DONE in convention by the Unanimous Consent of the States present the Seventeenth Day of September in the Year of our Lord one thousand seven hundred and Eighty seven and of the Independence of the United States of America the Twelfth. IN WITNESS whereof We have hereto subscribed our Names.

George Washington
President and Deputy from Virginia

[Signed also by the deputies of twelve States.]

New Hampshire
John Langdon
Nicholas Gilman

Massachusetts
Nathaniel Gorham
Rufus King

Connecticut
William Samuel Johnson
Roger Sherman

New York
Alexander Hamilton

New Jersey
William Livingston
David Brearley
William Paterson
Jonathan Dayton
Pennsylvania
Benjamin Franklin
Robert Morris
Thomas FitzSimons
James Wilson
Thomas Mifflin
George Clymer
Jared Ingersoll
Gouverneur Morris

**Obsolete.

Delaware
George Read
John Dickinson
Jacob Broom
Gunning Bedford Jr.
Richard Bassett

Maryland
James McHenry
Daniel Carroll
Dan of St. Thomas Jenifer

Virginia
John Blair
James Madison, Jr.

North Carolina
William Blount
Hugh Williamson
Richard Dobbs Spaight

South Carolina
John Rutledge
Charles Pinckney
Charles Cotesworth Pinckney
Pierce Butler

Georgia
William Few
Abraham Baldwin

Attest: William Jackson, Secretary

RATIFICATION OF THE CONSTITUTION

The Constitution was adopted by a convention of the States on September 17, 1787, and was subsequently ratified by the several States, on the following dates: Delaware, December 7, 1787; Pennsylvania, December 12, 1787; New Jersey, December 18, 1787; Georgia, January 2, 1788; Connecticut, January 9, 1788; Massachusetts, February 6, 1788; Maryland, April 28, 1788; South Carolina, May 23, 1788; New Hampshire, June 21, 1788; Virginia, June 25, 1788; New York, July 26, 1788; North Carolina, November 21, 1789; Rhode Island, May 29, 1790.

ARTICLES IN ADDITION TO, AND AMENDMENT OF, THE CONSTITUTION OF THE UNITED STATES OF AMERICA, PROPOSED BY CONGRESS, AND RATIFIED BY THE LEGISLATURES OF THE SEVERAL STATES PURSUANT TO THE FIFTH ARTICLE OF THE ORIGINAL CONSTITUTION

ARTICLE I*

Freedom of religion, speech, and assembly

Congress shall make no law respecting an establishment of religion, or prohibiting the free exercise thereof; or abridging the freedom of speech, or of the press; or the right of the people peaceably to assemble, and to petition the Government for a redress of grievances.

ARTICLE II

Militia and the right to bear arms

A well regulated militia, being necessary to the security of a free state, the right of the people to keep and bear arms, shall not be infringed.

---

*Only the 13th, 14th, 15th, and 16th articles of amendment had numbers assigned to them at the time of ratification.

ARTICLE III

Quartering of soldiers

No soldier shall, in time of peace be quartered in any house, without the consent of the Owner, nor in time of war, but in a manner to be prescribed by law.

ARTICLE IV

Unreasonable searches and seizures prohibited

The right of the people to be secure in their persons, houses, papers, and effects, against unreasonable searches and seizures, shall not be violated, and no Warrants shall issue, but upon probably cause, supported by Oath or affirmation, and particularly describing the place to be searched, and the persons or things to be seized.

ARTICLE V

Indictment by grand jury; no double jeopardy; due process of law; no self-incrimination; compensation for taking property

No person shall be held to answer for a capital, or otherwise infamous crime, unless on a presentment or indictment of a Grand Jury, except in cases arising in the land or naval forces, or in the Militia, when in actual service in time of War or public danger; nor shall any person be subject for the same offence to be twice put in jeopardy of life or limb; nor shall be compelled in any criminal case to be a witness against himself, nor be deprived of life, liberty, or property, without due process of law; nor shall private property be taken for public use, without just compensation.

ARTICLE VI

Guarantee of basic procedural rights in criminal prosecutions, e.g., jury trial, confrontation of witnesses

In all criminal prosecutions, the accused shall enjoy the right to a speedy and public trial, by an impartial jury of the State and district wherein the crime shall have been committed, which district shall have been previously ascertained by law, and to be informed of the nature and cause of the accusation; to be confronted with the witnesses against him; to have compulsory process for obtaining Witnesses in his favor, and to have the Assistance of Counsel for his defence.

ARTICLE VII

Jury trial in common law suits

In Suits at common law, where the value in controversy shall exceed twenty dollars, the right of trial by jury shall be preserved, and no fact tried by a jury, shall be otherwise reexamined in any Court of the United States, than according to the rules of the common law.

ARTICLE VIII

Excessive bail or fines, cruel and unusual punishments prohibited

Excessive bail shall not be required, nor excessive fines imposed, nor cruel and unusual punishments inflicted.

ARTICLE IX

Retention of rights by the people

The enumeration in the Constitution, of certain rights, shall not be construed to deny or disparage others retained by the people.

ARTICLE X

Reserved powers of the states

The powers not delegated to the United States by the Constitution nor prohibited by it to the States, are reserved to the States respectively, or to the people.

ARTICLE XI

Immunity of states from suits by citizens or aliens in national courts

The Judicial power of the United States shall not be construed to extend to any suit in law or equity, commenced or prosecuted against one of the United States by Citizens of another State, or by Citizens or Subjects of any Foreign State.

ARTICLE XII

Replaces third paragraph of Section 1, Article II. Principal provision requires separate ballots for President and Vice President and a majority electoral vote. Procedure to be followed it no candidate obtains a majority

The electors shall meet in their respective states and vote by ballot for President and Vice-President, one of whom, at least, shall not be an inhabitation of the same state with themselves; they shall name in their ballots the person voted for as President, and in distinct ballots the person voted for as Vice-President, and they shall make distinct lists of all persons voted for as President, and of all personas voted for as Vice-President, and of the number of votes for each, which lists they shall sign and certify, and transmit sealed to the seat of the government of the United States, directed to the President of the Senate;—The President of the Senate shall, in presence of the Senate and House of Representatives, open all the certificates and the votes shall then be counted;—The person having the greatest number of votes for President, shall be the President, if such number be a majority of the whole number of Electors appointed; and if no person have such majority, then from the persons having the highest numbers not exceeding three on the list of those voted for as President, the House of Representatives shall choose immediately, by ballot, the President. But in choosing the President, the votes shall be taken by states, the representation from each state having one vote; a quorum for this purpose shall consist of a member or members from two-thirds of the states, and a majority of all the states shall be necessary to a choice. [And if the House of Representatives shall not choose a President whenever the right of choice shall devolve upon them, before the fourth day of March next following, then the Vice-President shall act as President, as in the case of the death or other constitutional disability of the President.]* The person having the greatest number of votes as Vice-President, shall be the Vice-President, if such number be a majority of the whole number of Electors appointed, and if no person have a majority, then from the two highest numbers on the list, the Senate shall choose the Vice-President; a quorum for the purpose shall consist of two-thirds of the whole number of Senators, and a majority of the whole number shall be necessary to a choice. But no person constitutionally ineligible to the office of President shall be eligible to that of Vice-President of the United States.

ARTICLE XIII

Slavery and involuntary servitude prohibited

SECTION 1.   Neither slavery nor involuntary servitude, except as a punishment for crime whereof the party shall have been duly convicted, shall exist within the United States, or any place subject to their jurisdiction.

SECTION 2.   Congress shall have power to enforce this article by appropriate legislation.

---

*The part included in heavy brackets has been superseded by section 3 of the twentieth amendment.

ARTICLE XIV

Definition of United States and state citizenship; no state abridgment of privileges and immunities of United States citizens; no state denial of due process of law or equal protection of the laws to any person

SECTION 1.   All persons born or naturalized in the United States, and subject to the jurisdiction thereof, are citizens of the United States and the State wherein they reside. No State shall make or enforce any law which shall abridge the privileges or immunities of citizens of the United States; nor shall any State deprive any person of life, liberty, or property, without due process of law; nor deny to any person within its jurisdiction the equal protection of the laws.

Apportionment of Representatives among the states according to population, excluding untaxed Indians. Provision for reduction of representation under specified circumstances

SECTION 2.   Representatives shall be apportioned among the several States according to their respective numbers, counting the whole number of persons in each State, excluding Indians not taxed. But when the right to vote at any election for the choice of electors for President and Vice President of the United States, Representatives in Congress, the Executive and Judicial officers of a State, or the members of the Legislature thereof, is denied to any of the male inhabitants of such State, being twenty-one years of age, and citizens of the United State, or in any way abridged, except for participation in rebellion, or other crime, the basis of representation therein shall be reduced in the proportion which the number of such male citizens shall bear to the whole number of male citizens twenty-one years of age in such State.

Disqualification from office-holding by officials who, having taken an oath to support the constitution, engage in rebellion against the United States

SECTION 3.   No person shall be a Senator or Representative in Congress, or elector of President and Vice President, or hold any office, civil or military, under the United States, or under any State, who, having previously taken an oath, as a member of Congress, or as an officer of the United States, or as a member of any State legislature, or as an executive or judicial officer of any State, to support the Constitution of the United States, shall have engaged in insurrection or rebellion against the same, or given aid or comfort to the enemies thereof. But Congress may by a vote of two-thirds of each House, remove such disability.

Validity of public debt incurred for suppressing rebellion not to be questioned. All indebtedness incurred in support of rebellion illegal and void

SECTION 4.   The validity of the public debt of the United States, authorized by law, including debts incurred for payment of pensions and bounties for services in suppressing insurrection or rebellion, shall not be questioned. But neither the United States nor any State shall assume or pay any debt or obligation incurred in aid of insurrection or rebellion against the United States, or any claim for the loss or emancipation of any slave; but all such debts, obligations and claims shall be held illegal and void.

SECTION 5.   The Congress shall have power to enforce, by appropriate legislation, the provisions of this article.

ARTICLE XV

Right of citizens to vote not to be denied because of race, color, or previous condition of servitude

SECTION 1.   The right of citizens of the United States to vote shall not be denied or abridged by the United States or by any State on account of race, color, or previous condition of servitude.

SECTION 2.   The Congress shall have power to enforce this article by appropriate legislation.

ARTICLE XVI

Congress empowered to levy income taxes without apportionment among states on a population basis

The Congress shall have power to lay and collect taxes on incomes, from whatever source derived, without apportionment among the several States, and without regard to any census or enumeration.

ARTICLE XVII

Popular election of Senators for six year term by persons qualified to vote for members of the most numerous branch of the state legislature

The Senate of the United States shall be composed of two Senators from each state, elected by the people thereof, for six years; and each Senator shall have one vote. The electors in each State shall have the qualifications requisite for electors of the most numerous branch of the State legislature.

Procedure for filling vacancies in Senate

When vacancies happen in the representation of any State in the Senate, the executive authority of such State shall issue writs of election to fill such vacancies: *Provided*, That the legislature of any State may empower the executive thereof to make temporary appointments until the people fill the vacancies by election as the legislature may direct.

This amendment shall not be so construed as to affect the election or term of any Senator chosen before it becomes valid as part of the Constitution.

ARTICLE XVIII

Prohibition Amendment; repealed by Twenty-first Amendment

SECTION 1.   After one year from the ratification of this article the manufacture, sale, or transportation of intoxicating liquors within, the importation thereof into, or the exportation thereof from the United States and all territory subject to the jurisdiction thereof for beverage purposes is hereby prohibited.

SECTION 2.   The Congress and the several States shall have concurrent power to enforce this article by appropriate legislation.

SECTION 3.   This article shall be inoperative unless it shall have been ratified as an amendment to the Constitution by the legislatures of the several States, as provided in the Constitution, within seven years from the date of the submission hereof to the States by the Congress.*

ARTICLE XIX

Right of citizens to vote not to be denied because of sex

The right of citizens of the United States to vote shall not be denied or abridged by the United States or by any State on account of sex.

Congress shall have power to enforce this article by appropriate legislation.

ARTICLE XX

Ending of terms of President, Vice President, Senators, and Representatives

SECTION 1.   The terms of the President and Vice President shall end at noon on the 20th day of January, and the terms of Senators and Representatives at noon on the 3d day of January, of the years in which such terms would have ended if this article had not been ratified; and the terms of their successors shall then begin.

Beginning of required annual Congressional sessions

SECTION 2.   The Congress shall assemble at least once in every year, and such meeting shall begin at noon on the 3d day of January, unless they shall by law appoint a different day.

Procedure to be followed if President elect has died or no President has been chosen or qualified by beginning of the Presidential term. This amendment also deals with other contingencies

SECTION 3.   If, at the time fixed for the beginning of the term of the President, the President elect shall have died, the Vice President elect shall become President. If a President shall not have been chosen before the time fixed for the beginning of his term, or if the President elect shall have failed to qualify, then the Vice President elect shall act as President until a President shall have qualified; and the Congress may by law provide for the case wherein neither a President elect nor a

---

*Repealed by section 1 of the twenty-first amendment.

Vice President elect shall have qualified, declaring who shall then act as President, or the manner in which one who is to act shall be selected, and such person shall act accordingly until a President or Vice President shall have qualified.

SECTION 4.   The Congress may by law provide for the case of the death of any of the persons from whom the House of Representatives may choose a President whenever the right of choice shall have devolved upon them, and for the case of the death of any of the persons from whom the Senate may choose a Vice President whenever the right of choice shall have devolved upon them.

SECTION 5.   Sections 1 and 2 shall take effect on the 15th day of October following the ratification of this article.

SECTION 6.   This article shall be inoperative unless it shall have been ratified as an amendment to the Constitution by the legislatures of three-fourths of the several States within seven years from the date of its submission.

ARTICLE XXI

The Eighteenth Amendment establishing prohibition repealed

SECTION 1.   The eighteenth article of amendment to the Constitution of the United States is hereby repealed.

SECTION 2.   The transportation or importation into any State, Territory, or possession of the United States for delivery or use therein of intoxicating liquors, in violation of the laws thereof, is hereby prohibited.

SECTION 3.   This article shall be inoperative unless it shall have been ratified as an amendment to the Constitution by conventions in the several States, as provided in the Constitution, within seven years from the date of the submission hereof to the States by the Congress.

ARTICLE XXII

No person may be elected to Presidency for more than two terms

SECTION 1.   No person shall be elected to the office of the President more than twice, and no person who has held the office of President, or acted as President, for more than two years of a term to which some other person was elected President shall be elected to the office of the President more than once. But this article shall not apply to any person holding the office of President when this Article was proposed by the Congress, and shall not prevent any person who may be holding the office of President, or acting as President, during the term within which this Article becomes operative from holding the office of President or acting as President during the remainder of such term.

SECTION 2.   This article shall be inoperative unless it shall have been ratified as an amendment to the Constitution by the legislatures of three-fourths of the several States within seven years from the date of its submission to the States by the Congress.

ARTICLE XXIII

Allocation of presidential electors to District of Columbia

SECTION 1.   The District constituting the seat of Government of the United States shall appoint in such manner as the Congress may direct:

A number of electors of President and Vice President equal to the whole number of Senators and Representatives in Congress to which the District would be entitled if it were a State, but in no event more than the least populous State; they shall be in addition to those appointed by the States, but they shall be considered, for the purposes of the election of President and Vice President, to be electors appointed by a State; and they shall meet in the District and perform such duties as provided by the twelfth article of amendment.

SECTION 2.   The Congress shall have power to enforce this article by appropriate legislation.

ARTICLE XXIV

Right of citizens to vote in national elections not to be denied because of failure to pay taxes

SECTION 1.   The right of citizens of the United States to vote in any primary or other election for President or Vice President, for electors for President or Vice President, or for Senator or Representative in Congress, shall not be denied or abridged by the United States or any State by reason of failure to pay any poll tax or other tax.

SECTION 2.   The Congress shall have power to enforce this article by appropriate legislation.

ARTICLE XXV

Succession to the Presidency and Vice Presidency in case of vacancies

SECTION 1.   In case of the removal of the President from office or of his death or resignation, the Vice President shall become President.

SECTION 2.   Whenever there is a vacancy in the office of the Vice President, the President shall nominate a Vice President who shall take office upon confirmation by a majority vote of both Houses of Congress.

SECTION 3.   Whenever the President transmits to the President pro tempore of the Senate and the Speaker of the House of Representatives his written declaration that he is unable to discharge the powers and duties of his office, and until he transmits to them a written declaration to the contrary, such powers and duties shall be discharged by the Vice President as Acting President.

Presidential disability: procedure for determining when and for how long disability exists. Vice President to act as President for duration of disability

SECTION 4.   Whenever the Vice President and a majority of either the principal officers of the executive departments or of such other body as Congress may by law provide, transmit to the President pro tempore of the Senate and the Speaker of the House of Representatives their written declaration that the President is unable to discharge the powers and duties of his office, the Vice President shall immediately assume the powers and duties of the office as Acting President.

Thereafter, when the President transmits to the President pro tempore of the Senate and the Speaker of the House of Representatives his written declaration that no inability exists, he shall resume the powers and duties of his office unless the Vice President and a majority of either the principal officers of the executive department or of such other body as Congress may by law provide, transmit within four days to the President pro tempore of the Senate and the Speaker of the House of Representatives their written declaration that the President is unable to discharge the powers and duties of his office. Thereupon Congress shall decide the issue, assembling within forty-eight hours for that purpose if not in session. If the Congress, within twenty-one days after receipt of the latter written declaration, or, if Congress is not in session, within twenty-one days after Congress is required to assemble, determines by two-thirds vote of both Houses that the President is unable to discharge the powers and duties of his office, the Vice President shall continue to discharge the same as Acting President; otherwise, the President shall resume the powers and duties of his office.

ARTICLE XXVI

Citizens eighteen years or older not be denied suffrage because of age

SECTION 1.   The right of citizens of the United States, who are eighteen years of age or older, to vote shall not be denied or abridged by the United States or by any State on account of age.

SECTION 2.   The Congress shall have power to enforce this article by appropriate legislation.

ARTICLE XXVII

Congress may not raise its own pay.

No law varying the compensation for the services of the Senators and Representatives shall take effect until an election of Representatives shall have intervened.

INDEX

Tippecanoe, 100
Tlingit, 27
Tobacco industry, 263–264, 277
Town meeting, 39
Townsend, Charles, 46
Townsend Act, 46
Trade Act, 40–41
Transcontinental Railroad, 145
Treason, 74
Treaties:
　Clayton-Bulwer (1850), 125
　of Ghent (1814), 100
　Guadalupe Hidalgo (1848), 121–122
　Hay-Bunau Varilla, 171, 234
　Hay-Pauncefote, 171
　Intermediate Nuclear Forces, 246–247
　Jay (1795), 89, 91
　Kellogg-Briand (1928), 191
　Nuclear Test-Ban (1963), 218–219
　of Paris (1763), 44
　of Paris (1899), 165–167
　Pinckney (1795), 89
　Portsmouth (1905), 174
　of San Ildefonso, 44
　of Versailles (1918), 186
　Webster-Ashburton (1842), 119
Trenton, NJ, 56
Triangular trade, 41
Triple Alliance, 174
Truman, Harry S. (1884–1972), 197
　administration of, 207–210
　election, 206–207
Truman Doctrine, 208
Trusteeship Council, 205
Trusts, 171–172
TVA. *See* Tennessee Valley Authority
Tweed, William M. ("Boss"), 146
Tweed Ring, 146
Twentieth Amendment, 198
Twenty-First Amendment, 198
Twenty-Sixth Amendment, 198
Tyler, John (1790–1862), 118–119

U2 incident, 215–216
Unalienable rights, 51
Uncle Tom's Cabin (Stowe), 125
Underground Railroad, 127
Underground Tariff (1913), 181
Unicameral legislature, 40, 60
UNICEF. *See* United Nations Children's Fund
Union Pacific Railroad, 145
United Nations, 204–205, 269
United Nations Charter, 205

United Nations Children's Fund, 269
United Nations Population Fund, 278
Urban riots, 221
Ute, 26

Valley Forge, 54–55, 57
Van Buren, Martin (1782–1862), 118, 120, 123
　administration of, 116–117
　election, 116
"V.E. Day," 204
Venezuela, 173
Venezuelan boundary dispute, 161
Vespucci, Amerigo, 25, 28
Vice-President, 72
Vicksburg, 137
Vietminh, 214
Vietnam, 222, 225
Vincennes, 58
Virgin Islands, 183
Virginia Resolutions, 93
"V.J. Day," 204
Volstead Act, 180–181
Voting Rights Act (1965), 220

Wabash v. *Illinois*, 154
Wagner-Connery Act (1935), 199
Waldseemuller, Martin, 25
Wallace, George C., 224
Wallace, Henry, 206–207
War:
　of 1812, 100–101
　Civil. *See* Civil War
　Cold. *See* Cold War
　French and Indian, 43–44
　Korean (1950–1953), 210
　Mexican (1846–1848), 121
　Persian Gulf, 253–254
　Russo-Japanese, 174
　Seven Years', 43
　Six Days' (1967), 221
　Spanish-American, 165–166
　World I. *See* World War I
　World II. *See* World War II
War Hawks, 100
War Industries Board, 185
War on drugs, 251
"War on Poverty," 222
War Revenue Acts, 184
Warren Commission, 218
Washington, George (1732–1799), 43, 53–54, 64
　administration of, 86–89
　appointed Commander-in-Chief, 50
　election, 85

　Farewell Address, 89–90
　reelection, 85
Washington Conference, 189
Watergate Affair (1972), 227–229
Weaver, Gen. James, 149, 159
Webster, Daniel, 105, 116, 124
Webster-Ashburton Treaty (1842), 119
Weicker, Sen. Lowell, 227
Welfare reform, 262, 278
Wesberry v. *Sanders*, 220
West Bank, 243
West Berlin, 208
Whig party, 115
Whiskey Rebellion (1794), 86
Whiskey Ring, 145–146
White, Hugh L., 116
Whitewater investigations, 265
WHO. *See* World Health Organization
Wilderness Campaign, 138
Wilkie, Wendell, 187
Willard, Emma, 113
Williams, Roger, 35
Wilmot, David, 122
Wilmot Proviso, 122
Wilson, Woodrow (1856–1924)
　administration of, 180–187
　election and reelection, 179–180
Wilson-Gorman Tariff (1894), 162
Winnebago, 26
Winthrop, John, 35
Women's suffrage, 181
Works Projects Administration (1935), 198–199
World Health Organization, 269
World Trade Center, terrorist attacks against, 261, 275
World War I, 184–187
World War II, 201–205
WorldCom scandal, 273–274
WPA. *See* Works Projects Administration
Wrights, Frances, 113
Writs of Assistance, 45

XYZ Affair (1797), 91–92

Yalta Conference (1945), 205
Yellow press, 165
Yeltsen, Boris, 253
Yom Kippur War (1973), 229
Yorktown, 54, 59
Yugoslavia, 268

Zimmerman note, 183
Zuni, 26